THE BORDERS

A History of the Borders
from Earliest Times

THE BORDERS

*A History of the Borders
from Earliest Times*

****

Alistair Moffat

Deerpark Press
Selkirk

First published in Great Britain in 2002
by Deerpark Press

A CIP catalogue record for this book is available from the British
Library.

ISBN 0–9541979–0–9

Printed and bound in Great Britain by Martins the Printers, Spittal,
Berwick Upon Tweed.

Typeset by Trinity Typing, Wark, Northumberland.

Deerpark Press
The Henhouse,
Selkirk TD7 5EY.

Contents

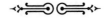

List of Illustrations

1. Eildon Hill North under snow.
2. The Mutiny Stones.
3. Scott's View.
4. Anglian fields at Midlem.
5. Jedburgh Abbey.
6. Melrose Abbey.
7. The decorated capital 'M' from the Kelso Abbey charter.
8. Kelso Abbey.
9. Lauder Common Riding.
10. A swing plough.
11. A ploughman and his bondager.
12. Workers in the Darning Flat at Gardiners' Mill, Selkirk.
13. Workers at Philiphaugh near Selkirk in 1890.
14. Gardeners and foresters at Philiphaugh in the 1890s.

Acknowledgements

I want to begin by thanking Walter Elliot. Without his kindness, wisdom, encouragement and good humour, this would have turned out to be even more of a marathon, and a much poorer thing at the end of it. Without the loan of countless books, the gift of priceless information ("it's like manure — spread it around") and the pleasure of frequent long blethers at Whinfield Road, I would still be writing this. As an inadequate mark of thanks, respect and affection, this book is dedicated to Walter. I hope he enjoys it.

George Rosie is a busy and gifted man but also that valuable thing, an interested non-Borderer, and I am grateful that he took time to read everything and offer some sagacious comments. I am particularly pleased to have the information on Walter Scott and Mark Twain, and on John Clay.

Dave Welsh also read every word and made it his business, as a professional historian 'marinaded in Border history', to examine every assertion with an occasionally withering rigour and at prodigious length. It must have been a considerable labour and this book is much the better for it. Thanks particularly for the ideas on Railway Time, Samuel Rutherford and the Border accents, and for much else besides.

My agent, David Godwin, was as ever a fount of encouragement and good sense. And thanks also to my friend Norman Davies. I hope some of the Notes make him smile. And I hope Cameron Pow enjoys the book.

With the help of the remarkable Jenny Corbett I was able to colour the early 20th century very vividly. Dave Welsh Snr, Mae Wilson, Walter Elliot and others also contributed tellingly, and James Stewart's precise testimony was invaluable.

I am also grateful to The Scottish Working People's History Trust and their secretary, Ian MacDougall, for allowing me to quote from 'Bondagers', an enormously important publication which casts a late evening light on life on the land in the early 20th century Border country. Douglas Hall edited the delightful 'Kalewater Miscellany' and I want to acknowledge his kindness in allowing me to use extracts. Willie Turnbull and Bill Pattison's 'Wartime Memories of Kelso' contains many gems, and one or two, with their generous permission, are on display in what follows.

Many other authors and publishers also gave permission to quote from their books and I gratefully acknowledge that here. Particularly I want to thank Mainstream Publishing for allowing me to quote from Edwin Muir's 'Scottish Journey', Professor D.E.R. Watt for passages from 'A History Book for Scots: Walter Bower's Scotichronicon', and Canongate Publishing for passages from 'The Journal of Sir Walter Scott', edited by W.E.K. Anderson. I also gratefully acknowledge quotation from Seamus Heaney's translation of 'Beowulf', 'A Taste of History' edited by Maggie Black, 'Life and Letters on the Roman Frontier' by Alan K. Bowman, 'Bede's Ecclesiastical History of the English People, edited by B. Colgrave and R.A.B. Mynors, 'Bede: History of the English Church and People' edited by Leo Shirley-Price, 'The Age of Bede' by Betty Radice, 'The Native Horses of Scotland by Andrew Fraser, the work of Michael Robson and his monograph on James Small, 'An Ingenious Mechanic of Scotland', and also Scottish Borders Council for allowing me to reproduce items from their stills library.

Helen Darling and her team at St Mary's Mill are a credit to the craft of librarianship and deserve thanks for their quiet courtesy. Thanks are due especially to Helen for alerting me to the excellent work of Clifford Gulvin.

When we converted this book into a television series, the director, Anne Buckland, brought a fresh eye to the content — and made me rewrite some of it, as usual. John Agnew filmed the Borders and Ken McNeil recorded what it sounds like with flair and accuracy, and Adam Moffat kept us all going, sometimes literally. Neil Robinson of Border Television commissioned the series with Sandy Ross of Scottish Television — thanks to both for your trust.

Riddell Graham of the Scottish Borders Tourist Board allowed me access to a very handy library of stills for the book and I'm grateful to him and those photographers who shot them.

The tolerance of my family is versatile. They still talked to me as though nothing was happening — when the book was going well, was stalled, or was a complete waste of everybody's time. Thanks and lots of love to Lindsay, Beth, Helen and Adam.

This book was born out of a question asked by Walter Elliot one day in Melrose. What follows must be one of the longest replies in history.

Alistair Moffat
Selkirk
20th November 2001.

To Walter Elliot

The Borders

1

Rivers Run Through

The winter of 1962/63 was long and bitter. Snow lay on the ground for months and the Tweed was frozen so thick that when Dr Davidson and his friends marked out a curling rink, they lit a brazier on the river-ice. Exotic episodes like that aside, everyone was sick of the weather, complaining about the slippy roads and paths, the frozen mess of grit and muck, and tired of shovelling away new falls of snow. Our fire was never out, banked up and smoored overnight, and even the coal fire in the upstairs big bedroom was lit when we went to bed.

But I was happy, very happy. In 1963 I finally got my dream job. There was no interview, no negotiation on pay and conditions, no need for previous experience and no opportunity to meet my employer. The present incumbent had decided to retire to make way for someone younger. At 15 he was due to leave school and learn a trade, apprenticed to a joiner. And at 12, it was thought that I was ready to take over. But all I really knew was that I was to report for work on the first Monday of the New Year, at 5am.

And so, at 4.30am on Monday 3rd of January 1963, I silenced the alarm, slid out from under the blankets onto the freezing linoleum and was into my clothes in less than a minute. My Ma was up, making sure that I was up in time for my first morning at my first regular job. She handed me a piece of hot buttered toast and told me to get a move on. I pulled on my anorak, folded the toast, put it in my pocket and stepped out into the icy night. Black as soot, this was not the morning but still the night before.

Delivering the Store milk was a plum job. The Store was the Kelso Co-operative and Wholesale Society and everybody, except the toffs, who were not members, and some folk in Roxburgh Street, got the Store milk. Gliding through the empty streets, the electric float made very little noise, only seeming to click and buzz faintly when it moved. The rattle of the metal milk crates was louder, and the sound of Tommy Pontin, the milkman, when he was whistling, which was all the time, was louder than everything.

Even though it was hard work and in the wintertime fingers frozen red and then numb (no gloves allowed because that meant only being able to pick up two or three bottles instead of eight), I liked the Store milk. Looking back from a distance of nearly 40 years, I can see how it was the job of my dreams. At 4.30 in the morning I felt that I saw the town before anyone else was up and doing, passed through the streets as they slept on, and watched lights go on in curtained windows as it awoke. I liked seeing the buildings quiet in the winter dark, mysterious and full of secrets. The ruins of Kelso Abbey stood black and tall against the eastern sky, and as the sun came up, it lit the bell tower, tipping it with yellow against the dark blue. When the abbey was built in the 12th century, it was easily the tallest building for many miles. Nine centuries later, it still was, and I liked that too. Empty, roofless and gutted now, penned in by iron railings, its walls soiled by countless pigeons, and with a scatter of headstones under the broken arches, the old church was a place of dreams. Seeing its great tower reach up in the early morning through a huddle of buildings and trees, it came alive for me when it was silent, in the half-dark, free from the 20th century which would drive, walk and chatter around its foot when the morning came.

I had heard stories of the abbey bells being cast into the nearby Tweed. When news came of approaching English armies, they were said to have been dragged along a track and thrown into the deep Maxwheel whirlpool where the Tweed turns sharply east towards Berwick and the sea. The summer before, we had been swimming in that part of the river, something strictly forbidden, and for good reason. We stood dripping in our trunks, helpless and horrified on the riverbank watching Bobby Armstrong being sucked into the Maxwheel and pulled down by the undercurrent. Screaming, knowing, he cartwheeled, skinny white legs momentarily in the air before going under for the last time. For weeks afterwards I thought about it, wondering what Bobby had seen in the deeps of the Maxwheel. There were tales of river tunnels, and in the run of wish-fulfilling illogic that pulls along a young imagination, I could see Bobby finding one, swimming up out of the mirk into the air and coming back to the light amongst the battlements of the Old Castle, Roxburgh Castle, whose ruins stood a mile to the west, across two rivers.

At the same time as I began to deliver the Store milk (did she plan this? — she was working in the accounts department at the Store at the same time), my Ma decided to take me in hand. At primary school I was apparently not a co-operative child and as a result, I found myself in the class where we made things, all day. Handicrafts, I think it was called; in one term we turned out raffia mats, and bits of old cork cut out in circles for teapots to sit on. It was great. Our teacher was a delicate wee woman who looked like Celia Johnson, wore a pink print smock and lived in a world of her own. Either turned towards the blackboard, writing and pointing, or looking at some distant vista out of the high windows, she seemed able to ignore the sporadic rioting in her classroom, the fights, the incessant racket made by the black-haired Romany kids shoved into our school for the winter, and the wee girl who sat behind me with her hand up, saying urgently, "Please Miss. Please Miss" just before she peed herself, every day.

My Ma made an appointment to see the Headmaster, with me dragged in behind her. After a short discussion which, thankfully, never seemed to mention me but dealt with the proposition that since my older and swotty sister clearly wasn't stupid, being Dux of the school and so on, then how come I was educationally sub-normal? All I remember was my Ma spitting on her hankie and rubbing my face and telling me to breath through my nose and not to look so gormless. The upshot was that the following week I found myself in the class where you never made things, did not riot, and did exactly what you were told, which was reading and writing. And history.

Around the same time, my Ma also dragged me all the way down Bowmont Street and in through the swing doors of the Carnegie Library to meet Mr Bird. A big man with a bald head, he wore tiny National Health specs that made him look like a kindly owl. At that time, since I didn't do any, I thought reading was impossible without specs. They were part of the equipment. "Now", he leaned over the lending counter to get a better look at the scruffy kid just frogmarched in by his Mother, "what about Richmal Crompton?" It seemed more like a question for him than for me. A Richmal Crompton might have been a bicycle or a make of cricket bat so far as I was concerned. I took 'Just William' home, but, even with my Ma checking on me every 5 minutes (I realise now that she was making sure that I could actually read), I could not make head nor tail of it. I was able to read the words but they made no sense. What language were these people speaking, on which planet did they live, and what was Violet Elizabeth Bott?

After a series of doomed attempts at Enid Blyton, Arthur Ransome and even, in desperation, Zane Grey, Mr Bird handed me a little brown, leather-bound book with a lion rampant crest tooled on the front. It turned out to be a history of medieval Scotland. I remember an early chapter entitled 'Troublous Times', and the others seemed to be a variation on the same theme. I cannot recall the book's title or the name of the author. But it was magical. Some of the things happened at Kelso Abbey, others in places I knew well, only a mile or two from my bedside lamp.

When I walked down through the dark streets to the Store milk depot, I could look over towards the hulk of the abbey tower rising above the rooftops and populate it from the pages of history books. In the empty town it was easy to imagine the names back into life, the hundreds of generations long vanished into the darkness of winters past. Now I knew who had bombarded the abbey with cannon in 1545 and destroyed all of the east end, who had founded it in 1128, and also that, like me, the monks had to get up in the middle of the night to go about their business. I knew that the Tweed had a bridge much further upriver than the modern crossing near the Maxwheel. About halfway through my milk round, there were deliveries to some houses on Chalkheugh Terrace which sat high above the Tweed looking out to the west, and to the overgrown ruins of the Old Castle, Roxburgh Castle, where kings had sat in judgement and seige engines rumbled. On the great river peninsula below there had been a medieval city, with named streets and houses, four churches and a royal mint, and it had all disappeared to nothing, not one stone left standing on another, only grass where the sheep and cattle browsed. When I left my job of dreams a few years later, the milkman, Tommy Pontin, said to Jimmy McCombie, my successor, that although I was reliable and always turned up, I was a bit slow on the deliveries. I expect he was right.

Tommy used to organise the round so that it ended near my house and allowed me some time to eat a breakfast, get changed for school and away on time. One of our last deliveries was never set down on the step, but handed over in person. Old Will Rutherford timed the opening of his front door to coincide exactly with my arrival and as I gave him his pint, his old collie always brushed past me out into the lane. Better known as Wull the Hird, he wore the sort of russet herringbone tweed suit given to estate workers as part of their fee, a matching bunnet, and carried a long crook with a horn handle he had carved himself. The Hird had worked high up in the Cheviots, and even though he had long since retired, he went nowhere without his dog, Blacker. "It was blacker than the other pups in the litter". Absolutely obedient, even to the quietest word or whistle, I never saw the collie on a lead, and never heard it bark. But it could fix you, eye to eye, in a long staring match. I once remarked to the Hird that Blacker seemed intelligent, for a sheepdog. "Intelligent?" he snorted, "Intelligent, is it? Ee think a' they can dae is herd sheep? That yin could knit ee a pullover."

Once the Hird and his dog had completed their morning walk (it got shorter and shorter as their arthritis got worse), and if the weather was fair, they stationed themselves at the foot of Forestfield, where it joins Inch Road. There was an old loupin'-on stane for Wull to sit down on and plenty of smells at the corner to interest the dog. As the world passed on its way, Wull greeted and chaffed people, sometimes making outrageous comments, many of which seemed to be addressed to his dog. "Will ee look at that?" he spluttered, when a lady with aspirations crossed Inch Road with, dear God, a West Highland Terrier wearing a wee tartan coat, "The dog's better put on than ee are, wumman!"

On Sunday mornings there was no milk delivery and in the summer I used to pick up the Hird's Sunday papers. He always asked me what I was reading, and I always told him, at length. Once I came across the story of Drythelm, a 7th century monk at Old Melrose who was fond of standing up to his neck in the freezing midwinter waters of the Tweed as a penance and a severe mortification of the flesh. "They're a' daft in Melrose", said the Hird, shaking his head. "Aye and strange craturs as well." As an example, he told me the story of Michael Scot, the Wizard. With clap of thunder and shaft of lightning, Scot had cloven the Eildon Hills in three. Buried in Melrose Abbey, for all the church disapproved of his black arts, his stone cist had been opened by curious young monks and Michael's book of spells removed. To this day no-one knows what happened to it.

Sometimes it seemed possible to hear Wull thinking, hear the connections tumble and click into alignment, like a cerebral fruit machine. "Ee were on about monks at Melrose the other week," he would start, and then, content with that link, embark on the story of

St Cuthbert. "He was a hird-laddie, like myself, and he saw visions up in the hills. Now, I can quite easily believe that." Once the Hird was in gear, the journey could be dizzy, labyrinthine. "What I want to know is that when he became a monk, what happened to his dog? If it was a guid yin, it wouldnae have left him or gone away with another hird. Did the monks have dogs? Maybe? They had sheep." These musings led to the definition of a good collie dog. And then the story of the Dumfriesshire shepherds who went out on the hills in the great storm of 1829. "They could smell the snaw coming", and with their dogs how they fought to bring down their hirsels off the hillsides before the sheep were engulfed in the drifts. Some men died on the hill, "and, you know something, their dogs stayed beside them. They could have got off and doon to the bottom shielings, but they stayed. They stayed."

In May 1959 a car came down our street. It wasn't the baker's van, the coal lorry or the red Post Office parcel delivery, it was a private car with black on white number plates bolted to the bumpers back and front. JR 4172 drew to a stately halt directly outside our house. And my Dad got out. He was beaming at us all, and I mean all, since half of the neighbours had appeared on the pavement to get a closer look. Pushing her way through the throng my Grannie hirpled forward and poked her stick at the pencil-thin tyres of the sort of car the Keystone Cops might have screeched to a halt in. "Who belongs this then?" My Dad grinned at her, "It's mine Ma".

For the first summer we never went anywhere in it. Or at least we didn't arrive at any destination, or make any holiday trips to faroff places. Instead we went for short hurls in the countryside. If it was a fine evening, my Dad would announce a hurl, we'd all pile in and usually drive south out of Kelso. Threading our way through the foothills of the Cheviots, he often followed a minor road running parallel with the Tweed Valley. Lit by a westering sun, the views were long, seemed never-ending, almost far enough to show the curvature of the earth. "There it is. The Inhabited World". But we never had any opportunity to get out and look, the car never stopped, no matter how much whoever needed a pee and we always got back home to 42 Inchmead Drive well before darkness, or even gloaming, came in. I suspect that my Dad was nervous in his first few months of car ownership; not wanting to cut the engine far up a country lane a long way from help, not trusting the battery to sustain lit headlamps, and certainly not keen to park JR 4172 outside any address but his own.

"Cruising at 30", my Dad sat back behind the wheel and smiled across at my Ma. We were on our way to Hawick, at last making a journey which involved getting out of the car. And even more than that, this was a trip where we stopped somewhere, did something, and then came home. That morning all of us had been scrubbed, dressed in our best, inspected and warned that nothing less than 'behaviour' would be tolerated. Ma looked grand in a new frock and Dad had been down to Jock Hume's to buy a new checked Van Heusen shirt to go with his checked sports jacket, his checked bunnet and the baggy grey trousers he called 'flannels'.

It was June and Hawick Common Riding Saturday. The horse races at the Mare were on and we were going. Born and raised in Hawick, my Ma saw JR 4172 as more than transport; it was a way of keeping in regular touch with her family. At the Mare, Auntie Mary, Auntie Daisy, Auntie Isa, Auntie Jean, Auntie Margaret and Uncle David, along with a couple of dozen cousins, had spread tartan rugs on the grass, set out a huge picnic and were sitting in the sunshine blethering, watching the jockeys leather their horses, blethering, pouring tea out of ancient cream-coloured thermoses, blethering, blethering, handing round ham sandwiches and busy being a large, old-fashioned extended Scottish family.

Stories, it seemed to me as a child that the Borders was nothing more than a mountainous pile of stories, a mass of unsorted jigsaw pieces sometimes shuffling together into a transient pattern, soon dissolving again into a chaos of names and places. But some of the stories stuck in my mind, who told me them and where. And gradually, as JR 4172 took us all over the Borders, I could see where some of them belonged and then in what order they should be thought about. At the Mare my aunties teased me for being a Kelso man, but they told me their stories because I was half-Hawick, and gave them edge and meaning because they wanted me to remember them.

"What though her lads are wild a wee,
And ill tae keep in order,
'Mang ither touns she bears the gree,
Hawick's Queen o' a' the Border"

When she recited that to me, there was a catch, unsuccessfully covered by a smile, in my Auntie Jean's voice. She meant it. It was the sum of all the stories, the outcome of all the suffering, what was left after the fun, the flags and the bunting came down at the end of the Hawick Common Riding. Tears filled up her eyes when Jean told the tale of Hornshole and the winning of the Flodden flag in 1514. These things happened. And for my Auntie Jean, they happened to her, to her people, in her place and they were part of the beating heart of now, of the Common Riding, and not uncertain or distant events from a misty landscape that belonged to the other country of the past.

"Teribus Ye Teri Odin,
Sons of Hawick that fell at Flodden"

In the desparate aftermath of that disastrous battle, a party of young men had gone out east from Hawick to intercept an English raiding party inbound to the town intent on destruction of all sorts. At Hornshole they clashed. In a roadside skirmish by the River Teviot, Hawick defeated mighty England and carried off their flag to prove it. Teribus Ye Teri Odin, the enigmatic town motto, is carved on the plinth of the Hawick Horse, a defiant sculpture that remembers Flodden and is the stone icon at the still centre of the Common Riding. Remembering a sorrow five hundred years old, Jean wept for Flodden and also for all those who had remembered it every year since, for all that experience in one place.

I was lucky to hear these things. JR 4172 delivered me to places and times when my own people, not yet made blasé or dissatisfied by the allures of mass-media, knew who they were and where that identity came from. Pride, softly spoken and clearly understood, was everything to the family sitting in the June sunshine on the tartan rugs at the Mare.

But sometimes that robust sense of identity depended on enmity, on defending it against outsiders. Battles, and not the modern long-range video-game version, were hard-fought affairs, men standing toe to toe, pushing, stabbing, close enough to smell the sweat, taste the blood and feel the fear. Either side of the border line, strings of bloody fights spatter over the pages of history. Border armies were personal, groups of brothers, cousins, neighbours, and men who depended for their lives on unspoken loyalty, and no-one ever taking a step back.

"Stand firm and sure,
For Jethart's here."

High on the Carter Bar where the modern road crosses one of the Cheviot watersheds, on the border between England and Scotland, the Scots were on the wrong end of a 16th century beating. Until, riding hard up the river valley, the men of Jedburgh arrived late to reinforce the Scots and scatter the English troopers, chasing them south down into Redesdale.

Dramatic reversals like that, the litany of Stirling Bridge, Bannock-burn, Flodden, Culloden and a dozen others draw a thick black line between us and the English, and build an easy fence for history to fall either side of. But, in truth, they tell only famous parts of a more complex and much richer story. Kings anxious and ambitious for their dynasties, wealthy landowners wanting more, and churchmen in search of greater glory for their God; these were the dynamics of national confrontation, the forces which brought armies to battlefields, the interests that stood to gain from victory and had the power to mitigate defeat, for themselves. Steel was sharpened and heads broken for the benefit of tiny groups of privileged people.

For me, these contrary thoughts had an unlikely beginning. The first time JR 4172 took us out of Scotland was more than an adventure. When we chugged across the Tweed Bridge between Coldstream and Cornhill, there was a squat roadside sign with a St George's Cross announcing ENGLAND. Nothing happened. No-one stopped us to ask what we thought we were doing. The colour of the road went from gunmetal tarmac to orange, but the hedges and fields were the same, the people in the village of Cornhill didn't spit as we passed, and there was no sign of Violet Elizabeth Bott.

Cruising at 30 allowed my sisters and I time to look at the countryside, read the signposts, and to point out nothing particularly exotic to each other. Double-declutching, my Dad changed down to get us up the hill to The Salutation Inn, where he told us he could see the sea. In the back that kept us busy until Longridge Towers where Barbara shoved Marjie and me out of the way to tell the front seat that she could definitely see the sea, and she saw it first. And what is more that the town on this side of it was Berwick Upon Tweed. It looked enormous. And it was full of English people.

There were so few cars on the roads in 1959 that passing another one was an event. No-one had yet bothered to regulate for them in small towns. And that meant that one of the many joys of JR 4172 was that Dad could park virtually anywhere. Pulling the complicated lever arrangement which flicked out a yellow indicator flag from a slot between the driver's and the rear doors, he drew in to the kerb by Stodart's Rum Puncheon, a restaurant at the Berwick end of the Tweed Bridge. I got out to look at the English. Expecting them to be different, to fail to understand me when I wanted to buy something in a shop, I was immediately on my guard. This was an enemy town. Anything could happen, and I was not to be disappointed.

It was Saturday morning and the Berwick market was in full cry. Stalls lined the High Street and under striped canvas canopies barkers shouted their bargains to a throng of shoppers. It seemed like a mad carnival, nothing at all like going for the messages. Wull the Hird had warned me about this sort of thing. He had been to Berwick once and bought a pair of socks in the market. "Shrunk in the first wash," he said, "Couldn't even have got them on my thumbs on a cauld day." I kept my hands plunged deep in my pockets, protecting my pennies against English trickery.

Forty years on, in the late Autumn of 2000, I drove down from Selkirk to Berwick Upon Tweed to have another look at the English. It was a slate grey day, the cloud cover and the North Sea merged into each other so completely that the vanishing point of the horizon was entirely lost. The world seemed folded in a chilly blanket. Pulled out of safe harbour by a tug, a tanker began to plough up and down through the choppy swell, and on Spittal Promenade, on the south bank of the Tweed estuary, a few dog walkers bent against the east wind. I bought a plastic cup of coffee from the cafe in Tony's Amusement Arcade and walked around the back to see if the iron drinking cup was still attached by a chain to a tap set into the wall. It was.

Spittal Trip was organised by Kelso's churches to allow the children of the town the opportunity to get out of it and visit somewhere different. The train windows were slid shut to jam officially sanctioned streamers, and on arrival at Tweedmouth Station, each child had a numbered and coloured badge tied to their lapels which entitled the wearer to a paper bag of buns and biscuits and a small bottle of Middlemas' lemonade. Then we were taken in a long crocodile to the beach to enjoy ourselves.

Unlike my labelled pals, I had been to Spittal, Berwick, the beaches down the coast at Scremerston (where we really did enjoy ourselves) many times in JR 4172 and I took an urbane, even slightly weary, view of the annual trip. What an irritating, supercilious child. I spoke to English people, and even went into Woolworths to buy toy soldiers on behalf of the more reticent. I liked England very much.

And walking around Tony's Amusement Arcade, down Berwick High Street, up to the King's Own Scottish Borderers barracks, I remembered why the town was so attractive. What made it different and exciting for a boy raised in the landlocked valleys of the Tweed basin was a simple thing; here was a working port, the smells and sounds of part of a maritime economy, the squawk of seagulls over the rooftops, a Customs House and Harbourmaster and the best fish and chips in the world. Ultimately it had nothing to do with the burghers of Berwick being English. As I grew older and a bit less supercilious, I came to understand that these people were Borderers like us, their experience and all of their history was intimately bound up with our own. And the St George's Cross and the ENGLAND sign were no more than coloured labels relatively recently attached. Outsiders often miss the point about Berwick's apparent isolation. The debate does not revolve around nationality, about whether or not the town ought be part of England or Scotland. What really matters is that Berwick should be clearly and consistently recognised as part of the Borders.

And this is something which needs to be stressed throughout the long story which follows this introduction. When Borderers both sides of the line look over their shoulders to Edinburgh or London, they see cultures and attitudes which differ far more sharply than those of Langholm and Longtown or Coldstream and Cornhill. And yet politics insisted on difference, and for a thousand years the peoples of the Border have been pulled apart by kings, churches and parliaments. Even though they shared the same climate, geography, diet, experience and hard-bitten sense of humour, they are now indelibly different peoples. As late as the 17th century the London Exchequeur wrote of 'English Borderers' and 'Scottish Borderers' with an exasperated emphasis on the second name. But now Carlisle is an English city inhabited by English citizens nominally attached to the Church of England and definitely situated in England while Hawick would be horrified if anyone suggested it was was not true-blue, 'Flower of Scotland', dyed in the wool Scots. In many important ways this is the story of how these people who shared so much came to be divided.

Coming back to live in the Borders after 30 years away felt like the resumption of an interupted conversation. People I hadn't seen in all that time greeted me as though we had spoken only the day before yesterday, and nothing much had happened meantime. All these years away (Wull the Hird always said that a day out of Kelso was a day wasted. What would he have said about the squandering of three decades?) I had been quietly circling the mountain of stories I had heard and read about the Borders, thinking about them when I thought I was thinking about something else. What held them together was, of course, a place. But what made them live was people. I came quickly to see that if the history of the Borders was not first, last and always about real people, then it was nothing much at all. Without the actions, words, tears, laughter and mistakes of people, stories soon dry up into the dusty arithmetic of history, of dates, numbered kings and annalists' lists. The reported remark of the austere 7th century monk, Drythelm, that he had been in colder places than the River Tweed in January comes racing across the centuries as absolutely authentic, the sound of a dour Borderer talking 1400 years ago. More recently there was the stubborn perfectionism of the Berwickshire blacksmith, James Small, rejecting prototype after prototype of his revolutionary cast-iron plough, and his refusal to patent the design and thereby restrict its use amongst his fellow Borderers, and ploughmen all over late 18th century Britain. The texture of Carr's Table Water Biscuits reflects the austerity and industry of the Carlisle Quaker family who founded the firm and throws a link right across the Borders to Eyemouth and the equally severe God worshipped by the North Sea fishermen.

Kings may have been distant but they were nevertheless important, and in the early period they are often all we hear of. However, the ordinary people of the past are the bedrock of this long and complicated story. And for a simple reason. They were our mothers and fathers, directly related to us in a clear line through uncounted generations. DNA testing all over Britain has taken samples from the remains of early peoples and compared it with our own. There is so little variation as to be statistically insignificant. And that means that across the human universe of nine or ten thousand years in this place, we are who we were. Outsiders came and they changed the society of the first settlers, the Old Peoples, first to Celtic, then Celto-Roman, then Christian, then English, then Gaelic, then Norse, then Norman, and on and on. The language spoken by the majority of Borderers changed at least three times and cultural habits more often. New people stamped new identities on the Old Peoples, but they did not replace them. We are who we were.

Everyone who has lived in the Borders has been profoundly influenced by geography as well as history. The rivers that run through the hills and plains might be frontiers now but for millenia they were connectors rather than limits. Before the idea of England began to compete with the idea of Scotland, the Tweed was a river that ran through the lives of Border people, guided them to the sea or up country, fed them and watered their fields.

The limitations of this book will be all too obvious, but its limits ought to be made clear from the outset. They begin with a line drawn from near Dunglass Church on the Berwickshire coastline up to Ecclaw Hill and then along the Lammermuir watershed ridges to Soutra, from there across Fala Moor to the ridge of the Moorfoot Hills, then to the head of the Eddleston Water valley north of Peebles and down the line of the A72 to Biggar. South of that line, the stories that follow will often bring in events in Galloway, Dumfries, Carlisle and the Eden Valley down to Penrith. Another line should be drawn from there across Stainmore, to the Tyne and Newcastle, 80 miles south of where we started on the North Sea coastline. This is a huge area, perhaps a twelfth of the land mass of Britain, and there is a great deal to say about the people who walked their lives under its skies.

The geographical scope of this book is easier to comprehend than the wash of history across the landscape. Because of the disruptive nature of political change, the early chapters deal with the wide area delineated above, but as the story progresses, the focus necessarily sharpens. From the medieval period onwards the area now known as the Scottish Borders moves into the centre of the narrative and stays there. This is a matter of practicality in a one-volume history. For the early period it makes sense to deal with both sides of the borderline for the good reason that it did not exist. But once the ideas of Scotland and England began to harden, and much more historical evidence becomes available, it is simply impossible to include everything of importance that happened on both sides of the line, or to the west of Langholm.

For clarity, a broadly chronological arrangement follows, although occasionally it will turn back on itself or jump ahead for what appear to me to be good reasons. But in order not to detour the narrative too frequently, there are a number of lengthy notes incorporated into the text but not necessarily the story. They can be skipped, or ignored, or read later. In any case they deal with vignettes, ideas, or events which were interesting and related to the history of the Borders, but did little to move matters along. For example a synopsis of the career of John Duns Scotus is included here as a note but since most of it happened outside of Duns, it has only an incidental place in the overall picture.

The observations of outsiders are sometimes helpful, particularly at times when the picture is blurred or uncertain. Their opinions are also worth having if they shed light on contemporary attitudes as did, for example, the Archbishop of Glasgow's 'Monition of Cursing' against the Border Reivers of the 16th century. But what has been rigorously excluded is the sort of outside validation often so eagerly sought and recorded, particularly in the last 200 years. Very recently a famous television game show host enjoyed a fishing holiday on the River Tweed and local journalists anxiously relayed his pleasant but patronising remarks about the Borders. Who cares? Over the last few decades there has been an abject and wince-making tendency for some Borderers, no doubt for what they believed were good reasons, to be pathetically grateful for anything positive said by famous, wealthy or influential visitors. Perhaps it was intended to create a needless sense of importance by transference, by the lending of names. In researching this book I began reading a promising-looking and well produced history of one of the Border towns, but sadly it set an immediate tone when the unctuous author started by showing around a well known Glasgow singer and setting down his favourable comments. He sounded like a native bearer in the train of a white sahib on a tour of a provincial backwater. I threw the book across my office and it slid under a bookcase, where it remains. We are not reservation Indians anxious for the good opinion of those who care little and know less about this place. We do not need them, any of them.

This story will show that we deserve the dignity of a long and eventful posterity, and that we do not require the approval of anyone else but our peers, our neighbours and all the uncounted generations who walked these hills and valleys before us. We are Borderers, and what we need is to understand better where we came from, and from that, to come to know who we are.

"Let them all say
What ere they may,
The gree goes aye
To Gala Water"

Wull the Hird might have sung the next verse of 'Braw, Braw Lads' but Mr Bird would not have approved. For, like many from an academic background, I suspect he would have prefered a cool, forensic approach, taking together all factors and shades of opinion to distill and produce a balanced and detached view.

What follows could never be that. I love this place, and this is the story of the people who made it.

2

The Wildwood

Four hundred generations ago, sometime around 6500BC, a small band of hunters pushed their boats out into the shallows of the Sunrise Salt Lake. Wading out as far as they could through the incoming breakers, six men carefully guided forward the sharp prows of their canoes so that they cut through the swell. Three men pushed each boat, and then the lightest scrambled on his belly aboard the stern and quickly made his way amidships to steady the dugout and allow the other two to flip simultaneously over the gunwales. Once they had found the birch-bark buckets to bail what water had been shipped in the launch, they took up their paddles and made for the calmer sea beyond the tidewash. It was a windless, sunny Spring morning and the hunters found it easy to turn the dugout canoes into a diagonal course to follow the coastline they knew well.

On the beach stood their people, many of them waving and calling out good luck. There were perhaps 70 of them on the waterline, the children playing advance and retreat with the waves. In front of the crowd, a few yards out into the warm salt water, their leader watched impassively as the canoes grew ever smaller on the face of the great lake. She was anxious and fearful.

From all her long experience, the Old Mother knew that this decision was not only right but inevitable. And it was better to act now, from strength, when something positive could be done, rather than later out of fear and weakness. On the night of the first full moon after the shortest day had been endured, she had gathered the strongest and most resourceful of her younger brothers and sisters, her sons and her daughters into to her log cabin. The winter had already been severe, and the worst of it was yet to come. As the Old Mother stared at the flames on the hearth, the special fire she had made with rowan logs (to protect her band), and hazel logs (for wisdom and guidance for her own thoughts) and green pine twigs from the King of the Trees of Wildwood (for resin-sweetness and spark) she slowly considered her thoughts. At the end of summer the low log walls of the cabin had been stuffed with turf and clay wattle, but the snell wind still found a way around the backs of the circle who sat around the magic fire. As she leaned forward to speak, one of her sons pulled the Old Mother's bear cloak snug around her shoulders. In more than 40 summers she had seen their hunting and gathering grounds change. When her father and his band came to this place, they had been alone at first, able to go where they pleased in search of food. And when others arrived, it was good. The young men and women could find partners from the new people and begin their own families, and perhaps even form their own independent bands. But after a time, the game was less and the food-plants, the fruits and berries not enough. Some moved on up the Rocky River into the interior, towards the Sunset Ridges in search of empty lands, and most important, bushes and trees whose fruits had only been harvested by the birds and hungry animals, and places where wild leaf and root plants grew in abundance.

The Old Mother smiled when she said what they all knew. There was food for the winter: stores of hazelnuts, smoked and dried fish, what could be harvested from the rocks on the shore where the Rocky River curled into the Salt Lake. And there were dried plants hanging in baskets from all the cabins. But it was not enough and the hungry moons of the late winter and early spring were still in front of them all. Old people were dying more easily than they should. That was perhaps in the natural order of things, but the Old Mother's smile faded when she talked of the children who had not survived the winter. The Gods of the Wildwood bent their snow-clad branches low in sadness to see that. Saplings should grow into tall trees and not wither and fall before their time. That only happened when the woodland was too crowded. And now it was itself suffering. The fires used to drive the game to the killing grounds had been too widespread, too destructive and it would take many summers for the cover to grow again and bring back the deer, the boar, the elk and particularly the great wild cattle, the aurochs. The Old Mother had heard that even in the lifetime of her father, reindeer and wild horses had been seen less and less, although some said that they went away out of the Wildwood to find open country where they could see for long distances, feel safe from their enemies like the lynx and the wolf, and have time to flee if they approached.

The Old Mother leaned forward out of her bear cloak to poker up her fire and pick up a bowl of warm nettle tea from the hearth. To the others she seemed to be shrinking, her beautiful buckskin tunic hung on gaunt shoulders, white hair in wispy pigtails and her teeth ground down to stumps as she opened her mouth to drink the tea.

Looking round at the faces lit by the flicker of the fire, she surprised them and grew animated, talking quickly with expressive hands and a questioning eye. For many moons the Old Mother had been considering what should be done, but before coming to the burden of it, they all needed to share her knowledge. The Land of the Great Bear, the country that lay directly under those stars of the northern sky was unknown. It was believed that the herds of reindeer and horses had gone that way, but nothing was certain. No-one had travelled there and come back with stories. But could it be so different from the mouth of the Rocky River? If the Wildwood stretched under the stars of the Bear, its Gods would have power. In the waters of the Sunrise Salt Lake, her father had told her that there were Seal Islands which lay on the path of a canoe journey to the Land of the Great Bear. If that was true, then there was food to be had, for once out of the water, it was easy to kill seals if you were quick.

Knowing how long it took for matters of this sort to grow in the minds of her people, the Old Mother suggested, but did not insist, that when the spring came a scouting party should take two canoes up the coastline to look for the Seal Islands, and perhaps to go beyond them. And then, to forestall any discussion, she rose as quickly as she could and made her way to the door of her cabin. Once outside in the moonlit clearing of the winter camp, the Old Mother took her oldest son's hand and then the hand of the oldest daughter. She motioned for all the others to join them in making a circle around the Tall Pine in the centre of the camp. Chanting in low rhythmic voices, they walked and danced in a sunwise direction around the great tree, looking up to its branches and beyond to the stars of the Great Bear.

The scouts made steady progress up the coastline, paddling in one unified stroke, not talking, concentrating on making headway. The men in each bow had fixed their gaze on certain landmarks, and by pulling harder for short bursts, they had kept both dugouts on course. The spring sun was climbing to its zenith, there was barely a whisper of a breeze, and the sea seemed warm. But with anxious backward glances, the two canoes were beginning to leave behind the familiar shapes of dunes, beaches, outcrops and the inland hills of the Sunset Ridges. They had come a long way from the mouth of the Rocky River and were moving slowly into the unknown.

With good pilotage the bow men had kept their canoes from coming to broadside on to the gentle swell and very little bailing had been needed. This was important because, on the beach, the Old Mother had given them a basket of fire. Inside a bark container, live embers had been carefully wrapped in green leaves and sealed well enough, it was hoped, to keep out the spray of the sea. In a separate bag there was tinder: wads of bog cotton, dried strips of tree fungus, dried grasses, twigs and mosses as well as a set of flints to strike a spark if the embers were soaked. Fire was vital to the hunters and they needed to be able to make it under almost any conditions.

Their dugouts protected their kit well. Carved from tall, straight and thick-trunked pine trees, they were almost 5 metres long and well adapted for inshore seaworthiness, the deposit of the skills of many generations. So that it would cut through the sea in a ploughing motion, with minimum resistance, the prow was sharply pointed and slightly undercut, and the gunwales left outshot to turn aside the wake, and if they got broadside on to the waves they were a first line of defence against swamping. Using a delicate flint chisel, the boatbuilder had engraved a pine branch and a cone, for good luck and good fishing, on the sides of the prow. These were the canoes of the Pine Tree People.

Far in the distance, to the landward, something had caught the attention of the one of the hunters. He shouted and pointed that he could see something, a high rock, higher than a seacliff, that seemed to rise singular and sheer out of the outline of the coast. Once they had set a course for the Rock, they became aware of something else appearing through the haze to the seaward side. There seemed to be a scatter of small islands lying in the Salt Lake opposite the position of the Rock. As they pulled their canoes through the waves and edged closer, they could make out two groups of islets, some no bigger than an outcrop, others with a flat surface. One group lay close to the Rock and the other further out towards the horizon. And then, with a shout, the sharp-eyed hunter in the stern of the leading canoe pointed out splashing, not waves, but splashing off the rocky coast of the largest islet. The Old Mother had been right. These were the Seal Islands.

The Salt Lake had passed the turn of low water and the scouting party got welcome relief from hours of paddling by allowing the indrawn tide to carry them towards the Rock that loomed high, backlit by the late afternoon sun, out of the water. Jumping into the shallows, they dragged the heavy canoes up the sandy beach as far as they could. When the tide refloated them, they would pull them further towards the dunes and then above the debris of the high water mark.

Unloading the canoes to make them lighter, each man took out a wooden framed backpack, picked up his spear and club, and unlashing the long hazel rods and leather tent cover from the gunwales, they spread them out to dry on the loose sand, weighting them down with large stones. With three left on the beach to tie up the precious boats with root fibre ropes, the others looked for a way up onto the summit of the Rock. In their packs they carried food, flint tools and knives, a net, leather drawstring shoes and a cloak woven from long strands of tough grasses, which was both waterproof and warm. They also had dried medicinal herbs and balls of antiseptic mosses for any cuts or wounds. But in the sunshine they needed no more than their buckskin tunics. Decorated with fringes of cut thongs on the arms and legs, beads and feathers, they were close fitting, and the trousers, sewn with sinews to allow flexibility, adapted to each man's shape.

From the long summit of the Rock the three hunters could see for a great distance. Behind them to the landward stretched a green sea of dense, unbroken forest ending in a horizon dominated by a low flat-topped hill. Shading their eyes against the glare they could see that it was Wildwood, the trees they knew; birch, willow, hazel, alder, pine, oak and elm. No finger of fire-smoke curled into the air above the tops. The Land of the Great Bear seemed empty. To seaward the line of the two groups of the Seal Islands strung out into the Salt Lake, with larger islets masking the smaller outcrops. None seemed large enough for even a small summer hunting camp, and on days when the sun did not shine and the wind blew, they would have been harsh places to keep a tent and a fire. Further up the coastline they could clearly see another, smaller rock that seemed to sit at the extremity of a low promontary further out to sea. But whether or not this rock was part of the land or an island, they could not tell at this distance.

The wind off the salt lake and the thin soil allowed little but bushes and scrub to grow on the low summit of the Rock where the hunters stood. As the three men pushed their way through to what seemed like a small break, all stopped dead in their tracks. On the ground a small circle of large stones had been set for a cooking fire. No charcoal or charred wood remained (that was useful) but this was an utterly unambiguous sign that others had been this way before. Perhaps last summer a party came after the seals and prefered a camp on the Rock to the precarious little islets.

On the beach the canoes had been made safe and a fire lit from the basket of embers. Expertly pushing the long hazel rods into the soft ground in a wide circle and leaning them so that they locked together at their tops, the hunters made the skeleton of their teepee. Then they wrapped the membrane of sewn skins around it and put their kit inside. As the sun fell behind them and moonrise took its place, glinting pale off the salt lake, the hunters talked over what to do. If others had been here before them, then, knowing the way, they would come again. The Old Mother had used all her wisdom when she said that they needed a new territory, somewhere under the Great Bear, a place no-one had ever seen. In the morning, if the weather was good, they would move on.

Every morning, when the sun had grown strong enough, and every evening before it dipped over the Sunset Ridges, the Old Mother climbed the lookout tree on the knoll above the winter camp. Her old bones made the ascent of the ladder a lengthy and breathless business, and when she at last gained the platform in the branches, she had to strain to focus on the wide expanse of the Salt Lake below. Even though her sight was beginning to fail, the Old Mother prefered to go up alone, without the company of a younger person with sharper eyes. No-one else in her band needed to know of her anxiety about the scouting party.

After climbing down on the morning of the fifth day after they had left, and making her way quietly back to the winter camp, she took a willow basket and stole away into the Wildwood, taking the path by the Rocky River. On her way, she stopped in several places to pick flowers, in familiar glades where what she wanted could always be found. Honeysuckle, ivy and rowan gradually filled her basket as she walked up the path by the sunlit river. After a time she came upon a grassy bank where a small spring broke into the open, trickled for a short way before crossing the path and joining the flow of the river. For the Old Mother, this was a sacred place, one of the mouths of the Earth out of which tumbled life-giving water.The gods of the Wildwood were near at this spring and in the stillness, they could hear your secret thoughts. Having made a three ply wreath from the twigs and flowers, she placed it on a ledge by the spring. The gods created these plants for their people to use and make their fears understood. With these three wound together, all signifying protection and the averting of evil, set near one of the mouths of the Earth, there could be no mistake. She only hoped that the gods were listening, were with her and her band.

After some moments in prayer, the old woman went off the path and into the denser parts of the wood to gather plants for food and medicine. Intent on scouring the ground, she found herself unconsciously approaching ever nearer to the clearing of the White Trees and the

Watermeetings. This was the place where other bands came to meet her own, where information and goods were exchanged, and a time when the younger ones looked for partners. Before the hunting began in earnest at the end of the summer, a fire-feast was held around the copse of tall birches. White wands were cut from the trees and given to the men who danced in deerskins and antler-masks around the flames.

The Old Mother emerged from the woods into the sunshine of the clearing, and looking around, saw that she was still quite alone. At several points on the perimeter stood the poles and high platforms of the raised death-beds where the bodies of ancestors were laid up for the gods of the Wildwood to see and for their birds to clean. She remembered when her father's body had been raised up. Her own time was coming but she did want to think of her own bones being taken up to lie on these death-beds; her band needed to move on and soon.

The reverie was shattered when she suddenly heard her name shouted somewhere along the path by the river. A young boy burst into the clearing to announce in breathless gasps that the scouts had returned. And they were all well, and they had a gift for the Old Mother.

Carefully unwrapping the birch-bark and leaf parcel, she found a rich red piece of roasted salmon. Encouraged by the scouts, she ate a mouthful and distributed the rest to the clamouring children. It tasted good. The scouts kissed and embraced the Old Mother and then went off with their women to rest, to wash and gather their thoughts on all they had experienced so that they could talk clearly at the evening meeting in the log cabin.

The rock they had seen sitting further out in the Salt Lake than the Great Rock had turned out to be part of a tidal island, and when the water was high, they made good passage between it and the mainland. Another day in the canoes beyond Tide Island, and they came upon something they had never seen the like of before. Between a high ridge on the farther side and a group of sandbanks nearer to them, they found themselves in the mouth of a huge river, many time larger than the outfall of the Rocky River. Seeing the power of its flow, they named it The Surger, as it poured its fresh waters into the Salt Lake. Broad enough to have islands in it, it seemed a mighty thing made by the gods. Woodland crept down to the banks on either side, and when they had ventured some headway up the great river, they came upon a watermeeting where even the tributary that joined the Surger was big, bigger than the Rocky River. Beaching the canoes on an island, they looked hard for the signs of a meeting place but could find none. Returning to the mouth, they climbed up a ridge and searched the horizon for fire-smoke but could see none. There were no paths through the dense and dank wood, and at every side they started wildfowl, seabirds off the treetops and game of every sort. At one moment they were sure they heard the booming of an auroch as it crashed through the bushes.

The estuary of the Surger teemed with fish and in the clear water they could see salmon swim. After a prayer for the wise fish, they speared four of them and roasted and feasted on them at their evening camp on the ridge. The excitement of the scouts' account was impossible for the Old Mother to ignore and the day after the meeting, she gave orders for the winter camp to be struck. The band would move for the summer hunting season to the mouth of the Surger. If the gods of the Wildwood wished to bless them with their bounty, they would stay. And if they did not, then they would return to the Rocky River to overwinter once again.

They stayed. The hunter-gatherers of the Old Mother's band were the first people to see the mouth of the Surger, to settle on its banks and to fish its waters. A year after they came, small groups paddled their canoes upriver and far into the interior and sometimes they were gone for the cycle of a whole moon. Two great watermeetings were found, and between them a remarkable sight, a place they called Threehills. But in all their travels, they saw no other human being.

In her 45th summer, having brought her band to a place in the Wildwood where the gods had smiled on them, the Old Mother died, gave her soul back to the great trees and her bones to the forest floor.

* * * *

These things happened. The places found by the Hunter-Gatherers on their voyages are not inventions, they are real and their names intended as renderings of how they might have seemed to them when they first saw them. And although no-one knows their names, and we have almost nothing of their language, we should try to remember the Hunter-Gatherers, to imagine them back into life, the first people who came here four hundred generations ago. For they are our mothers and fathers, and in many senses, we are their children.

THE IAPETUS OCEAN

Four and a half million years ago, the Borders was a much more emphatic border than it is now. Northern Scotland and Ulster once formed part of a huge North American landmass, while England was on the northern edge of a European bloc. Between them lay the Iapetus Ocean. A few hundred kilometres wide, what would become the landscape of the Borders was waiting to rise from its waters.

When these two great landmasses, or tectonic plates began to move towards each other in a process known as continental drift, they squeezed the Borders up out of the bed of the Iapetus Ocean. The angle at which the plates collided determined the south-west to north-east line of the Southern Upland and Cheviot ranges.

As the North American and European landmasses joined, they formed a massive continent which geologists have named 'Laurentia'. In time the Southern Uplands became detached to become offshore islands, and the remains of rock from that ancient period can still be seen near the mouth of the Tweed. During the same period the isolated old volcanoes we now recognise as the Eildons, Minto Hills, Ruberslaw, the Dunion, the Dirringtons and the Kelso Traps all began to be active, throwing out millions of tons of lava.

Ultimately Britain detached itself from Laurentia and it drifted across what became the Atlantic Ocean to form part of a European landmass.

But what these ancient geological events clearly demonstrate is a truth that has endured from near the beginnings of time; that the Borders came neither out of England or out of Scotland but appeared first as they have always remained, independent of either.

On the 8th of March 1997 The Times newspaper contained an article headlined "History Teacher Bones up on an Ancestor". Despite the sub-editor's arch attempt at jocularity, the burden of Nigel Hawkes' report was nothing less than epoch-making.

In 1903 the skeleton of a prehistoric man had been found in a cave in the Cheddar Gorge in south-west England. Much later, scientists had been able to determine the date of his death to the beginning of the 8th millenium BC, some time around 7900BC. Enough material from Cheddar Man's skeleton survived to allow sophisticated DNA testing to be carried out at Oxford University. His chromosome patterns were then compared with a sample of 20 people living in the area around the Gorge. In his article for The Times Nigel Hawkes reported that "To the astonishment of the scientists, a close match was found between Cheddar Man and Mr Adrian Targett", a 42 year-old history teacher at the Kings of Wessex Community School in nearby Cheddar village. The tests were exhaustive and allowed no statistical doubt that the descendent of a prehistoric man, who lived 10,000 years earlier, was thriving in almost exactly the same place as he had walked and hunted ten millenia before.

This test and others like it conducted in the Shetland Islands and, on a less detailed scale elsewhere in Britain, show something not only remarkable but also revolutionary. If the basic human stock of Britain has developed mainly from the first peoples who came here in the prehistoric period and that all of the cultural changes wrought thereafter were accomplished by relatively small groups of incomers (most of whom were men), then that proposition turns upside down the long-accepted belief that the British are a unique mixture, a 'mongrel race', an amalgam of all sorts of characteristics from Celtic through Anglo-Saxon, Norman and beyond. It is difficult to imagine someone more pure-bred than Mr Adrian Targett. And more, that there is an overwhelming likelihood that if DNA testing of comparable sophistication were repeated in the North of England and Scotland, where, historically, social mobility has been less than in the populous south, then we would find an even closer degree of inherited affinity with our prehistoric ancestors. In the Tweed Valley, there can be little doubt, we are the children of the Old Mother and the bands who came after hers.

18,000 years ago Scotland was buried under a vast sheet of ice 200 metres thick. Over many millions of years, there had been extreme fluctuations in the temperature of the Earth and plants, animals and perhaps even human beings may have flourished in what is now the Borders in some of these warmer intervals. But the last Ice Age obliterated any trace of life that might have pre-existed it, and as the domes of ice grew high above the Tweedsmuir Hills, the land was sterilised in its frozen grip.

3,000 years passed until, quite suddenly, the temperature began to rise. The great ice-sheets groaned and cracked and retreated northwards. In the short space of only a few hundred years, they had disappeared entirely. Torrents of meltwater shaped the landscape into river valleys, scoured the hills and in a time lasting only a few centuries, the warming tundra became home to a huge forest carpeting more than four fifths of the landmass. Pollen archaeology has found traces of the first species of native trees; oak, ash, elm, birch grew at altitudes up to 2000 feet while in the wetter places alder and willow appeared in abundance.

ICE AGES

The most recent Ice Age of 18,000 years ago, only a moment in the long history of the Earth, will probably not be the last. Stretching far back to the beginnings of the Earth around 4,600 million years ago, there appear to have been at least 12 Ice Ages, with some of the earliest lasting 100 million years. In what is known as the Cenozoic Era, the comparatively brief interval of the last 1.6 million years, seven episodes of glaciation have occured with up to 32% of the planetary surface covered in ice. Occuring at intervals of approximately 100,000 years, these recent Ice Ages have been interspersed with warmer periods when people may have been able to migrate north to what became the Borders before the first traceable bands of Hunter-Gatherers arrived around 6500BC. The current warm period began 10,000 years ago and it seems likely that it will end with another Ice Age, perhaps abruptly, at some unknowable point in the future.

With the retreat of the ice-sheets, an immense weight was lifted off the surface of the land in the Borders and it quickly began to rise, often by as much as 100 metres. At Dunbar in East Lothian, it is still rebounding at a rate of around 55cm per century.

Even at the peak of glaciation the central part of the North Sea remained unfrozen, although it had become a salt lake landlocked by tundra and ice connecting Britain and Scandinavia. When the temperatures continued to rise, the Sunrise Salt Lake was penetrated by the Atlantic in the north. And Britain became a long peninsula, with southern England still attached to the European continental bloc. Across this landbridge people came from the east and the south, and gradually funnelled northwards as conditions improved. By 6000 — 5500BC the bridge from Europe was inundated, the Sunrise Salt Lake became the North Sea and Britain became an island. There is evidence to show that for a time communications actually improved across the shallows of the English Channel, but eventually the breakdown of the landbridge meant that Britain became a difficult destination for peoples on the move. Unlike in the rest of mainland Europe, no great folk migrations tramped over this landscape in the way that, for example, the Barbarian tribes appeared out of the east during and after the period of the Roman Empire. Certainly the Rhine-Danube line was a brake on these folk-wanderings, but it presented a barrier far less formidable than the North

Sea and the English Channel. Some tribes, like the Vandals, turned
south away from the sea and penetrated down through south-western
France, into Spain (where they left the name (V)Andalucia) and on into
North Africa. Although invaders did come to Britain in successive waves,
much was accomplished by limited groups of determined men who
arrived at these shores in small boats. Geology, geography and the
technologies available at different historical periods argue strongly that
our country changed not through massive and radical displacements of
people when large, land-hungry groups of invaders expelled (where
could they go?) or killed the natives they had defeated in war, but
rather through much more complex and gradual processes of
acculturation. Over lengthy periods highly influential, probably
technologically more advanced elite groups changed native culture in
Britain, introduced more efficient ways of fighting, farming and thinking,
spoke new languages and re-shaped the landscape and its ownership.
And crucially, through their literacy and control of government, powerful
new elites had the ability to conjure an illusory sense of change since it
was clearly in their interests to make a decisive break with a past which
did not necessarily include them. This pattern has been repeated with
all the invaders who appear to have taken over Britain and changed it,
at a sword-stroke, from one thing to another. And the untidy truth is
that, for example, Norman England was not instantly created in 1066. It
took a long time for the Normans to become only a significant part of a
larger cultural mosaic.

All of these small groups of immigrants brought fundamental change
to the Old Peoples who were here first, but in a basic statistical sense,
they became part of them. In the Borders we we may speak a variety of
English, operate a system based on Roman law, acknowledge a church
that originated in the Near East and use Celtic names for our places,
but before all those things most of us are the direct descendants of the
Hunter-Gatherers of the Wildwood. That is where we come from.
Sometimes in the still of a soft evening on a woodland path, when a
game bird startles from the bushes, the voices of these people whisper
to us. And we should strain to hear them.

THE T-RIVERS

*Around most of the coastline of Britain, but particularly on the eastern,
many major rivers have similar names. Thames, Tees, Tyne, Tweed, Teviot,
Tay and Tain are all thought to come from the same root-word, Ta, Taus or
even Tavas. It means 'to flow' or even 'to surge'. Toponymists and philologists
accept that river-names are the oldest in the landscape. New peoples who
came to Britain tended to accept, for the sake of clarity and mutual intelligi-
bility, that the traditional name of a feature as vital as a river should not
change even if the language of most of the people did. And when some time
around 750BC, a P-Celtic language began to be widely spoken (it was the
ancestor of modern Welsh and therefore a language still recognisable to us
now) it absorbed the names of the T-Rivers into its vocabulary. It also adapted
others of less importance. The popular name 'Alauna', which mutated into
Ale, Allan Water, the Ellen in Cumbria and the Aln in Northumberland,*

probably had the sense of 'stream', or a shallow river that flowed over a bed
of rocks. A Rocky River.

It may well be that the names of the T-Rivers are the oldest words in
common daily use. When the scouts from the Hunter-Gatherer band of the Old
Mother found the Surger, they may have called it something like 'Tweed'.

Replacing the scrub and tundra left by the retreating ice-sheets, the
Wildwood began to carpet the Borders towards the end of the 8th
millenium, about the time Cheddar Man lay down to die in his cave
far to the south. Birch and hazel trees came first and were growing
widely by 7200BC. Oaks and elms were established by 6500 and 6000BC
and the warming climate allowed broadleaf trees to grow at high
altitudes, covering every hill in the Borders. The aspect must have
been jungle-like, green as far as the eye could see. In the lower-lying
and danker parts of the woodland, willow and alder grew so thickly
that a canopy developed. Darker and more humid than we may
imagine, the first Wildwood would have sometimes seemed a
threatening and mysterious place. There were no paths, other than
those made by animals, and thick undergrowth covered the rotting
deadwood and fallen timber.

The animals of the great woods survived either by browsing the
lush vegetation or by hunting. Wild boar rooted amongst the trees
while the massive aurochs, the wild cattle, grazed in the clearings and
ate tender leaves. The magnificent skull of an auroch was found in 1980
buried and preserved in a peat-bog near Selkirk. With a horn-spread of
four feet from indrawn tip to tip, it had clearly been a huge beast.
Almost as large was the Elk and its antler-spread could be even broader
than the auroch. Red and Roe deer prefered the cover of the trees, as
they do now in the managed pinewoods of the Borders, but ever alert
to danger, they did venture out into the upland clearings, at lochsides,
at the banks of streams and on the ridges where the wind kept the tree
cover sparse. In the valley bottoms beaver gnawed down trees to build
their dams, and at West Morriston near Earlston, there are remains of a
birchwood they felled some time around 5000BC.

Before the Hunter-Gatherers became their most deadly predator, the
animals of the wood, the fish and the birds were stalked and killed by
packs of wolves, the solitary lynx and smaller carnivores like the stoat
and weasel, while the brown bear would take what he could get from
the rivers and the trees. To capture and kill a predator of the Wildwood,
when a human hunter outwitted his animal rival, must have been
considered a great prize. And the Old Mother's bear cloak will have
been passed down the generations as a trophy.

THE AUROCHS

At Chillingham Park in North Northumberland, only a few miles from the
Rock at Bamburgh and the Seal Islands, the great wild cattle, the aurochs, still
roam. No longer crashing through the Wildwood in search of pasture, or being
hunted for its massive carcase, the auroch is now protected, introverted,
apparently inbred, and still very dangerous to approach.

In the 13th century the owners of Chillingham Castle built a park, and enclosed an area of the sort normally used to confine deer. But the reason for this great labour and expense was to make a place strong enough to contain a herd of wild cattle. It is difficult to imagine the 13th century Northumbrian nobility, however enlightened, as conservationists, but no other motive seems reasonable. For it seems certain now that the Wild White Cattle of Chillingham are the lineal descendants of the ancient auroch. Retaining the characteristic skull and horn shape and configuration that is very different from domestic cattle, their DNA has been tested and no comparable sample has been found. The blood grouping of the White Cattle is entirely unique in Western Europe. They are the last of the aurochs.

Forty or so strong, the herd has inbred for as long as records have been kept and likely for much longer. But the bloodline is kept pure by the emergence of a King Bull who impregnates all the cows until his reign is successfully challenged in a fight with a younger male, probably one of his sons.

In the severe winter of 1947, 20 of the White Cattle died and the herd was reduced to a precarious core of 8 cows and 5 bulls, and no calves. Despite great hunger, they refused to touch any artificial food offered to them, such as cattle cake and oats. The beasts died rather than eat it. Only meadow grass in summer and meadow hay in winter is ever eaten by the White Cattle, and the only shelter they seek is the lee side of a stand of trees. And the Foot and Mouth outbreak of 2001 virtually surrounded Chillingham, placing the aurochs in great danger. But they survived.

It is not wise to approach any of the herd. A cow will immediately attack someone near her calves, and because of their consistent ferocity, it is not possible to give the animals any veterinary attention at all. In the 300 acres of their kingdom, the aurochs are born, live, fight and die wild.

Because the Wildwood was difficult and obstructive country, and sometimes dangerously disorienting to penetrate too deeply, the first peoples entered it by water rather than overland. Clearly this created a distinctive pattern of settlement which has allowed archaeologists to follow the fragile and elusive evidence of the arrival of the Hunter-Gatherers. Waste from the manufacture of flint tools often gives away a campsite, and at the confluences of rivers, at what were prehistoric roadmeetings, substantial spoil heaps have been found. The junctions of Teviot and Tweed at Kelso, and Ettrick and Tweed between Galashiels and Selkirk seem to have been busy meeting places where exchange and trade, and social contact, might have taken place between different bands. More than a hundred campsites have been discovered in the Middle Tweed basin and nine of them have large flint spoilheaps and appear to have been well frequented.

The early peoples who came to the Borders travelled in boats, and over time, they may have used as least three different sorts of craft. Dugout canoes were well suited to inshore work up and down the coastlines and between islands. Manouevrable but heavy enough to sit down in a swell and hold the sea, they were not unsophisticated vessels hacked crudely out of thick logs by people who had only bone and flint tools at their hand. The great ocean-going dugout canoes of the Pacific coast Indians of Vancouver Island show how impressively these simple boats could develop. Until very recently the Vancouver Indians used technology similar to what was available to the Hunter-Gatherers of early Scotland, and yet their canoes could work in a big sea and, in groups, even take on the hunting of whales.

Better for inland travel in the shallow and irregular waters of rivers and streams were skin boats and bark canoes. An early outside observer of the British was the Roman historian Rufus Festus Avienius, and here he is repeating an ancient tradition;

"For these men know not to build their barks of pine and maple and do not shape their skiffs in fir, as the custom is, but, for a marvel, they fit out their boats with hides joined together and often traverse the wide sea on skins."

Although modern versions are now covered with canvas or other watertight fabric, skin boats are still made in the west of Ireland. There are two main sorts. Simpler and smaller is the coracle and it is built up in the shape of a large, circular basket usually out of hazel rods tied together with cord. The skin or canvas is then stretched over the frame, lashed to the edges and the whole thing is braced by a thwart which also acts as a bench. The essential joy of a coracle, and also its larger sea-going cousin, the more conventionally boat-shaped curragh, is that it is very light. Sitting on top of the water, it displaces only a few inches in a shallow river. And when rocks or rapids appear, one man can easily pick up a coracle and carry it forward to where the water is better. On hunting expeditions upriver curraghs may also have been used, and both types make an excellent temporary shelter when turned upside down.

The Forest Indians of the Eastern United States and Canada made canoes out of pieces of bark sewn together with fibre thread and the joints gummed with resin and attached to a light wooden frame. Sharing many of the advantages of the coracle and the curragh, bark canoes could be large at 4 to 5 metres long and able to take a substantial cargo of goods or people. Given the woodworking skills of the Hunter Gatherers in the Borders, it seems more than likely that they knew how to make bark boats.

The location of campsites on gravel river terraces, or near to lochs, were handy for canoe or coracle travel, for catching fish, water birds or larger animals when they came to drink. But there is evidence that experienced bands did not trust only to the vicissitudes of nature, the luck of the chase or a dependence on chance finds of plant food. North American Indians who lived on the banks of salmon rivers built permanent and complex systems of traps out of willow wands which required a great of work and materials, as well as considerable maintenance. But the traps guaranteed a protein-rich food supply for much of the year, particularly since fish could be easily preserved by smoking and drying. On the banks of the Tweed it is easy to see where and how similar arrangements could have been constructed, but because their materials were entirely perishable, even in the lifetimes of their users, none have survived.

YIDDIES

What has survived are the remains of rough stone jetties built out into the flow of the Tweed. Some are still visible under the surface near Norham Bridge and in the local dialect, they are called 'yiddies'. The idea was simple. Netting fish from the banks of a river is difficult since the current will always push the net back towards the bank where it will likely foul on vegetation. Essentially yiddies were long lines of large boulders projected into the current so that hunters could walk or wade out on them into the middle of the river. Behind the angle of the yiddie an area of slack water was created and the early peoples knew that salmon liked to swim into it, out of the strenuous current. They also knew that if they staked a net at the furthest extremity of a yiddie, the current would hold it in place against the body of slack water. When salmon swam out to feed in the current their gills became caught in the mesh.

This method of catching fish was used for millenia on the Tweed and at several sites number 8-shaped sinker stones have been found. They were attached to the bottom edges of the net. There is also evidence that the Hunter Gatherers used rods and lines.

When big animals were hunted in the Wildwood, it is unlikely that they were stalked or killed as individuals. This was a chancy and potentially wasteful method, unless a very young or old and infirm beast could be isolated. Game was driven. As happens now, lines of beaters would move through the undergrowth shouting and thrashing the bushes with sticks, pushing the game towards a killing ground where hunters waited to shoot arrows, throw spears or drive the animals over a natural feature like a river-cliff. Fire was sometimes set in the Wildwood for a similar purpose (or to create clearings where animals might come to graze and when archers could hope to pick one off) but the wind made its use for hunting unpredictable and even dangerously destructive. The use of bow and arrow allowed hunters to get close enough to browsing game to loose a fatal shot without warning, but again if the wind veered to the wrong direction, their smell could give away a hard-won position. Using natural herbal sources, Hunter Gatherers knew how to make a scent which masked a human smell, and could deceive animals for long enough for their killers to close in. A broken hunting bow was found in a peat bog at Rotten Bottom in the Tweedsmuir Hills in 1990, and, made out of yew wood, it is a beautiful and skillfully made object.

THE HUNTERS' TRYST

By 1970 the Eskdalemuir-Craik Forest had grown into the largest man-made wood in Europe. No-one knows exactly how many million trees grow over an area said to be substantially larger than Greater London. As the dense green canopy stretches across several horizons, it may be imagined that in some ways the Wildwood has returned. But in reality Eskdalemuir-Craik is less a great wood and much more an immense crop waiting to be harvested. The trees are packed together so tightly that in places the sun never penetrates the evergreen boughs and the floor of the forest is sterile.

Several species of plants and animals have fled, but one at least finds the forest a good place to live. The deer population has rocketed. Each year many hundreds have to be culled, sometimes 25% of all the animals. Using telescopic sights, marksmen shoot the deer at long range before carrying them out of the wood on all terrain vehicles.

The hunting may be high-tech now, but the activity itself has an unbroken history in this place. Almost buried by the eastern edges of the huge forest, there is a series of place-names which remember the deer-hunts of the Old Peoples. The Eildrig Burn trickles off Eildrig Hill, flows by Eilrig Cottage and the Eild Rig, before tipping into the Borthwick Water. It is a quiet place now, but generations ago it will have echoed to frantic shouts and screams, and the grass will have been soaked with blood. This dense concentration of names, and the particular configuration of the landscape, betrays one of the hunting grounds of the Hunter-Gatherers. Eildrig is from 'eileirg', a Celtic word for a defile — either natural or artificial. And it was the destination of a deer drive. Beaters strung out in a line attempted to push as many animals as possible (often others were mixed up in the mad rush — boar, foxes, all sorts of small creatures) towards the wide mouth of a funnel. Once in, they were driven to a narrow point where groups of hunters stood waiting for the kill. The most important hunter was given a place of honour, generally where he was most likely to make a kill. This was known as a 'sete' or 'seat'. Near Eilrig is Kingside Loch, a name that remembers a forgotten king who enjoyed the killing sete of honour.

If natural features such as cliffs were not available, a narrow valley of the right shape could be adapted. At Eildrig it looks as though the course of the burn was suitable. It has steep sides and before the drive began, the hunting party will have prepared the ground. A high fence was built at the top of a slope, and since adult wild deer can jump prodigious heights when badly frightened, it needed to be at least 7 feet tall. Living trees were often used with long stakes driven into any open ground between them. 'Palus' is the Latin word for stake, and it is the origin of pale, the precise English term for a deer fence. Branches were woven between the stakes and the trees to present as formidable a barrier as possible, and if thought necessary, a ditch was dug directly in front of the pale.

But it was important to give the fleeing animals the impression that the elrick was open at the narrow end so that they kept on coming. But as they passed, the hunters used arrows and spears to slaughter as many deer as possible. Any that escaped unhurt might be tripped and caught by nets laid on the grass. Hunting was a necessity, and not a sport.

The place where the hunters stood waiting to do their killing became known in Scotland as the Hunters' Tryst. In Edinburgh, buses travelling to the south of the city sometimes show that destination as a terminus. Where there was once an ancient Hunters' Tryst, there now stands a Safeways supermarket. And above Kelso there is a council house development known as Abbotseat.

The drama of the hunt and the stereotype of a fur-covered, flesh eating, bone-gnawing prehistoric man can be very misleading. Because bones survive better than the remains of vegetable or herbal matter, it is easy to imagine how Hunter-Gatherers came to be seen in that way. More accurately they should be called Gatherer-Hunters since it seems that between 50 and 90% of their diet was plant-based. They ate roots, leaves, seeds, stalks, fruit, nuts, flowers, gums, seaweed and fungi. These staples were all wild plants which still grow in the Border countryside but whose nutritional value has been ignored or simply forgotten. The roots of the silverweed, pignut, dandelion, wild parsnip and carrot were boiled or roasted or sometimes ground into meal to make a sort of brose. In 19th century Highland culture ancient, lightly disguised, pagan rituals surrounded the harvesting of wild carrots. It was done on a specific day, the Feast of St Michael on 29th September, and in a specific way. A three-sided mattock was used to uproot the more awkward, and its shape is thought to echo a pre-Christian association. In all sorts of settings and combinations three was a sacred number, but for pagan women, it represented a three-in-one goddess— the maiden, the mother and the crone. After the rituals of the harvest, the carrots were given to young men as signs of affection and good luck.

Sometimes feast days with equally faintly concealed pagan origins involved the baking of a cake or bannock, and this was done over a special fire of sacred woods such as rowan, oak, hazel and bramble. Other wood, like blackthorn and aspen were believed to be evil and were never used.

Hunter-Gatherers also ate salads and used wild sorrel, mint, rocket and much else, while nettles, Fat Hen leaves and wild cabbage were boiled. Nettles lose their sting when placed in hot water, and nettle tea was thought to act as a tonic, particularly for old people.

Hazel may have been a favourite wood for magic fires because of its great importance for Scotland's communities of Hunter-Gatherers. There exists powerful, and rare, archaeological evidence for the widespread and highly organised harvesting of hazelnuts, their processing and storage. On the tidal island of Oronsay in the Inner Hebrides, pits have been uncovered where huge quantities of nuts were roasted, and hundreds of thousands of charred shells left behind. Roasting greatly improves the flavour of hazelnuts as well enabling them to keep for long periods — throughout a winter. They could also be salted or made into a nourishing paste. But the sheer scale of the processing on Oronsay strongly suggests that hazel trees were being pruned and cultivated to ensure a high volume supply. Just in the way that salmon may have been caught in traps and yiddies in the Tweed, the Hunter-Gatherers managed the enviroment to suit their needs.

THE WISE FISH

Hazelnuts were thought to be nuggets of wisdom. Priest and poets believed that their powers and talents were enhanced by eating them, but there is a strange old story about how the salmon became the wisest of fish in the same way. Nine hazelnuts of knowledge fell into a sacred pool where the great silver fish swam. It ate the nuts and gained not only wisdom but also the distinctive red spots on its scales. In Gaelic culture this tradition has persisted in a surprising way. Am Bradan Mor, the Great Salmon, is still understood as a symbol of wisdom and learning and in a recent Gaelic-language television soap opera a fictional further education college was named after the Wise Fish.

However eccentrically applied, such beliefs are old, and it seems certain that the early peoples understood a great deal about the life of these magnificent creatures. From far out in the Atlantic Ocean where it has lived for up to four years, a Tweed salmon can find the river of its birth and swim up to the spawning grounds where new eggs are laid and young hatched. Even though scientists have tagged fish, conducted experiments and monitored the behaviour of large samples, there sits at the core of this epic navigational feat an essential mystery. The shape of the sea coastline and the distinctive smell of the native river are both thought to be waymarkers for their remarkable homecomings, but no behavioural studies have explained how the Wise Fish can find these places from a thousand miles out under the waters of mighty Atlantic. One theory believes that the salmon can see the stars of the night sky when they swim near the surface and that, in some unexplained way, their instincts for home are pulled along by the configurations of the heavens.

After they spawn, most fish die. But those that survive have been known to make the long journey across the ocean several times. Perhaps the Hunter Gatherers who lived on the banks of the Tweed recognised those who came back more than once, understood how far they had come, and called them wise for it. In any event, our culture still carries an echo of respect for these beautiful animals.

Every summer salmon are caught by hand at the mouth of the Surger. Nets are set out in small boats and then hauled in across the estuary by local fishermen. In an immensely long tradition, the fishery based at Tweedmouth harvests the fish in what has been a strictly regulated operation since records began. The names of the fishing stations on the tidal reaches of the Tweed are very old for that reason, most dating from the 12th century. Up to Norham, the names were attached with great precision, and sometimes intense argument between owners, to particular fishings on the river. These were very valuable and keenly patrolled. The dialect word for a salmon pool is a 'stell', and at Tweedmouth part of the estuary is 'Hallowstell' after the 7th century St Cuthbert, whose name made it a holy pool. 'Sandstell' is self-explanatory, but no-one now knows where pools got names like 'Gardo' or 'Calot Shad'.

At midsummer a Victorian rendition of a fertility festival is celebrated at Tweedmouth when The Salmon Queen is crowned before being paraded through the streets, and the happy old association between youth, fertility and the harvest reaffirmed.

In 1991 archaeologists made a remarkable find. High up in the Alps a prehistoric man was discovered frozen intact into the ice of a glacier. Probably stranded in a winter storm, he had died some time around 3,000BC. Beside him lay a wooden backpack which contained weapons, tools, birch bark containers (one of them had been used to carry live embers), and he also had with him a pair of draw-string leather shoes and a grass cloak. The man in the ice lived 3,000 years after the arrival of the Old Mother's band in the Tweed Valley, and his gear is likely to have been more sophisticated. But the basis of his technology was the same. For particular purposes he carried items made from the wood of 16 species of trees and had only one item with him made out of metal, a copper-headed axe. Also found in his pack and on his clothing were 30 different sorts of moss. Some had probably been picked up accidentally but others were deliberately brought along. Different mosses had specific properties, and into the modern period sphagnum was still being gathered for its antiseptic and coagulant qualities. Others were simply used as hygienic wipes, but what was interesting about their presence in the Iceman's pack is the fact that their use was part of everyday life, and they offer an echo of a huge hinterland of knowledge of the medicinal uses of wild plants. Hunter-Gatherers depended absolutely for their lives on a store of certain knowledge of the properties of plants, and their medical lore must have been impressive. 'Folk remedies' is the patronising label for what many people really see as ill-concealed New Agey mumbo-jumbo. But that is to deny long history and to ignore a valuable heritage.

WITCHES IN THE WILDWOOD

The medical plant lore of the prehistoric peoples of Britain was passed on from one generation to another for millenia. While methods of food production changed regularly and sometimes radically over time, diminishing a total dependence on the harvest of wild plants, fruits and nuts to something more partial and occasional, the eternal need for relief from discomfort or a cure for illness remained. Only the wealthy, and generally the urban wealthy at that, could afford what passed for modern medecine. As they had always done, everyone else depended on local healers whose experience and knowledge was often more effective than the new-fangled methods of medieval and early modern medical practice.

But in 1563 in England and 1591 in Scotland that benign continuum was brutally shattered and the ancient lore all but destroyed. The great witch hunts of the 16th and 17th centuries began. All over Britain, but with particular enthusiasm in Calvinist Scotland, witches were accused, rounded up, routinely and hideously tortured and thousands burned at the stake. 80% of the victims of the witchfinders were women. And it is seems very clear that most of those were local healers who used traditional infusions and decoctions of herbs and plants, or poultices and dressings, to treat their patients. Some of the women found it impossible to explain to their accusers why a cure worked, they only knew that it had always done. The pungent whiffs of pagan practice that surrounded some of their methods, the occasional ritual or form of words, can only have increased the sense of diabolical influence the witchfinders were so eager to detect as they did God's holy work.

A belief in witchcraft took a fierce hold in the Borders. In 1694 Lord Home of Renton "caused burn seven or eight" witches at Coldingham, and the casual inaccuracy of the report probably hides even uglier statistics. There was a dreadful execution at Jedburgh, the judicial seat of the county of Roxburgh, in 1696, and at Bullscleugh near Selkirk, a woman was burned over what appears to have been a standing stone associated with cultic practices of some unspecified sort. Even after the hysteria subsided in the early 18th century and the witchcraft statutes repealed in 1735, local populations still persecuted women suspected of some malefaction or other. In Carlisle someone nicknamed by the mob 'Madge Wildfire' was burned at Harraby to the south of the old city.

The effect of the terror was to destroy or drive deep underground a medical lore which had sustained uncounted generations since the time of the Hunter

Gatherers. But the obliteration was not quite total. For reasons of remoteness, of language and of institutional protection, the old practices survived in Gaelic Scotland. Few witchfinders penetrated more than the fringes of the Highlands, they found it difficult to manage even a quasi-legal process in two languages (when translation was probably difficult to organise amongst a reluctant population) and were in any case not supported by Gaelic-speaking society. Part of the reason for this was the high status of doctors and the respect for their knowledge which had been consistently fostered for centuries by clan chiefs and their leading families. The MacBeths or the Beatons, as they became better known, were the most distinguished and venerable dynasty of Highland doctors. It appears that they first came to Scotland in the dowry party of Aine of Connaught when she married Angus Og MacDonald, Lord of the Isles. This was the same man who brought the Islesmen and their Lochaber axes to Bannockburn in 1314. As hereditary physicians to the clans the Beatons flourished for 400 years. 19 branches of the family were in medical practice at one time and each king from Robert I Bruce to Charles I had a Beaton doctor in his service. Many of their manuscripts have survived to show eclectic influences, but one of the most profound was an encyclopaedic knowledge of the healing properties of plants.

When Gaelic Scotland began to wither in the 18th century and the power of the clans died away, the Beaton dynasty dispersed. But the knowledge of cures and reliefs continued, and much of it was deployed by women caring for people in their communities, neighbours and friends they knew and who trusted them. The writer, Mary Beith, has reconstituted a Highland materia medica and some of the names of the plants in her compendium have very ancient roots. Meadowsweet was used in baths to douse fevers and headaches, and in Gaelic it is 'lus Chu Chulainn' after the tradition that it was used by the Irish boy-warrior of the heroic age. The story of Cu-Chulainn may be more than 2,000 years old. And St John's Wort is known in the Highlands as 'achlasan Chaluim Chille', a strange name which means 'St Columba's oxterful'. There is a tradition that it was used as a poultice by the saint when he cured a young shepherd with what sounds like a nervous breakdown by placing it in the lad's armpit. In the absence of intravenous injections in the 6th century, the fastest places on the skin where substances can be absorbed into the bloodstream is either the armpit or the groin. Columba knew that, and the shades of a hundred generations standing behind him knew it too.

Because matters of precise distinction in the description of the natural world could be vital, and nowhere more so than in the selection of plants for herbal treatments when a mistake in colour or leaf-shape could prove at worst fatal, the language of the Hunter-Gatherers must have been rich. English, and American English in particular, is now an urban language which has lost the need to make fine judgements about the natural world (but has doubtless increased its lexical range in dealing with the complexities of human nature). But some sense of that old way of seeing the world can still be caught in Britain's Celtic languages. Scots Gaelic has a colour spectrum which is different and much more extensive than English because it derived over a long period from a rural culture's need to recognise the moods of the sea, the seasons of the land, the colour of animals and the complexions of the sky. Scots

English, the language of Robert Burns, also grew in the countryside and hints of its power can still be heard. Prosaically, and perhaps predictably, Scots has 32 near-synonyms for mud, and some, like glaur, clart, clatch and platch are in daily currency in a dreich Border winter.

An intimate affinity with the plants and trees of the Wildwood suggests powerfully that the Hunter-Gatherers found their gods there too. There is a clear northern European pagan tradition that men and women were created from trees, and well into the historic period the Norse saw their material and spiritual worlds entwined in the branches of the mighty Ash, Yggdrasil, the World Tree. In Scotland yew trees have been growing at places of burial for millenia, well before Christianity took its hold. The yew at Fortingall in Perthshire is thought to be 5,000 years old. When their bones were buried nearby the early peoples believed that the long roots of the yew would reach down into the soil and curl around them to suck up their souls into the branches for release. The evergreen leaves represented eternal life. And in the early farming communities of prehistoric Scotland, there is reason to believe that bodies were prepared for burial on raised platforms where the bones could be cleaned by the carrion feeders of the forest. Until recently North American Indians built death platforms for the same purpose.

A belief in life after death, or at least in some kind of transit of the soul is difficult to substantiate amongst the Hunter-Gatherers because so little has come down to us. In a midden of discarded seashells on the island of Oronsay, human fingers were found deliberately placed on seal flippers. And in western Europe, a Hunter-Gatherer burial was found where a woman had died in childbirth, and her tiny baby lay beside her, nestled in the wing of a swan. Looking up above the trees at the white birds in the evening sky, perhaps her father thought he could see his baby's soul fly on angel's wing. And after death on Oronsay, perhaps a sense that souls swam in the deeps of the world.

POLLEN

At Blackpool Moss near the farm of Nether Whitlaw, between Selkirk and St Boswells, scientists have been digging holes in the bog. They are looking for old pollen, thousands of years old if they can find it. Because they are anaerobic, wet areas of moss and marsh preserve organic material over very long periods. Decay needs oxygen and as layers of peat are laid down and compressed, vegetable matter and pollen becomes trapped and packed airtight. Radiocarbon dating can supply a chronology for these layers and allow scientists to quantify and date the pollen they find when corers are pushed down into the soft ground and samples extracted. Analysis of the pollen then tells a fascinating story — about land use, tree growth or tree felling, what crops were grown on arable land and so on.

Blackpool Moss is eloquent about the prehistoric landscape in the Borders — much more can be said about plants than people at this period. Leaving aside the scientific diagrams and data (which require considerable technical expertise to read and understand), it appears that the characteristic trees of the

Wildwood, the oak, hazel, elm and birch, began to be cleared around 4000BC. Some regeneration was re-cleared in the 3rd millenium BC and the immediate area, even though it sits up on the 250m contour, was used for cultivation from a very early date. People have farmed for a long time at Nether Whitlaw.

From the scatter of fragile evidence, a common-sense reading of the historical conditions and some reasonable analogy, it seems that the lives of the Hunter-Gatherers in the Borders may have been short, but they were far from brutish and nasty. As the climate grew warmer towards 4000BC, it is likely that food was plentiful for much of the time. And the seasonal nature of hunting, gathering and fishing allowed people time to do other things, or simply to rest, talk and consider the world. The Wildwood was not Edenic, but it was fruitful and the early peoples of the Borders grew out of it.

* * * *

The Axe-Priest was uneasy. Two summers ago he had come this way and felt the same sense of menace in the air. Even though the tree cover on the ridge was sparse, the path not difficult to follow, and there were places where the way ahead could be safely seen, he felt eyes on his back and heard bird calls that seemed too clear and too readily answered. And then, where the trees and bushes edged close to an uphill bend of the track, they silently appeared. It was as though they had always been in plain sight and only their movement betrayed human forms and allowed the priest at last to see them.

Falling in some distance behind were two men who did not look directly at him or make any attempt to gain ground. They carried spears, bows and flint axes, but seemed not to be shaping to use them. Two more moved in ahead of the priest and beyond the first screen of undergrowth beside the path, other shapes flitted between the trees. No-one spoke and no glances were exchanged. The Axe-Priest knew that they would smell his fear if he exhaled it, but in truth, it was their ignorance as much as the possibility of violence that concerned him. From the tattoos on their upper arms he could see that he was surrounded by men of the Wolf People. Pricked out on their skin were the outlines of blue-grey wolf tails, and their quivers were made of the shaggy pelts. Still predominantly hunters who covered the hills of the old Wildwood using generations of craft and instinct to find the upland deer, the boar of the valleys and even the giant beasts now rarely seen, the elk and auroch, these men still looked for their gods beside them, in the mystery of the woods, and in the secret places of the earth. The Wolf Tails had yet to understand the awesome and overarching power of the Sky Gods. And that was why the Axe-Priest was uneasy. They would not understand why he had come.

Wrapped in moss and each set inside a draw-string leather pouch, the axe-blades had been carefully fitted into his backpack. Three times three had been chosen by the High Priest; three sets of small blades highly polished until they gave off a dark lustre. Nine blades of the gods in the sacred union of three times three; the power of the axes came from their combinations, the way in which they worked together. For that is how they came to earth. Up in the Sky Quarries the miners took the rocks which hid the shape of the axes and always tried to find how the gods had fitted them together before they broke away what was not needed. When the Heaven-Fire melted the greenish rock, it infused it with power, with complexity and with mystery. These were the things the miners and their priests tried to understand, and the god-given reasons why the axes from the Sky Quarries were taken all over the Great Island.

In the green valleys beyond the quarries deep in the midst of the Lakeland mountains, the Deer People were used to meeting the solitary axe-priests on the ridgeways and by the rivers. Knowing that what they carried came from the gods, they were respectful, helpful, offering small gifts of food and good wishes. Shading his eyes against the strong sun and looking cautiously at his escort, the Axe-Priest knew that the Wolf Tails had never seen an axe of power before and had no conception of the importance of what he carried. Dressed lightly in buckskin, the hunters were intent on their journey, walking when it was level, jogging down slopes and all the time moving down the path into denser Wildwood. Making no sound past a footfall, the little procession came to the shoulder of a hill where a panorama unfolded. In the valley below lay two lakes, one was small and set before a much larger which stretched away towards sunrise. Near the Sky Quarries were many valleys like this, steep-sided and filled with the blessing of water.

It was mid-day and the summer sun had climbed to its zenith as the Wolf Tail escort reached the lakeside. A scatter of low cabins stood on a gravel terrace near a jetty and amidst them, dominating the scene, was an immense dead tree, its stark branches bare against the sky and the trunk stripped of bark. Like giant fruit, there appeared to be white objects hanging from it. As he drew closer the Axe-Priest could see that they were dozens of wolf skulls. Jaws agape, bone white and clinking in the breeze, the Wolf Tree told the ignorant in whose lands they travelled.

Taking two curraghs, the party crossed the small lake and reaching its end they quickly carried their boats to the larger and were underway in moments, pushed downwind by a stiff breeze. Still no-one spoke, but the Axe-Priest was reassured that while he was unquestionably a captive, no-one had challenged him either. Perhaps he had underestimated the hunters. Taking him ever deeper into the land of the Wolf, they seemed to know that he had serious business at his hand.

Through a mixture of portages and short river passages they descended quickly to the lower country. And after a time the riverbank landscape began to change. Where there had been Wildwood, there were clearings. And where there had been clearings, there was pasture and sometimes, beside it, a small patchwork of hurdle-fenced fields. But most striking were the riverside people and the buzz of their activity; children herding goats away from the fences and the crops behind them, men splitting long tree trunks with wedges, women stretching hides on a frame, older people carrying firewood. And beside the thatched longhouse, there was a cow tethered, its nose in a midden and a herd with his head clapped against its flank, milking.

As the curraghs passed all heads turned to stare, and as the Wolf Tails waved, the Axe-Priest stared intently back. Farmers with their mattocks and hoes, sheep, swine, cattle and goats cropping the grass with their ever-moving lips — these were the obvious tools that worked the land and, with the help of the Sky Gods, made it fertile every summer. But none of this would have come without the axe. What had tamed the mighty Wildwood, turned back the tide of the trees, was the power of the axe. It was the prime gift of the gods, and the reason why the axes of the Sky Quarries were a sacred understanding of the eternal debt of men.

When the river channel deepened, the curraghs moved swiftly in the downstream current to deliver the Wolf Tails to their destination. The Watermeetings was a place of power where the Surger was made stronger by his brother the Talking River. Across a flood plain they looked for each other, and then after flowing side by side, joined in an arrowhead and drove together on towards the sea. For a long way after their meeting, the waters did not mingle, and the crystal blue of the Surger ran beside the dark brown of the Talking River. But when they turned towards the sunrise near the foot of Threehills, they embraced each other, and became one.

At Watermeetings the great house sat on the skyline at the apex of a large clearing that reached up from the riverbank. On the hillside terraces there were many houses and much activity. The rattle and clack of flint-knapping echoed in the valley and several coracles arrived with large bundles of ash and hazel rods for the spear and arrowsmiths to work on. Pulling the curraghs out of the water, the Wolf Tails spoke for the first time, but not to the Axe-Priest. Instead they hailed their friends, chaffed at their children, and, almost as an afterthought, pointed out the great house on the summit of the ridge. To the priest this seemed to be a place of plenty and contentment. The gods were smiling on the Wolf People.

Perhaps there was a reason. When he had walked this way two summers ago the priest had listened to stories. In the circle of firelight, the old fathers had gone back over the whole history of the Wolf People, reaching almost beyond remembering, almost past the time of men. Reciting the names of the generations, recalling and fixing their by-names that told if they were tall, fair or fierce, the Axe-Priest watched and understood how their world appeared to them. High in the hills behind, sometimes in one piece of grey moorland, sometimes in another wooded dean, sometimes out of thick bushes, it was said that the river of the Wolf People rose. No-one can know exactly where, but it is there, up amongst the tops where the eagles wheel in the winds and the whaups cry. After the young river has trickled invisibly through mosses and clatches, often gurgling underground, always growing quietly stronger as its brothers join its flow, it gives birth to the seeds of the Wildwood, washes them into the earth, slakes the animals that grow out of it. And when the river of the Wolf People first carves its banks, begins talking, babbling over its rocks, it says the names of all who drank it, who set their boats on its surface and who watch it surge down to the sea. It carries off the ghosts of the past but it brings the children of the future down from the hills.

More than most of the tribes of the Great Island, the Wolf People understood who they were, bound together with the river that ran through their lives. No war had been needed to bring their families together, and no incoming group of new people had forced them to change their old ways. They had adapted because their river-ancestors would allow no other course. And the High-Chief in the house at Watermeetings was their Father, and they were his unquestioning children.

It turned out that hunting parties in the hills had been warned to look out for a stranger travelling alone and to bring him to the great house. Tall, heavily tattoed and wearing three rings of wolf teeth around his wrinkled neck, the High Chief was a humorous, courteous man. After greetings were exchanged in the cool gloom of the house, he abruptly dismissed his leading men, anxious that his visitor from the Lakelands should have food, rest and warm washing water before they spoke at length.

The feast was a sprawling affair, and sumptuous. From a central hearth and boiling pit, joints of pork were pulled, divided and distributed at the direction of the High Chief. With them went beakers of hot broth. And on wooden ashets sat piles of salted hazelnuts, lumps of crowdie cheese with flatbread and harder cakes of oatmeal, a mess of mushroom stewed with sharp juniper berries, collops of roasted venison with yoghourt mixed with honey and mint leaves, wrinkled apples, cloudberries, raspberries and small strawberries, and strips of smoked salmon wrapped around raw carrot sticks. And to drink there was crystal cool springwater mixed with mead.

In three nights the Summer Moon would wax its fullest, and the feast at the great house marked the start of the festivities. After the food had been cleared away, the High Chief and the Axe-Priest talked quietly of their bargain. The Wolf People would always be hunters and their river would always rise and grow strong in the Wildwood. But the gods were moving. When the first fire-clearings had become pasture for the deer and the hunters had learned how to feed them in the winter, find safe places for the does to drop their fawns, and kill the older ones without waste when the time came, these were signs that the gods were moving. When the small cattle first came, and the other quiet grazing animals, and the seed corn was sown, the ancestors of the High Chief knew how powerful the axe was to become. It was the instrument of the gods, of the Sky Gods who brought the sun, the rain and the winds to the new fields.

Taking a rush light and setting it closer to the hearth, the Axe-Priest laid three leather pouches before the old man and took out the precious axes. In the yellow light the lustrous green glinted over its smooth surface. The High Chief nodded and touched the axes. At the midnight ceremonies of the Summer Moon, they would appear, newly hefted and held high by the leading men.

Then, after more mead, the second part of the bargain was settled. In exchange the High Chief would arrange a journey, a safe passage. For many generations the priests of the Sky Quarries had looked towards the sunrise and dreamed that they would find the place where the first axes were dropped. When the Heaven-Fire melted on the jagged ridges of the Lakeland mountains, they knew that when the gods walked from the sunrise, the first, perfect axes fell on the hills nearest to the sea. There was a place, a huge mound called the Meeting Stones, where the axes had been buried. But no-one had ever tried to find them, until now.

For the festival of the Summer Moon many people would come to Watermeetings and the High Chief promised to send messages with some of them to his neighbours downriver, the Salmon People. The Wolf Tails could not accompany the Axe-Priest past the last boundary tree. Because they were his household warriors, it would not be right for the High Chief to send them into the country of another people. Instead he gave the priest parcels of small gifts for the leading men of the Salmon People and was careful to tell him their names so that they would know that they had met. Most important, a coracle packed with provisions was waiting at the jetties.

On the clear nights after the Summer Moon, the Axe-Priest used the starpoint hills to make the best calculation he could. The Meeting Stones lay a long way from the Surger, and although the fishermen from the Salmon people had guided him closer by pointing out tributaries with a good flow, he knew that he had a long journey through the dense interior. But he also knew the night sky well and after a few days of walking, he reached what he thought was the valley of the Meeting Stones.

For two months these uplands had been home to the herd boys and their flocks. Leaving the lowland pasture to grow hay for winter feed, and living in summer shielings in large groups of twenty or more, the shepherds followed their beasts with care and a wary eye. On the grey edges of the day wolves hunted these hills. Depending on their numbers to drive off an attack, and their stone stells for protection at night, the boys were always watchful. And they knew of the approach of the Axe-Priest, before he had even seen their flocks.

Above the valley stood many cairns filled with the bones of the dead. But the Meeting Stones were different. More than four times the height of a man and very long, the mound had taken many years to build. Larger stones had come from the nearby hills and others had been carried immense distances up here to the roof of the morning world.

As the herd-boys watched from the hillsides, the Axe-Priest laid down his pack and began to walk slowly around the circumference of the great mound, never taking his eyes off it. In a sunwise direction, he made three circuits. And then he sat for a time beside his pack, carefully taking things out of it. Once again he walked around the Meeting Stones, bending six times to set something small on the ground. Once the sun caught a dazzle point from what he carried. Although they could not make them out, these were the axes from the Sky Quarries. Finally the Axe Priest knelt, raised up his arms and turned his face up to the sky.

The Axe-Priest knew that the gods were close in this place. And in the morning, at sunrise, he would wait for their approach, and look for their guidance. In the sun's rays, the first axes would glow in the midst of the great mound of stones. And he would find them.

* * * *

When the evening sun falls behind the jagged ridge of the Langdale Pikes, it backlights them black against the sky. Looking west from Windermere and Ambleside, visitors sometimes notice this glowering horizon and remember that amongst the Beatrix Potter knicknacks and the Kendal Mint Cake, the Lakeland can still be a place of quiet majesty.

Six thousand years ago the Pikes did more than dominate the landscape. They loomed large in the thoughts of powerful men. High up near the summit ridge in difficult and dangerous places, there are ancient quarries of volcanic stone. Even though more easily accessible and workable deposits lie further down the slopes, the prehistoric miners prefered to climb up and hack the rock out of the highest outcrops they could find. No practical reason for this puzzling choice can be deduced.

Once the volcanic rock had been won from the high quarries, it was cut and fashioned into axehead-shaped pieces. Using abrasives, these were then polished until the stone gained a dull lustre. It is clear that the quality of the axes produced in this mysterious process was controlled in some highly organised, semi-industrial manner. For this was no bijou operation which rose and fell over a short period; at Langdale the debris of an astonishing number of discarded axeheads has been found, perhaps more than 75,000. The volume of successful output implied is difficult to calculate but the wide distribution of these distinctive polished axes all over Britain, including several found at sites in the Borders, suggests a trade running into six figures at least.

Many of the Langdale axes were small, too small to be of any practical use. And of the larger finds it appears that none show signs of ever having been used. Taking into account the inexplicable location of their quarries and the nature of their distribution, it looks as though the axes were used as gifts and also made as symbolic, sacred objects venerated in some unknown way in the religious ceremonies of the prehistoric peoples of Britain.

The symbolism must have been powerful. The Langdale axes first appear around 4000BC, the time when woodland clearance began in earnest. While the real work of tree cutting was done by large, razor-sharp flint axes, the celebration of their dramatic achievement might have focused on their polished cousins from the high quarries.

Pollen archaeology can be very precise in measuring the advance and retreat of species of plants and trees, and in doing so, say some less certain things about the role of human beings in the Wildwood. However, it is likely, judging from the measurable effects, that a number of factors were working to open up the landscape. Climate change and disease appear to have reduced the forest and in particular a sustained early episode of elm-tree blight felled many in the early part of the fourth millenium. But the principal impetus behind the slow destruction of the woods was both obvious and imprecise. Men and women were beginning to cut down trees in large numbers (and also to burn them back) in order to create clearings for pasture, cultivation and habitation. On the tops of Border hills shallow depressions can still be seen where old trees were uprooted by the wind and natural regeneration prevented by the immediate grazing of animals. This period saw the most radical and least well understood transition in human history.

Farming began in the fertile crescent of the Near East and slowly moved westwards over the European continent until it reached the Channel and North Sea coasts. It is impossible to know what happened at that point. Was there a sea-borne folk migration? Did significant numbers of new people somehow scramble into small boats bringing with them large domesticated animals and containers of seed corn? Perhaps. Or was there trade across the sea in new materials and new ideas? Or did the prehistoric peoples of Britain simply learn how to grow crops, tend flocks, and change much of their life-pattern without significant outside influence? The likely answer is a mixture of all these.

While the precise historical mechanisms must remain unknown, the general consequences of the transition from hunter-gathering to farming are more graspable. First and most important, a commitment to agricultural production on one particular area of land pinned a population to the map in a new way. In contrast to the old habit of moving comparatively freely around the Wildwood, groups of farmers began to settle on a piece of land which they worked, improved and most important, came to possess. The idea of the ownership of territory emerged. And with that, the further notion of good and less good land, which in turn implied competition, conflict, and winners and losers. And the new farming also prompted a substantial rise in the populations of particularly fertile areas, far greater than was possible amongst even the most efficient Hunter-Gatherers.

In good years farming created a surplus of food which allowed another radical departure. If everyone did not have to be involved all of the time in food production, then other roles could be created. Given the growth of competition for good territory, an early specialisation is likely to have been military. And in a parallel development, a hierarchical structure evolved under a leadership supported by a group of warriors.

The family bands of the Hunter-Gatherers gradually amalgamated into larger groups which might reasonably be seen as tribes. A shared territory implied a close network of blood relationships which ensured that a tribe was still regarded as an intimate unit. But inside it, people came to be treated differently. For example, matriarchy, or at least the leadership of the oldest, wisest and most experienced person, was supplanted by patriarchy. No doubt this change followed closely upon the rise of a male-dominated, warrior-based aristocracy.

PAINTS AND COLOURS

Because they left no written record, no maps and no signposts, it is impossible to know what name prehistoric Borderers gave to the place where they lived. In this they were no different from all of the early inhabitants of Britain. The first names were confered by outsiders who came from the literary cultures of the Mediterranean; the Greeks and the Romans.

But these were not necessarily alien labels since they often related to something observed by these curious outsiders. One of the earliest, and certainly the most defining, talked of the great native interest in paint and colour. A Greek sailor, Pytheas of Marseilles, called these islands 'Pretanike'. The name passed through several pairs of hands before being rubbed smooth into Britain. It comes from a native term and clumsily translates as 'The People of the Designs'. To the Greeks and Romans one of the most striking habits of the British was their fondness for painting their bodies with bright colours. And this was not confined to warpaint and decoration, there is evidence that prehistoric men and women liked to have their skin permanently tattooed.

The ancient palette available to early tattoo artists still survives and is to be found all around us in the natural world. Bright and permanent colours can be easily extracted from a wide range of plants commonly growing in the fields and hedgerows of the Borders. For example, the leaves of the iris give up a rich dark green, while its roots supply a matt black. Blaeberries make a purple dye, bog myrtle gives yellow and tormentil a bright red. There are dozens of other sources offering a spectrum of great subtlety. Far from being grey and muddy, the domestic lives of the early peoples were full of colour.

Sharpened bone needles were used to prick the skin and introduce the pigment in a pattern of dots set so close together as to present a solid bloc much in the way that tattoo artists still do. The designs were likely more standard than the eclectic mix of dedications and slogans available today, and the tribal names offer a clue as to what these might have been. Some refer to animal symbols. The Carvetii who lived around Carlisle translate as 'The Deer People', for example. When the formal and standard patterns used by the warriors of the North American Indian tribes to identify different groups is born in mind, it does not stretch credulity too far to imagine the tattoos of the Deer People involving an antler design, or some such. The Wolf Tails are of course an invention but their existence is not a fantasy.

This habit of body decoration continued in North Britain on into the historical period when the Romans described the tribes north of the Forth as 'The Picts' or Painted People. Many of the remarkable Pictish symbol stones show stylised carvings of animals such as bulls, geese, snakes and horses. And on the Borthwick Water, near Hawick, a beautiful Pictish carving of a fish, probably a salmon, has been found. Herodian, a snooty Roman historian of the 3rd century, wrote that the British went around 'for the most part naked', and that they tattooed their bodies with designs and pictures of animals. These animals were important, and their meaning may relate to tribal names, as well as to tattoo designs.

Once farming had established the domestication of animals and the shearing of sheep and goats enabled the production of textiles, the plant dye palette was adapted to make clothes more colourful. With its long history of textile production, the Borders never lost a cultural awareness of the importance of colour and the technological ability to produce it in quantity. Some Border dyes have become famous and associated with particular places and people — none more so than the particular shade of forest green worn by Hawick rugby players, the Robbie Dyes.

The gods were changing too. The Earth-Mother characteristics of Hunter-Gatherer beliefs gradually gave way to a concentration on fertility. This collection of ideas was far more intimately connected with farming and the delicate business of growing crops and domestic animals. And since its principal expression was the kindness or malice of the weather, men may have lifted their gaze from the trees of the great woods up to the sky. Just as an agricultural surplus enabled a role for warriors in a tribal society, it also allowed the development of a priestly class, (or at least priestly activity) people who understood something of the moods of the heavens, the transit of stars and the minds of their gods.

The farmers built religious monuments, mostly associated with burial, the afterlife and celestial ceremonies of some sort. The Mutiny Stones (known as 'The Meeting Stones' in the 19th century) lie on a ridge in the Lammermuir Hills, north-west of Duns. More than 85 metres long, between a minimum of 7.6m and 23m wide, and 2.5m high at the eastern end, it is a huge cairn shaped like a comet and its tail. The Stones were raised some time after 4000BC. In addition to its massive scale, what is striking about the monument is the complete absence of any evidence for burial. Sustained stone-robbing, including the construction of a sheep stell on the flank of the cairn, has reduced the size of the Mutiny Stones, but not radically disturbed its interesting orientation. Aligned north-east to south-west, it repeats the general shape of Borders geography. But more important, for several dawns after the full moon nearest to the summer solstice, the sun rises directly behind the eastern end of the cairn.

Not everyone stopped hunting around 4000BC. In fact no-one with any sense did. As new ways of producing food gradually introduced themselves and became more reliable, little of the old life will have been abandoned. Whatever cultivated crops, cows, sheep, goats or pigs could provide will always have been supplemented by the hunter's game bag, or the gatherer's basket. And an analysis of the noisome but highly informative contents of a blocked drain at the Roman camp at Bearsden in Glasgow shows that as late as the 1st century AD, wild plants, nuts and fruits still made up a very significant portion of a daily diet. The porridges and potages made common by the growth of cereals could be filling but tasteless fare, and wild berries and nuts were often used to supply much needed flavour and seasonal variety.

In the Borders the Hunters left their name on an ancient map. When Agricola, the Roman governor of Britannia, marched north in 79AD, he may have brought his son-in-law with him. The historian, Tacitus, wrote up an account of the campaign which not only added glory but also provided much completely new information about Southern Scotland. Most interesting is the list of the names of the native tribes. Occupying the central bloc of the Southern Uplands, from the mouth of the Ettrick and Yarrow valleys across to mid-Teviotdale, and then west over to

Annandale and the Nith, were the Selgovae. The name has a simple and unambiguous meaning and comes from the Celtic language root, 'seilg', to hunt. The Selgovae were the Hunters. And more than that it seems that their territory remained the hunting ground, the old Wildwood. Even allowing for the difficulty and inhospitability of the central hill country, there is nonetheless a surprising lack of prehistoric finds; few stone axes, cairns, cists or mounds, ceremonial sites, later forts. The population of this wilder area remained thin, even in the 3rd millenium BC when there was a general movement to higher ground.

But perhaps the Selgovae did develop a strong sense of their territory, even if they did take less enthusiastically to farming than their lowland neighbours to both east and west. The Catrail is a very long, discontinuous earthwork whose ditches run from north of Galashiels for 50 miles in a south-westerly direction before petering out in the wastes above Liddesdale. Perhaps this massive and enigmatic frontier began its life as the defined edge of the Wildwood. In any event, there is no doubt that the territory of the Selgovae developed, in a clear continuity in one place, into the greatest hunting reserve in medieval Britain, the Ettrick Forest.

ROOTING

In order to return to what they call 'continuous cover forestry', the Forestry Commission took a giant step backwards in February 2001. At Deerpark near Fochabers in Morayshire, they have reintroduced the boar into the Wildwood.

Although seeds dropping from Scots pines and other trees were germinating, natural regeneration of the woods had been patchy because a debris of moss, heather and dead branches was hampering the setting down of proper roots. The ground needed to be loosened up, or scarified. Apparently this had been obligingly done by wild boar for millenia, but something modern foresters had forgotten until now. Phil Whitfield, the Moray Forest district manager, was impressed, "Not only do we get a tough job done, but the standard of workmanship is exemplary. As well as scarifying the ground and munching their way through layers of roots and vegetation, the boars' dung fertilises the ground creating perfect conditions for young saplings to develop".

This and other initiatives encourage the thought that the sterile grip of managed forestry might be softening, and that the regiments of pines scarring Border hillsides might be allowed to fray at their sharp, rectilinear edges.

The Catrail follows the ridge above the confluence of the rivers Ettrick and Tweed and passes very close to a prehistoric fort known as the Rink. Sitting a hundred metres or so above the watermeetings, the site is not particularly elevated, but it is clearly visible from considerable distances. Most dramatically seen from the water, it dominates the last few miles of the course of the Ettrick. It was important for the house of a leader to be obvious in the landscape so that it could act as a physical focus of authority. The confluence of two wide and deep rivers naturally created a place of exchange and trade, and archaeologists have found strong evidence of intensive flint production over a long period at the Rink. Even now the gentle undulations of the fields below the old fort hint at the busy ghosts of a very distant past.

Climate change clearly helped the transition to farming. Milder and moister oceanic weather systems encouraged longer growing seasons, lusher grass and more widespread cultivation. And although pollen archaeology detects fluctuation — around 3100BC the Wildwood was regenerating faster than it was being destroyed — the general movement towards settled farming intensified over time. The effect of this can be seen not so much in direct evidence, such as an increase in the number and scale of farm sites themselves, but rather in what is implied. More successful food production increased population and this in turn led to larger and more ambitious religious monuments built by large groups of people with resources and time.

Before it rushes through the beautiful Neidpath gorge, the Tweed is joined by the Lyne Water. Although no great surging river, it brings something more to the watermeeting. The Lyne connected Upper Tweeddale to the head of the Clyde Valley, and through the Biggar Gap, people, animals and trade would come. From the north, down the valley of the Meldon Burn, there was access to the Lothians, and east, through the gorge, downstream to the Tweed basin. Lyne was a busy crossroads.

The prehistoric peoples of Britain made no distinction between politics, trade, religion, or indeed any other activity. And when a place had an economic importance, it tended to accrete every other sort as well. A few hundred metres before it joins the Tweed, the Lyne Water meets the Meldon Burn to form a raised river promontary of around 20 acres. Across the neck of this area a huge 600m long stockade was raised c2200BC. Massive posts standing between 3 and 4 metres in height enclosed a triangular precinct which was entered by a wide passage 25m long. What exactly happened inside the immense stockade cannot be clearly understood. But this general area was a particularly holy place in prehistory. Very near to the precinct were three burial cairns, two standing stones and the remnants of a long barrow. All that can be reasonably conjectured is that the stockade marked a Holy of Holies, a place different from the surrounding area by reason of its extreme sanctity. Unlike a Christian rood screen, or the inner sanctum of a classical temple, this very large 20 acre area seems not to be designed to exclude lay people, but rather expressly to include very many of them. But once inside, what they did is a mystery to us now.

Riverside communities living on fertile land built large monuments in the Borders, but nothing more than the shadows of most survive. Millenia of ploughing have almost completely obliterated henges at Sprouston, Springwood Park near Kelso, Ancrum, and Channelkirk. North of Kelso there is an intriguing juxtaposition where the henge at Mellerstain is aligned with three standing stones on Brotherstone Hill. The north-east to south-west axis is the same as with the Mutiny Stones.

Even though they are harder to remove than the ditches and posts of henges, the larger elements of stone circles and alignments, like those at Brotherstone, are still not numerous in the Borders. Perhaps the most atmospheric place, somewhere a fleeting sense of these forgotten mysteries might be had, is a small monument at Duddo in North Northumberland. Standing on a low ridge which looks both to the Cheviots and to the sea at Berwick, the stone circle is as carefully placed as any. But it is the stones themselves which take the place out of time. Five are large and over forty centuries have been chiselled into remarkable shapes by the wind. Fluted, pockmarked and even defaced by modern hands, they seem impervious to all that happens around them, stubborn and defiant. At the Duddo Stones it is impossible to feel anything other than a close affinity for the nameless people who dragged them overland and toiled to set them upright, forever.

Much less dramatic, but more prosaically human, is a series of discoveries in the Manor Valley, not far from the ceremonial complex at Lyne. Field walkers have come across scatters of heat-shattered stones, often in a horseshoe shape, sitting on a bed of soil containing large quantities of charcoal. These are known as burnt mounds, and they appear to have had two functions. Generally sited near streams, they were places where large volumes of water were boiled. A slab or wood-lined pit was filled and then large stones heated in a fire. The water could be brought quickly to the boil by placing the stones into the pit. It seems likely that quantities of hot food could be prepared by using this simple process that needed no metal pots or cauldrons. However, North American Indians also made burnt mounds for another purpose. Just as in Scandinavian saunas, the hot stones were used to make steam inside an enclosed space where people could sit comfortably. 25 mounds were found in the Manor Valley dating from around 2000BC, and their use does much to dismiss the notion that prehistoric peoples lived lives of filth, gloom and brutish ignorance. In fact the discovery of later polished bronze mirrors and tools for shaving and hair cutting foster an opposite view — that prehistoric peoples went to considerable trouble over their appearance.

When bronze technology came to be gradually adopted in the Borders, the new and stronger axes accelerated the process of woodland clearance markedly. But early Bronze age finds tend to be few and singular; an awl, a pin, a small dagger. The only substantial item which appears in the record in hoards, or indeed in any quantity, is the axe. Fourteen socketed axes were found at Kalemouth near Kelso, and another seven had been buried at Eildon Mid Hill. For the Borderers of three millenia ago, it appears that the axe never lost its fascination.

3

Language and Silence

If the day had been still and sunny, the effect would have been even more stunning, and certainly more frightening. In the spring of 79AD something far beyond the experience of almost all who watched it appeared in the Borders. Identically dressed and marching in tightly regulated columns, thousands of men tramped over the Cheviot Hills down into the Tweed Valley and made straight for the landmark Eildon Hills. With their armour and helmets glinting in the sunshine, red and yellow shields a river of colour flowing through the landscape, the sight of such a huge force of 10,000 men and riders will have been made much stranger, perhaps even otherworldly, by the fact that they all looked the same. Few watching had ever seen uniforms before, and to some the Roman army might have seemed to behave as one being, a giant articulated machine with thousands of men animating its head, body, arms and legs.

For those within a mile or two of the column, the effect will have been compounded by the strange noise made by the giant. Instead of the human sounds of talking or singing, uncountable marching feet beat out a dull and steady thud, thud, thud as they pounded along the tracks found by their scouts. Punctuated by an occasional parade-ground bark from the centurions who directed the column, the Romans marched in silence and, it appeared, without showing any sign of stopping.

Up on the ramparts of the sacred enclosure on Eildon Hill North, the king, his priests and warriors were watching. They knew that the Romans would come in the spring, but nothing had prepared them for the awesome sight that snaked through the trees towards them. Flanking and preceeding the column were detachments of cavalry sent to circle the advance and report any hostile movement, any possibility of hindrance up ahead. After the successful negotiations of the previous summer, no difficulties were expected, but Gnaeus Julius Agricola was an experienced and cautious general with good reason to mistrust the British tribes. As a young military tribune, he had seen the appalling slaughter and destruction of the Boudicca Revolt eighteen years before. And even though he believed that the Votadini would co-operate, and offer no resistance to his meticulously planned advance, the imperial government had also agreed a treaty with the Iceni of the south-east. In the event, that had meant nothing to Queen Boudicca.

In their battle order, the eagles in front and their commanders on horseback, it was important for the Roman column to impress, and to suppress any lingering thoughts of native resistance. The men of the Second Augusta and the Ninth Hispana were experienced soldiers and, knowing they were being watched, would have put on a stern show of imperial military power. When they reached the banks of the Tweed at the place identified by Agricola's surveyors, the centurions split the column formation into a very large square. On their command, each soldier set down his pack, took out an entrenching tool and began to cut into the turf. With the benefit of much practice and clockwork precision, it took the legionaries only two or three hours to dig a perimeter ditch and use the soil to set up a palisade. Inside, leather tents were unloaded from the baggage train and pitched in a rectilinear arrangement. And finally, if they were not on watch, the soldiers were allowed to fall out and unbuckle their armour.

None of the foregoing was recorded at the time in any text which has survived. And yet most of it is unarguable. There are plenty of extant descriptions of a Roman army on the march, historians know exactly what the legionaries wore and carried as standard kit, archaeologists can confirm marching camps all over Britain and their arrival at Newstead in 79AD is an undisputed fact. What is mysterious is the identity of the watchers. Who was standing on the ramparts of Eildon Hill North? Who were these kings, priests and warriors? When the legionary cavalry swept the river valleys in advance of Agricola's march, what did they think they might find?

For anyone genuinely interested in a history of the Borders, these are the central, but extremely difficult, questions. The Romans came, saw, conquered — and most of them went. Certainly they deserve a prime place in this narrative, but they must not be allowed to overwhelm it for 400 years. Or even worse, be allowed to start it. There is a long and dishonourable tradition of beginning histories of Britain with Julius Caesar's landing on the Channel coast in 55BC. Generally this remarkable dismissal is justified in windy phrases telling us that at this point, our island 'emerged into history' or 'came out of the shadows', or became 'part of the European mainstream'. It is as though nothing of any importance happened before the Romans decided to include us in their empire.

Border histories are no better. In his 'Roxburgh, Selkirk and Peebles', published in 1899 as part of the County Histories of Scotland, Sir George Douglas, Bart. has Agricola in the first sentence. In 'Border History' by George Ridpath (1848) his appearance is delayed — until the second sentence. The reasons for this stubborn tradition are both straightforward and sinister. Until recently, written records were the only sound currency for the historian, and after 79AD Agricola's campaign was reported by his son-in-law, Tacitus, in a Latin text which has come down to us. Other written sources exist to supplement and corroborate this and the Roman habit of leaving dated inscriptions and coins has also helped organise their occupation of Northern Britain into a reasonably coherent story.

These are the practical reasons why historians might have concentrated so relentlessly on what the Romans had to say about Britain and the Borders. But another, unstated set of attitudes bubbles under the surface of forensic objectivity. This is from the first page of George Ridpath's 'Border History'

"It is probable that, by these conquests of Agricola, the people inhabiting the country which afterwards became the borders between Scotland and England, together with the adjacent provinces betwixt the territories of the ancient Brigantes on the south, and the Friths of Forth and Clyde in the north, were brought into some degree of civilisation, and first taught to abandon their rude and wandering life, in order to dwell in towns and fixed habitations."

And here is the opening paragraph of Sir George Douglas' history;

'The Life of Agricola by Tacitus may be described as the false dawn of Border history. In that beautiful little monograph — a model of classical dignity and condensation of style, some of whose phrases have passed into stock quotations — the light of literature falls for the first time on our Border-land. But it falls there only to be withdrawn again, plunging the country which for the twinkling of an eye it had illuminated back into darkness for a thousand years.'

Now, when the assumptions rumbling around inside these, and other, similar ways of thinking are unpacked, a clear set of distinctions and preferences becomes obvious. It runs something like this. The Romans were civilised, more like us and as the recent owners of a large empire, we British can identify somewhat with their problems. Inasmuchas we can make them out through the gloom, the natives were, by contrast, primitive, not at all like us and if they made any impact on history, it was as a disruptive influence on the Pax Romana. A bit like the occasional episodes of irksome non-cooperation from those natives fortunate enough to be part of the Great British Empire.

While this may verge on caricature, the general lines are clear enough, and repeated over and over. But what is far from obvious is the logic of an astonishing mis-identification at the heart of the dichotomy. These pesky, ignorant and ignored natives, and not the Romans, were our ancestors, our people, us. The Romans came here and to scores of other places in search of empire, glory and money and they had no more interest in the Borders than the 19th century career diplomats who cut their teeth in the Indian Civil Service had in India. Their focus was elsewhere, back home. Why have we been so uninterested in who we were? The inescapable feeling is one of historical snobbery, that we would not have been seen dead with our ancestors.

BRITANNIA BARBARICA

The Greeks not only invented the word 'barbarian' from their equivalent of 'blah, blah, blah', but also the idea. When the mighty Persian Empire expanded westwards and was stopped at Thermopylae, Marathon and Salamis by the Greek city states, their resistance formed attitudes as well as battle-lines. Before the Persian Wars Greek culture shows little sense of a difference between themselves and other peoples. The Trojans seem to be more like the Greeks than unlike, and other outsiders sometimes acquire a god-like status, something in the way that the Aztecs treated the Spanish Conquistadores and their horses. But when the despots of the east, Darius and Xerxes, seriously threatened the existence of Athens, Sparta, Corinth and the other cities, attitudes changed sharply.

The great playwright, Aeschylus, had fought at the Battle of Marathon, and his play, 'The Persae', shows them as slitty-eyed, cruel, foreign, arrogant — and barbarian. The Greeks are, of course, the epitome of civilization.

This distinction runs like a poisoned thread through European history. Because of the pattern of migration and the funnel-like shape of Europe's geography, tribes, ethnic groups and nations have always feared and despised the peoples who live to the east. Like a set of evil dominoes our prejudice against the Germans (the Huns) is echoed in their feelings about the Slavs (Untermenschen) and in turn their views of those who live east of the Urals and so on, and on.

Allied to this is a deep-seated territorial fear of peoples who move. During the era of Die Volkerwanderung, the Folk Migrations of the early first millenium AD, the Roman Empire fought a long losing battle against peoples on the move, those who had no homeland. These fears still exist and the treatment meted out to the Gypsies, who arrived in Europe from India in the 11th century, continues a long and shameful tradition.

In Britain an intriguing series of attitude transfers took place over time. At first the Romans despised the native British as barbarians, and the informal name for Southern Scotland between the walls, an area sometimes included in the province and sometimes not, was Britannia Barbarica, or Barbarian Britain. In turn the native British may have called the Romans something like 'Y Rhufeiniwr' (phonetically, Roovanoor). When the Anglo-Saxons arrived, they assumed the role of the despised. But in the 7th century the Northumbrian kings managed to reverse the process by developing an aura of Romanitas, or Roman-ness, and the Celts of the west came to be seen as inferior.

English journalists have recently shown that these attitudes are still robustly alive; in The Sunday Times' in 1997, the restaurant critic, Adrian Gill, described the Welsh as 'dark, ugly, pugnacious little trolls', and on BBC television in March 2001 the quiz host, Anne Robinson, declared that the Welsh were 'irritating' and asked 'what are they for?'

But in the secret recesses of the Welsh language, there is an older version of history which goes back to the Anglo-Saxon invasions. The English are still the barbarians to the east, the despised Sais who have no knowledge of the glories of Yr Iaith Hen, the old language, and speak a version of 'blah, blah, blah' what the Welsh call Yr Iaith Fain — the thin language.

So, reviewing the available evidence, what can be said about the people who lived in the Borders in 79AD? First and most obvious, their story follows directly on what could be sensibly said about the first farmers and hunter-gatherers. That means going back at least a thousand years before the legions came and looking hard at how society was developing and changing in the course of the first millenium BC. And second, and most determinant, we need to remember that for much of this period these people spoke a language which we can understand, admittedly with some difficulty, and which was the ancestor of a modern language still spoken in Britain. From some time around the middle of the first millenium BC, a form of early Welsh was spoken in the Borders (and over the rest of Britain). This language survived unbroken to find expression as literature nearly 1500 years later, and more important, to find itself the vehicle of a coherent culture which we can recognise and which allows us to break the historical silence and build a strong sense of how life was lived in the Borders 2500 years ago.

This culture became known as Celtic, and much of it still exists. The handiest and most accurate modern definition of what Celtic means revolves around language, and the persistence of ancient speech communities in the west of Britain and Ireland. Inside the Gaelic and Welsh-speaking cultures of the west there exist long and unbroken traditions, habits and ways of seeing Britain which can help fill out the bare bones of the archaeology of the Borders for the 1st millenium BC.

Archaeologists first characterised the Celts as matchless metal-workers, and also located the origins of their culture in central Europe. At Halstatt in Austria artefacts from the period 750BC to 400BC have revealed a skill and sophistication not seen in Europe until that time. The slashing longsword known as the spatha is symbolic of a warrior-based Celtic society centred on defended hillforts. Their smiths could combine a hard iron spine with a softer cutting edge that could be honed razor-sharp to make the spatha an elegant and fearsome weapon. It was favoured by warriors fighting on horseback and was at its bloody best when a trooper used it to slash downwards on infantrymen. The Celts of Halstatt also made many other things; jewellery, horse-drawn chariots, coins and beautifully turned pottery. This much sought-after output made the central European Celts great traders, and it may be that it was through a mercantile network that their language spread quickly to the east and south, and most enduringly, to the west and Britain and Ireland.

Weapons like the spatha also made the Celts formidable; in 390BC they sacked the city of Rome, and in 270BC the Greek city of Delphi fell to them. Without much exaggeration, one historian has called them the first masters of Europe.

The only real difficulty with such a description is that it implies movement, or at least takeover of some kind. While that may have happened on the European mainland, as it did in the age of great folk migrations after the collapse of the Western Roman Empire, it is highly unlikely that large numbers of Celts sailed to Britain and Ireland on any sort of expedition. More credible is the slow process of acculturation. The British became Celts as the languages and their culture probably followed in the wake of trade around the coastline.

In any event the eventual outcome of contact was a thoroughly Celtic society in Britain and Ireland by the end of the 1st millenium BC. A picture of what that society was like can be pieced together from the archaeological record, from a close study of language and names, and also by sensible analogy with other Celtic cultures, including that of the 21st century.

No-one who visits the Borders can fail to notice the Eildon Hills. Standing out proud from the rolling farmland of the Tweed Valley, they dominate the landscape, finishing or featuring in almost every vista. Three peaks from the rim of an old volcano, the Eildons can be seen from most main routes, drawing the eye of every traveller towards them. The Romans chose them as a focal point, called the place Trimontium, which sounds very like the translation of a native name. Perhaps they were originally known as Trimynydd (Treeminuth) or Threehills. Just in the way that they do now, the Eildons fascinated the prehistoric peoples of the Tweed basin.

Around 1000BC these people began to protect themselves and their homes. Archaeologists have uncovered walls, ditches, stockades and banks enclosing settlements dating from that time. Clearly the considerable labour involved was undertaken for good reasons — and the only possible logic is that a wish for greater security grew out of increased risks of attack, dispossession and violent death. There are no records to show why people became more fearful and society more prone to conflict and competition. But there must be a strong likelihood that a rising population was fighting over the ownership of good agricultural land. However that may be, the older open settlements of round houses and enclosed fields of the sort excavated at Green Knowe in Peeblesshire were abandoned, and the long era of the hillforts began.

In the Borders there are hundreds of hillforts, many more than in the rest of Scotland. Their sites seems to follow the river-systems rather than seek out good, defensible places in the higher ground. That suggests a close relationship with a hinterland of pasture and fields, and the people who worked them. In that context it is difficult to resist the notion of a strong warrior-chief occupying a fort and offering protection and refuge in return for a tax in farming produce. The perimeters of many of the forts appear to require too many men to defend them like a rampart, and they may have been corrals to keep valuable beasts in one place while the fighting, or negotiation, went on in the open or at least in some sort of limited way like skirmishing or possibly single combat.

There are forts all over the Tweed basin but the map shows noticable clusters in the Teviot Valley, the Leader and the Upper Tweed above Peebles. Significantly in the hill country of the Ettrick and Yarrow, the territory of the Selgovae, there are very few. Generally the forts are small and appear to be domestic in nature, as though the thatched roundhouses of Green Knowe had been transposed to a hilltop. But a few others are quite different in scale. Eildon Hill North is not the highest of the three hills but its summit is flatter with a dramatic and uninterrupted aspect to the east and the sweep of the Tweed Valley to the sea. At the beginning of the first millenium BC a huge settlement was built on the hill. 300 hut platforms, with room for 200 more, were laid out on a 39 acre site inside a ditched perimeter skirting the summit for more than a mile. By far the largest hillfort in Scotland, it may occasionally have had a population of between 2000 and 3000, the equivalent of the town of Melrose lying at its foot. What sustained this huge settlement was its location. Impressive and singular (or rather triple) it stood not amongst a range of other hills but in an area of rich, riverside farmland on all sides. That was what made the hill particularly important and its rulers powerful. The name of Eildon Hill itself also hints at a long period of primacy and occupation. When the Old Welsh language became general in the Borders the hill had already been a focus for many generations. Eildon simply means the Old Fort.

The hut platforms on the summit measure 7 to 8 metres across and imply buildings big enough for between 6 and 10 people. Even on the top of a windy hill roundhouses could be comfortable, with a central hearth and screened off sections around the walls for sleeping and storage. But they must have been gloomy. Because there were no windows, all available light was needed and doorways faced east, towards the rising sun while eating and daytime tasks were done in the southern part of a house and sleeping in the north.

The houses on Eildon Hill North were not substantial buildings. Little evidence of the rock-cut post holes needed to support a large roof have been found and it appears that turf, wattle and wood were used rather than stone. These materials leave little trace. In this there is an implication that the hill was fully occupied only at certain times by a population that dispersed throughout the farming hinterland once business in the fort had been concluded. However, only 1% of the site has been excavated and the remains of larger and more impressive buildings may be waiting under the grass.

The everyday detail uncovered by archaeologists sometimes concentrates so closely on the practical as to forget the spiritual. This was a distinction not made by the early peoples of Britain; they did not divide their lives, as we do, into secular and religious sectors. Their beliefs informed everything they did. And if Eildon Hill North was thought to be a place of sanctity, then matters of comfort, the availability of building materials and any other quotidien consideration will have come a long way second in their thinking.

High places attracted prehistoric peoples. The megalithic monuments of the early farmers show a sustained and complex interest in astronomy and the calendar, and it may be that hills were simply an obvious way to get closer to the sky and its gods. Dramatic hills like the Eildons were only more obvious stairways to the stars, and some of the magic that swirled around their tops can still be understood. Shape-shifting mountains were thought to be sacred, and the veneration of Schiehallion in Perthshire is recorded in early modern tradition. The name 'Sidh Chailleann' means in Gaelic 'Fairy Hill of the Caledonians' or the Picts. Viewed from different standpoints, the mountain appears to change its shape quite radically — a thing which we can accept now, as users of rapid transport through our geography, but something which struck early peoples as magical. And as a single conical peak visible from many different aspects, Ruberslaw is also a shape-shifter. With three summits constantly changing their relationship to each other as a traveller approached or moved around them, the Eildons will have appeared even more otherworldly. And what will have particularly excited reverence was the patent fact that there are three hills. Three was a magic number and profound belief in its power can be found in many aspects of prehistoric religion. Shape-shifting encouraged the gods to use three names or take at least three different manifestations or be one part of a group of three. While these permutations (and not all are triplicities) seem to us to be confusing, even chaotic, they will have made sense of a sort we cannot now grasp. They had to, because understanding the minds of the gods was thought to be a matter of life and death for the Celts of Britain. The names of hundreds of their gods are known but the significance of only a very few are understood in any way. Two of them carried a club and seem to have required much propitiation to restrain their violent dispositions; Cernunnos was a horned being usually shown in a sitting posture, and Dagda was an immensely strong giant. Carlisle got its name from Lugh, the god of the crafts and arts so important to the Celts of Europe and other cities, such as Lyons, Leyden and Leon remember him. The word 'pony' may derive from Epona, the goddess of horses and fertility, and the Morrigan was a flesh-eating raven queen who stalked the dead on the battlefield. While it is difficult to visualise a pantheon of Celtic gods of the sort that the Greeks and Romans had, there are some general comments worth making. First and most obvious, these were not always benevolent deities and some, like Dagda and Cernunnos, could often be malicious. And as a result the Celts were anxious not so much to give thanks to their gods but to propitiate them with offerings and sacrifices. Some of these sacrifices were undoubtedly human. Bodies of people from the first millenium BC have been preserved in the acidic soil of peat bogs, and post mortems have revealed a ritual death. A man found in Lindow Moss in Cheshire (nicknamed Pete Marsh) was killed in a triple death; hit on the head twice with mortal force, throttled and his throat cut. There was no sign of restraint of any sort. It appears that Pete was a high status individual who did no manual work, and who may have been a priest himself, a Druid. And archaeologists believe that he went to his death willingly. In the mysterious ceremonies of the Celts of Britain, there is a palpable sense of an oppressive and fearful religious atmosphere which, with our Christian cultural background of love and forgiveness, we find difficult to comprehend or even feel comfortable with.

Place-names at the foot of the Eildon Hills remember more magic. Christianised now into St Mary's Well, Monks Well and St Dunstan's Well, or neutralised as Greenwells, or simply forgotten like the excavated wells near the Roman camp at Newstead, there is an extensive series of springs and wells which attracted the prehistoric priests and peoples of the 1st millenium BC. Watery places were seen as portals to the Otherworld, and for 3000 years wells have been venerated in Britain. Nowadays, without knowing why, we still propitiate these forgotten gods when we throw coins off bridges, and even in modern, high-rise hotels so-called water features in the foyer glint with silver offerings. Perhaps the most famous object to be thrown into a watery place was a sword. In the gilded medieval versions of the story, Sir Bedivere takes

Excaliber from the dying King Arthur and goes to a lakeside where he hurls it into the water. But just before it splashes into the surface, a hand and arm clothed in white samite reaches up and catches the hilt. It is a wonderful image and, surprisingly, one of the few authentic elements in the romantic renditions of the tale. Celtic priests threw many swords, shields and other metal artefacts into lochs and nowhere more enthusiastically than in the Borders.

In several places objects of great beauty have been found preserved in boggy areas or partially drained pools which used to be lochs. At Yetholm three magnificent bronze shields came to light which show how sophisticated the skills of smiths had become. The central boss is surrounded by concentric ribs which imitate the more practical wooden shields with rings of bronze studs. Using a repoussé technique where the rings on the side intended to be seen are carefully hammered out from the reverse, the smiths took care not to make a massively heavy shield which would be awkward to hold for any length of time. For it appears that the Yetholm shields were not intended for warfare; they are altogether too insubstantial to take or deflect a dunt of any weight. Rather it seems that they were made for a ceremonial use, and clearly a use which glorified or sanctified the wielder of weapons and the practicioners of warfare. After a time, the shields were given to the gods and either placed or thrown into a loch, possibly as a propitiation before a battle.

Massive hoards of metal have been found at Blackburn Mill near Chirnside in Berwickshire and at Eckford Moss near Kelso. These offerings were important occasions probably attended by large numbers of people. A small jetty was built so that a priest (this person may have also been the leader of a tribe, there is Irish evidence to show that kings had a religious role) could walk out to deeper parts of the loch to cast objects into it. At Eckford and Blackburn Mill these included cauldrons, dress fasteners, horse gear as well as weapons. In a bog near Stichill a bronze collar was was found. Intended to be worn like a piece of jewellry, it is perhaps the most beautiful artefact yet to re-emerge from the water. At Newstead there are hints of anxiety about the water gods. When wells outside the Roman camp were filled in, the priests were careful to placate them by placing animal sacrifices as well as metal in the shafts.

BOG BUTTER

Archaeologists have found wooden buckets or bark containers buried in peat bogs. They contain a hard, yellow substance. Some historians appear to be puzzled by it, wondering if it is a sacrifice like the swords and metalwork found in lochs, or a face cream, or hair oil. This is butter. Until the 19th century British crofters were making butter by an ancient method. And then, lest it spoil in the summer when milk was plentiful enough to allow its manufacture, they put it in strong containers and buried it in cool, peaty bog land. Sometimes they forgot where they had put it, forgot to dig it up, or died before they needed it.

In Orkney, until recently, butter was made by prehistoric methods. First milk was allowed to stand in a churn for two or three days until it thickened naturally. Then hot 'kirnin' stones were dropped in to speed the separation process. When the yellow butter had gathered at the top of the churn, it was carefully lifted out and the milk washed off with cold water. Any milk left in contact with the butter might have turned it sour. Then a knife was passed through to remove any animal hairs. After this simple process was complete, some butter was reserved for immediate use while the bulk of it was put into a wooden container. Sometimes as much as a hundredweight was stored at once, and in Ireland there was a habit of seasoning butter with wild garlic and leaving it in a bog-hole to mature, like cheese. Once a container was full, a deep hole was dug down until the peat felt cool enough to the touch. The bucket was then packed tight and buried. Prehistoric people understood the anaerobic qualities of peat-bogs and used them like long-term freezers. And like most of us, they sometimes forgot what they had put in the freezer.

In addition to throwing coins, our equivalent of the Yetholm shields and Stichill collar, into water, there was a strong tradition of 'visiting' wells in a ritual ceremony which persisted as late as the 19th century. These visits took place on significant days, May 1st and August 1st and at Colwell, near Chollerton in North Northumberland, a well was 'dressed' on Midsummer Sunday as late as the 1890s. This tradition still survives in the Peak District around the spa town of Buxton, and it involves elaborate arrangements of particular flowers and leaves of a certain colour being placed at the well, generally by women. Clearly pagan in origin and very ancient, the well-dressings have been sanitised and disguised as commemorations of saints and the alleged christian associations at each site.

These are memories of a powerful tradition that persuaded prehistoric people to throw into water their most precious objects; weapons, armour, pots and in one spectacular late example, coins. At the bottom of Coventina's Well on Hadrian's Wall, more than 13,000 were found. Evidence of metal-working on Eildon Hill North is clear and it may be that much of its output, such as the hoard of socketed axes found nearby, was intended for sacrifices associated with rituals on the hill.

Shape-shifting, and proximity to the gods and their holy wells are not the only reasons why Eildon Hill North should be seen as a magic mountain. The tradition of sanctity was powerful enough to reach into the medieval period and inform the famous tale of Thomas the Rhymer. Its proper telling belongs elsewhere in this narrative, but one determinant aspect was its location. The Queen of Elfland met True Thomas on Huntlie Bank as she rode down by the Eildon Tree. And it was there that they slipped through a crack in time to spend seven years in the Otherworld. For the 14th century listeners to the ballad of Thomas the Rhymer, Eidlon Hill North had lost little of its magic.

In 1000BC the first people to climb the hill to scoop out and level off the hut platforms and throw up the rampart were not Celts. By the time the Roman legions arrived in 79AD, they undoubtedly were. Exactly when and how their culture, and most crucially, their language changed is impossible to tell but the nature and pattern of the occupation of the hill might help to explain something of the process.

Between 800 and 400BC it appears that the great settlement was at least partially abandoned. Climate archaeology has shown those four centuries to have been a time of consistently high rainfall, much wetter than it ever been. 1100 feet up on Eildon Hill North, bad weather would have been even worse. And although only a small proportion of the site has been dug, it looks as though few people braved the rainstorms on the hill in the middle centuries of the first millenium BC.

ESKDALEMUIR WEATHER

Like the Hunter-Gatherers and Farmers of 6000 years ago, it may be that we are living in a period of climate change. The Eskdalemuir Weather Observatory has been keeping records since it was established in 1908. In the last 5 years it has recorded a series of extreme fluctuations. February 1997 was the wettest month since records began, in January 1996 there were only 9 hours of sunshine — in the whole month, and the blizzards of 5th and 6th February 1996 left 50cms of snow on the ground.

Taken together, and detached from their context, this list of grim statistics may indeed be a cause for serious concern. But the fact that they come from Eskdalemuir should be reassuring. It is a peculiarly Scottish institution. Founded in a place that regularly experiences some of the very worst weather in Britain, its function may be morale-boosting as well as scientific. If the weather is bad at Eskdalemuir, then that is as bad as it can get, and it is likely to be better everywhere else. In this important way, by regularly propping up the table of rainfall and temperature, it renders a service to the rest of the United Kingdom. And since no-one lives there except the meteorologists (who ought, in any case, to be interested in the weather, however bad), there is little sense of anyone suffering on our behalf. Here are some samples of the sort of statistics that swirl around the observatory.

* on 70% of mornings the cloud cover is total.

* there are 1130 hours of steady rain every year.

* frost has been recorded in every month of the year.

* there is ground frost on 112 nights annually.

* the evaporation from the surrounding forest is so great that the high humidity often makes it impossible to tell where the mist ends and the cloud begins.

Apart from the meteorological, there exist other sorts of evidence to shed some light on what the magic mountain was really used for. Festivals were important to the Celts. Four were held each year but not in the sort of January to December order that we might expect now. Each of them ultimately became saints or quarter days but their placing in the calendar was originally influenced by the activities and needs of cattle and sheep, and the crops grown to feed them and those who herded them.

Samhain was a festival held at the end of October and it was seen as the beginning of the Celtic year. As with all the festivals it was a time when fires were lit on hilltops and people climbed up to take part in religious rites, celebrations, dancing, story-telling, sports and much else. Toponomists offer corroboration in surviving Border place-names. Tinto Hill near Lamington takes its name from Teine for fire and it meant, simply, Fire Hill. At Samhain and at the other three festivals, the Celts believed that the barrier between the real and tangible world of the present and what they called the Otherworld of eternity were gossamer-thin, and that at any time, a man, woman or changeling child might be pulled through a crack in time and simply disappear. Part of the function of the Celtic priests who were called Druids was to protect their people from these fears and a favoured way in which they believed they succeeded was to build a charmed circle. We remember the phrase but forget where it comes from. The Celts were certain that the soul of a human being resided solely in the head, and for this reason they often decapitated their vanquished enemies and displayed their heads on poles. In north Britain this belief seems to have been exceptionally strong for more representations of Celtic heads have come to light than in the more populous south. The Druids used skulls in some way to ring the festival fires at Samhain with charm circles which were also known as ghost fences. We still do this today. Halloween is celebrated on October 31st, on Samhain Eve, when children carry hollowed out turnip lanterns with faces carved on the front and candles lit inside for dramatic effect. As witches and warlocks fly through the night sky, children will protect themselves with these direct descendents of Druid ghost fences.

When the great fires burned low on the festival hills and children began to fall asleep in their warm glow, adults would drink deep from their cups of beer, mead and wine and then take soot and ash from the edges of the dying fire and streak their faces in symbolic disguise. And then sometimes they would take a partner who was not the person they had children with and go off into the darkness to make love with them. This sort of structured sexual licence is the origin of guizing, and the spluttering fulmination of Kirk sessions all over Scotland well into the 18th century shows that this was a Celtic tradition that died very hard. Nowadays with the Kirk triumphant, or at least accepted, only children go guizing. The great fires of Samhain were shifted by London politics and the pyre of a Catholic plotter to November 5th, no doubt to the great relief of the Kirk and the zealous hypocrites who ran it.

That all of these rituals took place in the Borders, and well into the Middle Ages and beyond, there can be no doubt. Four times a year the Celts of the Tweed basin climbed their magic mountain. Before the warbands of the Angles funnelled up the Tweed Valley in the early 7th century, Eildon Hill North was a place of kings and priests. And when the Germanic invaders arrived they gave it a telling name. They called it Aeled-Dun, the Fire Hill. And at Samhain, and at Imbolc on February 1st when the ewes began to lactate and could be milked to feed hungry mouths, and at the feast of Beltane on May 1st whe the sun was waxing warm and growth began, and Lughnasa on August 1st when cows had calved and the first cut of hay was in, the people would climb Eildon Hill to celebrate, worship and also probably to pay their taxes. At the western foot of the hills lies some of the evidence for this. Firstly there are great earthworks which initially look defensive in character — and indeed one which stretches from Cauldshiels Loch all the way to the Ale Water at Blackchester Fort near Newhall is still called the Military Road and was undoubtedly oriented to protect Eildon Hill from attack from the south west. But the other earthworks zig-zag in many directions and the only explanation which fits is that they were large stock pens. Since wealth was measured by the Celts in cattle and tax partly paid in them, that is more than plausible. Two tangible remnants of the Celtic festivals themselves survived into the modern period. Lughnasa, or what became known as the Lammas Fair at Melrose was held until the late 17th century at the foot of the Eildons on the site of the golf course, amongst the complex of ancient earthworks. And over at the eastern foot of the hills, St Boswells Fair is another Celtic remnant which survived until the present day, albeit in a less than meaningful form. Originally it was held on August 1st but in the 19th century it was moved to mid July to avoid a clash with another Lughnasa Fair — Kelso Show.

The kings, or kingly priests, who ruled over Eildon Hill North are anonymous figures in the literal sense that their names are not known, but there are strong clues as to who they were. The name of the Selgovae was not the only one supplied by the Roman historian, Tacitus. Three other tribal groups are noted in his history; the Votadini, the Novantae and the Damnonii. A later geographer, Ptolemy, placed all four tribes on an eccentric version of the map of Britain and Ireland. The Selgovae were to be found in the Ettrick Forest and the Southern Uplands, and probably Annandale and Nithsdale. The Novantae were further west in Galloway, the Damnonii in the Clyde Valley, and the Votadini in the Lothians, the Tweed Valley and North Northumberland.

LEES, HIRSTS AND PIRNIES

Border place-names are pungent reminders of the Wildwood and how long it lasted. The Jedforest has little more substance now than a memory, and an approximate location in the Cheviot foothills to the south of Jedburgh, reaching as far east as Wooden near Eckford and Gateshaw near Morebattle. But once it covered an even wider area. And although propped up and decrepit, its oldest remnant, the Capon Tree, is still alive. On the Ordnance Survey the name of the Ettrick Forest is marked over a large tract of land where few trees grow. Placed between the Yarrow and Ettrick river valleys and over the Sundhope Heights, it looks oddly adrift on the map. And yet in its later appearance, the great forest did not necessarily imply a dense green canopy of trees. Rather it was a wild place, somewhere to hunt and also the home of wild men. In a strange echo of the past, supporters of Selkirk Rugby Club occasionally encourage their players at Philiphaugh with a roar, "Hawway the lads o' the Forest".

Not only have the names of the great woods of the Borders survived, but the descriptions of what small parts of them looked like can still be found on signposts and addresses. The suffix 'wood' is an obvious label; Oakwood is not ambiguous, but Threepwood is from the Middle English 'threpen' for disputed or debatable wood, and Hartwoodburn remembers the stags who leaped the streams that ribboned through the Wildwood. 'Hirst' in the likes of Ferniehirst Castle means a wooded knoll, and the commonly found 'lea' or 'lie' in Blainslie, Whitelea, or Mossilee denoted a place where there were no trees, a clearing. Perhaps because they were tall and could be seen from a distance, or were different in some way or merely isolated, single trees could be seen as landmarks, and Pirnie near Maxton simply stands for 'The Tree'. More detail can be read at Primside by Yetholm. It was 'the settlement by the white tree'.

These names were not invented by Tacitus or pulled out of a stock of standard Latin or Roman labels. They meant something. Toponymists have looked hard at Old Welsh and tentatively produced 'for the Novantae, the Vigorous People, for the Damnonii, the Deepeners or the Miners, and for the Selgovae, the Hunters. The derivation of the name of the last group, the Votadini, is more problematic. Tacitus' Latin rendering is easily converted into the original Old Welsh, Guotodin, but what it meant is difficult to parse. The most likely interpretation may reflect the low-lying nature of their territory in Lothian and the Borders. Guotodin may simply mean the People of the Broad Place.

The king who sat on Eildon Hill North was a Guotodin king. The archaeology from Traprain Law, another singular and large hillfort in the Lothians, and another Guotodin centre, shows many similarities with Eildon. But perhaps more telling is the recent discovery that it was occupied throughout the life of the Roman camp at Newstead, perhaps only half a mile from its foot. Only a friendly power, the Guotodin or, in a Latinised version, the Votadini, would have been tolerated so close to the main army depot north of Hadrian's Wall. And if the primary purpose of that site was religious rather than military, the commander at Newstead would have been comfortable with its use, and happy that a handy focus for tax collecting already existed.

The Guotodin kings who ruled after 400BC were confident. The defensive ramparts of Eildon Hill North were neither impressive nor intimidating. And the long perimeter of more than a mile would have required a very substantial force of determined warriors to keep it intact. Entrances were always weak points and archaeologists have found no fewer than five. Eildon Hill North's ramparts have the feel of a boundary rather than a wall, a means of separating a holy place from the rest of the temporal world below. Earlier pagan monuments like the henges at Sprouston and Mellerstain or the enclosure at Meldon Bridge have a sense of this separation, as do later Christian precincts at such as Old Melrose or Coldingham. This impression of a spiritual rampart is reinforced by the discovery of two pits dug under it. One contains the skeleton of a horse, the other a ewe. And it looks very much like these were sacrifices made before the back-breaking toil of digging the ditches and building the banks began.

By extension this sense of a sacred boundary around the summit of Eildon Hill North supports the notion of a Guotodin king with a priestly role, probably aided by a caste of holy men. An elite group may have lived permanently on the magic mountain, and on each of the Celtic festivals, their people climbed up to join them in rituals, sacrifices to the sky gods and celebrations.

Because these festivals likely involved the payment of the tithes or taxes needed to maintain a Priest-King, his holy men and his warband, the Guotodin people will have brought some of their wealth with them. If cattle and other livestock were driven into the earthwork pens at the foot of the three hills, then they doubtless presented a tempting target to enemies. The existence and orientation of the huge linear earthwork known as the Military Road suggests strongly that attack might have come from the south-west, from the territory of the Selgovae. The Military Road is different from other earthworks in the Borders. It is elaborate and important. And unlike other, simpler constructions of a ditch and bank, it has an arrangement of two ditches and two banks, or two ditches with the spoil heaped up between them into a single large bank. The Road runs for at least four and a half miles and was originally much longer, and also supported by three small forts at Rowchester, Blackchester and Cauldshiels Hill. The scale of this earthwork is unparalleled in the Tweed Basin, except by the settlement on the summit of Eildon Hill North. These two sites are clearly related and the purpose of the Military Road was to protect the kings on the hill.

But from what exactly? The arrangement and placing of the banks and ditches suggest a role similar to a modern set of anti-tank defences, a design intended to stop or slow a cavalry charge, or more likely, the advance of a squadron of chariots. Plenty of evidence exists for British and Irish Celtic society's use of war-chariots and there is no doubt that the Selgovae had them. The remains of the technology needed to build horsedrawn vehicles has been found in their territory.

At the foot of the steep slopes of Horsehope Craig in the Manor Valley near Peebles, a shepherd was working his dog in the spring of 1859. Amongst the scatter of the scree a dull glint caught his eye. Partly hidden by the smaller stones surrounding a very large boulder, he saw some small metal rings and a socketed axehead. Putting them in his pocket he walked down the Manor Water to Glenrath to find Mr Linton, the farmer. That afternoon both men went back to the scree and near the large boulder they found dozens of bronze objects, a prehistoric hoard. There were several axeheads, rings known as terrets (used to connect the leather straps of a bridle), various bands, and small mountings moulded with a design of concentric circles. When the objects were first examined by antiquarians, they were declared unique. Nothing like them had been found in Scotland, or Britain. And the only possible comparisons were with the metalwork of the Celtic cultures of Halstatt in central Europe. Dated around 750BC the mountings, rings and bands were recognised as the constituent pieces of a miniature wagon or cart, something made for display rather than use. And more, the circumstances of the find at Horsehope Craig suggested persuasively that the hoard of bronze had been buried as an offering, a sacrifice of precious objects to the gods of the earth. Just as weapons were later thrown into lochs at Yetholm and Eckford, so the Selgovae made an offering of what was central and precious to their culture — horse gear.

Other finds in the Borders have confirmed the use of two-horse chariots some time after 500BC. These were favoured in Britain because the original equestrian breeding stock appears to have been small. Two fast ponies hitched to a chariot was certainly a much more fearsome proposition than one cavalry trooper whose legs dangled close to the ground. In fact Celtic horsemanship was advanced and innovative. In order to give a charioteer the sort of response he needed at high speeds over uneven ground, the curb bit was developed. Smiths made an H-shaped piece of iron where the horizontal bar fitted into the pony's mouth and chains were attached to the top of the vertical bars. The idea was to create leverage on the lower jaw and allow the charioteer to pull the pony's head down and to either side. This gave quick control, and a well-schooled team would need only a flick of the reins to turn them instantly. In battle these skills might make a difference between life and death.

Chariots rarely carried only the driver. With both hands full of reins and both eyes on the terrain, he was scarcely in a position to fight. An archer and probably a spear-thrower stood beside him, with their feet braced on the flexible leather basket-work that formed the floor of the chariot. During the Boudicca Rebellion of 60/61AD British charioteers drove into the midst of the battle and their passengers appear to have alighted to fight.

Ponies were always well turned out for warfare; their coats groomed, their tails and manes plaited. But although charioteers will have taken a natural pride in the appearance of their teams, this was not a matter of show, but practicality. Tails were bound into tight bands so that they did not foul the harness or any part of the chariot or yoke, and manes were plaited to avoid any risk of becoming entangled in the long reins. Perhaps the most radical invention of Celtic blacksmiths was the horseshoe. Selgovan charioteers drove shod horses. Their tough little ponies had iron shoes fitted by the smiths because they needed them. North Britain was wet and hooves had to be protected from the often sodden ground. Horses only rarely get off their feet, and long exposure to dampness causes the foot to spread and soften, and it removes the horn's protective covering. When this happens the hoof splits, the feet become tender and the pony becomes useless.

Since the Celts began to develop equestrian technology 2500 years ago horses and horsemen have ridden through Border history. Across many centuries warlords have had the ability to put large numbers of men in the saddle in a morning, and deliver an army to battle in the afternoon. Hoofbeats have drummed an insistent rhythm across these hills and valleys — from the first faint echoes at Horsehope Craig, to the exploits of Celtic cavalry, the horsemen of the Guotodin and their greatest commander — Arthur, to the armoured knights of the Middle Ages, to the Border Reivers, then away from war to ploughshares and the pioneering development of landscape-changing technology pulled by the great Clydesdale horses, and finally to the memory of all of them sealed inside each of the Border Common Ridings when reminders of the horsemen of history ride through the summer towns and the hills behind them.

When the Romans encountered Celtic cavalry, they copied them and co-opted them. There were certainly southern British regiments in Agricola's army as it marched through the Tweed Valley in 79AD, but whether or not they were cavalry or infantry has gone unrecorded. After completing the first fort at Newstead, the Romans marched north to link with the western column. These troops had made their way up Annandale on the line of the modern A74, and then struck across towards the Forth on the line of the A702. These eastern and western lines of march were accomplished rapidly and designed to bottle up quickly the Selgovae and separate them from the Novantae. The later siting of forts at Beattock, Castledykes, Oakwood and Newstead itself show a policy of policing the mouths of valleys leading out of the Southern Uplands. From the first the Romans recognised the Selgovae as a formidable enemy, and they planned accordingly.

After coming together on the Forth, Agricola's army marched further north to engage the federation of tribes that ultimately became known as the Picts. At Mons Graupius, thought to be near Huntly in the northeast, they fought a battle which Tacitus claimed as a victory, but in reality seems to have been inconclusive. Methodical and thorough, Agricola brought his troops south and in 82AD the Novantae were reduced by a sea-borne expedition across the Solway Firth, launched from near Carlisle. Tacitus reports that Agricola considered an invasion of Ireland. Looking across the North Channel, he believed it could be managed with only a legion. However, these ambitions remained in the general's imagination, for in 84AD he was recalled to Rome. And a very short time afterwards all of his gains in Southern Scotland were abandoned as the Empire retreated south.

The Latin word 'limes' originally meant a path, but over time it gave us the English word limit because of the way in which the Romans began to use it at the limits of their empire. More precisely meaning a military road, the northern frontier of Britannia was built by Agricola between the Solway shore near Carlisle, through the Hexham Gap to the mouth of the Tyne and the harbour at South Shields. Known as the Stanegate, the original road connected a series of forts and Carlisle and Corbridge were initially the most important. Between them, at the interval of a day's march or 13 miles, lay two more forts at Nether Denton and Vindolanda (near Haltwhistle). Much further to the north, Newstead was abandoned in 87AD, but as the Stanegate was developing, imperial strategists decided soon after to re-occupy it. What became known as Dere Street connected Corbridge and Newstead allowing rapid communication between the evolving frontier and the outpost on the banks of the River Tweed.

After the retreat southwards the status of Newstead as a crucial forward position was enhanced. Already substantial at 10.5 acres when first built, it was remodelled and expanded to a very large 14.2 acres. The defences were also upgraded and the palisade raised from 4.7 metres to 8.5 and the rampart thickened from 7 metres to 13.7. To the watchers on Eildon Hill North the great Roman fort must have looked formidable, and those who marched and rode through its iron gates well organised and numerous. The garrison was unusual; a vexillation of legionary infantry and an ala of auxiliary cavalry. Legionaries were elite soldiers, well trained and equipped and with the added status of Roman citizens. Vexillations were subdivisions of legions and may have amounted to

500 or even 1000 men. Skilled at close-quarter, heavy battlefield fighting, the legionaries were generally sufficiently experienced and disciplined to take on larger forces and expect to defeat them. Roman commentators rarely doubt the courage of Celtic warriors but often fault their tactics which appeared mainly to consist of a furious charge. Determined and confident legionaries in a tight formation could absorb the shock of such a charge and inflict heavy casualties with their spears and the deadly short stabbing sword, the gladius.

The range of a vexillation of legionary infantry based at Newstead was limited to a maximum of 13 miles march a day, but the 'ala' or wing of cavalry could operate in a much wider radius. A full strength ala had 500 troopers and they were split into 16 units of 30, each under the command of a decurion. As their name implies a wing of cavalry protected a central core of legionary infantry from outflanking when they fought in concert on a battlefield. But the more likely strategic role of the Newstead ala was to split into units for scouting and skirmishing.

This garrison therefore had the ability to influence events at both a long and short range. Its relative strength and mix was a response to what the Romans saw as a continuing problem in constant need of policing — the Selgovae. At the foot of the Eildon Hills, near the confluence of several important valleys, in a place where the Ettrick, Yarrow, Gala Water and Leader all joined the Tweed, the commander at Newstead found himself in a pivotal position. But the likelihood is that he will have turned most often to the west, and that his scouts will have spent much time watching and waiting for signs of insurrection from the Selgovan kings and their warband.

By the time Newstead was rebuilt in 90AD, the Romans knew these cavalry warriors well. Twenty years earlier the Governor of Britannia, Q. Petilius Cerialis had attacked and subdued Venutius, a king of the Brigantes. His people occupied most of the uplands of the Pennine Chain, and they rarely ceased to contest imperial control of the north. Venutius compiled an alliance of northern hill peoples, what Tacitus called 'help from outside' (that is, help from outside the limits of the empire in 71AD) and marshalled his army at the hillfort of Stanwick near Scotch Corner. There can be little doubt that the Brigantian army included cavalry from the Selgovae and the Novantae of Galloway. At 16 acres in area the Stanwick fort must have had a very long perimeter that was difficult to defend. Under Cerialis, the Ninth Legion stormed the weak points of the ramparts, and after a hard fight, destroyed the Brigantian alliance. But prisoners will have been taken and more information extracted about what lay to the north of the Cheviots.

Excavations at the Stanwick fort have turned up evidence of the battle, and one particular group of objects is very interesting. In the defensive ditches near the gates skulls were found. Not the remains of casualties from Cerialis' charge, but older skulls which archaeologists believe had been placed on the gateway as a deterrent to the legionaries preparing to advance. These were all that was left of a Druid ghost fence.

At Newstead the Roman quartermaster depended on more everyday methods of ensuring security. Stone, wood, brick, nails and much else were needed to build the walls, barracks and stores of what became a military depot serving a wide area. Adjacent to the fort were large annexes and these soon housed suppliers and manufacturers of all sorts. This settlement was known as a vicus, and although merchants from all over the empire followed and supplied the army as it established new bases, many of those who came to live outside the fort will have come from the Tweed Valley. Archaeologist have found traces of the work of blacksmiths, bakers, potters, sandalmakers and glassworkers, and it is clear that trade and communication down Dere Street to the south and north and the River Tweed to the east was considerable. High-volume, heavy bulk items like wine are more likely to have arrived at Newstead by water than by road.

But what archaeologists cannot supply is much of a sense of what people at Newstead were like, how they thought, what their attitudes were. This in an intrinsic difficulty with the objects turned up by the shovel and trowel: they tell us a great deal but do not speak to us. At least not until a remarkable series of discoveries that began in 1973. Seventy miles south of Newstead, at a fort called Vindolanda on Hadrian's Wall, near Haltwhistle, Roman voices were found. More than 250 letters, lists, notes and official documents came to light miraculously preserved. Wafer-thin leaves of wood, no bigger than a modern postcard were used by Romans living at Vindolanda for all sorts of purposes. Letters were written directly onto the wood in ink, then scored down the centre, folded in half so that the script inside remained hidden and confidential (and preserved), and an address was written on the back of the right hand half. These letters, in particular, allow unique insights. Here is an invitation from Claudia Severa to her friend Sulpicia Lepidina, the wife of Flavius Cerialis, the commander at Vindolanda;

"Claudia Severa to her Lepidina greetings. On the third day before the Ides of September, sister, for the day of the celebration of my birthday, I give you a warm invitation to make sure that you come to us, to make the day more enjoyable for me by your arrival… Give my greetings to your Cerialis. My Aelius and my little son send him their greetings.
I shall expect you, sister. Farewell, sister, my dearest soul, as I hope to prosper, and hail. To Sulpicia Lepidina, (wife) of Cerialis, from Severa."

The atmosphere behind this formal but warm and human letter is redolent of what life was like in a similar modern circumstance — the British Raj in India; lonely, upper-class women posted with their husbands to one of the more distant parts of the empire, anxious to see each other, solicitous about their families, and perhaps a sense of maintaining civilised standards in trying circumstances. The habit of taking wives and families on military postings was relatively new, and not universally approved. The Old Republican virtues of discipline and tight-lipped sacrifice come through in this speech given by the historian Tacitus to an old senator, Caecina Severus;

"An entourage of women involves delays through luxury in peacetime and through panic in war. It turns the Roman army into the likeness of a procession of barbarians. Not only is the female sex weak and unable to bear hardship but, when it has the freedom, it is spiteful, ambitious and greedy for power. They disport themselves amongst the soldiers and have the centurions eating out of their hands."

The problem was that the Empire had expanded so fast and required so many soldiers to consolidate and police it, that flexibility was needed. If capable young men were to become high-ranking professional soldiers, serving long periods, then it was a substantial inhibition to both recruitment and subsequent morale to deny them a wife and family. During their 25 year term of service ordinary Roman soldiers were forbidden to marry but the lower ranks appear to have had wives, or at least women associated with them at Vindolanda. Thuttena is called 'soror', or sister, but it is a semi-formal term of endearment and meant that she was the partner of one of the soldiers. At the end of their service veterans were given Roman citizenship, their children were legitimised and also made citizens.

Sulpicia Lepidina's husband, Flavius Cerialis, was Prefect of the 9th Cohort of Batavians. Stationed at Vindolanda some time around 100AD, they came from the Low Countries, and as a recently conquered people, their levies were allowed to retain their noblemen as commanders. And it is therefore likely that Cerialis was himself a Batavian. Troops recruited from the edges of the Roman Empire were often posted to other peripheral areas. Imperial military planners may have believed that a recent frontier people might understand the circumstances on the borders of Britannia better. As a tribe from a northern latitude, the Batavians might have felt the cold and rain of a Border winter less keenly. But what is highly unlikely is that newly Romanised barbarians will have felt any empathy whatever for the native British living around the Stanegate. Former tribal warriors such as the Batavian cohort were in the process of becoming absorbed thoroughly into the huge and glittering framework of the Roman Empire. Opportunities, advancement, wealth, security, comfort and status stretched all the way from the Cheviot Hills to the Euphrates in the east and the Atlas Mountains in Africa. And few clearer examples of the rapid acculturation of former barbarians into Rome can exist than Flavius Cerialis, the Vindolanda commander.

In order to gain promotion to his rank, Flavius was required to be of equestrian status, which in turn demanded a property qualification of 400,000 sesterces. Compared to the annual pay of a legionary reckoned at 1200 sesterces, this was a huge sum. His name implies that Flavius, or perhaps his father, had been only recently admitted as a Roman citizen in the time of the Flavian emperors, 30 years before he came to Britain. In every sense he had arrived. The Vindolanda tablets have much to say about Cerialis' life and attitudes, and they show that he played the role of an upper-class Roman as if to the manner born.

His wife, Sulpicia Lepidina, also bears a revealing name and it appears that her family were also recently made citizens of Rome, possibly between 68 and 69AD, the short reign of the Emperor Sulpicius Galba. And like Flavius, she may have come from a recently Romanised barbarian society. The birthday invitation from Claudia Severa, and the earnestness expressed in it, is interesting. Her husband, Aelius Brocchus, was also a Batavian nobleman and the two families were often in contact on both social and professional business. After his posting to Britain, Brocchus became Prefect of a cavalry unit based in Pannonia, or modern Hungary, and this will have involved attaining equestrian status and becoming as wealthy as his friend, Flavius. Another correspondent was M. Caecilius September and he is also recorded as reaching the rank of Prefect, this time in Syria. Through all these relationships there is a palpable sense of ambitious young men and women intent on getting on in life, suffering far-flung postings in pursuit of career advancement.

At home in Vindolanda appearances had to be kept up. In addition to the thick woolen clothes like cloaks, vests and socks needed to keep warm as the east wind whistled through the Hexham Gap, the tablets show lists of more refined garments worn by Sulpicia Lepidina, her husband, children and their guests. They owned dainty pairs of sandals, as well as a particular type for wearing to the baths, and also fine tunics decorated with tapestry work, a 'cubitoria' or an outfit worn specially for dinner, and as a category for some of these clothes 'de synthesi' which meant that the items matched, possibly in different combinations. This was the varied wardrobe of people who aimed to remain sophisticated, no matter which godforsaken posting the army gave them. Even here, in the back of beyond with barbarians lurking only miles away, Sulpicia Lepidina, Flavius Cerialis and people of their social class dressed for dinner.

What they ate is also recorded in the Vindolanda tablets. Not surprisingly a much greater variety of butchermeat was available to the commander's table than ever made its way into the barracks. Ham, pork, beef and venison were all consumed, but there is a puzzling omission. Despite an archeological record showing a wide distribution of sheep, no lamb or mutton is mentioned. Perhaps that reflects a particular Batavian preference. The meat was seasoned with garlic, the ubiquitous Roman fish sauce, pickles, salt, olive oil and pepper. Few vegetables or fruits appear on Vindolanda's shopping lists, but there was plenty to drink and meals were washed down with cervesa, which translates as Celtic beer, vintage wine and mulsum, a drink made with wine and honey. Olives, wine and pepper clearly travelled long distances to reach the kitchens of Vindolanda.

But much of what the fort ate was grown locally, and the slaves who compiled the lists went to a local supplier or market and paid cash for what they bought. Here is an example;

"two gallons of bruised beans, 20 chickens, 100 apples, if you can find nice ones, a 100 or 200 eggs, if they are for sale there at a fair price..8 pints of fish sauce..a gallon of olives"

By 100AD a money economy is clearly in operation on the Stanegate and perhaps further north. It is difficult to imagine a reason why the slaves from the Newstead commander's praetorium did not go to market in the same way to bargain for fair prices from farmers or merchants in the Borders. That market was almost certainly held in the vicus, the civilian settlement outside the walls of Newstead. As well as merchants and suppliers, it also housed retired veterans from the army and there is some evidence of these men becoming involved in trade. How far cash extended through the economy is hard to judge but if primary producers were prepared to accept it, then the economic cycle would have been complete.

INFLATION

The Roman were very interested in money. Although coinage was invented by the Mesopotamians and developed by the Egyptians and Greeks, the Romans were the first to create an economy based purely on money. Around 300BC their first coins were closely related to livestock; the Latin word for money, is 'pecunia' and it is derived from 'pecus' for cattle, while 'denarius' meant 10 asses' worth. But once coins acquired an intrinsic value and began to be mass-produced in many centres, money drove imperial expansion as hard as political ambition. In 61BC, before his conquest of Gaul, Julius Caesar owed his bankers 25 million denarii, but after he had subdued and taxed what is now modern France, he made a fortune many times larger than his debts. Caesar's nephew, the first Emperor Augustus, used the expansion of the Empire to make himself by far the richest man the world had yet known.

In the 3rd and 4th centuries AD hundreds of millions of coins were being struck, and with the imperial budget running at 225 million denarii a year (mostly to pay the army, the civil service and to buy off the threats of barbarians on the frontier) it was inevitable that the quality of the coinage would become debased. There was not enough silver available in the Empire to make what was needed. And because the actual silver content of a denarius eventually became tiny, prices began to rise alarmingly. For an Empire run for profit and fuelled by cash, economic disaster loomed.

In 310AD the Emperor Diocletian issued his Edict on Prices. Listing common commodities with fixed prices alongside, he tried to halt the inflationary spiral by making it illegal. No-one, said the Edict, should pay more than 8 denarii for half a litre of wine or a pound of beef. Like modern attempts at price controls and wage freezes, it failed immediately. The market ultimately corrected the problem in a crude manner. Gold coins were reckoned as 'worth their weight in gold' according to current prices, and precious metals were increasingly used as tokens of exchange no matter that they came in the form of bowls, goblets or tableware.

The Roman Empire fell partly because it ceased to produce sound money and became less and less able to pay for itself.

In the period after 100AD the size of the frontier garrison on Hadrian's Wall began to grow until it reached 15,350 by the end of the century. The need for a large force of colonising soldiers implies a large population, but beyond that generalisation no sensible estimate can be produced. However, it is certain that the rapid introduction of such a huge new group will have greatly stimulated the Border economy. Taking into account wives, families and others, a modest figure of at the very least 30,000 needed to be fed and supplied with all manner of goods. The Vindolanda tablets mention a merchant called Metto, and in all likelihood he was a Borderer, perhaps the first to have his name mentioned in the written historical record. Metto sold parts for wheeled vehicles and he sent the fort a consignment of hubs, axles, spokes and seats. Given the well-attested native expertise at making wagons and chariots, these parts could have been manufactured in any number of locations, but it appears that the vehicles were assembled at Vindolanda. At the end of the list Metto notes that he has also sent 6 goatskins, and this probably confirms him as a merchant rather than a producer of cart parts negociating on behalf of his business alone. What is also clear is that he troubled to write decent Latin, something doubtless essential to commerce with the Roman army. The vici which grew up around forts would also have been predominantly Latin-speaking and those who came to them would need more than a few words to do their business. The massive presence of the army ensured a similarly deep penetration of the Latin language into the Border culture of the time.

Mention is made of two other men who might have been local entrepreneurs; Gavo supplied cloth and provisions, while Atrectus was a brewer making Celtic beer. It should be noted that the calorific content of beer was well known at this time and its chief value was as a food rather than an intoxicating drink. Although it was that too.

What these unique and invaluable splashes of light on life at Vindolanda show is a local economy responding to the needs of a large group of demanding colonists. And also to the particular wants of their elite, and these imply a good deal. Clearly there were dinner parties for senior people hosted in some style by Sulpicia Lepidina and Flavius Cerialis. And the luxury items these required will have stimulated contact and longer distance trade, doubtless through several agents, with primary producers in the Borders, who could use the speed and utility of a money economy to widen their activities.

DORMICE

The Romans considered mice a delicacy and ate them at banquets. Special pottery containers were made for keeping dormice and they were fed on acorns and chestnuts to fatten them up. In the summer they eat heartily to ensure they survive hibernation. Once the slaves had killed them, cooks gutted the mice and scooped out their flesh. This was then mixed with minced pork and stuffed back into the carcase. Skill was required to manage this properly but since fat dormice could grow up to 6 inches long, not counting the tail, a good deal could be shoved in. Big dormice must have been more than a mouthful.

Snails were also popular. Near towns and villas artificial islands were sometimes created for the express purpose of rearing them. Since snails always avoid water, these were effectively cages. Once they had grown large enough, slaves collected them in large pottery jars with airholes, and they were brought indoors for final fattening. Fed on milk, unfermented grape juice and wheat, they were taken out of their jars and into the kitchen at the point when they were too fat to get back into their shells. Helix Pomatia, or the Edible Roman snail, still slithers around the south of England — in peace.

Attitudes are harder to catch, but perhaps more comparisons with the British Raj are helpful. When upper-class Roman officers visited each other, they often went hunting and in one of his letters to Aelius Brocchus, Flavius Cerialis wrote; "if you love me brother, I ask that you send me some hunting nets". Only a few miles from Vindolanda, at Housesteads Fort there is a relief of a stag being hunted with a net. And on an altar found near Stanhope, about 15 miles south of Corbridge, is carved a telling inscription with a tone reminiscent of tiger-hunts in British India;

"Gaius Tetius Veturius Micianus, Prefect of the Sebosian cavalry regiment, on fulfillment of his vow willingly set up this [altar] for taking a wild boar of remarkable fineness which many of his predecessors had been unable to bag."

The Vindolanda tablets hardly ever mention the natives, but when there is something explicit, it is instructive about attitudes. This fragment seems to be part of a discussion about possible recruitment of British warriors into the Roman army.

"... the Britons are unprotected by armour. There are very many cavalry. The cavalry do not use swords nor do the wretched Britons mount in order to throw javelins."

This is the earliest confirmation, by outsiders, of the Celtic habit of fighting on horseback in the Borders (one of the reasons for the widespread wearing of trousers), and another fragment may sharpen the general reference to the Anavionenses, a tribe living in Annandale, possibly a sept of the Selgovae. But it is the use of 'Brittunculi' or 'wretched Britons' which resonates. Occupying soldiers have always refered to the natives as wogs, and the use of 'Brittunculi' belongs to that tradition — somewhat watered down by being written down in this case. The commander at Newstead and his officers and troops will have looked on eastern Borderers in a similar way; as a bunch of simple, illiterate, unsophisticated and sometime sly wogs. There is nothing surprising in this, except the passing observation of how inappropriate it is to begin a history of the Borders with the doings of the Romans.

The more reflective of the local population will have watched the new and massive movement of troops and goods, the building of stone structures from another civilisation, and listened to the instructions, perhaps disguised as advice, given to their kings by professional soldiers anxious to do an efficient job on behalf of an Empire which stretched limitless behind them. Two choices might have occured to thoughtful observers. Firstly Rome represented a glittering career, the Empire was filled with possibilities for the ambitious — look at the commander of the fort at Vindolanda whose stuck-up wife and family were no better 30 years ago than we are! Secondly the forts at Newstead and on the Stanegate represented another sort of opportunity — a sample of what might be available to those with the audacity and skill simply to take it by force.

Brigionus is certainly a Celtic name, and it seems likely that he was also a Borderer. In some unknown way he had approached Claudius

Karus, an officer at Vindolanda, and asked for help in, presumably, joining the army as more than a lowly recruit. Claudius then wrote to Flavius Cerialis;

"Claudius Karus to his Cerialis, greetings… Brigionus has requested me, my lord, to recommend him to you. I therefore ask, my lord, if you would be willing to support him in what he has requested of you. I ask that you think fit to commend him to Annius Equester, centurion in charge of the region, at Luguvalium, by doing which you will place me in debt to you both in his name and my own. I pray that you are enjoying the best of fortune and good health. Farewell brother."

Annius Equester was an important man and from Carlisle (Luguvalium), a place already thought of as central, he conducted the census. When the Romans consolidated a conquered area one of their first actions was to organise a census. The most famous involved Mary and Joseph travelling to Bethlehem. Accurate information was then used for the gathering of taxation. Annius Equester knew the local population well and would probably have dealt with hopefuls like Brigionus before. What happened to him is not known, but plenty of records exist of British units in the European Roman army.

In 105AD the second option was taken by the Selgovae. Their king rallied his warband, possibly in alliance with the Brigantes to the south, rode down the Tweed Valley and attacked Newstead in force. No account of the fighting survives, only the result. But it would have been surprising for the Selgovae to mount a successful seige and the likelihood is that they caught most of the garrison somewhere in the open, and then burned the fort. Archaeologists have found damaged armour and much abandoned equipment as well as many contemporary human bones. Leaving a charred ruin at its foot, the Selgovan king may have climbed Eildon Hill North to offer a sacrifice to the sky gods for his victory. Corbridge was also attacked and burned in 105AD, and the Romans expelled from Britain north of the Stanegate.

The Emperor Trajan was campaigning in Dacia at this time and may have depleted the British garrison, leaving only 3 legions in Britain. Selgovan military intelligence will have judged the summer of 105 a good time to attack and plunder the riches of large Roman forts and the settlements clustered around them.

In 117AD there was more trouble. The Brigantes of the Pennines, in another alliance with the Selgovae and the Novantae of Galloway, had risen in rebellion behind the Stanegate frontier, and were causing havoc in the north. A Roman commentator was unequivocal, "The Britons could not be kept under Roman control". The new Emperor, Hadrian, and his advisors wanted to protect the wealthy province of Britannia, and they determined on a radical solution. In 122 Hadrian visited Britain, inspected the Stanegate frontier and pronounced it inadequate. A great wall was to be built, running more than 70 miles from the mouth of the Tyne, through the Hexham Gap but on the higher ground north of the Stanegate, then on to Carlisle and beyond, for at least 26 miles down the Cumbrian coast. It was to prove an immense labour and is the largest Roman monument in Europe. Its construction is in large part a testament to the determination and ferocity of the Selgovae. For the military logic of Hadrian's Wall was not as a north-facing defensive rampart. Its design shows that it faced both ways, with the large southern vallum, or ditch, only bridged at forts. Two berms were excavated from a 10 foot deep and 20 foot wide ditch and the ground cleared so that there was a 120 foot wide area of open ground across which nothing could move unobserved. The Wall was designed from the outset as the core and conduit of an intensely militarised zone whose major purpose was to split the Brigantes from the Selgovae, and the other hostile tribes in the north.

Stanwix Fort was the command centre of Hadrian's Wall but it was not the earliest Roman foundation in the area. During the campaign of 71–74AD when the Brigantes were overrun at Stanwick in Yorkshire, Petilius Cerialis built a fort at Carlisle. Standing at a point where three rivers meet and also accessible to the important seaway of the Solway Firth, it was an excellent choice — but even better 2000 years ago than it appears now. What is now Carlisle Castle mount, the site of the Roman fort, was almost completely surrounded by flowing water and marshy ground. The River Eden used to have a southern channel, now diverted and dried up, and beyond the northern ramparts of the fort up to the confluence of the rivers Caldew and Eden was a treacherous bog.

The name of Luguvalium appears in the Vindolanda tablets and its adoption clearly implies the pre-existence of an earlier British fort on the site chosen by Petilius Cerialis. It means 'strong in the god, Lugh' and is a reference to the Celtic god of arts and crafts. By the 9th century the Old Welsh 'caer' for fortress had reasserted itself and the name settled down to the recognisable Caerluel. Directly traceable in this way, over almost 2000 years, Carlisle is certainly one of the oldest continuously used forms of the same place-name in Britain.

When the construction of Hadrian's Wall began Carlisle will have grown rapidly, and excavations during the redevelopment of the Lanes in the centre of the old city have turned up the foundations of massive Roman buildings. One measured 180 feet long by 34 feet wide. The discovery of Roman roadwork in the cathedral precinct and the orientation of other excavated buildings in the Lanes have located the forum around the area of its medieval successor, the Market Cross. In the 2nd century AD substantial new stone buildings were erected with the underfloor heating system known as the hypocaust. People with money to spend were coming to live in Carlisle.

The shape of the Roman town was broadly triangular and varied little until the early modern period. Since it was illegal to bury the dead inside the walls of Roman towns, the habit was to set up tombs by the roadside. Not only do these allow the line of the roads out of Carlisle to be plotted, but two in particular offer vaulable information. A Greek merchant, probably with a specialised trade who followed the Roman army as a supplier, died in the town at the same time as the Vindolanda tablets were being written and sent. His wife, Septima, left a valedictory verse;

"To the spirits of the departed
Flavius Antigonus Papias
a citizen of Greece, lived
60 years more or less, and
gave back to the Fates his
soul lent for that time,
Septima Do... set this up."

And later an elaborate tombstone with a sculpture of the deceased was found by the west road passing through Denton Holme. Wearing rich and expensive drapery, the lady sits on a high-backed armchair holding a circular fan and with a pet bird on her lap. A child stands beside her. It is a confident, stylish memorial to a luxurious way of life not seen again in Carlisle until the 20th century.

Some time around 250AD the town became a city. Created the Civitas Carvetiorum, or the capital place of the tribe of the Carvetii, Carlisle was prospering. Despite the fluctuations on the frontier in the 2nd century, its people and hinterland were functioning as the only substantial civic centre in Britain north of York. And as such Carlisle became a focus for Southern Scotland as well as for Cumbria.

But the original military stimulus for the growth of the city almost stalled. Before work on Hadrian's Wall was finished, it became clear that it was being built in the wrong place. Hadrian's successor, Antoninus Pius, decided to reoccupy Southern Scotland and build a new wall between the Forth and Clyde. Once again the Selgovae were at the root of these expensive and radical changes in imperial policy. Pausanias, a Greek travel writer, offers a sense of what happened;

"Antoninus Pius never willingly made war; but when the Moors took up arms he drove them out of all their territory... Also he deprived the Brigantes in Britain of most of their land because they too had begun aggression on the district of Genunia whose inhabitants are subject to Rome."

Now, Pausanias was writing of faraway places he was unlikely ever to visit and his use of names is very loose. The Brigantes had been part of the Empire for at least 60 years before Antoninus Pius' reign and more than a century before Pausanias was writing. But when it is remembered that in a huge empire of many different peoples, the name 'Brigantes' was sometimes confused for Britons, much in the way that English is for British nowadays, then the refence to tribes beyond Hadrian's Wall becomes clear. By 'the Brigantes' Pausanias means their allies, the Selgovae. Genunia is a lost name, but there are glimmers of meaning and it may refer to the warband of the Guotodin, or the Votadini, as the Romans knew them. The broad sense of the passage is clear, however, and it is that Hadrian's Wall stranded Rome's constant and valuable ally in Southern Scotland. It was too far south to be of any tactical help when the Selgovae attacked the Guotodin.

In 139AD Newstead was rebuilt and reoccupied as a depot on Dere Street, the main road north to the new frontier wall. And also as a

fighting base from which Roman forces sallied out to subdue the
Selgovae whose independence could no longer be tolerated in the rear
of the new border line in central Scotland. When enemies of the Empire
surrendered unconditionally their young men were immediately
conscripted into the army and shipped abroad. In 145AD Numeri
Brittonum, or British detachments, appeared on the Rhine frontier and
in all likelihood these were warriors from the Ettrick and Yarrow valleys
and the hills over to Annadale and Nithsdale. Perhaps some rose to the
rank of Prefect, like Flavius Cerialis. It is unlikely that any of them ever
found their way home again.

The new fort at Newstead was the largest yet at 16.6 acres. Acquiring
a stone wall for the first time, its garrison was also unprecedentedly
numerous with 2 cohorts of the Twentieth Legion providing a thousand
infantry and the Ala Augusta Vocontiorum, a crack cavalry regiment of
500 troopers recruited from southern France and northern Spain. The
Voconti were a Celtic tribe with a reputation for horsemanship. They
used the kinder snaffle bit in the mouths of their animals and may have
introduced it to the Borders. By the early 2nd century AD the Voconti
still spoke Gaulish, a Celtic language related to the speech of the
Selgovae. Perhaps these horse warriors could understand each other.

Trouble continued to flare in the 150s and 180s AD, and the Newstead
garrison must have lived a life on constant standby. The Emperor
Commodus sent Ulpius Marcellus, one of his ablest generals, to sort out
the chronic instability in Southern Scotland. After several punitive
expeditions mounted from the forts on Hadrian's Wall, order of some
kind seems to have been restored, although the campaign seems to
have prompted the Selgovae to make an alliance with the Maeatae, a
tribe based in the Ochil Hills, Strathallan and Strathearn. An uneasy
peace followed for a generation.

In 197 Clodius Albinus, the Governor of Britain, used the wealth
and the garrison of the province in a bid to become Emperor. He failed,
but in so doing removed troops from the Wall and, ever aware of
imperial politics, the Selgovae and Maeatae attacked and had to be
bought off with bribes. As they broke through it appears that they
damaged the Wall itself. This detail is a reminder of what a huge
propaganda — and psychological — effect this massive structure had.
To the British hill tribes in the north, it looked as though the Empire
could girdle the earth, tame nature and impose its will physically on
their ancestral lands.

Old, ill and irritated, the Emperor, Septimius Severus, arrived in
Britain in 208 with heavy reinforcements from the European army, and
also his sons, Caracalla and Geta, and his wife the Empress Julia Domna
in tow. The old man knew that his illness was incurable and he brought
his court with him, just in case. They set up at York and began to plan
campaigns in the north. But after several inconclusive seasons and the
reoccupation of Newstead, Septimius Severus died at York in 211. His
eventual heir, Caracalla, was pragmatic. After withdrawing troops from
the north, he determined on a different policy. Southern Scotland was
simply not worth the huge effort and steady haemorrhage of money
spent — particularly on Hadrian's Wall where the expense was truly

vast — and it was better to abandon any thoughts of permanent occupation. Better to concentrate completely on the protection of Britannia and to achieve this Caracalla's negociators began to formulate the terms of treaties. Details of these do not exist but the standard practice on troublesome frontiers seems to have been followed. In return for Roman withdrawal to the Wall, the payment of subsidies (generally in cash or precious metal) and an exchange of prisoners, the British agreed to refrain from tribal warfare and to use only supervised assembly points for large gatherings. In this way Roman influence in Southern Scotland was accepted in return for guaranteed autonomy. The strategic value to Rome was that the Votadini, the Selgovae (less reliably), the Novantae and the Damnonii of the Clyde Valley could act as buffer states between Britannia and the hostile tribes north of the Forth.

It worked. For almost a hundred years there was peace in Southern Scotland. Hadrian's Wall was used as a base for forces active to the north, but it appears that they did little but go on constant patrol. Subsidies were paid with some regularity. Near Meldon Bridge, at Edston, a hoard of 290 silver denarii has been found beside the remains of a Selgovan hillfort. The latest dated coin is 222AD. Outpost forts were garrisoned at Netherby, Bewcastle, Risingham and High Rochester. None were recommissioned north of the Cheviot watershed and Newstead appears finally to have fallen out of use, at least by the Roman army. No doubt other uses were found for its stone. Mounted scouts known as Exploratores were based at Netherby and Risingham and a vexillation called the Raetian Gaesati, javelin-men from the Alps, were assigned forward of the Wall as well as an infantry cohort, the Vardulli. The outpost forts were too small to accommodate all these groups at once and there must, therefore, have been a roster of permanent patrols in the Tweed Valley and the Southern Uplands. Inscriptions to the Raetian Gaesati and the Vardulli found at Jedburgh point to one regularly manned outpost, near a crossing of the Teviot, and another may have been located at Tweedmouth where contact by sea with South Shields would have been easy.

The Exploratores supervised meetings of tribesmen at licensed places in their territory. The Selgovae seem to have agreed on two. Roman maps identify Locus Maponis, which changed little in 2000 years into Lochmaben in Dumfriesshire, but the other, Locus Selgovensis, is much more difficult to pin down. It may have been at Meldon Bridge, an ancient and central site which retained its prestige up to the modern period and possibly the place where the Edston hoard was handed over. Until the 18th century the Peeblesshire Militia mustered on the adjacent Sheriff Muir.

Over in the west some sense of the life of the native population can be glimpsed around Carlisle. Altars inscribed to the god, Belatucadros, which translates as 'the bright, beautiful one', reveal a literate population who did not have much money — perhaps a lower middle class, well below the status of the commanders at Carlisle and Stanwix, and probably British. Belatucadros was a native god and the altars dedicated to him are primitive, commissioned by people with little spare cash and certainly not able to afford anything lavish. But they could compose a

Latin inscription, even though their daily speech was Old Welsh. This sort of bi-lingualism is common in colonies, particularly near military installations, and an aspect of it can still be observed amongst older people in the Gaelic-speaking areas of Ireland and Scotland. They speak one language which they rarely write and write another which they rarely speak.

Britain became part of a breakaway segment of the Empire based on Gaul between 260 and 273. And then under the admiral, Carausius, and his successor, Allectus, the province attempted independence again in the last decades of the 3rd century. As the politics of the imperial court became increasingly unstable and barbarians pressed harder on the frontiers, the 4th century saw several governors of Britain and generals stationed here making bids for the throne in Rome, and denuding the garrison to pursue their ambitions. These episodes were a traditional trigger for the Picts and others to raid in the south, and there are several reports which mention them. However, something of an entirely different magnitude happened in 367AD. The Barbarian Conspiracy burst over Britain. Co-ordinated in some unknown way, and giving the lie to the cliche of militarily unsophisticated savages hurling themselves in fury against Hadrian's Wall, the Picts, the Irish, the Attecotti (perhaps from the Western Isles), the Franks and the Saxons all attacked Britain and the northern coasts of Gaul at the same time. Stretched in every direction, imperial resistence collapsed or disappeared. For two years plundering bands roamed the countryside creating mayhem. Nectaridus, the Count of the Saxon Shore — in charge of defending the east coast, was killed and Fullofaudes, the Dux Britanniarum — the commander based at York, was either captured or beseiged.

MACSEN

The Welsh are still composing poetry and songs about a 4th century Spaniard who attempted to usurp the imperial throne from Roman Britain. 'Magnus Maximus o Gymru' is an early hero in Dafydd Iwan's anthem of Welshness, 'Yma O Hyd', or 'We're Still Here';

> *"You don't remember Macsen;*
> *No one here ever knew him.*
> *One thousand and six hundred years*
> *Is too long ago to recall.*
> *But Magnus Maximus left Wales*
> *In the year three hundred and eighty three.*
> *He left the nation as one.*
> *And today, just look at her!"*

Macsen is the Welsh rendering of his name and he appears in a remarkable poem known as 'The Dream of Macsen Wledig'. Dating from the 6th century, it tells a decorated but broadly accurate version of Magnus Maximus' imperial adventure. He gathered an army from the British Garrison, augmented it with native cavalry from Wales and Southern Scotland, and dealt with incursions from the Irish, and then fought a campaign in the north against the Picts.

> *Crossing to Europe, Macsen brought Gaul and Spain under his control. Finally drawn into battle against the legitimate emperor, Theodosius the Great (son of Count Theodosius), he was defeated and executed at Aquileia in northern Italy.*
>
> *British soldiers from Macsen's army may have settled in northern France and the wide incidence of the place-name, Bretteville, remembers them. However, some historians believe that a more enduring legacy became apparent in the Romanised Celtic kingdoms of Southern Scotland. In 383AD the prefects sent by Count Theodosius were probably still active, or their sons were. Not only was the charismatic Macsen seen as an early king of the Damnonii of Strathclyde, but there are also hints that he strengthened the buffer states between the Roman walls. Unless he took a positive role and had meaningful contact with the Celtic kings of Wales and Southern Scotland, it is difficult to account for the powerful, and enduring, memory of a Spanish general with ambitions to rule in Rome.*

In 369 a remarkable and highly effective and inventive soldier arrived in Britain with four regiments of the field army. Count Theodosius immediately rounded up gangs of raiders, regrouped the garrison, posted an immediate amnesty for deserters, and hurried north to sort out the defences of Hadrian's Wall. The Roman historian, Ammianus, records that Theodosius retook a place 'which owed allegiance to Rome' and was therefore not formally a province. 'He strengthened the wall which ran between Forth and Clyde' and much later it became known to antiquaries as 'Theodosius' Wall' rather than Antonine's. But most importantly, his review of the situation suggested a particular strategy. The previous year in North Africa an innovative solution had been found to a similar problem. To counter the raids of the Berber tribesmen, adjacent native kingdoms had been converted into military buffer states with Roman Prefects set over them. Count Theodosius did exactly the same thing in Southern Scotland, and at the beginning of the Strathclyde kinglists, the names of two of these men can be made out, just. Celticised, shortened and misspelt, they are almost undetectable, but Cluim was a Roman officer called Clemens, and there is another man called Cinhil or Quintilius, possibly his successor. In the kingdom of Rheged, the creation of the Novantae, one of the first and earliest rulers was Annwn, sometimes called Annwn Donadd, or Antonius Donatus. For the Northern Guotodin, based at Traprain Law, Catellius Decianus was made leader, and over the Southern Gododdin the first three kings were Tacit, Patern Pesrut and Aetern — all lacking the 'us' ending. 'Pesrut' is fascinating and it means 'the man with the red cloak', a Roman military office-holder of some kind. Even though their cognomens have been lost, these are singular, Mediterranean names which appear nowhere else. Each of these prefects will have been backed by a small force of, most likely, cavalry troopers.

After he had set up the buffer kingdoms and stiffened them with professional soldiers, Count Theodosius abandoned the outpost forts in the north but restored the Wall 'and its cities'. Around Carlisle and other towns in the south walls were strengthened. The Areani, the successors of the Exploratores, were disbanded. It seems that they had been treacherous, not only failing to warn of the Barbarian Conspiracy but also betraying military secrets to the enemy.

While the Picts continued to threaten from the north, Angles and Saxons began to land on the eastern coasts in ever greater numbers, and in 408 there was a severe raid. Constantine, yet another usurper Emperor from Britain, was ineffective in dealing with the barbarians and his officials were expelled. The only organised elements of government left were the cities and they managed to deal with the Anglo-Saxon raiders themselves, but in 410 their resources were thinning and they wrote to the legitimate Emperor, Honorius, to request help from Rome. Beleaguered in Italy, he could do nothing, and he replied with the advice that the British cities had to look to their own defences.

Honorius' letter is seen as the moment the Roman province of Britannia died. But in fact all that happened was that people stopped being paid. What had in any case become irregular payments to soldiers and officials ceased altogether. There was no longer any Roman garrison to withdraw and no imperial administration to pack its files. In the south few soldiers remained and mercenaries had to be hired for protection from raiders. But there were Roman armies available, although they had begun to wear a Celtic disguise. The three kingdoms of Southern Scotland, the legacy of Count Theodosius, quickly became an important focus. After Rome, in the 5th and 6th centuries, politics followed military clout and decisions affecting the whole of Britain were, for once, not made in the south east, but in the north, and some of them in the Borders.

4

Romanitas

In 870 the last of the British kingdoms of the North fell. The Damnonians of the Clyde Valley, first reported by Tacitus in 79AD, had evolved into the kingdom of Alclut, the Rock of the Clyde. Better known to us as Dumbarton, it was the seat of kings for at least 800 years, and probably longer. Late in its immense life the old kingdom came to be called Strathclyde, and with the adoption of the name for a local authority in 1974, it has reappeared on the map.

The Gaels to the north knew it by another, equally descriptive name. Dun Breatainn was the Fortress of the Britons, and rising sheer out of the waters of the Firth of Clyde, dominating a busy seaway, it must have impressed all who saw it.

In the Spring of 870 lookouts on the ramparts of the Rock saw something astonishing and terrifying. Rounding the headlands at Gourock Bay and making way into the inner firth was a huge fleet of warships, more than 200 keels could be counted. As they watched them approach, hauling down their sails and taking the oars, the lookouts must have felt the fear rise in their throats. Two hundred dreki, the dragon-ships of the Vikings were being rowed up the Clyde towards them. On their prows stood two Viking kings, Ivar and his brother Olaf, who had sailed out of their town at Dublin to capture Dumbarton Rock. Here is an extract from the Irish annals;

"In this year the kings of the Scandinavians beseiged Strathclyde, in Britain. They were four months beseiging it; and at last, after reducing the people who were inside by hunger and thirst (after the well that they had in their midst had dried up miraculously), they broke in upon them afterwards. And firstly all the riches that were in it were taken; [and also] a great host [was taken] out of it in captivity."

When they entered the stockade, the Vikings resisted the powerful temptation to slaughter those who had defied them for so long. Instead they packed their prisoners into the dragonships and sailed back to the slave-markets of Dublin. Slaving was perhaps the Vikings' most lucrative business and they supplied much of Europe in the 9th century. The flower of Strathclyde's nobility was auctioned in Dublin and then dispersed to other markets, but their kings appear to have escaped.

However, King Artgal, the son of Dumnogual, was later captured by the Dalriada Scots and on the advice of King Constantine I, the son of Kenneth macAlpin, he was put to death. If the Vikings wanted slaves, the expansionist Scots wanted the kingdom of Strathclyde. However, that was not the end of the dynasty. It seems that a member of the royal family of the Clyde became joint King of Scots after Constantine's death. Eochaid ruled with Giric until he was expelled in 889. In Scottish history such a fate generally signifies a total disappearance. But remarkably, what happened to Eochaid has been recorded, although Scottish records do not mention him again.

The Welsh Chronicle of the Princes, the Brut Y Tywysogion, notes that in 890;

"The men of Strathclyde, those that refused to unite with the English, had to depart from their country, and go to Gwynedd"

The Strathclyde exiles were given land in the Vale of Clwyd in north-east Wales on condition that they expelled the English living there. For the second time in their history they were being used as a buffer state against potential invaders. But the Welsh kings were sympathetic and even respectful. The three Old Welsh-speaking kingdoms of what they called the Old North, Yr Hen Ogledd, were seen as heroic and worthy. The kinglists of Southern Scotland only survived because the Welsh kings appropriated them and so that they could add greater antiquity and legitimacy, they prefixed them on the front of their own. The stories and traditions of the Old North survived too because the Strathclyde exiles brought them with them. In the circle of firelight the old heroes and their warbands were remembered as their exploits were recited by bards and listened to by their patrons. The stories were slowly absorbed into Welsh traditions, and after a time the Old North was thought by some to mean North Wales, and the Gwyr Y Gogledd, the Men of the North, became the men of Gwynedd. But the genealogies and the stories did endure because they found a place in Welsh history and they form, in large part, the basis for a history of Old Welsh-speaking Southern Scotland.

Many historians have mistrusted, resisted and even rejected the notion that this cultural transmission took place in any meaningful sense. And if it did, all that has really come down to us is myth-history, little more than unreliable, ramshackle traditions which, in any case, became so contaminated by the early history of Wales as to render them almost worthless in any serious consideration of the history of Scotland. Part of the reason for this reaction is linguistic. There persists an illogical impulse to believe that everything told or written in Welsh happened in Wales.

But this is to deny us a precious resource. If the stories of the Old North had not been carried south in the ships of the Strathclyde exiles and by others, and they had remained embedded in some form (perhaps in the Latin of the chroniclers or in Gaelic) in the culture of what is now Scotland, would they have been so undervalued and ignored? It seems unlikely.

However, that is not to say that the material preserved in Wales is easy to understand, offering a readymade version of events in the north. It is in fact very difficult to assess. There is a bewildering welter of names, very few dates and even fewer places. No coherent story is to be found, but rather a series of disconnected echoes of what happened in the decades after the young Emperor Honorius wrote to the cities of Britain telling them to expect no help from Rome and advising them to look to their own defences.

One of the most resonant echoes is to be heard in a nursery rhyme. Whether or not Old King Cole was a merry old soul keen on nocturnal fiddle concerts is not recorded, but his right name is. Old King Cole was a real person and the Welsh genealogies remember him as Coel Hen, or Old Cole, and they say that he was a great king. In reality he probably began as a career officer in the Roman army.

In the 3rd and 4th centuries AD an imperial administration anxious about the number of usurper emperors (who had tried to put the considerable weight of Britannia's resources behind their attempted coups) decided to split the province into two, then four parts, each under a different governor. The military structure was also devolved and grew increasingly defensive in nature. By the end of the 4th century the Count of the Britains (likely meaning all the provinces of Britain) was in charge of an ever-shrinking field army, the Count of the Saxon Shore commanded the eastern coastal defences, but in overall authority in the north was the Duke of the Britains. From the meagre evidence available it looks very much as though Coel Hen was the last Roman appointed Duke before 410AD.

When Honorius decided that he had to abandon the province, he wrote to the cities because there was no central colonial administration left. But when Coel Hen, or Coelius, the original Latin version of his name, heard of the change in policy, he was not left without a command. By 410, and some time before that, soldiering had become both native British and hereditary. No matter whatever fancy regimental titles continued to be used — archers from Syria or cavalry from Thrace — the truth was that they were staffed by Britons. When veterans retired, particularly when their last posting had been on Hadrian's Wall but also at other large forts, they tended to stay where they were, probably marry a local girl, and possibly live in the vicus and take up a trade which supplied the army. These men often encouraged their sons to join up, and perhaps expected some remittances from them to ease their old age. There is late evidence that families lived inside Roman forts, and that skills and probably kit, like helmets and armour, were passed on from father to son. When pay stopped coming from Rome in 410, what could they do but continue in the family business — of soldiering?

As Duke of the Britains Coel Hen had a problem. Now that his units no longer formed part of the imperial garrison of Britannia, what was their role to be? If a substantial and restless body of troops had been stationed in the north, then that could have been a volatile state of affairs. A curious document sheds some light on this. In 395 an administrator in Rome compiled the Notitia Dignitatum. Loosely translated as 'The Ascertaining of Ranks', its primary purpose was to set down the chain of military command in North Britain (and elsewhere) by listing officers, staffs and the units under their control. At face value it is impressive. Eleven regiments of cavalry and infantry appear to be based in Durham and Yorkshire and three others west of the Pennines, and then the entire garrison of Hadrian's Wall is set down with their forts in the correct geographical order. Lists of officers and units are also included separately for the Count of the Saxon Shore and the Count of the Britains' field army.

Detailed, apparently up to date in some areas, and clear about the organisation of the Wall, it is tempting to think that the Notitia Dignitatum represented a statistical reality in 395. If it did then very many troops were pulled out of Britain by the usurper emperors of the early 5th century, before 410. More than likely an imperial official compiled a list which presented a picture of maximum complement, of what should have been there, should have been available to protect the valuable province of Britannia in normal times. But it was not. Various estimates have been made of the forces listed in the Notitia and all are apparently substantial. But by the end of Roman rule in Britannia, the number of men on active service had dwindled away and those who wanted to had gone. In any event it should not be forgotten that the document is what it says it is, primarily a list of ranks rather than a report on the strength of units.

However that may be, Coel Hen's command will not have enjoyed anything like the putative numbers in the Notitia, and his army probably consisted of native British soldiers and also a few detachments of German mercenaries. Nevertheless that still made him a powerful man, the ruler of the north, both sides of the Pennines and up to the Wall and possibly beyond. Coel was experienced and used to responsibility and authority, and also a family man. The Welsh genealogies become heavily corrupted in places and Coel's wife is named as 'Stradwawl' which translates as 'Wall Road', and his daughter was 'Gwawl' or 'The Wall'. These sound like a confusion of areas of command with members of a family. The genealogies were transcribed by Welshmen distant in both time and space from the events after 410AD.

Coel's office as Duke of the Britains gave him an enormous tract of land, and the eight dynasties who claimed descent from him all ruled in that area of the north. It seems that after the old man's death his dominion disintegrated. But the memory of Rome remained powerful and did not dissipate for a long time. After the end of Britannia, Romanitas — or Roman-ness — was something much sought after by the new kings in Britain. The more Roman they appeared to be, the more legitimacy and authority was attached to them and their regime. And no-one showed more of a wish to identify with the political habits of the imperial past than Coel Hen's son-in-law.

The Welsh genealogies list him as 'Wledig' or 'The General' and give his reputation rather than his name. Cunedda (Kunetha) means 'Good Leader', and it is a pleasing paradox that this great man with no name should have as his sole historical memory a christian name, that of Kenneth. Even though he was a hero who originated from between the Roman walls, from what is now Southern Scotland, and did something unique and remarkable, we have forgotten Cunedda almost entirely. But the traditions in Wales are strong, the bards had much to sing of him, and together with a northern source they tell a fascinating story.

Some time around 425 to 430, not long after the end of the Roman province, Cunedda the General found himself at the head of a remarkable expedition. The military planners of what became the kingdom of the Gododdin in the south east quarter of Scotland and North Northumberland decided to be statesmanlike, to behave like the imperial Romans of the past. After 383 the usurper emperor Magnus Maximus had removed the garrisons from North Wales and the resulting gap in Britannia's defences had tempted outsiders to invade. The Irish from Leinster had occupied and settled in the Lleyn Peninsula (the names are cognate) and the natives had found it impossible to prevent this. With a large force of cavalry Cunedda was sent from the north to remove them, and he succeeded. In the whole history of the Western Roman Empire it was the only time when outsiders or so-called barbarians were ejected permanently. The history of Wales owes much to the General. And tradition underlines that debt by remembering the victory. For many generations in North Wales any deserted settlements or sheilings were known as 'Cytian yr Gwyddelod', the Huts of the Irish.

But the expedition was no simple matter. Logistically the movement of an army of cavalry is not easy; horses and spare remounts require a great deal of fodder and water, to say nothing of the troopers and their auxiliaries. Journey times between pre-selected and organised staging points will have had to be calculated and kept to. Such an exercise required planning and management. Perhaps they used the old Roman forts of Cumbria and Lancashire as stopovers where horses could graze in safety and troopers perhaps find roofed buildings for a dry bivouac. The system of Roman roads was still in working order and Cunedda's cavalry will have clattered on a good stone surface for much of the way. It is often forgotten how long the old straight roads lasted; as late as 1296 Edward I, King of England, was able to lead a 20 mile baggage train up Dere Street into Scotland. Cunedda's army was not an expeditionary force like Edward I's, and after they had despatched the Irish, they intended to settle on their lands. The campaign took a long time and the place-names of reconquered territory reflect that; Gwynedd is from Cunedda himself, Cardigan from his son Ceretic and Merioneth for a grandson who retained a Roman name, Marianus.

The army rode south from the Celtic kingdom of Gododdin to rescue Wales from the barbarians for several reasons, but one of the most compelling must have been practical. Clearly Gododdin was powerful and it was thought that the manpower could be spared to rescue North Wales. When Cunedda left the Tweed Valley, probably from the old fortress at Roxburgh where his grandfather, Paternus Pesrut, had been Prefect, he did not abandon the area. The genealogies note his successor as a 'son' of Coel Hen and they give him an interesting name. Unlike Cunedda's native British titles, this man prefered a Roman dignity and he called himself Germanianus. This was in imitation of the generals and emperors of the past who added a title to denote their conquests. For example, after the defeat of the British tribes in 43AD, Claudius called himself Britannicus and others did similar things. Germanianus was a king who triumphed over Germans in battle. But who were they?

In the early 5th century a group of Angles who had been employed as mercenaries by the Count of the Saxon Shore to protect the eastern coastline rebelled, and attempted to carve out territory in the East Riding of Yorkshire. Germanianus won victories against them and archaeology shows that thereafter they were confined to a very small area. Subdued they may have been at that time but this enclave would become the kingdom of Deira and one day the birthplace of great kings, the Northumbrians.

Germanianus ruled over the Tweed Valley and North Northumberland with one of his principal bases on Yeavering Bell near Wooler. His descendents would also rule a great kingdom and they too called it by a British name, Bryneich or Berneich. It would grow into Bernicia and its kings would also become the ancestors of the Northumbrian dynasties.

But that is to anticipate events — and by some distance. In the 440s both Cunedda and Germanianus were fighting barbarians beyond the limits of their own territory. And they were doing it for a reason we find hard to understand. But the reality for them was that they were acting as the defenders and inheritors of the Empire. In the West, Rome still stood, embattled and with most provinces overrun by tribes of invaders from the east, but an Emperor ruled and a Senate debated as they had for a thousand years. And perhaps the Romans would return, they had done so before.

What is particularly striking about Coel Hen, Cunedda and Germanianus is how quickly these men took control and how decisive their ability to act could be. In the European provinces of the Empire a powerful Celtic society did not re-emerge. Resistance to barbarian invaders was led by Romanised noblemen such as Aetius and Syagrius in Gaul. But the most vital of British leaders were native Celts and they came from the Tweed Valley and Southern Scotland, an area only occasionally part of the Empire and influenced by Rome rather than controlled by it. Perhaps that is the reason why the Borders became the focus of military and political power in Britain in the 5th century. Not, for once in our history, the south or the south-east of what is now England, but the lands between the Roman walls were the place where decisions affecting the future of all of Britain were taken.

THE DUKE OF BATTLES

No heroic figure from the immense sweep of British history has remained so alive in the popular imagination as Arthur. Each generation seems to devise a version of his story to suit their times, and in the late 20th century Luke Skywalker took the role of the young warrior and Obe Wan Kenobe became Merlin, the wise counsellor.

The historical origins of Arthur are complex and difficult to pin to a map. There is little doubt that he existed and made an impact on his time — why else would his name have survived so widely in story and place-name? The case for the historical Arthur having had his base of operations in the Borders is very compelling.

The actions of Cunedda and Germanianus, and the legacy of Count Theodosius show that the centre of British military and political power in the centuries following the Roman withdrawal from Britannia in 410 was in southern Scotland. Gildas wrote of a lull in the fighting between the Anglo-Saxon invaders and the native British which began around 500–510 and persisted to the time of his writing in 560. Fragments of the lost chronicle of North Britain, known as the Nennius text, describe a successful campaign led by Arthur against invaders, and several obscure place-names associated with those battles are listed. Toponymic research shows that 9 of Arthur's 13 battles took place between the Antonine Wall and Hadrian's Wall. From a line in 'Y Gododdin' poem, written in Edinburgh in 600, it is clear that Arthur's name was a by-word for bravery in the north at that early date, and also that his descendents were cavalry warriors.

The old medieval castle of Roxburgh, near Kelso, had a much longer history than its ruins suggest. Dark ages ditching at the west end and the shadow of more in the east offer clues. But when the historian and archaeologist, Walter Elliot, and others found hundreds of late Roman coins in a field across the River Teviot opposite Roxburgh, it became clear that the story went back even further.

Cavalry forts have special requirements and the castlemount and the wide haughland between the Tweed and the Teviot provide all of them. The river peninsula supplies protected and well-watered grazing for hundreds of horses, and the steep mount security for as many men. It is a near-perfect location. The ancient Celtic name of Roxburgh Castle was preserved and before the Angles came to change it, it was called Marchidun, in Old Welsh, the Horse Fort. Medieval and modern Arthurians would have prefered to call it Camelot.

Geography and political accident had much to do with the historical shift of power to the north, and both of these factors also served to protect the only Roman city in the Borders. Carlisle had grown in importance in the 4th century when it had become the capital of one of the four provinces of Britain, and it was still functioning as an urban centre as late as 685. Near the end of his exemplary life St Cuthbert visited Carlisle and was shown a Roman fountain still working. The anonymous author of an early biography of the saint reported;

"Cuthbert, leaning on his staff, was listening to Wagga the Reeve of Carlisle explaining to the Queen the Roman wall of the city."

And the Venerable Bede adds;

"… the citizens conducted him around the city walls to see a remarkable Roman fountain that was built into them."

As they showed the old monk and the Queen of Northumbria around the still-intact walls, their guides showed that they understood the history of Carlisle and the importance of a working fountain. It implies an acqueduct, a water supply system and drainage. And when a church dedicated to St Cuthbert was erected some time after 698, its alignment, still observable today, follows the street pattern of the Roman city. Much later, a large arched stone building was still standing when William of Malmesbury, the 12th century historian, described its inscription to Mars and Venus.

Carlisle was not the only civic survivor beyond 410. After the Barbarian Conspiracy of 367, Count Theodosius had ensured that the cities of Britain had adequate walls (and also towers at the angles to allow ballistas to rake their fire laterally along them). Undoubtedly their walls helped to protect St Albans well into the 5th century as well as Bath and Wroxeter. The cities of Roman Britain declined into ruins because their hinterlands eventually failed to provide enough food on a regular and reliable basis to feed their citizens. But in the Eden and Irthing valleys, there is good evidence that farming hinterlands continued to prosper unmolested for several generations after 410. At Old Penrith an inscription has been uncovered dedicated to Flavius Martius and he is described as a 'Senator' at Carlisle, while a milestone from Brougham talks of 'R.P.C.' the Respublica Civitas Carvetiorum, loosely 'the government of the capital of the tribe of the Carvetii'. Both finds indicate an important centre but their dates are not necessarily much later than 410. What takes the story of post-Roman Carlisle forward is something altogether unexpected.

St Patrick was born some time around 415 near Greenhead, between Haltwhistle and Brampton on the modern map, but near the Wall fort of Birdoswald on the old. The evidence for this blunt assertion does not come from a headstone or a birth certificate, but a process of reasonable deductions. Certain facts about Patrick are few but they do have the great merit of coming directly from the saint himself. He left two pieces of writing; the 'Confession' contains some autobiographical detail, and the 'Letter to Coroticus' has something to say about the politics of the north in the 5th century.

In the Confession there are some names, and these are very informative indeed. Patrick tells us that his father was Calpurnius and that he held office both in the church and in a city. Deacon literally means servant but in the context of early church life, it denoted a lay officer who may have attended to the secular affairs of a parish or diocese. But its use at least places Calpurnius as a Christian amongst other Christians in a church with an organised structure. And also a well-established church, for Patrick also says that his grandfather, Potitus, had been ordained a priest. For three generations this family had been Christians, going back perhaps to 360AD, and their church was sufficiently securely founded to have a bishop able to make new priests at that time. There were bishops in Britain as early as 314, and so the image of Potitus preaching and ministering to a congregation in the north 36 years later does not seem extravagant.

Patrick's father, Calpurnius, was a landowner wealthy enough to have male and female servants. The precise term for what he owned was a 'villula', or a small villa estate — and that fact alone locates Patrick's birth and upbringing in late Roman Britain. No villas or villulas existed in Ireland, for it remained independent of the Empire. But how is it possible to place Calpurnius' estate at Greenhead in the Irthing Valley, east of Brampton?

The historical context of Patrick's life, adventures and mission sets him somewhere near the north-west coast of Britannia in the 5th century AD, opposite the coast of the north of Ireland where he lived for two separate periods. Carlisle was the only Roman city in the north-west quarter of Britannia which at that time was a going concern. And Patrick's father's second official role means that his family had to live near a Roman city. In addition to being a deacon of the church, Calpurnius was also a decurion. This was something quite specific to Roman and post-Roman civic government. A civitas like Carlisle was run by a group known as the 'ordo', a body of around 100 men of means and standing who lived both in the city and also in the surrounding countryside. They were the decurions.

Patrick goes on to say that Calpurnius' villula is near a place called 'vicus bannavem taberniae', a name that seems to be partly corrupted. 'Vicus' is clear, and it was a settlement outside the walls of a Roman fort. The other element that reads clearly is 'bern', an Old Welsh name for a mountain pass. The only place in north-west Britannia which is simultaneously near a large fort and its vicus, a working Roman city and piece of geography that could bear the description of a mountain pass is at Greenhead. Near the fort of Birdoswald, the valley of the River Irthing narrows into a gorge which squeezes the road and the watercourse into a pass. Excavation on the south side of the river could possibly reveal the house of a small estate, and the birthplace of St Patrick.

In the Confession the familiar story of Ireland's patron saint is outlined. At the age of 15 or 16 (and bearing the British name Sochet or Sucat) he was captured in a slaving raid along with 'the male and female sevants of my father's house' and shipped down the Solway and across to the Antrim coast. After 6 years as a shepherd he escaped from captivity and walked a long way, probably to one of the Leinster ports. There he boarded a ship (exporting hunting dogs) and sailed for three days before making a second long journey on foot. The evidence suggests that Patrick travelled to France where he may have come in contact with the great St Martin of Tours, the founder of western monasticism.

At some point, possibly around 440, Patrick came back home to Britain and underwent formal training in the church. Now, this says a good deal about 5th century Carlisle. There is likely to have been a bishop at the head of an ecclesiastical organisation which supported Potitus as a priest, Calpurnius as a deacon, and could teach Patrick — in Latin. He cannot have expected to be confirmed as a deacon much before the age of 30, or to attain the next grade of presbyter or priest for another 5 years after that. While he was being trained in the familia of the Bishop of Carlisle, Patrick's father died and left him what he described as 'nobilitas mea', a mixture of inheritance and rank. This included not only the villula at Greenhead but also a town house in Carlisle and the rank of decurion of the city. By the time this happened, around 450, Patrick had decided to move on again, and so he sold all that his father had bequeathed him 'for the good of others'. Despite occasional raids by Irish slavers, Carlisle appears to have been a settled place with a thriving and expanding church under the protection of the Celtic kings of Rheged, the first generation descended from Coel Hen. Perhaps there was little to excite Patrick. When he sold his inheritance, he had resolved to use the cash to finance a mission to Ireland, the place where he had been enslaved.

Now, Patrick did not venture alone into a land of heathens, no matter how dramatic subsequent biographers have made his mission sound. There were groups of Christians in Ireland before 450, and it was to their invitation that he responded. Palladius was sent to the Irish in 431 by Pope Celestinus, and according to surving documents, he was successful. The cult of Patrick has obliterated the achievement of his predecessor. However, Palladius' ambit was in the south, centred on Leinster. Patrick went north, an area he already knew when he was a slave, and concentrated his efforts on Ulster, and the city of Armagh became closely identified with him and his subsequent cult. Bishops rarely went where there were no Christians at all and usually waited for an invitation before going into new territory to found a see. It seems likely that Patrick was invited by a small group in the north and in response to a general papal direction to make converts, a synod of British bishops chose to allow him to go to Ireland. The fact that he had the resources, through the sale of his father's estate, to mount a mission will have encouraged everyone concerned.

While he was bishop in Northern Ireland, around 470AD, St Patrick wrote an irritable letter to Coroticus, King of Strathclyde, to complain about the behaviour of his subjects. Evidently they had been raiding and enslaving the Irish whom Patrick had been working hard to convert, and if Christians behaved no better than pagans, what was the point? The saint develops a fine rage and fulminates that the Strathclyde men were not acting like;

"citizens of the holy Romans, but rather of the Devil, living in the enemy ways of the Barbarians."

Now, Patrick knew that the Damnonians had never been citizens of the Empire. He was refering to Coroticus himself, and his warriors, to the grandson of Quintilius the Prefect and the descendents of his cavalry troopers. Even though the province of Britannia had been abandoned 60 years before, in 410AD, and to all intents and practical purposes, had ceased to exist, Patrick still talked of Roman citizens on the Clyde, and of civilised standards of behaviour. Romania still lived in people's minds and Romanitas still meant something.

That was certainly true for people in Galloway and Southern Scotland when it came to commemoration. Several inscribed stones have been found which point to communities of early Christians who understood enough Latin to make statements about themselves and those important to them. They also adopted Latinised versions of their names even though none of them lived inside the boundaries of the former Empire. Viventius and Mavorius are named as 'Sacerdotes' or priests, and Ventidius is a sub-deacon. Many of the stones were found at Kirkmadrine and on the Whithorn peninsula in western Galloway, and this was the location of an early church which found enduring fame through the reputation of a charismatic bishop.

Ninian may have known Patrick's family for it seems likely that he was a member of the church in Carlisle in 400AD. Sent to Whithorn as bishop, he built a church known as Candida Casa, the White House, or the Shining White House. Meaning that it was made of stone and not wood, this structure marked an important connection, because its construction was thought to be 'in the Roman manner' in contrast to 'more Scottorum', the Irish manner, in wood. Archaeologists have uncovered a substantial ecclesiastical complex dating to Ninian's time. In a brilliant analysis of the Latinus stone, found near Whithorn, Charles Thomas has shown that it is not a tomb but the foundation stone of a church.

Like Patrick, Ninian was charged with a mission and the English historian, Bede, relates that he converted the southern Picts. Both the Novantae and the Selgovae were thought to be Picts by the Northumbrians and when they took over the see of Whithorn in the early 8th century two bishops gave themselves interesting names; Peohthelm means 'Leader of the Picts' and Peohtwine 'Friend of the Picts'. It seems that Ninian did not have far to go to find pagans — there were plenty in the Galloway hills.

The Northumbrians were anxious to promote the cult of Ninian and even though Whithorn suffered in the 9th and 10th centuries, the reputation of its saint was undimmed. A 12th century hagiography by Ailred, Abbot of Rievaulx in Yorkshire, ensured an enduring posterity and eventually, along with Columba, Andrew and Kentigern, Ninian was installed as one of the great saints of Scotland.

Christianity crept northwards from Carlisle up the valleys of the Southern Uplands and over their watersheds to the Tweed Basin. Inscribed stones mark its steady progress. Near where the Ralton Burn flows into the Liddel Water, about a mile north of Newcastleton, a drystane dyke was undercut by a flood and it toppled into the river. One of the stones was so large, nearly 6 foot long, that it stuck out above the water, and those who came to rebuild the dyke noticed writing carved on its surface. It read 'Hic Iacet Caranti Filii Cupitani', 'Here Lies Carantus, Son of Cupitanus', and archaeologists dated the stone to the 5th or 6th centuries. An object of that size is unlikely to have moved far, and the adoption of Latin names on a tombstone means that Christianity was seeping into the Borders through the western valleys.

In the 19th century another stone from the same period was found near Peebles, but sadly it has been lost, perhaps broken up or destroyed. However, the inscription was recorded and it told of ecclesiastical organisation for it said 'Locus Sancti Nicolae Episcopi', 'The Seat of St Nicolas, Bishop'. Another stone from Peebles recorded 'Neitano Sacerdos', 'Neithon the Priest'. Now, these inscriptions present a danger of over-interpretation, but what can be soberly asserted is that, as in Carlisle, there existed an organised church in the Borders at a very early date which was structured into recognisable canonical grades.

And also the presence of a bishop implies a number of churches in the area and possibly a number of parishes.

Support for this view lay in nearby ground. The Manor Valley is a very beautiful place. It runs south from the line of the Tweed near Peebles and ends at the source of the Manor Water, on Shielhope Head. There is, as they say, one road in and one road out. But the Manor is no historical cul-de-sac. In 1890 a slab of hard whinstone was pulled out of a small cairn on a hillside in the valley. On it were carved two words and a small cross. It appeared to be a tombstone and the finders took it down the hillside and set it next to St Gorgian's Cross. The name of Coninia was commemorated and she may have died in the 5th or 6th centuries. St Gorgian died before her, for he was an obscure Syrian martyr who met his maker around 350AD. The medieval parish church of Manor was dedicated to him and there exist traditions which take this association much further back into the past. Common sense also suggests an early dedication, perhaps in the 5th century when Gorgian's fame, such as it was, was still high.

In any case the continuity of Christianity in one place is impressive and the present church in the Manor Valley may have a long 1500 year history. But there is much more than a cross and a stone to see on the ground. Secular continuity at Manor is probably unique in Scotland, because it looks as though the pattern of landholding and the organisation of society has remained unchanged for a similar length of time.

The name of Manor is from the Old Welsh 'Maenor' and it had a specific and recorded meaning. A maenor was a collection of farms which formed a natural geographic, economic and administrative unit — in modern parlance, an estate. Manor's boundaries are clear, they are the watershed ridges of the surrounding hills, and the number of farms in the valley has not varied in a millenium. There were 13 in the early medieval period and 12 remain now, but according to the Second Statistical Account in 1845, 13 existed even at that late stage. The number and its consistency are important because they place the Manor Valley and its people in a cultural context which can be clearly understood from Welsh sources.

Hywel Dda was king of most of Wales in the 10th century, and he is remembered as Hywel the Good for a good reason. He caused Welsh folk law to be codified, and in so doing created a clear picture of how society worked. The law had been developing for centuries and the basic administrative units it regulated are very ancient. In the margin of the Book of St Chad, compiled c740, is a description of a maenor at a place called Llandybie, north of Llanelli. Society was pyramid-shaped with a king, his family, his warband and aristocrats at the top. They were the bonheddwyr, and the 'bon' element denotes ancestry or breeding just in the way that 'gens' prefixes 'gentleman'. Supporting them was a large unfree group, the Taeogion, and under them were Caethion, or slaves. These last were likely less numerous — in the Domesday Book of 1086 only 10% of the population were true slaves.

The basic unit of the maenor were the villages of the Taeogion and these were organised into groups of 7 in fertile lowland areas, and into 13 in upland districts like the Manor Valley in the Borders. Gwestfa, or food-rent, was owed by each settlement of Taeogion and the collection of this, as well as other matters like the allocation of land, was under the control of a powerful man called the Maer.

This office has survived in Scotland as a surname and in England as an office. Deriving from a Latin borrowing of 'Maior' or 'greater person', there are Mairs living at Scottish addresses, and Mayors presiding in English town halls. But these are not the only vestigial connections with an Old Welsh way of organising society in Southern Scotland. A collection of laws known as the 'Leges inter Brettos et Scotos' (the Laws between Britons and Scots) dates from the 10th century and it remembers much about the old ways. 'Galanas' is a Welsh term meaning blood price and it survived in practice in Scotland until very late. The Laws of Hywel Dda go into great detail, but the basic principle was that, in order to discourage violent revenge and wasteful feuding, the murderer of a person had to pay his value to the family or kindred of the victim, or the owner of a slave. The sliding scale of rates began with the king and each grade below was worth half of the son of the man above.

Women were worth less, a daughter half the galanas of her brother and a wife a third of that of her husband. But women were not wholly without rights and, unlike in English society, they had real status in law. If a husband was unfaithful, his wife received compensation and in the event of a divorce property was divided. Behind this lay a fundamental assumption in Welsh-speaking society that marriage was a contract and not a sacrament. But it could work the other way. If, immediately after marriage, a woman was discovered not to have been a virgin, the deceived husband could drag her out of the bedroom and, in front of the wedding guests, slit her shift open and shame her publicly.

Hywel's laws recognised that the act of marriage could take several forms in addition to a church wedding and one legacy of that way of thinking was the general absence of discrimination between legitimate and illegitimate children. Also, cohabitation ranked as formal marriage if it went beyond 7 years and a child 'begotten in brake or bush' was the responsibility of the father.

The Maer lived at the Maerdref and a likely candidate at Manor is the old fort of Cademuir near the mouth of the valley. This was the ingathering point for food-rents and the organisation of other services due in the maenor. These in turn were rendered to the king or to the bonheddwyr. In the 5th and 6th centuries the most important officer in the household of a Welsh-speaking king was the Penteulu, the Chief of the Warband. He went everywhere with the king, never left his side, for the warband was the basis of his power and the beating heart of authority. And in the Leges inter Brettos et Scotos this ancient relationship was remembered. The provision of food and lodging for a royal warband is listed as a service due. It was called the 'cylch' and its collection rigorously enforced.

The Leges also preserved an interesting variant on galanas known as 'cro'. It equates to the Irish Gaelic idea of 'enech', literally 'face' but really means honour, and there were elaborate laws in Ireland to deal with its loss and restitution. Honour and status within and amongst kindred groups was important. In the Irish law tracts of the 7th century an insult and the payment required to compensate for it was known as the 'enechruicce' or 'face-reddening'. If the giver of the insult ignored the 'law of the face', the bards had licence to subject him to public mockery so that amongst his peers his face fell further.

The whole force of traditional practices and dues in both the Scottish Leges and Hywel Dda's Laws is to support and service the idea of the kindred, help keep it stable and productive. There was no distinction between civil and criminal law, and no sharp relationship between crime and retributive punishment. Rather than the cutting off of a hand or the branding of a thief, restitution was what mattered, and that restitution was made to families and kindreds.

In the Manor Valley all of these things will have happened and were dealt with. Taxes were collected and fines paid. And the church seems to have inserted itself early into that cycle and took a proportion of much of what was rendered.

In both Welsh and Gaelic the words for a church are cognate, and 'eglwys' and 'eaglais' derive from the Latin 'ecclesia'. When Border place-names incorporate it, such as at Ecclefechan (the Little Church) in Dumfriesshire or Eccles in Berwickshire, it usually means that an early British church was founded there. And on the Ordnance Survey eccles names are often a strong toponymic clue to the remains of an old Celtic maenor. The skeletons of several can still be made out in North Northumberland because at an early stage they were given by the king of the Northumbrians to the church — some in the 7th century. And these places stayed in the hands of the clergy until Domesday in 1086 when they were recorded in writing.

But they were not called maenors. The English word 'shire' replaced the Celtic term although the core of the institution itself was largely unchanged. On the mainland opposite Lindisfarne was Islandshire, and Norhamshire neighboured it to the north. Over the Tweed lay Coldinghamshire and Berwickshire. In the 12th century the first three still belonged to the Bishop of Durham, and had retained their organisation and their shape. But Berwickshire had shifted its focus. The centre of the old shire had been at Eccles, much further west and the medieval nunnery with its large parish of three chapelries is a substantial shadow of its former status. Berwick means 'Barley-farm' and the suffix 'wic' denoted an outlying farm attached to a shire centre. There are many in the Borders; Hawick was the 'Hedge-farm' and may have been part of an old shire based on Jedburgh. The town clung on tenaciously to its status as a county capital when the new shire of Roxburgh was evolving in the Middle Ages and a powerful and ancient tradition possibly lay behind its acceptance as such by other, larger and more important towns. Borthwick means 'Byre-farm' and may have been part of the same unit as Hawick, while Fishwick is obvious and it may have belonged to Eccles. It is not clear how Berwick changed from being a dependent settlement to the shire capital, but its port and the growing trade through it may have had an influence.

In the Borders there is a lost shire whose nature and limits show a clear comparison and continuity with the Manor Valley and the maenor. The eccles name is buried under a more recent church but it is still recognisable. Kirk Yetholm is built on Eccles Cairn and a tradition existed in the 18th century that there was a dependent chapel nearby dedicated to St Etheldreda, the wife of King Ecgfrith of Northumbria. Around the Eccles Cairn are 12 upland farms which look very like they formed an old Celtic maenor. They lie in the Bowmont Valley and, as in Manor, many are still going concerns. Sourhope at the head of the Bowmont is joined by Shereburgh, Clifton, Staerough, Yetholm itself and Yetholm Mains, Shotton, Halterburn, and Mindrum, and there are three others with disappeared names not easily pinned on the map. Yetholmshire is a clearly defined geographical area and in 655 it belonged as a unit to King Oswy of Northumbria. In thanks for his victory over Penda of Mercia at the battle at the Winwaed Oswy gave the shire to the bishopric of Lindisfarne. The shadows of other ancient Border shires can be traced on the map. At the head of the Yarrow valley a clutch of Old Welsh place-names surround a possible upland centre at Chapelhope, there way be another at Phenzhopehaugh, and one at Bedrule between Jedburgh and Hawick.

The creation and increased policing of the Anglo-Scottish border on the line of the River Tweed loosened Lindisfarne/Durham's grip on Yetholmshire and in the 12th century King David I of Scotland granted it to Walter Corbet, a Norman knight in his service. But despite the changing politics around it, the old shire retained its unity. And even though four of its farms strayed over the border into England and another jurisdiction, Corbet was still recognised as their owner as they were part of the old administrative set-up. Mindrum was one of these and the place-name is the only ghost of the Celtic maenor left. It comes from 'mynydd', the Old Welsh word for mountain and may refer to the steep-sided Pawston Hill immediately behind the farm.

Like the maenors, shires retained certain common characteristics. The name of the chief official, the Maer, survived in Scotland for a time in the title of the great noblemen called Mormaers, but in the Borders the man in charge got the name 'Thane'. Like galanas, cro and cylch, other Old Welsh terms became embedded in later medieval habits and in the great and wealthy prince-bishopric of Durham the maenor makes a fleeting appearance. Cows given each year to the cathedral clergy were called in Latin 'vacca de metreth' and 'treth' is the Old Welsh word for tribute. But perhaps the most obvious and persistent survival of the maenors and their successor shires is the common grazing land that was attached to each. In Scotland this was called the muir or moor and at the head of the Manor Valley lies the Sheriffmuir on the banks of the Tweed. Yetholmshire's old common is still used and the area of haughland between Town Yetholm and Kirk Yetholm, on either side of the Bowmont Water, remains open and unfenced. In recent times gypsies have camped there and grazed their ponies. Unlike elsewhere, no-one in Yetholm minds, because people have brought their beasts to the haugh for a long time, perhaps 1500 years.

By the middle of the 6th century most of the native British were
Christians. Their conversion had been the work of dedicated priests moving
steadily north from established centres at Carlisle and in Galloway. A
fleeting notion of how these men spread the word of God has been
found at the village of Ednam, near Kelso. A bronze handbell, about
eight inches high, came to light and it may date from the period before
600AD when British churches were being established at places with
eccles names and elsewhere. But before a church could be founded and
built, it needed Christians to fill and support it. Travelling priests,
sometimes called 'peregrini' or pilgrims, said masses in the open air,
possibly at places already thought to be sacred from the pagan past,
such as wells, springs or river-meetings. To announce their presence, visiting
priests rang a bell around the houses and farms to rouse a congregation.

Ednam Kirk is old, and dedicated to the great saint of Lindisfarne,
Cuthbert. And the village has one of the oldest working mills in all of
the north. Ednam may have been a British foundation, perhaps attached
to Eccles only three miles away, but hard evidence for that is lost.

Evidence for anything in the crucial transitional period between 410
and 600 is very difficult to come by. The only native British record of
that time to survive in more than fragments was written by a priest
called Gildas. Later hagiographies remembered a tradition of him coming
from the north, possibly Carlisle, and his knowledge of the history and
politics of North Britain seems to be good. Gildas wrote a grumpy
book, 'On the Ruin of Britain', and in it he distributes the blame for the
loss of parts of the island to Germanic invaders. Sloth, foolishness and a
lack of Latin disabled kings and other powerful men from acting
decisively to eject the people he called 'the rascals' from British territory.
He begins with a rapid sketch of the history of Britain. Without
mentioning many names and giving virtually no dates, Gildas records
the harrying of Britain by the Picts and the Irish in the 5th century. The
raids became so severe that the British cities wrote to Aetius, the
Romanised nobleman leading resistance to barbarian incursions in Gaul.
Here is part of the letter;

"To Aetius, thrice consul, come the groans of the Britons... the barbarians
drive us into the sea, and the sea drives us back to the barbarians.
Between these, two deadly alternatives confront us, drowning or
slaughter."

The appeal was fruitless but it does show how persistent was the sense
of Britannia as part of the disintegrating Roman Empire in the west. To
gain some respite, Gildas says that Saxon mercenaries were hired to
defend 'the east side of the country'. After a time they mutinied and
demanded land. But then British military power reasserted itself and
with an emphatic victory at Mount Badon around the year 500, security
was established for perhaps two generations. It lasted until c550, the
time Gildas sat down to write his book.

And that is, more or less, all the general data that can be gleaned
from 'On the Ruin of Britain'. If Gildas had lived and worked at Carlisle
then the reference to the east side of the country can only mean Saxons

who were active on the Berwickshire or Northumberland coastline. An early Kentish Chronicle of the 8th century offers some help with the identity of these mercenaries;

"Hengist said to Vortigern…' Take my advice, and you will never fear conquest by any man or any people, for my people are strong. I will invite my son and his cousin, fine warriors, to fight against the Irish. Give them the lands of the north, next to the Wall'… He invited Octha and Ebissa with forty keels; when they had sailed round against the Picts and plundered the Orkneys, they came and occupied several districts beyond the 'Frenessican Sea', as far as the borders of the Picts."

Some of this, like the Frenessican Sea, is impenetrable, but the gist of it is plain. A southern, native leader called Vortigern had hired Saxons under the command of Hengist, and, with an eye on any opportunity, he had in turn found a job and some land in the north for his relatives. The expedition of Octha and Ebissa to Northumberland might be remembered in a collection of graves which cannot be dated, but are Anglo-Saxon in nature, and the temporary posting of Germanic warriors in the Nith Valley has left the place-name of Dumfries, the Fort of the Frisians.

ANGELN

Where did they come from? And why did they come? These questions about the origins of the Germanic tribes who invaded Britain after the Roman withdrawal are too rarely asked or answered. Perhaps understandably historians have prefered to concentrate on what they did when they got here.

According to Bede, Angles, Saxons and Jutes formed the racial makeup of the incomers but archaeologists add Frisians, Franks and Swedes to the list. Some of the tribes who sailed across the North Sea were originally neighbours. The Angles occupied the southern part of the Danish peninsula and some offshore islands while the Saxons lived in the lands between them and the mouth of the River Weser. The Jutes appear to have come from Jutland in northern Denmark, while the Frisians arrived from the necklace of islands off the Dutch coast, and the Franks from what is now France.

Archaeologists in northern Germany have discovered that some of the lands long settled by the Angles and Saxons were flooded in the 5th century by rising sea levels. Climate change may have forced some of the emigrants to seek dry lodging in Britain, but there were also other pressures. Europe is shaped like a funnel, and when peoples in Asia moved, a ripple effect could be felt as far away as the North Sea coast. The Angles, Saxons and Jutes and others came to Britain in a period known as 'Die Volkerwanderung', or 'The Folk Migrations' when many groups of people were on the move in search of land.

Gildas' Latin would grate on the ears of Classical scholars reared on Cicero and Virgil, but his style is interesting and it links him with St Patrick. Both men wrote in a manner which shows a late Roman rhetorical training. And the similarities strengthen the possibility of a school at Carlisle where a Latin education could still be had well into the 6th century. In essence Patrick and Gildas used the same classical structure for what they wrote. An introduction was followed by historical background, and then the outline of the main points of what they wanted to say, then some detail to back it up, and finally a summing-up and an epilogue which attempted to enlist the sympathies of the reader with the argument/narrative they set down.

What the Latin influences on Gildas and Patrick show is a protected enclave somewhere in the north where classical educational principles were still being passed on, still being valued. Without feeling any need to explain that he is refering to Latin and not his native tongue of Old Welsh, Gildas writes of 'nostra lingua', our language. But it was the church and its structures and mission which created an atmosphere in which nostra lingua could survive, and Christianity was a key element of Romanitas, something which further distinguished the overwhelmingly Christian Britons from the pagan Saxons. Gildas used another term which was equally eloquent about another shared attitude. In 'On the Ruin of Britain' he Latinised a Celtic root-word into 'Combrogi', and it refered to the British, the people with a shared border, the compatriots — and, by extension, the Citizens. This sense of the Roman past is, however, somewhat coloured in Gildas's writings. He is always careful to avoid confusing Romans with Britons, and it appears that the educated class he came from may have resented Roman rule and its historical failure. Latinity and Christianity are what he valued and perhaps the idea of Romanitas by 550 had developed into something more complex than a simple imitation of the habits and prestige of the Empire.

Octha and Ebissa are not noted again in the record, but at the same time as Gildas may have sat down to write in Carlisle, their descendents were stirring on the eastern coastline;

"In the year 547, Ida began his reign, which lasted for twelve years. From him the royal family of the Northumbrians derives its origin."

This passage occurs in the last chapter of the last book of 'The Ecclesiatical History of the English People'. Written by the Venerable Bede at the monastery of Monkwearmouth in 731, it is a masterpiece. Beautifully and clearly set out, well researched and intelligently expressed, it is also, unlike the groans of Gildas, a work of palpable optimism. Instead of attacking the misconduct of kings or priests and bemoaning the fall in civilised standards, Bede offers good examples for his readers to follow, tales of simple devotion and steadfastness to encourage them and only a mild irony when something amuses or displeases him.

And insofaras it is possible to tell, Bede is honest and straightforward, both in detail and in general. The title of the great work he wrote in his old age says exactly what it is, 'The Ecclesiastical History of the English People'. Definitely not a history of the place now called England and all who lived there up to the year 731, but a history of the English people and their church. Consequently Bede relates the story of the Roman occupation of Britannia, setting the Northumbrian kings in a pleasing continuum of Romanitas. However he has very little indeed to say about the majority of Old Welsh-speaking Celts who still lived in Northumbria and over much of the south of England. Bede is not writing their history — he is establishing the origins and progress of his kings, his people, the Northumbrians. Sadly his clarity of purpose has not been imitated by many of his successors. Modern English historians have confused his excellent history of the English people with their histories of England. And these are most certainly not the same thing.

ON THE RECKONING OF TIME

Given the sensitivities implicit in the debate at the Synod of Whitby in 664, it is not surprising that the Venerable Bede took great trouble over the dates in his 'Ecclesiastical History of the English People'. To make the sequence of events as clear as possible he adopted the AD system of dating which we use today. It was invented by Dionysius Exiguus (died 550AD) who worked out 1AD as the year in which Christ was both conceived and born. There is no evidence that he was correct and some that he got it wrong. According to the gospel writers Christ may have been born in the last year of the reign of Herod the Great, that is, 4BC. Or in the year of the first Roman census of Judaea, which was 6 to 7AD.

Bede wrote 'De temporum ratione', 'On the Reckoning of Time' in 725 to establish the AD system, to work out a table of dates for Easter up to 1063, and to sort out a chronology of world history to the reign of his contemporary, Leo the Isaurian, Emperor of Rome in the East at Constantinople. Romanitas affected chronological thinking and a popular alternative to AD dating was AUC; it stands for 'Ante Urbe Condita', 'from the founding of the city [of Rome]' in the 8th century BC. Regnal years were also used and in Spain and Portugal a system of counting dates from the Roman invasions of 39BC persisted until the 14th century.

Although AD was a concept created by someone else, it was Bede's adoption of it which led to its use in Europe and its ultimate ratification in 1048AD by Pope Leo IX.

Historians have written of the emergence of Bernicia in the 6th and 7th centuries as the first powerful expression of a particularly English polity in post-Roman Britain. By way of a parenthesis, they also note that the place-name of Bernicia is surprising in that it seems not to be English in origin, like Sussex, Essex or East Anglia. Bernicia is in fact an Old Welsh name. Bede simply reports that "in 547AD Ida began his reign". All of that is accurate, but it leaves one key question hanging in the air. Why did a new English, or Anglian king call his new kingdom by a Welsh or British name when his contemporaries in the south did not? A rapid survey of the maps of Australia or the USA will demonstrate that this is not what conquerors generally do. And why did Ida simply 'begin to reign' while all over the rest of England new Anglo-Saxon dynasties are busy killing in battle, ravaging and removing the previous owners?

Like St Patrick's birthplace at 'vicus bannavem taberniae' Bernicia comes from the Old Welsh root 'bern' for 'a gap, or mountain pass' and it derives from Bryneich or Berneich, the kingdom of the southern Gododdin ruled by Germanianus in the 440s. So that etymology gives Bernicia, 'the Land of the Mountain Pass'. At first sight this seems highly unlikely, a description of somewhere else. North Northumberland and the Tweed Valley do not abound in mountain passes. Even in the 6th century the rolling riverine hills and the dense woodland were altogether much less dramatic.

Except in one place, as will be argued presently. If Ida began to reign, according to the Venerable Bede, over a kingdom called by a Welsh or British name, then where did he rule it from? This at least is very clear. Ida took his wife's name, Bebba, and gave it to the great fortress which became the urbs regis, the royal city, and which we know as Bamburgh. Ida's people were originally sailors, or more correctly marines, who may have been descended from Octha and Ebissa or possibly arrivals in Northumberland from the south as hired coastal protection against the Picts from the north, and also other Germanic tribes from across the North Sea. The establishment of a naval base at Bamburgh and another on Holy Island makes every sort of logistical sense.

To make the process of Ida's transition from marine commander to the king of a British-named kingdom more understandable, we should turn to the alternative to Bede's very English history. This is the great heap of documents known as the History of the Britons. It was compiled by a Welsh-speaking monk called Nennius some time in the 8th century, perhaps 150 years after Ida lived. It is also the source of the Kentish Chronicle that related the original story of Octha and Ebissa. The History is no more than a collection of different documents arranged loosely in what Nennius believed was a chronological sequence. Disarmingly, he wrote in the preface, "I have made a heap of all I have found". There are sections dealing with a myth-history of Britain, tales of giants, Brutus the Trojan and a fair amount cribbed from a variety of classical sources. However, one particular group of related passages stands out as authentic and intermittently, very informative. Known as the North British Section, it strongly suggests that its source was a now lost history of the British kingdoms of the 5th and 6th centuries. The lost chronicles may have been written at Whithorn, although the fact that Nennius is a Latinised version of Ninian is no more than a co-incidence, or it may have been compiled in Glasgow where the long continuity of the Strathclyde kingship could more likely sustain such a project.

However that may be, the key passage for understanding what happened when Ida began to reign at Bamburgh reads simply, "Ida joined Din Guauroy to Berneich". Din Guauroy is Old Welsh for Bamburgh and Berneich for Bernicia, but the key word here is 'joined'. Not conquered, defeated in battle, overcome or ravaged like the other kings, but 'joined'.

From all of this evidence it appears that Bernicia was the name of a pre-existing British kingdom which Ida, from a position of power on the coast, took over, possibly in a bloodless coup, backed by a small Anglian elite and buttressed by the support of British warriors. And to make acceptance of his rule more immediately palatable, the name of the kingdom did not become Bamburgh but stayed as Bernicia. But where was Bernicia, the Land of the Mountain Pass?

Between 1952 and 1962 an archaeologist called Brian Hope Taylor excavated one of the most famous Anglo-Saxon sites in Britain. At Yeavering near Wooler, he discovered evidence of a large settlement. There were great feasting and meeting halls, and the largest was 80 feet long and 40 feet wide. With wall timbers sunk 8 feet into the ground, the great hall must have stood high on the little plateau above the River Glen. Carpenters and painters will have decorated its structure with carved heads and vivid motifs and pictures. Anglo-Saxon and Scandinavian halls had names, like ships, and Hrothgar, king of the Shieldings in the epic poem, Beowulf, called his Heorot. Beowulf was probably composed in the 8th century in Northumbria and here is Seamus Heaney's translation of the passage where Hrothgar decides to build his famous hall;

"... So his mind turned
to hall-building: he handed down orders
for men to work on a great mead-hall
meant to be a wonder of the world for ever;
it would be his throne-room and there he would dispense
his God-given goods to young and old —
but not the common land or peoples' lives.
Far and wide through the world, I have heard,
orders for work to adorn that wallstead
were sent to many peoples. And soon it stood there,
finished and ready, in full view,
the hall of halls. Heorot was the name
he had settled on it, whose utterance was law.
Nor did he renege, but doled out rings
and torques at the table. The hall towered,
its gables wide and high..."

Brian Hope Taylor also came across the only pagan Anglo-Saxon temple yet found in England, and a remarkable structure known as the Grandstand, and evidence of much activity. To all intents and purposes, Yeavering became the pre-eminent centre of Bernicia and the larger kingdom of Northumbria in the 7th century. Political decisions affecting the whole of Britain were taken in its painted halls and when the Mercians attacked Northumbria, they made straight for Yeavering to destroy what they saw as the heartbeat of the kingdom.

Nowadays, on the site of the royal capital of the most powerful English kingdom of the 7th century, there is nothing at all to be seen of its ancient glories, only two or three farms and a snell wind whipping off the Cheviots to bend the hawthorn hedges.

Brian Hope Taylor was surprised with the results of his dig at Yeavering. He found only a handful of Anglian objects, a tiny amount of their pottery and overwhelming evidence that it had been and to some extent remained a predominantly British site. There had been a very large Iron Age hillfort on the summit of Yeavering Bell, the domed hill that dominates the valley and looks over the Millfield Plain to the sea and to Bamburgh and Lindisfarne. The fort may have been occupied in the 5th century by Germanianus when he fought the first English settlers. And near the Northumbrian halls, Hope Taylor found the perimeter of a huge cattle corral which had certainly been in use as early as 450AD.

The reason why so few Anglian objects have been found is straight-forward. Yeavering was and remained the centre of the ancient British kingdom of Bernicia, and the evidence for this is difficult to resist. First of all, like that of Bernicia, the name of Yeavering was retained and not changed. It is also Old Welsh and comes from Gefrin, which means Goat-Hill. Bede did not even trouble to seek an English or Latinised version of the old name and he set it down simply as 'Ad Gefrin'. Brian Hope Taylor found no traces of defensive works around the great halls, no ramparts or stockades. That was because none were needed. Two kingdoms had come together in what appears to have been some sort of coalition and no enemies, no third parties, presented any immediate threat. The Grandstand is a unique structure for a unique political situation. Shaped like a wedge of pie, it imitated the tiered seating arrangements of a Roman amphitheatre. With the highest and longest curved row of seats at the top, eight more rows tapered down to the ground level where a dais was set for the king to sit on. This was a self-consciously Roman structure probably used for law-giving when one man told all of his leading people the same thing at the same time so that there could be no dubiety or argument. There were amphitheatres at York and Chester probably still extant and available as models for the designers of the Grandstand. But most obviously this construction signalled a particular commitment to communication — one culture communicating its ideas on kingship to another quite different culture which spoke a different language.

Meetings on the Grandstand are likely to have been as few and as short as possible. When the constant wind whistling down the valley buffeted the wooden stanchions, it must have been cold for those sitting and listening. And in general this place was far from ideal for a royal centre. The only credible reason for the Northumbrian kings to site one of their capital places at Yeavering was continuity. British kings had ruled Bernicia from there, and so that old habits of obedience and a clear recognition of royal authority could be maintained, Ida's successors sat in its draughty halls. When the period of transition was over, the site was abandoned and by the time Bede wrote his history in 731AD, it had been deserted for many years.

But perhaps one of the most compelling pieces of evidence for Yeavering as the centre of Bernicia is the simplest. The Land of the Mountain Pass stands at the mouth of one, the only one in the east. The narrow valley of the River Glen snakes back behind where the great halls and the Grandstand stood and into the Cheviot Hills to find its tributaries in the College Burn and the Bowmont Water. At Kirknewton, it squeezes between the steep sides of Homilton Hill and Kilham Hill before opening out again at the fertile farmland around Mindrum and old Yetholmshire. This is the only place in the eastern Cheviots and the

Tweed Basin where there is a genuine mountain pass connecting two places, the piece of geography that gave its name to Bernicia.

PAGANS

At Yeavering Brian Hope-Taylor discovered the only example of a pagan temple to survive in Britain to be built by the Angles. What went on inside the large building (17 feet across by 35 feet long) is essentially mysterious and the only substantial clue to the rituals was a pit full of ox-skulls and bones. From other evidence it appears that sacrifice was important.

The names of a few gods are known. Famously, the Anglo-Saxon pantheon, such as it has come down to us, gave us the names of some of our days. Wednesday is Woden's Day and he appears to be the paramount deity, closely related to the Norse Odin and the German Wotan, and also, interestingly, his characteristics are an exact mirror of those of the Celtic paramount god, Lugh.

Many Anglo-Saxon dynasties traced descent from Woden, and many also venerated Thunor, the sky-god of lightning who lent his name to Thursday. Friga was a goddess of love and she left us Friday while, in contrast, Tiw was a war-god who named Tuesday.

In his 'De temporum ratione' Bede lists some of the Anglo-Saxon pagan festivals. The most important appears to have been 'Modranect' or 'Mothers' Night' which was held on 25th December while 'Blodmonath' or 'Blood Month' was November when blood puddings were eaten following the autumn slaughter of beasts. Human sacrifice was part of these rituals and in Yorkshire archaeologists excavated the grave of a nobleman where a living woman had been thrown on top of the body, pinned down and then covered with rocks.

Paganism in Anglo-Saxon society seems not to have differed much from the way in which the pre-Christian Celts worshipped. Perhaps the survival of the name of Woden in an Old Welsh inscription on the plinth of the Hawick Horse is less surprising in that context; 'Teribus ye Teriodin', 'The Land of Death, the Land of Odin'.

Ida's coalition kingdom had a rocky beginning. After his death in 559AD, it appears to have broken up into small lordships. The names of kings appear in such rapid succession and for such short reigns, it looks as though there was mortal competition for the throne of Ida, and possibly several men held power in Bernicia simultaneously. Glappa died in 560, Adda in 568, Ealdric in 575, Theodoric in 579, Frithwald in 586, and when Aethelric finally put on the crown in the same year, it appears that he needed the active help of his son, Aethelfrith, in controlling the chaotic affairs of the kingdom.

Such as it is, the historical record shows no attempt by surrounding British kings in the north to take any political advantage of this instability. Instead the heirs of Coel Hen were too busy living up to the reputation awarded to them by Gildas in his book, 'On the Ruin of Britain'. In 573 Gildas' squabbling British kings fought a bloody battle amongst themselves. At a place called Arderydd in Old Welsh and Arthuret on the Ordnance Survey, the Christian kings of York defeated the pagan king of nearby Carlisle, Gwenddolau. It seems that one of his principal fortresses was at Carwhinley, or Caer-Gwenddolau. The slaughter was so great that it drove insane the bard known as Myrddin. According to a series of very early poems he fled into the Caledonian Forest to lead a life of mysticism and madness, and he fled into history as the Great Enchanter, Merlin.

The real victor of Arthuret was not the York kings but a man who was to become famous as the greatest British warrior of his generation, and the last seriously to challenge the growing power of the English. Soon after 573, Urien King of Rheged became Lord of Luguvalium, of Carlisle and Master of the Forest of Luel immediately to the south. The bards hailed him as 'Lord of the Cultivated Plain', a reference not only to the fertile Eden Valley to the south of the old Roman city but also to the fields between Annan and Nith. Carlisle was a substantial prize for Urien. To a king anxious to contrast his Romanitas with the ignorance of his barbarian enemies, nothing could be more eloquent than to rule from what was probably the last intact Roman town in Britain.

But Carlisle was not Urien's only centre of power. Rheged stretched from Dunragit, or Dun Rheged, in the west, near Stranraer and down as far as Rochdale in Lancashire. There were three main post-Roman fortresses in Galloway; Trusty's Hill near Gatehouse of Fleet, Tynron Doon in Dumfriesshire and Mote of Mark near Rockcliffe. The Mote has been excavated and the remains of a remarkably sophisticated culture uncovered. Metal work of great intricacy went on, there are considerable quantities of glass imported from the Rhineland and much else to show this was the seat of a powerful and wealthy king.

But perhaps the best sense of Urien and his court can be got from poetry. The King of Rheged is well remembered in Welsh because Taliesin, one of the greatest bards of the age, sang his praises. What follows is one of the oldest fragments of European vernacular literature;

> Urien of Echwyd, most liberal of Christian men
> Much do you give to men in this world,
> As you gather, so you dispense,
> Happy the Christian bards, so long as you live,
> Sovereign supreme, ruler all highest
> The stranger's refuge, strong champion in battle,
> This the English know when they tell tales.
> Death was theirs, rage and grief are theirs
> Burnt are their homes, bare are their bodies.
>
> Till I am old and failing
> In the grim doom of death
> I shall have no delight
> If my lips praise not Urien.

This can only be a poor translation of the fluid and alliterative Welsh, but it serves to make a number of points. First, the story of Urien has been ignored because it lived in the mouths of poets. Bards were indeed historians for the Celtic peoples of Britain, but they were not like the Venerable Bede, the sort of historian trusted and even revered by academics. And secondly it paints a king who was generous to his warriors, constantly rewarding them with gifts of gold and precious objects, and a society whose highest level had only the business of warfare in mind and was generally uninterested in politics of any other sort. Exactly like the kings portrayed in Beowulf — but not reported by Bede, in his measured prose, as such. Bards, mead and the tossing of gold trinkets amongst warriors appears to add up to unsophistication for us — in contrast with the pictures painted by Bede of the more statesmanlike and pious Northumbrians. These comparisons, when they are made at all, can be highly deceptive.

Finally, in his praise poem, Taliesin emphasises that Urien was a Christian, a force for civilisation, of Romanitas against the outsiders, the barbarians from across the North Sea.

Some time around 590, Urien and his counsellors determined to deal a telling blow to the barbarians. He drew together the armies of four British kings, and the manner in which he compiled and managed this difficult alliance makes it look as though he was very much the senior partner. Urien's elegy called him 'The Pillar of Britain' and praises him for his conquest of Bernicia. Real military success began when he and his son, Owain, defeated the Bernician king known to the bards as Fflamddwyn, the Firebrand. This was most likely Aethelric, a successor of Ida and the man who led four Bernician armies into Rheged. The bards sang that Urien and Owain destroyed the armies of Fflamddwyn 'on a Saturday morning in Argoed Llwyfein' or Leven Forest. There are still several Leven place-names around Bewcastle, a few miles north of Hadrian's Wall, astride the main route from Bernicia to Rheged.

The story is taken up by Nennius' history of the Britons and here is one of the key passages. It describes Urien's efforts to expel the English completely from North Britain;

"Hussa reigned 7 years. Four kings fought against him, Urien and Riderch Hen, and Gaullauc and Morcant. Theodoric fought bravely against the famous Urien and his sons. During that time, sometimes the enemy, sometimes our countrymen were victorious, and Urien blockaded them for 3 days on the island of Metcaud."

The date of the seige of Metcaud, the Island of Tides, better known now as Lindisfarne or Holy Island is between 589 and 593. Urien's allies were his neighbours; Riderch Hen was King of the Clyde who ruled from his impregnable fortress at Dumbarton, the Rock of the Clyde. Gaullauc's name may refer to his people since it derives from the Welsh word for the Roman wall, Guall. More likely Antonine than Hadrian's. Morcant was probably a Gododdin prince whose territory included North Northumberland. Irish annals add more armies to Urien's host at the seige of Metcaud. Aedan, King of the Dalriada Scots, was there, and his neighbour Fiachna, King of Ulster. The Irish bards sing Fiachna's praises for he took the stronghold of Bamburgh from the English, held some of their leading people hostage and put a garrison of Irish warriors inside the stockade.

From the ramparts of Bamburgh, the Irish could look north to Metcaud, the Island of Tides. They saw a long, low sandy place, no more than a few hundred acres. But at one end it is punctuated by a near-sheer rock by the sea's edge. The English had built a second fortress on this rock and given it the same name as Bamburgh. Named after Bebba, King Ida's queen, the castle rock of Holy Island has an old name still remembered, for it used to be called Bebloe's Rock. Below it, the Irish may have seen what their British allies called a llongphort, a ship camp. The English had probably beached their ships on the island as an insurance that defeat would not mean annihilation.

Opposite the island, at the mouth of the River Low, Urien and his allies had pitched their leather tents, found forage for their horses and men and settled down to wait, to blockade the English and starve them out, into their ships and away. What Urien had achieved was potentially immense. Like his predecessor, the great general Cunedda, he was about to expel the invading barbarians from the Empire. With Fiachna's help, he had bottled up Hussa and his warriors in a military cul-de-sac. Everyone knew that final victory over the English was close, and the minds of the allies will have turned to the aftermath. Urien was about to lead the British coalition to its greatest and most complete triumph, but what would stop him from becoming High King over all of North Britain? Only jealousy, it seemed. Here is the rest of the entry in the Nennius text;

"But while he was on the expedition, Urien was assassinated, on the initiative of Morcant, from jealousy, because his military skill and generalship surpassed that of all the other kings."

Morcant's immediate motive may have been the agreement of Urien with Fiachna that the Irish could occupy Bamburgh. If he was a prince of the Gododdin on the Tweed and north Northumberland, Morcant may have been resentful of that. In any case the assassination was a disaster. The British coalition immediately dissolved, the English escaped from their island prison, and the whole history of Britain turned decisively in a different direction. If Urien had lived, England may have developed as a smaller province of Saxons south of the River Trent, the capital city of all Britain might have become York, and we might all be speaking another language.

In 593 Owain, son of Urien, took vengeance of a sort for his father's killing. He fought against Fflamddwyn, Aethelric of Bernicia and defeated him again. Taliesin sang his praises;

"When Owain slew Fflamddwyn
It was no more than sleeping.
Sleeps now the wide host of England
With the light upon their eyes
And those who fled not far
Were braver than was need...

Splendid he was, in his many coloured armour,
Horses he gave to all who asked,
Gathering wealth like a miser
Freely he shared it for his soul's sake
The soul of Owain, son of Urien
May the Lord look upon its need."

But Owain's triumph was short-lived for he died soon after and was much lamented by the bards. With his passing, Rheged ceased to be a force in the politics of North Britain and virtually disappears from history — at least it seems to.

THE SONS OF PROPHECY

Owain ap Urien's name endured to become part of a strange and persistent Welsh tradition. As the Angles and Saxons overran more and more territory in the 7th and 8th centuries, the bards never allowed their people to forget that Welsh-speaking kings had once ruled in London. They called the new English-controlled parts of Britain Lloegr; it means 'The Lost Lands'. And in Dyfed, during the reign of Hywel Dda, a poem known as the 'Armes Prydein Vawr', 'the Prophecy of Great Britain' was composed. It called on the British of the north and west to unite with the Vikings under the banner of St David and expel the English forever from Britain.

Parallel with this was the hope for a Redeemer, 'Y Mab Darogan', 'the Son of Prophecy.' He would come to lead the Welsh back to their ancient glory, to victory over the hated Sais, the invading English who stole Britain from its rightful rulers. Eight sons of prophecy are mentioned consistently; Hiriell, Cynan, Cadwaladr, Arthur, Owain ap Urien, Owain Lawgoch, Owain Glyn Dwr and Henry Tudor.

For nearly a thousand years the Welsh yearned for a great leader; ordinary people gathered on hillsides to hear tales of the heroes and warbands of the past, of Cynan, Cadwaladr and Arthur, and to hear prophecy. Owain of Rheged gained fame in Wales because the bards kept his name alive as one of Y Mebyon Darogan who would ride out to defeat the English.

A series of severe reverses for the British followed Owain's death, and although battles lost or won are rarely conclusive, there were no more recorded victories for the Citizens after 593. Perhaps the worst setback was in 600AD at Catterick in North Yorkshire. The armies of Edinburgh joined with other British kingdoms to fight the Angles of the Yorkshire kingdom of Deira. The campaign is described in a long poem composed in Edinburgh by the bard, Aneirin, and it shares the name of the people who led the British, the Gododdin. The language is sometimes opaque and open to interpretation. But what seems clear is that the British army was primarily a highly mobile cavalry force that attempted to strike at the heart of the emerging English kingdoms.

Extravagant estimates have put the size of the host of the Gododdin alliance at 24,000. Even though warriors from Strathclyde, Kyle, Gwynedd in North Wales and the British kingdom of Elmet around Leeds were involved, this seems an impossibly large number. In the 6th

and 7th centuries and for a long time afterwards, kings fought with
warbands numbered in hundreds rather than thousands. The Anglo-
Saxon Chronicle is even more modest when it defines an army as more
than 30 men. The British were primarily cavalry warriors and while this
made them highly mobile and dangerous enemies, it did limit the size
of their hosts. Also it is misleading to think of armies as invaders of
occupiers of territory. What interested these men was the wealth or the
goods that land could produce rather than the land itself. The huge
territory of Rheged in Urien's time was no more than the extent of his
influence and ability to gather its wealth to himself. And thereafter
distribute it to his warband in his hall, like Hrothgar, king of the
Sheildings. There were no fixed frontiers around these early kingdoms
as such but rather limits — often limits dictated by logistics and geography.

The Gododdin poem is a fascinating document. Its vivid imagery
offers the first sustained impression of the lives and values of a British
warrior elite; what they admired, how they saw themselves and also
some sense of what they looked like. Honour in battle was absolutely
central and its maintenance as crucial as the elaborate 'laws of the face',
'the enechruicce', imply. This not only encompassed the raw courage in
the face of overwhelming odds but also a commitment to every other
warrior never to take a step back from the fight — the unbreakable
mutual loyalty of the brothers in arms, the warband. Here is a flavour
of the great poem;

"Wearing a brooch, in the front rank,
Bearing weapons in battle,
A mighty man in the fight before his death-day,
A champion in charge of the van of the armies;
There fell five times fifty before his blades,
Of the men of Deira and Bernicia,
a hundred score fell and were destroyed in a single hour.
He would sooner the wolves had his flesh than go to his own wedding,
He would rather be prey for the ravens than go to the altar;
He would sooner his blood flowed to the ground than get due burial,
Making return for his mead and the hosts in the hall.
Hyfeidd the Tall shall be honoured as long as there is a bard...

The retinue of Gododdin on rough-maned horses like swans,
With their harness drawn tight,
And attacking the troop in the van of the host,
Defending the woods and the mead of Eidyn....

The men went to Catreath, they were renowned,
Wine and mead from gold cups was their drink for a year,
In accordance with the honoured custom.
Three men and three score and three hundred,
Wearing gold torcs,
Of that hastened out after the choice drink,
None escaped but three,
Through feats of sword-play —

The two war-dogs of Aeron, and stubborn Cynon;
And I too, streaming with blood,
By grace of my brilliant poetry...

The men went to Catreath in column, raising the war-cry,
A force with steeds, blue armour and shields,
Javelins aloft and keen lances,
And bright mail-coats and swords.
He led, he burst through the armies,
And there fell five times fifty before his blades —
Rhufawn the Tall, who gave gold to the altar and fine presents to
the bard..."

On their way from Edinburgh to the battleground at Catterick it may be that the warband of Gododdin stayed overnight at Kelso. In the poem, one of the many great warriors noted is Cadrod Calchvynydd, sometimes rendered as Catrawt of Calchvynydd. The literal translation of the place-name is 'Chalk Hill' and that is the derivation of Kelso. Chalkheugh Terrace remembers the original Old Welsh name in a Scots version, and the chalky bank above the River Tweed was an unusual landmark visible from a distance. Aside from the references to Carlisle, this is the earliest mention of a native British settlement in the Borders. "I come from Kelso" is an ancient boast.

It used to be believed that the instigator of the expedition to Catterick was King Mynyddog Mwynvawr of Edinburgh, literally Mynyddog Big Money, often more decorously translated as Mynyddog the Wealthy or Luxurious. It has always seemed odd that unlike Urien, Owain or the Bernician kings, Mynyddog is never mentioned in any direct connection with the battle. An American scholar has recently pointed out that Mynyddog Mwynvawr could also translate as 'the wealthy mountain court' and may refer to the Gododdin fortress on Edinburgh's castle rock. This did not, however, leave the Gododdin without a leader. Here is Aneirin's description of Yrfai, Lord of Edinburgh, fighting at Catterick;

"It was usual for him to be mounted on a high-spirited horse defending Gododdin, at the forefront of the men eager for fighting. It was usual for him to be fleet like a deer. It was usual for him to attack Deira's retinue. It was usual for Golistan's son — though his father was no sovereign lord — that what he said was heeded. It was usual for the sake of the mountain court that shields be broken through and reddened before Yrfai, Lord of Eidyn".

Yrfai is called mab Golistan, the son of Golistan. This last is a Welsh rendition of Wulfstan, an Anglian name, and just as the Bernicians had British allies, it appears that the British may have had an Anglian military elite near the centre of power in Edinburgh.

Three years after their victory at Catterick, the Bernicians and Deirans won again at a place known as Degsastan. The victor was Aethelfrith and he had an interesting nickname. Am Fleisaur means the Trickster, or better, the Artful Dodger. For a general, this sounds like a compliment, but what is equally interesting is that Am Fleisaur is a Welsh name, probably confered by Aethelfrith's British allies.

Some scholars have maintained that Degsastan or Degsa's Stone shrivelled into the place-name, Dawston, in Liddesdale. But even though this valley was a busy through-route from the south west to the Tweed Basin, the location of this crucial battle is unlikely to have been there. In 1383 a Latin scholar of distinction, John of Fordun, published the 'Chronica gentis Scotorum', the Chronicle of the Scottish People. In it he gives a remarkably full account of the events leading up to Degsastan in 603. The British kings of the north had concluded an alliance with Aedan macGabrain, the king of the Dalriada Scots. Together they planned a pincer movement to crush Aethelfrith; the Scots were to attack from the north and the British from the south-west. According to Fordun, Aedan allowed his warband 'to burn and pillage through the fields and townships' of Bernician territory. As the Scots made their way back north with their portable loot, Aethelfrith chased and caught them at Addinston in upper Lauderdale. Addinston is a ground-down version of Degsastan. Lauderdale is a natural route for invasion of the Tweed Basin from the north, and where the roads divide at Carfraemill clearly an ancient place. Significantly, Carfrae means 'hill-fort' in Old Welsh. Finds of several cist cemetaries along its line show that what is now the A697 to the Tweed at Coldstream has been travelled for at least 1400 years. If Aedan macGabrain's warband was raiding in the Bernician lands in the lower Tweed and north Northumberland, then it is likely that Aethelfrith chased them along that old road and caught the Scots as they prepared to climb the watershed at Soutra Hill. Victory at Degsastan gave the English the Tweed Valley and provided a springboard for their capture of Edinburgh 30 years later.

Historians have described the Northumbrian advance over the whole of the North as unstoppable. They defeated British kings to the north and west and English kings to the south. Northumbrian kings became Bretwaldas, or 'Britain-rulers' and the focus of a national power settled on Bamburgh, Yeavering and north Yorkshire. At the battle of Chester Aethelfrith defeated a coalition of Welsh kings and when 1200 monks emerged from the monastery of Bangor y Coed to pray for a Christian victory over the pagans, he had them all slaughtered. Savagery as well as trickery characterised the reign of Aethelfrith, the Artful Dodger.

But within a generation, the atmosphere around these Northumbrian kings changed radically. Suddenly they appeared to grow out of their barbarity and into the role of High Kings of all Britain. They became Christians, cultured patrons of the arts and builders of a kingdom which was more than simply the outcome of the victories of their warbands. According to the English historian, Bede, the mission of St Paulinus and also St Augustine of Canterbury drew the Northumbrian kings into the church of Rome, and their foundation of monasteries created an atmosphere of learning and spiritual betterment.

Some of that is of course true, but as often with the Venerable Bede, he presents only a part of the story. What was also happening was a cultural exchange between the new kings of Northumbria and the old royal family of Rheged. Sometimes far from the clash of battle the mantle of Romanitas was being quietly passed from the old to the new.

Aethelfrith, the monk killer, was succeeded by another pagan, King Edwin. But events took place which set a different gloss on his reign. Bede reports that after some prevarication, he was converted to Christianity by the Vatican-approved St Paulinus, who followed his coup by converting thousands of Northumbrians at the royal palace at Yeavering in the foothills of the Cheviots. There is no reason to doubt this and the presence and the baptismal energy of the saint is remembered in a nearby place-name at Pallinsburn. But what Bede omits to say is that Edwin's initial reluctance was prompted by the fact that he had already been converted to Christianity from a distinct tradition — a Celtic tradition. In another fragment from the lost chronicle of North Britain, Nennius tells us something remarkable. It appears that Edwin was baptised by Rhun, the monkish brother of Owain, and the son of Urien of Rheged. Rhun may have been a bishop at Carlisle or Whithorn, but the entry into the church of a royal prince was by no means unusual and it became a tradition amongst Northumbrian kings. In fact one less than competent 7th century English king was forcibly tonsured and sent to a monastery to retire. But the point here is clear. The Celtic kingdoms of the Solway and Southern Scotland allowed post-Roman Christianity to develop and were instrumental in passing it on to the Northumbrians, and through them, to pagan Anglo-Saxon England. And Christianity was only the most obvious outward sign of Romanitas.

And yet inside the mechanics of this exchange there was a paradox developing which would come to a bloodless but supremely important conflict at the Synod of Whitby in 664. Edwin's successor, King Oswald of Northumbria sent not to Canterbury or Rome for help in the conversion and settlement of his kingdom, but to Iona. There were likely two reason for this. First and most obvious the existing Christian infrastructure, such as it was, had a great deal more in common with Celtic culture than with the south or Rome. All of the major 5th and 6th century figures in the north, Ninian, Patrick and Columba, came from that tradition. And secondly the Irish model of monasticism probably suited Oswald's strategic purposes more closely than the international corporation based at the Vatican. Large numbers of lay people, many of them married with families, were attached to Irish monasteries and included in the community as monks. In a practical reality they were farmers and stocksmen and the huge numbers of monks noted in the annals, like the 1200 slaughtered at Bangor by Aethelfrith, are the result of this sort of policy. For these reasons the Irish model offered Oswald a structure which would help him govern his kingdom as well as save the souls of his people.

But in 634 the Northumbrian king was unhappy. The prelate sent by Iona had proved a strict, ascetic disciplinarian, too severe and unbending. Aidan was sent to replace him, and he proved to be exactly the right man in the right place at the right time.

His achievements are generally listed as the foundation of the monasteries at Old Melrose, Coldingham and Lindisfarne, and the establishment of the premiere English episcopal see at Lindisfarne. This last is unarguable, but the first very doubtful.

Old Melrose shows every sign of having been an early Celtic foundation that pre-existed Aidan's arrival and perhaps even the Bernician victory at Degsastan. The choice of the site in a tight loop of the Tweed shows a fascinating and exotic influence, that of the early Christian fathers of the Near East. What mattered to them was the Kingdom of Heaven, and not the temporal world. In the 1st and 2nd centuries AD these ascetics fled from the persecutions, and the distractions, of the cities to find refuge in the deserts of Egypt, Palestine and Syria. There, like Christ, they hoped to find communion with God. The first Irish foundations of hermetic monks could not hope to use deserts to supply the same sense of isolation, and so they substituted the sea for the sands, and built their first cells in remote, storm-tossed places. Off the Kerry coast of south-west Ireland, the beehive cells perched on the inhospitable rocks of Skellig Michael are the most spectacular example of this devout need to withdraw from the world. The Irish went so far as to borrow the language of the Desert Fathers and called their monasteries 'diseartan', even though they were often surrounded by water. Dysart in Fife is one of several place-name memories of such places on the British mainland.

At Old Melrose the Tweed stands for the deserts of the sea as it serves almost to cut off this diseart from the distractions of the world, and a bank and a ditch complete the sacred defences where the waters fail to meet. On the cliffs that drop sheer to the North Sea, Coldingham more nearly approximates to Irish habits, while Lindisfarne's twice daily isolation by the tides might have seemed like God's providence, allowing contact but then cutting it. In addition to Old Melrose there are two shadow monasteries which may lie under the remains of medieval abbeys at Dryburgh and Kelso. In a calendar of Scottish saints, the 7th century St Modan is described as Abbot of Dryburgh, and there is also an early Northumbrian cross socket on the site. At Kelso it is clear that the removal of the unhappy Tironensian monks from Selkirk in 1128 caused a row over the fate of the old pre-existing church of St Mary. Local loyalty to the old kirk caused John, Bishop of Glasgow, to step in and sort it out.

Like the Irish hermits they admired so much, the monks in the Tweed Valley led ascetic lives devoted to contemplation, prayer and the mortification of the flesh. A rare and authentic-sounding glimpse into what life was really like in the Tweed Valley in the 7th century is given by Bede, and the vignette also offers the sound of a Borderer talking, the first reported conversation in our history;

"This man, Drythelm, was given a more secluded dwelling in the monastery [at Old Melrose] so that he could devote himself more freely to the service of his maker in unbroken prayer. And since this place stands on the bank of a river, he often used to enter it for severe bodily penance, and plunge repeatedly beneath the water while he recited psalms and prayers for as long as he could endure it, standing motionless with the water up to his loins and sometimes to his neck. When he returned to shore he never removed his dripping, chilly garments, but let them warm and dry on his body. And in winter, when the half-broken cakes of ice were swirling around him which he had broken to make a place to stand and dip himself in the water, those who saw him used to say: 'Brother Drythelm, it is wonderful how you can manage to bear such bitter cold'. To which he, being a man of simple disposition and self-restraint, would reply simply: 'I have known it colder'. And when they said: 'It is extraordinary that you are willing to practice such severe discipline', he used to answer: 'I have seen greater suffering'."

Echoing across the centuries, the tone of that is unmistakably of the Borders, the sort of conversation about the winter weather that could be had in Kelso Square.

DISGRACEFUL HAIR

How the monks at Old Melrose lived is difficult to visualise in the absence of much-needed archaeology. The historian, Walter Elliot, has surveyed the ground several times and established the location of the monastic vallum or ditch which separated the community from the rest of the world, and his preliminary findings show the remains of a substantial community living in and around a series of buildings, at least one of which appears to be a shrine. But past these assertions, it is not easy to say anything more about the site. Like Roxburgh Castle and the haugh to the east, Old Melrose urgently needs to be excavated. Both sites are of central importance to the history of the Tweed Valley.

However, Old Melrose is not a complete enigma. Sensible comparison with other, better documented places and a clear tracing of the transmission of ideas can be very illuminating.

St Ninian of Whithorn greatly admired St Martin of Tours. The church of Candida Casa had such strong associations with the Gaulish saint that Irish chroniclers called it 'Tigh Mhartainn', the 'House of Martin'. The reasons for this are straightforward. Ninian admired the work and ideas of St Martin because he was the first in Western Europe to adapt the practices of the ascetic monks of the Middle East who had modelled their lives on those of the Desert Fathers. This innovation did not make Martin popular with his fellow bishops. In the late 4th century, Gaul was still part of the Roman Empire and Christianity was almost exclusively based on the cities. St Martin appalled his urbane contemporaries by insisting on preaching in the countryside to pagans. 'Pagan' and 'peasant' are closely cognate words. When he came upon a pagan shrine the saint showed great physical courage by breaking it down and setting up a cross or a church in its place. In his 'Life of St Cuthbert' Bede has his hero do similar things. Martin's behaviour scandalised the bishops of Gaul who branded him as unfit for office and sniffed grandly at his 'insignificant appearance, his sordid garments and disgraceful hair.'

Soon after Martin died in 397 Sulpicius Severus wrote a life of the saint and it was widely circulated. Copies certainly made their way to Whithorn and Iona, and the book must have been known at Old Melrose. It may even have influenced the choice of location for the monastery. Here is Sulpicius' description of Marmoutier, a community founded by St Martin near the city of Tours;

> *"he [Martin] made himself a hermitage about two miles from the city. The place was so secluded and remote that it had all the solitude of the desert. On one side it was walled in by the rock-face of a high mountain, and the level ground that remained was enclosed by a gentle bend of the river Loire... His own cell was built of wood, as were those of many of his brethren; but many of them hollowed out shelters for themselves in the rock of the overhanging mountain."*

Perhaps the most decisive shift towards Romanitas occured during the reign of Oswy. At the Synod of Whitby in 664, he decided a dispute in favour of the Church of Rome and their method of calculating the date of Easter, ruling against the Celtic church of Iona and Ireland. This may seem a pettyfogging matter to us, but it was very important for reasons now forgotten. In order to avoid a clash with the Jewish feast of the Passover, Rome used a complicated formula to set the date of the holiday. And for reasons of remoteness the Celtic church had fallen into the habit of setting a different date which ignored the Passover. When King Oswy married Eanfled, a Kentish princess who kept the Roman dates, he found himself feasting alone on Easter Day, because according to his wife, it was still Palm Sunday. But there were difficulties more fundamental than domestic disharmony. In the 7th century Christians believed that Easter, their most important festival, was the occasion of a great battle between God and Satan. And for God to win that battle, all of his supporters, all Christians, had to pray for victory — at the same time. It was a matter of sheer numbers.

There were also other issues at stake. Monks from the Roman party shaved the crown of their heads, leaving hair growing above their foreheads and temples, in imitation of Christ's crown of thorns. The Celtic tonsure was different and cut over the crown of the head from ear to ear with the hair worn long at the back. It now seems certain that the Druids wore their hair in the same fashion and the Roman church will have sniffed at such whiffs of the pagan past.

In addition to the specific difference in the dating of Easter, a lack of uniformity in one location — Northumbria — where the two schools of liturgical thought actively clashed, there was another fundamental effect. Once a date for Easter had been fixed all of the other important festivals such as Lent, Ascension Day and Pentecost followed from it. Therefore the divergence was not only over one celebration, it meant two entirely different liturgical years.

So long as Celtic Christians confined themselves to the western edges of Britain and Ireland, the papacy could tolerate different practices and interpretations. But when Irish missionaries in particular began to become active in spreading the word of God in continental Europe, their uncatholic way of thinking approached too close for comfort. St Columbanus left his monastery at Bangor c590 with twelve companions. Together they founded many new communities such as those at Annegray, Luxeuil and Fontaines in France. Columbanus drew very many followers to him and refused to accept the authority of Frankish bishops or conform with their method of dating Easter. He finally settled in Italy and established the great monastery at Bobbio. The severity and asceticism of the Rule of St Columbanus was characteristic of the Celtic church and would have pleased a leathery old stick like Drythelm. Some sins carried a punishment of three years' fasting on bread and water only. So many Irish churches were founded in the Rhineland that in German they are known as the Schottenkirchen, the Scots (meaning Irish) churches.

EOSTRE

Easter is a mystery to most people, and no longer just a religious mystery. The question "When is Easter this year?" sends them scurrying to a diary to discover the date. Unlike Christmas it is a famously movable feast.

The Book of Common Prayer contains the formula. Easter Day is the first Sunday after the first full moon on or after 21st March. It is an old-fashioned way of reckoning time, and that sentence probably needs to be read twice by many. Even more complication sets in when the formula has to adapt to deal with clashes. If the first full moon following 21st March is on a Sunday, then Easter Day falls on the Sunday after that. This was to avoid clashing with the traditional date of the Jewish Passover. In most Mediterranean languages 'Easter' is a derivation of the Hebrew word 'Pesach' for Passover; 'Paques' in French, 'Pascua' in Spanish and even 'Pasg' in Welsh. Bede understood that the name of the pagan goddess of springtime, Eostre, had been adapted to become the English word 'Easter', but he saw no irony in that.

The move towards Rome confered more Romanitas on the Northumbrian kings and gained them legitimacy through the support of the papacy. But it could all have been entirely different. Before he married the Kentish princess, Eanfeld, King Oswy had another wife. This marriage was ignored by Bede who was anxious to underwrite the orthodoxy of the Northumbrian kings, but it was noticed in another fragment from Nennius. Some time around 635AD, before he succeeded to the throne, Oswy married a Rheged princess. Rieinmellt was the great granddaughter of Urien and her name means Queen of Lightning. She clearly attracted the young Oswy, but tragically died young, not long after their marriage. It may be that the ancient church at Hoddom in Dumfriesshire, visited by and dedicated to the British Saint Kentigern, was Oswy's monument to her. But had the Queen of Lightning lived, there would have been no Synod of Whitby. Iona could have taken precedence over Rome for much longer and the unpleasant St Augustine of Canterbury might have, with justice, lost the undeserved credit for the conversion of the English.

Edwin's successors developed this sense of continuity with the imperial past in their everyday business outside of churches. During royal progresses their retinue imitated Roman practices. Leading the procession into the king's estates was a standard bearer who carried a Roman insignia called a tufa, a winged orb intended to add dignity to what followed. The royal warband became the comitatus, the royal chaplain, the pontifex, and so on.

So far the fusion of Celtic and English Britain has only been hinted at — in the formation of Bernicia under Ida in 547, and the devopment of shires out of the model of the maenor. This process might be thought to be episodic and incidental. But with the reign of Oswy's son, Aldfrith, the determinant role of native British and Irish culture becomes much clearer.

After King Ecgfrith of Northumbria had overextended his ambition and was killed by the army of the Picts at the Battle of Nechtansmere near Forfar in 685, Aldfrith unexpectedly came to the throne. Modern scholars have hailed him as the father of the Northumbrian Renaissance. The learning and scholarship of the great monasteries at Jarrow and Monkwearmouth were made possible by Aldfrith. Magnificent sculpture began to appear in the wake of Northumbrian advances into Galloway and Cumbria, ultimately producing the Ruthwell and Bewcastle crosses. But scholars who celebrate Aldfrith's reign as the first flowering of a specifically English culture entirely fail to take into account the influences that lay behind it. To Bede the new king was 'vir doctissimus', 'a most learned man', to the historian, Eddius, 'rex sapientissimus', 'a most wise king', and to Alcuin of York he was 'rex et simul magister', 'both a king and a teacher at the same time'. Nothing like this had been written about any of his predecessors. But it is clear that Aldfrith's learning and wisdom had strong Celtic roots.

Before Ecgfrith's defeat and death at the hands of the Picts, Aldfrith had lived some years at the monastery of Malmesbury at the foot of the Cotswold Hills in Wiltshire. But in fact this most English of places was an Irish foundation. And Aldfrith's godfather and teacher, the great scholar and preacher Aldhelm, had been taught by the Irish monk, Maildubh. 'Malmesbury' is derived from an anglicisation of his name. The Irish Annals of Tigernach have something to say about the young Aldfrith. They hail him as a great Irish poet, writing in Irish Gaelic, and they give him a Gaelic name, "Altfrith mac Ossa, Fland Fina la Gaelhelv enaidh". 'Aldfrith son of Oswy, called Fland Fina by the Gaels, a learned man'. After receiving an education at Malmesbury, Aldfrith went to live in Ireland for two years. It seems likely that he went to stay with relatives, for his mother, according to Irish sources, was not Eanfled of Kent but a direct descendent of Irish High Kings, and the daughter of Cennfaelad Sapiens. He was the author of two of the earliest Irish law tracts, as well as the first vernacular grammar outside of the classical tradition in Europe. Cennfaelad was considered to be the father of Irish history.

Such was the intellectual atmosphere in which Aldfrith grew up and which prompted him to reign for 20 years with a wisdom and sensitivity that allowed a Northumbrian culture to flourish in an unprecedented way. It would be overstating the case to claim that this flowering was Celtic in its inspiration rather than Northumbrian, but equally myopic to deny what English historians from Bede to Sir Frank Stenton have denied for 1200 years — namely any Celtic involvement at all in what happened.

The lost kingdoms of Southern Scotland were not entirely removed from the pages of history, and their stories and achievements did not come to an abrupt end in the elegies of poets and their stanzas of disaster and defeat at Catterick and Degsastan. Rather, it seems that the stories and ways of thinking went underground or were appropriated by new and ambitious people.

5

Both Sides the Tweed

Wolves still roamed the Border hills, and even in the light summer nights in the Year of Our Lord 651, they would take a stray lamb if the shepherds did not keep a sharp eye for their grey shapes in the gloaming. While the other herd-laddies slept, snoring and whiffling quietly in the warm night air, Cuthbert and his dogs watched. Since he was a little boy he had had trouble sleeping, unable to settle, often in the grip of dreams, sometimes starting at demons waiting on the edge of his consciousness. Peering into the nightscape while others dozed beside him, his knees tucked up under his chin, Cuthbert's jumpiness made him a good shepherd. And the moon made it easier to see, the only real blackness was in the long shadows cast by the Brothers' Stones. Although people he knew and liked still came up to the hill to worship at the Stones, particularly when harvests were bad or there was plague abroad in the countryside, Cuthbert's mind had turned to Jesus Christ Almighty. And he shivered when he looked hard at the black shadows of the Stones.

Grazing inside the dyked enclosure, the sheep were quiet, and even though the devils in the old Stones scared him, Cuthbert felt his eyelids grow heavy and his head tilt slowly forward. The full moon seemed to go dim and slip behind a black cloud. In the depths of his slumber the boy began to hear music, it sounded like the chanting of the monks from over the Tweed at Melrose. And then the black cloud was suddenly pierced through with shafts of white light away to the east of Brotherstone Hill, towards the flat, dark-blue sea. The shafts seemed to carry uncountable thousands of angels. All of them shone with a brightness that lit the land below and each held open their arms in welcome. But not for Cuthbert. Far away a bright soul, a monk with his hands clasped in prayer, rose from the seashore to meet the angels. And as he reached their lowest ranks in the sky, they all turned with him to walk into glory.

The dog barked. Cuthbert snapped up his head and opened his eyes. The ewes were bleating loudly and the other herd-laddies were up and beating about the dykes with their crooks. The collies snarled, they could smell wolf. Looking back over his shoulder at the Brothers' Stones, Cuthbert saw six or seven grey shapes slink off into the darkness of the night.

Some days later news came to Melrose that the servant of God, Aidan, had died. He was Abbot of Lindisfarne, the Island of Tides, and a great and holy man. On the very night he died, Aidan's soul had ascended to heaven, said the brothers, and now he dwelt in the house of the Lord. Cuthbert was sure that he had seen a vision, had watched the old Abbot's spirit rise to meet the angels who had opened the gates of Heaven for him. Surely that meant that God had chosen him, had heard his prayers, and it was a sign that he should act. That day Cuthbert decided to enter the monastery at Melrose.

That is an embroidered version of a story first committed to writing around 720. At the express request of Bishop Eadfrid of Lindisfarne, the Venerable Bede did a great deal of research and then sat down to write a Life of St Cuthbert. In Chapter 4, he reported the saint seeing a vision of St Aidan ascending to Heaven. Because of Bede and other biographies, as well as several notices in different records, Cuthbert is the first Borderer to achieve a substantial historical personality. Bede had the advantage of eye-witness reports and stories heard at first hand because less than 40 years separated the death of Cuthbert from the writing of his life. Leaving aside Bede's political agenda, these circumstances make for a freshness and authenticity almost always absent from early saints' lives, many of which were composed in the medieval period, long after the death of the subject. Even though much of the content now seems routine for hagiography, and the miracles in particular are somewhat formulaic — shepherds tending their flocks at night had had visions long before Cuthbert saw the lights — there is a palpable sense of a real person; a pious, nervous, driven man. And perhaps because he was writing so close to the time of Cuthbert's life, Bede does include a good deal of valuable historical information amongst the tales of amazing events and exemplary acts.

By 651 the Tweed Basin was firmly under Bernician (or Anglian) control and cultural influence. Borderers were adapting to a new language, new methods of farming, the reorganisation of settlement — and most determinant, they were increasingly answering to new masters. Cuthbert, or Cuthbert's family, may have been one of them. Almost all early churchmen who rose to high office were aristocrats and Bede offers early indications that Cuthbert was the son of a powerful man. One of the first signs that God had noticed the boy was "when servants carried him outside in the fresh air." His knee had swelled up. In the distance Cuthbert saw a man on a white horse approaching. Because of his indisposition, the boy was unable to offer hospitality to the stranger. Nevertheless the man dismounted and prescribed a cure for the swollen knee. And then he went on his way. It transpired that the rider on the white horse was an angel and, like St Tobias, Cuthbert had been cured by divine intervention.

At Tynemouth a maritime disaster was in progress when monks bringing wood to the monastery there were swept out to sea on rafts. A great crowd of peasants stood on the shore jeering and shouting insults at both the stricken monks and their anxious brethren watching on the beach. Cuthbert arrived and tried to persuade the peasants to stop shouting and get down on their knees and pray for the men. The crowd turned on him;

"'Nobody is going to pray for them. Let not God raise a finger to help them! They have done away with all the old ways of worship and now nobody knows what to do'"

Cuthbert then fell on his knees and by the power of prayer pulled the rafts back to safety. This fascinating episode shows how insecure a hold Christianity had on ordinary people, and Bede had probably edited out comments along the lines of "If you monks are such devout Christians, why is your God going to kill you? After all that praying, shouldn't he save you by a miracle?" Which, of course, he did. The phrase "and now nobody knows what to do" is particularly interesting and may refer to difficult times — bad harvests, the plague, personal misfortunes and so on. Which God would deliver deliverance? The old gods or the new one? Plague is reported several times in Britain and the Borders in the 7th and 8th centuries and converts did apostasise when it struck.

Once Cuthbert had definitely decided to become a monk, he rode, carrying a spear, to the monastery in the loop of the Tweed now known as Old Melrose. Weapons and a horse were the accoutrements of a member of a wealthy family, one of the bonheddwyr. Prior Boisil was waiting to welcome the young nobleman, and when he arrived and

"gave his horse and spear to a servant (he had not yet put off secular dress), and went into the church to pray. Boisil had an intuition of the high degree of holiness to which the boy he had just been looking at would rise, and said just this single phrase to the monks with whom he was standing: 'Behold the servant of the Lord'."

It may be that Cuthbert's family had agreed to give land to Melrose for the support of the brothers and their devotions, and Boisil's presence at the gate to meet the young man and his somewhat ingratiating welcome recognised that generosity.

Tradition supports the notion that Cuthbert's origins were local. In his History of the Antiquities of Roxburghshire and Adjacent Districts (1859), Alexander Jeffrey reports that the saint was raised in the disappeared farmstead of Wranghame, at the foot of Brotherstone Hill. And there he visited his foster-mother, Kenspid. From this scrap hagiographers have wrought the image of an orphan shepherd-boy called by God as he tended his sheep in the Lauderdale Hills. The reality was that fosterage was much practised in Celtic Scotland (and amongst the clans in the Highlands as late as the 19th century) between noble families and their cadet branches. Boys were often raised from an early age by their relatives, sometimes a considerable distance from their place of birth, and the intention and result of this cultural habit was tremendous social cohesion and loyalty amongst kindred groups. Cuthbert was not an orphan but a wealthy landowner's son.

Some time after 651 Boisil contracted the plague at Melrose. Knowing that he had only a week or so to live (no doubt having observed the fate of others) he and Cuthbert read and discussed a book of the bible which could be managed in that limited time. Boisil had a commentary in 7 parts on St John the Evangelist and they read one each day until the Prior died. During that week it was said that Boisil, who had a reputation as a prophet, foretold to Cuthbert that he would one day be a bishop. But all the saint wanted was to live the life of a hermit;

"'If' he would [later] lament, 'I could live in a tiny dwelling on a rock in the ocean, surrounded by the swelling waves, cut off from the knowledge and sight of all, I would still not be free from the cares of this fleeting world not from the fear that somehow the love of money might snatch me away.'"

This is the longing of the Irish monks who so envied the ascetic life of the Desert Fathers and who built the 'diseartan' on Skellig Michael and Iona. After Boisil's death Cuthbert became Prior at Melrose and this could not have removed him from care. But a consolation was his solitary journeys around the hills and valleys of the Border country on missions of conversion and preaching. The extended passage that follows is one of the earliest extant descriptions of activity in the Borders unconnected with warfare. So complete is the Tweed Basin's absorption into Bernicia by 720, when Bede was writing, that he calls the natives 'the English';

"Outside [the monastery] in the world, he strove to convert people for miles around from their foolish ways to a delight in the promised joys of Heaven. Many who had the faith had profaned it by their works. Even while the plague was raging some had forgotten the mystery conferred on them in baptism and had fled to idols, as though incantations or amulets or any other diabolical rubbish could possibly avail against a punishment sent by God the Creator. To bring back both kinds of sinners he often did the rounds of the villages, sometimes on horseback, more often on foot, preaching the way of truth to those who had gone astray. Boisil did the same in his time. It was the custom at that time among the English people that if a priest or cleric came to a village everyone would obey his call and gather round to hear him preach. They would willingly listen and even more gladly put his words into practice as far as they had understood them. Such was his skill in teaching, such his power of driving his lessons home, and so gloriously did his angelic countenance shine forth, that none dared keep back from him even the closest secrets of their heart. They confessed every sin openly — indeed they thought he would know if they held anything back — and made amends by 'fruits worthy of repentance', as he commanded. He made a point of searching out those steep rugged places in the hills which other preachers dreaded to visit because of their poverty and squalor. This, to him, was a labour of love. He was so keen to preach that sometimes he would be away for a whole week or a fortnight, or even a month, living with the rough hill folk, preaching and calling them heavenwards by his example."

The sense of a Celtic atmosphere around Cuthbert is unmistakable, and unconsciously reinforced often in Bede's 'Life'. When invited to the monastery at Coldingham, the saint practiced the same sort of mortification of the flesh so enjoyed by the Melrose monk, Drythelm. In the dead of night he stole out of the dormitory and down to the beach. Wading into the deep water he prayed while up to his neck in the freezing North Sea. Apparently a young novice spied on Cuthbert and saw that when he finally regained the beach, two sea-otters

"bounded out of the water, stretched themselves out before him, warmed his feet with their breath, and tried to dry him on their fur. They finished, received his blessing, and slipped back to their watery home."

After the decision of the Synod of Whitby in 664 went against the Celtic faction, Colman, Bishop of Lindisfarne, abandoned his see (or was more likely ejected) and with 30 monks went to found a monastery in Ireland. Cuthbert was drafted in as Prior but it appears that he had some difficult in imposing his authority; "Some of the monks prefered the old way of life to the rule". Bubbling under the surface of Bede's narrative is a river of spite which carved a deep divide in the early church in Northumbria. The figure of St Wilfrid glowers across the chasm at Cuthbert, Aidan, Boisil and the unworldly hermits of Melrose.

Born at almost exactly the same time as Cuthbert but at the southern end of Northumbria, Wilfrid was an Anglian nobleman who appears to have become the friend and confidant of Queen Eanfled. She was the Kentish princess and bride of King Oswy whose preference for the Roman method of dating Easter began the process which led to the Synod of Whitby in 664. Eanfled made it possible for Wilfrid to be instructed at Lindisfarne while Aidan was still Abbot. But the regime was not to his taste and the 14 year-old did not accept the tonsure and become a monk. Instead, the Queen sent him to Kent to stay with her cousin King Erconberht. Rome was Wilfrid's ultimate goal and when he arrived in the holy city, he sought and received the Pope's blessing.

After taking the Roman tonsure and being formally ordained as a priest, Wilfrid found himself chief spokesman for the party of Queen Eanfled and the papacy at Whitby in 664. This was a tremendous opportunity for the young man and he grasped it. Chosen for his eloquence in English as well as his understanding of Latin, canon law and scripture, he made a persuasive case. "Do you think" Bede reports him as saying, "that a handful of people in one corner of the remotest of islands is to be prefered to the universal church of Christ which is spread throughout the world?" Remote from what? From the ancient pull of Rome, now the centre of Christendom, a new empire of faith.

King Oswy thought it politic to rule in favour of Rome. But an interesting conflict developed nevertheless. Wilfrid had been given the monastery at Ripon by Alchfrith, Oswy's son and sub-king of Deira in Yorkshire. Ripon had originally been founded as a daughter-house of Melrose by Abbot Eata and Cuthbert as guest-master. But when the Celtic cause was lost at Whitby, Alchfrith drove out the Melrose monks and gave the monastery to the coming man, Wilfrid.

A long and stormy career followed. Three times Wilfrid was removed from the Bishopric of Northumbria, and he fell out badly with two kings, Ecgfrith and Aldfrith, with two Archbishops of Canterbury, Theodore and Berhtwald, was imprisoned and went into exile at least twice. But as a sharp contrast to the devout and contemplative life of Cuthbert, Wilfrid's attitudes and behaviour are instructive. Aggressive and acquisitive, he thought himself a prince of the church and tried to make his episcopal see as large and wealthy as possible. When the new church (built 'more Romanorum', 'in the Roman style') at Ripon was consecrated, he threw a huge party with feasting for three days and in his sermon he was both ostentatious and triumphant;

"He went on to enumerate holy places in various parts of the country which the British clergy, fleeing from our own hostile sword, had deserted. God would indeed be pleased with the good kings for the gift of so much land to our bishop."

This boast was unusual, a rare notice of British eviction of any sort in the north. When Wilfrid died in 709 he divided his treasure amongst his retinue as though he were a secular king, and he made provision that his nominees succeeded in all the ecclesiastical offices he controlled. And he controlled many. In all this Wilfrid prefigured the worldly and highly political church of the Middle Ages when Popes could challenge and defeat with doctrine Holy Roman Emperors.

Meanwhile Cuthbert had retreated from the world. A reluctant Prior of Lindisfarne, he spent a great deal of time on Hobthrush Islet (now called St Cuthbert's Isle) which lay just off the coast of the island, by the priory. That proved too comfortable, and the saint decamped to Inner Farne, one of the Seal Islands, where he built a small oratory and accommodation for a few companions. Far from running the monastery as an active Prior, Cuthbert retreated further and further from the affairs of men. Visions and miracles flowed. Bede offers a clear sense of the thinking behind what seems to us now a strange and very harsh way of life;

"The Farne is an island far out to sea… [it] lies a few miles to the south east of Lindisfarne, cut off on the landward side by very deep water and facing, on the other side, out towards the limitless ocean. The island was haunted by devils; Cuthbert was the first man brave enough to live there alone. At the entry of our soldier of Christ armed with 'the helmet of salvation, the shield of faith and the sword of the spirit which is the word of God' the devil fled and his host of allies with him. Cuthbert, having routed the enemy, became monarch of the place, in token of which he built a city worthy of his power and put up houses to match. The structure was almost circular in plan, from four to five poles [about 25 metres] in diameter, and the walls on the outside were higher than a man. Out of piety he made the walls higher inside by cutting away the solid rock at the bottom, so that with only the sky to look at, eyes and thoughts might be kept from wandering and inspired to seek for higher things. This same wall he built not with cut stone or bricks and mortar but with rough stones and peat dug out of the enclosure itself. Some of these stones were so big that four men could hardly lift them, but with the help of angels he managed to fit them into the wall. There were two buildings, an oratory and one for living in. He finished off the walls inside and out by digging away a lot of the soil. The roofs were of rough-hewn timber and straw. Near the landing-place there was a bigger house for the visiting brethern to stay in, with a spring close by".

In 685 King Ecgfrith asked a reluctant Cuthbert to become Bishop of Lindisfarne. At the insistence of Theodore, Archbishop of Canterbury, the great Northumbrian see of Wilfrid had been divided into three; the other centres were at Hexham and York. Surprisingly the old hermit took to his new job as if to the manner born. When Ecgfrith led an army deep into the territory of the Picts in 685, Cuthbert prophesied disaster. Bede takes up the story;

"Cuthbert set off to Carlisle to speak to the Queen who had arranged to stay in her sister's convent to await the outcome of the war. The day after his arrival the citizens conducted him around the city walls to see a remarkable Roman fountain that was built into them. He was suddenly disturbed in spirit. He leaned heavily on his staff, turned his face dolefully to the wall, then straightening himself up and looking up into the sky, he sighed deeply and said almost in a whisper, 'Perhaps at this moment the battle is being decided'."

The old man clearly knew how to put on a performance. After his premonition, Cuthbert sought out the Queen for a quiet word of statesmanlike advice;

"Tomorrow being Sunday you cannot travel. Monday morning at daybreak leave in your chariot for the Royal City [Bamburgh]. Enter quickly for perhaps the king has been slain. Tomorrow I have been invited to a neighbouring monastery to dedicate the chapel but as soon as the dedication is over I shall follow you"

This episode shows the unworldly hermit at the centre of Northumbrian politics at a moment of crisis. Because Ecgfrith may have been slain (and since he most certainly had been at that point, this might be a piece of wisdom after the event) there was a danger of a palace coup and his Queen needed to look after her interests. It was sound advice. On his pastoral visit to Carlisle Cuthbert was treated with the great respect due to his office and it was a man called Wagga, the Reeve of the city who conducted the tour around the walls. Reeve is from 'Shire-Reeve' or Sheriff and it described a royal official. The fact that earlier in 685 Ecgfrith had made a gift to the Bishops of Lindisfarne of the old Roman city and land for fifteen miles around it — an immensely valuable donation — shows that when the Northumbrians took Carlisle from the descendents of Urien of Rheged, it was a royal possession at that time. And Wagga was also meeting his new master, Cuthbert. A memory of Ecgfrith's generosity may be the modern parish of St Cuthbert Without [the Walls] by Carlisle.

Before the Northumbrian defeat at Nechtansmere, Cuthbert had visited the Abbess Aelfflaed at the nunnery on Cocquet Island. They discussed the royal succession and who might be king after Ecgfrith. As the sister of Aldfrith, Aelfflaed had more than a passing interest in the issue. In fact she herself appears to have become an influential advisor on national politics, and when Cuthbert hinted that Aldfrith would succeed, he may have been recruiting her support by saying what the Abbess wanted to hear.

These episodes show an astute and worldly man at work, and they place Cuthbert astride both traditions in the Northumbrian church. By personal inclination and through his early teaching at Melrose, he was an ascetic Celt anxious to gain the kingdom of Heaven through strenuous regimes of extreme privation and piety in remote places. But at the end of his life when he became a bishop, he shows himself a political animal operating in a secular setting and hoping to have an influence (for the benefit of the church) on events. And at the end, remembering the dangers of disunity presented by the Easter controversy at the Synod of Whitby, the old man swallowed his personal preferences and warned all around him to be orthodox in their beliefs and practices.

AMAZING GRACE

The impression given in all his writings is that Bede was a sober, measured, punctilious and even-tempered soul. Only once does he really let fly. Here is part of chapter 10 of the Ecclesiastical History of the English People;

"... the Briton Pelagius spread far and wide his noxious and abominable teaching that man had no need of God's grace... St Augustine and other orthodox fathers quoted many thousand catholic authorities against them, but they refused to abandon their folly; on the contrary, their obstinacy was hardened by contradiction, and they refused to return to the true faith. Prosper the rhetorician has aptly expressed this in heroic verse:

> *'Against the great Augustine see him crawl,*
> *This wretched scribbler with his pen of gall!*
> *In what black caverns was this snakeling bred*
> *That from the dirt presumes to rear its head?*
> *Its food is grain that wave-washed Britain yields,*
> *Or the rank pasture of Campanian fields.'*

St Jerome did not trouble to write in Latin verse like Prosper, he was more direct and called Pelagius 'a fat hound weighed down by Scotch porridge'. The insult is interesting for it confirms the hated heretic's origins from either the north or the west of Britain. His name is a Latin version of 'Morgan' and it means 'son of the sea'. Perhaps Pelagius came from Strathclyde or the Solway. In 5th century Britain his ideas were certainly popular and their currency prompted two corrective visits from French bishops.

In Pelagius' lifetime (c360–420AD) matters of doctrine in the early Christian church were still fluid and only slowly hardening into the cast-iron precepts which sent many to a heretic's awful death in later centuries. The issue that prompted Bede's outburst revolved around the notion of Original Sin. Orthodox Christians like the great African theologian, St Augustine of Hippo, believed that the original sin of Adam and Eve in the Garden of Eden required all men and women to have the benefit of God's grace if they were to be saved and go to Heaven. Pelagius disagreed and thought that men could lead a virtuous life and through the exercise of their will, they could choose to avoid sin and gain salvation in that way.

This caused a tremendous row. To Augustine, Jerome and the other early fathers who lived amongst the chaos of the dying Roman Empire of the West with barbarians at the gates of their cities, it seemed that Divine Grace was all that could help them. Pelagius' common sense assertions (which appear to form much of the basis of the Protestant version of Christianity) forced Augustine to produce formulations of various aspects of dogma, including Grace, Original Sin and Predestination. Christianity clearly owes much to its argumentative heretics.

Cuthbert died in 20th March 687, and almost immediately his power began to grow. Eleven years after the monks buried him in the ground at Lindisfarne, his body was exhumed and found to be entirely uncorrupted, the limbs still flexible. No clearer sign from God was possible and so Cuthbert's body was, literally, raised to sainthood. A shrine was built to raise the coffin up on supports so that pilgrims could touch it while praying or get close enough for sanctity somehow to be transfered. At St Kentigern's shrine in Glasgow Cathedral, the coffin sat on a series of short pillars and pilgrims used to pray while putting their head between them.

When the Lindisfarne monks first raised up the shrine of St Cuthbert, Bishop Eadfrith began work on an object of great and enduring beauty. To commemorate the saint's life he wrote a Latin text of the four gospels and decorated it with sumptuous calligraphy and painting. The great illuminated manuscripts of the west were generally produced by teams of scribes who shared out the labour according to particular talents. But it appears that Bishop Eadfrith did all of the work on the Lindisfarne Gospels himself. It is an extraordinary achievement for one man, however gifted, and it strongly suggests a labour of love, a glorious work of art made out of devotion to Cuthbert.

A gospel book of such richness was no small undertaking. The vellum, or calfskin, needed was very considerable and many animals, perhaps 150, were slaughtered and skinned to provide the pages. Irish scribes believed that the finest vellum came from deliberately aborted calves. Eadfrith's palette for the illustrations sometimes travelled immense distances; lapis lazuli came from Afghanistan, indigo from the Mediterranean, kermes (carmine red) from North Africa and folium (pink) from the south of France. There was much to paint for the bishop designed his great book so that three fully decorated pages, a portrait of the gospel writer, a carpet page and an illuminated initial preceded each gospel. The work must have taken many years. At one point in its long production the book's pages may have travelled to Old Melrose. The Prior, Aediluald, is recorded as having been the binder and decorator of the covers. More likely, Melrose sponsored the work since Cuthbert was originally a son of the monastery.

Even though the other famous gospels of the period from Kells and Durrow in Ireland are profoundly Celtic in their look, Lindisfarne is much more influenced by the Mediterranean; Roman lettering, Byzantine painting, and a Near-Eastern style of decoration. The attention and money lavished on how the gospels looked betray their real function. Eadfrith's manuscript was never meant to be read. Rather it was an icon, a devotional object perhaps placed on an altar or simply shown to the faithful by a priest. For a religion based on the word of God and its interpretation, the use of a book as a symbol was entirely appropriate. And for Cuthbert the preacher they were a fitting memorial and have been closely associated with him and his cult for 1300 years.

BOOK LANGUAGE

Written records survive in all sorts of forms and several languages. In the period between 410 and 1113, most of what has come down to us exists in Latin, what Bede called Book-language, some in Old English, less in Old Welsh, a bit in Irish and Scots Gaelic, a few runes and a tiny amount in Tree Language. This last is more properly called Ogham and an example recently found as far west as Selkirk shows that it had a wider currency than many imagine. Like runes it was made in straight chisel strokes or knife cuts and the arrangement of its letters resembled the trunk of a tree and its branches. The whole inscription, generally a personal name, was the trunk and the letters attached or cut through it were like branches.

Runes derive from the Old English word 'run' and it has a sense of 'secret counsel', or esoteric knowledge, or even magic. This is a meaning still attached to it today, particularly in the phrase 'reading the runes'. Various Germanic peoples used them including the Vikings, the Angles and the Saxons. Because they were meant, like Ogham, to be cut in wood or stone, curves are avoided and the effect of a rune-row can look spikey, stark and forbidding.

In the Lindisfarne Gospels Bishop Eadfrith must have been tempted into self portraiture when he painted St Mark at his writing board with a sharpened reed pen and an ink-horn by him filled with iron-gall ink. This was a decoction of oak-apples and soot. The script used by scribes in writing Book-language varied according to a hierarchy of subject-matter. There were six basic styles — all imported from the Irish monasteries of the 6th and 7th centuries — and Insular Half-uncial was the grandest, and the least posh was Current Miniscule. The best light for writing belonged to God and most work was done out of doors in the cloisters of a monastery or even further afield if the day was sunny and calm. Bad weather and severe winters sometimes chilled the fingers of scribes so much that work was brought to a standstill. For the Christian religion, based on the Word of God, its copying and dissemination, this was no incidental difficulty.

Different hands and sometimes the shadow of a personality can be detected by experts in early manuscripts, and schools of writing traced through the teaching process. When one master in a scriptorium, or writing office in a monastery, taught many pupils, it is possible to see the connections in the style of the work.

Until the invention of the printing press and the portable book, the spread of knowledge and ideas depended heavily on good handwriting. And laborious copying was the only method of publication.

St Cuthbert's posthumous reputation grew because his genuinely pious life was well recorded (Bede was required to send his manuscript to Lindisfarne for checking before it could be copied and published) and when his shrine was removed to Durham Cathedral, the see became the most wealthy and widely landed in England. Pilgrims flocked to be near Cuthbert and both great and small gave gifts to the community who had care of him. The cult eventually enabled the Prince-Bishops of Durham to become the premier magnates in the north. An extraordinary achievement for the herd-laddie who saw visions on Brotherstone Hill.

In 1540 agents acting for King Hentry VIII in his attack on the church entered Durham Cathedral and broke the gilded shrine to pieces, completely destroying the structure around the coffin, ransacking the cupboards of relics and removing the Lindisfarne Gospels to London. The saint's body was hurriedly reburied in the precinct. Nearly 300 years later, in 1827, antiquarians dug into the grave believed to be Cuthbert's. And they found him. Inside a triple coffin lay a treasure; a wooden lid probably carved in 698, a gorgeous pectoral cross of gold and garnets, an ivory comb, a wooden travelling altar encased in silver, and a copy of St John' Gospel. All of these beautiful objects from Lindisfarne are unique in England and collectively they show at least two significant things. First and most obvious the hermit of Inner Farne enjoyed rich and expensive items, like the gold and garnet cross, which showed off his status as a bishop. And secondly the cultural influence apparent on everything buried in the coffin is cosmopolitan. The ivory for the comb is not from a walrus but an elephant, and the tone of the decorative work on the coffin lid, the altar and the pectoral cross is Mediterranean rather than Celtic. By the end of the 7th century Rome's influence was clearly overcoming that of Iona. It is, however, interesting to note that it was the Celtic simplicity of Cuthbert's life which caused his cult to grow so spectacularly. Wilfrid was also canonised and his view of the role of the church ultimately triumphed, but Cuthbert was loved.

In the Tweed Valley the power of Lindisfarne was also keenly felt. The extent of the early grants of lands to Lindisfarne is very telling, and it may offer a sense of the political structure that predated the rule of Bernician kings in the Tweed Valley.

What is known as the Terra Lindifarnensis reached up to the line of Dere Street where it stopped abruptly. With one large exception. All of the land between Teviot and Tweed right up to the confluence of the rivers at the fortress at Roxburgh is exempted. The Bernician kings made no gifts of land to Lindisfarne from that large triangle of territory. It looks as though a substantial person, able to hang on to his land, sat on top of the mound at Roxburgh for some time into the 7th century. At least until a man called Hroc, the Rook, came along to change the name to Roxburgh. Perhaps in that temporary postponement, there is a shadow of the old British kingdom of Calchvyndd?

In any event the line of Dere Street as a limit turned out also to be a temporary postponement. With such classic Anglian villages as Midlem and indeed Selkirk well to the west, it seems that good land was gradually reorganised and renamed, but not necessarily taken over. The line of the Catrail shows an interesting distribution of place-names with Old Welsh surviving in greater numbers to the west and Anglian to the east. It may represent a cultural frontier beyond which structures remained Celtic.

In the east, by the middle of the 7th century the low-lying and more productive areas of the Merse and Berwickshire had become predominantly English-speaking. The pattern of settlement was culturally distinctive; villages arranged around a green or a central street where markets were held, and behind the houses large gardens were laid out for private cultivation. In common ownership were the long strip-fields which were balloted for each year. The Angles ploughed up the smaller Celtic fields of the lower Tweed and replaced them with the oxgang, a long and narrow layout which allowed the heavy ox-powered plough to go on as far the lie of the land would allow until it was forced to turn in a wide and unproductive angle. The length of an oxgang was also reckoned by the time a team could plough without rest, although this must have been very variable. These ancient fields can still be seen behind Anglian villages in the Borders. At Midlem (Middle-ham) near Selkirk the arrangement shows up particularly well under a scatter of snow, since modern ploughing has largely left it intact. Two variants on a basic plan appear to have been used when Anglian villages were established. Midlem, Sprouston, Melrose, Bowden and Selkirk are laid out in a triangular arrangement while Lauder, Lilliesleaf and Hawick are single streets. Sometimes these are long, with houses arranged simply on either side and generally serviced by back lanes, which eventually got names like 'Back Row' or 'Back Side' when they developed into streets. On the green at Midlem, as an example, markets were held and goods sold. The lack of substantial finds of Anglian coins does not necessarily suggest that it was a barter economy. By the 9th century, the Northumbrian mints were producing very many more coins than elsewhere in England. These became known as 'stycas' and they were small and went down to low denominations. By 850 they were almost wholly minted in copper. This level of production implies a demand for coins from relatively ordinary people. Village houses and churches were mostly wooden and when a stone building went up, it was remarked upon. And none of these new settlements troubled to build stockades or ramparts. By the 8th century the Northumbrian kingdom had consolidated and although it lost primacy in England to Mercia and Offa, the man who built the Dyke, the vicissitudes of southern politics affected life in the Borders very little.

The 8th century saw an outflowering of religious sculpture which continues to dazzle all who see it. The Ruthwell Cross was raised some time between 730 and 750 at a village near the Solway shore, between Annan and Dumfries, and it is a remarkably sophisticated object. It stands six metres high and is covered with high relief carving and two excerpts from one of the very earliest English poems, 'The Dream of the Rood'. The cross was made in two sections of red sandstone and a marked difference in their colour shows that they were quarried from different places. But what seems an odd lapse of taste to us was not important to the sculptors who carved the biblical scenes on the shaft. They knew that they would be painted in the bright colours that can still be seen in the Lindisfarne Gospels.

Working together in a carefully conceived scheme the lines from 'The Dream of the Rood' and the carved and painted scenes tell a story of real coherence, a set of clear examples for a preacher to point to as he stood amongst a gathering at the cross. The central idea of the poem is that the Rood or the cross upon which Christ was crucified had a personality and was a witness to the events of the Passion. Lines from it are cut in Anglian runes on the narrow sides of the lower of the two stones of the shaft, and there is also Roman lettering on the broad sides, around the frames of the biblical scenes. A reader of the runes needs to move not from left to right in the way that the words are set out on this page but instead from right to left;

"Almighty God stripped himself.
When he willed to mount the gallows,
Courageous before all men,
[I dared not] bow…"

Moving from the lines of poetry to the sculptured reliefs, the first scene shows the crucifixion and then, reading up the cross-shaft, four more episodes from the gospels — the Annunciation, two miracles and the Visitation. The second quotation from the poem is then read on the other narrow side;

"I [lifted up] a powerful king —
The Lord of Heaven I dared not tilt.
Men insulted both of us together;
I was drenched with blood poured from the man's side."

And on the other broad side are more images of Christ and, significantly, a scene where the first monks, St Paul and St Anthony, break bread together in the desert. These were the early eastern saints, the Desert Fathers, so admired in the monasteries of the north and west of Britain and Ireland. In fact all of the scenes on this side of the cross are associated with the desert in some way or other.

The cross was not erected next to any known church at Ruthwell, but since the great church of St Kentigern at Hoddom is only 5 miles away, it may be that it acted as a waymarker for pilgrims. Place-names around the nunnery at Coldingham remember this habit of placing crosses at the approaches to a sanctified place; Applincross, Whitecross and Cairncross. By contrast at Jedburgh there is abundant archaeology but no names, not even the name of an early saint. The remains of no less than five 8th to 10th century crosses have been found. Some had been built into houses in the town, others used in the precinct of the medieval abbey. They appear to have been tall crosses with small heads and intricately carved shafts. A socket for one lies in the garden of Queen Mary's House while tradition asserts that another marked a crossing of the Jed at the foot of the Bongate. This last sounds like a pilgrims' cross. The presence of so many would alone signify an important site, but fragments of another object add even more mystery. Parts of a large and beautiful stone shrine, at least 5 feet long and three feet high, have been uncovered. A favourite Anglian sculptural motif, the inhabited vine scroll, has been used where animals — they are birds on the Jedburgh fragment — appear in a stylised representation of curling vegetation. Shaped like a house with a steep-pitched roof, the shrine was, more correctly, a cover intended to fit over the coffin of a saint. And in the case of Jedburgh's magnificently carved example, a very important saint. But who was he, or she?

Two candidates seem to be possible. The first is Boisil from Old Melrose, the friend of Cuthbert and the man who left his name on two Border villages, St Boswell's and Newtown St Boswell's. But, frankly, he appears to have been insufficiently important to warrant such richness, and in any case, his shrine ought to be at Melrose rather than Jedburgh. The other candidate is Cuthbert himself. For reasons which will become clear, his shrine moved in the 9th century and it may have rested a while on the banks of the Jed. The difficulty with that theory is that the shrine fragment has been dated too early, to the early 8th century, for its creation to fit with the much later dates of the saint's journeyings. What is clear, however, is that Jedburgh was an important ecclesiastical centre before 830 when Bishop Ecgred of Lindisfarne built a church at Gedwearde (or Jedworth). Confusingly Ecgred founded two churches and both were called Gedwearde. Here is the entry from Symeon of Durham;

"Ecgred, bishop of Lindisfarne, bestowed upon the holy confessor, Cuthbert, that vill [of Norham] with two others which he had founded, [both] called by the same name, Jedworth, with their appanages."

The appanages were substantial. They stretched "from Dune [the Dunion] to Teviotmouth, and thence to Wilton, and thence beyond the mountain eastwards". Another version of this entry talks of "the two Jedburghs, to the southern district of the Teviot." No church is mentioned in any of these notices, and certainly no 'eccles' name has survived in the locality, but this immense area may be the outline of old Jedburghshire. And the original central church may be buried under the medieval abbey.

THE RUIN

By the 8th century the Roman cities of Britain had ceased to function as large communities. Some were on sites continuously inhabited by smaller populations whose own buildings eroded and even erased what had stood there before. A ready re-use for quarried, squared-off and handily sized building stone could always be found. Roman altars were incorporated into the structure of Jedburgh Abbey and in Carlisle Cathedral the lighter grey stone seen in the clearstorey and one of the chapels was robbed from Hadrian's Wall and nearby Stanwix Fort and it contrasts very obviously with the red sandstone of the rest of the fabric.

The English and the native British were not contemptuous of Roman architecture. They simply had little use for it as it stood because their social structures were different, smaller in scale and rural. In fact a poem composed in Old English in the 8th century betrays a sense of awe, and even regret at what time and disuse had done to the old cities;

"The Ruin
Splendid this rampart is, though fate destroyed it,
The city buildings fell apart, the works
Of giants crumble. Tumbled are the towers,
Ruined are the roofs, and broken the barred gate,
Frost in the plaster, all the ceilings gape,
Torn and collapsed and eaten up by age."

While events in 8th century England preoccupied Northumbrian bishops and kings, events in the south seem not to have had much impact in the Tweed Basin. Internal dynastic politics did though. Here is another entry from the chronicler, Symeon of Durham;

"In the year 759 Aethelwold, who was also called Moll, began to reign on the Nones of August [5th].

And in the beginning of his third year, a very severe battle was fought near Eildon on the eighth before the Ides of August [6th]; and in it Oswin fell, after three days, on the first day of the week. And King Aethelwold, who was called Moll, gained the victory in the battle."

Since it took Aethelwald three days to defeat Oswin, a siege of some kind might have taken place, perhaps of Eildon Hill North. Or more likely at Old Melrose where the site is highly defensible.

In any case, the second half of the 8th century saw the Northumbrian kingship grow very unstable as the pressure from Offa's Mercians intensified. Bede dedicated his 'Ecclesiastical History of the English People' to King Ceolwulf who eventually resigned to become a monk at Lindisfarne, living there for nearly 30 years. His successor Eadberht reigned for 20 years before he too resigned to go into holy orders. But afterwards there appears to have been dynastic chaos. Between 758 and 799 at least nine kings (one of them twice) occupied the throne. Aethelwald Moll fought at Eildon Hill in 761 to quell what appears to have been a rebellion by Oswin, the second son of Eadhbert, a previous king of Northumbria. Oswin's power-base appears to have been centred in the Tweed Valley.

Aethelred was king when the Anglo-Saxon Chronicle reported trouble of an entirely different order for the year 793;

"In that year terrible portents appeared in Northumbria, and miserably afflicted the inhabitants; these were exceptional flashes of lightning and fiery dragons were seen flying in the air, and soon after in the same year the harrying of the heathen miserably destroyed God's church in Lindisfarne by rapine and slaughter."

The Vikings had sailed into history. 793 was the date of their first attack, but not their last. After the early raids, settlers came and the gradual takeover of the north radically altered the political balance, and almost destroyed the kingdom of Northumbria. The Vikings were not simply another set of acquisitive raiders and invaders. Their coming inspired real fear. Even when allowances are made for the two intimately connected facts that historical records were exclusively kept by churchmen and the pagan Vikings were fond of attacking undefended churches, there is no mistaking the sense of terror. At the same time as kings Ivar and Olaf were laying seige to Dumbarton Rock, the dragon-ships of another raiding party appeared off the Berwickshire coast. Here is an entry from the chronicle of Matthew Paris;

"Of the admirable deed of the holy abbess Ebba.

In the year of the Lord 870 an innumerable host of Danes landed in Scotland; and their leaders were Inguar and Hubba, men of terrible wickedness and unheard-of bravery. And they, striving to depopulate the territories of all England, slaughtered all the boys and old men whom they found, and commanded that the matrons, nuns and maidens should be given up to wantonness.

And when such plundering brutality had pervaded all territories of the kingdoms, Ebba, holy abbess of the cloister of Coldingham, feared that she too, to whom had been entrusted the care of government and the pastoral care, might be given up to the lust of pagans and lose her maiden chastity, along with the virgins under her rule; and she called together all the sisters into the chapter-house, and burst into speech in this wise, saying, "Recently have come into our parts the wickedest pagans, ignorant of any kind of humanity; and roaming through every part of this district they spare neither the sex of woman nor the age of child, and they destroy churches and churchmen, prostitute nuns, and break up and burn everything they come upon. Therefore if you decide to acquiesce in my advice, I conceive a sure hope that by divine mercy we may be able both to escape the fury of the barbarians and to preserve the chastity of perpetual virginity."

And when the whole congregation of virgins had undertaken with sure promises that they would in all things obey the commands of their mother, that abbess of admirable heroism showed before all the sisters an example of chastity not only advantageous for those nuns but also eternally to be followed by all succeeding virgins: she took a sharp knife and cut off her own nose and upper lip to the teeth, offering a dreadful spectacle of herself to all beholders. And since the whole congregation saw and admired this memorable deed, each one performed a similar act upon herself, and followed the example of her mother.

And after this had so taken place, when next morning dawned, the most wicked brigands came upon them, to give up to wantonness the holy women, and devoted to God; as also to plunder the monastery itself and burn it down in flames. But when they saw the abbess and each of the sisters so horribly mutilated, and saturated with their blood from the soles of their feet to their crowns, they retired from the place with haste, for it seemed to them too long to stay even for a short space there. But as they retired hence the aforesaid leaders commanded their evil satellites to set fire to and burn down the monastery with all its offices and with the nuns themselves.

And so the execution was fulfilled by the servants of iniquity, and the holy abbess and all the virgins with her attained most holily to the glory of martyrdom."

This grisly episode may not have been typical, and was probably so fully recorded for that reason, but the appalling actions of the Abbess Ebba and her nuns grew out of a fear of an even more dreadful fate at the hands of the pagan Vikings.

Increasingly they pressed on the kingdom of Northumbria. Having taken York and all of old Deira, the Vikings (or the Danes, as they came to be known in the late 9th century) moved further north. The Anglo-Saxon Chronicle takes up the story;

"In this year [876] the army [of Danes] went from Repton. And Halfdane went with part of the army into Northumbria, and took winter quarters by the River Tyne; and the army conquered the land, and often harried upon Picts and upon Strathclyde Welsh."

In the same year Lindisfarne was again attacked and the bishop took the momentous decision that the shrine of St Cuthbert could not remain in such an exposed and dangerous place any longer. The coffin was taken inland for refuge, probably by boat since its first resting-place was Norham. The Tweed was navigable by small craft for much of its length, at least as far as Peebles. Boatmen expected to have to make short portages when a rocky or shallow stretch prevented a safe draught. Norham was the first place where the river could be forded above Berwick, and its old name might have chilled the heart of the Abbess Ebba of Coldingham. Norham used to be called Ubbanford, or 'Hubba's Ford' — Hubba was one of the Danish sea-lords who raided the nunnery in 870.

After St Cuthbert had lain at Norham for a time he was moved again on several occasions, perhaps further and safer inland to the church at Jedburgh where the beautiful shrine was carved, and certainly to Ripon Abbey and thence to Chester-le-Street. Its final resting place was to be Durham Cathedral. Whatever the identity of the mysterious saint commemorated there, Jedburgh was an important place. Very close to Dere Street, at a crossing of the River Jed and with Teviotdale as its hinterland, it lay at a commercial hub. Anglo-Saxon and Anglo-Scandinavian coin finds from the 9th and 10th centuries have been discovered in two hoards in a field south of the Bongate, and in various locations scattered around the Market Square. The early history of Jedburgh is an intriguing puzzle made more and not less mysterious by the presence of a medieval abbey.

Hogback tombstones remember the less glorious or sacred resting places of Scandinavians in the Borders. There are seven in all, some complete, others in fragments. They are carved in the form of houses for the dead with shingle roofs and the representation of four walls. The best example is at Ancrum. Six foot four inches long, nearly two feet broad and a foot high, it is a substantial item of funerary sculpture. The principle of building in the shape of a house for a tomb is the same as that used in the design of the Jedburgh shrine. The curved roofline which gives the name 'hogback' was evidently typical of real Danish and Swedish houses of the period. Dating to the late 9th and early 10th centuries these graves mark the presence of Scandinavian incomers not only at Ancrum but also at Bedrule and Nisbet, with an outlier at Lempitlaw near Kelso. Six of the stones are found in village churchyards in a small triangle around Jedburgh.

While the Danish kingdom of York pushed hard on the Northumbrians from the south, there were powers in the north only too glad to take advantage of any weakness. The Gaelic-speaking kings of Alba had been slowly growing in influence, prestige and territory. King Kenneth macAlpin had burned the monastery at Old Melrose in 858 and apparently raided Northumbria on several occasions. It may be a measure of his ambition rather than any political reality when Gaelic chroniclers claimed that "he ruled the Tweed."

As Northumbrian power withered in Galloway their bishops at Whithorn came under increasing pressure. Badwulf, the successor of Peohtwine and Peohthelm, was consecrated to the see in 791 but he disappears entirely from the record in 803. In the 9th century Irish Vikings began to settle in Galloway and Cumbria and, surprisingly, to bring the Gaelic language to the northern shore of the Solway. As late as 915, however, the Northumbrians still clung on to Carlisle and the Eden Valley. Symeon of Durham records that between 910 and 915 a 'Princeps', an Ealdorman called Eadulf ruled in the old Roman city. But in the 10th century the Strathclyde kings, as clients of the Gaelic kings of Alba, took over Dumfries and Galloway and Carlisle and Cumbria in the aftermath of the collapse of Northumbrian power. Place-name evidence shows that this was more than a superficial political shift. Old Welsh reasserted itself as the native speech of Cumbria when Strathclyde took over — and that in turn shows how tenaciously the language had clung on in the north. In fact there seems to have been a vogue for the reassertion of Welsh culture towards the end of the 10th century. Old royal names like Riderch and Owain appear again and in Glasgow a vigourous religious life becomes apparent.

STRATHCLYDE

Of all the North British kingdoms Strathclyde lasted much the longest. Ruled by its own native dynasty until the Viking seige of Dumbarton Rock in 870 and the expulsion of Eochaid in 890, it carried on past these dates as a political entity. At the battle of Carham in 1018 King Owain of Strathclyde was the last to be so named. One of the reasons for this immense longevity was the little recognised Celtic practice of alternating kingship.

Descendents of Kenneth macAlpin (died 858) coalesced into two related sub-dynasties who agreed that alternate candidates should take turns to occupy the throne of the emerging kingdom of Scotland. In this way damaging internecine feuding was avoided. The difficulty with this remarkable agreement was the role of the heir apparent; what was he to do whilst he waited for the king of Scotland from the other dynasty to die? After 890 Strathclyde neatly solved the problem. Between then and 1018 the heir of the entire kingdom of Scotland was to be made King of Strathclyde. A similar process happens today with the Prince of Wales. In early Scotland, to give an example, Indulf (died 962) reigned over Strathclyde while King Malcom I was King of Scots, and when he died Indulf took his throne and Malcolm's son, Dub, moved into the vacant kingship of the Clyde.

In 927 the southern boundary of Strathclyde's influence reached down to Eamont Bridge near Penrith. That was the rendezvous chosen by Athelstan, the Wessex king in the process of asserting himself as the Bretwalda, the ruler of all England. He wanted a meeting with the Strathclyde and Scots kings to agree a relationship which would become much misused and misquoted in the future. The border between Athelstan's England and Scottish Cumbria was on the River Eamont which flowed out of Ullswater before joining the Eden, and thence up to the Rere Cross on Stainmore. But the Strathclyde and Scots kings had to recognise Athelstan's overlordship in return for that agreement on boundaries. No matter what would be asserted in centuries to come this relationship did not make the Scots kings dependent on the English kings for their realm. The Strathclyders and the Scots gave Athelstan what he wanted — his pretensions mattered little to them — in return for a quiet life.

In the old kingdom of Bernicia and Deira, the last known king, Aldred, ceased to reign in 927, 370 years after Ida had begun. Athelstan would have no other kings in England but himself and the Bernician royal family became the Earls of Bamburgh. At the same time Scottish sub-kings in Atholl, Moray and elsewhere were given the rank of Mormaers. The earliest title adopted by the Bernician kings is an interesting echo of the past. It was 'High Reeve' and Mormaer is an exact translation.

Ten years later the situation was different. Athelstan had seized the Viking kingdom of York and looked as though he had put himself in a strong position to threaten all of the north. By 937 Olaf Guthrifson, the Viking king of Dublin, had compiled an alliance including Constantine II of Scotland with Owain macDomhnuill, King of Strathclyde, Aralt, King of Man and several other Celtic kings. They sailed to fight Athelstan at Brunanburh, probably Bromborough near Liverpool, and were badly defeated by a smaller force. It was, mourned Celtic chroniclers, the last real chance to evict the English from Britain.

Athelstan and his dynasty took full advantage and gradually England rolled northwards. After Eric Bloodaxe had been removed, the Viking kingdom of York was turned into the Earldom of Northumbria, and these men, in turn, controlled the Earls of Bamburgh.

By 973 the Northumbrians were forced formally to accept what had probably been a fact for some time and they ceded Lothian to the Scottish kings. Raiding in the Tweed Valley became so frequent that it appears resistance to the Scots went on only at a local level. The Earls of Bamburgh and Northumbria had problems to the south.

Somewhere in one of the Perthshire glens, in 1005, Malcolm II macAlpin ambushed and killed his cousin Kenneth III and thereby secured the undisputed throne of the Kingdom of Alba. Immediately he gathered a host and invaded Northumbria, laying seige to Durham — but without lasting success. Ten years later, less headstrong and better organised, he made an alliance with Owain, the last King of Strathclyde, and in May 1018 in the woods of the narrow valley of the Caddon Water between Galashiels and Selkirk, they massed their host for the descent into the old kingdom of Bernicia.

Malcolm II knew that permanent control of the valuable villages of the Tweed Valley would enrich the revenues of the young kingdom of Alba and as the war-smoke billowed over the oak trees at Caddon Water, he and King Owain of Strathclyde, and their captains made their battle-plans with care.

Scouts had reported to Malcolm that Eadulf, Earl of Bamburgh, had reached the Tweed near Cornhill at the head of a force of Bernician spearmen. But the Scots king also knew that the new Danish over-king of England, the young Cnut, was distracted by a series of difficulties in imposing his rule. That meant Eadulf was fighting only for his ancient earldom, he had no forces from the English king and no certainty of his support even if he won.

Malcolm and Owain hurried down the Tweed to engage Eadulf as quickly as they could, and also, crucially, to choose their killing ground. In the early 11th century armies fought mainly on foot with forces of spearmen. And when two armies faced each other they formed a close-knit shield-wall before advancing, often only at a walk, to attack their enemy in hand to hand fighting. Over the tops of their long shields men stared into the eyes of their enemies, only inches apart, as they pushed and hacked at each other. They could smell each other's sweat, taste their blood and sense their fear. The greatest danger faced by a shield-wall formation was outflanking. If an enemy line was longer and there was space on the ground to do it, they could get behind a wall, roll it up and surround it. And that was when real slaughter took place.

And that is what seems to have happened to Eadulf's Bernicians on 26th May 1018 at the place they called 'aet Carrum'. Nowadays Carham is a sleepy hamlet of a dozen houses standing a hundred yards or so from a lazy bend in the meandering River Tweed. On the flat flood plain nearby, a thousand years ago, the grass was soaked with blood. Swinging their Lochaber axes, the wild Highlanders in Malcolm's host hacked the English shield-wall to pieces. Scenting slaughter and roaring their war-cries, they incited each other into 'freagarrachan' or 'rage-fits' and they climbed over the wrack of dying and screaming men and drove the defeated Bernicians into the Tweed or lifted them wriggling into the air on the points of their long spears. There was no mercy on that day and the chronicler Simeon of Durham recorded the carnage when he wrote; "all the people who dwelt between Tees and Tweed were well-nigh exterminated".

BY THE RIGHT

Pushing and shoving were as much a military skill as archery or horse-riding and in a battle such as Carham, those who pushed and shoved the harder were likely to do better. Since most people are right-handed and hold weapons in that hand while protecting themselves with a shield on the left, a pair of shield-walls locked together produced a curious effect. Almost every man in the line, because he was right-handed, tended to seek the protection of the shield held by the man on his right. In turn this reliance made him push his right-hand-man both forwards and sideways. Precisely the same tendency affected the opposing shield wall, and this would have sent both moving slowly in an anticlockwise direction on the battlefield. A bit like a scrum wheeling in rugby.

Reliable right-hand-men were important and the practice of the principals at Border common ridings having one (and a left hand man) is an echo of ancient battlecraft. This habit may also have given rise to the Best Man at marriage ceremonies standing on the right of the groom.

Although there is now no trace of the battle and no certainty about exactly where it was fought, Carham remembers it in another way. The village is almost precisely on the border between England and Scotland. That is the legacy of Malcolm's axemen and also a monument to King Owain of Strathclyde who was killed in the fighting. Carham in 1018 did not fix the border on the Tweed — the ambitions of the macAlpin dynasty reached far further, but in historical reality, it rarely moved after that date.

In order to grasp the historical realities behind this pivotal battle, relatively recent distinctions like Scots and English need to be set to one side. To the Borderers who stood up on the ridges on the south to watch the battle rage below them at Carham, the Bernician spearmen will have seemed far more familiar than the Gaelic-speaking Highlanders in Malcolm mac Alpin's host. For the people watching were themselves English-speaking Bernicians, on both sides of the Tweed. Over nearly half a millenium, from around 600 and into the 11th century, the history of the Borders was the history of Bernicia. They were one and the same place, and the attentions of a king of Scotland will have appeared both alien and unwelcome.

After Carham the influence of the macMalcolm kings and their control of the Border country shows up in a handful of Gaelic place-names like Glendearg and Cortleferry. But surprisingly these are found not in the fertile riverine farmlands of the east but in the upland areas of the west. It appears that Malcolm and his successors were more interested in the revenues from the English-speaking farmers of the Borders than in causing disturbance by removing these productive people off their lands.

Gaelic was rarely spoken in the Borders and English remained the speech of most groups of people in the 10th century. And in many important ways the area remained firmly in an Anglian cultural milieu. After 1066 and the invasion of William the Bastard, Gospatrick Earl of Northumbria fled north to take refuge at the court of Malcom III Canmore. Significantly a new earldom was created for this man out of the northern remnants of the old kingdom of Bernicia; Roxburghshire, Berwickshire and the Lothians. In 1072 Prior Aldwin of Winchcombe came north from the abbey at Evesham and settled in what seems to be the abandoned monastery at Old Melrose. Here is Symeon of Durham's report;

"But Aldwin left the monastery of Jarrow, having as the companion of his way and purpose Turgot, still in the garb of a cleric, but imitating in devotion and deed the life of the monks...
They came to the former monastery of Melrose, at that time a solitude; and delighting in the secluded habitation of that place began to live there [as monks] serving Christ.
But when their [monastic] life there had become known to the king of the Scots, Malcolm, to whom that pertained, they suffered at his hands grievous wrongs and persecutions for this cause, that, following the evangelic precept, they refused to swear fealty to him.
Meanwhile the venerable bishop Walcher besought, admonished and adjured them in frequent letters and mandates, and at last threatened that he with the clergy and all the people would excommunicate them in the presence of the most sacred body of St Cuthbert, unless they return to him and dwell under St Cuthbert."

The border was hardening. Even under the pious influence of his saintly wife, Margaret, Malcolm III would not under any circumstances allow the refounding of a monastery under Durham's control. And Durham utterly refused to allow its clerics to settle in a community it could not hope to govern effectively. Northern Bernicia was fast becoming Southern Scotland and Southern Bernicia was becoming Northern England. And a deadly faultline, the border, was widening between two groups of people who shared a common history and language.

The cathedral clergy at Durham continued, nevertheless, to claim ecclesiastical jurisdiction north of the Tweed. Insisting that Teviotdale and Jedburgh was theirs, they actually managed to hang on to Coldingham until the 14th century. And in 1080 a dramatic epilogue to Bernician politics was played out at Jedburgh. A church is at last mentioned, what must have been the home of the vine-scroll shrine and the focus of the crosses. Walcher, the Earl-Bishop of Durham who was so against the refounding of Old Melrose, was assassinated by a member of the exiled Gospatrick's family, Eadulf Rus. He fled to Jedburgh where, soon afterwards, retribution caught up with him and he himself was murdered. Some time before 1107, Turgot, the man who went with Aldwin to Melrose and by this time Archdeacon of Durham, still retained enough control over affairs at the church at Jedburgh to demand that Eadulf Rus' body be exhumed and cast out of the sanctified ground 'as if it were filth'.

The English speakers of the Borders and the Gaelic speakers of Galloway remembered a remnant of their shared Celtic history in a curious way. In his 'History and Antiquities of Roxburghshire and Adjacent Districts' (1859), Alexander Jeffrey notes that a class of servile fieldworkers were known in the Middle Ages as the 'cumerlach'. This term derives from 'Cymry', the Welsh word for the Welsh and is a clear echo of Old Welsh speakers in the Borders. In Galloway the same sort of people were known by a dialect word which, astonishingly, survived into the 19th century. 'Gossok' is from 'Gwas' which means 'servant' or 'lad'.

By the end of the 11th century the Tweed had become the eastern frontier between England and Scotland, whereas in the west the division remained more fluid for some time. In the far future the Borders would suffer very much from the presence of the border, but for the next two centuries, optimism, creativity and innovation were to be paramount. A golden age was dawning.

6

All the Faithful Sons of Holy Mother Church

Two kings sit in the loops of a capital 'M'. The beautifully decorated letter begins a long and fascinating document written and promulgated on behalf of the king in the right-hand loop. Fresh-faced, blond haired and eighteen years old, Malcolm IV almost wears a smile of satisfaction, as well he might, for the 'M' begins his own name. The document is a confirmation in 1159 of the gifts and rights originally confered on the abbot and monks of Kelso Abbey by the king in the left-hand loop. Grey-bearded, round-shouldered and slightly bent with age, David I sits holding the drawn sword of state in his right hand and an orb symbolising royal power in his left. Painted only six years after his death, the portrait was made by someone at Kelso who knew what the old king looked like. It is the first surviving likeness of a Scotsman, and it is fitting that it came down to us for David I was unquestionably a very great man.

Ailred, Abbot of the monastery of Rievaulx in Yorkshire, wrote a life of David, and in what feels like a genuinely affectionate account, he offers a familiar story of the personal impact of the powerful and charismatic;

"Finally if it happened that a priest or a knight or a monk, a rich man or poor man, citizen or foreigner, business man or countryman had conversation with him, he discoursed suitably and unassumingly with each concerning his business and duties in such a way that each one thought that he cared only for his affairs. And thus he sent them all away cheerful and edified."

Encounters with the famous are often reported nowadays in this way; "I felt as though I was the only person in the room." Or "He/she seemed to be talking only to me, intensely interested in what I had to say", say ordinary people breathlessly, and endlessly. Ailred's observations tell us that reactions to the presence of power have changed little over the centuries.

Born in 1084, the sixth son of King Malcolm III Canmore and the saintly Saxon Queen Margaret, David had few prospects. And these diminished nearly to nothing when his father and elder brother, Edward, were both killed on the same day in 1093. Riding through the hills north of Alnwick after raiding in Northumbria, they had been ambushed by the men of the Earl of Northumbria. When the disastrous news reached Edinburgh, Queen Margaret appears to have gone into shock, and it was said that she turned her face to the wall and died. With no king and no previously designated heir apparent, the native Scots earls took rapid advantage of the confusion and installed the 62 year-old younger brother of Malcolm. Donald III Ban had a Gaelic nickname, 'Ban' means 'Fair-headed', and he also had Gaelic instincts. Doubtless encouraged by his native supporters at court, King Donald 'drove out all the English who were with King Malcolm before'.

David macMalcolm was only 9 years old when his father was killed and his uncle Donald took the throne. There is no constitutional or cultural sense in which the old man was a usurper; Celtic kings could be succeeded by brothers and cousins even when their sons lived, for the habit of primogeniture was still alien in the north. But prudence persuaded David's older sister, Edith, called Maud or Matilda by her family, to take herself and her little brother out of the way and south to the court of William II Rufus, the son of William the Bastard, as contemporaries called him.

While Gaelic-speaking kings and English-backed pretenders fought over the throne of Scotland, David began to grow up in the thoroughly Norman-French atmosphere of the south. Even when his older brother, Edgar, took troops supplied by William II Rufus and challenged Donald III for his inheritance, David stayed put in England. Victorious in battle, Edgar eventually took the old man prisoner in 1099 and, in an act of knowing savagery, he had his eyes put out. No Celtic king could hope to rule if his vital faculties were in any important way impaired, and Edgar knew that blinding his uncle would do as much as killing him. Nearly 70, Donald III Ban suffered a miserable, blundering death in prison. But in 1100 respect for his former status compelled Edgar to allow the body of the old king to be buried with his ancestors on Iona.

When King William II Rufus was accidentally killed by a stray arrow while out hunting in the New Forest on the 2nd of August in the same year, events moved very quickly. On that particular day the circumstances for a coup d'etat were perfect. Henry, the dead king's younger brother, happened to be near at hand, and the generally accepted heir to the throne, Robert Curthose, was away, returning from the First Crusade. With a speed fuelled by adrenaline and opportunism, Henry had himself crowned within three days of the fatal accident. Issuing a coronation charter redressing the alleged abuses of his brother's reign, and incidentally rewarding his supporters, Henry quickly consolidated his precarious position by marrying Matilda, David macMalcolm's older sister. It was an excellent dynastic match, for Matilda was also the sister of the reigning king of Scotland, Edgar, and the niece of another Edgar, the Atheling, who had been proclaimed king in London by the retreating English after the battle at Hastings.

At the same time David macMalcolm became David fitzMalcolm. When his sister married the new English king, Henry I, the 16 year-old's world was transformed. Much romance has been written about the training of a Norman knight, some of the best by Sir Walter Scott, and ideas of chivalry ultimately developed into a vague, but generally honourable, code of conduct. However, at the end of the 11th and the dawn of the 12th century, the knightly instruction given to David fitzMalcolm was practical. Instead of the elaborate business of vigils spent in front of an altar and the learning of a complicated set of chivalrous principles, it involved the acquisition of fighting skills, an understanding of military tactics and strategy, and the inclusion in a close relationship of loyalty to a Christian king. These were lessons David would never forget.

Styled in documents as 'David, the brother of the Queen', he had little status past that of a supporter of the usurper king. The first years of Henry I's reign were stormy but successful. In 1101 he repelled Robert Curthose's invasion of England and by 1105 felt strong enough to move into Normandy. At the battle at Tinchebrai in 1106 he defeated Robert and took the Duchy of Normandy for his own. The Anglo-Norman realm of William the Bastard had been recreated.

It is not known if David fitzMalcolm fought beside his king against Robert Curthose on either occasion, but it is likely that he did. Henry gave him a small reward in Normandy, a lordship in the Cotentin, now known as the Cherbourg Peninsula. It may have been given for services rendered, land that became forfeit after Curthose's defeat. Significantly it lay in an area that would produce many names famous in Scottish medieval history. For example, the Cotentin village of Brix would mutate into de Brus, which later became Bruce. David fitzMalcolm's connections with north-western France ribboned throughout his long career and they tied together many strands which later coloured the history of the Borders of Scotland and England very deeply.

In 1102 another French family, the Montgomery Earls of Shrewsbury rebelled openly against the king. Henry acted decisively, seized their castles, abolished the earldom and gave their possessions to the loyalist family of de Clare. The Montgomerys and de Clares were Marcher Lords given huge tracts of land and great liberties on the borders of Wales. The English kings wanted to create a buffer between themselves and the Welsh princes, and gave license to the Marchers to build castles, and to invade and colonise at will. After several charges into Wales, large areas of the countryside were taken from native rulers, and wholesale cultural changes followed. Castles patterned the landscape, towns were created at Cardiff, Carmarthen and Haverfordwest, and colonists from both England and Flanders were settled, particularly in Pembroke which has never lost the characteristics of 'Little England beyond Wales'. Bernard, the Norman Bishop of St David's, dismissed the hermetic Welsh monasticism of the Celtic past and brought in the new orders from north-western France. In the early 12th century Benedictines, Cistercians and Augustinian Canons founded monasteries on the territories of the Marcher Lords. Tintern Abbey is perhaps the most famous of the early foundations.

David fitzMalcolm watched and learned. And in 1107 his chance came. His brother, Edgar, died. The king was only 26 but had not taken a wife and had no heirs. The kingdom of the Scots passed to his younger brother, Alexander, but there was to be something for David, something very substantial, for a huge tract of southern Scotland was bequeathed to him by King Edgar. At first the legacy was problematic. In a late variant on the alternating kingship arrangements of the 10th and early 11th centuries, Alexander had held the Tweed and lands in what was still called Cumbria, that is, Nithsdale and Annandale (as well as modern Cumbria) during the reign of his brother Edgar. He knew from his own experience how valuable David's inheritance could be and at first he refused to hand it over. His English brother-in-law had other ideas. Henry I promised to supply David with an army that could outnumber anything the Scottish king could put in the field, and Alexander sensibly relented.

Just as in the Marches of Wales it suited English royal policy very well to have a loyal supporter as a buffer between England and the kingdom of the Scots. William the Bastard had invaded at least twice in retaliation for Malcolm III Canmore's savage attacks which had taken fire and sword as far south as Cleveland and North Yorkshire. And in 1092 William II Rufus had invaded Cumbria, rebuilt the castle at Carlisle and determined to remove the north-west from Scottish ownership and influence by the exercise of sheer military clout. The Scottish kings could be troublesome, dangerously and expensively troublesome, and with his focus on business in France Henry I needed to secure the north. By installing David fitzMalcolm as a Marcher Lord in the Borders, he believed he had solved a chronic strategic problem.

There was every reason to think that David would serve Anglo-Norman interests well. He had spent his entire adolescence, his most impressionable years, at the royal court as it moved around England and Normandy. Fluent in French, schooled in Norman culture and steeped in the dynamic of dynastic politics, he was, as contemporary writers consistently assert, a most perfect knight. And with Alexander I relatively young and married, David's prospects as the sixth son of Malcolm III Canmore were possible, but not likely. At the Christmas court in London in 1113, Henry I gave David the best present in England. Matilda, the widow of Simon de Senlis, Earl of Huntingdon, Bedford and Northampton, and the daughter and heiress of Waltheof, Earl of Northumbria, was easily the richest and most widely landed woman in Britain. And, in an effort to cement their strategic bond even more tightly, the king gave Matilda to David in marriage. With his possessions in Normandy, Southern Scotland and now vast estates in the East Midlands of England, David had quickly become a substantial man. With such wealth anchored in the south, David was hardly likely to prejudice his new position by disloyalty on the Marches of Scotland. But to ensure against temptation, Henry I kept Matilda's other great inheritance, the Earldom of Northumbria, for himself.

One of Earl David's first acts was to issue a charter confirming the possessions of the Cluniac monastery founded in Northampton by his predecessor, Simon de Senlis. One of the witnesses to the document was a man who would become very influential in David's life and the development of government in 12th century Scotland. John is described simply as 'the Chaplain' of the Earl, but he appears to have been a close and constant advisor. At the same time as he assumed his English earldom, David did something innovative and determinant — something he had observed happening on the borders of Wales. In 1113 he invited a community of monks from a monastery in north-western France, a place called Tiron in the Forest of Perche near Chartres, to come to the Borders of Scotland to found a new church. When the 12 Tironensian monks, led by their Abbot Ralph (the number 13 being symbolic of Christ and his disciples) travelled from the Forest of Perche to the Forest of Selkirk, it was the first appearance of a reformed order anywhere in Britain. Probably on the informed advice of John the Chaplain, David chose to approach the Tironensians because he believed them to be dynamic and to possess the skills necessary to establish a new monastery in the wild up-country of his Scottish earldom.

St Bernard of Ponthieu was one of a number of pious men who felt a need to break away from what they saw as the decaying mainstream of European monasticism. Desiring a return to the three core vows of chastity, poverty and obedience, Bernard led a group of monks into the Forest of Perche to found a new, reformed church in 1109. Tiron lay near to south-eastern Normandy and the Duke was an early patron. And so, probably with the encouragement of King Henry and on the initiative of John the Chaplain, Earl David planted the Tironensians in the Border country.

It seems that he chose to bring the monks to Selkirk for a number of reasons. First and most obvious the place-name itself tells that there was a pre-existing church. The last element 'kirk' is self-explanatory, and the first 'Sel' is generally interpreted as deriving from 'sele', the Anglian word for a hall, or a manor house. Sometimes 'Sel' in Selkirk is seen as coming from 'schelch', Anglian for wood or wilderness. However tempting a geographical context the Ettrick Forest might be, the former reading of the place-name is much more likely since aerial photography shows the rectilinear outlines of an Anglian hall at Philiphaugh, on the flat riverside ground to the north-west of the modern town. It seems to be similar to but smaller than the examples at Sprouston and Yeavering. Before 1113 the kirk in Selkirk was almost certainly down at the banks of the Ettrick where there the shadow of a graveyard and the outline of what is likely to have been a church inside it. Another place-name offers corroboration. Kilncroft has nothing to with pottery and everything to do with very early churches. Old spellings drop the 'n', leaving 'Kilcroft' which derives from Gaelic and means 'the church's croft', or portion of land. 'Kil' comes originally from the Latin 'cella' or cell, and more accurately denotes the sort of hermetic church found downriver at Old Melrose. The Gaelic-speaking Columban monks who came from Iona with St Aidan in 651 liked riverside locations and the ancient church of Selkirk by the Ettrick may have been founded as an outlying hermitage. In any case Selkirk is an old name which holds inside it an even older story.

The French monks who came to the Hall-kirk will have been interested in its history. Continuity of sanctity was important, as was the need to find an existing church where the new community could carry out their devotional duties. Whatever its nature, stone or wood, and whatever its condition, deserted or occupied, the Tironensians existed primarily to worship God, to pray and to say mass. They needed a church in which they could properly do that and they will have used what they found on the banks of the Ettrick.

Scraps such as place-name evidence and the ghosts of aerial photography sustain a sketchy narrative for millenia of Border history before 1113. But Earl David's charter to the French monks of Selkirk offers something completely new, the first sustained and detailed sense of what life was like, how it was organised, and who organised it — in one small area. It is as though a single, brilliant spotlight has been suddenly switched on to splash light onto a tiny patch of an otherwise darkened landscape. Here is a translation of the complete document which carefully lists all of the gifts given by the Earl David to his French monks for the establishment of their monastery. This version probably dates from c1120;

"David, the Earl, son of Malcolm King of Scots, [gives] greetings to all of his friends, French, English and Scots, all of whom are sons of the holy Church of God. Let it be known to all those present and all those to come in the future that I have founded a certain monastery at Selkirk. That is an abbey in honour of St Mary and St John the Evangelist, and for the salvation of my soul, and of my father's and my mother's, that of my brothers and my sisters, and of all my ancestors. To this church of monks I have given in perpetual gift the land of Selkirk from exactly [where] a stream flows down from the hills and runs into the Yarrow [now called the Ettrick], as far as another stream which coming down from Crossinemara [probably Faldonside Loch], flows into the Tweed. And beyond that same stream which flows into Yarrow, a certain parcel of land by the road that leads from the castle to the abbey, and the Yarrow, that is, towards the old town. And in these places I have given the better part of the woods, the arable land and the fishings. And also the villages of Midlem, Bowden and Eildon and there the better part of the lands, the fishings, the woods and the arable lands. And also my whole lordship of Melrose, from the middle of the village, from the mid-point of the stream right up to the ditch, just as it divides and reaches the Tweed. And again [they will have] the better part of the fishings, the woods and the arable lands. And in Sprouston one carucate of land, and ten acres, and one part of a carucate pertaining to that. And in Berwick one carucate, and one measure below the church on the Tweed, and half of one fishing, and a seventh part of [the produce] of the mill, and 40 solidi [silver coins] from the annual tax revenue of the town. And in the town of Roxburgh one measure, and a seventh of the mills, and 40 solidi from the annual tax revenue, and a seventh part of the fishings. And a tenth of the cheese [production] of Galloway, and half of the tanned hides. And also another part of all the slaughtered animals belonging to me, and similarly part of the hooves, and a seventh of the hides of all the sheep and lambs, and a tenth of the stags and hinds which are brought to me by my huntsmen. And all my waters around Selkirk Common to be used for their own fishing as well as mine, and the pasture of the Common to be used by their men as for mine. And my woods to take and burn for their domestic use, as my men do. And in England at Hardingstone 80 acres of ground in my lordship, that is, with all that pertains to that lordship, and one measure of land pertaining to the lordship, and two cows with ten acres of grazing, and beyond that six and a half virgates [30 acres] of land, and six measures by the bridge at Northampton, and a certain island-meadow next to the village, and the mill of the village.

And I have confirmed that all of these things should be in the possession of the aforesaid monastery and its monks by free, perpetual and peaceful right, so that no-one succeeding me shall ask for anything other than prayers for the salvation of their soul.

This was done while King Henry reigned in England, and Alexander in Scotland, and John was Bishop of the Church in Glasgow, and Herbert Abbot of the said monastery.

These are the witnesses; the aforementioned Bishop John, Countess Matilda, Henry son of the Earl, Walter the Chaplain, Osbert the Chaplain, Alwyn the Chaplain, William nephew of the Earl, Robert de Bruis, Robert de Umfraville, Walter de Bolebec, Robert de Painton, Cospatric brother of Dalfin, Hugh de Moreville, Pagano de Braiosa, Robert Corbet, Reginald de Muscamp, Walter de Lindsey, Robert de Burneville, Cospatric the Sheriff, Cospatric son of Aldeve, Uchtred son of Scot, Macchus, Colbanus, Gillemichael, Odardo Sheriff of Bamburgh, Lyulf son of Uchtred, Radulph the Englishman, Aimar the Gallovidian, Roger de Leicester, Adam the Chamberlain."

Now, this is a dense, difficult and fascinating document. Condensed into the complex, clumsy and repetitious Latin of the Selkirk Charter are the cultural foundations of a new, Anglo-Norman world clearly built on the bedrock of the old. The main motivation for David's great generosity was less an appreciation of how a literate and well-organised community of monks might help him develop his inheritance in Southern Scotland, and far more an expression of the deepest piety. David was unquestionably devout and, as later charters say, a faithful son of Holy Mother Church. Perhaps significantly, his name was unusual for the times in its Biblical origin, and the term 'Christian name' very suitably derives from the growing habit of using scripture as a source in this way. When David repeatedly asserted that the new church at Selkirk had been founded and endowed for the salvation of his soul, he meant it, literally. In a secular age such as this, it can be difficult to appreciate the power of absolute belief and what it persuaded men to do. The prayers David bought so dearly would lift his soul, and the souls of his family up to Heaven and to eternal glory in the sight of God. For most of the last 2000 years in Western Europe the great influence of the church was based on the near-universal belief in these absolutes. When presented with documents like the Selkirk Charter it is tempting to relapse into modern pragmatism, even cynicism, and look for politics behind such extravegant expressions of piety. That is a mistake. No matter how many abuses crept into Western Christianity, the power of simple faith remained immense.

This clear continuity with the past meant that the old Celtic and Anglian saints of the Borders, Aidan, Boisil, Cuthbert and the others, were not rejected or devalued but supported and celebrated. The French monks at Selkirk may have dedicated their new abbey to Biblical figures, St Mary and St John the Evangelist, but they will have understood the sanctity of Old Melrose, only four miles downriver, and they will have respected it. Only four years before, the Tironensian founder, St Bernard of Ponthieu, had sought the peace and solitude of the Forest of Perche just as Aidan and his followers found a retreat from the world in a loop of the Tweed. In 1115 or 1116 David's own piety, and perhaps curiousity, took him to Tiron to meet St Bernard and see the woodland monastery for himself. Sadly the old abbot died before the Earl arrived. No doubt he, and probably John the Chaplain, prayed at Bernard's tomb and heard mass in his church.

Between 1113 and 1124 nine religious houses had connections with Earl, and later, King David as a benefactor of some sort, buying more prayers. However, he may have had it in mind to take his faith even further. Several Gaelic-speaking kings of the 9th and 10th centuries and also some Northumbrians as early as the 7th had occasionally abdicated and gone into monasteries to take holy orders and die there. This habit became more common amongst Anglo-Norman noblemen who sometimes endowed a church on condition that they be admitted to the community as novices as the end of their days drew near. This was known as taking vows 'ad succurrendum' which translates as 'in a great hurry'. Robert Avenel, Lord of Eskdale and Richard de Moreville of Lauderdale both became novices at Melrose and were buried under the floor of the church. Such privileges could be very expensive and in 1216 Sir Alan Mortimer made over half of his estate to the abbey on the island of Inchcolm if the monks would allow him to be buried in the church. This particular powerful belief represents another continuity with the Celtic past. Burial in holy ground was thought to cleanse the dead of their worldly sins and many believed that Iona had magic soil because Columba and many other saints had walked their lives on it. That, and the press of tradition, was the reason why 49 Scottish kings had been interred there — the last being Donald III Ban. David's royal patron, Henry I of England, lavishly endowed Reading Abbey and apparently made his burial in the church a condition of his gifts. Perhaps Earl David planned to enter a monastery, to die there and be buried in the magic soil. He showed every sign. Meanwhile many monks said many prayers for his immortal soul. In some examples wealthy supporters of a religious house would request even more than is in the Selkirk Charter and give money or goods so that the brothers would regularly pray for them 'for all time coming'.

MEASURING

The documents associated with Border monasteries and nunneries can be mysterious in at least one important regard. They are full of carefully specified units of measurement, almost all of which have passed out of common currency in this metric age. Some survive in the calculations of older people and in place-names. And often they were only local in their currency. Here is a reference chart;

1. Length

    A Scots mile, mentioned as late as Robert Burns' 'Tam O' Shanter' was indeed longer than the English equivalent, and measured 1,972 yards or 1,774 metres.

    A Scots inch was reckoned as the length of that part of an average man's thumb from the bottom of the nail to the centre of the first knuckle, or alternatively the length of three barley grains laid end on end.

    An ell was 36 inches or one yard, and this ancient measurement was still being used in the Border textile mills of the 20th century. Weavers on piece work were paid according to the number of ells they made, although the measurements had lengthened.

2. Land

    A Scots acre was not usually square but a long rectangle determined by the action of ploughing several rigs with an ox-team. It generally measured 282 yards (253.8 metres) long by 21 yards (18.9m) wide.

    An oxgang was 13 acres.

    A ploughgate was 8 oxgangs or 104 acres.

    A husbandland was the normal amount of arable land held by a peasant tenant, the sort of people who lived in the terrace of houses at Springwood Park near Kelso, and it was 2 oxgangs or 26 acres.

3. Volume.

    A boll was the unit of measurement for flour or unmilled grain and it was 12 gallons (54 litres). There were sixteen bolls to a chalder and a quarter of a boll was a firlot.

    Other commodities such as wax, lead or cheese was weighed by the stone which was 15 pounds in Scotland.

Even though we live in an age when almost everything comes in mass produced and very accurately measured containers, we should not assume that the calculation of amounts in the distant past was therefore approximate or slapdash. Land and the food it produced were the staffs of life and while regional variations in measuring both will have existed everyone concerned will have agreed on common standards at any point of exchange. Cheating was not tolerated and reports of the punishment and public humiliation of bakers who sold short weight loaves are not uncommon. In towns they were tied to a horse-drawn sled, a loaf slung around their necks and then pelted with refuse and worse as they ran the gauntlet of the street.

In addition to piety, literacy was a much prized attribute of the new foundations. As much as the content, the very existence of the Selkirk Charter marks a new departure. In the past land was held by customary right and an agreement on memory. But when William the Bastard demanded the Domesday survey of 1086, he changed the way in which people thought. Written title to land, duly witnessed and promulgated, quickly gained precedence over anything that anybody could remember or assert. If there was no documentary evidence to prove ownership of land, then there was no evidence. Unwritten customary rights did not disappear overnight (and in Celtic Britain and Ireland some still exist) but their basis became increasingly less sure.

In its careful perambulation around the boundaries of the land given by Earl David the Charter shows a settled and peopled landscape clearly capable of substantial production. A sense of that is available before this date, but towns in particular are recent and they developed strongly under David and his successors. Two are listed, Roxburgh and Berwick, and their existence is a key to understanding the landscape around them. For towns imply surplus agricultural production and trade. And while these two related activities do not mean prosperity for everyone involved, they do signal a move away from the subsistence farming of the past.

Castles, like the one noted at Selkirk, were also new. Now covered in dense woodland and situated on private land, it is difficult to imagine what Selkirk Castle looked like. Comparative evidence, both documentary and archaeological, and such investigation as can be managed in awkward conditions suggest the outline of a characteristic Norman motte and bailey construction. This was generally a Christmas pudding-shaped mound of earth topped by a wooden palisade and surrounded by a bailey, or lower enclosure, also protected by a palisade. These castles were quick to build, effective to use and they presented an obvious focus of a new and emphatic power in the landscape.

To the appearance of reformed monasteries, towns and castles in the Selkirk Charter, one more peculiarly Anglo-Norman institution can be added — the hunting reserve, the king's forest. When his huntsmen brought stags and hinds to David and they were passed on to the monks, they came from 'meos boscos', 'my woods'. The greatest royal wood in Scotland was the Ettrick Forest, the ancient lands of the Selgovae, the Hunters. Much later evidence will show that Anglo-Norman kings and nobles made elaborate provision for hunting — indeed, it appears that some thought of little else.

Place-names like Bowden, Midlem, Melrose, Sprouston, Eildon and the first historical mention of the Selkirk Common all strike an immediate chord of recognition with modern readers of David's charters. Less familiar are the English names like Hardingstone and Northampton. The distances between these pieces of productive land and Selkirk Abbey must mean that the income was realised in cash and transmitted to the Tironensian monks in that form. The grant of 80 solidi from the towns of Roxburgh and Berwick was a welcome and rare source of money, but the inclusion of the southern properties showed an early need for even more. Expenditure on the setting up of the new abbey will have been heaviest at the very beginning of its life and it appears that Earl David understood that.

The villages and farms given to the monks in the upper Tweed valley did not appear overnight. Clearly all of them were going concerns well before 1113, and perhaps the motte and bailey castle at Selkirk is the only real innovation. Even if the towns grew in importance in the 12th century, they must be the creation of the late 11th. It takes time for trading links to build, for primary producers to grow regular surpluses and ensure supplies, and most practically for a town to develop sufficient throughput to generate an income which could bear an annual tax of 40 solidi for the new abbey. Obviously Earl David did not conjure the landscape of the Selkirk Charter out of a formless chaos — although some historians make it appear that he did — but he did make the economy of Southern Scotland more dynamic.

The principal agents of change were the new men from the south, the Anglo-Norman knights from the East Midlands of England and also the Cotentin Peninsula in north-western France. Many of them appear as witnesses to the Charter; Robert de Bruis, Robert de Umfraville, Pagano de Braiosa, Walter de Bolebec, Robert de Painton, Hugh de Moreville, Robert Corbet, Reginald de Muscamp, Walter de Lindsey, Robert de Burneville, Odoardo Sheriff of Bamburgh and Radulph the Englishman. Amongst this large group of new men were some from the estates of the East Midlands, probably younger sons with little expectation of any substantial inheritance, as well as others from the south. What they all shared was a common origin — north-western France, and more particularly, the Cotentin Peninsula. The de Morevilles were prominent tenants in Huntingdon but before that they came from Brix and Nehon. The de Bruis family also held property in Huntingdon and had been near-neighbours of the de Morevilles. The Avenels came from Mortain, the de Soules from St Lo and the Stewarts had their beginnings in Brittany. When modern commentators notice that the upper classes in Scotland all seem to know each other, they are not mistaken, they have known each other for a long time.

Like the monks at Selkirk and Earl David the newcomers spoke French as their first language, and continued to do so for many generations. And the focus of their culture was French — even for Henry I the Duchy of Normandy was a more important possession than England and until the accession of Edward I in 1272 English kings looked across the Channel to Anjou, Aquitaine and Gascony before they thought about Britain. Several of David's followers, notably the Baliol family, held lands in three kingdoms, Scotland, England and France, and had obligations to three kings. What was essentially a French military and religious elite, inter-married, interdependent and international, became masters of an enormous area of Western Europe (and even the Holy Land after the crusades) and their ideas and material legacy remain with us at every hand. As pungent an ingredient in Border history as the Old Welsh-speaking kingdoms, the Romans, the Bernicians and Northumbrians, the Frenchmen who came north with David dominated politics for more than two centuries. It was not only the power and persistence of the institutions they created and developed, the reformed monasteries, the castles and towns, but also a series of new relationships which bound this group together into a homogenous, if not necessarily harmonious, whole. This system for thinking about society has become known as feudalism, and in Scotland it grew up first and most thoroughly in the Border country. And the most important single catalyst for that development was David.

ASHETS AND GIGOTS

The way the Normans pronounced their dialect of French had a pronounced impact on the English language. Everyday words like 'forest' kept the 's' inherited from the Latin 'foresta' but lost it in the French 'foret'. In his book 'Mother Tongue' Bill Bryson offers a fascinating list of examples of this sort of thing. Parisian French disliked the 'w' sound and so pronounced words like 'question', 'quitter' or 'quartier' with a hard 'k'. The Normans retained the 'w' sound and so we got kwestion, kwit and kwarter. Bryson points out that nearly all the words relating to the law are derived from Norman French and of a total of 10,000 borrowings, nearly three kwarters are still in use.

In the Borders our dialect contains several Norman-French words now obselete in the south, and most them are connected with meat, the food of the ruling class. 'Gigot' for leg of lamb is pure French but unintelligible over the counter of an English butcher's shop. 'Mince' is from the French word for thin and in England something called 'ground beef' is its equivalent, although that is changing. 'Poullie' for a young chicken is fading out of use in the Borders as is 'ashet' for the plate it was served on.

In 1124 Alexander I died without an heir and his younger brother, the sixth son of Malcolm III Canmore and Queen Margaret, succeeded to the throne. David I reigned for a surprisingly long time, until 1153. Forty years old on his accession, he survived until his 69th year, a long life in the early Middle Ages. A little more arithmetic reveals something very pertinent to the history of the Borders. From the time he prised his earldom out of the reluctant hands of his brother in 1107, until his death in Carlisle in 1153, David closely associated himself, his tremendous energy and his flair for innovation with Southern Scotland for 46 years, almost the span of two generations. Men were born, lived and died knowing no other authority but David's. And in all that long time he changed the face of the Borders more profoundly than anyone before or since.

By 1153 the Tweed Valley had been thoroughly feudalised. A network of obligations and relationships had been created between the immigrant and native lords and those beneath them who worked the land and produced all the food, and also between those lords and the king. Variations in this (admittedly oversimplified) structure included the new monastic foundations and the towns of Berwick, Roxburgh and Carlisle. In an obvious sense the Abbots, Priors and Prioresses along with the burgesses and mayors of the towns stood in a relationship similar to that of the great lords to the king and they had to answer for the corporations that appointed them. Although it should never be forgotten that the clerics also had to answer to the papacy in Rome and the mother house of their order, and this could easily give rise to a conflict of interest.

For the king, as head of state and commander-in-chief, the unit of assessment in a feudalised society was the knight's fee, or what it cost to maintain an armoured, mounted warrior. In the 12th century these men, astride their snorting destriers, were the elite battle troops of western Europe. And what made England a great medieval power was the ability to put very many knights in the field. Around the year 1150 estimates reckon that there were between 4,000 and 5,000 at the disposal of Henry II. David I understood that Scotland could not support anything like that number but he set about organising the creation of as many as possible. The realpolitik of the age told David that he could not hope to hold his independent kingdom for long if he did not modernise its army. The French witnesses of the Selkirk Charter were quickly enfeoffed with land in return for knight service; Robert de Bruis got Annandale for 10 knight's fees, Hugh de Moreville received Lauderdale on similar terms and Robert Corbet, Walter de Lindsey and Robert de Burneville became lesser landowners with lesser obligations. However, only two certain references to this process survive in documents dating from David I's reign. One concerns land at Athelstaneford in East Lothian and the other records the gift of land at Whitton and Lilliesleaf near Hawick. Walter of Ryedale or Riddell held his land for one knight's service " as one of my barons of that neighbourhood best and most freely holds his fief", says the charter. Clearly, exactly what this meant was well understood in the Borders. Incidentally Walter Riddell left his name on the hamlet west of Lilliesleaf, and between it and the Ale Water, not quite engulfed by pine woods, lie the remains of his motte and bailey castle now known, for some forgotten reason, as 'The General's Tower'. An important facet of this sort of arrangement made between the king and Walter Riddell was that he could pass his land on to his family by hereditary right. And primarily for that reason place-names in the Borders owe a good deal to French-speaking immigrants. Because these families often developed very long associations with particular places, the places became identified with them in an everyday parlance which eventually found its way onto the Ordnance Survey. For example, the farm of Sorrowlessfield near Earlston has, unfortunately, nothing to do with contentment and everything to do with the de Sorules family who were French friends of David I.

The process of feudalisation appears not to have involved the removal of native noble landowners, or at least nothing is recorded to that effect. In any case ten earldoms noted in 1050 were still held by the same families in 1150. And not all of the feudalisation of the Borders took place in the reign of David I. As early as 1095 to 1105 his elder brother, Edgar, gave part of the parish of Ednam, north-east of Kelso, to a man called Thor the Long. The charter says that the land was 'deserta' or waste, and there is an implication that no-one was turned out of their living as a result of the grant. Thor the Long is an interesting man and even though he has an Anglo-Scandinavian name and not a French one, he may have been a warrior owing service to the king for his land at Ednam.

What marked a radical change from the immediate past was David I's passionate commitment to the church. His mother, Queen Margaret, was canonised but all she really did was to bring Benedictine monks to Dunfermline, and his brother, Alexander I, introduced Augustinian Canons to Scone. For all that he did and gave to Holy Mother Church, David deserved to be sanctified several times over. Here is a good summary of the scale and range of his dedication from a man who knew him well, Ailred of Rievaulx;

"So deservedly he was seen as beloved by God and men. Clearly beloved of God, since immediately at the beginning of his reign he diligently practised the things that are of God in building churches, in founding monasteries, which he also endowed with properties and riches according to the needs of each. For although he found only three or four bishops in the whole kingdom of the Scots, while the rest of the churches were drifting aimlessly without a shepherd to the detriment of both morals and property, at his death he left nine bishoprics including both ancient ones that he had restored, and new ones that he erected. He also left monasteries of various orders, Cluniac, Cistercian, Tironensian, Arrouaisian, Praemonstratensian, order of Beauvais, namely Kelso, Melrose, Jedburgh, Newbattle, Holm Cultram, Dundrennan, the monastery of Holyrood Crag near Edinburgh, Cambuskenneth, Kinloss and a monastery of nuns near Berwick, and, as some say, a monastery of nuns of St Bartholomew near Carlisle, and Praemonstratensian canons of Newcastle and a monastery of Black Monks there, and another of nuns there, as appears in his prologue to the 'Statutes of the Burghs', and he also introduced thirteen monks from Canterbury to Dunfermline, and left many other monasteries fully staffed with brothers. When he was with them, he was like one of themselves, praising good deeds, and, if there chanced to emerge deeds less worthy of praise, modestly shutting his eyes to them, making himself available to all, concerned about everyone, giving generously, and asking nothing for himself."

In addition to this, David encouraged his barons to emulate the king's piety, and if they valued his favour (as well as their own salvation), they did. In the Borders Hugh de Moreville founded an abbey at Dryburgh in 1150, probably on the site of an ancient Celtic monastery, the Earl Cospatrick gave land for two houses of Cistercian nuns at the old church of Eccles and at Coldstream. Of uncertain origins, but certainly functioning in the first half of the 12th century, was a priory of Benedictine monks at Coldingham, the place where the Abbess Ebba and her nuns suffered, and also a hospital called Maison Dieu near Kelso.

Christianity was at least half a millenium old in the Borders by the time David became King of Scots, and his achievement was to superimpose a new ecclesiatical organisation. Before the arrival of the French monks from Tiron at Selkirk in 1113, it appears that various sorts of churches had the care of souls in the south of Scotland. The most prevalent type seems to have been the Anglian minster and at Jedburgh an important church was certainly established. A group of priests sharing a communal life based at that minster served a large parish, perhaps the natural agricultural hinterland of the settlement. 'Minster' is an English word deriving from the Latin 'monasterium' and that strongly suggests that these sorts of churches evolved from communities of monks. In the eastern Borders minsters were probably colonised from Lindisfarne, perhaps through its daughter-house at Old Melrose. And in the west the influence of Whithorn and Glasgow established old churches at places like Hoddom in Annandale. Other minsters in the Tweed basin were probably to be found at Stobo, Eccles and Edrom.

There were also hereditary priests whose presence and, presumably, old churches come to light in the 12th century. Disputes between them and the new bishops and abbots imposed by David I went on for some time, even into the 13th century. Even new landowners tried to oust hereditary priests and Ansketill Riddell, the son of Walter, made the mistake of picking on Uchtred of the church at Lilliesleaf. Even though he regarded the church as the property of his family, and was therefore guilty of nepotism, Uchtred took his case to the Papal courts in Rome and won. The place-name of Stow means 'Holy Place' and it was also the site of a very old church. Tradition insists that it held a relic of St Mary, a likeness of her painted by a contemporary. It also had the unusual status of sanctuary. Within the bounds of church land a fugitive might not be pursued further, but had to be dealt with by the church. Another ancient church, Coldingham, also had sanctuary rights, which are documented, and it seems that their ground was very extensive for once a man got inside the areas bounded by its crosses, and some these lie three miles from the Priory, he was safe for 37 days until the church dealt with him. The idea behind this seems to have been to create a cooling-off period. The presence of a large leper hospital inside Coldingham's bounds might also have discouraged pursuit. 'David, Keeper of the Lepers' at the hospital even had to bury his dead at a considerable distance from any other building. At Stow the hereditary office of priest was held by a man called Gilchrist, a Gaelic name which may have been his title, for it means 'Servant of Christ'. According to Alexander Jeffrey in his 'History and Antiquities of Roxburghshire and Adjacent Districts' (1845), the "Black Priest of that place enjoyed the privilege of Clan MacDuff". This probably meant that he had the ability to set a 'galanas' or murder price for someone seeking sanctuary which would go to the victim's family. The Bishop of St Andrews claimed this ancient and prestigious church and tried to remove Gilchrist and his family. Stow was ultimately incorporated in the see of St Andrews and its wide area of influence as a minster was reflected in the old county boundaries. Before reorganisation in 1974, Midlothian reached right down the Gala Water to Bowland, only two miles north of Galashiels.

When Thor the Long was given his land at Ednam by King Edgar, he built a church "in honour of St Cuthbert, and this church I have given, with a ploughgate of land, to God and St Cuthbert and his monks to be possessed for ever." This is very interesting because it shows that before David came to the Borders the religious focus was to the south, on Durham, the see of St Cuthbert and the successor of Lindisfarne. Not only is Thor the Long's dedication a memory of Bernicia, it also implies that what ecclesiastical structure there was in the Tweed Valley was managed from Durham, and doubtless in Durham's direct interest. David would use his new monastic foundations to change that focus radically.

The exhumation and expulsion of the body of Eadulf Rus from the minster of Jedburgh some time before 1107 on the orders of Turgot, Archdeacon of Durham shows how far north the power of the see of St Cuthbert extended and how late it persisted. In the Middle Ages Durham was beyond the grasp of ambitious Scottish kings and under assertive

bishops like Walcher and Ranulf Flambard the cathedral and its see
had become wealthy and powerful in its own right. In order to subdue
a rebellious local populace and resist the incursions of the Scots, William
the Bastard confered palatinate status on Durham. Sitting high on the
rocky peninsula in a lazy loop of the River Wear, the bishops became
the Prince-Bishops, able to enforce their will at all levels of society and
in all areas of activity; palatine status included the full ownership of
land, the right to levy taxes, to raise troops and to try all legal cases,
with no exemptions. They behaved like secular magnates — Ranulf
Flambard liked to have ladies in tight-fitting bodices serve his meals,
sniffed one monkish chronicler — and ruled like petty kings, because
that is exactly what they were. For even a King of Scotland, the Prince-
Bishops were formidable opponents.

Thor the Long's commitment of the church at Ednam to Durham at
some time between 1095 and 1105 was one of the last such recorded
gifts. In 1124 David revived the bishopric of Glasgow. the ancient see of
St Kentigern, and installed his faithful chaplain, John Achaius, as bishop.
Durham's claims to Jedburgh, Teviotdale and the upper Tweed were
repudiated and the introduction of the Tironensians directly from France
also established a new measure of independence from Durham. The
French monks were responsible to their remote mother-house at Tiron,
and obliged locally to their founder, the Earl and subsequently King
David. The see of St Cuthbert could have no possible claim to the
church at Selkirk and no locus in its affairs. Aside from their central
religious role, the new monastic orders clearly had many attractions for
the new king but their dependence on him and their independence
from Durham must have been chief amongst them. The abbeys at
Selkirk/Kelso, Melrose, Jedburgh and Dryburgh, as well as the nunneries
at Eccles, Coldstream and Berwick changed the social and political fabric
of the Borders and to understand something of how they did that, a
sharper focus is needed.

No monastery or nunnery was entirely typical. Each reformed order
had differences in their emphases, their practice and their effectiveness.
Nevertheless Melrose Abbey is a good example to examine; the monks
there kept a chronicle, they elected charismatic abbots, it was
economically dynamic, and on the edge of the small town it created, the
abbey precinct still stands somewhat apart with the outline of its
beautiful church visible against the green ridges north of the Tweed
and the big Border skies above them.

But it was not what David I intended. The original site he had
proposed for the monks lies two and a half miles to the east of where
they built their abbey. So that Old Melrose could be available for a new
colony, the king had made a deal with the Prince-Bishops of Durham
whereby he exchanged St Mary's at Berwick for the old monastery of St
Aidan. But it would not do. Even though there existed a powerful
continuity of sanctity with the holiest and most famous religious place
in the Borders, the first Abbot, Richard, and his followers prefered to
settle some way to the west of it at a location called Little Fordell. They
agreed to take the name of Melrose but refused to build in the loop of
the Tweed where Aidan, Boisil, Eata, Cuthbert and other saints had

worshipped God. No practical reasons appear to explain this. As at Selkirk there was a pre-existing church to allow services to be held before the abbey could be built. A ready water supply could not be closer to hand, arable land lay all around and good sources for building stone were not far away. And in any event the other three Border abbeys at Kelso, Jedburgh and Dryburgh were all content to establish themselves in the bends of rivers. Perhaps a mixture of spiritual and political motives prompted the Abbot Richard and King David to agree on a move to a new site. The Cistercians were an austere order who sought to be apart from the temporal world in a place where they could find God in peace. The Selkirk Charter spoke of a village at Melrose which David gave to the monks in 1113 and this must refer to a secular settlement beyond the precinct at Old Melrose, probably on what is now Ravenswood Farm. The Cistercians will have shied away from that and Ailred of Rievaulx described the early ethic of his order very neatly;

"Our food is scanty, our garments rough; our drink is from the stream and our sleep is often upon our book. Under our tired limbs there is but a hard mat; when sleep is sweetest we must rise at bell's bidding... Self will has no place; there is no moment for idleness or dissipation... Everywhere peace, everywhere serenity and a marvellous freedom from the tumult of the world."

Bishop John of Glasgow may have advised on the second reason to reject Old Melrose. If the new Cistercian abbey had been built on the site of a shrine of St Cuthbert it might have been drawn into the orbit of Durham, the resting-place of the saint's body and the focus of his immensely powerful cult.

At all events, the Chronicle of Melrose states, misleadingly, that "AD 1136 the Abbey of St Mary of Melrose was finished on Monday, being the second day of Easter Week, and its first Abbot was Richard." In fact the abbey took decades to build and this passage really signifies the completion and dedication of a temporary church erected at Little Fordell. Traces of wooden and stone structures put up for the monks and masons who arrived first have been found in excavations at Kelso and on the riverside at Jedburgh where the new abbey appears to have been built on the same awkward site as the Anglian minster.

After the dedication of a temporary church the next important task was to mark out the monastic enclosure, the area which became known as the abbey precinct. Because the Cistercians were a community who turned their backs on the world and looked inwards to God and his church, it was vital to be clear where the limits of that internal life began and ended. Precincts were bounded by ditches, banks, palings or walls, and some could be very extensive. At Melrose the monks probably had an open site at their disposal and they created a large rectangular area whose outline can still be seen. The abbey influenced the shape of the town profoundly and at the narrow south entrance to Abbey Street, the location of the south gate of the precinct, a clear sense of the western wall is visible for almost half a mile down to Annay Road. From that point, the likely location of the north gate, the boundary swings east across the Annay fields for three hundred yards before turning south across the Abbey Lade to where the east gate stood, and then on up to the High Road where it again turns to follow the modern street line westwards through the East Port before ending where it began at the corner of the Market Square.

Inside this long, looping boundary work began in 1136 on the abbey church. This was not what became the magnificent ruin now standing at Melrose. That is a 14th and 15th century creation and is the second medieval church on the same site. The first was destroyed by an English army in 1385. From the fragments which remain and the just-discernible ghost of an outline under the walls of the second church, it seems that the design was very plain, in the style of the two Cistercian abbeys in North Yorkshire at Rievaulx and Fountains. Cruciform in layout and austere in execution, it echoed the ethos of the reformed order. The other monastic buildings were arranged around a cloister, a covered walkway with a garden or open space in the centre. So that the height and bulk of the abbey church would not block out the sun, the cloister and the conventual buildings were usually attached to the south wall of an east/west alignment, but at Melrose this arrangement was reversed. The water supply from the Abbey Lade (from the River Tweed) flowed from the north and the monastic quarters needed drainage more than sunshine.

Off the cloister at Melrose lay the Chapter House, the large room where the community met each day to confess sins, suffer correction, discuss matters of abbey business and hear a chapter from the Rule of St Benedict read out. This last is the origin of the name. Between the Chapter House and the north transept of the abbey church was the Sacristy where the vestments, altar dressings, plates and chalices were stored. Monks officiating at mass robed in the Sacristy. Around the other two sides of the cloister stood the Refectory and the Kitchen, and the Warming Room, the only place where a fire was kept, other than for cooking. Even in the depths of a northern winter monks were allowed to remain there for short periods only. Above the east range was the Dormitory and it abutted the north transept to allow access to the church for night services. Stairs led directly from the Dormitory and each night when the bell rang at 1.30am for Matins the monks woke, lit their candles and made their way into the draughty, darkened church to worship God. Here is a table of the strict regime followed every day at Melrose Abbey.

1.30am	Service: Matins
3.00am	Service: Lauds
4.00am	Service: Prime. This was followed by mass and signalled the beginning of work in the monastery.
4.30am	Meeting of Chapter
7.00am	Work — likely in the scriptorium
9.00am	Service: Terce
11.00am	Service: Sext
	Lunch

12noon	Rest period — called 'siesta' after the previous service
	Service Nones
2.30pm	Work
6.00pm	Service: Vespers
	Supper
	Reading in the cloister
7.30pm	Service: Compline
8.00pm	Retire to bed.

This is the daily routine for the summer months. In winter the day began at 7am (although Matins was still kept at 1.30am) and ended at 4.30pm.

Outside the abbey precinct much trouble and energy was spent on manipulating the flow of the River Tweed into monastic service. A cauld thrown across the river at an angle diverted water into the Abbey Lade and the drainage system. In a recent dry summer unusually low water showed that the riverbank had been substantially shored up to prevent erosion and the river meandering. This helped to create a valuable meadow which is known locally as 'The Annay'. When the monks at Kelso, ten miles downriver, also built a massive cauld (so massive it was believed to be the work of the Wizard, Michael Scot) across the Tweed to funnel the flow into their mill race, the large islands created in the river were called 'The Annas', and at Jedburgh more monastic waterworks produced another riverbank meadow known as 'The Anna'. This is more than a coincidence. In Gaelic 'annaid' means 'church' or 'church land' and it may be that these three survivals remember very old ecclesiastical terminology and perhaps even a scatter of places held by Aidan's monks at Old Melrose. Two other, much more obvious, relics of the ancient patrimony of the Celtic monastery are to be found at St Boswell's and Bowden. Cuthbert's Prior and death-bed friend, St Boisil, took his own name from the Syrian monk, St Basil, and passed it on to St Boswell's. Early spellings of Bowden show Bothandene, and St Bothan was a close contemporary of Cuthbert and Boisil. Abbey St Bathan's also remembers him. Some of the grants of land to the new, reformed orders may have been owned by monks for many centuries before they received them formally from David.

Like the Celtic monks the 12th century Cistercians were ascetics, but unlike such practiced bathers as Drythelm and Cuthbert, they believed that washing was an unnecessary sensual pleasure and they confined their ablutions to a rinse of the face and hands once a day before lunch. On warm days Hierochloe odorata might have helped. Also called Holy Grass it was strewn on the stone or beaten earth floors of churches and when crushed underfoot it gave off the aromatic chemical called coumarin. Holy Grass is a rare plant but it still grows on some of the old granges of Kelso Abbey. Incense must also have been welcome and since churches were the only places where large indoor gatherings took place, liberal swinging of the censer will have kept bodily odours at bay. Before discipline relaxed in the later Middle Ages the lunch that followed hand washing was simple, scarce, mostly vegetarian and silent.

At mealtimes no conversation was allowed and only readings from scripture could be heard, but the brothers soon developed a sign language for essential communication. Like other orders the Cistercians followed strict dietary rules. Monks and priests were not allowed to eat the meat of four-legged animals, and for protein, when it was permitted at all, they depended on fish, cheese, eggs and poultry (only two legs). To meet these special needs many abbeys and nunneries dug fish-ponds, called stews, and bred carp and pike in them. The remains of stews can be clearly seen at Dryburgh Abbey and Eccles nunnery. Vehement arguments between monasteries and other parties often broke out over rights on the fishings of the Tweed and other rivers, and no doubt legal discourse was sharpened by the unhappy prospect of losing a tasty source of trout or salmon. Odd animals were classified as fish to allow the monks a clear conscience about eating them; because beavers had fishy tails they counted, as did barnacle geese and puffins because they were allegedly born at sea, like fish. As definitions became ever more ingenious and self-regulation weakened, monks began to enjoy 'pittances'. These were originally culinary treats paid for by small endowments of money; for example King Robert I gave cash to Melrose in 1326 so that the monks could enjoy a daily helping of rice cooked in the milk of almonds. Since both of these were imported foods this particular treat will have cost more than the usual pittance. And the popular image of big-bellied, rubicund monks has some historical basis.

COD

At Eyemouth the cod fishing is very ancient and the great fish hauled ashore turned out to be the perfect answer to the restrictions of a monastic diet and the problems of keeping food for long periods. The cod often swims inshore in shallow water and is easy to catch because it is so greedy. Eating anything, and moving through the water with his large mouth wide open, it will take a shiney metal lure as readily as a herring. The flesh of the cod is white, full of protein and it both salts and dries well.

The Melrose brothers had little opportunity to burn off the calories supplied by King Robert's rice puddings. Cistercian rules forbad them to do physical work and a large building to the west of the cloister is testament to the arrangements made to avoid exertion. Lay brothers, or 'conversi', were brought into the community on an associate basis to work the abbey farms and process what they produced. What is known as 'the lay brothers' range' was separated from the monks' cloister but its foundations show it to have been extensive, housing many more than the dormitory. Given better food, more sleep and excused some conventual duties, the lay brothers nevertheless took vows and worshipped in the abbey church. However, they continued to be separated even in the sight of God for their part of the nave was screened by a stone wall, the pulpitum, from the place nearer the crossing where the monks worshipped.

While others sweated in the fields, shielings and at the tanning pits behind the west range, the monks spent their time in prayer, contemplation and at their writing boards. The Chronicle of Melrose is the principal early monastic chronicle of Scotland. It falls into two parts and the first and earlier may have been written at Old Melrose since it relies on Anglo-Saxon sources. Dating from 1136 and the foundation of the abbey the second part includes many original entries and from around 1172 an analysis of the changes in handwriting suggest that the chronicle became a reasonably contemporary narrative. Whoever made the entries, which were no doubt approved by the Abbot or Prior, did his writing in the light of the cloister. Inside rooms had small windows and even on sunny days the light could be a strain on the eyes. And in the cloister the compiler of a chronicle would hear snippets of information and whispers of gossip.

The notion of Melrose as an intellectual centre is greatly reinforced by a fascinating manuscript known as 'On the Birth of St Cuthbert'. It relates the miracles of the saint and also asserts, bizarrely, that he was the son of an Irish king. By the time the Melrose author sat down in the cloister to write his hagiography anxieties about the power of Durham had clearly declined. Indeed the strange rationale behind 'On the Birth of St Cuthbert' appears to have been an unlikely but well-intentioned attempt to support his cult (and Melrose's close association with it) in the face of severe competition from that of the recent martyr, St Thomas a Becket. At Durham a gorgeously illustrated 'Life of St Cuthbert' was produced between 1170 and 1185 precisely to help counter the explosion in popularity of Becket's cult centred on Canterbury. And the Melrose scribe showed himself to be in the mainstream of contemporary controversy when he came up with the idea that St Cuthbert was really an Irish prince while Becket was only the son of a London merchant. Most monks were from upper class families whose interests and horizons could extend well beyond the quotidien business of making sure there was bread on the table and the other, equally basic questions concerning the mass of ordinary people. It is important to remember that the monks at Melrose and other large and wealthy communities were members of the elite group in Scotland and they shared agendas which would have impinged little beyond the cloister.

THE WIZARD

Part of the reason for the upsurge in philosophical thought in 13th century Europe was the rediscovery in the west of Aristotelian manuscripts which had been preserved in Arabic by Moslem scholars. One of the most important translators from Arabic into Latin worked at the University of Toledo in southern Spain in the first decade of the the 13th century and later in Palermo. His name was Michael Scot, and possibly born near Melrose, he got the name 'the Wizard'.

This happened as a result of a profound misunderstanding. Michael's namesake, Sir Walter Scott, had heard tales of alchemy and magic, and he knew that the early Italian Renaissance writer, Dante Alighieri, had placed Scot in the 8th Circle of Hell as an Enchanter. In fact Michael was nothing of the kind. Like many medieval scholars he travelled a great deal, often in search of patronage, and on arrival at Toledo, he was exposed to a dazzling array of new ideas and new texts, and the work of great Arab philosophers like Averroes. Interested in everything, he explored and translated from the complex worlds of astrology and alchemy. To dismiss these areas of intellectual enquiry as dubious wizardry is to rewrite history with a vengeance. Walter Scott should have understood that in the 13th century both alchemy and astrology, provided neither involved sorcery or any heretical ideas, were perfectly respectable, and even academic, disciplines. And they remained so for a long time. Chemistry grew out of alchemy, and, to give a good example, while Isaac Newton watched apples fall and formulated a theory of gravity, he still conducted alchemical experiments.

After Toledo Michael sailed to Sicily to take up teaching and translating work for two popes, Honorius III and Gregory IX. Offered the bishopric of Cashel in southern Ireland on an absentee basis, he declined for the eccentric reason that he did not understand Gaelic. Clearly an attractive and innovative thinker, Michael was then invited to join the court of the Holy Roman Emperor, Frederick II at Palermo. This was the acme of acclaim. Frederick was known as 'Stupor Mundi', the Wonder of the World, and his court contained some of the greatest talents of the age — including a man from the Borders.

Tradition insists that Michael Scot left the sunlit court of Palermo and at the end of his eventful life came back to Melrose where he was buried in the abbey precinct with his book of spells. In the Borders he is remembered, if at all, for nonsense, as the wizard who clove the Eildon Hills in three and threw 'a curb of stone across the Tweed' at Kelso where the monks built their great mill cauld. Which is a shame. For Michael's contribution to western philosophy was significant.

Outside, in the world, Melrose was counted as extremely wealthy. David I and his loyal courtiers had endowed the abbey with 5,000 acres in the immediate vicinity with villages at Darnick (a place-name with a 'wic' suffix, meaning 'hidden farm' and showing that it was an outlier of a lost Anglian shire), Newstead, Holydean and Melrose itself. On the south-facing slopes of Gattonside the monks kept orchards as well as cornfields. In fact, it happens that apples are all that remains of the Cistercian nunnery at Coldstream. The site of the buildings is lost under the modern town but the orchards still existed in 1877 when their unique variety of apples was recorded in Hardy's Botanical Guide.

In addition to the land close to the abbey, the monks held 17,000 acres of upland pasture in the Ettrick Forest, Lauderdale, Teviotdale and the Lammermuir Hills. The vast extent of their holdings can sometimes be gauged through an analysis of boundary disputes. It appears that previously understood and undocumented customary rights to common pasture were regularly challenged by Melrose. On the quadrant of hill country between Lauderdale and Gala Water, the moors were grazed by flocks belonging to a number of groups of people, but the Abbot and Chapter argued against the Men of Wedale, or Gala Water, that they should have exclusive rights. The dispute went in favour of Melrose, perhaps because the jurors swore their oaths in the abbey 'tremblingly and reverently' over the relics of the saints and in front of the king and his friend the abbot. A place-name remembers another land dispute in the same area. 'Threipwood' means 'disputed wood' and it was the object of contention between the abbey and Richard de Moreville of Lauderdale. Again the monks won and Threipwood became their wood.

Pasture was important because sheep became very important to the Cistercians. By the end of the 12th century they produced 5% of the total Scottish wool clip and according to the handbook of a 13th century Italian merchant, Francesco Pegalotti, it was of the highest quality. At its best price, he noted carefully, the woolpacks of Mirososso (Melrose) could easily outstrip those of Ghelzo (Kelso), Guldingamo (Coldingham) or Gridegorda (Jedburgh). Monastic sheep ranches were to be found all over the Border hills as many thousands of sheep devoured the pasture. The intensity of grazing was so great that express provision had to be made in the Bowmont Valley, amongst Kelso's holdings, to allow woodland to regenerate naturally. Once old trees blew down in the hills, sheep moved in and ate the saplings. The pock-marks of the shallow depressions of uprooted trees can still be seen in many places in the Cheviots.

Some of Melrose's wool was reserved for domestic use. The Cistercians were known as the White Monks because of their undyed woollen habits. Even in chilly Scottish winters the habit was all the early monks at the abbey were allowed to wear. They prayed, worked and slept in it — in fact, regulations for sleeping itself existed. Monks were to lie on their backs and keep their hands in view, folded across their chests.

At first, rules such as these were strictly enforced by the Abbot and his Prior, but when Melrose's possessions grew ever greater and her involvement in the outside world unavoidable, the list of office-holders in the abbey became longer until amost half the brothers had some administrative duty or other. This sort of regular contact with the 'tumult of the world' inevitably led to to temptation, secularisation and a relaxation of the strict monkish code. Because Abbots became, in effect, great barons they were often called upon by the king to participate in government in some way. Their European connections through the network of monastic orders, and to the papacy in Rome, provided ready-made channels for international diplomacy. This meant long absences and the running of the abbey was left in the hands of the Prior. Below him the hierarchy is less clear-cut; the other officers included the Sacrist who looked after ceremonial vestments and communion items, the Chamberlain kitted everyone out in everyday clothing, the Novice-Master was in charge of new entrants, the Almoner supervised charity work and gifts, the Guest-Master provided hospitality, the Infirmarer cared for the old and ill, while the Cellarer supplied food and drink.

The richer an abbey became the more there was to manage. And a system known as appropriation grew up and involved the nominal care of a large number of parishes. David I established the collection of teinds whereby a tenth of the produce of a parish was given to support the local neighbourhood church. Very often the landowners who endowed, and essentially owned parish churches were encouraged to give the teinds to an abbey or cathedral chapter for them to have and administer. This was hailed as an act of great piety. But eventually 85%

of parishes in Scotland were appropriated and the effect turned out to be very corrosive. The abbey or cathedral took all of the teinds to itself and appointed a curate or a vicar, sometimes at a tiny fee — certainly a great deal less than the value of the teinds. This impoverished the parishes and enriched the abbots, bishops and their great churches.

Melrose had fewer parish churches than Kelso, which took the teinds of no less than 40, but it did directly acquire a great deal of land in the 12th century. Once a gift of porperty was made to a religious house, it remained in its hands for a very long time. Secular ownership was much more prone to change and land could be divided, sold, lost, or bequeathed but church lands almost always remained part of the great religious estates and the multitude of place-names such as Chapelhill, Ladylands, Clerklands and so on remember that permanence.

Waltheof, the second Abbot of Melrose, was the step-brother of David I and he used his status to make the young abbey wealthy. Much of the produce of the granges, farms and villages, far too much to be used by even the greediest monks and lay brothers, must have been converted into cash and the buildings that went up after 1136 — unprecedented for the times in the Borders — absorbed enormous costs.

But Waltheof became famous for more than acquisitiveness. After an exemplary life and several recorded miracles, Waltheof was canonised and Melrose had her very own saint. Jocelin of Furness did what most saints needed and wrote a life of Waltheof recounting his goodness and enumerating the necessary miracles. Here is the story of one them;

"On one occasion when the calamity of a deadly famine threatened, a vast crowd of destitute people reckoned to number four thousand gathered at Melrose, and erected huts and tents for themselves in the fields and woods around the monastery to a distance of two miles. The abbot in his usual way went out with some of the brothers and the cellarer (called Thomas, who in fact and nickname was Good) to survey this great multitude. As he saw it, he joyfully said: 'What an awesome place is this! Truly this is the camp of the Lord'. And next he said: 'My heart goes out to these people; but I do not have to hand anything to set before them. We must see to it that they have food until the autumn, lest (God forbid!) they succumb to starvation.' The spirit filled the aforesaid cellarer since he was a man of compassion, and was for that reason very dear to the abbot, and he gave this answer to the saint: 'Dearest father, we have a great deal of livestock, cattle at pasture, sheep, wedders, and fat pigs, and no small amount of cheese and butter. We shall slaughter the animals, serve the rest of the products gladly, and dole it all out generously as food for them. Yet the shortage of bread touches and pains my heart, because with our corn nearly all exhausted, [only] a very small supply is still left in the barns of two of our granges, namely some wheat at Eildon kept for the use of the abbey community, and some rye at Gattonside reserved for the servants.' The good father was delighted at the cellarer's words; with bent head he gave him many thanks, and blessed him in the name of the Lord.

The abbot then made his way to the grange of Eildon along with the cellarer, and entering the barn he thrust the staff which he was carrying in his hand into a heap of sheaves; he genuflected, made the sign of the cross, blessed the crop there, and withdrew. Then he went away to Gattonside, and entered in the same way as he had done before, saying to the cellarer: 'Make a distribution now, and give both to us and to the poor with confidence, for God will make it grow, he will increase and multiply it to the extent necessary for our use and that of the poor.' What a remarkable event and a rare one! The corn which was stored in the corners of each barn and was thought to provide sufficent food for scarcely two weeks, stretched out for three months, as if it were inexhaustible. It remained at the same level (in imitation of the widow of Zarephath's handful of flour) until the gathering of the new harvest had been accomplished."

The people of the middle Tweed Valley seemed to be suffering in what were called 'the hungry months', June, July and August when the previous year's harvest was running out and the current year's not yet in. Also interesting to note is the provision of wheat for white bread for the monks, and the coarser rye bread for the lay brothers. As scions of the upper classes that sort of distinction will simply never have occured to the monks.

Waltheof had an importance to Melrose which far outran his ability to fill the empty bowls and pots of the peasantry. The church had always encouraged the cults of local saints; they were an early and credible substitute for a pantheon of pagan gods often associated with particular places such as springs, wells and river-meetings. And the relics of the likes of Waltheof and Cuthbert and others before him stood for the old magic — they were the equivalent of amulets, lucky charms and special prayers (always offered with candles because they were seen as a palpable symbol of prayers being lifted upwards to Heaven) on their feast days were only Christian versions of incantations on pagan festival days. Saintly relics were seen as a conduit for intercession, through prayers, with God and to be in their presence was somehow to be in the physical presence of the saint and through him, closer to the sight of the Almighty. The cult of relics quickly created the habit of pilgrimage and the church soon developed tariffs relating its effect on the chances of salvation. Difficult and awkward journeys to a shrine and large donations to the keepers of relics resulted in a shorter time in purgatory, the place where worldly sins were cleansed before souls ascended to Heaven.

St Waltheof was buried by the door of the Chapter House in the east range of the cloister at Melrose. So many pilgrims began to appear that the Cistercians were forced to remove the remains and house them in a shrine dedicated to their old abbot in the church. Melrose almost certainly held relics of St Cuthbert and perhaps others, and it soon became a focus of some substance. As Chaucer's Canterbury Tales shows, pilgrimage was a form of early tourism and money was made at Melrose out of those who came to pray to Waltheof and the other saints. As proof of their visit pilgrims could buy badges, and some pinned them to their wide-brimmed hats just in the same way badges are attached to baseball caps nowadays. At Melrose these took the form of a pun on the place-name with a malet and a rose depicted. Fragments of what is likely to have been St Waltheof's shrine were discovered in 1920 and they recall a gilded and painted structure of some size. They were a reminder that the interior at Melrose was far from gloomy. The walls were white, painted with limewash, and the architectural details and the sculpture were picked out in bright colours, while in bright weather the stained glass will have sparkled.

DUNCES

'Dunce' rather than 'Dunz' is the local, clearly ancient and correct pronunciation of the name of the former county town of Berwickshire. Dunces are named after Duns but not because the inhabitants lack intelligence, but rather because one of them became possibly the most brilliant philosopher of his day.

John Duns Scotus, or John of Duns, the Scot, was born sometime around 1266 and somewhere near Pavilion Lodge at Duns Castle, according to local tradition. Probably because he got his schooling at either the Franciscan friary of Berwick or Roxburgh, John took vows as a mendicant and then travelled to Oxford University to continue his studies. When he later went to Paris, the man from Duns found himself at the centre of European intellectual life. The 13th century saw the first sustained flowering of philosophy since the Greeks and Romans. In Paris the Dominican, St Thomas Aquinas, wrote and expounded his 'Summa Theologica' (The Summary of Theology) and the 'Summa Contra Gentiles' (On the Truth of the Catholic Faith). Essentially he produced a sprawling synthesis of almost all western philosophy to that date and showed how it was not incompatible with Christian beliefs. In what came to be called 'Thomism', a system of ideas adopted as doctrine by the Catholic Church and maintained as late as the Second Vatican Council of 1962–64, Aquinas brought together the ideas of Plato and Aristotle. In his considerations of intelligence, experience and sensory perception, he coined the phrase 'tabula rasa' or 'clean slate' for the as yet unfilled mind of a new born child.

By the time John Duns Scotus arrived in Paris, Thomas Aquinas was dead, but his ideas continued to shape the intellectual agenda. Perhaps because he was a naturally thrawn and sceptical Borderer, perhaps because as a Dominican Aquinas was easily seen as a rival to a Franciscan, and certainly because he could see real philosophical problems, Duns Scotus took serious issue with both the Summa Theologica and the Summa Contra Gentiles. Using brilliant semantic and metaphysical skills, he was scrupulous in his reasoning and consistently honest in his conclusions. For example, as a Christian he believed absolutely in the immortality of the soul but, as a philosopher, he admitted that he could not prove it. A highly complex and allusive scholastic thinker, Duns Scotus' most important works are not easily accessible, but for the persistent, they are, 'Quodlibetic Questions' (in Latin 'quodlibet' means 'that which pleases'), 'Questions in Metaphysics' and 'On the First Principle'. As interest in Christian philosophy declined, the subject-matter of Duns Scotus' work has attracted less and less attention, but the brilliance and technical brio of his methods of argument have been very influential, particularly in 20th century American thinking.

After his death in Cologne in 1308, those detractors who dismissed the conclusions of John Duns Scotus called his followers 'dunces'.

In the 13th century pilgrims also went in large numbers to Peebles. In 1261, in what must have been the staged presence of Alexander III, an object believed to be a piece of the True Cross was found. Apparently it rested on an inscribed stone, one of the earliest echoes of Christianity in the Borders six centuries before, which told of 'the seat of St Nicolas, bishop'. When the Cross Kirk was built to commemorate this event, the fragment of wood was put into a reliquary built into the south wall in such a way that it could be seen both inside and outside the church. The Cross Kirk proved to be very popular and to provide accommodation for pilgrims two hospitals were set up at Eshiels and Peebles itself.

Despite all of these medieval creations and sensations, the oldest and most sacred church in the Borders never lost its power. The Chronicle of Melrose records that in 1260 a man called Adam was the Keeper of the Chapel of St Cuthbert at Old Melrose, "having a full store of provisions laid up for him... by those poor persons who kept flooding to him... The rich also came to him and even the king of the land [Alexander III]". In 1322 the Bishop of Galloway offered an indulgence of 40 days remission from purgatory for pilgrims to Old Melrose and in 1437 the Pope, Martin V, sanctioned indulgences for those who went there. Despite the coming of the new monastic orders, the building of their immense churches and the power they held over the land and those who lived on it, and despite the diplomatic disapproval of St Cuthbert's cult based in the English cathedral at Durham, nothing could remove his memory in the Borders. Cuthbert was loved and that simple fact proved ineradicable.

What has been effaced, in a remarkable and total disappearance, is an entire Border town. Roxburgh is the first Scottish burgh to come on record, along with Berwick, in the Selkirk Charter given by the Earl David for the foundation of his new abbey. And yet there is now no trace of it to be seen, not one stone left standing upon another, nothing to suggest even exactly where it was. Roxburgh exists only in ink and vellum, in documents associated mainly with Kelso Abbey. A surprisingly complete picture of what the town was like emerges from the terse Latin of land grants and property boundaries. Three streets are named; the Headgate, King's Street and Market Street, and in 1150 the population was expanding so quickly that a new town had to be built (presumably) outside the walls or ditches. Medieval ruins can still be seen on the spectacular mound of Roxburgh Castle which lies astride the narrow neck of a river peninsula formed by the Tweed and the Teviot. The town lay to the east of the castle and the arrangement of its streets and houses almost certainly followed a familiar pattern, that of a main thoroughfare leading out of the castle gates and down to a church in the town. The parish church of St James comes on record in the 12th century and it lay near the banks of the Tweed about 500 yards east of the castlemount. A ruined fragment of the church and tombstones in its graveyard stood as late as the 18th century when the landowner, the Duke of Roxburghe, had them cleared out of the way of a horse-racing track. Documents relating to Dryburgh Abbey mention another church, Holy Sepulchre, which may have catered for the needs of an expanding population. In 1232 Franciscan Friars arrived at Roxburgh and such was the congestion in the town that they were forced to build their church outside the walls, near the River Teviot. Once again ruins survived into the 18th century when they were removed. All that remembers the Franciscans now are names; a house by the bridge over the river is called Friars' Cottage and the ground around it is Friars' Haugh. Medieval Roxburgh had schools, mintmasters and a bustling market where the racket of commerce and the speech of several languages rang out in a greeting or a bargain. All of its voices are silent now, all of its stories are lost in the grass where sheep and cattle graze and where, at race meetings, horses thunder between the jumps.

Over the Tweed in the ruined porch of Kelso Abbey lie two ghosts whose tombstones tell the story of why Roxburgh grew and prospered. "Here lies Johanna Bulloc who died in the year of our Lord 1371. Pray for her soul." is inscribed on the recto side of one, while on the verso is carved a pair of sheep shears. The other stone is from the graveyard by the Franciscan Friary of St Peter. All that can be made out on the face is the word 'mercer', or cloth merchant, but the stone itself is informative. It was orginally quarried from the distinctive 'pierre bleu' limestone which comes from the area around Tournai in Flanders. The lettering is done in the Lombardic style fashionable in 14th century Europe and the name of Roxburgh is misspelt, suggesting that the stone was carved as well as quarried in Flanders. These objects are all that survive from the disappeared town and both are testament to the reason for its fleeting existence, the wool trade.

Situated at the most significant river-meeting in the Borders, where Teviot meets Tweed, at a place where both could be safely forded in summer, only a few miles east of the great arterial north/south road of Dere Street, and hard by the Roman road from Craik Cross to Tweedmouth (which became the king's great highway from Annan to the Tweed valley), Roxburgh was always central. In the shadow of a mighty castle and surrounded by some of the most fertile and well-drained farmland in the Tweed Basin, the town was also commercially important. It is highly likely that there was a market at Roxburgh for some considerable time before 1113 when it came to light as a busy town. Archaeologists digging in the centre of Perth have found evidence that the town existed on that site as early as 1000, more than a century before any Scottish burgh came on record. What converted a local market serving an immediate hinterland into an international trading centre was the dynamic trade in wool and hides.

The stimulus for this change came from Flanders and Northern Italy where cloth and leather goods began to be produced in industrial quantities for re-export as well as domestic consumption. What created this demand for raw wool and hides was not new technology but the first effective deployment of merchant capital. Flemish and Italian merchants became very wealthy and powerful through taking control of supply, production and marketing. The only part of the integrated process that was beyond them was the actual rearing of sheep and cattle. In the Borders the reformed monastic orders and the new landowners did this on a sufficiently well-organised and predictable basis to feed consistently the production needs of Flanders and Northern Italy. The sequence was simple. Merchants from the cities of Bruges, Ghent and elsewhere had sufficient capital to buy bulk quantities of wool and hides at the summer and autumn markets at Roxburgh, and the abbeys of Melrose and Kelso could guarantee that these raw materials would be available, barring natural disaster, each year from their ranches in the Cheviots, the Ettrick Forest and the Lammermuirs. With 5% of the total Scottish wool clip — and that considered to be of the highest quality — the Cistercians at Melrose could act like a corporation and wield considerable power in the market-place. Monastic meekness had no place when hands were shaken on a deal with the Flemings. Because they also formed part of an independent international organisation, the Cistercian order itself, based at Citeaux in France, the Melrose monks were urbane and experienced negotiators with access to information on prices and conditions of trade in other wool-producing areas of Europe, and particularly in England. And at home, as their tenacity in pursuing boundary disputes testifies, they were also ruthless defenders of domestic production, sometimes driving small stocksmen out of business. For their part, the Flemings were desparate to buy and feed their cloth industry — in fact they joined a rebellion against Henry II of England in 1173/4 expressly 'to have his wool'. And in 1180 the Count of Flanders attempted to secure exclusive access to the output of Melrose's sheep ranches by granting the monastery freedom from all toll payments.

It cannot be a coincidence that flag-casting or ceremonial flag-waving takes place in Flemish towns and in Siena in Italy, as well as Selkirk in the Scottish Borders. And when surnames began to appear regularly in the 1500s, some Flemish-sounding names crop up, such as Mithag and Fleisher. The name of Fleming itself is also not uncommon. It may be that the bearers of these old names are descended from Flemish textile workers imported into the Borders through the contacts made by the wool trade.

Flocks and herds were driven to Roxburgh market on the hoof to be slaughtered and processed. The town operated like a busy abattoir and the haughland of the river peninsula would have been patterned with dozens of holding pens and the air filled with the bleat and low of animals all too aware of their fate. Every part of the killed beast was used. Cattle, for example, provided work for fleshers, tanners, horn carvers, leather workers, candlemakers and several other trades. Horn spoons and cups appear to have been in great demand. Indeed archaeologists digging at Perth have found evidence suggesting that cattle-processing was an appreciably larger business than the wool trade. At Roxburgh the balance may have tilted the other way. Once sheep had been clipped and slaughtered the merchants bargained for four basic products; raw wool bundled into bales known as woolpacks, woolfells or sheepskins, mutton and horn products. They paid in cash and in goods of equivalent value. No-one crossed the North Sea in an empty ship and a 13th century inventory of goods landed on the wooden wharves of Berwick is very instructive. A dazzling array of cargoes from Europe included sugar, pepper, cumin, onions, garlic, currants, ginger, almonds, rice, (perhaps bound for the pittances of Melrose) basil, alum, dyestuffs, metal pans, cauldrons, locks, timber and iron. But by far the greatest import was wine, and in 1263 King Alexander III imported for his personal and household use a staggering 44,856 gallons through Berwick. Business in the Borders was booming.

Across the North Sea, back in Flanders and Northern Italy, merchants fed the wool into their cloth production network. They used the putting-out system, paying for carding, spinning, weaving and finishing at piece rates. There is some evidence that these were tied to the retail price index of food. Production went on in hundreds of workshops in the towns and cities. Numbers employed could be very large and, for example, at Douai in the 13th century there were 150 merchant drapers each employing 100 people. Fine or highly finished heavy cloth production was a skilled craft and tended to be done in workshops run by master-weavers and drapers, while the less skilled work on coarser cloth was done in weavers' own tenement rooms or in their homes in the countryside. Demand for Flemish and Italian cloth soared in the 12th and 13th centuries. The European economy was expanding and the herd-laddies of the Cheviots and the Lammermuirs and their monastic masters quickly became part of that boom.

COINS

Coin derived from the identically spelled French word for 'corner' and it came from the process of royal tax gathering in Cornwall and Devon where the corners were clipped off tin ingots, and the little bits of metal, usually carrying a stamped mark, were called 'coins'.

The 40 solidi promised from the revenues of Roxburgh and Berwick in the Selkirk Charter is translated as 'shillings'. These coins formed part of the Carolingian system of Lsd. L was for libra or pound, s was for shilling, a twentieth part of a pound and d for denarius or penny, a twelfth part of a shilling. In old accounting, before 1970, 240 pennies theoretically made up one pound of silver. Those in modern British politics wishing to save the pound from the advance of the euro should perhaps remember that it was originally a European currency.

By David I's time silver pennies were being minted at Roxburgh and then subsequently elsewhere. Because they were made to the same standard and weight as English silver pennies, they were considered to be equivalent. In the Mellendean hoard found near Kelso all of the 890 coins discovered dated before 1296 and the vast majority (704) were English while 103 came from Flanders and only 65 were Scottish.

In Europe coinage was ultimately underpinned by the gold hyperperon of the Byzantine Emperors at Constantinople. Their standard and supply remained constant for centuries, well into the Middle Ages when they represented the hardest sort of currency. Byzantine coins also got the name 'bezants'.

As trade grew over longer distances silver pennies were minted all over Europe to various designs but a consistent weight. But William the Bastard insisted that controls were maintained for English pennies and the marks of the moneyer and the mint were die-stamped on the obverse so that those supplying underweight coins could be quickly found and punished.

Mintmasters were usually silversmiths or bullion dealers, or both, and they were granted a royal licence to act as moneyers. On one side of a coin the king's head was stamped and on the other was the mint mark. 'Wi:an:Roc' means William of Roxburgh.

In periods of intense and competitive economic activity, speed and cost of transport become crucial costs in the arithmetic of a merchant anxious for a good profit. At every possible opportunity in the Middle Ages bulk goods were moved by water transport. Merchant shipping between Berwick and the ports of the Rhine estuary was a relatively straightforward business, but what was difficult was the bringing of the woolpacks and the hides to the quayside. Roads to the east certainly existed, the Kelso Abbey documents record a 'via regis', the king's highway between Roxburgh and Berwick, and north/south traffic clattered happily along Dere Street. Other roads are mentioned in the Melrose collection; the 'Malchomisrode' sounds like another royal highway and it was the continuation of Dere Street north of the Tweed, while the 'Girthgate' left Melrose to join Dere Street as it climbed up to the watershed at Soutra. But road transport was slow, expensive and sometimes dangerous. Although it seems unfeasible to us now, the Flemings and their producers must have moved goods on the River Tweed, from Roxburgh twenty miles down to Berwick. Clues as to how they negotiated the shallows and the rocky rapids can be found in a backward glance at the craft that moved on the river thousands of years before, and also to a fascinating find on an archaeological dig in Aberdeen on the banks of the River Don. A medieval paddle used for a curragh or a coracle was found. With a displacement measured in inches, even when laden, curraghs would have provided an excellent means of taking Roxburgh wool and hides to Berwick. Even with short portages at awkward places the river journey would have been many times faster than one made on land. And in any case if the monks could contemplate and carry out the great hydraulic projects at the Melrose and Kelso caulds across the Tweed, the clearance of a channel in the river would have presented no difficulty. It appears that the Romans could do it, for a steering oar used on a barge was found during excavations at Newstead.

The link with Berwick was clearly determinant and both towns grew and prospered on the backs of Border sheep and cattle, and the financial acumen of Flemish and Italian merchants. Fifteen religious houses, all of them producers of wool and hides, held properties in Berwick and the foreign merchants maintained places of business. These resembled the 'factories' of English traders in colonial India, where a sort of diplomatic immunity was allowed, and where outsiders could live in communal safety. 'The Red Hall' was the name of the Flemish trading centre at Berwick and as many as 30 merchants operated out of it at one time. German merchants (doubtless this description included the Dutch) were to be found at 'The White Hall', and in Roxburgh a place called 'The Black Hall ' is listed but no particular nationality attached. Perhaps all foreigners used it.

When the wool trade began to expand in Europe, David I would unquestionably have been aware of its possibilities, he had observed its beginnings first hand at the court of Henry I, and therefore it seems likely that he quickly transformed the local market towns at Roxburgh and Berwick into something altogether more ambitious. There is no record of how he went about this in the Tweed Valley, but over at

Carlisle a new town was created in 1092 by William II Rufus himself and it offers a strong sense of how David may have acted. Here is the relevant entry in the Anglo-Saxon Chronicle;

"1092. In this year the king William travelled north to Carlisle with a very great army, and restored the town and raised the castle, and drove out Dolfin who earlier ruled the land there, and set the castle with his men, and afterwards returned south here, and sent very many peasants there with women and with livestock to live there and to till that land."

William was behaving exactly like the Marcher Lords of Wales when they created small urban enclaves protected by strong castles and which were able to process the output of the surrounding countryside. He even provided the farmers to make sure that there was output to process. When William's descendent, Edward I of England, conquered North Wales in the late 13th century, he did something very similar at Conwy, Beaumaris and Caernarfon. Always a powerful castle dominated towns peopled by English tradesmen and merchants. At Roxburgh and Berwick David was not in such a hostile setting but he did need to create a catalyst for the economy of the Borders and he needed new people to bring new ideas to the local market towns he found in 1107. Precisely how he did this is more than hinted at in a set of 17th century records of what William II Rufus did at his plantation town of Carlisle. The street pattern was laid out on the old and probably decayed Roman model, and the walls proudly shown to St Cuthbert by the Northumbrian Reeve, Wagga, were used as foundations for new fortifications. This passage from Hugh Todd's 'Account of the City and Diocese of Carlisle' (1699) explains;

"The English, the best and principal citizens were placed in the principal places of this city near to the market place and the church, and also in Richardgate and in Botchardgate. The Irish placed in the Vicus Hibernensium, dwelt there in cottages when it was waste, (the gate at the end of the street is called the Irishgate). The Flemings dwelt in Shaddongate (Shadwinggate) in the area called Vicus Flandrensis. The Frenchmen, or Normans dwelt in Castle Street (Vicus Francorum)."

The segregation of nationalities into quarters was an old idea and much used in the 12th century in England. The town plans of Carlisle and even Roxburgh and Berwick are known, at least in broad outline, but what these places actually looked like is much more elusive. Archaeology is difficult for the good and simple reason that modern towns are built on top of old ones, and the evidence is buried and likely to remain so. That is what makes the lack of investigation on the site of Roxburgh doubly frustrating. No buildings of any sort exist to prevent archaeology — only the thickness of some old turf lies between ignorance and enlightenment. However at Perth rescue digs in the 1970s made possible by delaying the interval between the demolition of old buildings and the erection of new have revealed a great deal of priceless information.

It appears that 12th century towns tended to nucleate around a regular market generally held on a street connecting two focal points, often a castle and a church. At Roxburgh the latter was the parish church of St James, which gave its name to a fair which lasted for nearly a thousand years, only being abandoned in the 1930s. But this development was not random and house-plots look as though they were regulated by what must, at that stage, have been a royal official, possibly a sheriff or his representative. Houses fronted on to a roughly metalled street, covered with gravel and small stones and also fouled by a good deal of rubbish, and behind them lay long and narrow gardens or backlands. These were reached by pends between the houses. Many old Scottish towns still retain these characteristic features and on the south side of South Street at St Andrews many of the backlands still exist in a recognisable form. Most 12th century town houses were one storey high, 9 to 10 yards long by 4 to 5 yards wide and with the gable end fronting on to the street. These houses were neither robust nor durable. To create the walls, stakes were driven into the ground and withies woven between them in the same way that hurdle fences are still constructed now. Mud, clay, straw or even dung was plastered on and allowed to dry so that the walls gained some solidity. Sometimes turf or peat was banked against them. Sometimes a ditch was dug along the projected line of posts and filled with loose stones before being topped with a crust of puddle clay. The idea was to mitigate rising damp. This rudimentary method of construction restricted the height of the walls to no more than 5 feet. Roofs were usually thatched and supported by a ridge pole slung between two uprights at either gable. Reached by the pend, doorways were set in one of the long walls and the doors themselves made out of wooden planking. In the centre of a clay, sand or gravel floor (covered with bracken, heather or straw and often mixed with meadowsweet to keep the smell managable) sat the focus of the house, the down-hearth. This was a stone hearth on which an open fire burned to provide heat, light and a means of cooking.

The construction of early medieval town houses, with wall-stakes in direct contact with the earth and therefore progressively rotting, did not allow a life longer than about 20 years. But many medieval towns suffered regularly devastating fires and a primary cause of these must have been sparks from the down-hearth floating up to a thatched roof on a windy day. Better-off families cooked in a cauldron attached to the ridge-pole by a chain, but most will have used large earthenware cooking pots shoved into the hot ashes of the fire on the down-hearth, or sat on a taller stone above the embers. Everyone ate potage. It was a vegetable soup thickened with cereals and sometimes flavoured with scraps of meat and bones. As it seethed, or boiled, on the hearth it was stirred occasionally with a spurtle to stop it burning or sticking to the sides. Flatbread was made much in the way that Indian restaurants produce nan bread. Unleavened ovals of dough were rolled out and set on a hot hearth stone and covered with an upturned pot. Oatcakes were baked in a similar way. Sometimes unlikely treats were caught and small animals like hedgehogs, squirrels or small birds were wrapped in wet clay and baked in the hottest part of the fire.

POTAGE

Here is a recipe for the universal medieval dish of potage taken from a manuscript in the British Library reprinted and explained in 'A Taste of History' edited by Maggie Black;

Ingredients
2lb of shin of beef
4 — 6 short pieces of marrow bone
4 pints of water
2 leeks
2 sticks of celery
2 onions
a quarter of a firm white cabbage
4 ounces of white breadcrumbs
a few saffron strands
2 teaspoons of salt
ground black pepper

Cut the meat into 2 inch cubes. Put in a stewpan with the bones and water. Bring to the boil and skim well. Reduce the heat and simmer, uncovered, for about 2 to 2 and a half hours. Meanwhile prepare the vegetables and boil in a separate pan, whole or in large pieces, for 10 minutes. Drain and cut into thick slices. When the beef is just about ready, remove the marrow bones and add the vegetables. Continue simmering until the vegetables are soft. Stir in the breadcrumbs, saffron and plenty of seasoning. Bring back to the boil, and cook for 2 to 3 minutes. Skim off any excess fat before serving.

In the Middle Ages this was eaten out of a wooden bowl with a bone spoon, if you had one, and accompanied with bread. The recipe is virtually identical (without the breadcrumbs and saffron) to what Bina Moffat called 'kail', because that vegetable was substituted for cabbage. Kail was generally thickened with dried pulses or barley tipped straight into the pot and allowed to simmer for at least eight or nine hours — the length of time someone was likely to be in the kitchen to watch it. When the meat was cooked, it was lifted out and served separately, perhaps with potatoes. Children in Kelso called it sloshy meat stew.

In the backlands at the byre-end of a town-house a milk cow was kept and, far from being slaughtered in a mass cull in the autumn, it seems that at Perth beasts were kept through the winter and fed on hay, straw, kale stalks and leaves — and whatever other scraps could be found. In some Border towns street names remember that urban dwellers kept animals in their houses. At Kelso the Tofts was where people lived and Croft Road was where animals were led out to each day to graze before being brought in again at night. These were breeding and milking stock. Rights of 'toft and croft' were zealously defended by towns and at Roxburgh the wide haughland of the river peninsula will have provided many acres of secure and well-drained pasture.

Drains found in the backlands in Perth show where animals were kept overnight, and these highlight a recurrent difficulty — the preservation of a clean water supply in towns. Water was often supplied by cisterns and wells which were not only in danger of being contaminated by animal faeces but also the sewage of the householders who sometimes dug cesspits in their restricted plots which were too close to a water supply. Typhoid and a host of other water-borne diseases raged through populations packed together in the streets of medieval Scotland and the lack of reliably clean water always inhibited the growth of towns, particularly when they expanded quickly. The widespread brewing of ale was partly a method of avoiding a doubtful water supply. In a quirky but determinant footnote from another historical period, the 18th century fashion for drinking tea helped to break the Malthusian cycle and allowed the great northern cities of the Industrial Revolution, Manchester, Leeds and the others, to grow rapidly without the breakout of decimating disease. Not only was water boiled before being drunk but tea itself had been considered a tonic drink in the Far East with mild antibiotic properties.

Beyond the walls or boundaries of Roxburgh, Carlisle and Berwick a suburban landscape extended. Rubbish dumps seem to have been little regulated, while industries that were either dangerous, such as blacksmithing with its fires and sparks, or disgusting, like tanning which used a concoction of dog turds, urine and other ingredients in the pits where leather was cured for long periods, were expelled from towns but allowed to remain nearby. Suburban housing also existed beyond the town limits and at Roxburgh, with its early new town, it was probably located to the east and south. where there was room to build. Archaeologists have uncovered a group of terraced farm cottages in what is now Springwood Park. Laid out along the road to the Teviot ford they date from the 12th century to the 14th and show evidence of economic health. Coins were found, and horseshoes. Crops such as barley, wheat, oats and rye were grown and stock kept, certainly sheep and cattle. The buildings and the farm were probably tenanted but they occupants did use cash and were wealthy enough to own horses. They were doubtless suppliers to both Kelso Abbey and the town of Roxburgh. Religious institutions, like the Franciscan Friars at the ford over the Teviot, sometimes prefered to be extramural. Others, like leper hospitals, were forced to be. It is not known if Maison Dieu, up on the ridge to the south of Roxburgh, was a leper colony but its association with and relative remoteness from a trading town suggests that it was.

The flimsy and combustible construction of 12th century town houses suggest a transience which we find hard to grasp. Modern towns present an altogether more solid and well-planted picture to mind than what the archaeologists found at Perth. Certainly wealthier medieval citizens built more robust houses and churches were made out of stone from an early date. But given the evidence of wattle, thatch and the sparks from a down-hearth, the withering of Roxburgh might be wondered at a little less. However, its total disappearance remains a tantalising enigma.

By contrast, Berwick seems never to have been anything but substantial, except for one crucial element. 31 out of 33 towns founded by Scottish kings were laid out in the shadow of a royal castle. Berwick's has been removed. Swept away by the 19th century railway station at the north end of the magnificent Tweed Bridge, all that remains of the castle are parts of the curtain wall. a 13th century tower and what was known as the 'White Wall' leading down from the site to the estuary. But unlike Roxburgh and Carlisle some sense of the 12th and 13th century government of the town has come down to us. A code of regulations known as the 'Laws of the Burghs' was probably compiled at Berwick, confirming its status as Scotland's wealthiest, most powerful and busy town. Apparently the annual value of its customs, the taxes paid on trade, were almost a quarter of those of the whole of England. In 1286 the revenue for Berwick was £2190 compared with £8800 for England.

The Laws of the Burghs were intended to apply throughout Scotland and other towns like Roxburgh and Carlisle (when it was included in Scotland) will have adopted its procedures. In the 12th century merchants began to develop some independence from royal authority in the sense that they were allowed to form a court which elected Provosts. From Michaelmas (29th September) each year four were elected to hold office for 12 months. The burgh court took the advice of 'probi homines' or 'worthy men' on who was suitable. The correct formal address for a Border Provost remembers a long past, and it is 'Worthy Provost'. By 1212 Berwick not only had burgesses, a court and provosts but also a common seal to append to its enactments. Towns were beginning to acquire political functions and characteristics. In 1238 the apparatus had developed even more when Alexander II wrote to 'The Mayor, the Provosts and the Commune of Berwick'. The Mayor was an interesting man. Robert de Bernham gave a fishing on the River Tweed to Melrose Abbey, probably a sweetener for Berwick's partner in the wool trade, and the gift was witnessed by 'the whole commune'. Robert's brother, David, was Alexander II's chamberlain at the time and it may be that his negotiating skills were instrumental in gaining more autonomy for the town. Because he needed to find two substantial sums for dowries for his sisters, the king was short of cash and David de Bernham, in charge of royal finances, may have suggested that the Mayor and burgesses of Berwick would be prepared to pay handsomely for a grant of communal privileges. The arrangement arrived at was attractive to both parties and a bargain struck at an annual payment of 500 merks. In 1191 London set up a structure for devolved municipal government and this seems to have been adopted at Berwick. A council of 24 'worthy men' elected their Mayor on an annual basis and after the grant of rights from the king, the commune bought land in the town from Simon Maunsel on which it built a hall called 'le Berefreit'. Used for the custody of prisoners and probably the place where the town bell was hung, it was the ancestor of the Tollbooth or Town Hall. The bell was needed to toll the hours for the regulation of trade, when it should begin and when it should end. Berwick Town Hall remains in the ownership of the Merchant Guild and not the local authority and the curfew bell still sounds for quarter of an hour every day except Sunday. In 1249 the Statutes of the Guild of Burgesses were drawn up and the entry fee set at 40 shillings so that only the wealthy could join. The Statutes sorted out rights and privileges amongst burgesses and chief amongst them concerned the wool trade. A virtual monoploy of the lucrative business was assured when they decreed that only a guild-brother (and, of course, stranger-merchants) might deal in wool, hides and finished cloth.

The shears carved on Johanna Bulloc's tombstone were a powerful symbol for the tale of the three cities of the Borders. Prompted by the king, stimulated by the hungry factories of Flanders, supplied by the new monasteries, the trade in wool and hides created a booming economy in the 12th and 13th century Border country.

All of this intense commercial activity undoubtedly engendered prosperity for all that time and for many people, but it was only possible in periods of relative peace. The looming shadows of the castles at Carlisle, Roxburgh and Berwick offered a daily reminder to merchants and craftsmen that they needed protection, but when each of them became instruments of war, trade shrank almost to nothing, the Flemish merchants looked elsewhere for their woolpacks and each of the towns became highly vulnerable targets.

Of David I's three major royal castles in the Borders only Carlisle has survived. Its immensely long military life came to an end in 1959 when the last garrison was withdrawn. From the time in 71–74AD when Petilius Cerialis built a fort at Luguvalium to the departure of the last soldiers 1,888 years later, there had been a manned military fortification on that site. The oldest feature is not the massive square stone keep begun by Henry I in 1122 and finished by David I, but the shape of the castle itself. Determined to some extent by the fall of the ground to the rivers Caldew and Eden, and the contours of the mound, the long curtain wall, enclosing barracks, an armoury, a parade ground and the inner bailey, probably echoes the original Roman layout very closely. A reminder of the early occupants of Carlisle Castle was found in the heavily defended inner gatehouse. Used as a lintel for a doorway between two rooms, a Roman altar dedicated to Jupiter, Minerva, Mars and Victory by a tribune of the 20th Legion had been cannibalised. The long perimeter of the Roman fort required a large garrison to defend it and William II Rufus and his medieval successors concentrated the most substantial defences in the western corner where their 12th century keep dominated a triangular area surrounded by a ditch, high walls and the inner gatehouse.

From an early stage Carlisle Castle was built in stone, much of it doubtless robbed from the Roman fort and from Stanwix and Hadrian's Wall across the Eden. Elsewhere the first Norman-French castles were made of earth and wood, more akin to the style of Dark Ages military architecture. Motte and bailey construction (the best example of the characteristic Christmas-pudding shaped mound can be seen at Hawick Moat, but the encircling bailey has disappeared) had several advantages; it was quick to build and required the import of no special materials or skills, and the resulting structure was impressive, glowering over the landscape, emphatic about who controlled it. However there is an interesting imbalance in the geographical distribution of mottes. Clearly they are early, likely the first structures erected by incoming Frenchmen granted land by David I and others. But even though the heaviest concentration of incomers was in the Tweed Basin, very few of these earth and timber castles were built there. The remains of only eight exist and all of these are to be found in the hill country to the west at Selkirk, Howden, Cavers, Hawick, Lilliesleaf, Liddel Water, Hermitage and Lauder, and not in the valuable and more fertile areas of the Merse. By contrast almost half of the 239 mottes in Scotland were in Dumfries and Galloway. This eccentric distribution must say something about conflict, or the lack of it, over land between incomers and natives. Certainly the heavy incidence in Galloway can be explained by the fact that the area was incorporated forcibly and late into the kingdom of the Scots, but the record is largely silent about the reception of Frenchmen in the central and eastern Borders. Even given the likelihood that some wait to be discovered under farmhouses or later medieval stone towers, the rarity of mottes may speak volumes about a relatively peaceful imposition of a new ruling elite on a booming rural economy with only sporadic problems in parts of the western hill country. Walter de Riddell's legal dispute with Uchtred, the hereditary priest of Lilliesleaf, might be seen as a contest between one landowning native aristocrat and an incomer, and their recourse to law as a relatively civilised means of settling differences which may have spilled over into unrecorded violence elsewhere. The facts that de Riddell built a motte and was in dispute with a local aristocrat cannot be unconnected.

At the same time as Carlisle's massive keep was started Roxburgh Castle began to assume the formidable presence only hinted at in the ruins hidden in the waist-high nettles, willowherb and bushes, and the many mature trees growing on this ignored, delapidated but enormously significant site. Once the strongest fortress on the entire Border, it was deliberately demolished for that reason in 1460 by the army of James II, who was killed when a cannon 'flew in flinders' near where he stood. Roxburgh was so well defended that the Scots would rather see it neutralised than risk it falling into the hands of the English. Between the Tweed to the north and the Teviot under the south walls, the castle sits on a mound 70 to 80 feet high and 350 feet wide by 800 long. Nature has undoubtedly been improved by great labour, particularly in the early part of the long life of this atmospheric place, but Roxburgh's great strength comes from its site.

By 1134 when the Chronicle of Melrose recorded that Malcolm macHeth, a northern claimant to the throne, had been imprisoned there, it was clear that Roxburgh had a keep, or central tower. And in 1128 the Church of St John inside the walls is noted. Like Carlisle there was a long perimeter to be defended and it looks as though the keep stood at the higher western end of the castlemount and the church would have been close by. Later expansions covered the whole area on top of the mound and many towers and barracks existed in the late Middle Ages. When the army of Henry VIII raided the Borders under the command of the Earl of Hertford in 1545, plans were made to rebuild part of Roxburgh Castle as a fort, and these have survived. More compact than earlier layouts, it focuses on the west end and when the English architect marked the largest tower as 'The Bell Tower', it looks very much as though it was raised on the foundations of David I's keep. As at Carlisle, it is nearly square in plan. And like its town lying to the east, Roxburgh Castle cries out for archaeology — even a sensitive clearance of vegetation and debris from the site would reveal a great deal.

At Berwick Castle no such opportunities exist. Trains trundle and wheeze through what was the great hall, and in the days of steam the ruins of the western curtain wall were almost black with soot. Platform One covers the place where Edward I of England sat in judgement on the Great Cause, the vexed issue of the succession to the Scots kingship. What can still be seen (permission is needed to enter the railway station from the other side of the tracks to take a closer look at the west wall) is supplemented by a brief description written in 1762;

"It [the castle] is environed on one side by the ditch of the town; on the other by one of the same breadth, flanked by many round towers and thick walls, which enclose a large palace, in the middle of which rises a lofty keep or donjon, capable of a long resistance, and commanding all the environs of the town."

When not at war castles had other important functions. David I needed Berwick, Roxburgh, Carlisle and the others to do duty as administrative centres, courts, hotels and well-maintained symbols of his authority — even when he was absent. Like 'Heorot' in Beowulf and the Anglian halls at Yeavering, the great hall of a castle was its heartbeat. In the early Middle Ages all of the king's retinue ate communally in the hall, it was also a living room for its owner, many lesser people slept on its floor or in adjacent closets, and it acted as a courtroom. Ailred of Rievaulx occasionally lapses into hagiography when he describes David I's dedication to ensuring justice for even the most humble (and sometimes unabashedly thrawn) but this passage does give a picture of one of the functions of a 12th century hall;

"I saw also with my own eyes, when sometimes he was ready to go hunting, and with his foot placed in the stirrup he was intending to mount his horse , that he withdrew his foot, left his horse and returned to his hall at the voice of a poor person demanding that audience be given to him, and he would not return to what he had planned on that day..[until]..he had heard the case for which he had been called kindly and patiently. It was his custom to sit at the door of the royal hall and to listen attentively to cases of poor people and old women, who were summoned on certain days from particular regions wherever they came from, and to strive hard to give satisfaction to each one. For often they argued with him and he with them, when he refused to accept the legal standing of a poor person contrary to justice, and when they refused to give assent to the reasoned argument which he demonstrated to them."

Only in Scotland would a king "often", according to Ailred, have to suffer backchat from thrawn old women unhappy with what he said to them.

Inside the hall there was usually a dais at one end where the king or the baron sat with his family and more important supporters on either side. He was the only person in the hall who sat on a chair with a high back. This eventually led to the convention of calling the most important person at a meeting 'the chairman' and the use of the phrase 'taking the chair'. Everyone else in a castle hall sat on benches, and the reason for this had as much to do with practicality as status. All royal or baronial furniture had to be easy to take apart so that it could be packed onto carts and taken to the next castle or palace. Tables were made out of boards and trestles and this cultural habit has left some interesting vocabulary; a sideboard was originally just that, a table at the side of a hall, and a cupboard was a table for cups. The French word for a sideboard was 'buffet' and the Yeomen of the Guard's popular name of 'Beefeaters' may derive from 'buffetier' the guards who sat at the side tables in the king's hall. The reason why furniture had to travel frequently was simple; a royal or large baronial household received much of its income in food and drink and they had to move from place to place to consume it. Almost everything went in a baggage train; kists full of napery, clothes, blankets, tapestries, plates and cutlery and sometimes even glass windows were taken out and replaced with wooden shutters when a castle was not being used by its owner.

Halls were heated by great fireplaces, sometimes more than one, and opposite the dais where the king sat in his chair, there stood a serving screen where dishes were sorted out and service organised. When the court occupied a castle many mouths had to be fed and the kitchens were constantly busy. Meat roasted on spits resting on firedogs and were turned and basted by scullions, laddies who did all of the menial tasks. In a stone building the large fires needed for roasting were less dangerous but even so, kitchens sometimes went up in flames. At Roxburgh Castle the Bakehouse (and Brewhouse) was in the south east corner, some distance from the keep and its great hall. This may have been inconvenient but it was prudent. Baking ovens were first heated by the simple expedient of lighting a fire inside them and then raking it out before inserting the bread dough on long-handled shovels called peels. Because of the volume of smouldering fuel, bakehouses often burned down and were usually separate buildings. As the story of St Waltheof and his barns at Gattonside and Eildon shows, wheat bread was reserved for the wealthy and brown or rye bread for the poorer sort. However there was a use for stale brown bread on the lord or king's table which has been remembered in a modern description of someone fond of their food. Four day old loaves of brown bread were cut into slices and a small indentation made in the middle. These were used as plates by the great and good and each course of a meal was served on a slice and then discarded (to be eaten later by the poor) as it disintegrated. Since those who used them spoke French these bread-plates were called 'tranches' or slices, but they were eventually anglicised into 'trenchers', and the term survives in the phrase 'trencher-man'. And the Gaelic word for a plate is 'trainnsear'.

More vocabulary underlines how the food each person ate was determined by social class. The best went to the king and barons in the Middle Ages, and the best food was meat. Live animals kept their English names of cow, sheep, deer and ox, but once they had been roasted on a spit, jointed and set on trenchers, they acquired the French-derived names of beef, veal, venison, mutton and bacon.

When the evening meal was over everyone slept either where they worked, in the warmth of the kitchens or the bakehouse, or where they had eaten, in the hall or in small wooden closets at the sides. Only the king or a baron had a bed-chamber and any privacy. His personal servants slept on a bed pulled out from under the royal bed or out in the corridor so that they were always near at hand and available. Life at court was lived in intimate and continual contact with other human beings. In such an atmosphere little could be kept secret and when, for example, men and women made love they either found privacy in what the laws of Hywel Dda called 'brake and bush' or they stayed indoors in the warmth and suffered the presence (and doubtless the occasional taunts) of their fellows with only darkness as a cloak.

As the Middle Ages wore on, the importance of the hall declined and more rooms were set aside for different and more private purposes. In modern house design the hall is now only the place for greeting visitors, hanging coats and connecting other, more used rooms.

When the king was not at Roxburgh Castle, it was not empty or peopled by a skeleton garrison. Two witnesses to the Selkirk Charter hint at what happened during the king's absence from royal castles. Government went on and at Bamburgh Odardo, called 'the Sheriff of Bamburgh', conducted it. He is joined in the witness-list by Cospatrick who became Sheriff of Roxburgh and was based at the castle. This was originally an Anglian institution and Wagga, at Carlisle with St Cuthbert in 685, was a prototype shire-reeve or sheriff. Royal officials who operated justice, military matters and rent collection in the name of the king, men like Odardo, were early civil servants and Cospatrick came from a family who had served the Bishops Palatine of Durham as sheriffs or thanes at Hexham. At Ednamshire Thor Longus sounds as though he was a thane of King Edgar's. In the Borders David I created four sheriffdoms at Roxburgh, Selkirk, Peebles and Berwick. The extent of their jurisdictions formed the shires which took those names and they kept their shape and ancient administrative purpose until the unhappy reorganisation of local government in 1974. By the time of his death in 1153 David I had brought nine sheriffdoms into being.

Little is known about Selkirk Castle, except that it belonged to David I. Like Roxburgh it is overgrown and obscured by trees, but at least place-names and geography tell part of its story and offer a reason why it was often occupied by the king. The large house at the western foot of Selkirk castlemount is known as The Haining and it comes from a Scots word meaning an enclosed area. To the south east lie the remains of the enclosure. A ditch and bank runs along the back of a ridge called the Deer Park, a piece of ground of around 60 acres. On the bank was the park pale or paling, raised to a height of 7 feet to prevent deer escaping. Near a royal castle, at the mouth of valleys leading into the heart of the Ettrick Forest, the Haining and the Deer Park are tangible relics of a medieval obsession.

Hunting had long gone on in the Southern Uplands, the lands of the Selgovae, the Hunters. But what the Frenchmen imported was the Carolingian idea of the 'Foresta', meaning a hunting reserve and not necessarily a large wood. By the time of the Selkirk Charter in 1113 to 1120 David I had organised his game reserves sufficiently to promise part of the bag to the new abbey, and in 1124 he established the Ettrick

Forest as a huge hunting ground. In 1136 the first explicit reference occurs when the new abbey at Melrose received gifts of privileges to pasture pigs and take timber "in my forests, that is, those at Selkirk and at Traquair". All the main characteristics of forest law were set down; hunting was forbidden to all except the king on pain of heavy fines (in England they took poaching more seriously and offenders were blinded and castrated), the timber was reserved, the pasture regulated and the whole set-up administered by sheriffs and royal foresters.

The methods used to kill wild beasts show Celtic origins. Game was driven by a 'tinchell' of beaters, and the Scots word derives from Gaelic 'timchioll' which means a circle. Men thrashed through the woods and brush, pushing the frightened animals towards the place where hunters waited with their weapons and dogs. This place was known as the 'tryst' or the 'set' and Abbotseat in Kelso might remember where one senior churchman and his retainers waited. All sorts of weapons were used but the most common were the hunting knife and crossbow which fired barbed arrows. Because many aristocratic hunters sat at the tryst on horseback the longbow was not practical. A short pointed sword was also sometimes used as well as axes, spears and clubs.

In the 15th century John Murray of Hangingshaw in the Yarrow Valley kept the king's hunting dogs. There were two sorts; sight and scent hounds. Also called 'running hounds' the former needed to be fast and medieval Scottish greyhounds were considered to be the best in Europe. A large and hairier variety also hunted and it resembled the Irish Wolfhound although it is unlikely that it ever took on wolves. Mastiffs were kept for that purpose and fitted with spiked collars to protect their necks from vulpine fangs. Scent-hounds worked on a leash and were trained not to bark. Known as 'rauchs' the most prized were sleuth-hounds and they sometimes trailed thieves and even rebels. Both Robert Bruce and William Wallace were hunted by sleuth-hounds.

Horns were heard ringing through the woods on hunting days and they became an integral part of the rituals and the excitement. Used to relay messages in a simple version of morse code with short and long blasts, they could also be distinctive. According to the medieval historian, John Barbour, his men could recognise Robert Bruce's horn as soon as they heard the first notes.

HAWKS, FALCONS AND TERCELS

Some time between 1165 and 1169 the men of Melrose Abbey tried to scare hawks and particularly sparrowhawks out of trees which they wanted to fell in Eskdale. The Norman-French family of the Avenels were furious and complained bitterly. Hawks were precious, they could be caught and trained by their falconers.

The generic name 'hawk' divides, of course, into two genders; the larger female is called a falcon and the smaller male, a tercel. There are also two methods of hunting. The Avenels wanted to preserve the sparrowhawks in Eskdale because, as short-winged hawks, they flew well in wooded country. Using surprise as well as sheer agility and sprinting speed, a sparrowhawk can overtake and kill its prey by gripping it with its needle-sharp talons. Long-winged hawks like the peregrine falcon hunt very differently. They climb high in the sky and circle slowly in the updraughts, watching for pigeons or ducks flying a long way below. When it sees its quarry, the peregrine snaps back its wings and dives at a speed estimated at 180 miles per hour. This astonishing drop is called 'the stoop' and the falcon and other long-winged hawks kill by a glancing blow delivered at terrific speed.

Hawks were often included in royal or knightly portraits of the later Middle Ages. Hooded to keep them calm and with jesses attached to their legs to keep them on the glove, these birds took years to train and were consequently considered to be very valuable and symbols of high status.

Recently a very beautiful but defaced relief sculpture of a hawking party was uncovered at Newstead and its style has persuaded archaeologists that it once adorned Melrose Abbey.

Hunting was enjoyed for the thrills of the chase and the food it supplied for the hall table, but it also had another function for the nobility. In an age when the elite battle troops were armoured knights, horsemanship was very important indeed and the ability to stay in the saddle a matter of life or death. Hunting taught young men to sit tight and with weapons in their hands, how to manoeuvre their horses with their legs.

These were skills perhaps fatally ignored by David I and his knights on 22nd August 1138. At the Battle of the Standard on Cowton Moor near Northallerton in Yorkshire the Scots dismounted and fought on foot. The ground may have not been good enough for horses because they English also left their destriers behind the lines. Thurstan, Archbishop of York, had mustered an army to repel David's invasion of the north and in the midst of its ranks the banners of St John of Beverly and St Wilfrid, the flamboyant 7th century Northumbrian bishop, were hauled up on high standards set on a 'machine' where everyone could see them. The day was a disaster for David. Having massed what the English chroniclers called 'an incredible army' of Norman knights, archers from Teviotdale (which included the Ettrick Forest), men of Lothian, Hebrideans and men from Lorne, a contingent from Moray and those warriors known as 'the Picts of Galloway', the king was defeated by a smaller force with, it appears, better discipline and a surer grasp of tactics. The Gallovidians begged David to allow them to form the front rank. The howling, barking and snarling of their war-dogs would terrify the English, their berserkers with their reckless courage would break through and they wanted the open ground in front of them so that they could charge. Roaring their Gaelic war-cries of 'Albannaich!' 'Albannaich!' — 'Men of Scotland' they raced towards the enemy. Ailred of Rievaulx takes up the story;

"But the southerns, since they were few, very wisely massed into one column. For the most vigorous knights were placed in the first front, and the lancers and archers so distributed through them that they were protected by the arms of the knights, and could with equally greater vigour and security either attack the enemy or receive his attack.

But the nobles who were of maturer age were arrayed (that they might support the others) around the royal banner, some being placed higher than the rest upon the machine itself.

Shield was joined to shield, side pressed to side; lances were raised with pennons unfurled, hauberks glittered in the brilliance of the sun; priests, white-clad in their sacred robes, went round the army with crosses and relics of the saints, and most becomingly fortified the people with prayer.

And at once the northern army left its position and advanced with spears erect. There followed the peal of clarions, the blare of trumpets, the clashing of spears striking one against the other...

And the column of Galwegians [Gallovidians] after their custom gave vent thrice to a yell of horrible sound, and attacked the southerns in such an onslaught that they compelled the first spearmen to forsake their post; but they were driven off again by the strength of the knights, and [the spearmen] recovered their courage and strength against the foe.

And when the frailty of the Scottish lances was mocked by the denseness of iron and wood they drew their swords and attempted to contend at close quarters. But the southern flies swarmed forth from the caves of their quivers, and flew like closest rain; and irksomely attacking the opponents' breasts, faces and eyes, very greatly impeded their attack.

Like a hedgehog with its quills, so you would see a Galwegian bristling all round with arrows, and none the less brandishing his sword and in blind madness rushing forward now smite a foe, now lash the air with useless strokes."

Probably because of the intensity of the English archery and the indiscipline of the Gallovidians, David lost a battle he should have won. But, better at diplomacy than the arts of war, he negotiated terms which gave him Cumbria and Northumberland. What he could not manage to achieve by force, he did by taking advantage of the dynastic chaos in England when King Stephen and the Empress Matilda fought over Henry I's legacy. And so for nearly 20 years the three cities of the Borders, Carlisle, Roxburgh and Berwick, and the whole Tweed Basin, including north Northumberland, found themselves in the same kingdom, undivided. It was to be a short respite.

By the time he reached Carlisle Castle in the Spring of 1153, the king was ill, and at 69, very old. When David I died in May of that year in his stone keep, it was more than 12 months since his only child to reach maturity, the Earl Henry, had himself passed away. Too unwell to do it himself David had asked MacDuff, the Earl of Fife, to conduct his grandson Malcolm around the kingdom as the rex designatus. As one historian has remarked, it looked less like the anointment of a successor and more like an election campaign. But Malcolm did succeed without opposition and although he made serious attempts to incorporate Galloway into his kingdom and in 1164 saw Somerled, the powerful King of the Isles, defeated, he was forced by Henry II to give up both Cumbria and Northumberland. By 1157 the border was once again on the Tweed and the watershed ridge of the Cheviot Hills.

The 12th century saw the zenith of Norman-French expansionism all over Europe. Adventurers under the command of Robert Guiscard had carved out a powerful duchy in the south of Italy and after 1100 created what became known as the Kingdom of the Two Sicilies. It lasted until the 19th century and the unification of Italy by Giuseppe Garibaldi. Ireland was invaded by a coalition of Welsh marcher lords led by Richard fitzGilbert, the Earl of Pembroke who was given the nickname 'Strongbow'. In 1095 the Pope, Urban II, preached the First Crusade and by the early years of the 12th century Norman-French kingdoms ruled on feudal principles had taken unlikely root in the valleys and deserts of Palestine and Syria. But the greatest, most formidable and widely landed of all was Henry II, king of England, Duke of Normandy, Duke of Aquitaine and personal owner, through his sons and his mother, Eleanor, of more than half of France, from the Pyrenees to the English Channel. Under his suzerainty England looked south and the Plantagenet kings saw their heartlands in the fertile fields and villages and great castles of France. Scottish kings were both part of that international feudal world — the chronicler, Walter of Coventry, noted that both Malcolm IV and his brother, William the Lion, 'profess themselves to be Frenchmen both in race and in manners, language and culture' — and a profound irritation to Henry II. Even though David I had dubbed and girded Henry a knight at Carlisle in 1149, there was little sense of loyalty or reciprocated affection in his dealings with Scottish kings. Malcolm IV sought the same honour from Henry as his grandfather had bestowed on him, but the English king kept him waiting until 1159.

Sadly and somewhat lamely the Scottish kings of the later 12th century seem to have been besotted with the idea of knighthood, knightly honour and the growing cluster of codes and rituals of chivalry. After William the Lion succeeded in 1165 he spent a great deal of time at Selkirk Castle indulging a fashionable passion for hunting and hawking. The chronicler, Jordan Fantosme, recognised the Scottish king's ill-disguised francophilia when he stated bluntly and disapprovingly that William held only foreigners dear and would never love his own people. But the games he wanted to play were dominated by a ruthlessness that appeared nowhere in the chivalric chansons or the tales of noble conduct. While pursuing his entirely legitimate claim to the earldom of Northumberland (held by the Scots until 1157) William carelessly allowed himself to be taken prisoner near Alnwick Castle in 1174. It turned out to be a personal and political disaster but Fantosme described the action as though it were a knightly tournament where honour rather than territory was at stake. The Scottish knights fought well, he reported, and named four of the best of them — and indeed there is more than a hint that William took the proceedings in a chivalric spirit. Henry II quickly disabused him of any lack of seriousness by first humiliating the Scots king when he had him led through Northampton with his feet tied under the belly of his horse, and then casting him like a criminal into the dungeons of Falaise Castle in Normandy. And the resulting treaty was punitive and highly costly with Roxburgh and Berwick occupied by English garissons until William bought them back for 10,000 merks in 1189 when Henry's son, Richard I, needed cash to go on crusade.

Despite the king's ineptitude, the 12th century saw the Norman-French settlement of the Borders established and its institutions begin to function. Both Malcolm and William made serious attempts to incorporate Galloway and the north of Scotland into the kingdom, and for their part the gaze of English kings was mostly fixed southwards on their lands in France and further afield. In these political circumstances the Borders suffered little and remained largely peaceful and prosperous.

But when Alexander II invaded Cumbria and Northumberland in 1215 in pursuit of his family's claims, King John of England hurried north at the head of a great army. His soldiers burned both Berwick and Roxburgh and carried havoc into the Tweed Valley. By 1221 relations had settled down sufficiently to allow Alexander to marry Joan, the sister of Henry III and into the diplomatic bargain the Scots received back David's old earldom of Huntingdon. Ultimately, in 1237, the border was mutually agreed by the Treaty of York which gave the Scots some lands in Cumbria in exchange for a renunciation of their claims to Northumberland. The Tweed-Cheviot line, with some minor adjustments remaining at the western end at the mouth of the Solway, became recognisably the border we see today — except that Berwick remained in Scotland.

What this meant in legal practice is amply demonstrated in a meeting which took place in 1245 between English and Scottish knights. The rendezvous was fixed at the Redden Burn, the point at which the border leaves the Tweed to march southwards to the Cheviot foothills. There still existed contentious areas and the purpose of the meeting was to sort them out. Hugh de Bolebec wrote to Henry III to report on proceedings, and naturally, his account is highly partial;

"I and the knights of Northumberland met the Justiciar of Lothian, David Lindsay, the earl of Dunbar, and many other Scottish knights at Reddenburn. Six English and six Scottish knights were elected as a jury to make a true perambulation of the march between the two kingdoms, and in particular between the lands of Carham (in England) and Hadden (in Scotland).

The six English knights, with one accord, immediately set off along the rightful and ancient marches between the two kingdoms, but the Scottish knights entirely disagreed and contradicted them. I and the Justiciar of Lothian thereupon decided to elect a second jury to reinforce the first. Once again the English knights agreed on the boundary and the Scots dissented.

Since the Scots had thus obstructed the business, I took it upon myself to empanel a third jury, this time of 24 English knights, who declared the true and ancient marches on oath. But when they started to make a perambulation of this line, the Justiciar and his fellow Scots forcibly prevented them, and stopped them carrying out the perambulation by threats."

The outcome of this dispute can still be seen. The line of the border follows an eccentric and meandering course, sometimes using natural features such as the Carham Burn and at other times cutting in straight lines across swathes of farmland. The people watching the two sets of knights riding to and fro, on both sides of Wark Common, must have wondered at the workings of distant diplomacy. They had grown up in what was essentially the same Bernician cultural atmosphere. Both sides of the imaginary line everyone spoke English, lived in shires, revered the same saints, ploughed their furrows and pastured the stock in the same way. But even as early as the 12th century forces to the north and south had begun to pull them apart as they grew into two distinct communities of English and Scots. In Scotland Alexander III developed the notion of a Celtic kingship to contrast with the Norman-French models of the recent past, and at his coronation in 1249 at Scone this was symbolised powerfully when a Gaelic-speaking seannachie recited his genealogy back to and beyond the Dalriada kings. And as early as the reign of Malcolm IV the phrase, 'kingdom of the Scots' came into currency. To the south of the Tweed a different differentiating device was used. Because the Northumbrians were so comparatively distant from London and a peripatetic royal court which spent much of its time even further away in France, the Prince-Bishops of Durham used their royal or palatine powers to help foster a meaningful border between two groups of similar sorts of people. In 1121 Bishop Ranulf Flambard built the mighty castle at Norham and described it as being 'on the border', and other sources used similar language to support that way of thinking about the Tweed Basin. And as concretely, the Prince-Bishops extended their influence by taking direct control of the old Lindisfarne shires of Norham, Islandshire and Bedlingtonshire. North Northumberland became North Durham and on Berwick Old Bridge there is a tangible reminder of that ancient division. The battlement above the sixth arch is higher than all the rest because it marks the midstream boundary between the County Palatine of North Durham and the town of Berwick. In administrative terms that border remained a reality until 1844.

The distinctions between Northumberland and the realm of the kings of the Scots were sharpened even further in the 12th century by the calculated political deployment of the cult of St Cuthbert. The great gifts given to Durham became known as 'St Cuthbert's Land' and the people who lived there, right up to the Tweed, got the unifying name of the 'Haliwerfolc', or 'the people of the saint'. This turned the focus of their identity southwards to the shrine and church of St Cuthbert and away from the memories of old Bernicia and the naturally holistic geography of the Tweed Valley.

THE BA' GREEN

Careful examination of the Ordnance Survey shows that the Anglo-Scottish border does not follow the midstream line of the Tweed from the Redden Burn down to Paxton Toll House where it stops being tidal and turns north to carve out a small hinterland for Berwick. East of the village of Wark it dips down into England to bring two or three acres of the southern bank into Scotland. No-one knows why this aberration occured.

19th century histories repeat an entertaining tradition which might explain. The piece of land in question used to be known as the Ba' Green, a place where an ancient version of handball was played. The same game is still enthusiastically contested between the Uppies (those who live above the Market Cross) and the

Doonies (those below) in the centre of Jedburgh each year. It appears to have few rules, but goals are scored and they are called 'hails'. At the Ba' Green near Wark the competition is said to have been international. Allegedly a team from Coldstream played against Wark and whoever won was awarded a small part of a country to hold for a year. But as Coldstream grew bigger and Wark shrank in importance (its castle now a formless ruin), the game became no contest and the Ba' Green stayed permanently in Scottish hands.

By the time of Alexander III the idea of Scotland ended at the Tweed and the Cheviot tops, and beyond them the Englishness of the Haliwerfolc was clearly understood. The king's concerns shifted from his borders to the vital issue of the succession for, by 1285, he had not yet fathered an heir. At the age of 44 he married the French noblewoman, Yolande de Dreux, in what seems like a self-consciously Celtic ceremony at Jedburgh. In the castle the wedding guests were entertained by Highland music and dancing and all appeared to be well with the royal world. But then a harbinger of the future was seen, the apparition of a figure who brought the celebrations to an abrupt end, just as history was about to bring to a close a golden age for the Borders which had begun almost two centuries before. Here is the relevant passage from Walter Bower's chronicle. the Scotichronicon;

"While everything was going on at the royal wedding according to due custom, a kind of show was put on in the form of a procession amongst the company who were reclining at table. At the head of this procession were skilled musicians with many sorts of pipe music including the wailing music of bagpipes, and behind them others splendidly performing a war-dance with intricate weaving in and out. Bringing up the rear was a figure regarding whom it was difficult to decide whether it was a man or an apparition. It seemed to glide like a ghost rather than walk on feet. When it looked as if he was disappearing from everyone's sight, the whole frenzied procession halted, the song died away, the music faded, and the dancing contingent froze suddenly and unexpectedly."

7

The Battlelands

On the night of 19th March 1286 King Alexander III was feasting and drinking with his cronies in the Great Hall of Edinburgh Castle when he announced that he had had enough of their company. He rose, perhaps unsteadily, from the high table and told them he wished to spend the night with his beautiful young bride, Queen Yolande. The immediate difficulty was that she was not in Edinburgh but at the royal manor of Kinghorn on the opposite shore of the Firth of Forth. But the king was adamant, a horse was saddled for him in the torchlight of the courtyard, and a party of esquires and attendants hastily assembled. By the time they had clattered over the cobbles of the castle and ridden to South Queensferry, a storm was brewing and strong winds were blowing up the Firth of Forth. The ferryman at first refused to row his king across but Alexander, no doubt still flushed with wine, insisted on seeing the beautiful Yolande, that night. When the boat finally reached North Queensferry and fresh horses were found, the weather began to worsen and the wind whipped spindrift off the firth. The burgesses begged the king to stay the night in warm lodgings and continue his journey in the morning. But Alexander would have none of it and he spurred his horse so quickly along the cliff path to Kinghorn that he became detached from his party. About a mile short of his castle, a strong gust of wind may have caught his mount broadside. The animal spooked, lost its footing and threw the king out of the saddle and over the cliffs to plunge to his death two hundred feet below. Next morning when his servants found Alexander's body on the beach, the last Gaelic King of Scotland was dead, and the male line of the macMalcolm dynasty was no more. He had left no heir except a little girl, the Maid of Norway, and the problems of the royal succession propelled Scotland into a long and destructive period of war with England. And for three centuries much of that war was fought in the fields and meadows of the Borders

At the same time as Alexander III was clattering out of the gates of Edinburgh Castle bound for his fateful crossing of the Firth of Forth, another horseman was making a much shorter journey through the stormy, rainswept night. On the 19th of March 1286, Thomas Rhymer of Earlston's pony picked its way carefully along the dark lane to the east end of the village. He had been summoned to dine with the Earl, in the Earl's castle by the Earl's toun. Once food and wine had been set down and the fire got roaring, Patrick, Earl of Dunbar asked his man, Thomas, if the morning would bring any important or interesting event. Even across the great distance of 6 centuries, a note of sarcasm is just detectable. But in a moment, Thomas Rhymer silenced the company and wiped the smirk off the Earl's face.

"Alas for tomorrow" he exclaimed, " a day of calamity and misery! Before the twelfth hour shall be heard a blast so vehement as shall exceed those of every former period — a blast that shall strike the nations with amazement — shall humble what is proud, and what is fierce shall level with the ground! The sorest wind and tempest that was ever heard of in Scotland!"

The following day was evidently fine, not a breath of wind and an open sky. The Earl of Dunbar and his companions turned their sarcasm into scepticism as they surveyed a Spring day in the Scottish Border country. What could daft Thomas Rhymer have been ranting about? But around mid-day the bucolic peace surrounding Earlston was shattered. Having ridden hard from Edinburgh down the Leader Valley, a breathless horseman arrived at Dunbar's castle bringing terrible news. Alexander III was dead and Scotland without a king. And the reputation of True Thomas, Thomas of Ercildoune, was sealed.

For nearly 4 centuries afterwards the prophecies of Thomas were copied again and again, and after the coming of the printing press and the invention of the portable book, their circulation leaped dramatically. His words were repeated by both the learned and the illiterate, his sayings became the stuff of politics, as important to the protagonists as religious belief and legal argument, and more influential on the course of events than we can now imagine. In short, before Walter Scott dazzled the world with the breadth of his imagination, True Thomas was quite simply the most famous Borderer who had ever lived.

In addition to his prophecies there are good grounds for believing that the Rhymer was the earliest Scottish poet writing in English, the forerunner of Henryson and Dunbar. According to Robert Mannyng, a 14th century English author, Thomas wrote 'The Romance of Sir Tristrem' some time in the second half of the 13th century. Sir Walter Scott edited and published a more modern version of the poem, and on coming across references to Thomas himself in the body of the text, he formed the view that the work had been orally transmitted to the author and embellished and improved in the process. Following 'The Minstrelsy of the Scottish Border' (1802–3) Scott's ear was well tuned to the rhythms of oral poetry and he certainly knew a thing or two about embellishing. But this assessment should command respect rather than be treated as a piece of wish-fulfillment (for fame for a fellow Border bard) on the part of Scott. It is more than likely that True Thomas was the first Scottish poet intelligible as such.

In order to understand more completely the story of the Rhymer and some of the reasons for his great fame, this narrative needs to rewind. Some time between 1068 and 1070 a man called Gospatrick emerged from the shadows to take a significant place in the historical record. He was a refugee from the extension of Norman power to Northumbria by William the Bastard, and indeed, is sometimes recorded as having been Earl of Northumbria. Malcolm III macAlpin, known as Ceann Mor, welcomed Gospatrick and gave him not only political asylum but also the royal shire of Dunbar to run. He was the great grandson of Malcom II, the victor of Carham, and therefore a distant relative of Ceann Mor. In order to function efficiently as a leader and organiser of men in his new charge at Dunbar, Gospatrick probably spoke at least three languages; Welsh, Gaelic and English. This was not uncommon in the Middle Ages but it is something which sits uncomfortably alongside our modern, monotonous adherence to monoglot English. At all events here is a man with a Welsh name depending on the favour of a Gaelic king and set in authority over a shire, an Anglian version of a Celtic structure imported into Scotland. A living distillate of some of the key ingredients of 11th century Scottishness. Gradually Gospatrick's shire became the earldom of Dunbar and March and his descendents became great landowners in the Lothians and the Borders. And they kept the name Gospatrick or Patrick. With one exception the first 8 earls of Dunbar all had that Christian name. It comes from the Welsh 'Gwas Padraig' or 'the Servant of Patrick'.

The Dunbars maintained a household appropriate to their great rank with all of the servants, aides and bodyguards still familiar to us through the archaic titles surrounding the present royal family. But there was one man whose role has been forgotten and whose contemporary importance was unmistakable. At the coronation of Alexander III, a man stood forward and in Gaelic he recited the young prince's genealogy in reverse order. He began 'Alasdair mac Alasdair mac Uilleam' and went right back into the mists of 5th century Dalriada and Fergus macErc. The point of this was not merely to impress, it was also to legitimise Alexander III as the rightful heir by his illustrious descent. This was important because Alexander was the first king to succeed peacefully and without challenge to the throne of Scotland by the right of primogeniture and not the principles of Celtic inheritance whereby the offspring of a common grandfather all had an equal right. And the self-consciously Gaelic atmosphere wreathed around the outdoor coronation at Scone was incidentally intended to mark out the event as distinctively Scottish rather anything resembling the accession of another Norman-French king.

The reciter of Alexander III's genealogy had a Gaelic title. He was a Seannachie, and each noble household in 13th century Scotland had one too since they paid at least as much attention to their legitimate inherited rights as the heirs to the kingship did. In the old Welsh-influenced south of Scotland, the Gaelic seannachies more resembled Welsh bards, and from Wales there is substantial evidence of their role. A common framework of stories, genealogies, beliefs and aspirations was understood and shared by the bards of powerful men. They were skilled poets and often musicians who underwent a long training and sometimes formed minor dynasties of their own as skills were passed on from father to son, and they could be men of property or even lesser nobility in their own right. The bards knew by heart a mass of stories and lore and their duties included the composition and performance of eulogies and elegies for their patrons, as well as much else in a less sonorous vein. Some of them were also mystics and renowned for their gifts of prophecy.

Now, this is something we sceptically misunderstand and tend to trivialise, but these seers or prophets were not medieval versions of newspaper horoscopes or the Gypsy Lady who sets up her caravan on St Boswells Green every fair week in the summer. Prophecy was the stuff of politics for more than 2 millenia and it reflected a particular mindset which greatly influenced events. Here are two relatively late examples of how this worked in practice.

The great Welsh hero, Owain Glyn Dwr, lived in an atmosphere of mysticism. In Henry IV Part One, Shakespeare understood this when he has Owen Glendower say, "I am not in the role of common men, I can call spirits from the vasty deep". In the years before he rose in rebellion against the English in 1400, itinerant bards sang that Owain was 'Y Mab Darogan', the Son of Prophecy. It was widely believed that after 800 years of oppression, the Welsh would throw back the English and could be kings in London again. Kept alive by the bards and their prophesies, this was a real aspiration for which ordinary people were ready to fight and die. The Welsh never forgot that their language was spoken over the whole island of Britain and throughout the Middle Ages they never lost faith that it would be again. Owain Glyn Dwr went everywhere with his bard and prophet, a fascinating man known as Crach Y Ffinant. He foretold that his master would die fighting under a black flag in Carmarthen, and as a direct result, Owain never campaigned there personally.

Crach Y Ffinant visited the Borders with Owain Gyn Dwr in 1385, and although he was only there on military business, the bard and his lord knew that they were in the Old North, Yr Hen Ogledd, the ancient homeland. But neither of them will have heard a word of native Welsh spoken. The language had died but its greatest prophet lived on in the disguised and widespread transmission of all that he had said and foretold, but no-one guessed what he really was. True Thomas Rhymer of Ercildoune was a bard smack in the middle of the rich Welsh language tradition of prophecy, but he has remained unrecognised as such because he spoke and wrote in English. Thomas was household bard to the Celtic/English Earls of Dunbar who acquired land in Earlston and built a castle there at the east end of the village. And, crucially, Earlston lay at the eastern edge of the quadrant of hills between the Leader and Gala Water valleys, the last heartland of Welsh speakers in the Borders. Towards the end of the 13th century older men and women may still have spoken 'Yr Iaith Hen', the Old Language. At the western end of Earlston, by the River Leader, Thomas owned property, perhaps even a small tower house that predated the ruin now on the site known as the Rhymer's Tower. Having become minor gentry, it may be that Thomas was one of a long line of hereditary bards who had served the house of Gospatrick since the 11th century and possibly before. His family was certainly important enough to witness documents associated with Dryburgh Abbey and wealthy enough to give lands in Earlston to the Trinitarian Hospital at Soutra in the 1290s. Thomas Rhymer — and that was almost certainly his surname since it was also his job, like Miller, or Baxter, or Turner — lived at a time of seismic change when the Wars of Independence ravaged the Border country for generations. And his prediction of the death of Alexander III thrust his skills and gifts into the centre of Scottish politics.

All of this background sets the famous ballad of Thomas the Rhymer in something of a different light. Certainly composed long after his death, some time around 1400, it sought to add to his tradition and reputation rather than offer a treatment of anything original. But it does clearly show the last glimmers of the evening of Welsh language culture in the Borders. Here are the first 5 verses;

> True Thomas lay on Huntlie bank;
> A ferlie he spied wi' his e'e;
> And there he saw a lady bright
> Come riding down by the Eildon Tree
>
> Her skirt was o' the grass-green silk
> Her mantle o' the velvet fine;
> At ilka tett o' her horse's mane,
> Hung fifty siller bells and nine.
>
> True Thomas he pu'd off his cap
> And louted low down on his knee
> 'Hail to thee Mary, Queen of Heaven!
> For thy peer on earth could never be.'
>
> 'O no, O no, Thomas' she said,
> 'That name does not belong to me;
> I'm but the Queen o' fair Elfland,
> That am hither come to visit thee.
>
> 'Harp and carp, Thomas' she said,
> 'Harp and carp along wi' me;
> And if ye dare to kiss my lips,
> Sure of your bodie I will be'

When the Queen found him, and it seems as though she was out looking for him, Thomas was lying on the flanks of the magic mountain of the Border Celts, on Huntly Bank by the Eildon Tree on Eildon Hill, a place where the barriers between the corporeal world and the Otherworld were blurred. Elfland is a sticky, sweet substitution for the altogether darker idea of eternity understood by the Celts. 'Harp and carp' says the beautiful Queen of Air and Darkness. 'Play and recite' she asks him. Do your job as a bard. And then, just as happened on Eildon Hill not so very long before Thomas lived, but much watered down in this version of the ballad, he found himself invited to kiss the lips and enjoy the body of a woman he did not know. Played down in all the versions printed since the prim sensibilities of Walter Scott first got hold of it, the sexual nature of the story bubbles just below the surface. And finally, Thomas is given a gift of prophecy by the beautiful Queen, and since it was a key function of an ancient Celtic priesthood to mediate between the gods and human beings, this transaction is absolutely consistent with a view of Thomas as a Celtic bard.

Back in the world of politics and power, the Earls of Dunbar and March were busy marrying well. Thomas Rhymer's patron, Earl Patrick, married Cecily Fraser who brought with her a dowry of lands in Inverness, and his son, also Patrick, married Marjorie Comyn who added lands in Aberdeenshire to the burgeoning Dunbar patrimony. But the most judicious union was his grandson's with the famous Black Agnes, daughter of Bruce's great commander, Thomas Randolph, Earl of Moray. Like father, like daughter and in 1339 Black Agnes commanded the defence of Dunbar Castle against the English. When her brother died without issue, she inherited the huge estates of Moray and Buchan and they subsequently passed into the control of the Dunbars who became one of the greatest landowning families in Scotland.

The spread of Dunbar power to the Highlands and the Moray coast and the nature of the uncertain times allowed the parallel spread of the prophecies of their servant Thomas Rhymer. And with extraordinary results. Over a period of four centuries, the man the Gaels called Tomas Reumhair became in essence a Celtic Messiah who would deliver them from servitude and reestablish the Gaelic hegemony over Scotland and even all Britain. Thomas exchanged the role of the prophet for that of Redeemer, and like Owain Glyn Dwr he was expected to lead the Celts back to their former glories. Bards used Tomas Reumhair's prophesies to support Montrose's campaigns in 1647, in 1715 Sileas na Ceapaich recited to the Jacobite clansmen "Thomas says in his prophecy that it's the Gaels who will win the victory!" and in 1745 Prince Charles' army was known as 'the Rhymer's children'. This messianic role is a direct borrowing from the Welsh language traditions which Thomas caught the end of in the late 13th century, but which was still clearly recognised and a part of political thought in lowland Scotland in the early 14th and in the Highlands as late as the mid 18th.

Very gradually Thomas' prophesies fell out of currency and now most people only know him through the Ballad of Thomas the Rhymer. This has been sweetened up and watered down to such an extent that the insipid faerie-land it inhabits seems like an invention of Beatrix Potter rather than something which had the power to cross a ghost-fence, materialise in the 'shapeless air' or pull a man through a crack in time. And Thomas himself, as a figure in the historical landscape, has been largely forgotten, and his importance misunderstood or trivialised.

The longer term political impact of the event he predicted in 1286, the accidental death of the 45 year-old Alexander III, did not become immediately apparent. Even though both of his sons had died, David in 1281 and Alexander in 1283, the king had moved quickly to designate his infant grandaughter as his heir. The Maid of Norway was the child of King Erik II and Alexander's daughter, Margaret. At the age of three, on the death of her grandfather, she became Queen Margaret of Scotland.

What became known as the Community of the Realm, the barons, the great churchmen and the burgesses, quickly accepted the succession of a little girl none of them had ever seen. There was no longer even a conduit through whom sympathetic communication might easily be effected since the Maid's mother, Margaret, had died giving birth to the child. She was a little Norwegian princess who could have no idea of the state to which fate had brought her.

Nevertheless, the Community of the Realm acted with confidence and despatch. To counter the very real threat of an attempt on the throne from Robert Bruce, Lord of Annandale and grandson of William the Lion's brother, Earl David of Huntingdon, six Guardians were appointed. Two earls, two bishops and two powerful lesser barons represented not only a cross-section of the ruling elite but also both the north and south of Scotland. Duncan, Earl of Fife, William Fraser, Bishop of St Andrews and Alexander Comyn, Earl of Buchan could control the area north of the Forth while in the south Robert Wishart, Bishop of Glasgow, James the Steward and John Comyn of Badenoch were powerful enough to follow their directions with force if need be.

In the name of the Community of the Realm the Guardians embarked on government; new ecclesiastical and judicial appointments were made, arrangements for defence undertaken and relations with other countries cultivated. At the tender age of only three the Maid was much too young to travel to Scotland and undergo the solemn rituals of coronation. She would have had no idea what was going on. It was sensibly decided to wait until Queen Margaret was a little older and more robust.

In the Border countryside these concerns were far from the minds of ordinary people. Certainly they knew that the king had died and that True Thomas of Earlston had prophesied it, but the high politics of the succession, the dangerous ambitions of the Bruces and the government of the Guardians barely touched them. Their lives beat out the steady rhythm of the seasons. They hoped that the Maid would come safely over the sea, but they hoped for a good harvest even more, and a mild winter as well. What none of them could know, except perhaps Thomas Rhymer, was that between 1286 and 1296 they were living in a high summer of peace and productivity, the closing years of a golden age begun by David I when he brought his French monks to Selkirk in 1113.

The high summer of the late 13th century is no mere metaphor. Between 1100 and 1300 the weather was significantly warmer than it is now. Meteorologists call the period 'the medieval climatic optimum' and by contrast the 500 years after the end of the 13th century gets the name 'The Little Ice Age'. Forensic evidence such as tree-ring measurements (often from timbers used for the construction of medieval buildings), and the analysis of cores taken from glaciers and from lake and ocean sediments show that average temperatures were at least 2 degrees centigrade higher than today's and that rainfall was sufficiently consistent to allow productive growing seasons. Summers were longer and warmer, and, given what can be gleaned from sparse evidence, harvests reasonably reliable. Good weather was very important to an overwhelmingly agricultural society in all sorts of ways. For example, if two or even three cuts of hay were available in the low-lying areas, and at the same time upland pasture good enough to provide five or six months of grazing, then many animals could have been sustained by medieval Border farmers — certainly enough to create the large surpluses that trafficked through the wool and hide trading towns of Roxburgh and Berwick. And a plentiful supply of hay meant that, contrary to the conventional wisdom, the onset of winter did not see a widespread cull of animals.

Specific documentary and archaeological evidence for the longer medieval summers in the Borders is hard to come by. Only extreme weather such as floods or storms merited the notice of the chronicler at Melrose, and there can have been very limited appreciation of progessive trends. However, in the Lammermuir and Cheviot Hills the folds and shadows of cultivation terraces and runrig fields can still be seen. Created in the 12th and 13th centuries and apparently abandoned after 1300, they were used to grow crops of cereals, mainly oats. Some of these fields are found at altitudes of 1200 feet — places where modern crops would simply fail to ripen. Another, more ephemeral, fragment supports the notion of longer and warmer growing seasons. The Gaelic word for the month of February literally translates as 'The First Month of Spring'. In the 12th and 13th centuries perhaps it was.

THE LITTLE ICE AGE

The sustained deterioration in the weather between 1300 and 1850 may not have been a single episode. Cold and wet summers, particularly in 1315 and 1316, were a feature of the 14th century, but not a consistent one in the 15th. Nevertheless conditions were bad enough to force the abandonment of the Norse colony on Greenland which had been established during the medieval climatic optimum. Glacier measurements in the Alps show significant surges of bad summers and cold winters in the 1590s, 1690s and 1810s. During William Shakespeare's time ice fairs on the frozen Thames were common.

Air bubbles trapped in ice have much to tell about the historical atmosphere since stratification allows them to be dated with some precision. Dust content is a guide to weather turbulence and high acidity can point to an intense period of volcanic activity.

One of the more persuasive modern explanations of the wide variety of climate pattern is the process known as 'weather-blocking'. The temperate areas of the Earth, like Britain, have changeable weather because the upper-air streams prevailing from the west bring Atlantic systems. These are influenced by both northerly and southerly patterns, depending on the season of the year. Sometimes the flow of the upper-air streams becomes blocked by masses of cold or warm air and pressure systems become trapped and stay over one land-mass for long periods, causing harsh winters or heat waves.

One speculative consequence of the sustained improvement in the weather might have been the relatively bloodless introduction of the Norman-French families brought to the Borders by David I. Better climate allowed more widespread cultivation, and if more land was available, then pressure on it might have been less intense. Balanced against that notion are hints of upland clearances of hill farmers — particularly in the disputes contested so vigorously by the monks of Melrose Abbey. To make way for large-scale grazing grounds people may have been cleared off their land in the same way as Highland crofters suffered in the 19th century.

Six month summers not only pushed farming to upland limits in the Lammermuirs and Cheviots, it also increased the population. From 1100 to 1300 it may have doubled to a figure of 1 million for the whole of Scotland. However, given the scarcity of the evidence, these statistics represent little more than informed guesswork, and they often work back from later data. In 1755, before the agricultural and industrial revolutions changed Scotland from an overwhelmingly rural to an overwhelmingly urban country, 5.6% of the total population lived in the eastern Border counties. If these percentages were broadly applicable in 1300 and they are divided into the medieval population figure of 1 million, the following breakdowns are possible. Roxburghshire was the most populous county with 2.7% or 27,000 people, then Berwickshire (excluding Berwick, which was English by 1755) with 1.9% or 19,000. Selkirkshire was the least settled county in the whole of Scotland with only 0.3% or 3,000 inhabitants, while in Peeblesshire 0.7% repesented 7,000. That adds up to an overall total of 56,000.

Even though they are only approximations, these numbers are central to the process of piecing together a picture of life in the Borders at the end of the 13th century. 90% of the population lived on the land in 1300 (and in 1755) and the average density per square mile was 35. Allowing for the anomaly of Berwick and the effect of the Ettrick Forest in depressing Selkirkshire to such low levels, it looks as though the rural landscape was a busy one. In more intensively farmed arable areas of the lower Tweed Basin the density might have been as high as 50. Compared with the modern countryside, medieval farms teemed with human activity. But even with the press of all these people the Borders was quiet and green seven centuries ago. The loudest artificial sound was the peal of the abbey bells ringing the canonical hours. No other mechanical noise could be regularly heard and the air was filled not with the whine and thrum of engines but the with the distant bleat of ewes on a hillside and the cry of whaups wheeling in the updraughts. And given the number of people who worked the fields, there would often have been the chance of a blether, a laugh, the exchange of news, the telling of old stories. And at night, under the moon and stars the brightest light came from an open fire or a torch, or candle. When there was no moon or the cloud cover was thick, the countryside was black-dark, and no-one ventured outside willingly. Looking back to that time, the intensity and body-warmth of early medieval Border society must have been palpable.

In towns people lived even more cheek-by-jowl, but the scale of these settlements was small. If 10% of the population of Roxburghshire lived in towns then that leaves only 2,700 inhabitants between Roxburgh, Jedburgh and Melrose, to say nothing of other, lesser places like Kelso and Hawick. The largest town was certainly Roxburgh but a sensible allowance for other places leaves a population in the town of approximately 1,500 and 200 to 300 houses at the very most. Berwick is more problematic. The 1755 figures omit any mention of the burgh and the only useful statistic seems highly inflated. When Edward I beseiged Berwick in 1296 chroniclers agree that his army slaughtered about 7,000 people, mainly men. Now, farmers and others from the surrounding countryside will have undoubtedly sought refuge in the town as the English advanced along the north bank of the Tweed. If the chroniclers' figure is reliable — and there seems to be general agreement — and equivalent numbers of women and children can be added to the total that makes at least 28,000 — clearly an impossibility in the context of other calculations. That high figure represents the entire 19,000 population of Berwickshire and 9,000 citizens of Berwick. What seems a reasonable estimate, based on English examples, is a more modest resident population of between 4,000 and 5,000. Berwick was certainly bigger than Roxburgh, and if the volume of trade suggested by comparative customs figures is correct at a quarter of all business done through English ports, then a very substantial town is clearly implied.

MUNICIPAL SIN

In addition to the expulsion of dangerous or noxious trades, Scottish towns also kicked brothels out beyond the walls. Perhaps it was thought that passion would set the thatch aflame. In France and Germany these premises were known as 'womens' quarters'. Compelled to contribute to tax income in some euphemised fashion, and to wear a distinguishing badge, a ribbon, bonnet or cloak, prostitutes were licensed in the 12th and 13th century towns.

When crusaders returned from the Near East, having experienced the pleasures of bathing in brothels, they began to demand something similar in Britain. A bath with a prostitute became known as a 'stew' and by 1100 several had been set up outside London's walls. As a busy port Berwick will have made similar arrangements for stews, and probably Roxburgh did too.

Prostitutes always followed large armies and these women, sometimes called 'strollers' were an accepted fact of military life and provision was made for them. As both Scots and English armies crossed and recrossed the Borders, these professional women trailed behind.

Aside from burgesses, the two other constituents of the Community of the Realm bear some statistical examination. In later medieval Scotland there were fewer than 4,000 men and women in holy orders. Allowing for some decline and the particular concentration of great monastic houses in the Borders, estimates suggests that 500 monks, nuns, canons, priests and friars were supported by the local economy. The deposit of all those rents, services and gifts are of course the great churches themselves. Not even large castles like Roxburgh and Norham could compare with the scale and splendour of Kelso, Melrose, Dryburgh and Jedburgh abbeys. Not only were they by far the largest buildings in the landscape, they also enclosed interior spaces which soared above and amazed those who entered the church for the first time. To ordinary people God's glory was not a theological abstract but the reason why these awesome buildings rose up to touch the heavens.

Estimates of the size of the final and most powerful estate of the Community of the Realm are also worth examination. Noble families made up 1% of the population of late medieval Scotland and in the Borders that meant nearly 600 more people who did not till the soil or tend flocks, but rather enjoyed the fruits of the land through the exercise of ownership, the management of property and the presence of military power behind it. The number of households is difficult to know but if an average family of 5 or 6 is assumed then around 100 castles, towers, houses and halls could be found in the eastern counties.

What can be said about the people who supported all of this arithmetic, the farmers who supplied the burgesses in their towns, prayed in the parish kirks of the great abbeys and paid their rents to the lairds? Between 1290 and 1300 when it decided to reorganise the administration of its vast estates, Kelso Abbey and its scriptorium provides some answers. The Rent Roll of the properties and their tenants is a lengthy document and it offers a sustained picture of the rural lives of ordinary people at the close of the 13th century. Perhaps as a consequence of the mercantile workings of the wool trade the Abbot and Chapter of Kelso appeared to want the substitution of cash rents for those traditionally paid in labour services. In the Rent Roll approximately half of their 3,000 acres of arable land was granted to tenants who paid annual sums of cash and amounts of produce.

Rural settlements seem to have taken the form of townships, somewhat in the way modern crofting communities in the Highlands and Islands are organised where houses string out along a common track with plenty of space between each one. In the Borders, townships got the later name of 'fermtouns'. A 'ferm' or 'firma' was a cash payment made by a 'fermour' or 'firmarius' for the lease of a piece of land over a longer period than the usual yearly rental. Tenure might be granted by Kelso Abbey for three to five years, or even in some cases as a liferent which could become heritable.

The fermtouns came together for a simple purpose — to supply the resources for a plough team. In the Middle Ages 8 oxen were usually needed to pull the heavy wooden plough through the earth and the farmers living in a fermtoun combined to provide them. Tidy formulae offer the sense of a structure whereby a husbandman cultivated two oxgangs and was therefore bound to provide two oxen for the team needed to plough a ploughgate. And a ploughgate, or 120 English acres or 104 Scots acres, was the amount of arable land that could be managed by one plough team and therefore produce enough food for one fermtoun. In reality there was wide variety. Some soils were light enough to be worked by 6-oxen ploughs, other husbandmen were wealthy enough to own a whole team, and so on. Generally fermtouns and the land immediately around them were enclosed to keep beasts out when crops were growing and their muck was not needed. Houses resembled those in towns and the longhouses excavated at Springwood Park near Kelso were likely typical. In Scotland the infields were called either the 'inbye' or the 'crofts', and they were cultivated much in the same way as domestic gardens are nowadays, without rest and refreshed by mucking or fertiliser of some other sort.

Because all agricultural work was done by hand with the aid of draught animals, the system of runrig developed. Rigs, or ridge-and-furrow in England, could be very long but, on average, were 18 to 36 feet wide and separated by ditches on either side. The fall of the ground could be considerable with the crown sometimes 3 feet higher than the ditch. Particular patterns of ploughing created the rigs and the great strength of the ox-teams made it possible to maintain them year after year. The furrow-slice was always turned towards the crown and when a furrow or 'fur' had been ploughed, the team were turned to work in the opposite direction and turn the earth to meet what had already been done.

In the Borders rigs were always ploughed with the grain of the land to ensure good drainage. On a sloping field the ditches ran down to the lowest point where water naturally collected. By contrast, in the south of England, ploughing was directed across the slope to catch and hold the lighter rainfall. Before the mass drainage programmes of the 19th century, soil could be very heavy and when it was dry, the old Scotch plough created a great deal of friction when it turned the slice. Ox-teams of eight were yoked two by two in line ahead and when the leading pair reached the bottom of a rig, they began to turn in a wide arc before the plough was out of the furrow. This action explains the characteristic s-shape of the medieval rigs occasionally visible in the Borders.

Once ploughing and mucking was done and the furrow-slices had dried and tilthed a little (a dry breeze is considered the best sort of weather), the rigs were harrowed in preparation for sowing. Oats, bere (a four-row barley) and some wheat were planted. At 18 to 36 feet the width of the rigs is well adapted for the hand-broadcasting of seedcorn. And also, three hopeful months later, for harvesting. Depending on the size of the rig 3 to 4 shearers could work line abreast. In what must have been back-breaking work they cut the ripened corn with toothed sickles called 'heuks' in the Borders. The medieval method of harvesting was still current in the 16th century and it involved grasping a handful of stalks and cutting in a sawing motion towards the shearer's body. Contrary to popular imagination scythes were not used to harvest corn but to cut hay, and the reason for that was economy. The swinging motion of the large blade of a scythe could knock precious ears of corn in all directions whereas the careful use of a heuk wasted little. Behind a line of shearers the bandster worked. Using twists of corn stalks, he laid down bands on the stubble ground where cut sheaves could be laid on top. When each was filled he tied the stooks together and set them upright. Sometimes a good bandster could work two adjacent rigs.

When the exhausted shearers finally reached the bottom of the last rig, they paused to acknowledge the final few sheaves. Everyone gathered round and drinks were often taken to celebrate what is called in English 'Harvest Home' and in the Borders 'Hairst Hame'. The last stalks were woven into corn dollies and set up in a barn or wherever the harvest celebration proper was to take place. Incidentally corn 'dolly' has nothing to do with childrens' toys, it comes from 'idol' and must represent a distant memory of a Celtic past.

The corn was dried for milling in kilns built in most townships but for the poorer sort of people ancient methods had still to suffice. 'Graddaning' involved the delicate business of burning the chaff off the grains. Always done by women working in pairs it meant setting fire to a handful of oats and watching carefully to see when the chaff was burned off before tamping it out on the ground. The other woman raked the ears to check if they had indeed lost their chaff and had not been badly charred. When sufficient had been burned, the grain was put into a large wooden tub and gently trodden on to complete the process before being finally winnowed on a threshing floor. Some longhouses had a floor built into them with two doors forenent so that a breeze could whistle through and carry off the chaff.

The Kelso Abbey Rent Roll of 1290 to 1300 has much to say about the working of arable land and comparatively less notice is taken of pasture. This is surprising because Kelso's sheep flock was large at 7,000 to 8,000 head. Many hirsels were hefted to the hills around the Bowmont Valley, the ancient Anglian Yetholmshire, where rows of medieval cultivation rigs can still be seen, particularly in the evenings when the sun slants low enough to throw shadows. Kelso's large arable holdings no doubt supplied the needs of the monks more than adequately, and the substantial surplus was sold at Roxburgh and Kelso's markets, as well as at other outlets closer to their widely scattered estates. Given the amount of upland tillage, there is more than a suggestion in the Kelso records that cultivation may have been close to its limits, and a further rise in population insupportable without technological change.

Wool and hides were very attractive products to the monks because they represented a cash crop. By 1300 Melrose was maintaining a huge flock of 12,000 head and the Cistercians in Scotland had 20% of the total wool clip, much of it of the highest quality. So that they could plan the exploitation of this great resource, the monks at Melrose began selling futures. Exactly as commodity brokers in London and New York do now, they sold their wool clips at fixed prices before the shearers began their work. Often the Cistercians entered into long-term contracts with Flemish and other European merchants which could mean a lower price per woolpack but represented a guaranteed income over several years. Occasionally, in bad times when the clip was sparse, Melrose went into the wool market as a buyer, anxious for the fleeces of other producers to make up their contracted volume for the export trade.

SPINNING AND WEAVING

When Border woolpacks arrived in Flanders from Berwick they entered a production line. In the quayside warehouses women first sorted the fleeces into different grades, paying special attention to their origin, and men removed the more obvious bits of muck. The wool was then put out to home-based workers who washed, carded and spun it into yarn. Women always did the preparatory work and this habit gave rise to words and phrases like 'the distaff side' and 'spinster'. What accelerated the demand for Border wool dramatically was the introduction of the spinning wheel in the 13th century. Probably originating in China, its use created an even more industrial process. Before being given to the weavers the yarn was sized with melted fat or butter.

Pairs of men worked the looms, throwing the shuttle from one to another and alternately pressing down the pedals to push the weft into place. Cloth then went to be fulled in troughs of alkaline earth, hot water and urine. The next stage was washing (or 'waulking' in Scotland — the origin of the place-name Walkerburn) and this was done by groups of men trampling in large tubs.

After it was dyed, the cloth was stretched on tenterhooks, then teazled with thistles to raise the nap, and finally trimmed with shears. Only then was it ready for sale — at a value as much as twenty times what the monks of Melrose or Kelso were paid.

Such was the demand for pasture that Alexander II was forced to disafforest his royal hunting grounds of Gala Water and Lauderdale so that the hills could be given over to sheep rather than game. And the commercial pressures from European cloth producers drove Melrose into several bitter disputes over grazing rights which had the effect of cutting into an ancient journey. Known as transhumance it involved the driving of flocks and herds from lowland fields up to higher pasture for the summer. Since, literally, a time out of mind, communities had divided, and young men herded their flocks from what in the Highlands is still called 'the winter-town' up to the shielings of 'the spring-town' in the hills and moorland. Many of the upland cultivation rigs were ploughed and planted by herd-laddies who stayed with their beasts long enough to harvest the oats and other crops. Not fenced or dyked in any way, the summer grazings were held in common right — as they still are at Selkirk and other Border burghs. The spring-towns were known as shielings in the south of Scotland and the frequent presence of 'shiel' or 'shiels' in place-names remembers where some of them were. Galashiels is only the most famous.

Even though the herds had to be constantly wary, for wolf packs still hunted in the hills — Weststruther in Berwickshire means 'Wolf's stream' — there is a striking sense that the atmosphere around life at the shielings was different, less serious than in the winter-town. Living their lives outdoors, in the long and warm summer evenings, young people amused themselves with stories and music and echoes of the crack and laughter have come down to us in the shape of the Border Ballads. What has survived is a later rendition of the bardic traditions of Thomas Rhymer and others whose names are now lost to us. At the shielings something close to the ballads was sung or recited. Perhaps because it does not concern battles or cattle-raiders, or deeds of derring-do, the old song 'The Dowie Dens of Yarrow' carries some sense of the romance of the long evenings in the spring-towns of the Border hills. Here are some of the verses;

"At Dryhope lived a lady fair,
The fairest flower in Yarrow,
And she refused nine noble men
For a servan' lad in Gala.

Her father said that he should fight
The nine lords all tomorrow,
And that he that should the victor be
Would get the Rose of Yarrow."

The servant-lad was killed and his body flung into the Yarrow Water.
His lover rode the hills looking for him;

"But she wandered east, so did she wast,
And searched the forest thorough,
Until she spied her ain true love,
Lyin' deeply drowned in Yarrow"

She pulled him from the water and took his body back to Dryhope. Her
father was not sympathetic and assured her that she would wed well;

"Haud your ain tongue, my faither dear,
I canna help my sorrow;
A fairer flower ne'er sprang in May
Than I hae lost in Yarrow.

I meant to make my bed fu' wide,
But you may make it narrow,
For now I've nane to be my guide
But a deid man drowned in Yarrow.

And aye she screighed, and cried, Alas!
Till her heart did break wi' sorrow,
And sank into her faither's arms
'Mang the dowie dens o' Yarrow."

The geography of the Borders, with its river valleys and sheltering hills,
is well suited to transhumance. In northern Berwickshire some parish
boundaries include low-lying arable lands before looping up into the
Lammermuirs to take in summer pasture. The annual journey from the
winter-town could be long if a fermtoun was distant from its upland
common and much gear had to be taken. Pack transport in the Middle
Ages was mostly human with back-panniers made from willow withies,
or even woven grass for cargoes such as grain. Ropes of spruce roots,
twisted grasses or heather sat across the upper chest and secured
panniers carried on the back. This was technology entirely unchanged
from the time of the Hunter-Gatherers. Ponies were sometimes used to
take heavier items slung across a wooden pack-saddle and the oxen
needed to plough the high fields worked hard to pull sledges or solid-
wheeled carts called ox-wains.

After lambing the sheep were also driven up to the hill pastures to
allow hay to grow on the lowland fields. Herds built low, turf-dyked
enclosures for ewe-milking. These were the 'yowe-milkin' buchts' and
they were used by young lasses who had walked up from the winter-
town. Sheep's cheese was made from the rich and pungent milk, and

no doubt before they made their way back in the light evenings, there was much 'laughin' and daffin'' between the herds and the ewe-milkers.

Back in the winter-town those left behind kept the birds off the growing crops and made sure the milk cow's tether was fast in the ground. They spent time re-water and windproofing their houses. The 'Redd' or the 'redding up', as Borders dialect calls spring-cleaning, still goes on in many farms after the beasts are turned out for the summer. At harvest time some of the herds returned to the lowlands to make sure that all the corn was safely in, but August was too early to bring the flocks down off the hills, and after the corn-dollies were made, they went back up-country.

The Kelso Rent Roll records few personal names but elsewhere in the documents the identity of farmers and herds can occasionally be found. In 1280 Andrew Fraser from the Berwickshire village of Gordon gave the following to the abbey;

"three acres of pasture in the lordship of Gordon, with [i.e. including] Adam, son of Henry del Hoga, my neyf and all his issue. And with pasture in the same lordship for 400 sheep and all their issue."

Adam and Henry del Hoga were not slaves but unfree men, that is, farmers bound to the land they cultivated and obliged to render goods and services to their feudal superior — be it Andrew Fraser or the Abbot of Kelso. In the Middle Ages country people fell into three broad groups; the free tenants, like Fraser, dependent peasants like the del Hogas, and a class of landless cottars who sold their labour for cash or food, or both. The only overall term for a peasant used in the Kelso documents is 'nativus' or 'neyf', the origin of the slang word 'nyaff'.

By 1290 the Maid of Norway was seven years old, and it was thought a good time to bring the lass over to her kingdom of Scotland for the coronation. At Birgham, a village on the north side of the Tweed, about halfway between Kelso and Coldstream, Scottish barons met with English envoys to discuss a dynastic marriage. Edward I of England unquestionably coveted Scotland, but his resources had been severely stretched by his thorough defeat and conquest of the Welsh in the 1280s. With vast loans from the Italian bankers of Lucca, some of them secured on the English wool clip, huge English armies had taken the field, and squadrons of sappers, masons and woodcutters had followed them to colonise Wales. Castles were raised at Conwy, Beaumaris, Caernarfon and elsewhere, and walled bastide towns attached to them. Edward had won Wales, but at a tremendous price — a price he could not afford to pay for Scotland. Dynastic marriage between the Maid of Norway and his heir, Edward of Caernarfon, was cheaper, neater and would have proved just as effective.

At Birgham a nervous treaty was made. The Scots insisted on all sorts of clauses and forms of words designed to protect their independence, but they were nullified by the catch-all English qualification;

"Saving the right of our said lord [Edward I] and of any other whomsoever, which has pertained to him, or to any other, on the marches, or elsewhere, over these things in question before the time of the present agreement, or which in any right way ought to pertain in future".

In other, simpler, words, Edward would have his way whatever the Scots thought they had insisted upon and safeguarded. To the Melrose chronicler matters looked ominous, and he cast his gaze south to colonised Wales 'under the yoke of the English'. Anthony Bek, the Prince-Bishop of Durham, was appointed to act as 'lieutenant' in Scotland on behalf of the Maid and Edward of Caernarfon, but in reality, and the Scottish magnates greatly resented this, he was the English king's agent. The surrender of Roxburgh and Berwick castles, and certain others, was demanded, but the Scots managed to persuade Edward to wait until the Maid arrived in Scotland.

She never came. The little girl died in Orkney, at that time still Norwegian territory under the control of her father. By October 1290 rumours of the Maid's death were circulating in the south and powerful factions began to stir. Jean de Bailleul was a Norman-French magnate with substantial lands in France, England and, by relatively recent marriage, in Scotland. Although better known to history as John Baliol, he almost certainly never knew himself as that, using the French version of his name in documents. He acted quickly and gave, as a sweetener, to Anthony Bek of Durham certain lands in Northumberland belonging to the Scottish crown, signing himself, 'heir of the kingdom of Scotland'. For their part the de Bruces persuaded the Guardians of Scotland that they had no right to make a king. Looking north from London Edward I could see that the game was being played into his hands.

In 1291 English royal clerks were rummaging around chronicles and land documents anxiously searching for legal references to Edward I or any previous king of England as the feudal overlord of Scotland. More practically the king sent cash to Newcastle to buy friends or soldiers, whichever suited the occasion best, and his fleet made ready to blockade Scottish ports. By 2nd June Edward was on the Tweed at Norham Castle. In what was seen as a joint parliament, held in Norham Kirk, the only available building large enough to hold all parties, Edward accepted the Scots' invitation that he should sit as president of a court to decide who ought to be sovereign after the Maid's death. All of the proceedings were, as usual, conducted in French — on both sides. And the attitudes of the Scots delegates must have been coloured by the presence of the English fleet anchored in Berwick Roads and the substantial armed retinues of the 67 English barons who had come to Norham with Edward. The king put it to the Scots and the 'bons gents' they represented that he should be recognised as their legal overlord. They asked for time to consider the question and withdrew. After three weeks' deliberation, the Scots attempted to stall by replying that they

"have no power to reply to your [Edward's] statement, lacking a lord [king] to whom the demand ought to be addressed... for he, and no other, will have power to reply and act in the matter."

Edward's lawyers were ready for the equivocation and they quickly countered that if the Scottish parliament could not answer that basic question, then the claimants for the Scottish crown certainly could — for one amongst them was surely a king.

There is some evidence that Edward's agents encouraged a large number of competitors for the throne of Scotland, and no doubt about what their answer would be to the question of English suzerainty. A 'yes' was unanimous — what possible chance of success did any competitor have if they rejected the claims of the king who would judge which man should take the crown?

When these procedural matters were clarified, Roxburgh, Jedburgh and Berwick castles were surrendered to the English and Edward embarked on a tour of Scotland to receive oaths of fealty. By 2nd August he was in Berwick Castle to hear the claims of the competitors, and particularly those of the most likely, Robert de Bruce and Jean de Bailleul. Arguments in what became known as 'The Great Cause' were complex, and an adjournment was granted to Count Florent V of Holland to discover an obscure document which would prove his claim. It lasted a whole year and the court did not reconvene in Berwick until June 1292. During that period it seems that Edward I's lawyers seriously considered his own claims as a distant descendent of Malcom III Ceann Mor and his English Queen Margaret. By 6th November the court of 104 auditors had decided that Jean de Bailleul should be king of Scotland, and eleven days later Edward I formally confirmed their judgement. The crown of the macMalcolms, a Gaelic-speaking dynasty descended from the Dalriadan Ard-Righrean of the 6th century, had passed to a Norman-French family from Normandy. At the Christmas court in Newcastle the new king knelt to an English king to do homage for Scotland. It was not a dignified settlement but perhaps it would ensure peace.

King Jean reigned for four difficult years. Using feudal argument and legal procedure, Edward repeatedly undermined his authority. The Treaty of Birgham was repudiated and Jean forced to appear before the English court to justify his decisions in Scotland. Because he was given no more respect and place than any of Edward's barons, the Scottish king was put in an impossible position and serious trouble became inevitable. Matters finally came to head in 1294 when the presence of King Jean was demanded at the head of a Scottish army to campaign in France on behalf of his suzerain, the King of England. A year later a council of 12 Scottish magnates took government out of Jean's hands and immediately forced up the political temperature by concluding an alliance with Philip IV of France, the enemy of Edward I. War was a certainty.

In the summer of 1296 the English king once more appeared on the banks of the Tweed. At Wark Castle his captains mustered a tremendous army of 25,000 foot soldiers (including 11,000 Welshmen, many of them expert archers) and 4,000 cavalry, with more than 1000 heavily armoured knights. Reports that their baggage train was strung out for 20 miles along Dere Street cannot have been exaggerated. They were joined by the Prince-Bishop of Durham, Anthony Bek, who supplied another 1000 foot and 500 cavalry. In defence of Jean I's kingdom, the Scots could not hope to put an army of even half that size in the field, and their French allies were too pre-occupied and too remote to help. Nevertheless the

Scots mustered at the ancient hosting-place of Caddonlea, near Galashiels, with the intention not of confronting Edward but launching a flanking raid into Northumberland. Scots soldiers had not fought in a serious campaign for two generations and the avoiding tactics were prudent. The feast of Easter was celebrated by the English court at Wark before preparations began for the fording of the Tweed, just below the Cistercian nunnery at Coldstream. This could be a dangerous crossing but apparently only one soldier was swept away by the current. After a day's march along the king's highway, which had carried woolpacks the year before from Roxburgh market to Berwick's quays, the English vanguard arrived at St Leonard's, another Cistercian nunnery which stood outside the town. Edward used the chapter house as his headquarters to direct the seige of Scotland's largest and most prosperous burgh.

BUCKLERS AND BALDRICKS

Heavy armour was expensive and worn only by medieval knights who could afford it. Perhaps less than 10% of Edward I's army in 1296 would have worn metal armour able to resist a well-aimed blow or arrow. Most men had padded jackets made of boiled leather and studded to keep the padding evenly distributed. Chain mail was expensive, but it did last and some will have been inherited a shirt from their fathers. Other men had only a leather cap to protect them.

Foot soldiers carried a small wooden shield known as a buckler, and properly used it could deflect rather than parry a spear or sword thrust. Knives and swords were slung from a belt called a baldrick.

Made from an inexpensive wooden shaft tipped with a metal point of some kind, which might keep attackers away from unprotected bodies, spears or pikes were popular. A Border variant was the Jethart Stave; it had a single-edged blade shaped like a meat cleaver.

Meanwhile the supporting English fleet had coasted up from Newcastle and lay at anchor once again in Berwick Roads. On the morning of 13th April, in what may have been a tactical feint, the captains of the fleet made ready and on the indrawn tide, sailed into the Tweed estuary to attack the town. The garrison rushed to repel the English marines who attempted to scramble ashore from three ships which had been run aground on the sandbanks known as Calot Shad. Scots chroniclers later claimed that all three were destroyed. However, this was probably nothing more than a sideshow. After publicly knighting Henry Percy and a few other northern noblemen, Edward gave orders for his massive army to charge the defences of Berwick. Evidently these were no more than 'a ditch and a barricade of boards', and some knights simply rode straight over them. The seige took only a few hours, but the sack of the town went on for three days. Seven thousand people were slaughtered — some modern estimates have run as high as 11,000 — including 30 Flemish merchants in their factory, the Red Hall which was described as a 'tower'. A chronicler wrote "blood streamed from the bodies of the slain so copiously that mills could be turned by its flow". A grisly signal flashed through all Scotland — those who resisted the power of

Edward could expect a similar fate, and no mercy. After houses had been ransacked and all possible portable loot removed, the English evacuated the streets, torching the thatched houses as they went. Berwick was burned to the ground, and Edward's strategists made plans for the building of a bastide town like those in North Wales at Conwy and Caernarfon. Following the same model, English colonists were to be brought to settle in Berwick and Berwick would be brought into England. When the town fell, the castle's garrison surrendered and Edward's victory was swift, brutal and complete.

Four weeks after the fall of Berwick the English were at Dunbar beseiging the castle of Thomas Rhymer's master, the Earl of Dunbar and March. As ever the fleet shadowed the advance and lay at anchor in the mouth of Belhaven Bay. A relieving force sent in the name of King Jean was destroyed and Edward pressed on northwards in pursuit of the retreating Scots. At Kincardine Castle, Jean surrendered and was forced, in effect, to resign his throne. In a ceremony normally reserved for treasonable knights, Edward insisted that he be publicly humiliated. At Montrose Jean was dragged into the market place and in front of the assembled English barons, his knightly girdle was removed, his surcoat, blazoned with the royal arms of Scotland, was ripped off, the royal signet ring torn from his finger and his great seal broken in pieces. No doubt to a roar of laughter from his barons, Edward commented, in French, 'a man does good business when he rids himself of a turd'.

Plain Jean was carted off to imprisonment with his son, named Edward — in doubtful taste, in the Tower of London. In 1298 he declared, with some enthusiasm, that he wanted nothing more to do with Scotland or the Scots since he believed them to be both malicious and deceitful. A year later a deal was brokered to allow the transfer of Jean into the custody of the Pope, and soon after he retired to his estates in northern France, at Bailleul, where he died gratefully far from the kingdom he had tried to rule and close to the place he naturally called home.

Edward I based his government of Scotland at Berwick and an exchequeur, or treasury, was set up to gather the fruits and rentals of a defeated nation. Hundreds of prominent Scots had appended their seals to a document pledging fealty to the English king; so many were stuck on that it got the name 'The Ragman Roll'. Since he had not the cash to build new and modern castles as he had in Wales, Edward operated a policy of occupying all of the important existing castles in Scotland. Roxburgh, Jedburgh and Berwick controlled much of the Borders and their garrisons policed what became an English pale for the following twenty years. The effective writ of the Governors of Scotland only extended to the immediate vicinity of most castles north of the Forth and west of Edinburgh, but in the Tweed Basin English control was much more thorough. In a 60 mile radius of Berwick, rents were paid, at least in part, to maintain the occupying forces.

In 1297 William Wallace exploded into history. He led an ever-growing army of disaffected Scots and by July scouts were reporting to the English commanders at Roxburgh and Jedburgh that 'he lay with a great company in the Forest of Selkirk'. After a stunning victory at Stirling Bridge, his supporters proclaimed Wallace as sole 'Guardian of

Scotland' at 'the Forest Kirk', which must mean Old Selkirk Kirk whose shell stands near the hidden remains of Selkirk Castle. The image of elusive, will o' the wisp guerrilla fighters emerging from the greenwood without warning to attack authority was popular at the end of the 13th century, and the modern parallels drawn between Wallace in the Ettrick Forest and Robin of Sherwood are entirely appropriate. Both heroes hid in royal forests and defended the causes of rightful kings. In all his time as Guardian, Wallace was careful to emphasise that he acted in the name of King Jean.

HOODOLOGY

The fear of William Wallace 'lying with a great company in the Ettrick Forest' and the efforts of 14th century English captains to cut down the Jedforest and other Border woods betray a well-developed medieval anxiety about outlaws in the greenwood. The legend of Robin Hood is only the most famous manifestation of this.

Plays and ballads about Robin were in popular currency in the Middle Ages and several early Scottish historians place events in the 13th century Border country. Andrew de Wynton asserts that in 1283;

"Litil Iohun and Robert Hude
Waythmen war commendit gude
In Inglewood and Bernnysdaile
Thai oyssit at this time thar trawale"

Inglewood Forest lies just to the south of Carlisle and, remembering Old Welsh etymology, Bernnysdaile or Barnsdale might refer to the Irthing Valley and the Hexham Gap.

Be that as it may, Sir Walter Scott did much in his novel 'Ivanhoe' to fix the modern complexion of the story. He wrote that it took place during the reign of King Richard I, in the England of the 1190s, and adopts as a theme the tensions between the disinherited Saxon, Ivanhoe, and the Norman, Sir Brian de Bois-Guilbert. Interestingly Scott paints the evil Prince John as speaking only French and having no English, while good King Richard is bilingual. The tale is wrapped up at one of Robin Hood's greenwood fastnesses with Ivanhoe triumphant while Richard I smiles benignly.

The myth of Wallace was powerful. It even survived his catastrophic error in taking on the English in an open set-piece battle at Falkirk in 1298, as well as the historical fact that it was Robert de Bruce who really developed the arts of guerrilla warfare in Scotland at that time. Wallace was an early hero whose fame was celebrated in 14th and 15th century historiography, but the power behind his story was not the elemental cry for 'Freedom!' uttered by Mel Gibson in the film 'Braveheart'. That is largely an anachronism. Support for Wallace, and for his talented ally, Andrew Moray (whose tragic death from wounds suffered at Stirling Bridge proved a genuine turning-point), materialised for 13th century reasons. Edward I had severed the fundamental tenet of feudal society. In return for the rendering of rents in kind, cash and services, feudal inferiors had a right to expect protection from their feudal superior. Instead of providing that, Edward behaved brutally and summarily, ruling Scotland like a tyrant. For these simple reasons fewer and fewer Scots could be persuaded to join the English cause on a sustained basis and, in the end, the conquest won so quickly could not be consolidated.

Nevertheless, Edward I was determined to dominate Scotland and between 1296 and his death in 1307 at Burgh on Sands near Carlisle, he came north with an army every year except three. Even on his deathbed, he wanted to carry on and he begged his son to boil the flesh off his bones so that they could accompany his soldiers up the north road. The effect of this near-constant state of war in the Borders was literally devastating. In the first decades of the 14th century it appears that a sudden deterioration in the weather led to a series of bad harvests. From 1300 to 1315 the combination of wet summers and incessant military activity must have been very destructive, and there was famine by 1316. The words of an anonymous Scots poet looking back on the death of Alexander III and its consequences are eloquent;

"Since Alexander our king was dead
That Scotland left in love and peace,
Away fled abundance of ale and bread,
Of wine and wax, of pleasure and glee.
The gold it was all changed to lead,
The fruit it fails on every tree..."

In 1309 Edward II is recorded authorising 'his burgesses of Roxburgh' to raise a tax so that they could replace the ditch and paling defences of the town with a stone wall. And dated three years later, a series of remarkable documents offers a telling insight into the complexities and dangers of contemporary life in the sheriffdoms of Roxburgh and Berwick. As the power of Robert de Bruce was growing, his agents demanded blackmail in the form of protection payments from landowners in the Borders in return for the usual guarantee not to attack their property. When enough cash was paid to the right people, a truce was obtained and farmers could get on with the business of producing food. The problem with this arrangement was that the English commanders constantly frustrated it by refusing to pay their share of the blackmail. Behind the secure walls of Roxburgh, Jedburgh and Berwick, why should they? And they also compounded the difficulty by hindering estate-owners in the countryside from paying up even when they wanted to. In fact they repeatedly confiscated the cattle and other goods brought to Roxburgh and other markets by known supporters of Robert de Bruce. Reprisals for these violations were greatly feared and no doubt carried out. In London Edward II took a dim view of all of this and, in an astonishing reversal of the expected, he criticised his own garrison commanders for attacking his enemies and making life difficult for English supporters in the Borders. In a surprising manner Edward II showed that he had grasped something which eluded his father. Protection was being offered to Scots in an area which might reasonably expect to remain in English hands. And the feudal contract was thereby being remade. This episode also illustrates directly how difficult life had become for ordinary people after 1296. The fruit was indeed failing on every tree.

Robert de Bruce had also learned lessons from his predecessors. Although it was anachronistic to talk of patriotism, and loyalties in the Borders were a matter of practicality rather than inclination, it became increasingly clear in the years leading up to Bannockburn, in 1314, that the idea of Scotland as a nation was gaining wider currency. The Guardians had derived their authority from the Community of the Realm of Scotland and while that had a very narrow base, it did at least exist as a notion distinct from any community of the realm in England, or anywhere else for that matter. And it widened the method of government from an autocracy to a small oligarchy. Amidst the uncertainties and ruin of the Wars of Independence this sense of collective national identity developed quickly and by 1320 it had found expression in a dramatic and rightly famous document. But in the Declaration of Arbroath the important bit is not the most quoted, but the passage that makes clear that the Community of the Realm of Scotland had not only achieved expression independent of a king, and the fact that it even visualised a time when it could be in conflict with him. If ever King Robert should;

"turn aside from the task that he has begun, and yield Scotland or us to the English king or people, we should cast [him] out as the enemy of us all, as subverter of our rights and of his own, and should choose another king to defend our freedom; for so long as a hundred of us are left alive, we will yield in no least way to English dominion. We fight not for glory, nor for wealth nor honours; but only and alone we fight for freedom, which no good man surrenders but with his life."

This passage has become an icon of nationalism in Scotland. For the Borders it reads like a death sentence. Scotland was hammered into nationhood by the Wars of Independence, but the anvil of its forging was the Border countryside. And the Borders has never recovered from that historical curse. As the line drawn between Berwick in the east and the Solway mouth in the west hardened into a national frontier so the communities on either side suffered as national conflict rumbled across their fields and villages. This was warfare often directed from long distances, and carried on by people with no connections to the place where they fought, looted and burned. One example amongst thousands suffices to underscore the point. In pursuit of a dynastic marriage prompted by the needs of international diplomacy, Henry VIII sent an earl from Hertfordshire north with a force of Spanish gunners in 1545 to blow Kelso Abbey to bits — because it had the great misfortune to lie close to the English border.

On a less sonorous note, myth-history began to foster a sense of differentness. At the battle of Dunbar in 1296 the defenders of the castle shouted at the English that they would cut off their tails. Evidently nothing made a 13th century Englishman more angry than that strange taunt. Abbot Walter Bower, the author of the Scotichronicon, repeats a widely held belief that the English had tails and were blighted with them for showing disrespect to St Augustine and, later, to St Thomas a Becket. The tails were called 'muggles'. Entertaining stories like these achieved the sort of popular currency denied to the Declaration of Arbroath, but in many ways were just as powerful an expression of nationalist sentiment.

Robert de Bruce was careful to recognise the importance of the Community of the Realm and pointedly consulted his barons and leading churchmen frequently on matters of policy. And his skill as a strategist won the extraordinary victory at Bannockburn where, although massively outnumbered, he out-thought the over-confident English barons. However, the battle was only decisive in establishing Bruce on the throne, and despite a popular wish to believe otherwise, it did not bring the Wars of Independence to a close. In 1319 and 1322 Edward II invaded again and wasted the countryside as far north as Leith. A truce was eventually negotiated (and greatly facilitated by Edward's domestic difficulties) and it held until after Robert de Bruce's death in 1328. By that time Roxburgh and Berwick had been recovered and customs statistics show that the port had regained its pre-eminence as the leading exporter of wool. Even after the immense slaughter and burning of 1296 Berwick had rebuilt quickly and under English occupation, the export trade continued to function. A more pressing problem was felt at sea. During periods of hostility between Scotland and England merchant ships bound for Flanders and the Rhine estuary were often the prey of officially sanctioned English pirates. Habitually hugging the English coastline down as far as Dunwich and Yarmouth before striking east across the open sea, the Flemish ships were easy meat. And overland, records of safe-conducts granted to English and Scots merchants wishing to trade in either country show almost total breakdown in the early 14th century. Between 1296 and 1348 only 3 were granted to English applicants and none to Scots. These figures almost certainly disguise a good deal of informal activity, but just how much is impossible to discover.

The upshot of the Wars of Independence and their long aftermath are clear, however, and that was the rupture and the occasional near-total eclipse of the economy of the Border country — what had been the hub of commerce and the intensively cultivated bread-basket of Scotland must, after many summer campaigns when soldiers stole, trampled or burned the harvest, have more resembled a desert. What fates befell ordinary Borderers are not difficult to imagine.

When Robert I died his heir was a four year-old child, David II. Fears of another succession crisis were fed by the ambitions of Edward Balliol, the son and heir of King Jean. With the encouragement of Edward III of England he assembled an expeditionary force drawn from the group known as 'The Disinherited'. These were Scots (and English) noblemen who supported the English or Balliol or both and had been removed from their estates and driven out of Scotland by King Robert de Bruce. Edward promised restitution and also sought it for himself. A fleet of 88 ships sailed north out of the Humber estuary. At Dupplin Moor near Perth, the small expeditionary force defeated a larger and badly led Scots army, and Balliol went on to Scone to claim his father's crown and have himself anointed as King Edward I of Scotland. As part of a prior arrangment he immediately granted the sheriffdoms of Roxburgh and Berwick to Edward III 'for all time coming'. Perpetuity was to last a long time. From 1334, with one short break when Alexander Ramsey took the castle by stealth, until 1460 Roxburgh remained continuously in English hands. Berwick was never recovered. It ceased to be a Scottish royal burgh in 1338 and was formally ceded to England in 1482. Like Gibraltar, it sits on its headland looking out to sea, and with its back turned against its natural hinterland, its ancient links severed with its sister-town of Roxburgh. The long English occupation proved corrosive as it broke the Borders economy in half and while Berwick shrank into irrelevance, Roxburgh spiralled into decline and, by the 16th century, total extinction.

After Balliol's unexpected success at Dupplin Moor, Edward III launched an all-out war of destruction on Scotland. Even more brutal than his grandfather and with no thought whatever of winning over support in Scotland, he arrived under the walls of Berwick in 1333. The town held out for a month behind its new walls, and Edward's frustrations (and no doubt the logistics of feeding a large army not on the move) got the better of him. Shadowed as usual by the fleet, the English army invaded as far north as Scone, but this was no military progress but a deliberate trail of destruction where pillage replaced politics. Burdened with loot, Edward eventually returned to find Berwick still holding out. His captains arranged a truce. In return for a pledge that the town would surrender if a relieving army did not appear within a matter of days, the governor, Sir Alexander Seton, gave up a number of hostages including his sons, Thomas and Alexander. With no regard for the agreed terms of the truce, Edward ordered a gallows to be built across the Tweed from the town walls, just out of bowshot but in full view of the defenders. Seton's son were produced, bound and stood on stools with nooses around their necks. Edward then demanded the immediate surrender of Berwick — or not only would Thomas and Alexander die but two more hostages, each day, would wriggle on the end of an English rope in front of their parents and friends. It is said that Lady Seton turned her husband away from the battlements as the stools were kicked away from under their childrens' feet. On the southern end of Old Berwick Bridge is a place still called 'Hang a Dyke Nook'.

A relieving Scots army appeared north of the town and Edward met them at Halidon Hill. English archery was in its deadly pomp in the 1330s and so many Scots fell under the murderous hail of arrows that some commentators believed the battle to be definitive, a signal for the end of cross-border warfare. Placed in front of the lines of knights and men-at-arms at Halidon Hill, the archers operated in a new formation called 'the harrow'. This involved forming up in pointed echelons which allowed men to shoot to their flanks as well as directly ahead. The longer English bow could shoot arrows higher into the air and let gravity impart a terrific impact on those unfortunate enough to be underneath.

THE ROYAL COMPANY OF ARCHERS

The longbow is the principal weapon of the Royal Company of Archers, the Queen's Body Guard for Scotland, and its use is still practised by members. 400 are active and there is also a non-active retired list. The Company is mostly on duty when the Queen has ceremonial duties in Scotland.

Various 'arrows' or archery competitions are held and with medals dating back to 1603, the Musselburgh Arrow may be the oldest. Others are held in Edinburgh, Montrose, Biggar, Peebles and Selkirk. The latter was revived in 1818 at the suggestion of Sir Walter Scott. In 1995 Lieutenant Colonel A.P.W. Campbell won the Silver Arrow.

The members of The Royal Company are not usually young men and most are retired soldiers or professional people — members of the Scottish 'establishment'. Some observers deride as irrelevant and Ruritanian the sight of white-haired, elderly gents in green uniforms with flamboyant long feathers in their bonnets marching around Edinburgh, occasionally unsteadily, clutching longbows. That would a harsh judgement, for the existence of the Archers remembers long traditions.

Of the 400 active Royal Archers, about 60 are shooting members who compete regularly for the silver arrows. Shoots are organised into 'ends' where the target is set 180 yards away. Each archer looses two arrows and points are scored if it is hit. In a recent photograph of an arrow held at Holyrood Palace, no-one appears to have hit what is an admittedly small target. Whoever is nearest is awarded a point. Competitions consist of 12 ends.

In 1835 the magistrates of Selkirk proposed to open the competition for the silver arrow to all-comers and The Royal Company took great umbrage, refusing to surrender possession of the prize. However, peace was made and the Archers visit Selkirk every six years to shoot.

In an echo of the more deadly competitions fought between Scots and English archers at Halidon Hill, Neville's Cross and elsewhere, The Royal Company have a triennial fixture against the Woodmen of the Forest of Arden.

Between 1296 and 1513 Border history was dominated by the effects and outcomes of battles, and also by the brooding presence of castles. Towns huddled their walls for protection, men came to them for justice, and as a focus of political power they naturally drew the attentions of invading armies. Despite Edward III's appalling actions, the defenders of Berwick were able to keep the English at bay for a long period, certainly more than a month. History has not recorded much of the detail of the battle for Berwick, but the chronicler at Lanercost Priory either saw for himself the progress of the seige of Carlisle in 1315, or knew someone who had. In the aftermath of victory at Bannockburn, King Robert de Bruce brought his army under the walls of the city. Its defences were similar to those of Berwick with a strong castle integrated into a circuit of walls. And both towns had determined commanders. Sir Alexander Seton's equivalent was a remarkable man, Sir Andrew de Harcla.

When Bruce's army crossed Hadrian's Wall in 1315, de Harcla watched from the battlements. His men had thrown down the bridge over the River Eden and the Scots would have to ford it to approach the city. It would be a dangerous business for the river was in spate, brown and swollen with floodwater. But no matter what disaster befell the enemy, de Harcla's garrison was bound to be massively outnumbered. At his command he had only 4 knights, 50 men-at-arms, 15 esquires, 30 hobelars (light cavalry), 150 archers and each of the three city gates had a detachment of 60 archers to defend it. In addition the townspeople would do their best to help the defenders and man the long circuit of Carlisle's walls with whatever weaponry they could muster. Burgesses at Berwick, Roxburgh and Carlisle were all legally bound to give the service of 'watch and ward' in times of crisis.

Here is the passage from the Lanercost Chronicle;

"On every day of the seige they assaulted one of the three gates of the city, sometimes all three at once; but never without loss, because there were discharged upon them from the walls such dense volleys of darts and arrows, likewise stones, that they asked one another whether stones bred and multiplied within the walls. Now on the fifth day of the seige they set up a machine for casting stones, next to the church of Holy Trinity, where their king stationed himself, and they cast great stones continually against the wall, but they did little or no injury to those within, except that they killed one man. But there were seven or eight similar machines within the city, besides other engines of war which are called 'Springalds' for discharging long darts, and staves with sockets for casting stones, which caused great fear and damage to those outside. Meanwhile, however, the Scots set up a certain great berefrai like a great tower, which was considerably higher than the city walls. On perceiving this, the carpenters of the city erected upon a tower of the wall against which that engine must come if it had ever reached the wall, a wooden tower loftier than the other; but neither that engine nor any other ever reached the wall, because, when it was being drawn on wheels over the wet and swampy ground, having stuck there through its overweight, it could neither be taken any further nor do any harm. Moreover the Scots had many long ladders, which they brought with them for scaling the wall in different places simultanneously; also a sow for mining the town wall, had they been able; but neither sow nor ladders availed them aught. Also they made great numbers of fascines [bundles] of corn and herbage to fill the moat outside the wall on the east side, so they might pass over dry-shod. Also they made long bridges of logs running on wheels, such as being strongly and swiftly drawn with rope might reach across the width of the moat. But during all the time the Scots were on the ground neither fascines sufficed to fill the moat, nor those wooden bridges to cross the ditch, but sank to the depths by their own weight."

Even though it was July the rain had been incessant, so bad that instead of ripening, the crops rotted in the fields. The seige engines stuck fast in the mud, all of the attempts to fill in the moat or the ditches were washed away, and after eleven frustrating days the Scots retreated back across the Roman wall and made their way northwards. Nevertheless, their efforts to take Carlisle and the defenders' to prevent them offer a

great deal of information about seige warfare in the 14th century, something which became wearily familiar to generations of Borderers.

The first motte and bailey castles, like the Lovell stronghold at
Hawick, were built out of earth and wood and they were vulnerable to
an incendiary missile bombardment before a frontal assault, usually at
the gates, by a charging army of beseigers. Defenders threw wet hides
over their thatched roofs to deflect fire-arrows, but what generally
decided the outcome of the seige of a motte and bailey were the numbers
and determination of the men on either side. After the First Crusade in
1099, English and Scots noblemen returned with tales of massive stone
castles which had been near-impossible to capture. And later crusaders
saw an array of seige-engines which impressed them very much. These
were the direct descendants of Roman equipment whose basic
technology had been developed by the generals and engineers of the
Eastern Roman Empire based at Byzantium. In essence they had changed
very little. Given French names by their western users, they operated
on the principles of tension, torsion and counterpoise. The trebuchet,
mangonel and ballista were all designed to project stones at or over the
high walls of a town or castle. Because of their actions missiles could
only damage the roofs of towers or the upper parts of walls. But modern
experiments with a trebuchet have shown that even inexperienced
engineers can quickly learn to direct their stones very accurately.
However, at Carlisle in 1315 the Scots made little impression and only
succeeded in killing one man. The beseiged had longbows and
crossbows. The latter were slow to load, involving the mechanical
rewinding of the bowstring with a racheted handle, and they were
more effective in seiges than in the fury and turmoil of the battlefield.
Carlisle was evidently equipped with 'springalds' and these were larger
crossbows fixed on the ramparts, able to traverse from side to side and
tilt up and down. Springalds delivered longer and more destructive
bolts which could pierce armour. Small ballistas, described in the
Lanercost account as 'staves with sockets', also rained down missiles
on the Scots below the walls. Height was a great advantage and castles
were always sited to allow defenders to shoot downwards, as well as to
enjoy a vantage point from which events could be observed and
anticipated.

The principal attribute of a stone castle was a simple one — thick
walls. Three metres was the average but some masons extended the
base to five metres and more. If they could get closer in to the walls,
three options were available to the attackers. At the gateways, the
weakest point of any castle or town wall, battering rams were used. At
Carlisle the ditching, which had defended most sorts of fortress for
millenia, appears to have kept the Scots away from the gates. When
sappers could approach the walls, they often attempted to undermine
them. Bruce had brought a 'sow' with him and this was a mobile screen
designed to trundle up to the base of the walls and protect the sappers
from missiles dropped from the battlements. These tactics were often
effective until military architects developed an ingenious means to
counter them. What was called a 'batter' was built onto the bottom
course of a stone wall. It was a sloping stone abutment which had the

dual purpose of keeping sappers away from the foundations but also allowed defenders to drop stones, boiling water and other things straight down onto the batter so that they would ricochet off it and penetrate inside the protecting sow. Around the outside walls of the Inner Bailey at Carlisle the batters can still be clearly seen. But no use was made of them. The ditches and moat were enough to keep the Scots at bay. And the seige-tower or 'berefrai' was countered by the construction of something similar inside the walls to meet it. In the event the heavy rain made that tactic unnecessary since the berefrai stuck fast in the mud.

Sir Andrew de Harcla's spirited defence of Carlisle restored English morale after the disaster at Bannockburn. and in 1322 Edward II made him Earl of Carlisle. But his triumph turned out to be short-lived. In an extraordinary episode which proved a harbinger of things to come in the Borders, de Harcla went secretly to Lochmaben to meet King Robert de Bruce and to conclude a peace treaty between England and Scotland even though he had no commission from the king to do so. He had no faith in Edward II and no expectation that he could defend Carlisle and so, like many Borderers after him, he simply took matters into his own hands. Events moved very quickly. De Harcla was surprised and captured inside Carlisle Castle and tried by the king's Justiciar, Sir Gafrid de Scope. He handed down the hideous sentence reserved for traitors. Tied to a hurdle, de Harcla was dragged for a mile and a half to the gallows at Harraby. In front of the usual large crowd, he was stripped of his clothes and hanged by the neck until almost, but not quite, unconscious. Skillful executioners could judge these matters expertly. Then de Harcla was taken down from the gallows and tied to a butcher's table. The executioner first cut off his private parts and held them up to the crowd, and then with a hooked knife he ripped open the man's abdomen, while he still lived and could see what was happening, and pulled out his stomach and intestines. They were burned before de Harcla's eyes. Only then was he put out of his misery and beheaded. Having been hung and drawn, the body was quartered and the bits set up for display on city gates, including those at Carlisle which had been so stoutly defended against Robert de Bruce.

In 1346 David II was busy planning to follow in his father's footsteps and lead an invading army into Cumberland. Four years before, Alexander Ramsay had recaptured Roxburgh Castle and successful raids had been mounted into Northumberland while Edward III was distracted by war in France. David II had concluded an alliance with the French king, Philip VI, who needed the help of the Scots after his stunning defeat at Crecy. Raiding and blackmailing in Cumberland was organised from the Scots' temporary headquarters at Lanercost Priory before David moved camp to Bear Park near the city of Durham. While out on reconnaissance his scouts were surprised by an English army mustered by William de la Zouche, Archbishop of York, and once again the Scots were tormented into defeat by English archery. King David was badly wounded in the face by an arrow, and even though he resisted doggedly, knocking out the teeth of one of his attackers, he was taken prisoner by the English.

CRECY

Two months before the Scots lost at the Battle of Neville's Cross, Edward III won a remarkable victory. At Crecy in north-eastern France 12,000 English soldiers defeated a French army three times its size. The longbow was absolutely decisive.

More than half of the English army were archers, 7,000 of the total, and their skill proved deadly. Using the harrow formation pioneered at Halidon Hill, Edward III arrayed his small force in a battle-line 2000 yards long on the summit of a gentle ridge near the town of Crecy-en-Ponthieu. Three battalions of dismounted knights, men at arms and spearmen were interspersed amongst the archers. Facing them was a massive medieval host bristling with the lances of thousands of armoured knights.

The fighting began at 4pm with a dense flight of arrows into the French ranks. Because the English longbow was indeed long at more than 6 foot and with a draw weight of 80 to 120 pounds it could send arrows 250 to 300 yards. Bowmen practiced a great deal and were adept at loosing heavy showers of arrows at a near-constant rate. Each English archer carried 2 sheaves, 48 in all, onto the battlefield, and having stuck them point down into the ground, could shoot at a rate of ten per minute. Fletchers made huge numbers of arrows, and provided the ranks of bowmen could be kept supplied, the rate of rapid fire could be maintained for a long time before men tired. The technique was to launch a volley high into the air, allowing for any breeze, so that gravity would add force as the arrows fell. When an enemy retreated out of range, boys sometimes ran forward to pick up any which had missed. It was estimated that more than half a million arrows were shot at Crecy.

The French responded in the only way they knew how, by launching charges of mounted armoured knights. Betwen 14 and 16 were made. Standing behind their sharpened stakes in the harrow formation bowmen shot at the charging horses and with their hooked halberds the infantry pulled the knights out of the saddle. The day ended with futile chivalric gestures which smacked of incomprehension and frustration. The blind King of Bohemia was fighting on the French side and he was led into the thick of the fighting roped to several of his knights. As his horse went down all he could hear was the whoosh of English arrows.

The Battle of Neville's Cross was disastrous. King Edward Balliol set out from Carlisle on an expedition to 'recover his realm', David II was held captive for 11 years, and the English re-occupied Berwickshire, Roxburghshire, Peeblesshire and Dumfries. Once Edward III had concluded his successful campaigns in France he could turn northwards, like his father and grandfather before him, and give his full attention to Scotland. Storm clouds were gathering.

King Edward Balliol could find no support even though Scotland had been deprived of a king, and contrary to expectation, the English did not invade. Instead, something far more devastating visited itself on the whole of Britain. In June 1348 the Black Death reached the southern coasts of England. Brought by Gascon sailors — the epidemic was raging through the English-held city of Bordeaux — it took its first victims in the village of Melcombe on Weymouth Bay. Fleas from black rats and humans carried the bacillus and when they bit, they regurgitated it straight into the bloodstream. Flea faeces could also transmit the disease and two sets of symptoms confirmed its rapid onset. When it infected the lymph glands, sufferers experienced hard swellings, or buboes, in the groin and under the armpits. And when the bubonic plague affected the lungs, victims hacked up a deadly bloody mucus. Four days after the appearance of symptoms people died — and in Britain in 1348–49 they died in huge numbers. Between a third and half of the entire population perished within 18 months of the arrival of the 'great pestilence' at Melcombe.

At first the Black Death was thought to be confined south of the Tweed and no doubt it was those Scots who believed that the English had tails who called it 'the foul English pestilence'. The Tweed was used as a natural cordon sanitaire and the few bridges and fords were closely guarded to prevent travellers from the south crossing, and ferry boats were drawn up on the Scottish shore. By 1349 the plague had yet to reach Scotland, and an army mustered at Caddonlea near Galashiels to invade and take advantage of the devastation of the south. The logic must have been that the Scots were naturally immune — simply because they had the good fortune to be Scots. Of course, they were not. The disease suddenly erupted amongst the campfires at Caddonlea, probably brought by mercenary soldiers. And the army panicked and scattered.

The plague raged through the Borders, and the south east of Scotland was worst affected with at least a third of the population struck down. Townspeople perished more quickly but in a densely settled countryside the chances of infection were not significantly reduced. Some fermtouns will have been deserted, others decimated, with sheep and cattle wandering over the unharvested rigs, and unmilked cows lowing in pain.

At Kelso Abbey one of the monks translated 'A Noble Treatise Against the Pestilence' written by John of Bordeaux. No doubt it was read avidly. Here is the introductory paragraph;

"Here begins a noble treatise made by a good physician, John of Burdouse, for medecine against the pestilence illness. And it is departed [arranged] in 4 parts; the first part tells how a man shall keep himself in time of Pestilence so that he shall not become ill, the second chapter tells how his sickness comes, the third chapter tells of medecine against his illness, the fourth tells how he shall be kept."

A mixture of common sense, advice on personal hygiene and some medieval medical theory (it was believed that the bacillus was airborne, carried on a 'miasma' of foul air), the treatise tries to be clinical but succeeds only in sounding understandably desperate. In conclusion John of Bordeaux offers no guarantee of survival and urges prayer and consolation in the power of God's grace.

The more pessimistic saw the Black Death as only another, admittedly cataclysmic, episode in a predictable cycle. Famine in 1315–16 was followed by a long period of cattle and sheep disease known as murrain, and the initial sweep of the plague was not the last. Further visitations came in 1361, 1379, 1392, 1401–3, 1430–32, 1439 and 1455. All sorts of jeremiads attempted to provide explanations of these repeated manifestations of the wrath of God; they ranged from the increasing laxity of the monastic orders to the habit of fashionable women of 'wearing clothes so tight that they wore a fox-tail hanging down inside their skirts to hide their arses'.

The longer-term effects of the Black Death were much more tangible. The drastic decline by 30% of the population of the Borders caused a crucial shift in the balance of economic relationships. Labour was scarce and so rents went down. Reduced demand for food drove down prices. And consequently a smaller acreage of land remained under cultivation. These factors tilted the balance of power towards the agricultural labour force and removed some from the secular and ecclesiatical landlords. All of Europe suffered from the Black Death and trade inevitably declined. Merchants became less dominant in the government of towns like Berwick and craft associations began to incorporate into guilds. And successive appearances of plague must have reduced Roxburgh to little more than a village by the beginning of the 15th century.

A direct consequence of the fiasco at Neville's Cross in 1346 was that David II was captured and offered for ransom. Embarrasingly the Scots could not come up with the 100,000 merks demanded and their king remained a prisoner for 11 years. Meanwhile, the Tweed Basin, Selkirk Forest and Peeblesshire stayed in English hands, and when the Treaty of Berwick came to be agreed in 1357 for the release of David II, that occupation was confirmed. Scotland got its king back but lost huge swathes of its southern territories. The new treaty was handy for Edward III of England because the earlier grant of his puppet, Edward Balliol, no longer had even an arguable legal force. Realising that the ransom for a king recognised by him would be higher and wanting the Scots to settle the business soon, for he needed the cash for his wars in France, Edward demanded and received the abdication of King Edward I Balliol at Roxburgh Castle in 1356. Like his father, King Jean, he retired to his home in Bailleul in northern France.

The end of the de Bailleul interest in Scotland and the failure of 'the Disinherited' to reclaim their lands created the conditions for the rise of a new set of names. Chief amongst them was Douglas. Sir James had been a vigorous supporter of King Robert de Bruce and was rewarded with the forests of Selkirk, Traquair and Ettrick in 1321–22. His cousin, Sir Archibald Douglas, also received land in the south, as did two more de Bruce captains, Thomas Randolph and Robert the Stewart. The sensible policy of placing the interests of his supporters immediately next to the Border, and next to his enemies, worked well for Robert de Bruce. When the king became progressively more and more unwell and began to die of leprosy, Sir James Douglas marshalled a substantial army of men who were not only protecting his kingdom of Scotland, but their newly acquired possessions as well. And at the little-known battle of Linthaughlee near Jedburgh, they defeated and scattered a large English army of 10,000. The problem with the wide Border lands of the Douglases and others is that they often became the pawns of international diplomacy. When the English reoccupied the south of Scotland after the battle of Neville's Cross in 1346, the new Scots aristocracy lost a great deal, and when these forfeitures were formalised in the Treaty of Berwick, their only resort was to illegal action. Unauthorised raiding of English-held land began soon after 1357, and by 1364 the Chamberlain at Berwick reported to the London Exchequer that no rents could be collected at Hawick because of the devastation caused by the Scots. Having abandoned their claims in Selkirkshire and Peeblesshire to the Douglases and others, the English administration at Berwick concentrated its efforts on holding the more fertile and lower-lying lands of the Teviot and Tweed valleys. Control was anchored by a string of strongly defended castles from Roxburgh and Jedburgh in the west to Wark, Norham, and Berwick along the river.

MORE MAYOR

Most modern inhabitants see themselves as Berwickers rather than either English or Scots — although according to the town historian, F.M. Cowe, a significant group favour a return to Scotland since they feel neglected by London. For centuries the status of Berwick has been unsatisfactory.

On June 7th 2001 a referendum was held in the town potentially to take advantage of new legislation which allows local municipal government to elect a full-time, salaried mayor. Only London has so far done this. Apparently because it thought that a town of only 26,000 could not afford the £100,000 needed to sustain the mayoral office, a resounding 'no' was recorded by Berwick. Nevertheless the attempt to revive the great office held by powerful men like Robert de Bernham was salutary, indicative of a new discomfort at a capital city at Edinburgh, close to the town in miles but very distant in politics. A resurgent Scotland might leave Berwick even more isolated. Perhaps a referendum is too blunt an instrument to cut through an ancient dilemma. The issue is not about full-time mayors, or Scottishness or Englishness, but rather, how Berwick can reconnect with its natural hinterland, the Border country.

The Scottish reconquest of Berwickshire began to gather momentum in 1369 when the Earl of Dunbar and March reclaimed his ancient possessions around Earlston. The Humes and the Pringles assisted and by 1371 the only places in Berwickshire still returning rents to the Berwick Chamberlain lay inside a radius of no more than 5 miles of the town. South of the line of the Tweed, and after the confluence at Kelso, the line of the Teviot, Roxburghshire was all occupied in 1357. Once again the reconquest crept forward. In 1369 Makerston was in Scots hands, but Ednam and Kelso remained English. Gradually the area of occupation was whittled down to Roxburgh Castle, its immediate environs and a strip of land between it and Jedburgh Castle. The new Scottish king, Robert II, could not officially sanction the retaking of the Borders since its loss had been agreed, with several other things, in an international treaty. But he certainly approved and was seen to reward those who led the raids. His diplomats could also complain about English retaliation and this took place mainly in Berwickshire. Warning of the approach of a company of hostile soldiers (and to many Borderers both sides were hostile) was flashed around the countryside by means of bale-fires, and here is an early 15th century set of instructions for a form of signalling of some sophistication. The variations show that raiding was a frequent feature of life. The original Scots is reproduced here because it seems to contain the first recognisable echo of Border dialect;

"A baile is warnyng of ther cumyng, quhat power whatever thai be of. Twa bailes togedder at anis, thai cumyng in deide. Fower balis, ilk ane besyde uther and all at anys as fower candills sal be suthfast knowledge that thai ar of gret power and menys"

in English;

"The [burning] of a bale is warning of their coming, whatever size [the force] might be. Two bales [burnt] together at the same time means that they are certainly coming. Four bales, each beside the other and [burnt] all at once like four candles, are a sign of certain knowledge that they are of great power and menace."

In 1373 William, by this time Earl of Douglas, was in protracted dispute with the English keeper of Jedburgh Castle, Henry Percy. The Scots demanded the return of the Jedforest, a wide area of wild land between the town and the Cheviot watershed which was centred on the valley of the Jed and its tributaries. This was a symbolic turning-point. The occupying English forces had always feared the forests of the Borders, had been anxious about the ability of Scots to use them as sanctuaries and guerilla bases. Before the battle at Linthaughlee in 1326 the invading commander, Sir Thomas Richmond, equipped his army with axes "to hew down the forest itself, which was one of the securest retreats of their enemies". Later, in 1386, another English general, John of Gaunt, allegedly requistioned as many as 80,000 axes for his soldiers to cut down the woodland and lay the countryside bare. Pollen archaeology has revealed substantial deforestation in the Borders in the 14th century.

The only real royal intervention in the reconquest was historic. In 1377 Robert II expelled the Durham monks from Coldingham Priory and replaced them with Benedictines from his monastery at Dunfermline. The last remnant of St Cuthbert's Land north of the Tweed was removed after seven centuries near the old diseart on the cliffs above the North Sea. Even God's saints began to acquire nationalities.

The English still held Roxburgh and Berwick castles, and in 1385 the young king who had faced down the leaders of the Peasants' revolt four years before, Richard II, came north at the head of huge army. The Earl of Douglas had taken Wark Castle and parts of Northumberland and the English garrisons on the Tweed and Jed were looking isolated. Richard had 14,000 soldiers with him, the largest army seen in the north since Halidon Hill, and they carried the banner of St Cuthbert. At Hoselaw, south of the Tweed near Kelso, they camped and lit 'a thousand fires' on the rigs above the river. King Richard raised his uncles to the dukedoms of Buckingham and Cambridge before advancing up the valley. The Scots scorched the earth in front of them and, perhaps in frustration, the king ordered the destruction of Melrose and Dryburgh abbeys.

The immediate pretext for burning the Border abbeys was political; the Scots Church supported the Avignonese Anti-Pope, Clement VII, while the English remained faithful to the Roman Pope, Urban VI. This was not a matter of theological preference during the course of the Great Schism of the Western Church but rather a function of Scotland's renewal of the alliance with France. The Avignonese Anti-Popes were always French nominees and any support from abroad, however nominal, bolstered their dubious legitimacy. But the real reason for Richard II's invasion of southern Scotland was punitive; he wanted to deliver a sharp reminder to the Scots that England would not tolerate trouble from the north, particularly as part of the strategy of an alliance which sandwiched and created the very real possibility of war on two fronts. The Melrose monks were wealthy enough to afford to remit the papal taxation known as Peter's Pence to Avignon and Richard's destruction of the abbey was a blunt warning to both parties. With a clear note of regret the Walsingham chronicler recorded the English invaded "saving nothing and burning down with the fiery flames God's temples and holy places, to wit the monasteries of Melrose, Dryburgh and Newbattle." Subsequent historians have added this to the fact that Richard II almost immediately agreed to pay something towards the rebuilding and come up with a sense that somehow the English felt guilty about their destructive rampage. This is to interpret 14th history with 21st century values. Richard II helped to rebuild Melrose because he believed that the south of Scotland was once again in the hands of its rightful and legal owners, and that Melrose was his. The new abbey would pay its Peter's Pence to the Pope in Rome, as was proper and a part of English foreign policy and the English king would pay something towards the rebuilding of his property.

There is no question that English continued to view the Teviot and Tweed valleys as their territory, albeit contested. At Roxburgh Castle they were prepared to spend a great deal of cash and effort to maintain a dominating presence rather than a token garrison cowering behind the old castle's mighty walls. In 1378 Richard II's chancery contracted a master-mason, John Lewyn, to carry out extensive repairs and refurbishments to the fabric of the fortress. The contract survives and it shows how large and formidable Roxburgh had become;

"This contract is made between the King and John Lewyn, master mason. It testifies that Lewyn will do the following works at Roxburgh Castle. That is: a stone and lime wall fortifying the side of the castle [starting] from the Watchtower end and towards the north and south right up to the other wall of the castle. And [Lewyn will build] three towers, one of them fifty feet in height above the ground, and the walls of these towers shall be six feet thick. Of these three towers, one will be in the middle while another will join on to the old wall of the castle in the north and the third will join it in the south. The middle tower will have a gate and two vaulted rooms, each of which will be twenty feet long and eleven and a half feet wide. Above the gate and the two rooms will be a hall forty feet long. There will be three fireplaces in the hall and above it there will be a private room with a fireplace.

There will be a barbican [gatehouse] in front of the gate, ten feet long inside with a vaulted archway. The walls of the barbican will be five feet thick and a total height of twelve feet above and below the ground, and they will be fortified inside and outside. In the tower on the south wall there will be a vaulted larder and above it a vaulted kitchen with three fireplaces, and above the kitchen a private room with one fireplace. And in the tower in the north wall there will be four rooms, each one on top of the other with a private room and a fireplace. Two of the four rooms will be vaulted. There will be dwelling-houses [barracks] along the walls between the towers, these will be twenty-four feet in length and eighteen feet wide. And the wall between the middle tower and the other two towers will be thirty feet high and all of ten and a half feet thick [so that there can be] vaulted passage-ways four and a half feet wide in the middle of the wall leading from the middle tower to the other two towers.

And John Lewyn will build up to a height of thirty feet the old walls of the castle on both sides [north and south] that is, from the two towers in the south, and in the north right along to the donjon [the keep]. In the middle of each of these walls there will be a turret ten feet higher than the built up wall and there will be similar turrets, each six feet square, in the battlements."

At Melrose rebuilding was underway very soon after the summer of 1385 and in 1389 the English administration at Berwick allocated money for the work by reducing the customs duty due on each sack of wool by two shillings for up to 1000 sacks. The fact that the Melrose monks attempted to increase their quota by several hundred sacks shows that an organised clip was again possible, and that their sheep ranches could recover quickly from the recurrent tramp of soldiers across Border hills and valleys. With a figure of 45,000 hides exported in 1378 the Scottish Exchequeur Rolls add to the impression of a recovering economy.

The architecture of Melrose's new kirk mirrors political change — and who was paying. For the years immediately following Richard II's invasion, while Roxburgh Castle was being strengthened and English control over Roxburghshire and Berwickshire being reasserted, the work on the abbey was done by English masons. The surviving stone tracery of the windows in the Presbytery (the eastern end of the nave, beyond the crossing) is executed in the English perpendicular style and it has been compared to contemporary work done at Beverley St Mary in Yorkshire. When the Scots began to regain control of the Tweed Valley, there is a perceptible shift to a more European manner. Around 1400 the Parisian master-mason known as John Morow (or Jean Moreau) had charge of the building work at Melrose and his hand can be seen in the south transept and the side chapels of the nave.

The clack of malet on chisel was heard at Melrose for much of the following two centuries. No doubt there were long pauses in the work when little was done — probably as a result of a lack of funds and the interesting truth is that the new kirk was never finished. By the mid 15th century the habit of letting monastic property for cash rents rather than working it with the large community of lay brothers had reduced the need for accommodation in the church. The lay brothers' choir had been at the west end of the old building, and the new one was never completed.

Despite its ruinous state, despite the ugly alterations made to house the 17th century parish kirk, despite the stone-robbing and despite the defacing of the scuplture by, to quote the 18th century travel writer, Thomas Pennant, "the stupid zeal of covenanting bigots", Melrose Abbey is glorious, surely the most beautiful medieval church in all Scotland. And beautiful for what it is now, not for what it was or might have been.

Quarried from the nearby Eildon Hills, the stone is strikingly coloured with warm rose-tints, yellows and severe greys. In the evenings of sunny days the old kirk seems to glow with subtle pigment, shadow and form. The architecture is masterly — positive and assured. In contrast to the dour mass of Kelso Abbey's surviving west end, the piers at Melrose's crossing are slender and elegant, virtuoso pieces of medieval engineering. But what brings the building to life more than any imaginative leap back in time and gives more pleasure even than its fabric, is the sculpture. A mixture of formal and hieratic, complex and playful, it shows a series of genuinely artistic minds at work. Not since the Lindisfarne Gospels and the mysterious shrine of Jedburgh minster had religious art in the Borders reached the heights achieved at Melrose in the late 14th century.

Even though the heads have been defaced, the representation of the Virgin and Child set on a niche attached to a high buttress on the south side is a confident piece of carving. The massing of the figures is managed with real skill — St Mary leans forward a little with her baby so that those looking from below can see her better — and the handling of the drapery of her shift is deft. Positioned in line with the pulpitum, the stone screen inside the church which separated the monks from the lay brothers, the statue of the Virgin and Child is a reminder that like all Cistercian houses, and incidentally all of the Border abbeys, Melrose is dedicated to St Mary.

Around the wall-heads and the niches the abbey is decorated with great zest and occasional humour. Cleverly carved representations of miserable sinners support the now-empty pedestals of saints with inscribed captions such as "He suffered because he himself willed it" or "Fear the Lord" or "When Jesus comes the shadows will pass". Gargoyles include a famous pig playing the bagpipes and several others of an altogether more sinister cast. With frog-like bodies and grimacing heads, one of them a skull, these are incubuses set on the outside of the church to ward off evil. Coming from a long tradition rooted in a Celtic past some of these sculptures have a primitive, idolic feel and on a small number of older Irish churches, examples even appear to be pornographic. The Sheela-na-Gig sculptures are female forms with exaggerated breasts, pulled-apart pudenda, and clear pagan origins.

The roof of the Presbytery at Melrose survived both the Reformation and even the zealous Covenanters, and it offers a sense of how the monks and their contemporaries saw the decorative figures made for the new church. Nine of the bosses covering the jointing of the ribs of the vaulting are carved with representations of 8 saints surrounding the Holy Trinity. The sharp-eyed can read these sculptures but centuries of cultural change have robbed us of the means fully to understand them. Stories of the saints used to be integral to the lives of every sort of person; before the Reformation we celebrated saints' days in far greater numbers than the four national days (St Patrick, St David, St Andrew and St George) held now, we prayed to saints with particular attributes for particular reasons, and we often revered local saints as a more immediate connection to God. Above all, we knew what happened in the lives of saints, believed in their miracles and grieved at the details of their martyrdom. Melrose is literally covered with stories, most of which we no longer understand, and the roof bosses of the Presbytery are a good illustration of that loss.

Around the Holy Trinity the saints are shown with their attributes so that those looking up could quickly identify them, and cue the story in their memory. This iconographic shorthand is worth exploring in some detail. That St Peter, the first in the circle, holds the keys of the kingdom of Heaven is perhaps still understood, but how many know that the symbol of the Cross Keys, used mainly on pub signs, is a reference to him? Next, St Bartholomew carries a knife which reminds how he suffered martyrdom by being flayed alive in 44AD. With his X-shaped cross St Andrew is the most recongnisable, and the 'crux decussata' was used to martyr him at Patras in Greece. Andrew is also patron saint of Greece. St Matthias was the apostle who took the place of Judas Iscariot, and is shown carrying an axe, the instrument of his martyrdom by decapitation. The sword in St Paul's hand reminds those reading the circle that he was also beheaded — in Rome on the orders of the Emperor Nero, when the saint had the temerity to convert his favourite concubine. It was said that milk flowed from his severed head and that the swordsman was moved immediately to conversion. St James the Great holds the staff and scrip or bag carried by pilgrims and the reference here is to his magnificent shrine at Santiago de Compostela in northern Spain, and also to Melrose itself where the relics of St Waltheof and St Cuthbert and perhaps others attracted many. Next to him St James the Less carries a club which was not the instrument of his martyrdom but perhaps a reminder of the tradition that he was Jesus' younger brother and his attempted defence of Christ in the Garden at Gethsemane. St Thomas completes the circle around the Holy Trinity and his spear is a symbol of the crucifixion, which he attended, and the moment when the Roman soldier thrust it into Christ's side. Master-masons always liked to see St Thomas somewhere in a great church since he was the patron saint of builders and his more usual attribute is a builder's set-square.

Saints, their powers, the example of their lives and their sometimes strange stories enriched Christian belief for ordinary people. Not only did they replace a pantheon of pagan gods in the 5th and 6th centuries with something comfortingly similar, they could also intercede and help a closer identification with what could seem like a distant God. The continuing popularity of the St Christopher pendant for travellers is a relict of an old way of thinking, but the meaning of the richness to be seen all over Melrose is now largely lost to us.

SAINTED

In the middle of the 12th century Pope Alexander II asserted the exclusive right of the papacy to make saints. Up until then the situation had been unregulated with the Cornish in particular making very free with holy honours.

The process instituted by the medieval popes has changed little. It begins with the spontaneous growth of a posthumous cult around the life and works of an outstandingly pious person, often a priest, nun, bishop or even a pope. An application is then made to 'The Congregation for the Causes of Saints' and the Vatican bureaucracy rumbles into action. Sometimes it can take centuries. A miracle is needed, and supporters of the cult figure try to bring one about by praying that he or she will intercede with God. Any incident thought to be related to the prayers, such as a recovery from a serious or fatal illness, is then investigated by the Congregation. If the miracle is substantiated, then the cult figure advances to become beatified. Such demi-saints are permitted the title 'The Blessed'. A second miracle is required to translate the beatified to sainthood and if that is thought to have occured, a case is prepared to go before the Congregation court. A 'Postulator' argues for and a figure known as 'The Devil's Advocate' against. Only after a candidate has survived this test is sainthood confered.

All of this paraphenalia may seem impossibly arcane and credulous to some, but in catholic countries the saints continue to protect their flocks and intercede with God on behalf of all sorts of people. Astronauts are advised to pray to St Joseph Cupertino, advertising executives to St Bernadine of Siena and broadcasters to St Gabriel.

Some more ancient saints have fared less well. Etheldreda, the wife of the Northumbrian king, Ecgfrith, had a chapel dedicated to her near Yetholm and under the French version of her name, St Audrey, she became very popular in the south of England during the Middle Ages. Held on her birthday, St Audrey's Fair at Ely became famous for the fine quality of the jewellery and silk scarves on sale. Sadly these were supplanted by cheap imitations and the word 'tawdry' was given to the English language by a contraction of 'St Audrey'.

When the great window at the east end of Melrose was filled with stained glass, it would have lit the Presbytery with speckles of coloured light, and on the special days of the saints above, as they looked down on the earthly, it would have seemed a particularly peaceful and holy place. And yet the window is named after a Border warlord who was buried near the high altar after a famous and violent death. The body of Earl James Douglas was brought here after the Battle of Otterburn in 1388 and interred in the holiest place at Melrose, a place where the sanctified soil would wash away his mortal sins.

The Scots had waited three years to exact vengeance for the burning of Melrose and the wasting of the Borders, and when Richard II of England began to quarrel with the uncles he had ennobled at Hoselaw in 1385, an opportunity seemed to present itself. With Douglas at the head of a small army, the Scots struck deep into Northumberland, the territory of the Percy family and they reached Newcastle virtually unopposed. After a few skirmishes and the organised collection of as much portable loot as could be found, they turned back homewards up the north road. Henry Percy, nicknamed Harry Hotspur by Shakespeare, quickly marshalled an army of 9,000 and marched through a whole day and into the evening until he caught the Scots at Otterburn in Redesdale. Under the light of a harvest moon, battle was joined.

The earliest extant Border ballad tells the story. Parts of 'The Battle of Otterburn' date from the 15th century but the best known version remains that collected by Walter Scott in his 'Minstrelsy of the Scottish Border'. The first verse is stirring;

> "It fell about the Lammas tide,
> When the muir-men win their hay,
> The doughty Douglas bound him to ride
> Into England, to drive a prey."

More hunting metaphors, elaborate chivalric language and the mores of the 16th century combine in the rest of the poem to describe how even though Douglas was killed, Percy lost the battle and was forced to yield to a dead man. In a historical reality Otterburn was a routine Border battle fought between powerful barons avid for loot and prestige, and what makes it singular is the survival of the ballad. And what makes it ominous is the celebration, glorification and romanticisation of all matters martial in the culture of the Border country. These were values bound to remain paramount for more than 200 years.

> "This deed was done at Otterburn,
> About the breaking of the day;
> Earl Douglas was buried at the braken bush,
> And the Percy led captive away."

By 1400 the Black Douglases had built a patrimony which covered much of the Borders. In addition to the Forests of Selkirk and Ettrick, they owned the old royal village of Sprouston, as well as Browndean, Eskdale, Lauderdale and large estates in Teviotdale. In their slipstream their supporters also grew prosperous and powerful; the Humes became great barons in Berwickshire, the Hoppringles (later shortened to Pringle) were in Lauderdale and the Scotts and Kers in Teviotdale.

Despite the press of Douglas power, Roxburgh, Jedburgh and Berwick castles continued in the hands of English garrisons. In 1394 Sir William Inglis took Jedburgh Castle briefly before the English Keeper, Sir Thomas Strother, regained it. In a strange episode the two adversaries fought a duel, perhaps on a point of personal honour. At Rulehaugh, in front of the Earls of Douglas and Northumberland, Inglis killed Strother, apparently after only a few minutes. But the English kept Jedburgh and for reasons now obscure, Robert III rewarded Sir William Inglis with the old barony of Manor, near Peebles. Finally, the castle fell to Sir William Douglas of Drumlanrig in 1408 and it was decided to destroy it entirely rather than suffer the risk of English re-occupation.

In 1406 another Scots king was captured and held to ransom by the English. James I, had been sent to France for his safety, but his ship was captured en route by pirates off Flamborough Head. Delivered to

Henry IV as a prisoner, he remained in captivity for 18 years. His brother, the Duke of Albany, became Regent of Scotland.

King or no king, it made little difference to ordinary Borderers who continued to suffer the familiar pattern of raid and counter-raid. Roxburgh Castle's garrison seemed undismayed by the loss of neighbouring Jedburgh, and after Sir William Douglas of Drumlanrig burned the town of Roxburgh in 1411, they retaliated vigorously. The Keeper of Roxburgh, Sir Robert de Umfraville, attacked Jedburgh on a fair day, when the town was packed with people and produce, seized all the plunder his men could carry and set the town ablaze. A year later the towns of Hawick, Lauder, Selkirk and Jedburgh again were burned by de Umfraville. Even with an English presence reduced to only Roxburgh and Berwick, life for ordinary people must often have been made miserable by the ebb and flow of international politics. Because the Regent of Scotland decided on a French alliance, a cottar living in the Tweed Valley could regularly expect to pay a heavy price.

Ordinary people took refuge in their faith and prayed that the depradations of war would not touch them too often, that the harvest could be safely gathered in and that their beasts would not be stolen by foraging soldiers. And they also took refuge in their traditions and their stories. The pre-Christian Celtic culture of the Borders lasted long beyond the withering of the Welsh language, and around the fireside farmers and their families told tales from a past which refused to be forgotten.

Borderers believed that the Celtic Otherworld was near at hand, even domestic in its manifestations. In farm places invisible beings known as brownies were thought to be powerful and, provided that they were treated properly and fed well with bowls of porridge and cream, their influence could be benign. Helpful sprites, they worked unseen, often at night, to ensure a successful lambing and a good hairst. In the 15th century Border country such a view of the world should not be thought irrational or even strange. When skirmishing parties of soldiers could erupt out of nowhere to destroy a life's work, and worse, the forces of fate or happenstance dominated the attitudes of most people. Alongside these grim realities, the unrealities of brownies will simply not have occured to those who needed all the help and comfort they could get.

Indoors, away from the outside world, the spirit known as 'the Wag at the Wa'' sat with a family around the hearth and the cooking fire, unseen but listening, unheard but influential. A widespread belief in an Otherworld was a pre-Christian legacy which appeared to co-exist comfortably with the teachings of the great churches of the Borders. Certainly such a Celtic mythology required no greater effort of faith than the mysteries of the mass or the miracles of the saints celebrated at Melrose Abbey.

By the time James Hogg was writing, in the late 18th and early 19th centuries, these pagan traditions were very ancient and ran unquestioned with the grain of Border society. In 1801 he corresponded with Walter Scott about the immense span of the oral transmission of stories and the beliefs implicit in them;

"Till this present age, the poor illiterate people in these glens, knew of no other entertainment, in the long winter nights, that repeating, and listening to, the feats of their ancestors, recorded in songs, which I believe to be handed down, from father to son, for many generations."

In point of fact women were crucial to this process. In the last century collectors of folk songs and stories in the Gaelic Highlands and Islands depended heavily on the memories and musical skills of women who ensured the survival of much that would have been lost. James Hogg's own mother, Meg Laidlaw, was a major source for Walter Scott's 'Minstrelsy of the Scottish Border' and in the 19th century Nancy Brockie of Bemersyde could remember songs and stories from a distant past.

A central difficulty with our understanding of these traditions is that they fly on gossamer wings. The sickly sweetness of 'Faerie' or 'Fairyland' disguises a much more textured, robust and genuinely mystical view of the unseen world beside us. Victorian obsessions with scantily-clad little girls and boys have their own dark beginnings, but their imagery successfully overlaid an old sense of parallel worlds and misunderstood the nature of contact between them. For many Borderers these contacts were real, regular and took place at particular places. Thomas Rhymer lay on Huntly Bank on Eildon Hill, the magic mountain, to meet the Queen of the Otherworld but it was not the only portal through which mortal men and women could pass. The ballad of Tam Lane or Tam Lin is impossible to date accurately, since it lived for so long in the mouths and memories of ordinary people before being written down in the early 18th century, but its themes and language march in time with the story of True Thomas. Here is an abridged translation;

> "The king forbad his maidens a'
> That wore gold in their hair
> To come and go by Carterhaugh,
> For the young Tam Lin is there.
> And those that go by Carterhaugh
> From them he takes a wad [payment],
> Either their rings or green mantles
> Or else their maidenheads.
> So Janet has kilted her green mantle
> Just a little above her knee,
> And she has gone to Carterhaugh
> Just as fast as she could flee.
> She had not pulled a double rose,
> A rose but three or four,
> When up and spoke this young Tam Lin,
> Crying 'Lady pull no more!'
> 'How dare you pull those flowers!
> How dare you break those wands!
> How dare you come to Carterhaugh
> Withouten my command!'"

Fair Janet loses her maidenhead to Tam and becomes pregnant. He tells her;

> "'I was once a mortal knight
> I was hunting here one day,
> I did fall off from my horse,
> The Fairy Queen stole me away'"

They make plans to rescue Tam as the Faeries ride on Halloween, or Samhain Eve, and Janet pulls him off his horse and back through a crack in time into the land of the living.

Janet met Tam Lin at Carterhaugh Woods near Selkirk, and recently the traditional site of 'Tam Lane's Well' has been restored. To ordinary people certain real locations could be unreal, dangerous places where lives were utterly changed, perhaps even lost. But there was no mystery in the air around Carterhaugh, a beautiful and atmospheric place by the River Ettrick on the edge of the Duke of Buccleuch's policies at Bowhill. Everyone understood what went on, and what the risks were.

Like 'The Dowie Dens o' Yarrow' and the ballad of Thomas the Rhymer, the story of Tam Lin is not about the clatter, clash and blood of battle, what Walter Scott called 'the big, bow-wow stuff'. Rather, it deals with passion, love and freedom and focuses on the character of Fair Janet, her determination to make love to Tam and then to rescue him. As such the ballads may have had more resonance in the hearts and minds of women, and particularly women like Meg Laidlaw and Nancy Brockie. Perhaps that is why it survived.

Beyond the winter evenings and the tales told in the flicker of firelight, politics continued its deadly play over the Borders landscape. In 1428 James I renewed the alliance with France, and eight years later he arrived with an army at Roxburgh Castle. John Lewyn's refurbishments had been followed by another set of expensive and extensive repairs in 1419 when 500 stones of iron were sent up from England to make new gates. After a fortnight below Roxburgh's walls, James' seige engines could make no impression and when serious disagreements broke out in the Scottish camp, he was forced into a humiliating retreat. A year later James was murdered by aristocratic conspirators at Perth.

The subsequent minority of James II was dogged by the high-handed doings of powerful barons, primarily the Black Douglases. In essence, war was declared between the crown and its unbiddable subjects, and given that no credible alternative to the Stewart dynasty was ever seriously promoted by the Douglases, there could be only one eventual outcome. In 1455 the Earls of Douglas were attainted for treason, and the last act of the civil war took place in the Borders. At Arkinholm, an old name for Langholm, a small band of 200 men led by the Laird of Johnstone came across the Earl's three brothers and their retinues. One was killed, another later executed and the third fled to England to join the Black Douglas in exile.

War was changing in 15th century Scotland. Guns would change everything, from military tactics to fortifications, and James II was fascinated by them. During the campaigns against the Douglases the efforts of his commanders were much helped by "the gret gun the quhilk a Frenchman shot richt wele". One of the few fruits of the French alliance was the import of expertise, both in operating cannon and making them. There is some evidence of the manufacture of artillery at Galashiels. In 1442 the Exchequeur Rolls record the visit of Mr Nicolas, a carpenter, to 'Galowayschiels' concerning the wooden carriage for one of the king's great guns. And the place name of 'Gun Knowe' implies more than a passing involvement in making ordnance. The term 'barrel' comes from the early methods. Essentially a long tube was fashioned by fastening together a series of wrought-iron strips or strakes and banding them with hoops — like a barrel.

Guns got pet names, and in Scotland Mons Meg is the most famous. But perhaps the great bombard known as 'The Lion' was the most destructive. In 1460 James II brought his army to Roxburgh Castle and to smash its thick walls, the huge gun was set up in a trench. A chronicler takes up the story;

"King James hauing sik plesure in dischargeng gret gunis past til a place far fra the armie to recreat him selfe in schuiting gret pieces, quhairof he was verie expert, bot the piece appeiringlie, with ouer sair a chairge, flies in flinderis, with a part of quhilk, strukne in the hench or he was war, quhairof (allace) he dies".

Thomas Rhymer's prophecy that only a dead man would win Roxburgh Castle came true. The widowed Queen Mary of Gueldres rushed her son across the Tweed to Kelso Abbey where, in the presence of most of the Scottish magnates, the little boy was consecrated and crowned at the high altar. At great cost the Scots finally took the castle almost 200 years after it had been lost, and expelled the last English occupying force from the Tweed Valley — except for that of Berwick. With the fall of Roxburgh, the Wars of Independence came to an end. Like Jedburgh the great castle was 'doung to the ground' lest it fall again into the hands of the English. Little more than a ruin, 'the castle and the place called the castlestead' was granted to Walter Ker of Cessford in 1488. The town had shrivelled to a village and the market in wool and hides diverted elsewhere. Roxburgh was a spectacular casualty of international politics, but at least the ancient fortress did not decline into the shadows of history before it had killed a king.

CHIVALRY

There existed no medieval codes of chivalry as such, but rather a set of widely understood ideals which found their way into courtly writings and had some force amongst the military upper classes. However, it has to be said that the most successful warriors of the period, Edward I and Edward III of England, ignored chivalry. The execution of the sons of Sir Alexander Seton opposite the walls of Berwick outraged contemporaries and at the famous Battle of Crecy in 1346, the English concentrated on killing instead of making honourable prisoners of any who yielded.

Broadly, the ideals of military prowess were expected to be dignified by a sense of justice tempered by mercy. Above all else knights should always show total loyalty, and a betrayal of feudal oaths made to the king was answered by the terrible punishment of hanging, drawing and quartering. Humility was prefered to boastfulness, and largesse to the lower orders and the church considered attractive.

French intellectuals were very interested in the idea of the perfect knight and in his writings Chretien de Troyes wound chivalry around the tales of Arthur, an anachronism from which the Celtic warlord never really escaped.

Guns would decide the fate of another Stewart monarch. James II's grandson, James IV, would fall at Flodden field because he and his generals failed to grasp their importance. On 9th September 1513 the first battle in British history to begin with an artillery exchange was fought, and partly because their guns were not readily adaptable for battlefield use, the Scots lost the day, disastrously.

Once again the alliance with France induced a Scottish king to invade England. Having lost the towns of Tournai and Therouanne to Henry VIII, whose ambition appeared boundless, the French were desperate to distract the English and divide their resources, and James IV was implored 'to advance a yard into England'. There was enthusiasm in Scotland to take advantage of what appeared to be an opportunity. Contingents of Highlanders and Lowlanders, most Scottish magnates and the king himself combined into an army of more than 20,000, the largest to march out of Scotland for many generations.

Because they planned to beseige Norham Castle, 17 large wheeled bombards were hauled on bogeys in the baggage train. From emplacements still visible on the Scottish side of the Tweed near Ladykirk, James' gunners pounded Norham with huge gunstones, and within 6 days the castle fell. Etal, Wark and Ford were also taken.

Meanwhile the 70 year-old Earl of Surrey raised an army in England's northern counties. And remembering local allegiances, he took up the banner of St Cuthbert from Durham Cathedral. At Alnwick the army mustered, and a curious exchange began between Surrey and James IV. Couched in the elaborate language of chivalry, a message was brought to the Scottish camp by the Rougemont Pursuivant. Politely, the English general enquired if the Scots were prepared to do battle on the 9th of September some time between 12 noon and 3pm. The Islay Herald was despatched to the English camp with an equally polite message saying that these arrangements were agreeable.

On the 5th of September James IV led the Scots from Ford Castle, where it is said that he dallied with its keeper, Lady Heron, and across the nearby bridge over the River Till. Where the Cheviot Hills peter out into folds and ridges, the Scots chose a naturally well defended site to encamp. Between three hills with a commanding view to the east and south, the direction from which the English were bound to approach, their captains were careful to build a fortified enclosure with an artillery trench defending the only weak point, a narrow gulley. Lookouts on Flodden Hill saw the English advance from the south-east. Formed into three battalions and protected by mounted flankers and scouts, they

moved slowly into the Milfield plain where they halted. They decided
to pitch their tents at Barmoor which, being slightly elevated, offered
adequate visibility of the surrounding contryside. Once he had received
intelligence of the heavily defended position of the Scots, the Earl of
Surrey sent the Rougemont Pursuivant on another errand, this time less
polite, to complain that James IV was acting in an unchivalrous manner.
His invitation to do battle was intended to bring the armies together on
open ground, on the level playing field of Milfield Plain. Refusing to
admit the herald into his presence, James sent word to Surrey that he
would do as he pleased.

On the morning of 9th September the Scots saw that the English army
of 20,000 men was moving again, but not towards their position. Across
the Till, out of range of James' guns, Surrey appeared to be leading his
forces northwards to the Tweed. Scottish bombards were trained on
Ford Bridge but the English skirted it and, in a fit of chivalrous disgust,
looked as though they were leaving the field. To the Scots captains it
may have appeared as though they were shaping to cross the Tweed at
the Coldstream fords and raid into Berwickshire in an attempt to outflank
James IV's advance.

Before they reached the river, the English suddenly swung westwards
and crossed the Till, the vanguard and the artillery across Twizel Bridge
and the bulk of horse and foot at Straw Ford, less than a mile upstream.
Very soon Surrey's army would lie between the Scots and Scotland,
cutting off any line of retreat. James IV and his generals rushed to
occupy Branxton Hill and deny their enemies the advantage of the high
ground. But the heavy bombards trained on Ford Bridge and those in
the trench near West Flodden could not move quickly. Expecting to use
artillery against the walls of Norham, Wark and the other castles, the
Scots had brought only seige pieces. Lighter, more manouevrable and
smaller calibre cannon had been embarked onto the ships of the fleet.
And crucially, so had the gunnery experts sent by the French. The
English did, however, have battlefield weapons, landed by ship at
Newcastle on 30th August, and as important, experienced German
bombadiers to fire them

When Surrey approached Branxton, he was forced to use his guns to
rake the Scottish ranks arrayed on the hillside. Showers of rain and
strong winds prevented effective archery. But the guns did enough. By
contrast such Scottish bombards as were deployed could not be trained
to fire on a low trajectory downhill, and their gunstone shot whistled
over the heads of the English. After an intense exchange the Scots
gunnery-master was killed and all their bombards silenced. Determined
to attack, James IV had no option but to advance downhill.

It had rained often since the seige of Norham two weeks before and
the ground was very wet, even boggy and treacherous in places. No
sustained headlong charge was possible, even when some Scots threw
off their shoes to fight barefoot or in their stocking soles, and the densely
packed schiltroms must have developed fatal gaps. At 17 foot 6 inches
in length the Scots had difficulty in controlling their new pikes. They
were much better in defence, planted in the ground and presenting a
bristling hedge to oncoming cavalry. At 9 foot, and with axe and spear

heads, the English halberds, by contrast, swung and thrust to good effect.

In the van of his men, charging on foot "after the custom of the nation" James IV ran down Branxton Hill and tore into the thick of the halberds. Pedro de Ayala, the Spanish ambassador, said of him "he is not a good captain because he begins to fight before he has given his orders". But James' immense physical courage almost succeeded. Reaching to within a spear's length of the position of the Earl of Surrey, who at 70 did not lead from the front but directed matters from the rear, the charge of the Scottish king almost broke through the English centre. The Highlanders on his right flank were routed, and after driving back the men of Cheshire and Lancashire, the Borderers on the left were contained by Lord Dacre and his 1,500 Border cavalry. After some hours of desparate hand to hand fighting, the king's centre was rolled up and surrounded. All each exhausted man could do was to exact a dear price for his own life.

Under the wrack of dead and dying men James' body was found by Lord Dacre and taken to Berwick Castle where Scots prisoners identified it. From there it was shipped south to lie for many years in the Charterhouse at Sheen, west of London. An archbishop, a bishop, 9 earls, 2 abbots and 14 great lords died at Flodden, but English casualties were also very heavy. Surrey's army was badly battered, very short of food and the weather made everything more difficult. No attempt to follow up the expensive success at Flodden was undertaken. Nor could any effort be made to avenge the defeat.

Artillery predicted the course of the battle, and the death of James IV decided its outcome. Despite popular belief to the contrary, the number of Scottish Borderers who died was likely smaller than casualties from other contingents, since, after scattering the battalion opposing them on the left and being contained by English reinforcements, they left the field. On the morning of the following day, 10th September, Lord Hume led his Borderers back to Flodden to offer to continue the battle, but they were driven off by cannon fire. Because of the intensity of the fighting and the damage done to Surrey's forces, Hume must have reckoned Flodden still to be winnable.

Others were waiting on the periphery. Having circled the battlefield like hungry scavengers, the 'banditti' of Teviotdale and Tynedale attacked the English camp, rifling tents and stealing horses. And later the baggage train of the retreating Scots was shadowed by troops of horsemen, but nothing came of it. These incidents were a sour foretaste of the aftermath of Flodden in the Border country. The days of the Reivers were dawning.

8

Riding Times

Most photographs are taken *from* the Cheviots, rather than *of* them. Unlike the spectacular sea and lochside mountains of the Scottish Highlands, these hills are not the stuff of easy composition. Not high, jagged, dramatic, or reflecting on the glassy surface of the water, or piercing the white clouds gathering around their majestic heads, the Border hills appear stolid and undistinguished, folding endlessly away into the distance, grey-green, one humped summit much like another. Photographers prefer to use them as a frame, pointing their lens downhill at the distant Teviot or Tweed valleys, at the lush greenery, the summer trees or the homely geometry of farms, dykes and field fences.

The view in the opposite direction seems uninviting. In the heart of the Cheviots, up on the watershed ridge, the wind is relentless, often eye-watering — even on fine days. Ever-present, it has buffed the hills smooth and rounded, whipping the long grass flat, inhibiting the natural growth of trees except in the steep-sided hopes where willow scrub and thorns take decades to reach any height. On the northern slopes of the Cheviot itself there are cultivated regiments of black-green pinewoods in tidy rows by the College Burn. One of the smaller plantations almost touches the Border fence and the Ordnance Survey notes that it hides a short tributary of the College called Smeddum Sike. In Scots, smeddum means 'force of character, mettle, spirit'. More map-reading reveals a well-named landscape. What appears not to be singular features at all have not only attracted place-names but, it seems, a hidden history; Meg's Cleuch, Blair's Hole, Carlin Tooth. Echoes of the steps of people on these deserted hills are just audible. Other names are descriptive, Swineside, Crooked Sike, Black Cleuch, and merely record the use and observation of the land. Some are more precise. King's Seat, Butt Roads, Deer Cleuch and Deer Doups probably commemorate old hunting grounds.

Gradually and grudgingly the hills begin to come alive, begin to give up secrets, to tell stories. For the drama of the Cheviots is different from the majestic mountains of the far north. Unlike theirs, it is human. And paradoxically it lies in the relentless bleakness, in the treachery of their moorlands and mosses, and the fact that for all of the 16th century and a long time before that, this was the landscape of larceny.

The Border Reivers rode through the Cheviot Hills into history. From Teviotdale and Liddesdale they raided down into England, sometimes as far south as Yorkshire. And from Redesdale and Coquetdale they forayed north into the Tweed Valley, sometimes over the Lammermuirs and beyond. And Scots and English stole from each other, regardless of nominal nationality. These were the Riding Times, and in modern European history they have no parallel.

Over a huge area of mainland Britain, either side of the Cheviot Hills, perhaps a tenth of the landmass of Britain, there existed a society which lived entirely beyond the laws of England and Scotland, which successfully and persistently ignored royal or central government, kept its own ancient culture intact, gave familiar words and concepts to the language of crime, and created little except trouble and indelibly famous stories.

What lay at the heart of the Riding Times was something blunt and simple — the raid itself. Reivers stole anything portable that might be of value but mainly they went out after livestock; cattle, sheep and horses. Borrowing the parlance of the American West, they were rustlers. The most concise description of a raid by a contemporary commentator is worth quoting at the outset for it goes to the core of what mattered to 16th century Border society, both the raiders and the raided. John Leslie, the Bishop of Ross, described by one 20th century author as 'the best of the Papists', probably travelled to the Borders more than once and when he included what follows in his 'History of Scotland' of 1572–76, he clearly knew what he was talking about. This translation from Leslie's Latin was made by the English antiquarian, William Camden;

"They sally out of their own borders, in the night, in troops, through unfrequented by-ways, and many intricate windings. All the day time, they refresh themselves and their horses, in lurking holes they had pitched upon before, till they arrive at the dark in those places they have a design upon. As soon as they have seized upon the booty, they, in like manner, return home in the night, through blind ways, and fetching many a compass [taking circuitous routes]. The more skillful any captain is to pass through these wild deserts, crooked turnings and deep precipices, in the thickest mists and darkness, his reputation is the greater, and he is looked upon as a man of an excellent head.

And they are so very cunning, that they seldom have their booty taken from them... unless sometimes, when, by the help of bloodhounds following them exactly upon the tract, they may chance to fall into the hands of their adversaries. When being taken, they have so much persuasive eloquence, and so many smooth insinuating words at command, that if they do not move their judges, nay, and even their adversaries (notwithstanding the severity of their natures), to have mercy, yet they incite them to admiration and compassion."

The origins of reiving are much older than Leslie's history. The seeds of lawlessness were planted, sometimes deliberately, in the greenhouse of international politics. In 1249 customary arrangements for cross-border justice were codified in 'The Laws of the Marches'. Recognising that an open frontier between two different jurisdictions would lead to a need for agreed procedures and joint action on disputes between their subjects, Scots and English kings co-operated to create a legal apparatus different from those administered from London and Edinburgh. Traditional meeting-places along the line of the frontier were to witness regular courts where cases were heard and judgements made. As it is now, oath-swearing was intergral to hearings. Anyone making an accusation against the subject of another realm had to be prepared to support it by solemnly swearing that his statements were true. The Laws of the Marches specified only four exemptions; the Kings of England and Scotland and the Bishops of St Andrews and Durham. Other, lesser officials stood in and, significantly, the proxy for the Bishop of St Andrews was the priest of the sanctuary of Stow. Such an important role for someone who appears to be only a parish priest must be a memory of the antiquity and sanctity of the former Anglian minster.

In times of relative peace March Law appeared to work well enough, and in 1297 a further layer was added for its administration when the first Wardens were appointed. Three on each side of the border worked in pairs. The jurisdiction of the Warden of the Scottish East March ran from Berwick to the Redden Burn and was answered by the English East March and its Warden on the opposite bank of the Tweed. Warden-meetings were held at Norham Ford and Redden. The boundary of the Scottish Middle March followed the Redden Burn up into the Cheviots and along the border ridges to near Kershopefoot and faced the English Middle March which covered Coquetdale, Redesdale and Tynedale. This pair of wardens usually met at the Redeswire, near Carter Bar. And finally the two West Marches encompassed Dumfriesshire and parts of Galloway, and Cumberland and Westmoreland. Meetings were held at Gretna, Lochmabenstane and Rockcliffe. The exception to this neat arrangement was the lonely valley of Liddesdale. For reasons which will be become clear, it needed its own Keeper.

After the Wars of Independence ushered in what proved to be centuries of warfare in the Borders, the March Wardens became increasingly busy. The dislocation of war and the remoteness and weakness of central government created the conditions which allowed the rise of the reivers. The causes of crime amongst the Border Scots were well understood by Bishop Leslie;

"[They] assume to themselves the greatest habits of licence… For as, in time of war, they are readily reduced to extreme poverty by the almost daily inroads of the enemy, so, on the restoration of peace, they entirely neglect to cultivate their lands, though fertile, from the fear of the fruits of their labour being immediately destroyed by a new war. Whence it happens that they seek their subsistence by robberies, or rather by plundering and rapine, for they are particularly averse to the shedding of blood; nor do they much concern themselves whether it be from the Scots or English that they rob and plunder."

And amongst the English Borderers William Camden observed similar attitudes in 1549 when he wrote;

"The chief [dales] are Tynedale and Redesdale, a country that William the Conqueror did not subdue, retaining to this day the ancient laws and customs. These Highlanders are famous for thieving; they are all bred up and live by theft. They come down from these dales into the low countries, and carry away horses and cattle so cunningly, that it will be hard for any to get them or their cattle, except they be acquainted with some master thief, who for some money may help them to their stolen goods, or deceive them."

Perceptive as ever, Camden touched on the other set of conditions which fostered the growth of organised crime amongst the people of the Border hills. The ancient laws and customs he observed are a clear survival from a very long past. The hillmen of Southern Scotland and Northern England whom "William the Conqueror did not subdue" were also a source of endless trouble to the Romans, persuading them to go to the extraordinary length of building a wall to divide and contain them (in fact there was a serious and costed proposal in the mid 16th century to rebuild Hadrian's Wall — at £30,000 it seemed like a bargain). Seen from a historical perspective the essence of the society of the Border Reivers was undoubtedly Celtic, with clear cultural links to the clans of Highland Scotland, and the laws and customs of Wales and Ireland. When a 16th century horizon erupted with horsemen, they rode with the ghosts of an immense past beside them, reaching back to the tribesmen who tormented the garrison of Hadrian's Wall, and beyond them to the Selgovae, the Hunters of the Border hills.

If the Reivers had not forgotten Old Welsh, or spoke Gaelic and not English, then there would have been little to mistake in their identity. But a comparison between the well attested characteristics of those Celtic societies who did hang on to their languages and the English-speaking Borderers turns out to be very telling.

From the time of the Greeks and Romans onwards commentators were struck by the fascination of the Celts for war and all its habits and practices. Thought to be 'war-mad', needlessly bellicose and impetuous, this set of characteristics still finds currency amongst the cliches of the fiery and passionate Celt. Here is another passage from Camden;

"In the wastes... you may see as it were the ancient nomads, a martial kind of men who, from the month of April into August, lie out scattering and summering with their cattle, in little cottages here and there, which they call shiels and shielings."

Others support this view and two examples add detail. At the Battle of Flodden in 1513, Thomas Howard, the son of the Earl of Surrey, was much impressed by the warlike nature of Scottish Borderers; " the boldest men, and the hottest, that ever I saw any nation". And the medieval French historian, Jean Froissart, had much to say about Borderers. They were;

"good men of war, for when they meet there is a hard fight without sparing: there is no 'Ho!' between them as long as spears, swords, axes or daggers will endure, but lay each upon other."

Camden thought that Borderers were like nomads, and the comparison is informative. Like many in central Africa and elsewhere, Celtic societies set great store on the value of cattle and, in general, early peoples often expressed concepts of wealth through counting the number of cows they owned. The language of money grew out of this custom and the Latin 'pecus' for a cow is the derivation of 'pecunia' for cash. The earliest recorded epic tale from Ireland, the 'Tain Bo Cuailgne' translates as 'The Cattle Raid of Cooley', and its hero, Cuchulainn, exerts himself greatly to protect the brown bull belonging to the King of Ulster. Scottish Gaels have developed a unique colour spectrum to differentiate their cattle as they are ingathered off the hillsides, and the most loving term of endearment in the language is 'm'eudail' and it literally means 'my cattle'.

As stocksmen Borderers lived for most of the year outdoors in their shielings and the sense of them as tribal herdsmen is sharpened by several descriptions of their houses and villages. They were very primitive and could be built in three or four hours around a frame of stakes shoved into the ground, walled by divots of turf and roofed with branches. Bishop Leslie commented that Borderers lived in "sheephouses and lodges... of whose burning they are not sore solaced".

The Celts were feared throughout the Roman and Greek world as skillful cavalry warriors, and they even worshipped horses, particularly the fertility goddess, Epona, a mare whose name may be the origin of the word 'pony'. And like them, Borderers lived in the saddle, and horses stood at the core of their lives. Even a modern dictionary makes the connection. The words 'riding' and 'raiding' have the same derivation from a Northern English form of an Old English word 'rad' meaning 'a riding'. The most feared and nefarious family in the Borders was the Armstrongs of Liddesdale and when a contemporary commentator described them as 'ever-riding', he meant 'ever-raiding'. By the 15th century a 'raid' had acquired the specific gloss of 'a military expedition on horseback', and by 1600, when reiving ceased, the term fell out of use. Predictably it was revived by Walter Scott in 'The Lay of the Last Minstrel' in 1805.

WORDS

The reivers created nothing except trouble, and vocabulary. 'Blackmail' was their most notorious coining. The extraction of protection money with menaces is doubtless as old as time, but what the reivers contributed was the term itself. 'Mail' means rent and, for example, 'grassmail' was paid for the lease of pasture. And so blackmail literally means 'black rent' and it was perfected by the Grahams in the West Marches. Reaching a degree of organisation only possible in lawless conditions, they kept a public record of all those farmers paying blackmail in the parish churches of Arthuret and Canonbie.

'Red-handed' meant what it means now, being caught in the act, and Walter Scott revived its use in his novel 'Ivanhoe', published in 1819. Crimes were committed by bands of raiders who got the name 'gang'. This was a common word in Middle English for a group of men, but Borderers attached a criminal gloss which it has never lost. 'Gear' was what they stole and although

that word requires context to associate it specifically with the activities of a
gang, there was no shortage of examples in the 16th century.
    'Reiver' itself is interesting. It now has an exclusively historical meaning
but it can be found in ominous words like 'bereaved' and 'bereft'. It derives
from the Old English 'reafian' which first occurs in 'Beowulf' in the 8th
century. If the great epic was indeed composed in Bernicia, then that points of
a long period of usage for 'reiving' in the Borders.

In Galashiels a bronze sculpture outside the old town hall gives an impressively faithful sense of what the horses of the reivers looked like. Frozen at the point of leaping into the gallop, the pony looks much too small for the heavily armed and armoured man in the saddle. His feet dangle well below its belly, and modern equestrian standards would frown on such an unequal combination. Sadly it has long been impossible to recreate a living version of the Gala sculpture and discover whether or not these little ponies really could carry such burdens. The breed of horses ridden by the reivers became extinct in the 19th century. As a result of negligence, even forgetfulness, the Galloway pony has disappeared from Border hillsides. However, a good deal of information about these shaggy little horses has outlived them. Better known as the Galloway Nag, and mentioned both by Shakespeare and Scott, it was described in 1858 by William Youatt;

"A horse between thirteen and fourteen hands in height is called a Galloway, from a beautiful breed of little horses once found in the south of Scotland, on the shore of the Solway Firth, but now sadly degenerated, and almost lost.
    The pure Galloway was said to be nearly fourteen hands high, and sometimes more; of a bright bay or brown, with black legs, small head and neck, and peculiarly deep and clean legs. Its qualities were speed, stoutness, and surefootedness over a very rugged and mountainous country."

Another writer, Professor Low, also caught the last few generations of Galloway Nags ('nag' used to mean simply a small riding horse, and had no pejorative overtone in the 16th century) and he had something to add about their origins;

"They exceeded the pony size and were greatly valued for their activity and bottom... Besides this part of Scotland [the south] was a country of forays during the rude border wars of the times, when a more agile race than the ordinary pack-horse was naturally sought for; and all along the borders of the two kingdoms, a class [breed] of similar properties existed. Many of the true Galloways of the western counties were handsome, and their general characteristic was activity, and the power of enduring fatigue."

What was most important to the Border Reivers was stamina, the ability of their Galloways to travel long distances over the most difficult and treacherous terrain. And often to do it at night, preferably a soot-black, moonless night. Much of the cattle-stealing was done in the winter time, between October and December when the beasts still had the remains of their summer condition and could be driven for many miles. The Cheviot Hills, their mosses, hidden defiles and wind-whipped tops can be a miserable, even dangerous environment when the easterlies blow off the North Sea. Surefootedness in the summer light is one thing, but a pony able to find its way through the hills in the black of a freezing winter night, with a fully armed rider on its back, is quite another. There is good evidence that the winters of the 1590s were appreciably more severe and longer. Given that reiving reached its height in that decade, the skill and 'bottom' of the Galloways is to be marvelled at.

An 18th century Scottish doctor called Anderson seems to have done his rounds on the back of a Galloway. Clearly very fond of the horse, he remembered;

"In point of elegance of shape, it was a perfect picture; and in disposition was gentle and compliant. It moved almost with a wish, and never tired. I rode this little creature for twenty-five years, and twice in that time I rode a hundred and fifty miles at a stretch, without stopping except to bait [eat], and that not for above an hour at a time. It came in at the last stage with as much ease and alacrity as it travelled the first. I could have undertaken to have performed on this beast, when it was in its prime, sixty miles a day for a twelvemonth, running without any extraordinary exertion."

Once their Galloways had taken the reivers to the beasts they had fixed to steal, their job changed. They had to be agile enough to round up a herd of black or brown cattle in the dark and show all the nimbleness of an American Quarterhorse in keeping the pack together. The skills and versatility of these little animals was amazing, and their central importance to the business of reiving is sometimes missed. In the same way that their dragon-ships delivered the Vikings into surprising places where they could raid and escape with relative impunity, so the Galloways took Borderers on extraordinary journeys far from their homes and allowed them to appear, it seemed, out of nowhere.

There is one place where the Galloway Nags still gallop, but it is a long way from the Cheviots. In the 18th century these hardy ponies were exported through the port of Bristol to Canada and several herds still roam the windswept wastes of Newfoundland. Perhaps they feel at home.

HOOFPRINTS

Horses have galloped through Border history for millenia. Up until the advent of the mass-produced motor car, horses were seen every day in every city, town, village and country place in Britain. Horsepower used to pull along our daily lives. In the last 50 years the sound of hooves clopping along the streets and lanes has been almost completely stilled. For most people to see a horse is an event. And to be able to ride one a great and unusual skill. Horses have disappeared from our lives.

Except in the Borders. Horses are everywhere and their ratio to people in the Scottish counties is high and estimates vary between 1 to 5 and 1 to 20. In the corridor of river valley and rolling hill country between Galashiels and Hawick, horses almost certainly outnumber people. There are two main reasons for this. First, the annual common ridings usually involve cavalcades of hundreds of riders, many of whom spend their summer weekends in the saddle riding not only the bounds of their own town but also supporting others as well. And these are not members of a wealthy elite able to afford pasture, stabling, tack and all the other expensive items associated with horses. What keeps this remnant of equestrian culture very much alive and thriving is the fact that it is sustained by large groups of ordinary people willing to devote all of their spare cash and energy to spending time in the saddle. The common ridings form the core of Border cultural identity and horses stand at the heart of them.

Foxhunting also sustains unbroken traditions of horsemanship. When deer became scarce in the 17th century and woodland cover more sparse, hunters began to ride out with packs of hounds after the fox, a pest usually unceremoniously despatched by farmers. By the 19th century the sport had become popular and the Gilbert and Sullivan-style rituals and terminology developed. Hunting pink is perhaps one of the few authentic traditions since it is only worn by men because it imitates early military uniforms and recalls the enthusiasm of 18th century cavalry officers for the chase. Six hunts are active in the Tweed Basin and once again their supporters are not an elite of red-faced toffs yelling 'Yoicks!' and 'Tally-ho!'(although they certainly exist) but a cross-section of ordinary Borderers.

The scale of a raid depended on its target. If a small number of cows, sheep or horses was involved then as few as six or eight riders picked their way through the midnight moss. But if a great laird had decided to put 2,000 men in the saddle, there was no need, or even possibility, to move anywhere quietly and without detection. A raid began at a muster-point, and using the familiar language of the hunt, this was called a tryst. Cairns, river-meetings and other features were used, and since those who gathered from longer distances might arrive after the main party had left, directions were sometimes cut into the turf. At Frogden, near Kelso, there existed a circle of stones around a patch of smooth turf where a reiver could write with his sword. Speed was important and the Maxwells of the Scottish West March reckoned to have 250 in the saddle in half an hour. When the Scotts of Buccleuch planned a huge raid into the English Middle March in 1532, 3,000 riders were galloping south on the same day as the muster was called.

This ability to create an army out of nowhere in a morning not only made the great reiver warlords immensely and immediately powerful, it also alarmed central government deeply. Just as the Highland clans could rally quickly behind the cause of a catholic king, because of ancient and unquestioned bonds of blood and service, so the Borderers could have, at any time, swung behind a rebellion or coup of some sort and galloped hard to Edinburgh for the reckoning. It must have been a substantial comfort to successive Stewart kings that Borderers never found any cause worth uniting and fighting for, except their own.

Reivers carried a variety of weapons and most men could afford an eight to ten foot wooden lance tipped with a steel point. Used both for flat-out charging like an armoured knight and sometimes also thrown like a javelin, riders were expert at skirmishing with them, showing the skills now seen with polo ponies. Dirks or daggers (called 'whingers') were common and many carried a basket-hilted sword. A well-tried tactic was to charge full-tilt towards an enemy, parry his stroke with a small wooden shield or a drawn dagger, and as he was passing cut quickly at his neck or shoulder. When faced with adversaries on foot, reivers slashed down and cuts suffered to the head and face got the grim nickname 'a Lockerbie lick', after the Johnstones attacked the town in 1593. The better-off rider could afford a pair of pistols known as daggs. They were heavy, had only one shot, were impossible to reload on horseback and they took decades to replace the simple power of the bow and arrow. However, a small crossbow, called a latch, was carried behind the saddle and it was light enough to be shot with one hand.

Protection from blows concentrated on the head and upper body. Steel bonnets were almost universal and a quilted jack, sometimes with small steel plates sewn into it, was worn on the abdomen. Some of the better-off had 'backs and breasts', or steel breast plates, but they were a mixed blessing being heavy and significantly limiting the speed and endurance of a pony. Poorer riders wore two sheepskins with the fleece side turned inwards. This must have been suffocatingly warm but such padding did deflect slashing blows, particularly when bits of bone and horn were sewn on the shoulders and arms. The business of riding also affected what could be worn to protect the legs and while long jack-boots helped, some wound brass or pewter wire around their thighs to deflect a cutting stroke.

WHITE MEATS

Because they could forage better and were generally less trouble, ewes were often used for milking more than cows in the 16th century Border country. A variety of hard white cheese was made which kept for a long time and was occasionally so hard that it had to be soaked and beaten with a hammer before it was edible. Dairy products of this sort were known as white meats.

In common with other stock-rearing cultures the Border reivers lived on a diet of white meats, some red meat and cereals. Jean Froissart observed them carrying food with them;

"Under the flaps of his saddle each man carries a broad plate of metal, behind the saddle a little bag of oatmeal... they place the plate over the fire, mix with water their oatmeal, and when the plate is heated, they put a little of the paste upon it and make a thin cake like a cracknel or biscuit, which they eat to warm their stomachs."

There is no better accompaniment for cheese than a good, rough oatcake, and perhaps that is a judgement passed on by DNA rather than an acquired taste. It is sad to reflect that in the river valleys of the Tweed, Teviot and Eden only one or two regional cheeses are made. A similar area in France would produce thirty or forty varieties with their biggest market being local. In the Borders we seem content with sweaty red cheddar from New Zealand.

At Warden-meetings, or truce days, large groups of reivers attended, fully armed. The Laws of the March had ordained that justice between English and Scots would be done and that the Wardens of the Marches would preside. On 7th July 1575 a meeting had been fixed at the Redeswire, near the point at which the modern road crosses the Carter Bar. At the head of a huge cavalcade from Coquetdale, Redesdale and Tynedale rode old Sir John Forster, the Warden of the English Middle March. One of the rare English Borderers to be appointed by Elizabeth I, his reputation was no better than it should have been. Wardens were not well paid and many, particularly on the Scots side where the Wardenship tended to stay in the same families, were in fact great reivers themselves when the opportunity presented itself. Also fixers and extortionists, in the contemporary phrase 'they winked at' the criminal actions of their kinsmen and neighbours, providing they got their cut. Forster was near 70 when his pony trotted up onto the ridge of the Redeswire and he had a lifetime of robbery and corruption behind him.

The Scots were led by Sir John Carmichael, not a Warden but the Keeper of Liddesdale, and a man with a reputation entirely opposite to Forster's. It was to prove a combustible mixture.

At the moment when both cavalcades caught first sight of each other, they halted. Generally this was a formality but its original purpose was to offer each group the opportunity to weigh up the size of the other, and pick out the identity of who might be attending. If one was heavily outnumbered (a limit of 1,000 a side was eventually agreed) then a warden might refuse the meeting and turn his pony around. If all seemed well the Wardens and their immediate entourage advanced into the middle ground between the cavalcades. There they exchanged guarantees and fixed a truce to last until sunrise on the day after, or longer if needed. When all was settled the Wardens both raised their hands to signal to their followers to come on. They were supposed also to embrace. Perhaps some did.

Tense situations are well dealt with by this sort of predictable formality and the bureaucracy involved was designed to defuse problems before they flared. Bills of complaint naming malefactors were exchanged in advance of the truce days and each warden was bound to produce the accused. Three methods of adjudication evolved. With six from the English side selected by the Scottish Warden and vice-versa, juries of 12 men heard cases. Sometimes a matter could be dealt with on the Warden's 'honour', that is, an accused could be acquitted if his Warden was prepared to swear to his innocence. In addition an accused could call on the oaths of an avower to support the truth of his denials.

Verdicts dealt mostly in the currency of reparation rather than physical punishment. Goods or livestock stolen were compensated for by the formula of 'double and sawfey'. Convicted or confessed (some did — no doubt for tactical reasons) thieves were bound to pay double the value of the goods stolen and an amount of 'sawfey' for the insult of taking them in the first place. Precisely this legal formula exists in the Laws of Hywell Dda, a Welsh king who reigned in the 10th century and who compiled a codex of customary Celtic law. 'Sawfey' is even a corruption of the Welsh term, 'sarhaed', which means 'a fine for injury'.

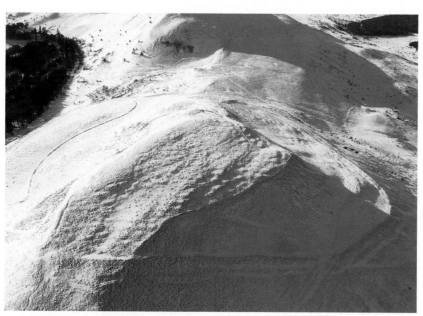

1. Eildon Hill North under a scatter of snow showing clearly a pattern of perhaps 500 circular stances for prehistoric huts.
Reproduced courtesy of Scottish Borders Council.

2. The Mutiny Stones in the Lammermuir Hills. Beside the long cairn is a sheep stell built out of stones robbed from the monument.
Reproduced courtesy of Scottish Borders Council.

3. The familiar Scott's View showing the three Eildon peaks in the distance,
and the ploughed field in the foreground is the centre of the site of the
ancient monastery of Old Melrose.
Photograph by Ken McGregor.

4. Aerial photograph of the ridges of ancient Anglian fields near Midlem
shows up what is invisible on the ground.
Reproduced courtesy of Scottish Borders Council.

5. The ruins of Jedburgh Abbey.
Reproduced courtesy of Scottish Borders Tourist Board.

6. The ruins of the late 14th and early 15th century rebuilding of
Melrose Abbey.
Reproduced courtesy of Scottish Borders Tourist Board.

7. The decorated capital 'M' from the foundation charter of Kelso Abbey. On
the left sits the bearded King David and beside him his grandson, Malcolm IV,
the Maiden.

8. The riders following the Lauder Cornet wear 20th century dress but out on the common they look like light cavalry from another age.
Reproduced courtesy of Scottish Borders Tourist Board.

9. A 19th century swing plough made on the principles pioneered by James Small.
Reproduced courtesy of Scottish Borders Council.

10. A ploughman rides home in the evening accompanied by his bondager.
Reproduced courtesy of the Robert D. Clapperton Trust, Selkirk.

11. Workers in the darning flat at Gardiners Mill, Selkirk.
Reproduced courtesy of the Robert D. Clapperton Trust, Selkirk.

12. A group of workers employed in the renovation of Philiphaugh, Selkirk, in 1890.
Reproduced courtesy of the Robert D. Clapperton Trust, Selkirk.

13. The gardeners and foresters at Philiphaugh in the 1890s.
Reproduced courtesy of the Robert D. Clapperton Trust, Selkirk.

14. Kelso Abbey from the north.
Photograph by Ken McGregor.

Central to all of this was the idea of honour, in the sense of having a reputation for truthfulness and for keeping a promise made. Perjury was taken seriously and the punishment for it was known as 'bauchling and reproaching'. At Warden-meetings proven liars or oath-breakers were loudly and publicly vilified by bauchlers who carried a glove on the end of a lance to point at the man in question, or they showed a picture of him or blew their hunting horns to pick him out. This could be an incendiary procedure and it so often led to trouble that it was suspended after 1562 when fighting broke out yet again. Honour was important in Border society and its protection or destruction inside a legal apparatus once again mirrors a Celtic example. In Irish texts of the 9th century 'enechruicce' or 'face-reddening' was recognised as a punishment and all sorts of enforcements were arranged around the notion of of dishonouring, and playing a central role were the bards. They were adept at the composition of mocking and belittling verses, and some remnants survive in the corpus of the Border Ballads. At the Redeswire in 1575 name-calling began when it was realised that an accused man had not appeared. An English Borderer, Harry Robson of the Falstone, was absent and his production was the responsibility of old Sir John Forster. And when he in turn was accused of failing to do his duty, tempers began to fray. The Scots Keeper, Carmichael, and the old man entered upon a shouting match which quickly ignited violence, it seems, from the English side. The Tynedale men loosed a flight of arrows at the Scots and battle was joined despite the efforts of Forster and Carmichael to restrain their men and restore order. A contingent from the town of Jedburgh arrived (giving rise to their anthem whose chorus is 'Stand firm and sure for Jethart's here') and many Englishmen were taken captive. The incident became known as 'The Raid of the Redeswire' and it is said to have been the last battle fought between the two nationalities. The authorship of the ballad that followed is unknown, but it is certain that he was a Scottish bard. Here is the last verse;

> "Who did invent that day of play,
> We need not fear to find him soon:
> For Sir John Forster, I dare well say,
> Made us this noisome afternoon.
> Not that I speak preceislie out,
> That he supposed it would be perril;
> But pride and breaking out of feuid,
> Garr'd Tindaill lads begin the quarrel."

The tale of Thomas the Rhymer shows that the bardic tradition was alive in the river valleys of the Borders in the late 13th century. In the hills the old traditions were likely stronger. Certainly the legacy is powerful. Described by an American critic as 'unsurpassed by any in the world' the Border Ballads are justly famous. The best have an energy and accuracy which still stirs the imagination half a millenium after they evolved. Many refer to real people and real incidents and the atmosphere around the tales of the raiders in the night and battles lost and won is unmistakably that of martial glory. These were the deeds of hard driving men in hard riding times, and the language of defiance and raw courage may not fit 21st century attitudes, but it is impressive for all that.

One incident and one short example of a ballad will illustrate. By October 1566 the Earl of Bothwell had become Mary Queen of Scots' lover and he was anxious to impress. Hermitage Castle in Liddesdale was his and he used it as a prison to hold a gang of Elliots he had lately rounded up. On the hunt for more of the same surname, he came upon Jock of the Park, also called Little Jock Elliot. Bothwell shot him out of the saddle and dismounting, he walked over to administer the coup de grace. In an instant Elliot was all over the Earl, stabbing him in the face, chest and hand. With difficulty the wounded man escaped and made for the safety of Hermitage Castle. But while he had been away, the Elliot prisoners had overpowered the garrison and the bleeding Bothwell found himself negotiating with them to be allowed back into his own castle. The first line of the resulting ballad has gone into the Scots language, and the Scots' pysche;

"Wha daur meddle wi' me?
Wha daur meddle wi' me?
My name is Little Jock Elliot,
And wha daur meddle wi' me?

I've vanquished the Queen's Lieutenant,
And garr'd her troopers to flee:
My name is Little Jock Elliot,
And wha daur meddle wi' me?"

The Border Ballads existed exclusively in an oral medium until Walter Scott, with much help, collected them into 'The Minstrelsy of the Scottish Border' in 1802–3. Many of his contributors were women who had become the memory of that culture rather than its creators. That role belonged to an entirely forgotten and anonymous group of people, the lost Celtic bards of the Border.

BALLET

Border ballads extol the virtues and courage of martial men engaged on deeds of dangerous glory. The etymology of the word 'ballad' is surprising. It comes from the Old Provencal 'ballada' meaning 'a song for dancing' which in turn is from the Latin 'ballare' for 'to dance'. This is also the derivation of 'ballet', as in Swan Lake. A ballet rather than a ballad based on the tales of the Border reivers might be entertaining and 'The Ballet of the Outlaw Murray', for example, might produce a new slant on a familiar story.

There were hundreds of Jock Elliots and the identity of Jock of the Park is only probable and not certain. Like the Highlanders and the Welsh, Border reivers used a limited number of surnames and even fewer Christian names to go around with them. To confuse matters even more the same families tended to repeat the same Christian names again and again for generations. What made recognition easier — or possible in some cases — was the retention of the patronymic. In the Gaelic Highlands this was taken by outsiders to be a surname when 'mac' was attached to Donald, for example, and in Wales when 'ap' or 'son of' was imperfectly welded to Rhys to become Price, or 'ap' to Hywell to become Powell. Through some unknowable process Borderers had fixed early on distinctive surnames — Armstrong, Scott, Elliot, Carleton, Fenwick, Ker and about a dozen other major 'names' — but what cleared matters up for those who needed to know was the prefixing of old-fashioned patronyms. So, an unspecific Jock Elliot could become Sim's Jock Elliot, or Jock the son of Simon, or if that was not enough, Davie's Sim's Jock Elliot. Sometimes matronymics were used to make Meg's Jock Elliot better known.

Just as memorable were additional names, something originally called 'an eke-name', an extra name which ultimately mutated into 'nickname'. Ill Will Armstrong, Nebless Clem Croser, Bangtail Armstrong, Buggerback Elliot and his brother, Dog-Pyntle are famous for their nicknames rather than who they were. Almost certainly who they were, in such a close society, was intimately bound up with what they were called. Others are even more mysterious; evidently several men got the nickname 'Sweet-milk', and one 'As-it-luiks'. In his unsurpassable 'The Steel Bonnets', George MacDonald Fraser pointed out the similarity between these last and the American Indian way of naming warriors — Crazy Horse and so on. Taking into account the nomadic life of a Border society which lived outdoors on horseback, the parallels do not end with names.

Names were important to Borderers (they still are) because they stood obviously for family, the binding agent amongst all the disorder and chaos visited upon and created by the reivers. Like the Highland clans, each name had a chief or a Heidsman, and some controlled very large forces of horsemen. Loyalty to a family was expected to be absolute. In the absence of law and order and the ineffectual presence of a weak or remote central government, it was all the security that most people had. These bonds of blood were powerful and durable. The Elizabethan playwright, Ben Jonson, walked all the way from London to Dumfriesshire to visit the lands of his ancestors, the Johnstones. In order to distinguish himself from all the other Johnstones in London, Ben had changed the spelling himself.

Feud was an inevitable corollary of such tight-knit intensity. Families on the same side of the border often fell out over some slight or other, sometimes even branches of the same family. The Kers of Cessford evidently hated the Kers of Ferniehirst. But the longest-lasting feud in British history was fought between the Maxwells and the Johnstones and their satellite 'names'. They alternated the wardenship of the Scottish West March between them and, depending on who was in the ascendant, perpetrated some appalling atrocities of vengeance. Allied to the Maxwells were the Moffats, a particularly unpleasant bunch, and having murdered a gang of Johnstones, they proceded to decapitate them. And after putting their heads in a sack, the Moffat Heidsman is said to have uttered, "There you are then, Johnstones, ye can a' greet thegither now."

The original offence, quickly forgotten, took more than 80 years to resolve and involved at least one pitched battle, at Dryfe Sands in 1593. When Lord Maxwell met the Heidsman of the Johnstones in 1608 to discuss the terms of a reconciliation, the talks ended after a short time. Maxwell had shot Johnstone twice in the back.

Duels, or single combats, sometimes settled matters. The place-name 'Tourneyholme' at the junction of the Kershope Burn and the Liddel Water remembers how often this piece of neutral territory was used. Precise times and instructions, particularly on the question of armour and the nature and number of weapons, were issued and sometimes set down on paper in an indenture. Opponents often fought on horseback and occasionally in pairs. The second fighter became known simply as the second, but in 18th and 19th century duelling he ceased to be involved in the contest. When the Earl of Bothwell fought Ker of Cessford, they laid about each other for two hours without result. After agreeing that both were too tired to continue, the seconds carried on and the Earl's man was slashed across the cheek.

When they fought, which was often, families roared into the melee with their war-cries. These were often the names of their muster-points and the Cranstons shouted 'Henwoodie!', the Maxwells 'Wardlaw! Wardlaw!', while others used surnames as rallying calls, 'A Hume! A Hume!' or 'Shafto! Shafto!' Where brothers and cousins fought side by side, few will have held back, for nothing meant more than family and no-one questioned why they were in battle. The worst that could happen, worse even than death, was to be expelled, to become, in the parlance of the Border, 'a broken man'. At the end of the 16th century some of these joined together into a surrogate family to form a notorious gang known as 'Sandie's Bairns'.

THE SCOTTISH MAFIA

When the Arabs conquered Sicily in the 9th century many natives took to the hills to become outlaws who herded flocks of sheep, goats and cattle. After the Norman and then the Spanish conquests these groups formed themselves into tight family units bound by intense loyalty. Vendetta, or feuding, became common and by the early modern period they had developed sophisticated techniques of blackmail and protection racketeering. 'Mafia' is a Sicilian dialect word which is the exact equivalent of 'smeddum', and it also means 'boldness, mettle, or spirit'.

At peace the inheritances of Celtic culture were equally patent. Partibility, or the division of a man's land between all of his sons, was the curse of medieval Wales, a legal custom exploited to the full by Edward I in his war against Llywelyn II in the 13th century. It survived well into the 16th amongst the reivers, particularly on the English side where it was known as 'gavelkind'. William Camden noted that over time the division of land had reached a point where sons inherited entirely uneconomic units, far too small to support even one person. In the way that these things often happen in England, gavelkind was not abolished until 1928. This parallel survival was not helped by another similarity with the

Welsh law codes. Illegitimate children 'begotten in brake and bush' were usually recognised, and provision made for them in wills and the surname confered.

THE BA' AND THE BELL

Football was popular amongst the reivers and in such notices as exist, it is usually refered to as 'the ba''. Wat Armstrong of Liddesdale is remembered as 'the best at thieve craft or the ba'', and his surname reckoned themselves great players. In 1599 the first six-a-side match in history was played at Bewcastle with the Armstrongs of Whithaugh supplying one of the teams. The Earl of Bothwell was a keen footballer and there is a record of violent disagreement between him and an opponent, the Master of Marishal. No code of rules has come down to us and no doubt they varied a great deal with some games lasting from dawn to dusk.

Horse-racing was more straightforward, with clear winners and losers. Well beloved by the Border reivers, race meetings were occasions for betting, plotting and even fighting. Prizes won by the fastest combination were known as 'bells' and this tradition is carried on in the races associated with common ridings. The Peebles Bell is perhaps the most prestigious.

First and before all else, families such as the Armstrongs considered themselves Armstrongs, Carletons considered themselves Carletons. Nationality came a long way second, for these peoples on either side of the Cheviots shared common understandings and cultural habits which long predated the drawing of the frontier line. Even though it was forbidden except under licence from the wardens, there was a great deal of intermarriage between English and Scottish Borderers. This cemented cross-border alliances which both troubled and occasionally puzzled governments in Edinburgh and London. So little did it matter to them that some men bargained with their nationality. In 1550 Sandie Armstrong threatened to become a Scotsman if the English wardens could not protect him and his property. And in 1528 Sim Armstrong even went so far as to advise the Earl of Northumberland that the King of England ought to rule in the Scottish Borders since the bureaucrats in Edinburgh were useless.

One incident suffices to demonstrate the casual disdain of Borderers for the causes of the kings of England and Scotland. At the Battle of Pinkie in 1547 a sharp-eyed observer noticed that in addition to their crosses of St Andrew and St George, both sets of Borderers wore a great deal of extra identification; kerchiefs worn like armbands and letters embroidered on their hats. Worse, their national badges were sewn on so loosely that "a puff of wind might have blown them from their breasts". But most embarassing was the discovery that, standing within a spear's length of each other, in the midst of a furious battle, Scots and English Borderers were talking to each other. When they realised that they had been observed, both lots made some show of running at each other and "they strike few strokes but by assent and appointment."

Away from the din and clatter of battle the monks of the Border abbeys continued to seek spiritual peace in the quiet contemplation and worship of God. War burst in on them, and far more often after 1300 than before. But the great churches survived and even after the destruction of Melrose by Richard II's army in 1385, the abbey was rebuilt in great splendour. In 1927 a document came to light in the Vatican archives which paints a detailed picture of a Border abbey as it looked in 1517, in what turned out to be the late evening of its long life. John Duncan was a priest associated with the bishopric of Glasgow and his description of the great church at Kelso is both illuminating and elegiac;

"The church or monastery of Calco took its name from the small town of that name by which it stands. Its dedication is to St Mary... It is in the diocese of St Andrews, but is wholly exempt from any jurisdiction of the archbishop and is directly subject to the Apostolic See... It lies on the bank of a certain stream which is called in their language the Tweed and which today divides Scotland from the English...

The monastery itself is double, for not only is it conventual, having a convent of monks, but it is also a ministry; for it possesses a wide parish with the accompanying cure of souls which the abbot is accustomed to exercise through a secular presbyter-vicar, removable at his pleasure. The Abbot exercises episcopal jurisdiction over his parishioners himself.

The church, in size and shape, resembles that of St Augustine de Urbe, except that at each end it has two high chapels on each side, like wings, which give the church the likeness of a double cross. Its fabric is of squared grey stone, and it is very old indeed. It has three doorways, one towards the west, in the fore-part, and the other two are at the sides. It is divided into three naves by a double row of columns. The entire roof of the church is wooden, and its outer covering is of leaden sheets. The ground within is partly paved with stone and partly floored with bare earth. It has two towers, one at the first entrance to the church, the other in the inner part at the choir; both are square in plan and are crowned by pyramidal roofs like the tower of the Basilica of St Peter. The first contains many sweet-sounding bells, the other at the choir, is empty on account of decay and age. The church is divided by a transverse wall into two parts; the outer part is open to all, especially parishioners both women and men, who hear masses and receive all sacraments from their parochial vicar. The other part, the back of the church, takes only monks who chant and celebrate the Divine Office. Laymen do not go in except at the time of Divine Service, and then only men; but on some of the more solemn festivals of the year women are also admitted. In this furthest-back part, at the head of the church, there is an old wooden choir.

The high altar is at the head of the choir, facing east, and on this several choral masses are celebrated daily, both by monks and by secular chaplains. In the middle of the church, on that wall which divides the monks from the parishioners, there is a platform of wood; here stands the altar of the Holy Rood, on which the body of Christ is reserved and assiduously worshipped, and there is the great worship and devotion of the parishioners. On the same platform there is also an organ of tin.

The sacristy is on the right-hand side of the choir; in it are kept a silver cross, many chalices and vessels of silver, and other sufficiently precious ornaments belonging to the altar and the priests, as well as the mitre and pastoral staff.

The cemetery is on the north, large and square, and enclosed with a low wall to keep out beasts. It is joined to the church. The cloister, or home of the monks, is on the south and is also joined to the church; it is spacious and square in shape, and is partly covered with lead and partly unroofed through the fury and impiety of enemies. In the cloister there is, on the one side, the chapter-house and the dormitory and on the other, two refectories, a greater and lesser. The cloister has a wide court round which are many houses and lodgings; there also are guest quarters common to both English and Scots. There are granaries and other places where merchants and the neighbours store their corn, wares and goods and keep them safe from enemies. There is also an orchard and a beautiful garden.

In the cloister there is usually the Abbot, the Prior and the Superior; and in time of peace thirty six or forty professed monks reside there. The town... contains not more than sixty dwellings and is subject to the Abbot in respect of both temporal and spiritual jurisdiction. Nearly all the inhabitants are husbandmen and cultivators of the fields of the monastery, and none of them pays tithe or dues; on the contrary they receive payment from the Abbot, that they may be able to withstand and repel from the monastery the continual attacks of enemies.

The Abbey has, in addition, three or four other hamlets under it from which it receives tithes. It also holds the patronage of many parish churches from the vicars of which it receives part of the fruits. The Abbot's house is separate from that of the monks, but their table is in common.

Its value is somewhat uncertain because of the continual raids and pillaging of enemies and robbers, but by common opinion it is estimated at 1,500 ducats or thereabouts: and its fruits consist in church dues, tithes, provisions and rentals."

Despite the fury and impiety of raiders, the churches of the Borders were not lurching into an irreversible decay of both moral and architectural fabric, and thereby making the Reformation inevitable. That view allows informed hindsight too much play. In other European countries which remained catholic, churches needed reforming but did not suffer a Reformation. In Scotland the historical narrative did not have to lead to John Knox, Andrew Melville and the creation of the Kirk, the Church of Scotland.

Certainly there was laxity and even abuse amongst the monastic orders. Monastic houses had a reputation as grasping landlords. The Abbot of the Cistercian Abbey of Coupar Angus was compelled to scold his brothers at Melrose because they had moved out of the communal dormitory and into houses where they kept private gardens. But these domestic transgressions were nothing compared with the gross excesses of some English monks which made them such an easy target for the 16th century movement to dissolve the monasteries.

In fact in Scotland there appeared to be a revival of interest in the conventual life and by the 1550s the number of novices was increasing and the abbeys were reviving. In 1505 the people of Jedburgh joined with local lairds to endow a new foundation of Observantine Friars. A large church and cloister was built to house the preaching and teaching order, and within its walls scholarship had a brief flowering. In 1513 the Jedburgh Friar, Adam Bell, wrote a philosophical work, 'The Wheel of Time'.

It spun quickly for Jedburgh. By 1523 Henry VIII had gone to war with France, and to keep the Scots from interfering, Surrey, the victor of Flodden, sent parties of English Borderers from Redesdale and Tynedale raiding into the Teviot and Tweed Valleys. Jedburgh was burned and parts of Kelso Abbey destroyed. Although the English government was the main sponsor of the 1523 raids, the English Borderers, of course, had their own interests. After the Battle of Flodden, Dand Ker of Ferniehirst had thrown out the legitimate Abbot of Kelso and installed his brother Tam. This outrageous coup pulled the unfortunate abbey into the world of the reivers and made it a proper target for attack. In 1523 the Abbot's house was demolished, the gatehouse thrown down, the dormitory burned and the lead stripped off the roof and shipped to Wark Castle. The Scots attempted a half-hearted retaliation and Dand Ker led an attack on Wark, probably anxious to recover his brother's lead.

PORTABLE BOOKS

The monks who sat at their copying boards in the cloisters of Border abbeys usually produced large format books which were bulky, very heavy and expensive (in man hours) to produce. In the Middle Ages readers went to read books which stayed in the same place. This restricted the spread of literacy very much and allowed it to remain a near-exclusive prerogative of the church.

In 1507 a Selkirk man, Walter Chepman, and Androw Myllar set up the first printing press in Scotland in Edinburgh's Cowgate. Their royal patent permitted them to print law books, liturgical works, acts of parliament, and chronicles. Part of the dynamic of the Reformation was the notion of the priesthood of all believers and to become more than a doctrine, it required a programme of mass literacy to enable personal reading of the Bible. While John Knox's insistence on a school in every parish supplied the necessary skills, the successors of Chepman and Myllar supplied the texts, principally affordable editions of the New Testament for ordinary people to read without the help of a priest.

James V could only observe what was happening in the south of his kingdom. He was 11, in the hands of the Regent, the Duke of Albany and between 1526 and 1528, was held a virtual prisoner by Archibald Douglas, the Earl of Angus. When he escaped the 17 year-old was determined to establish his independence as emphatically as possible, and one of the first acts of his personal rule was to mount a judicial expedition to the Borders. Better known as justice ayres, these were full-scale military exercises where a large force of soldiers marched down from Edinburgh to base themselves at Jedburgh or Dumfries. From there they scoured the countryside for known criminals and brought them to trial. Strenuous efforts were made and justice ayres were often timed to co-incide with a full moon so that police action would not be suspended by darkness. Between 1513 and 1603 more than 80 justice ayres visited the Borders but few had any lasting impact. When he rode down the Leader Valley in the summer of 1529 the young king was determined to change that.

That winter the reivers had been out often, lifting cattle in Cumberland and Northumberland. Anxious to develop good relations with his uncle, Henry VIII, James had been embarassed by these raids, and particularly by the antics of the Armstrongs. He had summoned Border Heidsmen to Edinburgh, Buccleuch, Ker, Hume, Maxwell, Johnstone and several others, and promptly thrown them in jail. Adam Scott of Tushielaw and William Cockburne of Henderland were both executed in Edinburgh. James had 10,000 men at his back, and he was determined to bring the Armstrongs to book.

The greatest and most notorious reiver of the day, a man who could put hundreds and perhaps thousands in the saddle, was Johnny Armstrong of Gilnockie. So devastatingly successful had he been in forays into England that Henry VIII had made a special point of asking James to deal with him. Two months after the executions of Scott and Cockburne a deer hunt was organised in the Teviot Valley. It may be that by the stratagem of sending a letter of safe-conduct to him, James V invited Johnny Armstrong to join him at Carlenrig near Hawick. Borderers, and particularly those with a well-advertised criminal record, were wary of the blandishments of Scots kings and solid assurances of some sort must have been forthcoming. Dressed in his best clothes, riding with only fifty of his men, suspecting nothing, Armstrong was brought into the royal presence. Amazed at the reiver's finery, the King remarked "What wants yon knave that a king should have!" Perhaps Johnny had been cocky, disrespectful. Amongst independent-minded Borderers there has always been a pleasing disdain for those thought to be their betters. In the kirkyard at Carlenrig Chapel, the king's men began to close in on Armstrong and his entourage. As it dawned on him that he had been deceived, the reiver started talking — for his life. Missing the subtleties of the political reality behind his situation, he shouted to James V, "King Harry would downweigh my best horse with gold to know that I was condemned to die this day." It was true, Henry VIII would have paid dearly — that was the whole point. When his hands were tied, a noose slipped around his neck, the rope slung around a stout branch and he was set on his pony, Armstrong made a last, desperate plea. But the King turned his back and Johnny roared after him in fury, "What a fool I was to seek grace at a graceless face!" And then a serjeant whacked the pony's backside.

All of the reivers were strung up and hanged from 'growand trees' in Carlenrig kirkyard and one, Sandie Scott, was burned alive in retribution for his torching a house while a mother and child were still inside. Johnny Armstrong appears to have had eloquence, style and courage. Perhaps that is why almost immediately he became a hero, a reiver who allegedly only raided in England, was good to his people and just in his own way, and so on. It was all nonsense. Like most of his kind, he stole, burned and killed on both sides of the border.

SCOTS LAW

Along with a separate education system and the Church of Scotland, Scots Law completed a collection of institutions which made us different from the English, and sustained a distinct culture apart from the English. When taxed with the question of precisely what those legal differences are, even the most patriotic countenance can cloud over. No Procurators Fiscal south of the Tweed? Advocates and not barristers? There is some awareness of fancy names but little sure popular grasp of fundamentals.

The historical truth is that there was, in fact, little difference between Scots and English law in the Middle Ages. Aside from a few Celtic survivals like galanas and cylch, Scoto-Norman law was very like Anglo-Norman law. Criminals and litigants could expect broadly similar treatment on both banks of the Tweed.

What really began to stimulate difference was the disastrous battle at Flodden, and an astute Pope. After 1513 James V was strapped for cash and he appealed to Pope Paul III for a portion of the church in Scotland's revenue. Born Alessandro Farnese and nicknamed 'Cardinal Petticoat', Paul III was the brother of a papal concubine, an enthusiastic promoter of his family to ecclesiastical office and a devoted patron of both Michelangelo and Titian. And he was also a brilliant innovator, putting in train the reforming Council of Trent and underwriting those fierce agents of the Counter-Reformation, the Jesuits. When Scotland's king pleaded, in 1531, that he was broke, Paul saw an opportunity. He would agree to advance James a tithe of church revenue if he would establish a College of Justice. Based on a Roman model, complete with senators and other paraphenalia, it would act to import the principles of Canon Law into Scotland. As the Reformation began to take significant hold in northern Europe, Vatican strategists needed to create as many institutional links as possible with countries like Scotland.

The College of Justice contained 15 full-time judges and, despite the Scottish reformation of 1559–60, it remained in being to develop as a dynamic focus for modernisation. From that time onwards Scots Law grew away from English Common Law and it has never lost its 16th century Roman roots.

When Henry VIII began in earnest on the dissolution of the monasteries and broke with the Church of Rome so that he could be free to marry Ann Boleyn, a series of rebellions began to break out all over the northern counties. What became known as 'The Pilgrimage of Grace' was triggered by the attacks on the smaller monasteries. Taking the five wounds of Christ as their emblem, the rebels called themselves pilgrims and soon substantial forces rose all over the north. On 3rd November 1536, 15,000 had assembled at Burford Oke, only 7 miles from Carlisle. They were persuaded to disband but Sir Thomas Clifford, the son of the Warden of the English West March made the mistake of sending Border reivers to harry the rebels. Another uprising was sparked and put down only with great difficulty. The English monasteries duly ceased to exist and much of their wealth reverted to the crown. The English did have a

Reformation but it did not come about for theological reasons — politics drove the creation of the Church of England, and would destroy the catholic church in the Borders.

In 1545 the Earl of Hertford landed at Coldingham with 12,000 men. What was called 'The Rough Wooing' was about to become very rough indeed. In order to intimidate the Scots into agreeing to a dynastic marriage between Henry VIII's heir, Edward, and the infant Mary Queen of Scots, the English had begun to raid into the Borders in 1543. But they also brought other means of persuasion. Dangling generous pensions in front of many Heidsmen, Henry's agents hoped to organise a pro-English party inside Scotland. Those who accepted (and these were overwhelmingly people living near the border and therefore in greatest jeopardy) were counted as 'assured Scots', and more than a thousand swore oaths of loyalty to Henry before taking his money, probably for the sake of some peace.

When the French and catholic factions at the Scottish court brokered an alternative betrothal to the Dauphin, Francis, Henry was enraged. The year before Mary had been promised to Edward. Vengeance would be his, and if the Borders could not be bought then, by God, the place would suffer.

The Henrician Reformation and the dissolution of the monasteries made the still-catholic abbeys of the Tweed Valley obvious prey and Hertford led his men to Kelso to begin their work. The idea was to fortify the abbey as a military base, but a courageous band of Scots were determined, against immense odds, to make it difficult. Here is Hertford's report;

"From the camp at Kelso, 11th September 1545, at night. Please it your Royal Majesty to understand that upon Wednesday at 2 o'clock in the afternoon, I, Earl of Hertford, with your majesty's army did arrive here afore Kelso... and immediately upon arrival a certain number of Spaniards [mercenaries], without my appointment [approval], gave of their own courage an assault with their harquebuces to the Abbey but when I perceived the same to be too little purpose for the winning of it I caused them to retire and thought best to summon the House [i.e. the defenders of the abbey], which I did forthwith... and such are were within the same being in number one hundred Scots persons whereof twelve were monks... did refuse to render and deliver it. Whereupon I caused the same to be approached out of hand with ordinance and within an hour a great breach was made... the Scots bye and bye driven into the steeple but the way being so dangerous and of good strength and night being at hand, I decided to leave the assault till morning, setting good watch at night about the House. Which was not well kept what a dozen of the Scots in the dark of night escaped by ropes out of back windows and corners with no little danger to their lives. When the day was come the Steeple was soon assaulted. It was immediately won and as many Scots as were within slain."

After the conclusion of the seige Hertford ordered the fabric of the old abbey to be destroyed by fire and by undermining 'so that the enemy may have little use for it'. The trail of vengeance next led to Jedburgh where the abbey and the new Franciscan friary went up in flames. Six towers were also burned and these were the property of local lairds. Jedburgh must have resembled a miniature version of the Tuscan town of San Gimignano where many of the 16th century towers of the nobility have survived to dominate the horizon.

The Hertford Raid was immensely destructive; 287 towns, villages, farms and churches were attacked and burned. Since the Wars of Independence began in 1296 the Borders had suffered grievously and regularly but nothing approached the disastrous scale of events in 1545.

When the Scottish Reformation began to unfold in 1559–60, the Border abbeys were ruined shadows of their ancient glory. And their communities were in no condition to offer much of an argument to John Knox and his zealots. Since the beginning of the 16th century the revenues of most abbeys had been granted to commendators, absentee superiors who installed proxies to oversee such organisation as was left. James V made three of his bastard sons commendators in the Borders. Revenue was all that mattered to these men and the great landed wealth of the religious houses was granted away as heritable tenures for lay people who could afford to buy them. The tenants of the outlying Melrose granges at Lessudden (the east end of modern St Boswells), Newtoun (St Boswells), Newstead and Gattonside pooled their resources for the large down payment needed to secure tenure, and made provision for the annual payment of feu-duty thereafter. These farmers were not typical and the bulk of the estates of Kelso and Jedburgh went not to those who lived on them but those who wanted to buy them.

Monastic lands shrivelled but did not disappear all at once. The rights and relationships of the monks were too tightly woven into the fabric of Border life for them to be disentangled overnight. And nor were the monks summarily cast out beyond the precincts. Those who wished to end their lives in monastic vows were allowed to do so. In the 1560s at Melrose several old men stayed on, and in 1587 it was reported, "the haill monkis of the monasterie of the abbey of Kelso ar deciessit."

ICONOCLASM

The first, plain Cistercian church at Melrose reflected the order's early distaste for elaborate imagery and display. The second could not have been more different in tone; flamboyant and festooned with sculpture from floor to roof.

Idols or graven (meaning carved) images were abhorrent to the emerging Protestant church and particularly to the Scottish followers of Jean Calvin of Geneva. The word of God expressed in the Bible was central to their spare, conceptual grasp of true Christianity and the statues of Christ, the Virgin Mary and countless other figures smacked of the Old Testament's repeated disapproval of idolatry. Reformers smashed the faces of graven images to take away their power, and also destroyed much stained glass. The latter is truly a lost glory, for no contemporary illustrations of the great windows exist.

The reformed religion was slow to take hold in the Borders. Many lairds, such as Hume of Blackadder and Ker of Ferniehirst, stubbornly stayed with Rome, and sustained recusancy was recorded at Ashkirk, Hassendean, Greenlaw, Nenthorn, Ednam and Old Roxburgh where the church of St James still held mass for its few communicants. Religious life certainly changed for most ordinary people, but perhaps less dramatically than might be supposed. Many new Protestant ministers and readers were converted priests or monks, and those abbeys which had acted as parish churches continued to do so. The iconoclasts defaced what they saw as idolatrous and all painting and much sculpture perished. What could not be easily reached or was architecturally integral generally had the faces knocked off with hammers. But aside from these losses, the progress to a Protestant salvation differed at first only in the details from the old road.

For the reivers religion had never been a high priority. The first encounter since baptism for some came when they 'sang neck-verse at Harribee', the gallows hill south of Carlisle where they stood on a stool with a noose around their necks listening to a priest recite the Miserere or the 51st psalm. Up in the hills, far from prying eyes, itenerant catholic priests carried on making their rounds amongst the shielings for many years after 1560. These dedicated men were known as 'book-a-bosom' parsons and they performed the hatch, match and despatch rituals needed by the riding families.

In the low-lying river valleys where settlement was denser, conversion proceeded and Protestant ministers took over the important churches. One of the most acute teething troubles of the infant Church of Scotland was the short supply of new ministers. Converted catholic priests and monks were a handy stopgap, and while their change of heart may often have been genuine, some will simply have moved with the times. These attitudes made them suspect and most were appointed only as readers, a junior sort of minister.

Those lairds who could afford larger houses, stone-built towers or even castles sometimes recognised the new religion publicly, but in the privacy of their chapels, they remained quietly faithful to Rome.

Other leading families, particularly in the Tweed Valley, appear to have embraced the Reformation more readily. The Pringles of Smailholm Tower were clients of the Douglases and appointed as Master Rangers of the Tweed Ward of the Royal Forest of Ettrick. The grand title brought some handy revenue and bought a great deal of influence for the Pringles. In the 1580s Andrew Pringle appropriated one of the south aisles of the former abbey of Melrose, wishing to use it as a burial plot for his family.

At Smailholm the Pringles built a very well preserved example of a Border Peel Tower. As the frontier became militarised and grew ever more lawless, the better-off raised defensive towers and the remains of hundreds can be found all over the Borders, from Dumfriesshire and Cumberland and the North Sea coast. The description 'Peel' comes from the Latin 'palus' for a wooden stake, which also produced 'pale'. It came into currency because government legislation required Borderers to create outer defence walls of ditches, thorn hedges and paling stockades.

The Pringle chose a commanding site at Smailholm. From the top of the tower the views are long, uninterupted and extend to the foothills of the Cheviots far to the south. In the short wall-walk on the roof there is a watchman's seat nestled in against the chimney breast for some welcome warmth on long winter nights. Beside him there is a recess for a lantern and near at hand will have been an unlit bale-fire. When the beacon blazed on Smailholm's top, half the Borders saw it.

The architecture of the tower is blunt and simple. When the watchman roared that raiders were coming everyone gathered up their goods (beasts would have been driven off to some cover), rushed into the tower and bolted the thick wooden door. Behind it was a stout iron gate known as a 'yett' and above it a slit in the wall for a gun-loop to allow fire on attackers hammering at the door. Walls were very thick and windows small, but towers could not hope to withstand a seige, only the brief attentions of raiders who generally did not linger very long.

But they did want what, and often who, was inside. Ordinance would have made short work of most Peel Towers but fast-moving bands of reivers could not cart cannons around easily. The most common tactic was to fire the door, and perhaps get some way inside. Sometimes that made 'scumfishing' possible, this was the odd name given to the practice of smoking out defendants with bundles of wet straw billowing up the interior. If raiders gained the ground floor they were forced to fight their way up a spiral staircase where design was against them. Not only were defenders always at least one step above them, but the clockwise turn of the stairs allowed them to keep their unguarded left side to the inside wall, and gave them free play with a sword on the outside. And to make matters even more difficult, there was often a 'trip-step', one built with a much higher riser than the rest.

Occasionally attackers used scaling ladders and once they had gained the roof they would then remove it and drop down onto the top floor of the tower. But the best tactic of all was surprise. Sir Thomas Carleton of Cumberland raided into the Scottish West March in 1547 with encouragement from a government still stubbornly intent on 'Rough Wooing'. When he approached Lochwood Tower, a Johnstone stronghold, Carleton set his forces cannily. Like Smailholm, Lochwood had an outer barmekin wall (replacing the paling of earlier times) protecting the tower and enclosing some ancillary buildings. Carleton made a record of his raid and in it he related how, at night, his men "stole close into the house within the barnekin, and took the wenches, and kept them secure in the house till daylight". The reivers discovered that only two men and a girl were in the locked tower and, making sure that no-one made a sound, they waited patiently for the dawn. Finally, up on the wall-walk a man appeared, dressed only in a shirt. He looked around to see that all was well and shouted down to the girl to open the door. "Our men brake too soon", wrote Carleton, because the girl spotted them and almost got the door bolted before they could barge in and take Lochwood Tower without a blow being struck.

Smailholm also suffered in the Rough Wooing. One dark night in November 1544 raiders from Tynedale and Redesdale "with certain assured Scots took up Smailholm [village] and Smailholm Craig and took away 100 prisoners, brought away 600 cattle, 100 horses and much household furnishings". Two more attacks followed until John Pringle was himself forced to swear the oath to King Henry and become an assured Scot, promising not to interfere with future English raids and, presumably, not light his beacon.

In Tynedale and Redesdale Bastle Houses were more popular, and affordable, than towers. Getting their name from 'bastille', the French word for a fortified house, that is exactly what they were. Built of solid stone walls with a vaulted 'pend' on the ground for cattle and a first floor for people. The upper part was generally reached by a ladder or an outside stair. Bastles are unique in Britain and all lie within twenty miles of the frontier.

By the mid 17th century the Pringles had become too grand for the grim old tower at Smailholm and they moved into Galashiels to build Old Gala House. Auld Watt Scott of Harden bought the place and it stayed in his family until the 19th century. As a 'wee, sick laddie', suffering what was probably an attack of poliomyelitis, a three year-old Walter Scott was brought down from smokey Edinburgh to stay with his grandfather and his Aunt Janet at Sandyknowe Farm, just below Smailholm Tower. The wee boy came for many summers and listened to his aunt recite tales and stories from memory. Like Meg Laidlaw and Nancy Brockie, Janet Scott knew the long story of the Border by heart, and no doubt spoke and sang from the same place. To the young Scott she passed on the adjacent glories and excitements of his ancestral past. The wee, sick laddie needed only to look up behind the farmhouse at the great tower 'standing stark and upright like a warden' to feel his chest swell at a martial past that was so authentic and touched him so deeply that he inhabited it for the rest of his life. In many important ways Smailholm and Miss Janet Scott were the making of the great novelist — not so much his inspiration as a living affirmation of who he really was, the descendant of the Bold Buccleuch, Auld Wat of Harden and other members of the ruthless gang of criminals who had despoiled and almost destroyed the countryside Scott gazed at through the windows of Sandyknowe farmhouse.

On spring days when the sun begins to wester behind the Eildon Hills, the view to eastward from Smailholm Tower can be breath-taking. The Tweed valley opens wide between the dark heads of the Cheviots to the south and the softer roll of the Lammermuirs to the north. Too far away, perhaps thirty miles, to see clearly, the North Sea shimmers under a haze, only implied by a flat horizon.

At the mouth of the Tweed, Berwick sits quiet, brooding on the past. More than any other in Britain, war has shaped this town. Reminders of conflict, fear and politics appear around almost every corner. Visitors approaching the Tweed bridges from the south see ramparts reaching down to the quayside. From the north the A1 used to pass under the massive portals of the Scotsgate, and until 1964 there was a garrison of soldiers in Berwick.

If the frontier had remained peaceful then Berwick's destiny should have been commercial rather than martial. With a burgeoning agrarian

economy producing valuable surpluses in her deep hinterland and
trafficking them through a mercantile apparatus growing in
sophistication and contantly widening its web of contacts, Berwick's
future should have been rosey. A seafaring link to northern Germany,
the Low Countries, Scandinavia, the Baltic and Russia, the town might
have developed into a major British city and if the borderline had become
nothing more potent than a cultural curiousity through an earlier union
of the crowns, rather a dangerous military fact, perhaps Berwick would
have become Scotland's largest city, playing a southern Glasgow to
royal Edinburgh. Looked at from a Border perspective, Bannockburn
was a disaster. If Edward II had defeated Robert de Bruce, then Scotland
might have moved closer politically to England, or, more likely, the
frontier would have shifted safely north to the Lammermuirs. In either
case the Border economy would have survived intact, perhaps even
prospered, and the fatal disconnection of Berwick might not have taken
place.

Between 1147 and 1482 the town changed hands no fewer than 13
times. Often it was sacked and its inhabitants killed or driven out, and
on several occasions it had to withstand seiges without result — except
the continuing inhibition to expansion and trade.

After Richard, Duke of Gloucester (later Richard III), took Berwick
in 1482 the Scots were persuaded to recognise political realities and on
24th August in the same year, they formally ceded the town to King
Edward IV of England. It was one of the darkest days in the history of
the Borders. Buffer territory was agreed between the town and the
frontier and the Berwick Bounds formed a pale extending three miles
inland. In 1550 the garrison is first recorded completing 'the riding of
the Bounds' when the integrity of the boundary markers was checked
and any instance of Scottish encroachment pushed back. Just below
Mordington House the border runs along the Bailies' Burn, a memory
of the ancient process. This is an early historical notice of what must be
amongst the most revered and loved traditions of the Scottish Border
country, the annual common riding. After 1609 the Mayor and
Corporation of Berwick clambered onto their horses and spent a summer
morning riding the Berwick Bounds. Now they hire a bus to make the
short trip — but they still do it, every year.

The farms of the Bounds were intended as an overland supply of
food in the likely event of hostility with Scotland. Even though this
turned out to be a less frequent event after the Battle of Flodden, the
English crown continued to see the town as key possession. What
complicated matters was the conflict between the old and new religions,
a shifting strategic situation whose twists and turns eventually
produced something remarkable in Berwick. When the catholic Queen
Mary Tudor married King Philip of Spain, war was declared on France.
In January 1558 Calais was beseiged and the last outpost of the English
European Empire fell within a week. Berwick was seen as a northern
Calais, a fortress town in a hostile country that, by rights, ought to
belong to England. And England was determined to hang on to it.
Scotland was a traditional, if generally ill-advised, ally of France and
England was often at war with France. As ever this left open the usual

possibility of a two-pronged attack, or the necessity to anticipate one and thereby dissipate English forces by leaving enough in reserve to secure the northern frontier. Berwick would be a bastion against the Scots.

Artillery had begun to govern the thinking of military architects and in the 1550s work was undertaken on a truly massive ring of defences for Berwick. Only days after the fall of Calais in 1558, a plan was commissioned from an Italian designer, Portarini, and Sir Richard Lee put in charge of the construction work which was to get underway immediately.

The 16th century walls survive intact and they show how central Berwick was to English foreign policy. Completed during the reign of Elizabeth I the defences were by far the most expensive project paid for by the notoriously parsimonious queen. The cost was a staggering £128,648.

The simplest single reason for the survival of Berwick's walls is their sheer mass. Designed to resist cannon-fire, they consist of stout stone walls infilled with earth to make them very thick indeed, in some places thirty feet across. A well-directed barrage would certainly damage such a wall but could never hope to breach it. Even more substantial were the bastions. Shaped like compressed arrowheads projecting from the curtain wall, there are five facing to the landward side of the town, the direction from which trouble might approach. Cannon placed on the broad wall-heads, or cavaliers, of the bastions had an uninterupted field of fire on attackers attempting to negotiate the ditches in front of the defences. Artillery was poor at dealing with an enemy who had fought their way close in to the walls of a fortress, and to cure this shortcoming an ingenious solution was devised at Berwick. Behind the barbs of the compressed arrowhead of each bastion sit two pairs of cannon sited so that they can fire parallel with the curtain wall, and be able to rake any soldiers who got close. These flankers ensured that there could be no unprotected ground.

By 1570 her huge walls had made Berwick virtually impregnable, and, after such an enormous outlay of cash to ensure that, they probably sealed the town forever inside the English state.

MARIE D'ECOSSE

The series of treaties known collectively as the Auld Alliance did Scotland little practical good and the Borders much harm. Diplomatic ties briefly threatened to harden into something much more concrete in the late 1550s, and the huge ramparts at Berwick can be seen as an English reaction. With the accidental death of Henri II of France in a jousting match in July 1559, Mary Queen of Scots suddenly became Marie, La Reine de France when her husband succeeded as Francis II. At her marriage celebrations the arms of England and Ireland were displayed and Mary was hailed as the Queen of Four Kingdoms, it being generally recognised that she had an excellent claim to Elizabeth I's throne. Despite the Treaty of Edinburgh between England and France in 1560, Mary remained an incendiary figure capable of igniting all sorts of fears in the mind of her cousin, Elizabeth.

As Elizabeth I's reign wore on it became increasingly clear that she would not marry and that there would be no heir 'of her body'. James VI of Scotland, her cousin's son, came to be seen as the likely successor and in 1586 he was, like the assured Scots of the Rough Wooing, made a pensioner of the English crown. In what was probably Scotland's first propaganda campaign to be mediated by the printing press, images of James as a competent, even exemplary sovereign began to circulate widely from Edinburgh. Depicted as Solomon the Wise Ruler, Augustus, Patron of the Arts, Brutus the Unifier of Britain, and Arthur the re-founder of the old British Kingdom, it was rumoured that if he succeeded Elizabeth to become King of England as well as Scotland, James would change his name to Arthur.

The problem with all of this image-building was the Borders, and in particular the activities of the reivers. In the 1590s a prolonged spell of bad weather had produced a string of bad harvests and this was partly instrumental in driving criminal activity to new depths. Far from being a competent king fit to govern England, James looked as though he lacked the wit to control a few bandits on the Borders. Having appointed some of her kinsmen as March Wardens, Elizabeth I was extremely well informed about the antics of reivers on both sides of the line. What might have saved James' royal blushes was the patent fact that she had enjoyed just as little success in curbing the bad behaviour of her own people.

ESMÉ

Esmé Stuart was a man, probably the lover of the young James VI. Arriving from France as the Sieur d'Aubigne, he dazzled the king and within a short period they became very close. In March 1580 James made Esmé Earl of Lennox and a year later Duke. From a Borders perspective his affair with the impressionable king was a stroke of good fortune. Stuart secured the arrest of the Regent Morton, an efficient administrator who had mounted three effective judicial expeditions to the Borders from 1575 to 1578, and had him executed on 'The Maiden', a guillotine brought to Edinburgh by the Regent himself.

Gay relationships are rarely explicitly mentioned in the historical record, but statistics dictate that there must have been gay reivers. Nicknames offer strong hints; Buggerback Elliot, Bangtail Armstrong.

The intensity of raiding had been increasing since the 1570s. In the winter of 1589–90, Liddesdale raiders were foraying out stealing and burning on at least one night of every week. Over ten years one family-group of Elliots is reckoned to have mounted 40 raids and stolen 3,000 head of cattle, £1000 worth of goods, burned 60 buildings, killed 14 men and taken 146 prisoners. These figures are extracted from reported activity, and there may have been a great deal more which escaped the written record. With so much opportunity the techniques of the reivers were honed to razor sharpness. Because they knew that their return journey could be the most dangerous part of any raid, they began to use the device of ambush very effectively. Laden with stolen goods and slowed by herds of beasts, their chances of being caught by pursuers were high. Many had sleuthhounds able to pick up a trail quickly (some reivers slaughtered a beast to distract the dogs) and the march law of 'Hot Trod' allowed those who had been raided to chase reivers over the border in either direction. To counter this difficult problem incoming bands would split into two groups. One would ride and lift the cattle they had marked while the other would wait, hidden by darkness, in a suitably narrow place on the pre-agreed route back home. Once the stolen beasts were herded through, the second party waited to ambush the pursuers. This simple tactic was perfected by the Armstrongs and copied widely by other riding families.

Less subtlety was needed when a great raid was planned. After meeting at their muster-point thousands of riders travelled in the open, often on Dere Street, and descended into a valley to occupy it for some days. The main body headquartered itself on a village or somewhere men and horses could be easily provisioned, and then sent out satellite parties to lift the livestock and goods from outlying farms. Sometimes parts of the main group waited along the trails to ambush any pursuing the forayers.

On 24th March 1603 Sir Robert Carey began a journey which would consign the great and small raids to history as fast as his horses could gallop. A kinsman of Elizabeth I and appointed by her as Warden of the English Middle March, he attended the old queen through her last few days, all the while keeping in touch with Holyrood Palace by letter. Determined to carry the news of Elizabeth's death northwards and be the first to tell James VI that he was also James I, Carey had organised a relay of post-horses to be put on constant alert for his immediate use, at any time. He had travelled the north road often and could fairly claim to know it intimately. For a huge wager of £2000 Carey had walked all the way from London to Berwick in 12 days. When Elizabeth died on the morning of 24th March, he was in the saddle in minutes, spurring his horse north out of London. His sister, Philadelphia, had pulled a ring from the dead queen's finger and rushed to give it to Carey as a token of good faith. The ring had been a gift from James VI.

Reaching Doncaster on the first night, he awoke early and made good progress to reach Berwick by nightfall. With good fortune Edinburgh should be possible by the following afternoon. But somewhere in Berwickshire Carey fell from his horse and while he lay on the ground it kicked him in the head. Spattered with mud and blood, he clattered into the inner courtyard at Holyrood on the Saturday evening only 60 hours after leaving London. Even though James VI had gone to bed, Carey was rushed in to give him the news he had been waiting for all his life. Proof was supplied when the ring taken from the dead queen's finger was produced.

"Ill Week" followed the news of Elizabeth's demise and James' succession. There existed a tradition that all the laws of a kingdom were suspended between the death of a monarch and the proclamation of the next. Be that as it may, the Border reivers embarked on a feverish period of raiding when almost every band of active criminals in the West March was out on horseback. Grahams, Armstrongs and Elliots launched full-scale raids into Cumbria, lifting more than 5,000 head of cattle. Ill Week was more than likely a last flourish. Borderers were more politically acute than most, especially when questions of English/ Scottish relations were at issue, and they probably reckoned that the accession of James VI to the English throne could seriously cramp their independent style.

And they were right. Almost immediately the new King of Great Britain acted to suppress organised criminality in the Borders. A commission of ten was appointed, five Scots and five English, to sit in Carlisle from where a comprehensive police action was directed — on both sides of a redundant frontier. March law, the wardenships and the six marches were dissolved while large mounted squadrons roamed the countryside at will to search out and detain known reivers. The Grahams had been particularly active during Ill Week and they were singled out for special attention. Those not hanged without trial, a notorious process known as 'Jethart Justice', were deported to Ireland. Many Armstrongs, Johnstones, Elliots (as many as 3,000 of this surname are thought to have fled) and others followed them across the North Channel to form an ethnic group known as the Ulster Scots. Confusingly, this group also included families of English Borderers. Some stayed only a generation or so before moving on to North America where they were very successful. Eleven of the first fifteen presidents of the USA were of Ulster Scots ancestry and, in his 'The Steel Bonnets' George MacDonald Fraser makes the astute observation that high office could still be inhabited by direct descendants of Border reivers when, in 1968, President Johnson handed over office at the inauguration of President Nixon, a ceremony observed by Billy Graham and Neil Armstrong.

As James VI and I's pacification of the Borders began several Heidsmen saw clearly which way the political wind was blowing and they turned with enthusiasm on their own people, exploding the bonds of family loyalty which had endured for generations. Many must have gasped in astonishment at what went on. Sir George Hume hanged 140 and Scott of Buccleuch absented himself in 'the Belgic Wars' in the Low Countries before returning to hang and drown many without trial. The pacification of the frontier meant that land was worth having and a hanged reiver was a dispossessed one whose property reverted to the perpetrators of the king's justice — even if they themselves had been only lately on the other side of the law. The iron yetts of peel towers were to be reforged into ploughshares and the most potent weapon of Border reiving, the Galloway Nag, was to be removed from the landscape. A law was enacted forbidding the ownership of a horse worth more than £30 Scots, which in practical terms meant only a pack-horse or a draught animal. The carrying of arms was strictly proscribed and, with no cross-border redoubt to run to, the reivers who ignored the law could be hunted and hanged. Each time a man was caught and the case against him appeared to be doubtful the same answer always came back from Carlisle — hang him. By 1609 the mounted police force had rounded up what they believed were the last of the known criminals in the West March and these were despatched in a mass hanging at Dumfries. King James no doubt nodded with satisfaction when a report was delivered to London in the same year saying that the commission 'has purgit the Borders of all the chiefest malefactors, robbers and brigands."

Brutal it may have been, summary in its execution and no doubt often mistaken, but James VI and I had succeeded in achieving something beyond his predecessors. In a grand and slightly precious gesture of British statesmanship, the Border counties were to be renamed 'The Middle Shires' with their capital at Carlisle. Before 1296 when the border between England and Scotland shifted and was only occasionally contentious, the Tweed Basin, the Eden Valley and Dumfriesshire had prospered. When the frontier became a dangerous place, when the kings of England and Scotland continually contended across it, the Border withered and grew notorious as the resort of thieves and lawlessness. After 1603 when the united crown attempted to erase the line from the map, there appeared a chance of revival if not rebirth. The other directions taken by British history and three hundred years of damage and dislocation probably made a second golden age impossible. But at least there would be peace, and with that the clouds of war over the Borders would finally lift.

9

Dangerous Rapture

In 1637 the Borders saw 37 executions. No-one could remember such a peaceful time. The police action against the reivers had largely concluded in the 1620s and the Commission sitting in Carlisle disbanded. Slowly and cautiously farmers, stocksmen, villagers and townspeople began to change age-old attitudes; they looked to the horizon for changes in the weather instead of blazing beacons heralding troops of horsemen, they expected rather than hoped to see out a winter without raids and, most of all, they disengaged their society from the corrosive patterns of organised crime and re-entered the everyday politics of England and Scotland.

Since the Scottish Reformation had taken hold in 1559–60 those politics brought radical change to the Borders. The lives of ordinary people were profoundly affected by the thinking of the Kirk and the new directions taken by its charismatic leaders. Apart from its insistence on universal orthodoxy the old Catholic Church failed to live up to its literal meaning. Far from being wide-ranging, Catholicism had long stood for the polar opposite. Compared to the relative inclusiveness of Protestantism, Catholicism had deliberately concentrated knowledge and power in the hands of a priestly caste, part of whose role was to exclude the mass of ordinary people from all but a passive observance. In order to preserve the mystery of divine office, the great monastic churches of the Borders had kept lay worshippers out and if, as at Kelso Abbey, they allowed parishioners in at all, they were separated from the monks' choir and the high altar by a solid screen which prevented them even from seeing what went on far less taking any active part. Central to the ideology of the Reformation was something wholly different and new — the notion of the priesthood of all believers, and the breaking of the church's monopoly of direct contact with God and the parallel role of intercession. Priests would no longer hold the keys of the Kingdom of Heaven, for salvation could be attained by faith alone.

John Knox led a group known as 'the six Johns' who produced a manifesto listing what, in practical terms, the reformed church would do. 'The Book of Discipline' was drafted in 1560–61 and it is a text absolutely central to any clear understanding of modern Scotland. Embedded in every clause is a variant or an elaboration on a new idea described by Knox as 'a godly commonwealth', a forging of church and state into one homogenous entity. And much of its thinking was heavily influenced by the work of European reformers such as Jean Calvin. Each citizen of Christ's Kingdom of Scotland had responsibilities and these are laid out with grim, uncompromising precision. After some necessarily negative admonitions on the abolition of saints' days, "all those that the Papists invented" and some directions on the suppression of idolatry, Knox sets forth the constitution of the godly commonwealth. Ministers are to be elected by their parish congregations, the Kirk is to provide for the deserving poor, Kirk sessions are to be elected with authority to police the moral conduct of both the parishioners and the minister, and Superintendants are to replace the bishops in the administration of dioceses.

But arguably the most important and far-reaching provision of all was the following clause. Like the rest of 'The Book of Discipline' it is addressed to their 'Honours', the Lords of the Congregation, who had taken government out of the hands of the Regent, Queen Mary of Guise in 1559–60;

"Seeing that God hath determined that his Church here in earth shall be taught not by angels but by men… of necessity therefore we judge it, that every several church have a Schoolmaster appointed, such a one as is able, at least, to teach Grammar, and the Latin tongue, if the town be of any reputation. If it be upland [rural] where the people convene to doctrine but once in the week, then must either the Reader or the Minister there appointed, take care over the children and youth of the parish, to instruct them in their first rudiments, and especially in the Catechism, as we have it now translated in the Book of Common Order, called the Order of Geneva. And further, we think it expedient that in every notable town, and especially in the town of the Superintendant, [there] be erected a College, in which the Arts, at least Logic and Rhetoric, together with the Tongues [Latin, Greek and possibly Hebrew], be read by sufficient masters…

The Grammar Schools and of the Tongues being erected as we have said, next we think it necessary there be three Universities in this whole Realm, established in the towns accustomed. The first in St Andrews, the second in Glasgow and the third in Aberdeen…"

Central to this central clause was the aim of universal literacy. If the priesthood of all believers was to take meaningful shape, then all believers had to be able to read the scriptures for themselves without the help of priests or ministers, to understand the psalms and learn to recite the catechism. For Knox and the reformed church the high road to Scotland's salvation lay through learning your letters.

GRAMMAR

Latin and Greek are now little taught in Scotland's schools, and Hebrew hardly at all. With the recent demise of religious education, these grievous losses have created a generation of students with scant knowledge of either the classical tradition or the Christian heritage of Western Europe. This means that much of our history and art is mysterious to younger people. The Bible stories and beliefs behind, for example, Michelangelo's Sixtine Chapel ceiling are no longer understood and the manifold legal and political legacies of the Roman Empire are well-nigh invisible. This is not merely a shame or a matter for regret but a yawning educational deficit.

In the 1960s and 70s Scottish universities demanded a document called 'The Attestation of Fitness'. Proof of examination passes in Latin, Mathematics and English were sent to Kinburn House in St Andrews, and for a fee of ten shillings and sixpence a certificate was returned without which it was impossible to matriculate in Scotland. Sic transit scientia.

The rallying cry 'a school in every parish' did not ring out over a deserted educational landscape. Many schools had been established by the pre-Reformation church in Scotland. Friars were particularly interested in education and at Jedburgh the brief life of the community founded in 1505 almost certainly saw the employment of the first in a long line of dominies for Jedburgh Grammar School. At Selkirk the grammar school was run by William Brydin, who also doubled as parish priest and town clerk. There were also much older schools at Roxburgh, Berwick and Carlisle, although outside the large towns it is more difficult to find evidence of medieval foundations.

What Knox envisaged was of an entirely different order. Education provided on a universal basis was seen as an absolute religious necessity and the Kirk never ceased to strive for its fulfillment. But literacy without books would save no souls and the drive for open access to schooling needed to be met by a busy publishing and printing industry. Edinburgh in particular developed an unprecedented output of affordable portable books. These could be catalogued into six broad categories; religious works, Latin grammars, catechisms in Scots, books of psalms, histories and chronicles and literature in Scots. Print runs were often long. In 1622 one bookseller had for sale 1,500 bound Latin textbooks and a further 39,000 in sheets which could be trimmed and bound on demand. Another held in stock 2,300 small bound books in English and 42,000 in sheets. High volume meant low prices and Henry Charteris, an Edinburgh publisher-bookseller, offered editions of Jean Calvin's catechism at twopence a copy. Bibles were a more formidable publishing proposition and significant numbers of these did not find their way into private hands until the 1650s.

BIBLE BILL

The publisher William Collins was an ardent and active supporter of the 19th century radical evangelist, Thomas Chalmers, and with his brother, Charles Chalmers, he set up in business in 1819. An early Collins speciality was the production of inexpensive bibles for mass consumption. Like John Knox, Andrew Melville and the early reformers, Chalmers and Collins believed that godliness was close to literacy and the ability to read the word of God directly, without gloss or interpretation was a matter of salvation or damnation. Merged into the publishing house of Harper-Collins, the company retains a base in Glasgow and remains a mass producer of the scriptures.

By the early 17th century the reformed church had succeeded in setting up or taking over more than 700 schools in Scotland. Regardless of social class, all children in each parish between the ages of 5 to 7 and 10 to 11 were to be instructed in reading, writing, arithmetic and Latin where possible. Several sets of school rules survive and they outline a long school day. Children attended 6 days a week, from sunrise to sunset in the short days of winter and from 7am to 6pm, with breaks for breakfast, lunch and periods of recreation, in the summer. They sat on benches in one room if there was a schoolhouse, or in the church if there was not. Homework was often given out and the most common form was the overnight learning of passages of scripture by heart for recital the following day. Failure to recall the set text could be painful. "The master shall inflict punishment, striking some on the leg with a birch wand, belt or pair of tawse, others on the hips as their fault deserves, but none at any time or in any case on the head or cheeks".

TAWSE

At one time in the not too distant past the Fife town of Lochgelly was a name that struck fear into the hearts of Scottish schoolchildren. Lochgelly was where the tawse was made. A thick leather strap approximately 20 inches long it had a grip formed at one end, while at the business end what were known as 'tawse-taes'. To inflict even greater pain the designers at Lochgelly had the idea to split the end of the strap into two parts, and for reasons clear only to physicists and those on the receiving end, it hurt a lot more than a solid single strap. Scottish schoolteachers were also split on the matter of the tawse — not on the moral issue of its use, but how to use it best. Some favoured the tawing of a single hand held out by an erring pupil, but with a wide and high take-back over the shoulder, the chances of missing and self-inflicting a minor injury on the leg were high. A boy who 'jouked' and made the teacher miss was usually awarded 'a dooble tawin''. Others demanded that both hands be held out, one over the other, so that even an inaccurate blow might catch a pupil on the wrists, often more painful. The verb 'to taw' is still found in Scots dictionaries but no longer in Scots classrooms.

Teachers were also instructed to encourage and praise where appropriate and there appears to have been a genuine wish to see diligent and clever children progress. This was made possible by a coherent structure for further education put in place by Knox and the reforming ministers. Those 'apt to learn' could progress to a grammar school to acquire the Latin necessary to gain entry to the colleges in the towns and Scotland's three universities. Here is another passage from a later version, in English, of the Book of Discipline;

"If they be found apt to letters and learning, then they may not (we mean neither the sons of the rich not yet the sons of the poor) be permitted to reject learning, but must be charged to continue their study, so that the Commonwealth may have some comfort by them"

One of the main reasons for this was that the Commonwealth was expected to pay. The Kirk originally hoped that the revenues from the estates of the pre-Reformation church would provide for the new education system but, predictably, powerful secular interests, mainly the baronage, got there first and precious little was left. In 1561–62 an arrangement was made to allow one third of the old revenues to go to the crown and thence to the Kirk. What little survived that fiscal journey was wholly inadequate and most parishes were left to fend for themselves. Which, astonishingly, they did. Many heritors, or landowners, helped by contributing a little cash and in-kind payments such as land or property for the creation and upkeep of schools.

The 1633 Education Act laid down a defining principle of the Scottish system which forged a distinctive attitude. Unlike in England, every parishioner, not just those with children, was compelled to pay for the maintainance of a school. A 'stent' or local tax was levied to pay for the stipend of a schoolmaster and provide for the upkeep of a school, if one existed, and the building of one if it did not. Sometimes this proved extremely difficult to translate into fact. At Ednam, near Kelso, there were in 1627 "620 catechisable persons [members of the church] with a school very poorly provided and most... unable to pay school wages." Despite early difficulties it was the sense of a community responsibility for education which nourished the notion that educated people should return some comfort to the common weal — even if most of those educated were boys.

When late 20th century governments began to compel students to pay for higher education this ancient contract was broken, and the real and recent sense of contributing something, of giving back to a community which sustained a free education system for all may have been consigned, through short-sightedness and an ignorance of Scotland's history, to oblivion.

By the early 17th century mass literacy was becoming a political reality. As Knox prayed it would, it did create a godly commonwealth and, perhaps for the first time in Scotland's history it put the fire of religious zeal into the hearts of many ordinary men and women. Before the Reformation they believed unquestioningly in God and the alternative of eternal damnation, performed the rituals and paid the tithes in return for an assisted passage to salvation. After 1560 belief was not diminished but enhanced by direct access to the scriptures — believers were able to read and understand the sacred word of the Lord God Almighty. This process admitted them to the inner values of a religious life they had only observed in the past. And such intimate knowledge of the transcending beauties of the Bible fuelled the creation of the stunning cultural achievement of the Scottish education system, but it also created a marked propensity to religious rapture in the minds of many people, what turned out to be a dangerous rapture.

When Charles I attempted to enlarge the Union of the Crowns into religious uniformity between England and Scotland by imposing the English Prayer Book and reintroducing bishops into the Kirk, presbyterian Scotland would have none of it. Rioting broke out in Edinburgh and at Greyfriars Kirkyard the National Covenant of 1638 was signed by barons, lairds, townspeople and ministers. Copies were distributed for signature to other parts of Scotland. Both sides began to arm. And Borderers must instinctively have flinched, fearing the return of a bloody past.

Described by a contemporary as 'the auld wee crooked soldier' General Alexander Leslie had risen through the hard school of mercenary service in Europe. While in the armies of King Gustavus Adolphus of Sweden and his psalm-singing troopers of the Thirty Years War, Leslie had organised a signing of the National Covenant by Scots mercenaries under his command in Germany. By late 1638 war seemed to be inevitable and a contingent of battle-hard Scots docked at Leith with the auld, wee crooked soldier on board. Immediately Leslie put preparations in train for what became known as the First War of the Covenant.

In late May 1639 word had come that Charles I had raised an army and was marching on Berwick. Leslie led a detachment of 4,000 Covenanters south to meet him and by 4th June they were in Kelso. On hearing of the approach of royalist cavalry, orders were given for Kelso to be defended by entrenchments (some of their remains can be seen in the Broomlands estate to the east of the town). The Earl of Holland advanced with a large force of 13 troops of cavalry, 3,000 infantry and 4 field cannon, but the strength of Leslie's defences persuaded him to fall back. The following day the Kelso detachment made for Duns where they joined up with the rest of the Covenanter army. Aerial photography shows clearly where Leslie sited their camp. On the summit of Duns Law there are well-defined outlines of a large rectangular area surrounded by ditching with small bastions at each corner where cannon were mounted. Robert Baillie was Principal of Glasgow University in 1638 and also a chaplain to the Covenanter army. He left an excellent description of the camp on Duns Law, as well as a powerful sense of the army itself — a godly commonwealth at war to defend its right to salvation;

"It would have done you good to cast your eyes across our brave and rich hill, as oft I did, with great contentment and joy. I furnished to half a dozen good fellows muskets and pikes, and to my boy a broadsword. I carried myself, as the fashion was, a broadsword, and a couple of Dutch pistols at my saddle; but I promise, for the offence of no man, except a robber by the way; for it was our part alone to pray and preach for the encouragement of our countrymen, which I did to my power most cheerfully. Our hill was garnished on the top, towards the south and east, with our mounted cannon, well near to the number of forty, great and small. Our regiments lay on the side of the hill, almost round about: the place was not a mile in circle — a pretty round rising in a declivity, without steepness, to the height of a bowshot; on the top somewhat plain; about a quarter of a mile in length, and as much in breadth, as I remember, capable of tents for 40,000 men. The colonels lay in canvas lodges, high and wide; their captains about them in lesser ones; the soldiers all about in huts of timber, covered with divot or straw. Our colonels were for the most part noblemen... our captains for the most part barons or gentlemen of good note; our lieutenants almost all soldiers who had served overseas in good charges. Every company had, flying at the captain's tent door, a brave new colour stamped with the Scottish arms, and this motto, FOR CHRIST'S CROWN AND COVENANT in golden letters. Our general had a brave royal tent but it was not set up; his constant guard was some hundreds of our lawyers, musketeers, under Durie and Hope's command, all the way standing in good arms, with cocked matches, before his gate, well apparelled. He [Leslie] lay at the foot of the hill in the castle [Duns Castle]… Our soldiers were all lusty and full of courage; the most of them stout young ploughmen; great cheerfulness in the face of all… Had you lent your ear in the morning, or especially in the evening, and heard in the tents the sound of some singing psalms, some praying and some reading scripture, you would have been refreshed: true, there was swearing, and cursing, and brawling, in some quarters, whereat we were grieved; but we hoped, if our camp had been a little settled, to have gotten some way for these misorders; for all of any fashion did regret, and all did promise to contribute their best endeavours for helping all abuses. For myself, I never found my mind in better temper than it was in all that time from I came from home, till my head was again homeward; for I was as a man that had taken my leave from the world, and was resolved to die in that service without return. I found the favour of God shining upon me, and a sweet, meek, humble, yet strong and vehement spirit leading me all along; but I was no sooner in my way westward, after the conclusion of peace, than my old security returned."

Regiments of lawyers, psalm-singing ploughmen and even a naive regret that soldiers were given to swearing — Bailie's description, as well as his own demeanour, was that of an army of religious zealots. Armed rapture. A landslip near the camp uncovered a slew of round pebbles — God had revealed bullets to fire at the enemy! The colonel of the lawyers' regiment, Sir Thomas Hope of Craighall, was an aggressive and sagacious advocate who kept a journal on Duns Law which enumerated the number of times an Unseen Voice spoke privately to him.

The National Covenant was more than a declaration of rights, it was a signed agreement between Scotland and God. It meant what it said — at great and tedious length — that Scotland was a nation covenanted to God, a chosen people with a unique relationship with the Almighty. This was the absolute belief, the dangerous rapture which persuaded lawyers and university principals onto the battlefield, and which would spill much blood in the Borders in the decades after 1638.

LEX REX

One of the most influential writers and ideologues of the Covenant was Samuel Rutherford. Born at Nisbet and educated at Jedburgh Grammar School, he developed radical thinking on one of the central issues of contention between the late 17th century Kirk and the Stewart monarchy. His book, 'Lex Rex', argued that no king possessed a divine right to rule; "Every man is freeborn, No person emerges from the womb in a state of civil subjection to any King, Prince or Judge." Authority, said Rutherford, derived from the people and not from God.

Leslie's careful planning and impressive show on the summit of Duns Law persuaded Charles I to seek compromise rather than conflict. The Treaty of Berwick was agreed and the armies withdrew from the Borders.

A year later Leslie's troops were once again tramping through the Tweed Valley. Charles I had no intention of honouring the agreements made in the Treaty of Berwick and he called his first parliament to Westminster for 11 years to vote subsidy for an army to deal with the Scottish Covenanting rebels. The 'Short Parliament' refused to supply the money and Leslie's forces met little opposition, brushing aside Lord Conway's troopers at Newburn on the Tyne. They occupied Newcastle and forced the king into another humiliating truce. As the constitutional crisis in London deepened the Scots saw a clear opportunity to extend the godly commonwealth to include all of the British Isles and Ireland. For the Parliamentarian side the English civil war had begun badly and John Pym, one of their leaders, argued persuasively for an agreement with Scotland. Since they stood to lose much by a royalist victory the Covenanters were natural allies. The Solemn League and Covenant of 1643 promised 20,000 Scottish troops for the Parliamentary cause in return for the conversion of England, Wales and Ireland to presbyterianism. Alexander Leslie and his namesake David Leslie, another experienced mercenary who had returned from the Thirty Years War in 1640, commanded the Scots at the Battle of Marston Moor near York, and helped to win a victory in 1644 which turned the tide of the war in favour of the Parliament. Forty one burgesses from Selkirk fought against Prince Rupert and the royalist army. They had left the town to join the Buccleuch regiment in Hawick "for the expedition to England, for the relief of Protestants there, borne down through the tyranny and cruelty of the Papists" according to the minutes of Selkirk Town Council.

However, difficulties were brewing in the north and David Leslie was forced to return to Scotland. James Graham, the Marquis of Montrose, was the most brilliant commander in all the royalist armies. Having defected from the Covenanting cause, he was appointed officer commanding the king's forces in Scotland. From the royalist stronghold of Carlisle he rode north with only three companions to raise an army. Reinforced by Alasdair MacColla, a scion of the southern branch of Clan Donald, and a small force of 2,000 Highlanders, Montrose embarked on a brilliant campaign. In thirteen months he won six consecutive victories against Covenanting armies. Key to his success was an ancient tactic, the all-out Highland charge. It succeeded even against well-armed and well-organised opposition. Muskets were unreliable, slow to re-load and once the first volley had been fired, a charge of Highlanders screaming their war-cries and racing across the heather could reach and cut to pieces lines of infantry with only bayonets to parry the slashing blows of the claymores.

By late 1645 Alasdair MacColla had led his clansmen west to attack their old enemies, the Campbells. Montrose needed new recruits to carry on the war and he swung his depleted army south to the Borders. The royalist Lords Traquair, Hume and Roxburgh had promised support but when Montrose reached Kelso, he discovered that Hume and Roxburgh had contrived to be 'captured' by Covenanting troops. Lord Linton and the Marquis of Douglas did turn up with a few horsemen . However these added little to Montrose's small force which numbered only a thousand or so with five hundred camp followers when he reached Selkirk in 12th September 1645.

David Leslie had 6,000 Covenanter cavalry at his back and, as matters unfolded, surprise on his side. Even though Montrose had chosen good, defensible ground at Philiphaugh by the River Ettrick, it was always going to be an unequal contest. Thick early morning mist on 13th September compounded Montrose's difficulties. He knew that they were coming against him but had no idea that the Covenanters had moved quickly up from England and were very close to his positions at Philiphaugh. Once the royalist army had been located, Borderers in Leslie's army advised an outflanking manoeuvre and 2,000 troopers were sent, completely undetected, around Howden Hill to come at the royalists' undefended rear while Leslie himself led a frontal assault. When defeat became inevitable Montrose was led, forcibly, off the field and his party rode hard for Peebles, the north road and safety.

Determined to stay true to their infamous battle-cry of 'Jesus and No Quarter', Covenanting troops then fell into an extended frenzy of killing. Irish mercenaries who surrendered on David Leslie's assurance that their lives would be spared were slaughtered. And many female camp followers were also cut down on the battlefield. Chaplains urged the troops, some of them Borderers, to cut down the idolatrous Papists and purge the godly commonwealth of their abominable presence. More camp followers, mainly Irishwomen and their children, had been held under guard with about 100 Irish soldiers at Newark Castle, more than a mile from Philiphaugh. In cold blood, some time after the battle had ended, the chaplains once more whipped up the bloodlust of the Covenanters. An eyewitness recorded the appalling scenes at Newark;

"There were many big with child, yet none of them were spared but all cut in pieces with such savage and inhumane cruelty... for they ripped up the bellies of the women with their swords till the fruit of their womb, some in embryo, some perfectly formed, some crawling for life and some ready for birth, fell down upon the ground weltering in the gory blood of their mangled mothers."

Others were shot nearby at Slain Men's Lea and more prisoners held in Selkirk Jail had to wait three months while the burgesses raised cash to buy the bullets and powder to shoot them too.

GUSTAVUS ADOLPHUS

When Scott of Buccleuch led 2,000 of his men to 'fight in the Belgic wars' in 1603, he was carrying on a long tradition. Scots mercenaries had fought in Europe at least since the 15th century and the heavily armoured Highland infantry known as the Gallowglasses were in the service of native Irish kings throughout the Middle Ages.

By definition mercenaries fight for payment but the 25,000 Scots who marched through Northern Europe on the side of 'the Protestant Cause' between

1625 and 1632 appear to have had a genuine affinity and a common cause with their co-religionists. In the middle phase of the Thirty Years War King Gustavus Adolphus of Sweden commanded the Protestant armies and enjoyed repeated success against the Catholic princes. During what was one of the bloodiest and most destructive conflicts in European history, he was often impressed with the steadfastness and grit of his Scots mercenaries. Alexander Leslie was promoted to the rank of Field Marshal in the Swedish army.

The brilliant campaign of James Graham, Marquis of Montrose, also depended on mercenaries. The major reason why he won six consecutive victories against much larger Covenanting armies was that the men led by Alasdair MacColla were battle-hard, highly experienced soldiers. They had fought in Ulster in 1641–42 and also in Flanders in the army of the King of Spain. Veterans such as these were much sought after and when they found themselves on the losing side the victors often enlisted them, after some negotiation. When David Leslie gave the Adjutant of the Irish at Philiphaugh his assurance that their lives would be spared, it was an agreement made between professional soldiers. And it may have been in Leslie's mind to offer them some employment. When the crazy amateur Covenanter troops murdered them and their women, it grossly offended not only common humanity but also the business ethics of mercenary warfare.

David Leslie's army had laid a long seige around the royalist city of Carlisle from October 1644 to June 1645. Such was the strength of the ancient defences that a garrison of 700 held 4,000 at bay for 9 months and only surrendered when King Charles was defeated at Naseby. Commissioners reported to parliament that Carlisle was "the model of misery and desolation". In fact the city had yet to recover from the long-term depredations of the reivers on the local economy. In 1617 Bishop Snowden told King James VI and I;

"The city of Carlisle is in great ruin, and extreme poverty, partly because the Lieutenant (Governor) is not there resident, and partly for that the inhabitants exercise themselves in no arts or trades, neither have they other means of livelihood besides fishing. In the country at large many of the meaner sort live dispersedly in cottages, or little farms, scarcely sufficient for their necessary maintenance, whereby idleness, thefts and robberies are occasioned."

Reiving was still troublesome to the north of England and a tax was raised from the heritors of Cumberland to pay for a small mounted police force to discourage raiders. It had some effect but an act of parliament in 1662 showed that the border was still being used as a means of avoiding justice and that 'moss-troopers' were active in Northumberland and Cumberland.

National politics also continued to cross and re-cross the border after the establishment of parliamentary rule and the execution of Charles I. Oliver Cromwell felt strong enough to renege on the terms of the Solemn League and Covenant and after the Scots accepted the restoration of Charles II in 1648 (when he signed the National Covenant), he invaded Scotland and heavily defeated David Leslie's army at Dunbar. General

George Monck was left as the Parliamentary governor of Scotland, the 'Commissioner for Scots Affairs'. He emerged as a pivotal figure after Cromwell's death and the subsequent failure of his son, Richard, to hold down the office of Lord Protector. With an army under his command, Monck was correctly identified as a king-maker. In October 1659 he told his senior officers in Edinburgh that he was opposed to the use of military force to influence parliament. Given the course of events, this was a mysterious utterance. An army junta in London had dismissed the Rump Parliament, but it had later been allowed to reconvene under the protection of dissident units of the London garrison. Watching events closely from Edinburgh Monck realised that chaos was not far off and the blandishments of the royalist party grew ever more attractive. In December 1659 army command headquarters for Scotland was moved to Coldstream on the north bank of the Tweed, where Monck's own regiment was based. Every member of the Westminster parliament knew that the moment the army in Scotland crossed the river, it left its area of proper jurisdiction and changed from a garrison force into a political instrument. Over Christmas in Coldstream General Monck waited and brooded. If his soldiers forded the rain-swollen Tweed, they would have to march on London and impose a new government — parliamentary, or a king and parliament. On New Year's Day with their colours fluttering under grey January skies, Monck's regiment led his army through Coldstream and marched into history as the Coldstream Guards. By 3rd February 1660 they were in London, and 11 days later they mustered on Tower Hill. Captains roared orders to lay down their arms so that they could be formally disbanded — and then after a moment, they roared again that the soldiers should pick them up again as The Lord General's Regiment of Foot Guards, the Coldstream Guards. To the rattle of drums hats were thrown in the air and all shouted "God Save King Charles the Second!". By May a king reigned again in London.

MATCHLOCKS AND FLINTLOCKS

17th century matchlock muskets had serious design flaws. In addition to taking a long time to load, the lit match, a smouldering cord-end held in a small vice above the firing plate or pan, sometimes set off the gunpowder accidentally and if it was raining might not set it off at all. Sometimes there was 'a flash in the pan' and at other times a musket went off 'half-cock'. One of the reasons why the Three Musketeers wore such rakishly broad-brimmed hats was to keep the rain off the firing mechanisms of their weapons as they aimed them. Musketeers also wore a bandolier with cartridge cases hung on it. They contained measured charges of gunpowder. After firing a first volley they tipped a new charge down the barrel, followed it with a wad and then used a ramrod to pack it tight. And then they pushed a lead musket ball down. For speed musketeers carried the balls in their mouths. Speed was important. Depending on the weapon and the wind, the range of a musket was about 200 yards. Highland armies used to wait for government musketeers to fire their first volley and then they charged. Racing across the heather, fuelled by adrenalin, a Highlander could cover 200 yards in less than 25 seconds.

The earliest design of bayonet also had problems. The plug-bayonet was shoved into the muzzle of a musket, which obviously prevented it from being fired a second time. At Killiecrankie in 1689 the Cameronians and the other government regiments could not remove their bayonets because dampness had swelled them and stuck them fast in their muskets. Nevertheless someone managed to pull it out and get a volley off for it was a stray bullet that killed the charismatic Jacobite commander, Viscount Dundee. The credit for the fatal bullet was claimed by Ringan Oliver, a well-known Border Covenanter and marksman. Without Dundee's leadership the rebellion quickly fizzled out.

Flintlocks were an improvement. To ignite the gunpowder a spark was created by an action which drove a flint against a metal plate. Accidental discharge was rare and rain did not affect the performance. Ready made cartridges with gunpowder and a ball wrapped in greased paper meant that only one operation was needed to load the gun. At Culloden in 1746 the government soldiers had flintlocks and side-fitting bayonets.

Monck hoped that the Restoration brought about by his Coldstream Guards would herald a period of stability and consolidation after all the damage and cost of the Civil War. In Scotland the reign of Charles II began something entirely other, it signalled a reign of terror, a domestic, self-inflicted terror that haunted the Borders with a dreadful vengeance. Between 1661 and 1662 three hundred women and some men were burned at the stake for witchcraft — and this is almost certainly a gross underestimate. It was a hideous death suffered for no good reason by more than 4,500 people in Scotland between 1590 and 1680, and insisted on by a population who sincerely believed that they were bound to perpetrate scarcely imaginable barbarities in the best interests of a godly commonwealth. The witch-burnings of 17th century Scotland were as much a consequence of the dangerous rapture of the Reformation as the parish schools and the Wars of the Covenant, and they were carried out with sadistic enthusiasm in the Scottish Borders. South of the Tweed a much larger population burned far fewer witches and behaved with comparative restraint. While the townspeople of Lauder, Stow, Selkirk, Jedburgh and other places regularly sanctioned the torture and hideous murder of hundreds of women and men, their English neighbours largely refused to join in the frenzy. While Scotland burned more than 4,500 in the 17th century, only 500 died at the stake in England — proportionately a huge difference. In fact some commentators believe the total Scottish figure to be a serious underestimate.

In 1563 the interest in witches first stirred when the Protestant Parliament in Edinburgh passed an act outlawing witchcraft on pain of death. Several Protestant countries in Europe enacted similar legislation at approximately the same period. If the Reformation thoroughly Christianised entire populations for the first time, then many remnants of pagan practices, particularly those associated with folk medicine and healing, will have suddenly appeared to stand outside a strict orthodoxy policed not by a priest but a whole community. And many healers were women. Systematic teaching and exposure to sermons in vernacular languages (instead of impenetrable Latin) will have given many people a powerful sense of responsibilty for their own salvation. Logically this realisation could and did also comprehend an opposite moral position — the total rejection of God and the worship of the Devil. As Protestant societies all over northern Europe began to fear the Satanic enemy within, and often associate his working with the remnants of pre-Christian religious practice, witch-burning broke out in many places, but with markedly less enthusiasm in England.

WITCHFINDER GENERAL

In 17th century Germany witchhunting developed like a frenzied epidemic. Dr Benedict Carpzov wrote a textbook, Practica rerum criminalium, on the proper conduct of witch trials. Evidently a bible-reading, god-fearing man he was nevertheless involved in the death of a staggering 20,000 people over his long career. The Bishop of Bamberg, a town near Nuremberg in southern Germany, had a special witch-house built with a torture chamber decorated with biblical texts. In ten years he had 600 witches burned. From 1500 to 1700 in Germany alone perhaps a million people were tried, tortured and killed because they were thought to be witches. Historians find this extraordinary phenomenon difficult to explain, and the only agreed common factor appears to be the parallel development of the Reformation.

Protestant Scots saw Devil-worship slightly differently. Clearly a godly commonwealth demanded the thorough rooting out of witches, but a deadly ingredient was added to the brew by King James VI. His morbid terrors and perverted interests led him to take part personally in witch trials. In 1591 Agnes Sampson of North Berwick was dragged before the king and a gathering of his nobles at Holyrood Palace to be interogated. Despite her appalling treatment she stoutly denied the charges and James sent her back to prison "there to receive such torture as has been lately provided for witches". Agnes Sampson was hanged by the neck, choking and vomiting for an hour before finally producing a confession.

James VI and I contributed more than a lurid interest in witch trials. In 1597 he published a book 'Daemonologie', a best-seller which outlined the notion of the demonic pact. In essence this saw a witch as a servant and devotee of the Devil — a Diabolic rather than a Christian, someone committed to work for the triumph of evil over godliness. In Scotland it was a crime to be a witch, whereas in England it was forbidden to commit acts of witchcraft. The more open-ended Scottish charge caught up many more unfortunates and could easily be used as a tool of spite or social exclusion.

Most accusations of witchcraft appear to have arisen as a result of quarrels or disputes within a community. Something of that sort may have led to the arrest of Catie Lees of Torwoodlee near Galashiels in 1630. She was taken to the tolbooth at Lauder to suffer dreadful indignities and torture. Willam Lees, her terrified husband, was reported to be 'content' that his wife was to be tried by 'pricking'. Once inside the tolbooth Catie was stripped naked and had all her hair shaved off. Then two 'watchers' threw her into a filthy cell to shiver in solitary confinement and rattled the bars regularly to keep her awake. Two days of total sleep deprivation was enough to extract a delirious confession, the details often supplied by the accusers. If nothing was forthcoming a professional witch-pricker was summoned. Catie Lees would have had her hands tied above her head to a hook or a beam and her whole body lifted off the floor of the cell. It was believed that the Devil's hellish power came from below, from the earth and was transmitted through witches' contact with it. Then a man with a long and needle-sharp brass pin probed Catie's naked body in search of blemishes, any mark which could be identified as 'the Devil's mark' or 'the Devil's nip'. Once a mole or a large freckle had been found, the pin was shoved in hard. If no pain was felt or blood shed then the suspect was certainly a witch.

In 1649 the Kirk Session at Stow appointed a committee to examine witches and James Kincaid of Tranent, the most infamous witch-pricker of 17th century Scotland, was sent for. On both James Henrison and his wife, Marion, of Stow Townhead he found the marks of Satan and "gave an oath before the Session that they were great witches". Marion Henrison was burned at the stake but the Kirk Session records show that her husband somehow survived the indictment since he was certainly still alive in 1650.

In the same year Robert or Hob Grieve was imprisoned and tortured in Lauder tolbooth where he confessed that he was the Devil's chief agent in the Leader Valley. Thumbscrews were often used to extract confessions and another favoured method was to lock a victim in the stocks so that only their lower legs protruded. Iron bars were then laid across them and the tremendous weight was excruciating. Twenty years before, Hob Grieve's wife had been burned for witchcraft in Lauder and it appears that through his own misery he gained some measure of vengeance. Under examination (i.e. torture) he gave up the names of many local women who were stripped, pricked and executed by hanging. Astonishingly one woman forgave her accusers on the scaffold and another said that she had only confessed so that she could end her unhappy life. Margaret Dunham was an innkeeper in Lauder and the costs of her trial, torture and execution were meticulously detailed and deducted from the value of the estate she had left to her children. The two watchers who had kept her awake, the services of the pricker, the sackcloth she wore on the scaffold and the wood for its construction added up to £27. There was money to be made out of this hideous business. John Kincaid was paid six shillings a day and a bonus of £6 Scots for every witch he confirmed. And he confirmed plenty.

Confessions were very important because, in strict legal terms, a witch could not be burned without a commission from the Privy Council in Edinburgh. Sometime this could be difficult to acquire and when Cromwell's forces occupied Scotland after the battle of Dunbar in late 1650, many cases were summarily dismissed. And from 1670 onwards the Privy Council showed less inclination to accept confessions obtained under torture, and judges who did not hesitate to impose heavy sentences on religious radicals often described witch-prickers as 'villains and cheats'. Sir Walter Scott's researches led him to believe that all manner of chicanery regularly took place. For example, witch-prickers were said to use retractable pins which, of course, caused no pain and drew no blood. Accused women were aware of official scepticism and some bravely defied local courts and Kirk Sessions. In 1606 Isobel Falconer of Eyemouth successfully petitioned the Privy Council in Edinburgh to the effect that the sheriff-depute of Berwickshire was not competent to try such a serious case, and in 1634 Elizabeth Bathgate, also of Eyemouth, obtained release from the Edinburgh tolbooth because the court at Duns which convicted her was incompetent.

However, a great deal went on unnoticed by the Privy Council. In the Borders witches were sometimes tried by water ordeal. This seems to have been a medieval practice enthusiastically carried on into the 17th century. A suspect was stripped naked, bent double and tied in the shape of a St Andrews Cross with her right thumb attached to her left big toe and vice-versa. And then, as the crowd roared, she was thrown into a 'hell-pot' or deep pool. Flotation showed guilt and drowning a dubious innocence.

Burning was most common because it was seen as a method of completely extirpating the existence of a witch. Most women were 'virreit' or strangled, at least into unconsciousness, before the fires were lit around them, but others suffered the appalling fate of being burned 'quick' or alive. At Greenlaw a witch was dragged to the stake at Gibbet Lea to be burned quick and when she begged for a drink from the River Blackadder, the crowd shouted no — the drier she is the better she'll burn. In 1608 in Edinburgh a group of perhaps eight witches were tied to stakes to be burned alive. Wood, peat, coals and tar barrels were piled around the screaming women and set alight. The fire burned through the bonds of three of them and, covered in horrific burns, they broke free and ran out of the blazing inferno only to be caught by the crowd and thrown back in.

By the early 18th century the witch-hunts had virtually ceased with only sporadic instances reported. Janet White of the Yarrow Valley was accused in 1721 of witchcraft when she burned the clothes of a sick child while muttering an incantation. Janet vehemently denied the latter and said to the Kirk Session that the child's parents had agreed to the burning of the clothes. No action seems to have been taken. The witchcraft acts in Scotland were repealed by the united Westminster parliament in 1736 but it is significant that this was only done on the initiative of English MPs and not Scots.

Patrick Hamilton, George Wishart and the handful of other reformers who were burned at the stake, and the Covenanters cut down in the 17th century are too readily seen as the obvious martyrs of the Scottish Reformation. That is an incomplete view. The heaviest civilian casualties of the creation of a godly commonwealth were the 4,500 and more who suffered a hideous death at the hands of the pious.

Few witch trials were reported in the north of England and the burning of a woman with the suspicious name of 'Madge Wildfire' at Harraby near Carlise in the early 18th century was notable because it occured at all. The suspicion is that the name might represent a tradition rather than an event. English Borderers had a markedly less obsessive interest in religion and certainly did not see themselves as members of a godly commonwealth — they were more concerned to wring a living from the windswept fells south of the frontier. The dales of Cumberland, Westmoreland and North Northumberland are less fertile than the lush river valleys of Tweed, Teviot and Annan, and the life of an English stock farmer could be hard. Not only was the land poor and the weather often inclement, but politics and economic competition also pressed heavy on the sheep farmers and graziers of northern England.

The 17th century saw the gradual erosion of rights to common land, even in the more remote back country of the Cheviot Hills. Effective law enforcement and the decline of the reiver war-lords made land valuable again and what had been described as 'waste' became desirable. Hill country around Tynedale, Redesdale, Liddesdale and Coquetdale could be made productive if it was related to the boggy valley bottoms, and that required a consolidation of ownership. Little cultivation was possible in the valleys but in summer, when the stock had been driven up to the high pasture, abundant, good-quality meadow hay could be cut to sustain the beasts through the winter. Using various quasi-legal devices that were always backed by the threat of force, powerful lords and gentry began to appropriate more and more common land. Selkirk owned a vast common of 22,000 acres and on three occasions, in 1536, 1607 and 1656, there were serious outbreaks of violence as townspeople fought the lairds' men to protect their rights. In the South Common the Earl of Roxburgh forced a division in 1678 which gave him a great deal of land around Bowden and Whitmuir. In 1695 an act of parliament formalised these land grabs and communities on both sides of the border slowly lost their commons. It could be a long and barely discernible process of attrition from one generation to the next and it took until 1777 for Hawick to give up most of her rights.

The other pressure on Border stocksmen was economic. As the general menace of reiving declined into sporadic outbreaks, and England and Scotland drew closer after 1603, Highland cattle drovers began to sell their beef to English markets. Agriculture in the north was unable to produce enough winter feed to prevent the annual late Autumn cull, and in the late summer while their beasts still had good condition, Highlanders drove them to markets, or trysts, at Falkirk and elsewhere. After a bargain had been struck the goods were once again on the move south. Government officials hoped to collect substantial customs dues by canalising the cattle drives through Gretna and Carlisle, Kelso, Jedburgh and Duns. Dues were high at £10 Scots per head and £5 for a calf, and many drovers attempted to evade payment. This took them through the hills on some of the old reiving routes (which had become known as 'thief roads') and down into England by slow stages. To protect their feet from hard surfaces and allow them to graze as they went, cattle were driven on grass as much as possible. In the Borders turf dykes known as 'raiks' were built 50 to 100 feet apart to provide a through-way for herds and to keep them off crops and valuable grazing. In the open ridge country of the Cheviots drovers chose different 'streams' for their cows, for the traffic could be so heavy that the ground remained boggy and churned up for days as different consignments of animals passed through. To keep condition on them, cattle were driven slowly with frequent stops to graze and few drovers expected them to cover more than ten or twelve miles a day. At overnight 'stances' or 'stands', which were always near a burn, watches were kept in relays. While large-scale raiding had stopped, a few cows were sometimes detached from a grazing herd that had been allowed to disperse too loosely.

BLACK PUDDINGS

En route from the Highlands to the Falkirk trysts cattle drovers made black puddings. Using the sharp point of a small knife they would open a minor blood vessel on an animal and drain off some of its blood before stopping the flow with sphagnum moss or somesuch. Mixing it with oatmeal, fat and onions they concocted the 'marag dubh', the black pudding.

Charles Macleod of Stornoway make the best black pudding in the world (phone number 01851 702445 for mail order) and when one of the present proprietors, Iain Macleod, was asked for the secret of their astonishing quality, he made the vague but reassuring reply, "We're very choosey about what goes into it". Macleod is the most common name on the island of Lewis and visitors to Stornoway anxious to acquire a black pudding are advised to ask for directions to Charlie Barley's.

Some Borderers became drovers — the skills of cattle-herding and cattle-stealing had much in common, and some Border cows, particularly from Galloway, found their way to English markets. But the vast majority of the beasts came from the Highlands. They were attractive to London dealers because they were cheap to buy and could easily undercut the price of English beef. Northern English graziers petitioned for higher customs duties on Scots cattle, saying that;

"the cattle being fed, maintained and fatted with far less charge than can possibly be done in England, they filled and quit the markets and undersell those of English breed."

Sheep were a better crop for Borderers on both sides of the Cheviots and the 17th century saw some resumption of the intensive sheep-rearing pioneered by the medieval Border abbeys. And techniques were timeless. Shepherds were still careful to have their ewes tupped as late as possible, even into November, so that they would lamb in the warmer months of March and April. From February ewes were milked in 'buchts' and many remote place-names such as Buchtrig, Bughtknowe and Butterbucht remember the practice. Before shearing the sheep were washed in a dub or pool and then branded with a 'smit' or mark. Autumn saw animals brought down from the hills to have their backs smeared with a mixture of butter and tar to keep parasites at bay, a time-consuming process repeated even when their fleeces began to grow back in. The mixture was applied to 'the shed' where a fleece divides, and it was reckoned that sheep saw far more butter than humans ever did.

The shepherd's calendar counted the days of a hard life in the northern fells but to more urbane visitors the people appeared quaint and backward. In 1676 a grand personage made his way from Newcastle to Carlisle through the Hexham Gap. Chief Justice Sir Francis North's journey was recorded by his nephew, Roger North, a man who had clearly forgotten (if indeed he ever knew) how dangerous reiver society had been;

"Here his lordship saw the true image of a Border country. The tenants of the several manors are bound to guard the judges through their precincts; and out of it they would not go, no not an inch, to save the souls of them. They were comical sort of people riding on nags, as they called their small horses, with long beards, cloaks and long broadswords with basket hilts, hanging in broad belts, that their legs and swords almost touched the ground. And every one in his turn, with his short cloak and other equipage, came up cheek by jowl and talked with my lord judge. His lordship was very well pleased with their discourse, for they were great antiquarians in their own bounds…"

Parochialism and a powerful sense of history was already characterising Borderers; two themes which will increasingly insist on their place in this narrative. At least the Chief Justice's escort remained, as ever in the Borders, unimpressed by status and he had the good sense, unlike his nephew, to listen to their stories and take pleasure from them.

Forty miles as the crow flies north from the Hexham Gap religious rapture was again at work. After the restoration of the Stuarts bishops had again been forced on the Kirk and despite several attempts at reconciliation, a significant part of the Covenanting movement stubbornly remained outside the established church. Congregations met in the open air, often in remote places with less risk of interference, and the attendance at these field conventicles could be huge. Some in Galloway attracted 10,000 worshippers.

In 1679 the Archbishop of St Andrews, James Sharp, was murdered and a Covenanting army defeated a government force at Drumclog near Strathaven. Having pitched camp at Bothwell Bridge in Lanarkshire, their cause drew support from many shades of Covenanting belief. The most militant were the followers of a preacher, Richard Cameron, who quickly became known as the Cameronians. Heavily defeated by the Duke of Monmouth at Bothwell Bridge, the Covenanters scattered and many took to the hills. The 1680s were called 'The Killing Times' because around 180 martyrs lost their lives. Field conventicles in the Borders drew large congregations and the area around Gateshaw, by the Kale Water near Morebattle, is still known as 'the Singing Braes'. Alexander Peden was an Ayrshire preacher who often toured the southern counties and his conventicles were so memorable that they attracted three separate place-names; Peden's Pulpit high on the slopes of Ruberslaw near Hawick, Peden's Cleuch at Southdean near Jedburgh and Peden's Stone at Castleton.

GATESHAW BRAES

Religious dissent at the village of Morebattle near Kelso did not end with the establishment of the Presbyterian Church of Scotland after the accession of William of Orange and Queen Mary in 1668. When the church became vacant in 1723 the Duke of Roxburghe (elevated from an earldom after the union of 1707 and gaining an 'e') had the legal right to nominate the new minister. James Christie of Berwickshire was chosen but the congregation wanted Andrew Tait who had been preaching to them since the death of the previous incumbent. After two years of wrangling matters boiled over in 1725 when the ministers of the Presbytery (the surrounding churches) arrived at Morebattle Kirk with Christie in tow. There was a rammy in the kirkyard led by a hefty local man nicknamed 'Nub of Bowmont'. Evidently he carried a large club and roared at the assembled crowd to remember their Covenanting past.

Christie was eventually inducted, but soon afterwards a substantial part of the Morebattle congregation seceded from the Church of Scotland. With no church building to hand they held open-air services on Gateshaw Braes. On 28th September 1737 people walked and rode from all parts of the Borders to take part in what was, essentially, a field conventicle. By 1739 Gateshaw (not Morebattle) acquired a full-time minister of the Secessionist Church, John Hunter. The centenary of his arrival was celebrated in 1839 with a huge conventicle at which no fewer than four sermons were delivered and all of the reasons for the original secession and the manifold charges against the established Church of Scotland were rehearsed in great detail. A further set of anniversaries were marked in 1889, 1939 and 1989. The theology and politics of the Covenanting movement and the Secession of 1737 might be imperfectly remembered now, but the thrawn spirit of dissent lives on.

In the towns religious dissent was more difficult to conceal but even so, house conventicles were popular. Contemporary records appear, at first glance, to suggest that town life itself was becoming more popular. The 17th century saw the granting of 17 charters to establish burghs of barony in the Scottish Borders; this was additional to the 9 burghs of barony and 4 royal burghs already in existence. In essence a charter allowed a local nobleman to set up a centre where markets and fairs could be held, and revenue gained from them. The monopolies of royal burghs were relaxed in 1674 to accommodate these initiatives. Genuine towns like Melrose, Kelso, Eyemouth, Duns, Hawick and Galashiels developed as small urban centres because there existed economic stimuli which encouraged growth, but most of the other burghs of barony were in fact speculations. Hamlets such as Rutherford, Longnewton, Linton and Smailholm have remained small, never blossoming into the sort of lucrative towns envisaged by the barons who secured their charters.

RUTHERFORD

Even though Lord Rutherford's charter to erect the hamlet of Rutherford into a burgh of barony failed to encourage much house-building or trade, it did mean that the identity and location of his family remained clearer than most. The Borders telephone directory lists one of the most memorable addresses in Britain; John Rutherford, Rutherford Lodge, Rutherford.

Interest in trade and its profits was not confined to ambitious Border lairds. In 1695 the Company of Scotland was set up to found colonies in the New World and open up markets independent of England or English interference. An enormous amount of money was raised, perhaps a quarter of all the cash wealth of Scotland. Colonies on the Darien or Panama isthmus were proposed. As the narrow finger of land separating the Pacific Ocean from the Caribbean and the Atlantic, the location of a trading settlement at Darien made every sort of logistical sense. Two expeditions were fitted out and sailed from Leith. And both ended in disaster. Disease in the mosquito-ridden mangrove swamps killed hundreds, the English colonists in the West Indies refused essential provisions and the Spanish forced 'New Edinburgh' to surrender in 1700.

CAMERONIANS

Richard Cameron was hailed as 'The Lion of the Covenant' and his followers remained faithful to his Covenanting ideals even after he was caught and killed by dragoons in 1680. On the accession of William of Orange and Queen Mary, the Earl of Angus raised the 26th Regiment of Foot from the followers of Cameron, and they became famous in British military history as the Cameronians. The regiment fought with great bravery in the defeat by the Jacobites at Killiecrankie and over a 300 year existence they amassed 113 battle honours and produced a remarkable number of generals. Faced with amalgamation with another regiment the Cameronians chose to disband in 1959. The emotional ceremony was held at a field conventicle in Lanarkshire.

Scotland was broke. Border lairds had invested many thousands of pounds and several burghs, such as Selkirk, had contributed £500. All of it was lost. The Darien disaster created a political as well as an economic crisis and some in Scotland saw a union of the parliaments as the only possible solution. Radical constitutional change would allow access to English markets and English colonies and prevent any future damage from protectionism. If England had co-operated, Darien would not have failed. In 1705 the debate was sharpened when the English parliament proposed the Alien Act. This measure would cause major disruption to cross-border trade by treating all Scots as aliens, as though they were French or Spanish. It was a flat-out piece of blackmail that would have made an Armstrong or an Elliot proud. Anti-English sentiment swelled, and if a popular vote had been possible, union with England would have found little support.

By contrast the English parliament was weary of Scottish problems and particularly anxious to avoid destructive dynastic dispute when the childless Queen Anne died. A united British parliament behind a united British crown worn by a prince of the Protestant house of Hanover was the ideal direction for history to take. An independent Scotland might choose to follow another road, as it did when Charles II was proclaimed King of Scots in 1648, and precipitate Britain into further warfare. Jacobite kings loomed like a menacing spectre at enemy courts across the Channel.

Money was found to compensate for the Darien disaster and 'the Equivalent' was promised in return for support for union with England. £398,085 and ten shillings was to be distributed to shareholders in the Company of Scotland. The proposal for union remained deeply unpopular in the streets of Edinburgh but the cash and the removal of the threat of the Alien Act persuaded many in the Scottish Parliament. When matters came to voting in 1706 a group known as the Squadrone Volante (the Flying Squadron) made the difference. Led by Border landowners, in the shape of the Marquis of Tweeddale and the Earl of Roxburgh, they opted to treat for union with England. Roxburgh was pragmatic about the reasons why;

"The motives will be, trade with most, Hanover with some, ease and security with others, together with a general aversion to civil discords, intolerable poverty and the constant oppression of a bad ministry".

When union came in 1707 Scotland's keystone cultural institutions of Kirk, education and the law were preserved. They were enough to maintain the border as a reality, to ensure that English and Scots Borderers continued to grow away from each other. The Union of the Parliaments and the creation of a unitary state did not signal a return to the ancient communities of interest and James VI and I's romantic 'Middle Shires' remained the southern and northern counties of different countries. By 1707 too much history had happened.

10

Day In, Day Out

When the evening sun slants low in the west and the heat is off the day, a breeze riffles through a green hay park carrying the murmur of distant voices clear across the valley from a farm steading. A child shrieks to counterpoint the bass notes of lowing cattle grazing in the summer air after a six month winter in the byre, and further down the valley the clop of a trotting horse fades in and out of hearing. Thorn hedges cast long shadows over the tidy pattern of fields and parks and on the western hillsides drystane dykes snake up to the ridges, a memory of backbreaking labour on cold, windswept days. In the distance, surveying all below, sits the Big Hoose, framed by its policies and an avenue of lime trees new into leaf.

There are moments in the Borders when the past settles back on the land and makes the present seem like another country. Only two or three generations ago, within the inherited memory of most families, Scotland was quiet and green. Before the ceaseless drone of traffic, the din of cities and the rattle of machinery taught us to listen less and make even more noise, the voices of the past could be plainly heard, chattering and laughing, complaining and weeping, and all talking of the same thing. Two hundred years ago farming was everyone's business.

But the Border country we sometimes glimpse on summer evenings is not a timeless Arcadia. The fields, the thorn hedges and hardwood shelter belts, the steading, the Big Hoose and its policies are not old. What seems to us like an Edenic, even eternal Borders landscape was created in the late 18th and 19th centuries, the result of changes which swept medieval agriculture off the face of the land and put in its place progress, embodied in the new and sometimes radical precepts of the improvers.

Parts of that vision of progress only came into focus slowly in the 18th century, while others appeared all in a rush, particularly in the 1760s and beyond when new technology was rapidly developed. The story of the invention of the Borders landscape is therefore a patchwork. Many areas and many people remained conservative, only adopting new methods as the old life became unviable, and by contrast, others saw the future in starker terms and, often self-consciously, set the pace for change. A patchwork story is perhaps best understood through the eyes of people who experienced the creation of the new landscape and left behind a clear sense of how they saw it. As the 18th century wore on, it grew increasingly rich in written records but one of the most fascinating happens to be very early and very complete. Lady Grisell Baillie's Household Book was compiled between 1692 and 1733. Mostly it exists in long lists of items set against their cost, but occasionally there are passages of discourse on matters important to Lady Grisell; education, the correct behaviour of a butler, a proper record of recent history and much else. The house most often recorded by the Household Book also survives. Mellerstain, near Gordon in western Berwickshire, is one of the most beautiful big hooses in Britain and Grisell saw it begin life in 1725.

The simple, even severe, classical lines of the house and its terraced gardens are little more than ten miles from Lady Baillie's birthplace, but a far cry from her own beginnings. She was the daughter of Sir Patrick Hume, a committed Presbyterian who resisted the efforts of Charles II to bring Scotland into closer religious conformity with England. His friend, Robert Baillie of Jerviswood, was arrested in London for treason in 1684 and brought to Edinburgh where he was imprisoned in the Tollbooth and probably tortured. His jailors may have taken to their work with some relish since Baillie was the great-grandson of John Knox. Fearing for his own freedom but anxious to communicate with his friend, Patrick Hume sent messages with his twelve year-old daughter, Grisell, who apparently behaved with remarkable maturity and courage. When a fellow prisoner, William Carstares, had his thumbs crushed by the 'thumbikins' and confessed that he and Baillie had been part of a plot to assassinate Charles II, the end came swiftly. Despite having been seriously ill with a protracted fever, Baillie was dragged in his nightshirt to the Court of Session where he was sentenced to be hung, drawn and quartered later the same day. Recalled to Edinburgh from university in Europe, George Baillie went to see his father in the Tollbooth. "If ye have a strong heart ye may go and see me nagled", said Robert to his son, "but if ye have not a heart for it, ye may stay away".

THUMBIKINS

As a legitimate legal practice torture was treated with an insouciance we find puzzling. The thumbikins or thumbscrews were handy, could be fitted into a coat pocket and applied with ease. The mechanical operation resembled that of a nutcracker. A three or four inch iron bar had three holes pierced and a separate three-pronged element of the same size inserted through them. The central rod was screwed and when the victim's thumbs or fingers were sandwiched between the bars, a small turnkey spanner was applied to a nut to close them together in order to inflict excruciating pain. Since they made little mess (except when victims vomited or voided their bowels or bladder) and were easy to carry around and use, thumbikins sometimes came in handy in the courtroom to extract whatever a judge wanted to hear.

William Carstares became Principal of Glasgow University and in an audience King William of Orange asked him about the thumbikins used on him in the Edinburgh Tolbooth. At their next meeting Carstares produced a set and a curious king inserted his thumbs between the bars to gain some idea of how they worked. Evidently Carstares offered to screw it up.

When news of the execution reached Berwickshire Sir Patrick Hume immediately went into hiding. In the teeth of a bitterly cold January he first found refuge in the Hume family vault in Polwarth kirkyard, near Duns. Each night Grisell stole out of Redbraes Castle, found her way down to the Howe Burn and then up and over to the kirk with a parcel of food for her shivering father. Evidently dragoons were watching the castle but after a month's privation in the vault, Grisell helped Sir Patrick slip into Redbraes where he hid under the floorboards whenever detection threatened. Finally the Humes escaped to Holland and the city of Utrecht where they were joined by George Baillie of Jerviswood.

As James II attempted to drag an unwilling Britain back to catholicism, secret negotiations began with his son-in-law, Prince William of Orange. Both George Baillie and Patrick Hume's son, also Patrick, had joined the prince's horseguards and they were part of his invasion force in 1688. As soon as William was established on the throne, his supporters were rewarded. Hume became Earl of Marchmont and Baillie was elected MP for Berwickshire. In 1692 Lady Grisell Hume became Lady Grisell Baillie, the couple moved to set up house at Whitesyde where an old fortified tower house stood on a ridge looking south to the Cheviots, and she began the first page of her Household Book. By all accounts it was a love-match and their daughter remembered;

"They never had the shadow of a quarrel or misunderstanding or dryness betwixt them, not for a moment. He never went abroad but she went to the window to look after him; and so she did that very day the last time he was abroad, never taking her eyes from him as long as he was in sight."

George Baillie was badly stung by the Darien disaster, having invested £1000, and he was said to resent deeply the destructive role of the English. However, when the balance began to swing in the direction of political union with England, he quickly saw its advantages, both personal and historical. With Roxburgh and Johnston, Baillie was one of the leaders of the Squadrone Volante who recognised union as a means of securing the Hanoverian succession, the opening of trade and the preservation of the Presbyterian religion. Having seen his father 'nagled' for his beliefs by a neo-catholic king, this last may have been of the greatest importance for Baillie. But like the others he also hoped to profit by the union — and he did, handsomely. Sent to Westminster as one of the 42 Scottish MPs, he was quickly appointed to the lucrative office of Commissioner for Trade and he enjoyed the substantial salary for 7 years.

Evidence of Baillie's determination to see George, Elector of Hanover, succeed after the sudden death of Queen Anne is to be found in Lady Grisell's Household Book. The entry for 15th May 1715 records a payment of £4, four shillings and sixpence for a gun and 30 swords, and on 18th September of the same year a further £18 and four shillings for 29 guns and bayonets and a barrel of gunpowder weighing 7 and a half stones. Ironically all of these weapons probably fell into the hands of the Highland army when a detachment looted the tower at Whitesyde on their way to proclaim James VII at the market cross of Wester Kelso.

This first substantial Jacobite Rebellion proved to be little more than a hiccup in the steady rise of George Baillie. George I appointed him a Lord of the Admiralty and a Lord of the Treasury, both positions attracting high salaries and powerful influence. Grisell's accounts reflected their enhanced status with notes of luxury items, musical instruments and so on, and also a sense of the circles they moved in. Some entries are very direct in their language; "29th December 1715 Drinkmoney £1, one shilling and sixpence" or "To lose at cards at Lord Lowden's 8 shillings" or " an opera ticket 8 shillings."

However, much of this expenditure was incidental. The Baillies devoted huge resources to the creation of a new house, renaming the site Mellerstain. In view of the pacification of the Border, the union of the parliaments and the confident expectation of continued prestige, the old fortified tower house of Whitesyde was no longer appropriate. Something altogether grander began to grow in Grisell's mind. The pre-eminent architect in Scotland was William Adam and in 1724 his services were engaged. Conceived on a truly grand scale, he designed one of the first big hooses in the Borders.

The site of the old tower was very commanding with sweeping prospects across the Tweed Valley to the Cheviot ridge, and it was decided to build the new house adjacent to it. Initially planned in two or three stages, the east pavilion was finished first (no doubt while the Baillies continued to live in Whitesyde) before a west wing went up to house the servants. William Adam also laid out the gardens and reorganised the geography to enhance the already magnificent view. The River Eden was canalised and dammed to form a long rectangular lake and on the first ridge of any eminence beyond it, a square turreted Gothick folly was built. Called the Hundy Mundy Tower, it has small window and archway openings to enhance the sense of distance from Mellerstain House. The overall effect is spectacular — and entirely unlike anything seen in the Borders until that date. It is undoubtedly more than a co-incidence that William Adam also designed the first version of Floors Castle for George Baillie's fellow member of the Squadrone Volante, the Duke of Roxburghe. Begun before Mellerstain, in 1721, there was no need to build a Hundy Mundy Tower, for Floors already had real romantic ruins set before it in the tumbled shapes of Kelso Abbey, Roxburgh Castle and St James' Church. Just as the tangible effects of being too close to a hostile border could be seen in the destruction of the ancient churches and the castle and the disappearance of the burgh, so the advantages for a few people of political union with England were all too obvious at Floors and Mellerstain.

EDNAM RULES

The author of 'Rule Britannia' was born at Ednam, near Kelso in 1700. James Thomson was the son of the minister and he was educated at Jedburgh Grammar School and Edinburgh University. Abandoning his divinity studies, Thomson went to London to make a career as a dramatist. He succeeded and with another expatriate Scot, David Malloch (who changed his name to the more anglicised 'Mallet') he wrote 'The Masque of Alfred' in 1740 and it included the song 'Rule Britannia'.

Thomson's enthusiasm for Britishness extended to a wholehearted adoption of the English language and a rejection of his native Scots. His long poem 'The Four Seasons' ransacks the dictionary in anxious pursuit of dramatic effect. Here are the opening lines of 'Winter';

"For see! where Winter comes, himself, confest,
Striding the gloomy Blast. First rains obscure
Drive thro' the mingling Skies, with Tempest foul;
Beat on the Mountain's Brow, and shake the Woods,
That sounding, wave below."

Modern readers find this sort of thing difficult to like but that should not cloud the undoubted fact that it was popular and influential in its day. James Thomson is commemorated by a statue in Westminster Abbey and an obelisk monument in a field between Ednam and Kelso.

These opulent palaces marked a decisive break with the past in more than architectural terms. Those who lived in them quickly began to see themselves as a group far apart from the rest of Border society. In 1726 William Adam wrote to George Baillie to say that he proposed to lower the floor of the kitchen in the servants' wing to five feet below the window sills and it "is so much better that it prevents those in the kitchen and scullery from looking into the gardens". In her Household Book Lady Grisell sets down 37 separate directions for her butler, including "You must keep yourself very clean" as well as a complicated system of signs designed to let him know when to clear away one course of a meal before bringing in another, and so on and on. Because of his role as a Westminster MP and in government, George Baillie and his wife were in London a great deal and no doubt in her directions to her household Grisell aped the manners of the sophisticates she met there, passing on what she observed to her servants. However, it is likely that when they did speak, Grisell and her butler spoke in Border Scots. Remembered as a talented songwriter, she certainly wrote in Scots and although only two of her compositions survive, one, "Werena my heart licht I wad die", was approvingly quoted by Robert Burns and shows genuine talent. But the common thread of language would be broken over time as the speech of Border aristocrats became indistinguishable from their English equivalents.

BORDER BLETHER

While homogeneity of speech drew together one stratum of society, divergence divided another. The abrupt change in modern accents between Cornhill and Coldstream, and Longtown and Langholm is puzzling.. There can be few places in Europe where such a sudden change takes place — and the change is radical. Northern Northumbrians and Cumbrians sound like people a long way to the south of them, and completely unlike their Scots-speaking neighbours. That people who live so near each other and share so much history and culture should have such differing talk is perhaps a result of the great changes wrought in 16th century Scotland by the Reformation. John Knox's Book of Discipline

> *created a distinctive sort of schooling and his church a different sort of worship.*
> *And perhaps these two central cultural shifts polarised Border society so*
> *profoundly that Scottish Borderers turned their backs on their neighbours and*
> *began to sound Scottish, and English Borderers looked south and began to*
> *sound English.*

When Grisell Baillie looked out of the windows of Mellerstain House she must have smiled at the confected drama of the view. Like herself it was beautiful, and it showed the power of her family to create something wholly new out of a few hundred acres of Border geography. But most of all it was testament to the distance travelled by the determined wee lassie who had taken messages into the dark heart of the Edinburgh Tollbooth and parcels of food to her father hiding in Polwarth kirkyard. Grisell Baillie never forgot the desperate days of her childhood and in the Household Book she went to considerable trouble to set down what she judged a correct record of the death of 'My Father-in-law', Robert Baillie of Jerviswood. Just as the geography around Mellerstain was altered to suit her needs, so posterity was set right by this formidable woman.

Beyond the Hundy Mundy Tower life on the land for those less fortunate than Grisell went on much as before. In 1700 95% of the Border population lived on the land and everyone had an umbilical connection to it. Since the Middle Ages methods of farming had changed little and the open landscape of scattered fermtouns, ox-ploughed runrig and rough pasture would have been immediately recognisable to a Melrose monk or a Berwick burgess. Arable land was still divided into inbye rigs under constant cultivation, like a modern vegetable garden, and outbye where crops were grown on a basic rotation before the land was allowed to fall fallow and recover its fertility. Beyond the heid-dyke lay the muir or the common where beasts went for summer grazing and farmers found fuel and building materials. The inbye was regularly mucked by the droppings of beasts, and after cropping, cows, sheep and goats were allowed to glean the stubble and deposit more fertiliser. Rights to the common grazing were controlled by a reckoning process known as souming (a derivative of 'sum') which related the amount of arable worked by an individual farmer to the number of beasts he could release onto the common. The more arable, the more beasts he could graze, and the more muck they dropped — it was a matter of elementary balance.

The only substantial enclosures seen on the old landscape were the heid-dykes separating the common grazing from the ploughed rigs, and also a few small turf or stone walls around the farmhouse to keep cattle and sheep out of the corn-store when they were inbye for the winter. Farms were not laid out in a clear and tidy pattern, as they are now. Thistles and corn cockle grew everywhere and were harvested for winter fodder. Stones had been tumbled for centuries into the ditches between the rigs which were often choked with weeds. Shelter from the winter winds was often scarce since there were few big trees to bield houses or stock. In fact the early 18th century Border country saw such a dearth of woodland that one of the first tree nurseries in Scotland was set up in 1729 at Hassendean, near Hawick.

Farmhouses had also changed little since the Middle Ages, with the basic longhouse shape and organisation of dwelling area end on to a byre and perhaps a barn. Sometimes the dwelling-house end had been more emphatically demarcated from the byre and barn by a passageway called a 'through-gang'. It connected the front and back doors, or the midden or rubbish tip on one side of the house with the yard on the other. The constant fire was the domestic focus. In more basic houses it still burned on a central hearth and the reek found its way out through a hole in the thatch or turf roof. Everyone sat, ate and slept around the fire as their ancestors had done for millenia. And even now, these memories are still alive — for many people who live in centrally heated towns and cities the flicker, warmth and smell of a real fire is what turns a house into a home. Sitting quiet after supper, staring almost hypnotically into the flames is the unconscious inheritance of uncounted generations. Stories, songs, arguments and complaints were all heard in the circle of firelight that warmed an 18th century family group. What a husband and wife did for privacy can only be guessed at. Given the Calvinist atmosphere of the times, they must either have waited until the children were asleep before making love, or in the summer months found a place outside far from the curious eyes and ears of youngsters.

Although these houses seem to us unimaginably primitive they supplied the basic life-sustaining elements needed by hard-labouring people. Nowadays we rarely experience the intense chill of a winter storm, are rarely soaked through or bone-weary from physical work, and we are not often so hungry that our bodies shake from lack of calories. Enough food, warmth and shelter could be found in these smokey 18th century houses and after a long day out on the rigs, such elementary comforts will have made the darkest cot-house seem like a welcome refuge.

The poet's sister, Dorothy Wordsworth, spent some days in a Highland blackhouse in 1803. Like Border cottages it had a fire in the middle of the floor and no actual chimney but rather a hole in the thatch. Despite the palpable sense of early tourism, her remarks offer some notion of what these interiors were like;

"... when I sat down in the chimney corner of her smokey biggin' I thought I had never been more comfortable in my life. Coleridge had been there long enough to have a pan of coffee boiling for us... We caressed our cups of coffee, laughing like children at the strange atmosphere in which we were: the smoke came in gusts, and spread along the walls and above our heads in the chimney [i.e. the hole in the roof] where the hens were roosting like light clouds in the sky. We laughed and laughed again, in spite of the smarting of our eyes, yet had a quieter pleasure in observing the beauty of the beams and rafters gleaming between the clouds of smoke... When we had eaten our supper we sat about half an hour, and I think I never felt so deeply the blessing of a hospitable welcome and a warm fire."

At Mellerstain Lady Grisell Baillie suffered few of the privations of ordinary people. Much of her time was taken up with the organisation of supplies, of 'purvey', for the dinner table. Long lists of items in the Household Book show a wide variety of cuisine when the Baillies were in London, sturgeon, broccoli, asparagus, oranges and much else. But at Mellerstain they dined on more homely fare. In the west wing kitchen, where William Adam had lowered the floor, the Baillie's cook went through a similar routine day in, day out. First thing in the morning she riddled the fire in the basket grate and shouted on one of the servant lassies to bring in more fuel. Once a blaze crackled, a black cauldron filled with three gallons of water was hoisted onto the swee-hook and swung over the flames. Big chunks of meat and bones went in next and they were followed by a few onions stuck with cloves and finally a bouquet garni of herbs tied with a twist of string was added. Onions were a favourite Border vegetable. Some roasted them on the edge of the fire in their skins, particularly when they were less than fresh, and others chopped them finely to add to a bowl of brose. After the cook had stirred the boiling broth she knocked down the fire to embers and put a lid on the cauldron to keep out any soot that might fall down the lum. Then fresh vegetables were chopped, soaked barley and peas drained and bits of hen cut up. By mid-morning the meat had boiled through and with a skewer cook lifted it out of the broth and set to one side on an ashet to cool. Then the mixture was strained to remove the herbs and any other unwelcome bits. After tipping in the vegetables, grain and chicken, salt was added and a few fresh leaves of mint, parsley or nettle might be sprinkled on before the lid was replaced. Recipes for what is now called Scotch Broth differ little from this, and the ever-simmering stockpot shows some French influence on Scottish cookery. The pot-au-feu is a tradition that reaches across the social spectrum from chateaux to humble dwellings.

While the broth was finishing, cook set a flat girdle pan to heat up over the fire. Then she started to prepare oatcakes and bannocks. Both used the same basic paste of oatmeal and water with salt and butter or fat to taste. Thinner than bannocks, oatcakes were cooked on one side only on the girdle before being set leaning on a stone by the fire to toast. Cooking on both sides made them too tough and too wearing on the teeth. Bannocks could be made with barley flour as well as oatmeal and had milk added to make them softer and thicker. As an addition or alternative, dumplings were sometimes boiled in the broth but the favoured clootie dumpling was usually made as a separate dish. A mixture of flour, suet and milk was wrapped in a clout or cloth (leaving enough room for expansion) and boiled for three or four hours depending on its size. After having been dipped in a luggie of cold water, the cooked clootie was put in front of the fire to dry and develop a skin. It was eaten in slices like a loaf of bread and when cold could be fried in some fat on the girdle.

STOVIES

Scotland is a winter country and it likes filling and warming food to keep out the cold. After all 'calorie' comes from the Latin 'calor' for heat. Stovies are the perfect dish for a cold night. A thick-bottomed cast-iron pan produces the best results;

* *Put in a generous dollop of dripping to melt.*
* *Add three or four chopped onions and soften them.*
* *Slice ten medium tatties (a mealy variety if available) and place them on top of the onions.*
* *Add enough water to cover the onions but not much of the tatties (about half a pint will do) and then put on a tight lid and simmer for an hour. While the tatties cook gently in the onion and dripping steam, shoogle the pan occasionally to prevent sticking.*

Stovies are one of the few remaining cross-border cultural ties. They are made in northern England under an alias, Pan Haggerty, but taste exactly the same. Which is grand.

In 'Humphrey Clinker', his novel of 1771, the Scottish writer Tobias Smollet left a record of the daily diet of ordinary people;

"Their breakfast is a kind of hasty pudding of oatmeal, or peasemeal eaten with milk. They have commonly potage to dinner composed of kail or cole, leeks, barley or big (a form of barley) and this is reinforced with bread and cheese made with skimmed milk. At night they sup on sowens flummery of oatmeal."

Leaving aside the meat and spices, it is striking how similar the food eaten at Mellerstain was to that of the farm workers of the countryside around. The menu may seem dull and unpalatably repetitive but it was filling, it did sustain hard manual work and it turns out that, according to modern dieticians, it was also very healthy. Certainly a history of endless bannocks, dumplings and broth created a singular cultural attitude to food amongst most Scots. Here is James Hogg of Ettrick writing in the 1820s about what he liked to eat;

"I like to bring the whole power of my stomach to bear on vittles that's worthy o't, and no fritter't away on side dishes, such as patés and trash of that sort."

The national preference for large quantities of filling foods, for stodge, continues but now, with refined wheat flour and a heavy use of fat, it is much less healthy and likely a cause of widespread heart disease amongst a largely sedentary population in Scotland. The hard work has stopped but the particular appetite has persisted and the fact that bakers' shops far outnumber fruit shops in Scottish towns is a historical legacy, not an accident or an expression of new preferences.

During the 18th century the way in which people ate their food gradually changed. In the decades immediately after 1700 all of the members of a farm community ate together, the farmer, his family and any who worked for him. A Selkirkshire farmer who died in 1745 left a detailed list of his movable possessions, and they are eloquent about the way he and his lived. It is worth quoting in full:

"Four beds, two fitgangs [long stools], three big and four small chests, one aumrie [small cupboard], two cupboards, a wool wheel, a lint wheel, a clack reel, a big table, an oval table, a long settle, six chairs, four stools, two meal arks, three tubs, a flesh boat, four butter kits, three cogs, six milk bowies, two stoups, two kail pots and a kettle, a brass pan, a salt fatt [vat], a brander, a girdle, a ladle, a sowens sieve, a babrick [baking board], a meal skep [straw container], two basins, a pewter stoup and jug, six pewter plates, three trenchers and a dish of earthenware, eleven wooden trenchers, six plates, six wooden caups [bowls], twelve horn spoons, six dozen bottles, a crook and clips for hanging pots above the fire, a pair of tongs and flesh hook."

By the standards of the day the Selkirk farmer was well-off and his many possessions describe the everyday routines of a life on the land. At mealtimes he sat at the end of his big table with his family on either side and his three male and three female servants at its foot. As at Mellerstain broth was the staple of their dinner, eaten with bannocks and oatcakes and supped out of wooden bowls with horn spoons. If meat was available the farmer would cut it up and dish it out on trenchers to be eaten without the aid of cutlery. In essence early 18th century farmers and their families ate what they grew and ate it off what local craftsmen could make out of locally grown materials such as horn and timber.

Although the pattern of service varied considerably (it is said that the cultural difference between hill farming and arable in Roxburghshire was much greater than that between English and Scots methods either side of the Tweed) it is possible to make some generalisations about workers in Borders agriculture. A hind was contracted on the basis of supplying another man with whom he could manage all the ploughing needed on a certain acreage. In return he got a house, quantities of oats and barley and enough ground to sow corn for his family and to keep one or two cows. His wife and children were expected to work with him at busy times such as harvest, ploughing and hay-making. Not surprisingly a half-hind received half the wages of a hind but he got more oats, particularly if he had a family. Seasonal workers, sometimes called 'taskers', were taken on as needed. In the upland farms shepherds were hired on a similar basis to hinds and instead of land to grow corn, they were allowed a 'pack' of up to 40 sheep of their own. Some of these conditions of employment died very hard and hirds were still allowed a pack in the latter half of the 20th century on Border hill farms.

The old agriculture was not inherently wasteful or particularly inefficient. Late 18th century improvers were fond of going into print with their progressive schemes and techniques and they often took sideswipes at what they saw as outdated and even mistaken methods. The reality is that the old ways worked well enough for a subsistence agriculture, only producing a surplus in good years and suffering the occasional bad harvest.

HEADS IN THE CLOUDS

Lady Grisell Baillie's daughter, also Grisell, married an eccentric man. Sir Alexander Murray of Stanhope, on the upper reaches of the Tweed near Peebles, was an ardent supporter of the new agricultural methods. Anxious to make his own unique contribution, he studied ancient history to see what could be gleaned from those who had farmed the Tweedsmuir Hills before him. When he came across cultivation ridges on the flanks of the hills, he concluded that it was humidity which had persuaded farmers to sow crops at these altitudes. After all, were the hills not often obscured by low cloud and inside these clouds crops had clearly flourished, a long time ago? In addition, some advantages in the science of irrigation might be procured by studying the weather at the tops of hills, where so many of these ancient peoples had lived and thrived. Unsuccessful experiments were conducted in the hills of Ardnamurchan, the area of mainland Britain subject to the highest annual rainfall.

Undaunted, Murray also planned a mining village in the Tweed Valley optimistically named 'New York'. Local people became so incensed at his madcap schemes that there were plots against his life. In 1743, long after Lady Grisell had fled home to the sanity of Mellerstain, Sir Alexander cheated the plotters and died in his bed, no doubt dreaming of glory.

Two factors created conditions for change. First and most fundamentally attitudes shifted from seeing land as a resource for producing fighting men to one which believed that it was valuable in itself for what it could grow. And secondly Scotland's population had been increasing steadily from 1500 and farming needed to feed more mouths. And greater productivity meant that landlords could squeeze more rental income out of their tenantry. Methods of husbandry quietly advanced in the early 1700s with an increased use of lime as a fertiliser, better management of crop rotations, the breaking in of new ground, longer leases to tenants to encourage improvement and an expansion of rural market centres.

Two trends within that context were more marked. A hundred years before they began in the Highlands, large scale clearances of cottars and their families took place in the Borders, and indeed right across the Lowlands. At the village of Longnewton in Roxburghshire (which attempted to become a burgh in the 17th century) the Earl of Lothian wanted to combine a number of small tenancies into one substantial farm. Some time after 1785 John Younger recalled what happened. His father had 14 acres with a house but all the land was to be absorbed into the new farm. Younger senior was only allowed to keep the rental of the house because he was a time-served shoemaker whose trade was thought valuable. But his dykes were thrown down and the land ploughed up to the walls of the house. Even the family hens were shot. Over a very short period the village of Longnewton virtually disappeared with twenty houses contracting into one farm. All that remains of the settlement is an isolated roadside graveyard sheltered by ancient yew and broadleaf trees.

Elsewhere the change was even more abrupt. Commercial sheep farming in the Lammermuirs saw the levelling of many cottar houses and the only hint of the existence of these turf and wood structures is often an old rowan tree growing in the corner of a field. Large numbers of people were involved in the Border clearances. In the 1690s 60% of the rural population of Berwickshire were cottars, and across the Tweed the percentage was also very high. Thomas Pennant, an early travel writer, rode through the Borders in 1772, crossing into England at the Reddenburn. As he made his way along the south bank of the river, he grew increasingly indignant at what he saw;

"All this country is open, destitute of trees, and almost even of hedges, for hedges are in their infancy in these parts, as it is not above seven or eight years since they have been introduced. The land is fertile, swells into gentle risings, and is rich in corn. It is miserably depopulated; a few great farmhouses, and hamlets, appear rarely scattered over the vast tracts.... A humour fatal to the commonwealth prevails over many parts of the north, of flinging numbers of small tenements [tenancies] into a large one, in order to save the expense of building; or perhaps to avoid the multiplicity of receipts, lay a whole country into a sheepwalk. These devour poor mens' houses, and expel the ancient inhabitants from their firesides, to seek their bread in a strange land. I have heard of a character... that is too infamous to be overlooked; which has so little feeling as to depopulate a village of two hundred souls, and to level their houses to the ground; to destroy eight or ten farmhouses on an estate of a thousand a year; for the sake of turning almost the whole into a sheepwalk. There he lives, and there may he long live his own tormentor, detesting, detested by all mankind! Wark and Learmonth, once considerable places, are now scarcely inhabited."

What hastened the removal of cottar families from their smallholdings was a second development which gathered pace in the 18th century. In 1500 half of Scotland was considered to be common land available for use by local people but owned by no one individual. For cottars the common was a vital resource providing peat, turf, roofing materials such as bracken or heather, stone, some timber and rough grazing. But as demand for food surpluses slowly grew and landowners attempted to increase their output, pressure mounted on what some saw as waste ground. In 1695 the Scottish parliament passed an act allowing common land to be divided amongst the landowners of a parish if a majority agreed. And, of course, many did. In the Borders the burghs had rights to substantial commons and surrounding lairds began in the 18th century to argue that they were entitled to enclose and keep all or part of what had been open for centuries. At Hawick the Duke of Buccleuch pressed hard on the hill country to the south of the town, lying between the Teviot and the Slitrig, claiming that as Baron of Hawick he owned the whole common. Arguments both legal and physical raged for some time before arbritration awarded the Duke 30% of the land, mostly that part south of the Fenwick burn. The burgh enclosed what remained with fences and dykes and in 1794 announced that there was no longer any need for common ridings. Ancient passions refused to accept this ruling, the marches continued to be ridden and crowds lining Hawick

High Street still roar 'Aye in common!' after the Cornet rides by with the burgh flag.

SMALLHOLDINGS

Historical wrongs are rarely righted, but the descendants of the victims of the Border clearances did get some redress at the beginning of the 20th century. The much better known Highland clearances prompted the Crofters Act of 1886 which secured tenure and fixed fair rentals. Its powers were extended by the Congested Districts Act of 1897, which, in turn, set up the Congested Districts Board (eventually this became the Board and then Department of Agriculture) to deal with matters of landholding in rural areas. The Board had the power to buy land, by compulsory purchase if necessary, and create smallholdings. These were defined as "an area of land... sufficient to employ the whole labour of a man and his family and not enough to necessitate the employment of hired labour."

In 1905 the Liberal government pushed through more legislation in the same vein and, despite opposition from Conservative MPs such as H.J. Tennant of Berwickshire, the Small Landholders (Scotland) Act came into being in 1911. Demand for land increased markedly after the First World War and by 1923 there were 1729 smallholdings being farmed in southern Scotland. In eastern Berwickshire 95 came into being with a concentration of 61 at Foulden. Poultry farming, pig-keeping and market gardening were popular, and the community at Foulden developed so cohesively that a village hall was quickly built and remains well used. No-one, however, has yet advertised the weekly dance as A Cottar's Saturday Night.

Elsewhere in the Borders small groups of cottars could not hope to wield as much collective power as burghs like Hawick or Selkirk and the wholesale disappearance of the commons quickened the pace of dispossession. Some landowners, like the Dukes of Buccleuch, made strenuous efforts to organise employment for cleared families. Planned villages at Newcastleton, Langholm and Swinton were set up as centres for cloth production. And despite the scale and summary nature of the Border clearances, little objection or disturbance has been recorded. While that does not mean that none took place, the pain of removal for the cottars may have been eased by the plentiful opportunities for work which began to materialise in the 18th century.

GRESS

Girse, gersume, naitur girss, gress or just plain grass is deceptive. It all looks much the same, but in the improved farming, it was most certainly not. With a liberal mixture of weeds, herbs and wildflowers the old meadow pasture had what farmers call a 'mattress' under its top growth — a good hold on the soil gained through many years of non-disturbance. And it was the best sort of pasture. The mixed content provided grazing animals with high quality fodder and a strong dose of health-preserving herbs and vitamins.

However, the need to rotate crops and shift animals around to get the benefit of their dung led to a demand for quick-growing sown grasses which could also be taken as a hay crop. Most are a mixture of cocksfoot, a pasture grass which grows purplish spikelets when left for hay, timothy was named after Timothy Hanson an American farmer who developed it in South Carolina in the 1720s, ryegrass which is thick-bladed and found on lawns and cricket pitches, and clover which is technically classed as leguminous, or vegetable-like. Sweet vernal grass is the variety that gives off the glorious smell of new-mown hay. Nevertheless farmers no longer sow it for fodder because it contains coumarin, a chemical producing a lovely smell but a bitter taste in the mouths of grazing beasts.

In the inventory of the Selkirkshire farmer who died in 1745 only three items are not related to the storage, preparation and eating of food, or to sleeping and sitting. His wool wheel was used for the spinning of home produced wool into yarn, and the clack reel for winding the finished product onto bobbins. Homespun cloth was mostly made by local weavers working in a village or a farm in the early 18th century and because of the gap in technology, only one loom was needed to use up the output of several spinners. Women did the work at home (hence the term 'spinster') because its repetitiveness allowed them to do other chores such as cooking or child-minding at the same time. The major problem with spinning was snapping. As the yarn twisted off the distaff a good deal of female spit was needed to keep it moist and pliable. Badly diagnosed illnesses amongst cottar women were sometimes thought to originate from a lack of saliva whereas, in fact, sitting in a damp cottage all day was likely the real cause.

The third item in the inventory was a lint wheel, and it supplies incidental evidence for an industry which grew quickly in the 18th century Border country. Lint or flax was grown by many farmers and often it formed part of the in-kind arrangements made when workers were hired. At Over Whitlaw, between Selkirk and St Boswells, the farmer had an obligation to sow lint (a capful of seed) for spinning by his cottars, as well for the use of his own household. Place-names all over the Borders remember a crop which has now been entirely discarded; flax or lint was grown and processed at the likes of Linthill near Lilliesleaf, Lintalee near Jedburgh and Lintburn in Berwickshire and in many other places.

Part of the reason for the surge in flax production in Lowland Scotland was the establishment of an active, well-funded and well-organised body called the Board of Trustees for Manufacture. Set up in 1727 with an annual budget of £6,000, its remit was to improve Scottish linen and woolen production, and the Scottish fisheries. After the union of 1707 there was a determination both to fight back against English commercial competition and also to take advantage of the opening up of English and foreign markets. So successful were the efforts of the Board that by 1772 more than 20,000 Scots were employed in turning out 13 million yards of linen, the majority of it for export. It was easily the nation's largest manufacturing industry.

THE BRITISH LINEN BANK

In 1746 the British Linen Company was founded with the specific purpose of making Scottish linen independent of both German and Dutch cloth by introducing a system of quality control and providing substantial credit. Linen stamped by the company's representative was to be a guarantee of the best and half of the company's capital of £100,000 was to be available immediately for investment, while the Royal Bank of Scotland weighed in with more credit if needed.

The venture did not go well. The price of flax fluctuated, import duties on Dutch and German linen were reduced and the removal of government subsidies for growers — all these factors made for a less than rosey picture. However, the banking activities of the company had fared much better. Promissory notes had been issued to agents and weavers and in 1765 the Royal Bank recognised the British Linen Company as a bank. Others were not so accommodating and in the 1770s there was a 'note war' when the Bank of Scotland refused to accept British Linen banknotes. It was not until 1906 that the company finally changed its name to the British Linen Bank. And in March 1971 it merged with its old rival, the Bank of Scotland. In the guise of a merchant bank, called British Linen Assets, it regained a form of independence in 1999.

Most Border towns and parishes produced linen but Melrose quickly became pre-eminent, achieving an annual output of more than 33,000 yards. The Rev. James Brown, minister of Melrose Parish Kirk, enthusiastically supported the industry and helped to set up a large bleachfield (several Border towns have retained the place-name) to dry and whiten the cloth on the west side of Weirhill where the 19th century parish church now stands. Melrose linen became well known and much of it was sold in London.

The looms in the town represented the end-point of a long and complex process which involved many farms in the surrounding countryside. Flax was considered a hungry crop which quickly drained goodness from the ground. Farmers had to be subsidised and encouraged to grow it locally because the cost of importing yarn from Holland made Scottish linen expensive. Many were persuaded and gradually a steady supply was forthcoming.

Flax had to be harvested by hand rather than with heuks or scythes. Because the whole plant was needed to make yarn, workers had to pull up each stem by the roots. Then it was tied in bunches and soaked in water for weeks to soften it. Lint-holes or flax stanks on modern farms are often mistaken for duck ponds. At Over Whitlaw it is likely that that clear pools in the adjacent mosses were used. After the 'retting' or soaking process was over the bunches were washed and beaten to break down the plant further into fibrous strands. The flax was then pulled through a heckle, a board with rows of long iron teeth sticking out of it. The men who did this difficult and tiring work were called hecklers and often worked in groups in a heckling shed. When demand for yarn was acute, wages were high and groups of men could often afford to pay someone to read to them while they went about their tedious business. Newspapers and pamphlets were a favoured source of information and distraction and these workers became so well informed that at public and political gatherings they were liable to ask pointed and disconcerting questions. As the term passed into common usage, hecklers developed an awkward reputation which saw their name outlast their trade when mechanisation took over. In the Borders the volume of flax needed to sustain the weavers soon led to the design and construction of simple water-powered lintmills.

The Melrose linen weavers saw output gradually decline in the later decades of the 18th century until, in 1784, only 17,792 yards were produced. Part of the reason for this was a skill shortage. Galashiels had begun to grow and several local investors had set up woollen mills driven by the fast-flowing Gala Water as it neared its junction with the Tweed.

Work in these embryonic industrial processes was hard, and despite the hecklers' interest in literary diversion, the opportunities for time off and relaxation were few and far between. The reforming Church of Scotland had abolished most of the old saints days which formed a pattern of regular breaks from work. Most people toiled for six days a week with the Sabbath strictly enforced as the Lord's Day. However, secular traditions did survive in some Border towns and country districts, and the likes of common ridings did involve a holiday for ordinary people. And in the 18th century evidence of a widespread interest in sport begins to come to light.

Not surprisingly horse-racing was keenly supported in the Borders. More regular meetings appear to have been held in the Tweed, Teviot and Eden valleys than elsewhere in Scotland or the north of England. The oldest racing trophies in Britain are the Carlisle Bells of 1590 and 1597. Almost exclusively, meetings were held on high moorland sites which were either sheep pasture or town common land or both. Caverton Edge race course near Kelso is now obliterated by the trees of the Bowmont Forest and no traces remain of the races held at Blakelaw further to the south. Selkirk and Hawick held meetings at Gala Rig and Pelmanrig respectively and both were areas of common land which still see what are now called 'flapping' races during the common ridings. A memory of what the early meets might have looked like stirs when the Standard Bearer or Cornet takes part in an amateur gallop with his supporters down one stretch of the track. All arms, legs, whips and what the equestrian manuals politely call 'voice-aids', the contestants thunder towards the finish line with great gusto and in high contrast to the sleek thoroughbreds and professional jockeys who sit near-motionless in the saddle. Lamberton Races, near Berwick, were held on a moor with stunning views out over the North Sea, and Jedburgh held their meetings at a now lost location called 'Jedburgh Edge'. The choice of all these windy places was made on practical grounds. The high moorland was open and unfenced, and all that was needed in preparation was the setting out of rudimentary markers for the course and the clearing of sheep off the track.

An entry in Lady Grisell Baillie's Household Book offers a domestic contrast to the drama of the Border horse races. In 1710 she recorded payments made to Tam Youll for 15 and a half days work on her 'boulling green'. This was a reasonably sedate game both ladies and gentlemen could play, and the spelling suggests a French influence. Perhaps the version Grisell knew was like modern boules.

Ordinary people were fond of a vigorous variant of bowls. Border place-names remember a game which is now long extinct. Bullets or Lang Bullets was played in many places, and certainly at the Bullet Loan in Kelso. Also known as road-bowls, it had simple rules. The basic idea was to throw a ball (about the size of a modern cricket ball) along a track to a predetermined fixed object like a large tree or prominent building taking as few throws as possible. Metalled roads were best because their hard surface imparted bounce to the ball and sent it on further. It was so popular at the end of the 15th century that a Hawick priest, John Irland, warned young men that it was better to practice archery than 'bowlis'. Kelso's Bullet Loan has been overshadowed and diminished by the new Hunter's Bridge but in order to allow sustained passages of play it must have been longer, possibly incorporating Drying House Lane. The game of bullets declined in the last few decades of the 18th century. According to John Hardy, a contemporary Berwickshire historian, the roads became too busy and throwing a ball along them could be dangerous. In any case, he noted, farm workers no longer had the time to play since the improved agriculture demanded more of their time throughout the year.

In Border towns and villages the 'ba'' was tremendously popular. Without the benefit of accurate records it is difficult to tell if this was the same game played in the time of the reivers and by the likes of the Earl of Bothwell and Willie Armstrong, but it seems likely. Some time in the mid 18th century what was a version of football changed to be called, quite specifically, handba. Apparently fitba had simply become too dangerous. The origins of rugby football surely lie somewhere in this period rather than with the over-simple notion that William Webb-Ellis invented the game in a headstrong moment at Rugby School when he picked up the ball during a football game.

Ba or handba was played at Hawick, St Boswells, Ancrum and as late as the 1930s at Lilliesleaf. At Duns, on the Friday night of Reiver's Week, the local version of a common riding, a genuinely old tradition of playing handba is kept alive. At 6pm, after shopkeepers have boarded up their ground-floor windows, a team of married men take on the bachelors of the town. Three ba's are competed for in the square. In Selkirk a version of handba was linked to another popular sport, cockfighting. Modern sensibilities are offended by the thought of animals being forced to fight to the death for entertainment but in the 18th century even children were encouraged to be involved. Boys brought along a cock to the parish school, and under the supervision of the Chief Magistrate of the burgh, sitting at the headmaster's desk, the spurred birds were put into the circle to fight. Losers had their necks wrung and were flung in the corner as an in-kind payment to the teachers. The boy with the winning bird was crowned the 'King' or 'Cock of the School'. He then had to produce a handba and take part in an unusual handicap race. After the cockfight all of the boys walked down to the West Port and assembled while the Cock of the School went on with his handba to stand at the gate of the Haining, the local big hoose, about 80 yards down the hill. At a given signal they all set off with the boys in hot pursuit of the carrier of the handba. If he could reach the Howden Burn, a mile or so distant, and throw the ba over it before being caught, then he added another triumph to his victory at cockfighting.

WHITE FEATHERS

James Palmer, the first editor of the Kelso Chronicle, ran a campaign against cockfighting. A particularly unpleasant aspect of this was the tradition on Shrove Tuesday or Fastern's E'en when schoolboys tied a cock (one that refused to fight) to a post and stoned it to death. The thrower of the fatal stone got to keep the carcase.

Cockfighting became so popular in Glasgow that a building went up in Hope Street in 1835 specifically designed to accommodate cockpits. 280 people, including handlers, feeders and judges, could fit in and all sorts of men — from servants to aristocrats — gambled much on the outcome.

All manner of phrases or sayings derive from this cruel sport. 'Showing the white feather' as a sign of cowardice came from the belief that a white feather in a cock's tail betrayed poor breeding stock, not a characteristic of a real gamebird. Belgium was the cockpit of Europe for many centuries. Aggressive birds were cocksure and so on. 'Cock-up' appears to have a different origin. It comes from printing slang, and when a lead letter slug sat up proud in an old letterpress forme, it was called a 'cock up'.

The most famous handba game in the Borders is still contested in Jedburgh. Two games are played between two teams of variable size. The Callants' Ba' is held at Candlemass on February 2nd and the Mens' Ba on Fastern's E'en, known as Shrove Tuesday in England. At the Mercat Cross the teams gather for the start of play. Despite Jedburgh's geography and sloping site the 'Uppies' team consists of men born in the town south of a line drawn from the car park at the end of the Friars in Exchange Street to the Mercat Cross and on the Deans Close in the Canongate, as well as those born outside of Jedburgh who first entered the town by a southern road, from Newcastle, the Dunion, Oxnam or Lanton. The same precision applies to the 'Doonies' who must have been born north of the line or first entered Jedburgh by the Edinburgh road, the Monklaw road, or the Ulston road. The size of the teams is limited only by the male population of the town and hundreds have been known to take part.

Precision begins to waver when the rules of the Jethart Handba are considered. To begin with, they are not published and those who play appear to know all they need to know without any instruction. The only general injunction is that no-one should be intentionally injured. Games became so robust that in 1848 attempts were made to abolish the ba but the sheriff court sensibly denied the application.

What happens on the day can be spectacular. A stitched leather ba stuffed with straw has ribbons attached and is thrown up in the air above the teams at the Mercat Cross. An immense scrum follows and sometimes a man breaks free with the ba and hares off through the streets. Scoring is marginally clearer than the rules of play. A goal is scored when a ba is 'hailed' in the correct place. For the Uppies, hails are won when the ba is thrown over the railings surrounding Jedburgh Castle grounds. But not just any part of the railings, only those to the left of the main gates and before they turn into a stone wall. The Doonies score when they roll the ba over the course of an invisible stream. Under one of Jedburgh's streets the Skiprunning Burn runs into the Jed Water. However, hails are not the only way to win. If a ba is held underwater in the correct part of the Jed and the stitching is cut, then that counts. A cut is not as valuable as a hail but two cuts are better than one hail. 'Smuggling' is a time-honoured means of extracting the ba from the inevitable scrum. Generally this involves two players working together. One runs from the scrum pretending that he has the ba while the other slinks off in another direction with it hidden in his clothing. Smugglers sometimes lie writhing on the ground after the manner of professional footballers claiming that they are injured and that they have had enough. Under the pretence of going home, the smuggler will leave the ba at a prearranged spot for his partner to collect while the other team are searching the town for what they assume is a lost ba. Suspected smugglers must submit to a vigorous search (this can be uncomfortable) by the opposite team. No officials exist to arbitrate between the Uppies and the Doonies and, surprisingly, decisions about particular incidents are debated and agreed by teams on the day. Darkness eventually brings play to a close when the welcoming lights of public houses begin to twinkle in the gloaming.

The Jethart Handba is an amazing sight, an entirely unselfconscious piece of history played out with undimmed passion. Visitors to the town, whether they come by either the Newcastle or Edinburgh roads, are not advised to take part.

FASTERN'S E'EN

'Carnival' literally means 'farewell to meat' and Fastern's E'en was one, being held on the last Tuesday before Lent. While the wealthy splashed out on a meat-dominated banquet, ordinary people took to the streets to play handba or go to the cockpit. At the Duns handba the object was to hail the ball in either the pulpit of the parish kirk or in the happer (grain hopper) of the mill. The latter was much prefered since the merry miller gave the winning team pork and dumplings. Special foot-wide bannocks were also made and the flavour of the miller's was unmatched. Toasted over the burning seeds of shelled oats, it must have been both smokey and rich.

The Kirk cast a baleful stare at these popular festivals and did what they could to soften and 'civilise' them. Cockfighting as a prelude to the ba has disappeared but the social function of the game as a way of blowing off steam and indulging in some excess before the strictures of Lent has been wisely left as it is. The towns and country districts of the 18th century Borders found themselves securely in the grip of the Kirk; its powers and functions were very wide-ranging, judicial and civil as well as religious. The nature of Scots Calvinism made it so. Society was divided into two contrasting parts; the Elect who were bound for glory in the afterlife and the Reprobate who were destined to burn in the fires of Hell. To the Elect godly discipline and self-control were vital — in fact these virtues defined them as the Elect, and the Kirk was their context and community.

As John Knox and his associates had prescribed in The Book of Discipline, the parish was run not by the minister but by the elders of the Kirk Session. These men were elected for life and their responsibilities reached into every part of their parishioners' existence. They were charged to collect and distribute the poor funds and to examine claimants for relief very closely. In a real and immediate sense this gave them power over life and death by destitution. Education was controlled by the Kirk with, it appears, the full support of most communities. In 1790 it was said that the parish of Yetholm's 'parents will submit to considerable privations rather than not send their children to school'. Perhaps the Kirk Session's most visible role was their close supervision of the moral behaviour of their parishioners — and their minister. In effect this could mean almost anything, and the court of the Kirk Session heard cases of theft, assault, and wife-beating as well as fornication, adultery, blasphemy and breaking the Sabbath. They acted as the basic court of justice in Scotland and could refer cases upwards to the Sheriff Court if their competence was in doubt, or the seriousness of the offence was obviously beyond them. By 1750, though, the old men of the Kirk Session had narrowed their focus considerably and most of their cases concerned sexual transgressions of one sort or another. For example, anyone found guilty of fornication was fined, rebuked and forced to do public penance. Erring parishioners were forced to sit or kneel on the repentance stool in church in front of their neighbours while the minister harangued them, or worse, were locked into an iron neck-collar called 'the jougs' which was usually attached to the wall of the parish kirk. One repeated offender was locked in the jougs at Coldstream for six successive Sundays. In Jedburgh the parish minister, the Rev. Paul Methven, was found guilty of adultery and forced to stand on the repentance stool in his own kirk, wearing sackcloth, on successive Sundays. A Kelso woman put in the stocks as late as 1834 attracted huge crowds. Fornicators were tied to ducking stools and plunged into the Tweed several times before being released.

However, the impression of tight-lipped Scottish presbyterian morality needs qualification. The Kirk Sessions also acted to protect young women as well as censure them. If an erring young man had absconded to another parish to avoid his responsibilities, then a Kirk Session could track him down and persuade even a distant parish to force him to acknowledge the infant and pay for its upkeep. This was to avoid too many (and there were many) illegitimate children becoming a burden on the parish. Funds were very limited and the elders wanted them to stretch as far as possible to cover cases of unavoidable hardship. And if a young man could be made to pay, he should. Social justice of a sort motivated these men as well as a smug prurience.

The most acute pain of most of the punishments imposed was public humiliation, something keenly felt in small urban or rural communities. And it was designed to act as a deterrent against breaking the rules — and depleting the poor relief fund. Such was the power of the Kirk in the 18th century that anyone moving from one parish to another required to carry a 'testificat' or certificate of good behaviour, or otherwise. These could take the form of kirk tokens or badges signifying people of good character — or not. Sins could follow people around.

Of course, the gentry were not so closely subject to the justice of the old men of the Kirk Session and their moral conduct passed largely without comment from the pulpit. And if they did transgress, then the matter could often be settled by a cash payment. Underpinning this deference was cold politics. In 1712 the Westminster parliament pushed through the Patronage Act which allowed landowners to 'prefer' a new minister when a vacancy arose. In the Borders a small group of powerful noblemen, including the Dukes of Roxburghe and Buccleuch and the Earl of Lothian, had the right to choose the minister for many parishes. This act struck at the heart of Scottish Presbyterianism, but it did not lead to the violent reactions of the 17th century even though the Covenanting days and the Killing Times were fresh memories for a generation of mature adults. It needed the General Assembly of 1731 to persuade some that matters had gone too far. It decided that the selection of ministers should have nothing to do with congregations and be a matter only for landowners and the Kirk Session. Two years later a breakaway group of some substance emerged. In 1733 the General Assembly expelled a group of ministers led by Ebenezer Erskine who believed that the Kirk had strayed too far from from its rigorous Calvinist origins. The Secession Kirk was adopted with enthusiasm in Morebattle and several other places, including Midlem and Selkirk, where the Covenanting flame still flickered, but it was never a mass movement.

The Toleration Act of 1712 saw the creation of the Scottish Episcopal Church out of the remnants of Charles II's attempts to impose bishops on the Kirk in the 1670s and 80s. This infuriated Presbyterians already nettled by the Patronage Act and many regarded the official sanction of what amounted to Anglican worship in Scotland as a betrayal of the Act of Union. What quickly became known as the English Kirk was established in most Border towns and traditionally it has enjoyed the support of the minor gentry.

The breakaway Relief Kirk was founded on more liberal principles than the Secession and in 1752 Thomas Gillespie led a large group of like-minded ministers out of the Church of Scotland and in 10 years their following had grown to 100,000. By the end of the 18th century more than 30% of Scots worshipped in dissenting churches or were catholics. This fragmentation inevitably slackened the iron grip of Kirk Sessions and fatally fractured the monolith of the Calvinist society of the Elect. By the 1760s there was more than one way to get to Heaven.

BURGHERS AND ANTI-BURGHERS

The issue of patronage divided the Church of Scotland so often in the 18th century that by 1800 a bewildering spectrum of sects had appeared. For reasons of convenience Kelso contained the kirks or meeting houses of most of them, and 75% of the population of Jedburgh did not worship in the Church of Scotland. Here is the relevant passage from the 1793 Statistical Account for Kelso;

> *"Besides the established church (the parish church), and an Episcopal chapel, there are a number of sects, each of which has a house for public worship, and some of them are even elegant. These are the kirk of Relief, Burghers, Antiburghers, Cameronians, Methodists and Quakers. There are three Roman Catholics and one Jew in the parish. The major part of the inhabitants, particularly of the genteel class, attend the parish church and the Episcopal Chapel. The meeting-houses are chiefly supported by the inhabitants of different parishes in the vicinity. This place, being centrical and convenient, induces them to build here."*
>
> *By 1744 the Secession Kirk had 30 congregations in the south of Scotland, but in that year it split over the issue of the Burgess Oath which prominent members were required to swear to a secular authority and which, some argued, bolstered the legitimacy of the Church of Scotland, which they believed to be illegitimate. Therefore the Burgher Secession Kirk was set up alongside the Anti-Burghers. Further disagreement led to yet another split over the state's support of the Church of Scotland, and the Auld Licht Burghers and Anti-Burghers appeared with the New Licht Burghers and Anti-Burghers. Ultimately both sects of the New Lichts decided to forget the origin of the second disagreement and merged into the United Secession Church (New Licht).*
>
> *Kelso also had a Relief Kirk, which did not split, and the Cameronians, Methodists, Baptists and Quakers seem to have remained united. Reunification of most of the Presbyterian sects came in 1900 and 1929, with the diehard Auld Lichts of the Secession Kirk holding out until 1956. The 'Wee Frees' of the Highlands and Islands remain doggedly outside the Church of Scotland and have continued the happy tradition of splits and factions up to the present day.*

Secular developments also eroded the Kirk's certainty. The mid 18th century saw the historical and philosophical phenomenon known as the Scottish Enlightenment. Mellerstain House and Floors Castle had imported the new architectural ideas into the Borders, and, amongst the landowning elite, also established one of the Enlightenment's fundamental precepts; namely that nature could and should be at man's disposal, and not the other way around. Philosophers and scientists such as David Hume, Adam Smith and James Hutton all insisted on the primacy of reason and order, and these ideas found themselves quickly applied to Scotland's most important occupation — agriculture. While his deep interest in geology was fed by acute observation of rock strata at Siccar Point on the North Sea coast near Cockburnspath and at Jedburgh, James Hutton was also a farmer who brought innovative ideas to his estates in Berwickshire. Several of his landowning neighbours shared his scientific approach and one of the most influential was Henry Home, who was born at Kames, near Swinton, not far from Polwarth kirkyard where his namesake hid from the dragoons. On his appointment to the Scottish bench Home took the title Lord Kames but he spent a great deal of time on his Borders farm. Enlightenment ideas about the improvement of agriculture found eloquent expression in his very influential 'The Gentleman Farmer', published in 1776. Like many of his fellow improvers

Kames thought and wrote in propagandist terms and tended to present the new methods in a revolutionary tone. In fact improvements had been quietly happening since the late 17th century.

Famously introduced from America, potatoes took some time to become commercially popular but they were planted as a field crop in Berwickshire by the 1740s. Turnips or neeps also caught on and their principal value was as winter fodder, and sheep could survive on them for months, eating them directly out of the ground. Kail, a green winter vegetable from the brassica family, had the singular virtue for Scots that it actually benefited from periods of hard frost with the flavour becoming distinctly spicey. Originally introduced from Holland, its popularity became such that broth began to be called kail and sometimes the word was substituted for food generally. To keep hungry wintering beasts away from the crops (although nothing could be done about the birds apart from an abject scarecrow) a kailyard was built close to farmhouses and cottages, and it gave its name to a couthy brand of cosy Scottish fiction much read in the 19th and 20th century.

BAGIES AND LEEKS

In bread, pie and cake-obsessed Scotland the nearest thing we have to national vegetables are the leek and the neep. Bashed neeps accompany champit tatties, haggis and too much whisky at Burns Suppers. The yellow turnip is known as a swede in England for the excellent reason that the agricultural improvers of the 18th century introduced it from Sweden. A memory of the source of this new crop is preserved in Border dialect. 'Rotbagga' is the Swedish word for neep, and it survives in the Tweed Valley as 'bagie'.

Cock-a-leekie soup often precedes the bashed neeps and it appears to have been an 18th century variant on the standard broth produced on every Scots hearth. To reflect cultural preferences leeks divided into two sub-varieties. The English liked the more tender lower white part of the leek, the blanch, and were less keen on the fibrous green leaves, the green flag. As in so many things the Scots took an opposite view, developing a long-flagged and short-blanched variety. The reason for this was a particular liking for green broth.

The Welsh, it is said, will eat either sort. On a March Saturday in 1965 the Provost of Hawick was speaking at a civic reception for a visiting Welsh rugby team when he felt compelled to talk to them about leeks. He made a comparison between the Cock-a-leekie soup they had just eaten and the Scottish rugby team. To the baffled Welshmen he explained that neither was any good without a lot of green in it. Green is, of course, the colour of the Hawick rugby strip.

Improvement was often forced on tenants by progressive landlords when they agreed new leases. These could be very prescriptive. When Andrew Plummer rented Over Whitlaw farm to Robert Greig, he told him what to grow and even when;

"The Tenant is to be restricted from taking any part of the farm above two successive white crops [such as neeps] then a green crop [such as kail] which shall be succeeded by a crop of barley laid off with a sufficient quantity of rye grass and clover"

And the amount of land Greig could plough in the last four years of his fifteen year tenancy was restricted to 70 acres, presumably so that the remainder of the arable land could recover its fertility.

New crops needed better ground. First and most basic was a programme of enclosure to keep grazing beasts out of sown land, and incidentally to mark out ownership clearly and unambiguously. A map of the Borders made between 1747 and 1755 by General Roy shows that this process was very slow and that the bulk of the land was still open runrig and common, with enclosed areas only showing up close to the big hooses and the mains farms. Many of these were actually grazing parks used for fattening cattle and lambs. Dykes were prefered to hedges because they did not harbour hungry birds, and when stoney fields were systematically cleared (often by itinerant gangs) materials could not be closer to hand. Where stone was scarce ditches were dug and beech or hawthorn planted on the upcast. Both quick-growing their boughs could be half-cut and pleached sideways to create a dense barrier and also a handy bield for animals. Up at St Mary's Loch in Selkirkshire sparse thorn hedges planted across the prevailing wind are the only shelter for hardy sheep.

CHEVIOT SHEEP

The best meat-sheep in Britain was bred at the farm of Robert Bakewell (1725– 95) in Leicestershire. The New Leicester was crossed with Border sheep in the 1760s to create the Cheviot, a bigger animal hardy enough to withstand a winter on the hills. They were so successful that Highland landlords cleared thousands of crofters off their holdings to make way for flocks of Cheviots. Sometimes Border shepherds went north to heft the animals to new hills. 'Na Caoirich Mora' or 'The Big Sheep' were hated by Highlanders who saw their cattle driven off and replaced by these imports from the south. 1792 was remembered as 'Am Bliadhna nan Caoirich Mora', 'The Year of the Sheep' because violence broke out in Ross-shire when hundreds of crofters attempted to remove the flocks from the glens.

Dykes and hedges defined the landscape in a new geometry, and they also forced roads and tracks to travel around their perimeter. Many minor roads in the Borders still wind around field-ends in what seem like extraordinary detours to drivers used to motorways. Well-travelled tracks were often upgraded to metalled roads in the mid 18th century, and between 1790 and 1815 the new Turnpike Trusts spent £2 to 3 million in Scotland to improve surfaces, sort out drainage and build bridges. This had a side-effect of providing jobs for dispossessed cottars over a lengthy period, and even when the era of intensive road-making was over, their creation spawned another new trade. Some cottars became carters and busy 18th century routes remember the business with place-names like Carter Bar or the Carter's Rest at Jedburgh. A two-wheeled vehicle yoked to a single horse got the name 'the Scotch Cart' and it was very popular.

Carters were the goods vehicles of the new agriculture and they rarely travelled unladen. One of their most steady loads was straight-sawn timber. The development of mechanical saws had replaced the old techniques of splitting tree trunks into uneven beams with wedges And even though the impact of these new materials on the lives of everyone was dramatic, it has often been ignored. Building works immediately benefited from the availability of quantities of squared-off joisting all cut to the same length and width. Many two-storey farmhouses date from the 1770s and slates replaced thatch as straight purlins were fitted to take the sarking needed to accommodate them. The new fashion for courtyard steadings found rapid expression as barns, cartsheds and stables all went up quickly with the liberal use of the new timber. On a more humble level farm workers also saw their domestic lives transformed. As the likes of the Carron Ironworks turned out affordable nails, hinges and latches, ordinary people began to acquire what we would recognise as furniture. Most basic was the box-bed. These large structures could be moved around to create small partitioned spaces where privacy was possible, and they also signalled the end of communal sleeping around the hearth. Tables, benches, cupboards and shelving all became available to make daily life easier. This appetite for joiner-work not only created jobs but also attracted bulk imports of Scandinavian timber to feed the sawmills.

Despite the advances, improved agriculture was hampered by the backwardness of a central process. Ploughing was still done in the old way with the big wooden Scotch plough pulled by teams of oxen or horses. And the rigs were still in place, mainly because no better solution to to drainage had been found. Both enclosure and new cropping were severely inhibited by these old methods and arrangements. And ploughing was labour-intensive and therefore expensive. A team of at least four oxen (sometimes as many as eight were needed) or four horses was led and urged on by a goadman, the plough was directed by the ploughman holding the stilts, sometimes another man had to put his weight on the beam to keep the share in the ground, and behind them was a group of women and bairns who bashed down the bigger clods of earth or pulled out weeds not covered with the furrow-slice. As many as eight people could be involved. Robert Burns ploughed with a goadman whose job also included using a pattle or stick to clear away stones and weeds choking the gap between the coulter and the ploughshare. John Lambie was the goadman who chased the mouse with a pattle when its nest was turned up by Burns.

BORDER BACCY

The American War of Independence (1775–83) deprived Britain of an addiction. Virginia and other tobaccos were imported into Glasgow in such small quantities that the price rocketed to two shillings a pound. Mr Jackson, an enterprising Kelso farmer, managed to raise a crop of the weed and sell it at a handsome profit. The street-name in Kelso of Drying-House Lane has nothing to do with clothes, it commemorates a building where the tobacco leaves were dried. The new crop caught on so well that there was scarcely a farm in Roxburghshire and Selkirkshire where it was not planted the year after Jackson's success. Sadly providence intervened, the weather was terrible and most Border baccy was ruined. A coup de grace was administered by the Westminster government when they decided that it was illegal to grow the weed in Britain and they bought up and destroyed what little had survived the wet spring.

The old Scotch plough has been described as a heavy wooden wedge that needed to be dragged through the ground by the brute force of at least four beasts. It was slow, expensive and inefficient and considered a brake on progressive farming.

On the road to Blackadder Mount farm in central Berwickshire, two groups of buildings hide behind the beech hedges. A cottage has been made out of the west end of each of the ranges by the roadside but the remainder is empty, semi-derelict and overgrown with willowherb, rowan and a tangle of scrub. The architecture is formal, though, with severely pitched gables, regular fenestration and a pleasing symmetry in the design. These are not tumbledown ruins but the abandoned remains of serious business. In the southern range of one set, which forms a courtyard with the u-shaped northern buildings, there is a high double doorway cut into the gable end, big enough for a large modern van to pass through. Inside sits the reason for this little complex of buildings. Just discernible in the gloom of a summer interior is the massive lum of a blacksmith's forge. A huge yellow sandstone mantle, beautifully chiselled and squared, projects from red sandstone mountings with flues cut into them. Below the lum is a half-broken fireplace that once reached waist-height. The forge was clearly large enough to heat substantial items of metalwork.

The man who bellowed the coals into red-heat and clattered his hammer off the anvils thought a great deal about the problems of the old Scotch plough. All of its difficulties were obvious to a young Berwickshire ploughwright. His powers of observation were acute, his grasp of design theory and scientific method tenacious, and his inventiveness bore the stamp of genius. James Small was unquestionably a great man, certainly one of the greatest Borderers who ever lived. And yet his name is now almost entirely forgotten and his epoch-making achievement largely unrecognised. James Small invented the modern plough and his genius changed the landscape forever.

Some time around 1740 Small was born at Upsettlington, a few miles south of Blackadder Mount, on the opposite bank of the Tweed from Norham Castle. His birthdate and origins are obscure but certainly rooted in agriculture; his father was a farmer and James served his time as an apprentice to a carpenter and ploughmaker at the village of Hutton in the 1750s. Like many ambitious young Scots Small took himself to England and found employment as 'an operative mechanic' in 1758 in Doncaster where he no doubt advanced his skills and knowledge. Prompted by some initial discovery or conceptual breakthrough, the young man returned to Berwickshire in 1764 and was immediately set up in business at Blackadder Mount. No record exists of exactly what took place to encourage such a move but it seems likely that Small had hit on the basic principle behind the new plough and decided to come home to develop it. Despite having no capital to invest he had little difficulty in convincing a patron to support him. In his account of Small's life of 1812, John Sinclair takes up the story;

"John Renton Esq., of Lammerton, a zealous promoter of the agriculture of this country, saw at once this man to be the only individual wanted to accomplish its prosperity. Mr Renton, therefore, immediately settled him at Blackatter Mount; erected all the necessary buildings for a smith and carpenter's manufactory; set him a-going with cash, and gave him credit; and forthwith twenty, and sometimes upwards, of carpenters, six or eight blacksmiths, and many other hands, were constantly employed. Hence issued out numbers of ploughs, carts, wagons large and small, and all the different implements of husbandry, in abundance. Small's plough was particularly admired, and is sought after at this day. The plough previously used here was drawn either by four horses, or four oxen and two horses, with hard labour; and in quantity ploughed it fell far short of the present two-horse plough without any driver [goadman]."

As often with world-changing inventions what made Small's plough revolutionary was a simple idea. The old Scotch plough had an iron-tipped wooden ploughshare which turned up a furrow-slice which was pushed to the side by a separate component known as a mouldboard. This was made of wood and fixed more or less flat-sided. The construction and alignment of these elements created a great deal of friction and needed the musclepower of many beasts to pull it. When it did go through the ground, the furrow was not deep and the mouldboard did not turn over the furrow-slice completely. As a result a small army of plough-followers was needed to pull out weeds from under the slice and bash down big clods with a mel. And because the ploughframe and mouldboard were made of wood they wore out quickly as stones scarted at their surfaces and they often broke down.

James Small designed a mouldboard and ploughshare as one piece and changed the alignment and shape so that it turned over the furrow-slice completely. Crucially he abandoned wood and had the new plough cast in iron at the Carron Ironworks at Falkirk. The effect was indeed revolutionary. Because the new screwed shape (essentially the same shape as modern ploughs) encountered less friction, it could delve deeper and stay in the ground without difficulty. And it could also turn over a bigger furrow-slice so completely that it buried the weeds and mulched them as additional fertiliser. And because less friction allowed the plough to cut the sod more easily, it needed fewer animals to pull it. It turned out that two strong horses could do the job well and since a ploughman with the long reins wrapped around his hands gripping the stilts could also steer them, no goadman was needed. By reducing ploughing to a one-man operation Small's invention had, therefore, a dramatic effect on agricultural labour patterns.

In 'The Gentleman Farmer' Small's Berwickshire neighbour, Lord Kames, was effusive;

"Of all the ploughs fitted for a cultivated soil free of stones I boldly recommend a plough introduced into Scotland about twelve years ago by James Small in Blackadder Mount, Berwickshire, which is now in great request; and with great reason, as it avoids all the defects of the Scotch plough".

As with most successful iniatives which seem to appear overnight the new plough actually took much time and effort to perfect. Despite Kames' enthusiasm its introduction to Scottish agriculture was slow and patchy. And far from making James Small a wealthy man, his invention left him broke, occasionally imprisoned for indebtedness and sent him to an exhausted early grave in 1793. It was only after his death that the scale and importance of what had been created in the workshops at Blackadder Mount was realised. Here is the judgement, made in 1796, of a contemporary Berwickshire farmer, Alexander Lowe;

"He [Small] from his own genius, and the hints he got, improved it [the plough] much from time to time, and it is now in general use in the county, except in some of the highland parts of Lammermoor, where the old Scotch plough is still used… It is drawn by two horses, the common strength applied to every two horse plough in the county, except on high and banky lands, where oxen are used behind the horses."

James Small made no money from his plough for at least two obvious reasons. First, he did not patent the design, and in fact wrote and published (at a loss) a 'Treatise on Ploughs and Wheel Carriages' in 1784 which was essentially an instruction manual on how to build the new plough. The dedication is to Alexander Renton of Lammerton 'as a testimony of respect and gratitude for that countenance and protection so long afforded' and it offers a clue as to why Small did not move to safeguard his invention. It may have been a condition of the Rentons' sponsorship that the plough be generally available and not limited by patent so that agriculture as a whole could benefit. Or perhaps Small felt so obligated to his supporters that he believed he could not attempt to profit so extravegantly by his work. And if he did he would have to pay them back in some way. In the treatise his deference is painfully evident, "My situation in life has deprived me of many advantages of theoretical learning", and those who knew him thought Small "distinguished by simplicity of behaviour, and modesty in his pretensions". When a new edition of the treatise was published in 1802 with the help of the Farming Society of Ireland "the public interest, though attended with much detriment to their own personal interests" of the Small family was noted in the preface.

The second reason why Small lost money was simple. He was a hopeless businessman and a brilliant and demanding inventor and craftsman. One example suffices to illustrate. At the request of the Duke of Buccleuch wooden models of the new plough were sent in 1786 to the secretary of an agricultural society based in Bath. The designs were greeted with great enthusiasm but far from stimulating a flow of orders from the south-west of England, it seems that Small was never even paid for the models. Uninhibited by patent law the ploughs were no doubt widely copied in the west country.

When contemporaries saw James Small at work they remarked on the single-minded focus he brought to the job. As he perfected the shape of the cast-iron plough he built mouldboards out of soft wood and had them pulled through the ground so that he could log the points of hardest wear. When information from these trials was carefully collated, the design was modified again and again. Many expensive prototypes were summarily discarded and sometimes even smashed by Small as his frustrations boiled over. All of this research cost a great deal of money and as the list of employees funded by the Rentons shows, substantial wage bills had to be found every week. Frequently in debt, he even went to prison and in 1788 the Board of Trustees and Manufactures stepped in to give £50 to Small's son, John, who was jointly responsible for the business. Worn out, broke and certain that his work would make the lives of those who lived on the land easier, James Small died at the approximate age of 53 in 1793. Perhaps more than any Scotsman he could truly claim that his monument lay around him. Many individuals and groups contributed to the invention of the modern rural landscape, but none more so than James Small. His passion overcame even the stolid conservatism of Border farm workers and John Sinclair remembered a telling episode;

"The late Mr Lumsdaine of Blanerne was one of the first who ordered the new improved plough, but his servants did all they could to prejudice their master against it, pretending it did not go well, etc. Small was then obliged to appear in the field himself, and taking the plough into his own hand, he proved to Mr Lumsdaine and all his ploughmen how well it could work. Had he not been a good ploughman, as well as an able mechanic, he could not thus have triumphed over those who opposed the introduction of his improvements."

THE KELSO CHRONICLE

The newspaper business thrives in Scotland. As a society we devour them, reading more per capita than any other European country. They are also an old business with its origins in the mid 18th century. Of those still available on the newstands today, the Aberdeen Press and Journal is the oldest, dating from 1747. Then comes the Kelso Chronicle of 1783, the Glasgow Herald (now The Herald) a few weeks later and The Scotsman in 1817.

The first editor of one of Britain's oldest newspapers was a remarkable man called James Palmer, and his office still stands in Bridge Street in Kelso. Much impressed by the ideology of the American Revolution of 1775–83 and a supporter of both the French Revolution of 1789 and the Irish Rebellion of 1798, he was not popular with the gentry. And from time to time Palmer found himself in Jethart Jail on some charge or other. Despite this his paper survived, even thrived. However a conservative rival appeared in 1797, supported by the establishment and printed and published by the Ballantyne brothers. Walter Scott was an early contributor, and in 1799 an advertisement was inserted in the Kelso Mail for the let of the empty premises lately used by Mr James Small at Blackadder Mount.

But had Small not been able to yoke good horses to his plough, all of the hard work would have been in vain and the Blanerne men left distinctly unimpressed. Coal, Covenanting and carting all came together in the 17th and 18th centuries to produce the perfect engine for the iron plough, the Clydesdale horse. Draught horses had been used on Border farms for centuries but generally these were tough little ponies whose musculature and conformation had managed most jobs, but they had to work in combinations of at least four to pull an old Scotch plough through the heavy soil. Robert Burns and John Lambie yoked a four-team and coaxed them through the work. When one of more of the horses grew too old and exhausted, they trained new ones to fit in. The phrase 'old stager' remembers this. Inexperienced horses were yoked next to an old stager — one that had learned its job pulling a stagecoach. More intelligent, neater-footed and companionable than teams of oxen, plough horses took roles which help to visualise how the ploughman saw his work. The inside two who walked in the previous furrow were called by Burns 'fur-afore' for the leading horse and 'fur-ahint' for the second. On the unploughed land the leader was 'lan-afore' and the second 'lan-ahint'. New horses generally went ahint. Even though the team was led by the goadman the ploughman used a repertoire of spoken commands to guide them. Some of these are familiar to us through watching cowboy films where the stagecoach drivers used the same basic sounds; 'hawp' means move to the right, 'wynd' to the left, the clicking noise 'tsick-tsick' means go on and 'pproo' or 'whoa' means stop.

These skills became even more important as Small's plough came into use, but the horses changed. Heavier-built animals who had big feet and could generate power through legs collected under a well muscled hindquarters and big shoulders were needed. The Lanarkshire coal industry, much of it owned by the Dukes of Hamilton, had similar requirements. The small pack-horses with panniers slung over a pack-saddle could not satisfy the increasing demand for coal and big horses were urgently required to pull three ton carts along the improved roads. The Dukes of Hamilton had been supporters of the National Covenant and therefore of William of Orange in 1688. That European connection helped to solve the carting difficulties of the lucrative coal trade. Big Brabant stallions were brought from Prince William's lands in Flanders to cover local mares and gradually the Clydesdale breed evolved. The Statistical Account of 1793 summarises the historical impact of this initiative;

"Rutherglen Fairs are famous for the finest draught horses in Europe... About a century ago an ancestor of the Duke of Hamilton brought six coach horses from Flanders... They were all handsome black stallions. The surrounding farmers gladly bred from them, and the cross with the Scotch horse procured a breed superior to either, which has been improved by careful breeding. Great attention is paid to colour, softness and hardness of hair, length of body, breast, and shoulders of their breeders [meaning stallions]. Every farm has four or six mares. The colts are mostly sold at the fairs of Lanark or Carnwath. They excel in the plough, the cart, and the wagon".

After Small's plough had become widely adopted, Scottish agriculture was driven by horsepower. In addition to the plough, the heavy horses pulled harrows, carts and turned rudimentary machinery. They were much more intelligent and versatile than oxen and ploughmen often formed strong bonds with these huge animals. Some could weigh more than a ton and everyone involved knew that no-one could force them to do anything they did not want to do. Farm hinds became known as horsemen or ploughmen and the fact that one man could work alone in the field revolutionised the organisation of agricultural labour. Numbers employed were reduced but as more land was brought into use and the rural economy expanded, there was still plenty of work. Women and children did all the jobs on a farm not involving the use of horses, such as milking, weeding, singling and herding. The stables became the focus and each ploughman spent a good deal of time there, looking after his horses, washing their legs after work, grooming the sweat off their flanks, feeding them and forging a close partnership in shared service. If a ploughman's horses went on well, then so did he.

THE HORSEMAN'S WORD

Initiation ceremonies associated with ploughmen were carried out all over lowland Scotland, including the Borders. Young lads were brought blindfold to a barn and forced to kneel at the feet of the First Horseman. Secrecy was of the essence as they recited the oath, "Hele, conceal, never reveal; neither write nor dite not recite nor cut nor carve, nor write in the sand."

When the blindfolds were taken off and a dram handed round, the Horseman casually offered the boys a pen and paper so that they could write down the oath in case they forgot it. Any who accepted were expelled immediately. For those alive to the ruse, they stayed and entered upon a world of inherited horse-lore. What feeds to give and when. How to add herbal mixture to induce docility and obedience, and much else of real worth.

At the end of the ceremonies the initiates were taken, after a great deal of whisky, to the darkest part of the barn. There a shadowy figure sat and when pushed close, the young lads heard him whisper to each in turn the Horseman's Word. It was 'Eno' or 'One' backwards, and it symbolised the essence of partnership between man and horse.

Once the fields had been ploughed and sown, they were often harvested by large itinerant gangs of shearers from the Highlands. Mostly women, they came to the Lowlands with their heuks in the late summer. As the southern corn ripened first they began work in Berwickshire and the Tweed Valley before moving northwards to Lothian, Fife, the Mearns and the Moray Firth coast. Often when they bent to their work, the women sang and some Border farmers employed a piper to play for them. After the cut sheaves had been led in on the field wagons, the process of threshing by flail began. Once again the production line was bottlenecked by old methods — until Andrew Meikle of East Lothian produced a workable threshing mill in 1788. It fed the sheaves through rollers into a revolving drum which used centrifugal force to detach the grain and horsepower to turn it. And forty years later Patrick Bell developed a mechanical reaper pushed by Clydesdale horses, and so completed what amounted to a rapid mechanisation of cereal farming.

DUNURE FOOTPRINT

Clydesdale horses became big business. The possession of a good stallion could make a breeder very wealthy indeed. Dunure Footprint is thought to have been the greatest sire in Clydesdale history. Born in 1908 by another famous sire, Baron of Buchlyvie, Footprint's powers were truly prodigious. Before the era of frozen sperm and artificial insemination, this amazing stallion fathered more than 5,000 foals during his long career. In his prime Dunure Footprint could cover a mare every two hours, day and night, at the height of the breeding season. What kept the stallion hard at work were frequent drinks of milk mixed with raw, beaten eggs, and the encouragement of his groom. Footprint's output was very lucrative for his owner, William Dunlop. Each time he covered a mare, its owner paid £60 for the privilege. By the end of the breeding season the stallion was exhausted, and although he could still manage to serve a mare presented to him, he fell off her after the deed was done. Dunure Footprint's sons and daughters dominated Clydesdale horse showing and breeding in the decades between the two world wars. No doubt the old fella died happy.

After millenia of repetition, cultivation changed over an astonishingly short period. The everyday lives of most agricultural workers improved along with methods. Their food became more varied and nourishing, and in 1798 families living on Roxburghshire farms enjoyed bread, oatmeal, potatoes, milk, cheese, eggs, salt herring, salted meat and no doubt as much kail as they could grow. For farmers politics took a hand and the long period of the Napoleonic Wars turned many of them into gentlemen. Britain was forced to rely on domestic food production entirely and that necessity naturally forced up prices. Some grand farmhouses were built and inhabited by men and women who found that they had less and less in common with the workers, or 'farm servants' as they came to be called, who lived in the row of cottages down the track. The improved agriculture swept away more than old methods, it also altered attitudes and stratified social class in a way all too recognisable in the Borders today.

The most famous Scottish ploughman who ever lived, Robert Burns, owned a copy of James Small's treatise, but he never made use of it. Working alone in an outbye field with only his horses for company was not a prospect Burns ever relished. For him the body warmth, the crack and the shared experience was a necessary compensation for the hard, hard work of farming. In 1791 he finally gave up the land he loved so much and turned his back on the improvers who were changing the landscape that had made him.

11

Walter Scott and the Kindred Ground

Just as James Small helped to invent a Border landscape that seems well-rooted and ancient to us now, so Walter Scott invented a romantic past which is readily accepted as only a little more than the truth. Tragic Jacobites, ingenious wizards, comical rustics, ill-fated lovers and honourable reivers ride through the pages of 'The Lay of the Last Minstrel', 'Marmion' and the Waverley Novels to deliver to us an impossible posterity wrapped in the brilliance of Scott's narrative gifts and the absolute authenticity of his sense of place. In the early 19th century the Border country ceased to be an everyday sort of place and became instead the geography of Walter Scott's imagination. In the same way that William Wordsworth set a fictional sheen on the Lake District, or James MacPherson's Ossian poems on the mountains and islands of the Scottish Highlands, Scott's romances and epics created the Scott Country, a place made more and more real by 200 years' repetition of his stories and the ideas inside them. To many outsiders Walter Scott invented the Borders, and increasingly, his pungent gloss on all that experience in one place has been accepted and endorsed by insiders. After all, who but a dull curmudgeon would reject the offer of a heroic past, particularly if some of those heroes really existed? Even though they were not all Scott cracked them up to be — they might have been.

More soberly the notorious conservatism of the Scottish Borders, encapsulated in the phrase 'aye-been' (always been so — and therefore no reason to change), has acquired some of its smugness from Scott's inventiveness and endorsement. But the uncomfortable truth is that what's aye been is in fact quite recent.

The popular acceptance of a romantic past for the Borders had its beginnings in popular belief. Walter Scott did not publish his first work of historical fiction until 1805 when 'The Lay of the Last Minstrel' appeared. For most of his life before that he had been listening to Border ballads, the narrative poetry and song which had built into a rich oral tradition that seemed to be robustly alive at the end of the 18th century. Because Scott's romances grew out of what people told, recited and sang to him, it can be no suprise that when he later replayed (in different settings) what he heard as a young person in the likes of 'Marmion', 'The Lady of the Lake', 'Waverley' and the rest of his substantial opus it

found such ready acceptance. When his interest grew and he first went
to Liddesdale to listen to and write down the ballads still in currency
there, he was guided by a fellow lawyer, Robert Shortreed. Much later
Shortreed made this perceptive comment to J.G. Lockhart, Scott's biographer;

"He was *makkin' himsell* a' the time, but he didnae ken maybe what he
was about till years had passed. At first he thought o' little, I dare say,
but the queerness and the fun."

The making of Walter Scott probably began with an illness. Some time in
1773 while barely a toddler, what appears to have been poliomyelitis
struck him down and severely impaired his developing mobility. The left
leg was worst affected. His father, also Walter Scott, was an Edinburgh
lawyer living in the midst of the teeming city and, believing that country
air could only help his son recover, 'the wee sick laddie' was sent to
Sandyknowe Farm, the home of his grandfather. The farmhouse sat at
the foot of Smailholm Tower near Kelso. Robert Scott died when Walter
was only four but the boy retained vivid memories of the old farmer. All
sorts of folk-cures for the lameness were tried and once the flayed carcase
of a sheep was wrapped around him while it was still warm and the old
man coaxed Walter to crawl across the floor of the farmhouse parlour.
But mostly what he remembered were stories. Forced by his illness to sit
indoors for long periods Walter listened to tales told by his grandfather,
his Auntie Jenny and Sandy Ormistoun, the cow-bailie at Sandyknowe.
Much of what they knew had been passed on to them in an unbroken
oral tradition stretching back to the days of the reivers and even beyond.
A small amount of published material was available and Auntie Jenny
read to Walter from Allan Ramsay's 'Tea-Table Miscellany', a five volume
collection of traditional songs and ballads which appeared between 1724
and 1737. Sometimes Ramsay altered the material to suit what he
considered to be 18th century tastes. Even so, Jenny's edition was only a
printed version of material similar to the sort of thing she, Robert Scott
and Sandy Ormistoun could summon up from their own memories —
which were prodigious compared to those of the 21st century. Sitting
happed up in a blanket by the winter fire at Sandyknowe, the young
Scott drank it all in and never forgot it. In the introduction to Canto III of
'Marmion' he remembered how his grandfather and the big skies of the
Border landscape had shaped his mind;

> "Still, with vain fondness, could I trace
> Anew, each kind familiar face,
> That brighten'd at our evening fire!
> From the thatch'd mansion's grey-hair'd Sire,
> Wise without learning, plain and good,
> And sprung of Scotland's gentler blood;...
>
> Thus while I ape the measure wild
> Of tales that charm'd me yet a child,
> Rude though they be, still with the chime
> Return the thoughts of early time;

And feelings, roused in life's first day,
Glow in the line, and prompt the lay.
Then rise those crags, that mountain tower,
Which charm'd my fancy's wakening hour.
Though no broad river swept along,
To claim, perchance, heroic song;
Though sigh'd no groves in summer gale,
To prompt of love a softer tale;
Though scarce a puny streamlet's
Claim'd homage from a shepherd's reed;
Yet was poetic impulse given,
By green hill and clear blue heaven."

What made the stories even more vivid was the place where they were told. Up behind the farmhouse sat the ruin of Smailholm Tower, the mountain tower, and Scott's imagination animated it as old Sandy Ormistoun whispered tales of long ago;

"And still I thought that shatter'd tower
The mightiest work of human power;
And marvell'd as the aged hind
With some strange tale bewitch'd my mind,
Of forayers, who, with headlong force,
Down from that strength had spurr'd their horse,
Their southern rapine to renew
Far in the distant Cheviot blue,
And, home returning, fill'd the hall
With revel, wassel-rout, and brawl.
Methought that still with trump and clang,
The gateway's broken arches rang;
Methought grim features, seam'd with scars,
Glared through the windows rusty bars,
And ever, by the winter hearth,
Old tales I heard of woe or mirth,
Of lovers' slights, of ladies' charms,
Of witches spells, of warriors' arms;
Of patriot battles, won of old
By Wallace wight and Bruce the bold;
Of later fields of feud and fight,
When, pouring from their Highland height,
The Scottish clans, in headlong sway,
Had swept the scarlet ranks away."

Published in 1808 after the success of 'The Lay of the Last Minstrel', 'Marmion' was a phenomenal success. The Border country became internationally famous — Scott found a huge and loyal readership in the USA — and Smailholm Tower was visited by Wordsworth, Washington Irving and painted by J.M.W. Turner. At nearly two hundred years' distance it can be difficult to comprehend the immense impact made by Scott's writing.

LETTERPRESS

Walter Scott's working day often began early. At his desk by 6am, he wrote with a quill pen on quarto sheets and by 9am and breakfast time, he reckoned to have 'broken the neck' of the day's work. As with many people Scott's handwriting deteriorated with age and towards the end of his exhausted life, when working quickly, his manuscripts could be difficult to decipher. After he had finished a piece of work it was sent to copyists who produced legible versions and appear to have tidied up the material a good deal. Then it went to James Ballantyne for printing and another editing process. In 1817 he dispatched the manuscript of 'Rob Roy' with these relieved lines;

> *"With great joy*
> *I send you Roy.*
> *'Twas a tough job,*
> *But we're done with Rob."*

The Kelso shop which turned out 'The Minstrelsy of the Scottish Border' has disappeared but at Innerleithen Robert Smail's Printing Works survives intact in the care of the National Trust for Scotland and it offers a powerful sense of how Scott's work was produced.

The very first printed books were made in the Far East with 'The Diamond Sutra' appearing in 868 and the works of Confucius in 953. Each page and all the characters on it were carved out of single wooden blocks. And even though this meant a comparatively rapid production and circulation of one book, it was also somewhat wasteful. In 1439 in Strasbourg Johann Gutenberg began to use single-cut letters to make up lines of type. After production was finished, these could be broken down and re-used to create other books. Letterpress printing carried on unchanged in its essentials until the middle of the 19th century. And these essentials can be seen at Smail's Printing Works.

When, for example, Walter Scott's copy was received, compositors began to upmake lines of type in the caseroom or composing room. Taking a stick (somewhat like the wooden tray for Scrabble letters but with a screwed vice to keep them tight) in hand, each compositor worked from a case of loose type. Letters were slotted on to the stick both upside down and in mirror image — some older printers can still read lines of set type as fast as printed copy. Then the lines were set into a galley, tied with page-cord and checked. This involves making a galley-proof which is generally hand-pulled in a simple machine so that compositors can quickly look for mistakes. Then whole pages are hammered into a large frame called a chase. Areas of type are fixed by 'furniture' or wedges which can be screwed tight, and then everything is tapped flat with a mallet and wooden planer to make sure there are no 'cock-ups'.

Many thousands of fonts are in use. A standard word-processor offers fifty or so. But the most popular remains one of the oldest. In 1470 when Nicolaus Jenson designed the first typeface not to resemble handwriting (called Gothic or black-letter), he called it 'roman letter' and variations of it are widely used.

Printing could be a lucrative business and, like Robert Smail's (who published a newspaper and much else), some printers were also publishers and even booksellers. Walter Scott made several attempts to set up the Ballantyne Brothers as publishers, and he became a sleeping partner. Their business acumen was not sharp and although they did a great deal of work while Scott's popularity climbed and the print-runs of his books grew, he was published by Archibald Constable of Edinburgh. Determined to keep the prolific Scott on his list, he offered large advances for future work. These were paid in the form of promissory bills which Scott discounted for cash immediately upon receipt. The building of Abbotsford and the acquisition of land around it consumed enormous amounts of money. Constable himself depended on promissory bills from his London agent, the biggest outlet for Scott's books, Hurst, Robinson and Company. All of them were heavily mortgaged to the author's future output. In 1825 Hurst, Robinson speculated disastrously in the English hop harvest — for reasons best known to their directors — and they lost a great deal of cash. Their business crumbled. They were unable to honour the bills granted to Constable who, in turn, could not honour the bills held by those who had paid Scott cash. Owing £256,000 Constable declared himself bankrupt and paid 2/9 in the pound. With debts of £116,858,11s and 3d Scott could have done the same. But he refused and vowed to pay off all his debts. 'My own right hand will do it' he declared, and between 1826 and 1832 he killed himself with hard, constant work. By 1834 £90,000 had been paid off and the remainder by 1848.

Because of his disability the wee laddie was often in the company of adults and occasionally they told him of their own experiences when they touched on great events of the recent past. An uncle who came to visit at Sandyknowe, Mr Curle of Yetbyre, had been in Carlisle when 19 Jacobite prisoners were tried and hanged in October 1746, only 30 years before. He told the tale of young John MacNaughton, an Edinburgh watchmaker who rode as a courier for the Pretender's captains. Accused of killing a dragoon colonel at Prestonpans (who was actually cut out of the saddle by the claymore of a Cameron clansman) he was contantly pressed to turn King's Evidence against his comrades. Even when MacNaughton was on the scaffold and the hangman had tied him to the sledge to await execution, he refused to betray anyone. The chaplain of the Manchester Regiment, Thomas Coppoch, had been tried in his cassock and when sentence of death was passed, he cried out "Never mind boys, for if Our Saviour were here these fellows would condemn him!" And perhaps most poignantly, the tale of the unknown prisoner who composed the ballad 'Loch Lomond' while waiting in Carlisle jail for the day of his execution and to take the low road home in his grave. What child could not listen in rapt silence to these stories and not be deeply affected by them?

In 1776 the family decided to send Walter to Bath to take the curative waters in an expensive effort to help him recover better health. Auntie Jenny went too and they stayed for a year when the wee laddie seems to have been well enough to learn to read, write and go out to his first theatrical performance. It was 'As You Like It'. After their return Walter spent a good deal of time in Kelso, living first at Garden Cottage (now, of course, Waverley Cottage), in the shadow of the abbey and close to the Tweed. At Kelso Grammar School James Ballantyne was a fellow scholar and the two formed a firm friendship that lasted a lifetime, bringing great success as well as desperate financial ruin.

Scott's fascination for ballads and the oral history of the Borders led him to his first great project. After Edinburgh University and a period studying for the Scottish bar, he made his way in 1792 to his uncle Robert's house at Rosebank in Kelso. In the autumn of that year, he went to Liddesdale with Robert Shortreed to begin work on what would become 'The Minstrelsy of the Scottish Border'. Always a great patriot, Scott may have been prompted by the popularity of Thomas Percy's 'Reliques of Ancient English Poetry' to convert his love for the old ballads into something more concrete. Scotland had a great tradition too and should not be outdone.

Seven expeditions, or 'raids' as Scott liked to call them, were made towards the end of the 1790s as the work gathered pace. Many women were what modern scholars call 'tradition-bearers' and they could recall a large body of material which they generally sang. One of these was Margaret or Meg Laidlaw of Ettrickhall Farm in the Ettrick Forest. Like many notable Border women she appears to have retained her maiden name and is rarely refered to as Margaret Hogg. Her son James inherited her love of the ballads and entertained his own aspirations as a poet. In 1794 his first published poem was included in 'The Scots Magazine and General Intelligencer' and in 1800 he connected with the popular mood at the onset of the Napoleonic Wars when his marching song 'Donald MacDonald' became popular. But what turned James Hogg's fortunes was his meeting with Walter Scott through the help he supplied in compiling 'The Minstrelsy of the Scottish Border'.

THE SCOTS MAGAZINES

Walter Scott's concern for the preservation of Scottishness was not a new phenomenon. After the union of 1707 others worried about the loss of political and cultural focus to London, and in 1739 'The Scots Magazine and General Intelligencer' was founded to reduce dependence on news from the capital of the new Britain. As a counter-balance to the 'Gentleman's Magazine', it came into being with the promise that 'our countrymen might have the production of every month sooner, cheaper and better collected than before'. The Scots Magazine reported Scottish affairs and was rewarded with a substantial circulation. The editors invented a births, marriages and deaths column, an innovation imitated by every newspaper since.

By the 1800s rivals had begun to appear, cresting an upsurge in Edinburgh printing and publishing and the popularity of Scott, Hogg and others. Archibald Constable, the publisher of the Waverley Novels, realised that there was a public appetite for magazines, review articles and regular columns, and after buying The Scots Magazine in 1801, he also set up 'The Edinburgh Review' in 1802. What made Constable's approach different was that he maintained a distance between himself, as the publisher, and the editor. And he held his readership by making sure that his magazines appeared regularly.

Another Edinburgh bookseller and publisher, William Blackwood, launched a new magazine in 1817. Originally entitled 'The Edinburgh Monthly Magazine' it soon became known as 'Blackwood's Magazine', and it developed into a rival for Constable's output. Needing a sensation to bring the new magazine to the attention of the reading public, James Hogg supplied the idea

of the notorious 'Chaldee Manuscript'. Pretending to be the translation of a
lost book of the Old Testament discovered in the suitably remote Bibliotheque
Nationale de Paris (in his recent novel 'The Evening of the World', the Borders-
based novelist Allan Massie reveals a fondness for a similar device) the
manuscript launched an ill-disguised all-out attack on the Edinburgh Review
and its supporters. One of the first circulation wars had begun.

The Edinburgh Review survived Blackwood's blast and was published
regularly until 1929. Blackwood's Magazine went on until 1980, but the
oldest of all, The Scots Magazine, continues to publish and is now owned by
D.C. Thomson of Dundee.

Hogg was no uncritical acolyte though, and for his part he 'sorely tried'
Scott while remaining doubtful of his treatment of some of the balladry
he recorded. Not as doubtful as his mother, Meg Laidlaw, whose reaction
to the publication of the Minstrelsy became famous;

"The sangs were made for singing, no' for prenting and now they'll
never be sung again: and furthermore… they're no' setten doun richt
nor prentit richt."

When the recorded versions of the ballads were recited from the pages of
the Minstrelsy it seems that these grumbles had some substance. According
to James Hogg, Scott's rendition of 'Jamie Telfer in the Fair Dodhead'
was greeted with cries of 'Changed! Changed!' when read out to a Border
audience. Evidently certain passages which presented the ancestors of
Scott's patrons, the Dukes of Buccleuch, in an unsympathetic light were
turned into examples of their sagacity and bravery, and he also converted
the saviours of Jamie Telfer from Elliots into Scotts.

But more seriously, the growing impulse to polarise the past
expressed in the ballads on either side of the border, as Scots versus
English and vice versa, becomes very clear in the Ballad of Johnnie
Armstrong. Reliable evidence confirms that Armstrong behaved exactly
like most English and Scots reivers in that he stole from whoever and
wherever he could. It mattered not a jot to him or his family where any
of their victims lived, south or north of the frontier. Sim Armstrong, the
Laird of Whithaugh and Johnnie's kinsman, boasted that his people
burned churches in Scotland as well as despoiling property on the
English side. Despite this Armstrong was quickly painted as a patriot,
and writing only 35 years after James V had hanged the reiver at
Carlenrig, the historian Robert Lindsay of Pitscottie offers this remarkable
view in his 'The Historie and Cronicles of Scotland';

"After this hunting the King hanged Johne Armstrang, Laird of Kilnokie,
which many Scottish men heavily lamented, for he was a redoubted
man, and as good a Chieftain as ever was upon the Borders, either of
Scotland or of England. And albeit he was a loose living man, and
sustained the number of twenty four well horsed able gentlemen with
him, yet he never molested no Scottish man. But it is said, from the
Scottish Border to Newcastle of England, there was not one of whatsoever
estate but paid to this Johne Armstrang a tribute, to be free of his cumber".

Much of the basis of the ballad is taken from Lindsay's account of what happened at Carlenrig, and this in turn imparts the distinctly patriotic tone which found its way into wide currency through 'The Minstrelsy of the Scottish Border'. Walter Scott relied heavily on 'The Historie' for some of his historical novels and he certainly did not invent the Robin Hood-like persona of the outlaw. But nor did he qualify it even though his knowledge of Border history was much more sophisticated than this simplistic view. In fact the introduction contains this unqualified observation;

"the common people of the high parts of Teviotdale, Liddesdale, and the country adjacent, hold the memory of Johnie Armstrang in very high respect."

Why the descendants of those who had suffered at the hands of Armstrong should hold him in such regard is a historical mystery.

Lindsay's relabelling of history suited Scott's own passions very well. Nourished by the sort of stories told by Mr Curle of the Jacobites at Carlisle, he had become a self-confessed cultural patriot. Politically a Tory, he approved grudgingly of the union of 1707 while publicly worrying about the potential loss of Scottishness, of 'what makes Scotland Scotland'. The phrase 'The Borders' also changed its sense at around this time as it came gradually to signify only the Scottish side of the frontier, rather than the area encompassed by the March wardenries of the 16th century.

JOHN LEYDEN

It was said that Walter Scott could not mention the name of his brilliant friend, John Leyden, without weeping. The son of a shepherd, Leyden was born in 1775 at the village of Denholm near Hawick, and on the green stands a monument to this remarkable man. It looks oddly like a miniature version of the Scott Monument in Edinburgh.

'The Minstrelsy of the Scottish Border' benefited from Leyden's great scholarship. The master of 9 languages (36 by his death) he contributed both collected ballads and an essay 'A Dissertation on Faery Superstition' to the second volume, as well as writing his own poems. 'Scenes of Infancy' about his early life in the Teviot Valley is the best known.

Like Mungo Park, Leyden was fascinated by faraway places. In April 1803 he left the Borders to take up a civil service job in India where he became immersed in the cultures of the East. His 'A Comparative Vocabulary of the Barma, Malayu and Thai Languages' was published in 1810.

The Earl of Minto took Leyden along as an interpreter on an expedition against the Dutch colonies of the East Indies. In August 1811 Minto's ships made landfall on Java, and having heard that there was a substantial library of rare manuscripts nearby, and anxious to get to them before they were destroyed, Leyden jumped into the sea and was amongst the first to wade ashore. He then spent the day in soaking clothes examining the manuscripts in a damp warehouse. A fever took hold and he died, some said of curiousity, three days later.

As his literary career advanced from success to success, Scott became more and more interested in the Highlands and Highlanders. What could be more profoundly Scottish than the Gaidhealtachd where they spoke a language unintelligible to the English (the fact that it was also unitelligible to many Scots was an inconvenience to be glossed over) and cleaved to an ancient culture which seemed to have the twin attractions of distance and incomprehension? This absorption in Gaelic Scotland solved a creative difficulty for Scott the patriotic writer in that he understood very well that Scottish and English Borderers had too much in common to allow much play for the wider appositions of Scottishness and Englishness. There was no difficulty of that sort with the Highlands, and in 'The Lady of the Lake', 'Waverley', 'Rob Roy' and several other pieces, he used those starker cultural differences to great dramatic effect. The invention of Rob Roy — against most of the historical evidence — as a sort of Highland rogue (captured on screen with a practiced twinkle by Richard Todd in the 1950s feature film) is a particular triumph of the imagination.

In the novel about the 1745 Jacobite Rebellion, 'Waverley or 'Tis Sixty Years Since', there is a fascinating insight into how Scott's attraction to the Highlands was working on his mind and how he conceived the whole of Scotland. Using the material supplied by Mr Curle of Yetbyre and others, he has Edward Waverley visit Euan Maccombich in Carlisle jail where he awaits execution. The condemned man utters a macabre thought about what the authorities will do with his severed head;

"I hope they will set it on the Scotch gate,… that I may look, even after death, to the blue hills of mine own country which I love so dearly."

In order to see the hills of his own country Maccombich would have needed preternatural posthumous eyesight. The Highland line lies a long way north of Carlisle, and the blue hills of the Borders stand between. Of course Scott knew that, but his poet's licence and determination to paint all Scotland tartan overrode common sense.

In 1822 more myth-making of a similar sort got underway in spectacular fashion. It was proposed that George IV should pay a state visit to Scotland, something no reigning monarch had done since the days of Charles II. Master of ceremonies was to be Walter Scott, and the occasion turned out to be fascinating, one of the greatest publicity stunts in British history. In essence Scott conceived it as a tartan-wrapped celebration of all things Highland, with the Highlands even more obviously standing for the whole of Scotland. Only 76 years after Jacobites were being hanged at Carlisle and the clans emasculated and pacified, Scott persuaded the portly King George into a Royal Stewart kilt (worn some distance above the knee over flesh-coloured tights) and most of the Scottish gentry into the tartan spuriously prescribed for them. It was a triumph that seemed to fool many people, but by no means all. Scott's own son-in-law, J.G. Lockhart, muttered that the whole thing was 'a hallucination' and a travesty. Apparently all Scots had become Highlanders and the tartan could and should be worn from Dumfries to Duns, and all over the Lowlands. It was only a matter of finding the correct sett for the branch of whichever Highland clan the Browns, Smiths, Elliots, Armstrongs, Kerrs or whoevers were somehow associated with, or even descended from. It is surely a measure of Scott's showmanship, skill and judgement of public mood and taste that the hallucination has been vigorously maintained ever since. From 1822 all Scots have worn tartan, sporrans and dirks on special occasions without inhibition or even so much as a blush.

DAD'S ARMY

The only parts of Europe to escape domination by the whirlwind force that was Napoleon Bonaparte were Scandinavia, Russia, the Ottoman Empire and Britain. Russia was to prove his nemesis, but had the planned invasion of 1803–4 gone ahead Napoleon may well have found the battle for Britain his political and military undoing. In addition to the regular army there was other, formidable opposition. The Volunteer Movement was a late 18th century version of the Home Guard and it was immensely popular, attracting huge numbers of men to its ranks who were too old or unable (this was before the era of conscription) to serve in the army. Fears of invasion or revolution were far from imaginary; naval mutinies at Spithead and the Nore in 1797–8 coincided with the French-backed Irish Rebellion led by Wolfe Tone, Father John Murphy, Henry Joy McCracken and others.

After war was declared against France in 1792, Walter Scott joined the Edinburgh Volunteer Light Dragoons and was elected as Paymaster, Quartermaster and Secretary. His enthusiasm and comradely humour earned him the nickname of 'Earl Walter', and his lameness appears not to have inhibited his horsemanship. After 1803 he transfered to the Midlothian Yeomanry Cavalry. Where they could afford it the Volunteers dressed themselves in the height of contemporary military fashion with high-collared blue swallow-tail coats over white waistcoats and breeches, and riding boots. Some even wore bearskin caps, and they tended to be very generous with ranks and titles. The Volunteers were nevertheless serious, and they mustered often to listen to their officers and drill in as much order as they could manage. Several Border towns have Volunteer Halls or Parks to remember all that activity.

As Napoleon's invasion force kicked their heels at Boulogne in 1803–4, an ancient early warning system was revived in the Borders. On hills and high points bale fires were maintained and constantly manned so that if the French landed on the North Sea coastline (or any other) the whole countryside would know in minutes. It had worked well in the days of the reivers and would do again if the French dared set foot on a British shore.

On 31st January 1804 the system went spectacularly into action. A Volunteer sergeant new to the Borders, but as keen and dedicated as anyone, was put in charge of the bale-fire on Hume Castle in Berwickshire. Peering into the winter darkness, he was certain he saw the flames of a coastal beacon at Dowlaw in North Northumberland. Immediately he fired the bale at Hume Castle. Peniel Heugh and the Dunion saw it and flared in moments. And then the alarm crackled rapidly through the Borders as Caverton Edge and Crumhaugh Hill went up and more beacons were lit down Teviotdale, Ettrick and Yarrow. When Volunteers saw the hilltop fires, the adrenalin must have pumped as they clambered into their uniforms, buckled on their swords and grabbed muskets and scrambled to their muster-points. The same Lord Minto who took John Leyden to the East Indies swam his horse across the swollen Teviot to reach his men at Jedburgh. Walter Scott was in Cumberland when the Hume Castle bale flared and he rode 100 miles to join the Midlothian Yeomanry Cavalry at Dalkeith. The countryside that flew past him was in uproar and Napoleon's cuirassiers were expected to come clattering along the Berwick road at any moment.

They did not. No-one did. What the unfortunate sergeant at Hume Castle had seen was not a bale-fire on Dowlaw, but the everyday work of some Northumbrian charcoal burners. The mounds of wood needed to make good charcoal were built to burn slowly and retain a tremendous heat inside — and not to emit long togues of flame. But this one did. It appears that the dim glow of a mound sparked what became known as The False Alarm of 1804. It was an episode worthy of 'Dad's Army'.

While Walter Scott was re-inventing Scotland to keep it Scottish — by any means — what was happening to the oral culture of the Borders, the place and phenomenon that had first set fire to his brilliant imagination? As the son of Meg Laidlaw, a 'tradition-bearer' who had many ballads by heart, and a farmer, James Hogg was much more of a natural inheritor of that culture than Scott ever could be. In a real sense he carried it on with new poetry which borrowed from old idioms. 'The Queen's Wake' was published in 1813 and it made Hogg famous. Born in the Ettrick Valley into direct and sustained experience of life on the land, Hogg's was an authentic and vibrant voice, more a successor to Robert Burns than a protege of Walter Scott. His 'The Private Memoirs and Confessions of a Justified Sinner' is still considered a masterpiece and his 'Kilmeny', a poem in 'The Queen's Wake' collection, a virtuoso display of great skill and invention. But to the Borders Hogg bequeathed a more obvious and tangible legacy. His enthusiasm for sport of all sorts gave rise to the first of the summer 'games' which are not exclusively associated with the common ridings, or particular holidays. In 1827 the St Ronan's Games were launched at Innerleithen at Hogg's instigation. With the help of Scott, Lockhart and some Edinburgh literary friends, a celebration of what he called 'manly exertions' was organised in the summer of that year. Hogg himself was an all-rounder, good at foot-racing, wrestling, fishing, curling and archery, but his motivation went far beyond that to what he detected as contemporary social problems. In the wake of the agricultural revolution many people were leaving the land to find employment in the textile mills of the growing towns. Hogg worried about the effects of social dislocation as the old life on the land changed abruptly and sometimes bafflingly. For many who went from the hills and the fields into the clattering cacophony of the mills, it must have bewildering. Hogg sympathised and, engagingly, he also wanted people to have more fun. The sports included in the programme of the first St Ronan's Games were self-consciously traditional; races, archery, lifting and throwing heavy weights and throwing the hammer. Some of this was borrowed from the events that lay at the heart of traditional Highland games, but much of it represented a return to the excitements and entertainments of a Borders past. And

Hogg put a considerable amount of money where his mouth was by funding many of the prizes himself and persuading wealthy friends to stump up.

MUNGO'S BUM

At the end of Selkirk High Street stands a statue that tells a wonderful, strange and moving story. Set into the wall of the Co-op supermarket is a panel adding more information to the brief inscriptions on the plinth. Flanked by four bronzed Africans, Mungo Park looks out eastwards over the sheltering hills of his native Selkirkshire. Born in 1771 at Foulsheils in the Yarrow Valley Park studied medicine and, through a chance family connection, came into contact with Sir Joseph Banks, a founder of the Africa Association. Despite his youth — he was only 24 — Banks appointed Mungo to lead an expedition into the dark, unmapped heart of Africa to find the source of the great river Niger.

With six African companions he plunged into an entirely unexplored interior, taking with him food for only two days, some goods to trade for more supplies, a compass and sextant, firearms and an umbrella. And a great deal of courage. Sensibly Park kept his group small and native — only 7 men could scarcely be seen as hostile. Nevertheless they endured much, suffering hunger, thirst and ill-treatment at the hands of the Moslem tribes of what is now Mali. Because he was the only white man any of these tribesmen had ever seen, Park was the subject of humiliating curiousity. So that they could marvel at his milk-white Border skin, the Moslem chieftains forced him to strip off his clothes and bare all. The opening scenes of T. Coraghessan Boyle's novel about Mungo Park, entitled 'Water Music', offer a vivid dramatisation of these awkward episodes.

Park's own 'Travels into the Interior of Africa', published in 1799, gave an excellent account of the expedition and comprehensive mapping survey of the upper reaches of the Niger, showing that the river begins its long journey to the ocean by flowing eastwards. Perhaps that is why the statue at the end of Selkirk High Street looks east.

Two and a half years passed since his departure and many had given up Park for dead. When he knocked on the front door of his family home at Foulshiels near Selkirk, his younger brother said, "That'll be our Mungo". Not having mentioned him at all up to that point, he went on to add, "I saw him getting out of the coach in the square."

After some years doctoring in Peebles, and striking up a friendship with Walter Scott, Park itched to be back in Africa to finish the work he had begun on the Upper Niger. In 1805 a large expedition of 40 Europeans, many of them soldiers, left for what is now Nigeria with Mungo at their head. Almost immediately things went wrong. Decimated by malaria and dysentry the party was reduced to only 5 as their boat began the long journey downstream. At the rapids of Bussa the boat either foundered or was ambushed, and Park drowned or killed.

Back in Selkirk his family refused to believe that Mungo was dead. He had survived before. Encouraged by wild tales that he was being held captive somewhere in the interior, his son Thomas Park left for West Africa in 1826 to mount a search. On the western plinth of the Selkirk statue there is a commemoration of Thomas' desperate journey. He died somewhere in the Gold Coast in October 1827.

Another entertainment dear to Hogg's heart was routed via his stomach, and also connected with St Ronan's Well. In the novel of the same name Walter Scott described a regular meeting of gastronomes catered for by Meg Dods, landlady of the Cleikum Inn. The fictional Meg went on to write an actual book. In order to create 'The Cook and Housewife's Manual' a writer called Christian Isobel Johnstone took on the persona of Meg, and the recipes offer the first real extended sense of traditional Scottish food. The cultural context for this self-conscious revivalism was to be found in the notorious literary periodical known as Blackwood's Magazine. 'Noctes Ambrosianae' was a regular column set in the Ambrose Tavern in Edinburgh's New Town. Much was said about the food consumed on these evenings and a good deal of that by the Ettrick Shepherd, a semi-fictionalised identity created for James Hogg by John Wilson, the editor of the magazine. Painted as a decent but ignorant old rustic with a thick streak of patriotism running through him, Hogg, along with his cronies, prefered good, plain Scottish cooking with none of the side-dishes and bits and pieces of the fashionable European cuisine of their neighbours. Ashets of beef, lamb, roasted fowl, oysters, mashed potato, and toasted cheese were all served at once — with none of this nonsense about hors d'oeuvres, entrees and the like. Best of all was the broth, the ancient soup that had sustained generations of Borderers. Beside it the new 'brown' and 'white' soups were insipid;

"That's hotch-potch — and that's cocky-leeky — the twa best soups in natur. Broon soup's moss water — and white soup's like scaudded milk wi' worms in't. But see, sirs, hoo the ladle stauns o' itsel in the potch — and I wish Mr Tickler [a crony] could see himsel noo in a glass, curlin' up his nose, wi' his een glistenin, and his mouth watering, at the sight and smell o' the leeky."

BORDER COLLIES

The Ettrick Shepherd may have been an urban fiction but the real James Hogg knew a great deal about real shepherding. In 1807 he persuaded Archibald Constable to publish 'The Shepherd's Guide: being a practical treatise on the diseases of sheep', and his 'Shepherd's Calendar' includes much useful material. But most striking was Hogg's fascination and affection for his collie-dogs. Here are the first three verses of 'The Author's Address to his Auld Dog Hector' of 1807;

"Come, my auld, towzy trusty friend;
Waur gaurs ye look sae douth and wae?
D'ye think my favour's at and end,
Because thy head is turnin' grey?

Although thy feet begin to fail,
Their best were spent in serving me;
An' can I grudge thy wee bit meal,
some comfort in thy age to gi' e?

> *For mony a day, frae sun to sun,*
> *We've toil'd and helpit ane anither;*
> *An' mony a thousand mile thou'st run,*
> *To keep my thraward flocks thegither."*

Pastoral dogs were originally used to protect flocks and herds from wolves, but as the sheep economy took hold in the Borders and the threat of predators receded, dog-working became more sophisticated. And James Hogg did not underestimate the value of these animals;

"Without the shepherd's dog, the whole of the open mountainous land in Scotland would not be worth a sixpence. It would require more hands to manage a stock of sheep, gather them from the hills, force them into houses and folds, and drive them to markets, than the profits of the whole stock were capable of maintaining."

All over Britain there were many different breeds of pastoral dogs, with wide regional variation, but towards the end of the 19th century the Border Collie became dominant. Historians agree that a Northumbrian farmer, Adam Telfer, bred the first true Border Collie and that the recognised pedigree descends from his dog.

Shepherds reckon the abilities of a good working dog to reside in obedience and intelligence. A collie able to think for itself while doing instantly what it is told is a good combination. Commands are shouted or signalled by blasts on a whistle, which carries further and better in the wind. 'Come bye' generally means 'circle a flock to the left', 'Way bye' is 'circle to the right' and 'Come in ahint' to 'move directly behind a flock'. But most hirds use their own vocabulary; 'Time!' for 'slow down!', 'That'll do' for 'stop' and so son. All of these commands are used in the 'gather'. This is the basic job of the collie and involves gathering the sheep off the hillsides in a flock around the hird. Border Collies rarely bark and use other devices to move the sheep in the desired direction. In essence the dog mimics the movements of a predator, contantly implying threat. 'Eye' is important. Hirds like a dog with a strong eye, meaning that it fixes a flock with a stare and holds it during a movement. 'Clapping' is when a dog drops low with its belly brushing the grass and creeping forward much in the way that big cats stalk their prey on the African grasslands. And if an aggressive ewe turns to challenge a dog, it must be able to retaliate by gripping the fleece in its teeth and forcing the animal back into the pack.

The first recorded sheepdog trials held in Britain were at Bala in mid-Wales in 1873. Breeding stock was constantly improving and agricultural shows saw keenly contested dog classes from that time onwards. After the First World War the name 'Border Collie' was adopted to denote working dogs as opposed to those bred for showing.

James Hogg's family were reputedly angry at the columns in Blackwood's Magazine and the way they portrayed 'the Ettrick Shepherd', although it appears that he himself thought it all very funny. The formidable Tibbie Shiel, who kept a famous inn at the head of St Mary's Loch, was an early and long time friend of Hogg. Her comments on his literary output could only come from a Borderer. She thought he 'was a gey sensible man for a' the nonsense he wrat'. The reaction of Meg Laidlaw (his formidable mother who gave Walter Scott a piece of her mind when 'The Minstrelsy of the Scottish Border' was published) to Hogg's own work is not recorded. But her comments to Scott did contain an important general truth. By writing down the ballads he changed them (not only in a textual sense), and by publishing them he did take them out of the mouths of ordinary people. But however regrettable it was to Meg Laidlaw, this was a tradition that was bound for change. The economies of publishing, the growth of a popular appetite for books, widespread literacy and an increasing need for fresh material — all these and more were bound to touch on a primarily oral tradition, and ultimately marginalise it. But Meg was wrong if she thought that ballads would cease to be composed — James Hogg's output alone showed great vitality for old forms and old skills — it was rather that they would find their way into the cultural bloodstream on printed paper rather than through the memories and mouths of poets and singers. In short, Border culture was commercialised by Scott, Hogg and others who came after them. That marked a significant departure and may have distanced the begetters of that cultural output, turning many into consumers rather than creators or participants, but it did not necessarily devalue it.

Running alongside this process was another dynamic. The literary productions of Hogg, Scott, John Leyden and later, Andrew Lang and a dozen or so others did make Border culture much more concrete. By writing down ballads, stories and novels, all that experience became fixed at the time of its creation rather than remaining endlessly fluid in the way that an oral culture can be. And that relative fixedness also managed a second decisive shift. Slowly and often subtly, building up over the decades of Scott's greatest output and for many years after his death in 1832, the atmosphere around Border history changed. Stories need drama and change to animate them sufficiently to hold an audience, and that tended to premiate, say, the era of the reivers over the more everyday triumphs of the likes of St Aidan, the burgesses of medieval Berwick, or James Small. That much is obvious in the way that Borderers continue to label themselves and, to an extent, libel themselves. Recently when a racey title for a new rugby team was sought, they were immediately called 'The Border Reivers', and when they amalgamated with the Edinburgh team, they did not adopt the name of a venerable rugby club and logically retitle themselves 'The Edinburgh Borderers' or some such. Instead the meaningless 'Edinburgh Reivers' came into existence. We have far more worthy heroes than these horse-riding thieves, but Scott and others attached an indelible glamour to them. James Hogg was deeply implicated in this and his 'Lock the Door, Lariston' also arranged the action along national lines. Even though the author dismissed it as ' having no merit whatsoever, excepting a jingle of names, which Sir Walter's good taste rendered popular', he is unquestionably wrong. It is a splendidly vibrant piece of popular writing. And that is an important point. If these writers had been less talented then our view of the past might not have been distorted by such powerful imaginations.

"Lock the door, Lariston, lion of Liddesdale,
Lock the door, Lariston, Lowther comes on,
The Armstrongs are flying,
Their widows are crying,
The Castletown's burning, and Oliver's gone;

Lock the door, Lariston — high on the weather gleam
See how the Saxon plumes bob on the sky,
Yeoman and carbinier,
Billman and halberdier;
Fierce is the foray, far is the cry.

Bewcastle brandishes high his broad scimitar,
Ridley is riding his fleet-footed grey,
Hedley and Howard there,
Wandale and Windermere —
Lock the door, Lariston, hold them at bay.

Why doest thou smile, noble Elliot of Lariston?
Why do the joy-candles gleam in thine eye?
Thou bold Border ranger,
Beware of thy danger —
Thy foes are relentless, determined and nigh.

Jock Elliot raised up his steel bonnet and lookit,
His hand grasped the sword with a nervous embrace;
'Ah, welcome, brave foemen,
On earth there are no men
More gallant to meet in the foray or chase!

'Little know you of the hearts I have hidden here,
Little know you of the moss-troopers might,
Lindhope and Sorby, true,
Sundhope and Milburn too,
Gentle in manner, but lions in fight!

I've Mangerton, Gornberry, Raeburn and Natherby,
Old Sim of Whitram, and all his array:
Come all Northumberland,
Teesdale and Cumberland,
Here at the Breaken Tower end shall the fray'.

Scowl'd the broad sun o'er the links of green Liddesdale,
Red as the beacon-light tipp'd he the wold;
Many a bold martial eye
Mirror'd that morning sky,
Never more oped on his orbit of gold!

Shrill was the bugle's note, dreadful the warrior shout,
Lances and halberds in splinters were borne;

Halberk and hauberk then,
Braved the claymore in vain,
Buckler and armlet in shivers were shorn.

See how they wane, the proud files of the Windermere,
Howard — Ah! woe to thy hopes of the day!
Hear the wild welkin rend,
While the Scots shouts ascend,
Elliot of Lariston, Elliot for aye!

12

The Singing Country

Family holidays can be formative and the parents of John Ruskin, the 19th century art critic and academic, were wealthy enough to afford annual tours to what were considered the more picturesque parts of Britain. Like most cultured people they admired the work of Samuel Coleridge, the Wordsworths and Walter Scott. These tastes led naturally to holidays in the Lake District and the Scottish Border country. After 1870 John Ruskin made his home at Brantwood on Coniston Water and from there visited the Borders at least once. Romantic idealism often informed his observations but rarely to the point of distortion, and when he wrote about the culture he met in the Borders — and Ruskin was keenly interested in popular culture — there is only a tinge of hyperbole;

"The Border district of Scotland was… of all districts of the inhabited world, pre-eminently the singing country — that which most naturally expressed its noble thoughts and passions in song."

Through the enormous and all-pervasive influence of Scott, and a continued and determined process of revivalism which sustained itself through a period of profound economic and social change in the 19th century, the Borders could easily claim never to have given up the description of 'The Singing Country'. Old songs were still sung and as a new identity for the emerging towns was created, these were adapted and new ones written. John Ruskin was better travelled than most, but the pre-eminence of a ballad culture in the Tweed basin over the entire "inhabited world" appears to be a very large claim. But it probably seemed that way to a Victorian writer largely because of the work and life of Walter Scott.

Other cultures in Britain produced much music and song, but the output of Welsh, Scots and Irish Gaelic bards was a closed world to Ruskin and the English literary establishment. Duncan Ban MacIntyre, one of the greatest ever Gaelic poets, lived virtually unnoticed in early 19th century Edinburgh and worked (in what was to become a High-land tradition in the Lowlands) as a policeman in the City Guard. Iolo Morgannwg was re-inventing, or often simply inventing, the Welsh bardic traditions of the Middle Ages and beyond — and composing magnificent work in the process. But in an atmosphere where educated Englishmen (and Scots) were more likely to learn Italian or classical Greek than a Celtic language, the mighty cadences of Iolo's poetry fell on deaf ears east of Offa's Dyke, and Duncan Ban's paean to the majesty of Ben Dorain was understood by few south of Perth. What prompted Ruskin's comment about Borders culture was presentation, through the work of Scott and others, and the fact that it existed in English, or at least in a recognisable dialect of Northern English.

As he doggedly worked himself to exhaustion and an early grave, after 1826 brought financial ruin, the laird of Abbotsford became something of a national treasure. His heroic attempt to act honourably and pay off his vast debts certainly endeared Scott to his loyal public who continued to buy his novels and biographies even though their quality had become patchy as a consequence of the grinding need for sheer quantity. As he turned out money-making copy, such as his massive 9 volume 'Life of Napoleon Buonaparte', Walter Scott's health worsened despite the fact that he was still in his late fifties. In particular his childhood lameness proved increasingly bothersome. On 15th February 1830 he was struck by what appears to have been a series of cerebral haemorrhages which affected both mobility and speech. But he recovered and kept on writing. A contemporary newspaper cartoon shows how concerned and informed the reading public were about the situation; it depicts Death in the shape of a skeleton barging into the study at Abbotsford to find the great man at his desk. The skeleton exclaims "Eh! bless me, I thought by the papers some of my people had dispatched this man". In 1831 the government became involved and offered Scott the use of a navy frigate, HMS Barham, to take him to wherever his health might improve. With the prospect of a winter to come medical opinion persuaded Scott to sail south to the warmth of the Mediterranean with his children Anne and Walter. By the time they reached Naples in the spring of 1832, however, there was a marked deterioration in Scott's health, but his spirit — and his self-critical faculties — fared better. Here is an entry in his journal, dated 26th January;

"This day arrived, for the first time indeed, answer to last post end of December, arrived an epistle from Caddell [Robert Caddell, publisher] full of good tidings. 'Castle Dangerous' and 'Sir Robert of Paris', neither of whom I deemed sea-worthy have performed 2 voyages, that is each sold off about £3400 and the same of the current year. It proves what I have thought almost impossible, that I might write myself [clear]. But as yet my spell holds fast. I have besides two or three good things in which I may advance with spirit."

Despite his optimism and determination, Scott suffered another stroke and it was decided to get him home to Abbotsford as speedily and as comfortably as possible. J.G. Lockhart met the party in London, and after three weeks' respite at the St James Hotel in Jermyn Street, he and his father-in-law boarded a steamer bound for Edinburgh. On 11th July they began Scott's last journey to the Borders. In his biography Lockhart notes that for much of the time Scott seemed confused and uncertain of where he was, but when they took the road down from Middleton Moor;

"he began to gaze about him, and by degrees it was obvious that he was recognising the features of that familiar landscape. Presently he murmured a name or two — 'Gala Water, surely — Buckholm — Torwoodlee'. As we rounded the hill at Ladhope, and the outline of the Eildons burst on him, he became greatly excited, and when turning himself on the couch his eye caught at length his own towers, at the distance of a mile, he sprang up with a cry of delight."

When the coach reached Abbotsford itself, Willie Laidlaw stood waiting by the main door. For many years he had served Scott as factor on his estates and become a firm friend. Confusion cleared again. "Ha! Willie Laidlaw! O man, how often have I thought of you."

According to Lockhart there were summer days when Scott could be taken outside by the beloved Tweed, but when, on 17th July, he was set once more in front of his desk, his power deserted him;

"'Now give me for my pen, and leave me for a little to myself'. Sophia [his daughter] put the pen into his hand, and he endeavoured to close his fingers upon it, but they refused their office — it dropped on the paper. He sank back among his pillows, silent tears rolling down his cheeks."

For a man who had created worlds with his pen, it was a bitter loss. On 21st September, a warm day at Abbotsford when the windows were opened to admit a cooling breeze, Walter Scott died. He was only 61. In peaceful moments he may have been able to reflect on an immense life. Not only had Scott changed the face of literature, inventing new genres in the shape of the historical novel and the short story as well as the phenomenon of the best-selling author, he had also changed the Borders completely. His influence would ramify into every recess of Border life, from the economics of textile production, to the forging of an indelible self-image that would find expression in the iconography of the common ridings (the St Ronan's Festival at Innerleithen is even named after a Scott novel), in Border rugby, the growing tourist industry and much else.

WARMONGER SCOTT

When Walter Scott died he was enthusiastically mourned in the southern states of the United States. Newspapers from Richmond to Atlanta and New Orleans published black-bordered editions in 1832 containing long obituaries, and it was remarked that the demise of presidents caused less of a stir. And according to Mark Twain, Scott's influence in the south was so profound that it was a major cause of the American Civil War. In his autobiographical 'Life on the Mississippi', published in 1883, Twain considers the freedoms confered by the American and French Revolutions and then goes on;

"Then comes Sir Walter Scott with his enchantments, and by his single might checks this wave of progress, and even turns it back; sets the world in love with dreams and phantoms; with decayed and swinish forms of religion; with decayed and degraded systems of government; with the silliness and emptiness, sham grandeurs, sham gauds, and sham chivalries of a brainless and worthless, long vanished society. He did measureless harm; more real and lasting harm, perhaps, than any other individual that ever wrote. "

Genuinely angry, Twain continues;

"It was Sir Walter Scott that made every gentleman in the South a Major or a Colonel or a General or a Judge, before the war, and it was he, also, that made these gentlemen value these bogus decorations… Sir Walter had so large a hand in making the Southern character, as it existed before the war, that he is in great measure responsible for the war. It seems a little harsh towards a dead man to say that we never should have had any war but for Sir Walter, and yet something of a plausible argument might, perhaps, be made in support of that wild proposition."

It was the triumph of a singular imagination, unquestionably a literary genius and unmistakably a heroic figure. Near the Volunteer Hall in Galashiels sits a granite bust of Scott and on the plinth the sculptor has chiselled, 'O Great and Gallant Scott'. For a man who never struck a blow in anger, it seems an odd motto. But there are many definitions of courage and a mental toughness allied to a protean capacity for hard work converted Scott's talent into genius. He cast a mighty shadow over the 19th and 20th century Border country and its history is impossible to understand fully without taking frequent account of his many influences. In several important ways we are all Scott's heirs. And in one particular his work was to have a profound impact on the lives of succeeding generations of Borderers, many of whom would never read a word he wrote. Scott had a busy eye for detail and one of those sowed a very fertile seed.

Hodden grey, or homespun grey, was a thick, coarse, undyed and warm cloth often found on the backs of ordinary people. But it was not always a uniform colour of grey. At some point in the distant past country weavers had taken the natural shades of raw wool and worked the warp and weft to create a rectilinear pattern of white and brown/black squares known as checks. It was a good way to convert what nature provided into a tidy, obviously man-made arrangement rather than attempt the impossible feat of creating a one-colour finish without the aid of dyes. These hodden grey weaves became known as 'Shepherd's Checks' or 'Shepherd's Plaid' and many were glad of them on a bitter winter day.

At Bowhill House, near Selkirk, there is a glass case containing early editions of 'The Lay of the Last Minstrel', 'The Life of Napoleon Buonaparte', some manuscripts and bits and pieces of memorabilia. The books are set against two large swathes of Shepherd's Checks which are described as the plaids worn by Sir Walter Scott and his friend James Hogg. While the cloth behind the glass looks well-pressed and suspiciously new, there is no doubt as to the truth of the general assertion that both men wore plaids of this exact sort. Portraits exist of Hogg and Scott draped in the grey check, and their work contains several references to what became known as Galashiels Grey. On the back of the success of Scott (and to a lesser extent of Hogg) the Shepherd's Plaid became fashionable in the 1820s and the weavers of Galashiels found themselves very busy.

But it was still a small business. The Manufacturers' Corporation of Galashiels was formed in 1777 with 23 members, most of whom were weavers. In Melrose, where the linen industry was centred, there were 140 looms working at that time. In 1780 the Corporation bought a machine known as a 'Teazing Willy', which was used to work the raw wool into a state where it could be more easily spun. A Cloth Hall was built in 1791 to provide a covered market-place where the Gala weavers could sell their output. And the first textile mill was built soon afterwards by a man with an appropriate name. 'Mercer' means 'cloth-finisher' or more generally 'cloth merchant', and George Mercer rented a site in 1800 at Wilderhaugh (wild deer haugh) where he could build a wheel by the bank of the fast-flowing Gala Water. Very few mills are located by the stately Tweed, most prefered to be on its tributaries as they rush from the hills. Mercer fitted out a waulk-mill at Wilderhaugh, a finishing mill where cloth was thickened.

The textile trade was further bolstered by the philanthropy of the Rev. Dr David Douglas who put his private fortune at the disposal of the Galashiels Manufacturers 'when trade was slack'. No bigot, he also invested in the Buckholmside Brewing Company which aimed to provide good ale for the people of Gala 'as the wells were foul'.

From the early 19th century Galashiels might have developed as small-scale textile town producing a modest amount of checked cloth. The influence of Scott and the acumen of two cloth merchants intervened to change that prospect. Amongst the papers of the Manufacturers' Corporation of Galashiels exists a fascinating document which shows exactly what happened. It is a memoir written by Archibald Craig and it relates the set of circumstances which began to convert Galashiels from a weavers' village into a textile manufacturing town.

"It was in the autumn of 1829 that I returned to Edinburgh by way of Liverpool from London, and upon landing at Glasgow a rather conspicuous object attracted my attention among the crowd on the Broomielaw, namely, a man dressed in a pair of black and white large-checked trousers. In the present day [1874] such an article of dress would not have been noticed, but when I explain that at that period nothing was worn for trousers except plain colours such as drabs, greys and blacks, the effect of such a marked change of dress will be better understood.

I think it highly probable that this man's trousers were made from either his grandfather's plaid, or his grandmother's shawl, as the white was so well 'smoked', not with sulphur, however, but with an age of peat reek, which by no means improved the appearance. I had not been many weeks in Edinburgh, however, before another pair or two of a smaller and more modest size of check were to be seen, and these I ascertained were made out of travelling cloaks. About four or five years previous to 1829 shepherd check cloaks, not unlike the Inverness capes of the present day, were much worn by gentlemen for wraps, and it was out of these cloaks that the trousers were made.

Shortly afterwards I had an enquiry from London for 'a coarse woollen black and white check stuff made in Scotland, and expected to be wanted for trousers', and requesting some patterns to be forwarded. This was easier asked than performed, as at that time these goods were only made in plaids, with borders and fringes. However, cutting a small piece from the seam of a cloak, it was forwarded… It turned out to be the article required, and an order for half a dozen pieces was received. These were soon made, and were, I believe, the first Scotch tweeds that were sent to London in bulk. They were introduced into influential quarters, and increased orders followed rapidly, and the firm with which I am connected had about a monopoly of the trade in London in these goods for a considerable time."

Archibald Craig went on to explain how new designs were found to prevent the boom in demand for shepherd's check from being only a short-lived vogue;

"It happened that one of the manufacturers had made a quantity of these checks, but the white was so impure and dirty-looking from being mixed with grey wool that they would not sell. In the circumstances a happy idea struck someone, that if they were dipped in brown dye it would hide the fault and produce a brown and black check. The idea was acted upon, and on the 'new style' being sent to London they sold rapidly, and fresh orders were sent for more of the same pattern. These brown and black checks were succeeded by blue and black, then green and black and these again by broken and large checks in all the above colourings, and at every change of pattern a fresh impetus was given to the trade. After these checks had run their day they were succeeded by the same colourings in tweels, black and white, black and brown, etc., a good variety of new patterns and colourings following each other."

BORDER RANGER

In common with much of rural Scotland, many emigrants left the Tweed valley in the course of the 19th century. John Clay moved from the Borders to another frontier to become one of the men who won the west, or at least helped to buy it. Born at Ladykirk, opposite Norham on the Scots side of the Tweed, he left his father's farm at Kerchesters and found employment as the agent of the Scottish American Investment Trust. Based in Edinburgh's Charlotte Square, this was a ruthless combination of financial interests intent on buying up the rights to ranch cattle over huge tracts of the American West. They engaged John Clay to travel to the USA and visit ranches in order to assess their value. If he believed the business to be worthwhile and not run by a crooked hustler or rustler, he cabled Edinburgh to buy. And if he was unimpressed he counselled them (and himself) to move on. With such power at his hand, Clay must have had a high old time.

> *Many of the cattlemen he dealt with were Scots and they included the notorious Stewart family of Montana. Their methods of dealing with known and suspected rustlers would have made a Border reiver proud. The vigilante group called 'Stewart's Stranglers' lynched at least 100 men, many more than were killed by the Daltons, the James Gang and the other infamous outlaw gangs put together.*
>
> *John Clay recorded much of this in his 'My Life on the Range' published in 1924 in Chicago, but surprisingly he never forgot the tranquility of his early days on the banks of the Tweed, and in 'Old Times Recalled', he rhapsodised about a lost Arcadia.*

The promotion of Border cloth by Walter Scott and James Hogg was initially a happy cultural accident, but both men were anxious to see the textile business prosper. At a dinner held at the Fleece Inn in 1821 the Manufacturers' Corporation of Galashiels invited them to celebrate, and when asked for a song, Sir Walter obliged with, it was thought, a passable rendition of 'Tarry Oo'. Describing the process of converting 'oo' or wool into cloth, it offers an appropriate anthem for the history of Galashiels sung by a man instrumental in changing it;

"Tarry Oo, Tarry Oo
Tarry Oo is ill to spin
Caird it weel, caird it weel
Caird it weel ere ye begin
When 'tis cairded, row'd and spun
Then the work is halflins done
But when woven, drest and clean
It may be cleading for a queen."

A year after his dinner in Gala, Scott was busy organising an event which would provide even more work for the weavers who supped with him. It was decided that the new king, George IV, would undertake a state visit to Scotland and that the whole affair should be conceived and organised by the great novelist, Sir Walter Scott. In August 1822 the populace of Edinburgh gathered at the port of Leith to witness an astonishing sight. The portly king had been persuaded into a Royal Stewart kilt and bonneted and plaided for two colourful weeks, he attended tartan-covered extravaganzas of many sorts, balls, pageants and ceremonies — most of them conjured up from Scott's romantic imagination rather than any authentic set of Highland traditions. George IV was the first reigning monarch to visit Scotland since Charles II in 1651, and no matter how daft he looked, the middle and upper classes anxiously followed suit and climbed into kilts and plaids for the occasion. Offstage, J.G. Lockhart muttered that his father-in-law "has made us appear to be a nation of Highlanders, and the bagpipe and the tartan are the order of the day". Behind the flummery Scott appears to have retained a hard-headed common sense and no illustrations exist of him clothed in anything other than his Shepherd's plaid and sensible breeks.

An expatriate club, the Highland Society of London, had written to clan chiefs in 1815 asking them to send a sample of their clan tartan to be registered and deposited. To many this was a baffling request since they had no idea that any such thing existed. But tartan manufacturers were often happy to supply a pattern (many were simply numbered or carried place-names for identification) for them to adopt, and many so-called traditional setts date from this period. Following the pantomimic state visit of George IV, the popularity of tartan surged tremendously and the notion that particular surnames had a 'right' to particular patterns added a unique marketing twist. This was developed by the remarkable Sobieski-Stewart brothers, John and Charles-Edward. Claiming to be descendents of Bonnie Prince Charlie, they compiled an allegedly ancient list of clan tartans in a book with the sonorous title of 'Vestiarum Scoticum'. Clearly bogus and much consulted, it is the origin of several of today's 'clan' setts. Queen Victoria and Prince Albert carried royal patronage of tartan on to new levels. The walls of Balmoral were covered in the stuff and, as ever, the monarchy established an almost mandatory trend for the clothes of courtiers and high society which was enthusiastically aped by the lower orders.

All of this was meat and drink to Border cloth manufacturers. After all, tartan was no more than an elaborate and colourful version of the checked fabrics they were used to turning out. While royal patronage inserted Border products into the centre of London society, their further exploitation was greatly stimulated by an enterprising expatriate Scot who ran a fashionable tailoring business in Regent Street. James Locke visited Galashiels in 1830 or 1832 to meet weavers and mill owners and discuss how they might advance their business. At first he met obdurate conservatism. When Locke explained that he needed a pattern book in tweed and tartan, the Gala manufacturers were not helpful; "We shall never forget the look we got, and the difficulties we had to overcome before our suggestion was agreed to". Armed with his hard-won pattern books and versions of the newly designed ancient tartans, Locke expanded his business with real flair, although he was careful to note that the original fashion item inspired by Walter Scott was still a staple;

"We had been long familiar with the 'shepherd's maud', and, we believe, were the first to wear one in town. [Locke almost always uses the royal 'we']. Well do we remember, about 1833, going down High Holborn on a Sunday morning with a whole host of admiring followers behind us. What lots of these were made in the next ten years for travelling purposes. The maud was an article that added much to the Scotch trade, and they were soon produced in all the clan tartans. We remember to have sold one for a bedcover to the present Pope, and Lady Franklin gave one to all the officers of the ships going to seek for the North-West Passage.

Ladies' shawls were a very extensive branch for about ten years. Every manufacturer in Galashiels made these goods for the Glasgow and London markets. At first they were made of Cheviot wool, but soon the cry got up for finer qualities. For many years these shawls were only made in six-quarter to eight-quarter [sizes] in all the clan patterns, and also in fancies of every kind, made out of the finest fleeces.

We well remember making a pattern which became a great favourite, it was called the 'Blair Athole'. In 1842, when the Queen first went to Scotland, we proposed to ourselves a new shawl. We took the large 'Murray' and incorporated it with the 'Victoria'. Could it have been patented, it would have been a fortune. From this came nearly all what have been termed the 'Dress Clan' pattern in shawls."

Tartan has never gone out of fashion and is still made in Gala even though much of the traditional textile industry has withered. Through his novels, and particularly 'Waverley' which dealt with the 1745 Rebellion, Walter Scott made its popularity politically possible. Neutralising the seditious, barbarous and anarchic Highlander in a cloying web of romance, he then frisked him for most of his portable iconography and through the antics of George IV in Edinburgh delivered tartan and tartanry into the heart of fashionable society, where it has remained.

In London Locke and his dandyish friends wore jackets and trousers made up from Border cloth, and gradually the fashion of having both in the same pattern evolved. When the Prince of Wales wore a 'suit' with matching jacket and trousers, an enduring sartorial vogue was set and 'suit-lengths' were turned out in volume by the Galashiels manufacturers. Clearly a showman and a gifted entrepreneur alive to every opportunity, Locke even went so far as to coin a new name for the checked cloth produced in the Borders. An oft-repeated tale insists that when he received a package of 'tweel' (or twill) from Galashiels in 1847, the Regent Street tailor somehow misread the label and wrote back asking for a consignment of 'tweed'. Given that the recipient of the fabled parcel was an expatriate Scot, a successful tailor and a visitor to Gala, none of this makes any sense. He knew fine what tweel was and where the Tweed flowed. 'Tweed' cloth was almost certainly Locke's deliberate invention, a smart piece of marketing which clearly branded cloth made in the Tweed valley and associated it with the most famous Tweedsider in recent history, Sir Walter Scott.

More and more opportunties arose and it appears that Locke was instrumental in introducing tweed to a social set who would in time come to be described by it — as 'tweedy'. Even though he probably overstates his role, the relation described between demand in London and supply from Galashiels is clear enough.

"When gentlemen of the rod and gun began to enquire for that which would resemble the shooting ground, we had nothing of the kind, neither was there any in the market. We wrote to a Galashiels house for a 'range', but they replied they had never heard of such an article. By the following post we requested them just to imitate Buckholm Hill which overshadowed them, at this time in beautiful bloom. A boy was despatched to bring some heather. Now, when a handful of this was squashed together it had different shades varying with the seasons. This proved to be the very thing we wanted, and led to the introduction of a variety of colourings before unknown. This was the origin of heather mixtures."

Galashiels was transformed by the efforts of Walter Scott, James Locke, Archibald Craig and others. Dorothy Wordsworth, the sister of the poet, was in the town in 1803 and disappointed to observe the beginnings of a change from picturesque to industrial;

"A pretty place it has once been, but a manufactory has been established there; and a townish bustle and ugly stone houses are now taking the place of the brown-roofed thatched cottages, of which a great number remain."

Three mills were turning when Miss Wordsworth visited, taking their power from the mill-lades running off the Gala Water. By the time Scott and Hogg were dining at the Fleece Inn with the Manufacturers in 1821, there were ten mills and many outworkers spinning and weaving in their cottages. 1830 to 1850 was a period of expansion and prosperity for the town and at the Crystal Palace Exhibition of 1851, four first class medals were awarded to Galashiels cloth makers.

GRACE DARLING

At about 4am on 7th September 1838 tremendous seas and gale force winds drove the steamship Forfarshire onto the deadly rocks of the Farne Islands off the Northumberland coast. The ship immediately broke in two and at least 43 people were plunged into the deeps to their deaths. As dawn broke through the storm clouds, Grace Darling, the daughter of the keeper of the Longstone Lighthouse on the easternmost Farne, saw the outline of the wreck and searched through the swirling mirk with a telescope for any sign of survivors. At about 7am she saw some movement on the black rocks and with her father, she rowed out into the mountainous seas to attempt a rescue. Taking a leeward but lengthy course they made two trips and saved nine people, including a Mrs Dawson who carried her two dead children in her arms.

A week later the Newcastle Journal carried a full account of the episode which stressed that it was Grace who had persuaded her father, William Darling, to put to sea. The story was picked up by the London Times which asked "Is there in the whole field of history, or of fiction even, one instance of female heroism to compare for one moment with this?" Grace Darling immediately became the subject of hysterical admiration. Incredibly, tourists came to the Farnes to see her, to beg for locks of her hair. Offers of marriage poured in, awards, decorations, a London theatre offered a starring role in "Wreck at Sea" for £50 per week, William Wordsworth was moved to write a eulogy and she was made 'National Heroine of Japan'. There is now a Grace Darling Museum at Bamburgh.

But the museum is also a monument to a story which spun out of control, a very early example of how newspapers can create a perception which obscures much of the truth. What really happened was buried under all the adulation. As with many jobs in 19th century Britain, lighthousekeeping involved the whole family, although only one man was paid. When the Forfarshire struck Big Harcar Rock at 4am, Mrs Darling was on watch while her husband slept, and Grace had helped her father the day before to lash their rowing boat in safety from the coming storm. Her brother, William Darling Jr, was also part of the family business, and it was by no means unusual for Grace to be scanning the seascape with a telescope. In "Grace Darling — Her True Story" written in 1880 by her sister, Thomasin, and a Mr Daniel Atkinson, it is made clear that William Darling Snr decided to attempt a rescue because he believed that neither the North Sunderland or Bamburgh lifeboats would launch in such a fierce storm. His rowing boat was the only chance for the Forfarshire. And since his son was away, only Grace was available to row with him.

What she did was indeed heroic, but not quite as heroic as the newspapers made out. In fact Grace seems to have been embarassed at all the fuss and it may have contributed to her early death in 1841, three years after the wreck

The organisation of the tweed industry was dictated by the long and difficult process of converting the fleeces of Border sheep into bolts of Border cloth. For the sake of clarity, this is best set out in stages;

Sorting. When shorn fleeces bought by a mill owner arrived from the valleys, they were usually dirty, even though hirds always washed their sheep before the clip. But often this was only a dunk in a pond or pool in a stream or river. Burrs, tics and sheep-shit made sorting an unpleasant job, and the 'tarry oo' sung about by Walter Scott was a reference to the habit rubbing a tar and butter mixture onto the skins of sheep to inhibit insect infestation. Each fleece was generally divided, with the cleanest wool coming from the neck and the shoulders and the dirtiest from the hind quarters. As it was dumped into different bins, sorters also tried to keep coarse and fine wool separate.

Scouring. Long metal troughs were filled a solution of cold, soapy water and after the wool was tipped in workers trod on it and sometimes used their hands to rub out the more tenacious muck. This was a long, cold and sometimes miserable job which only ended when the wool rinsed clear. Then it was dried slowly so that it did not become brittle. Similar care is taken nowadays when washing and drying a woollen jumper.

Blending. After cleaning, wool was carefully re-sorted according to quality and character so that consistent yarn could be produced by the spinners. Coarse, soft, shiny or black/brown wool was divided into different bins.

Teazing. To keep sheep dry on a winter hillside, wool is naturally impregnated with a fat known as lanolin. Washing removes this, leaving the wool too slippy and silky to allow it to stick and twine together when yarn is spun. Teazing pulls out the fibre into a rougher state and when oil is added later (rape-seed oil or olive oil for more expensive yarn) tangles are unravelled. This was the stage in the process done by the original Teazing Willy bought by the Galashiels Manufacturers in 1780.

Carding. Using two plates studded with fine teeth working against each other, this operation converts the mass of wool into usable strands.

Spinning. Carded wool was generally sent out of the mill to home workers who spun the strands into yarn. The essence of spinning is to twist the wool, like very fine rope, so that it gains both length and strength. Most was done on cottage wheels of the sort still turned out nowadays as ornaments, but in 1798 there were eight hand-turned spinning jennies in Gala, mostly in spinners' lofts, and these machines could spin several threads at once. By 1814 the first water powered spinning mules were installed in mills and they changed the patterns of textile production by drawing spinners out of their houses and into what were early 'manufactories' or factories. The development of the textile industry fluctuated dramatically with the pace and incidence of technological change. Sometimes mechanical looms outstripped the ability of spinners to supply them with yarn, and at other times there was a surplus of yarn as weaving lagged behind.

At this stage of the process yarn was often dyed, but the ancient techniques and knowledge employed properly belong in the finishing stage.

Weaving. In 1823 there were 130 looms in Gala operated by 100 weavers and some apprentices. All of the work was done at home and this simple fact inhibited the pace of innovation — but probably maintained quality.

First the warp was prepared. A highly skilled job, it involved tying onto the wooden rollers of a loom hundreds of threads which would run lengthways through a bolt of cloth. Winding the yarn off bobbins a warper arranged the threads into odd and even groups which moved up and down as a weaver passed the shuttle between them. In Gala, tweed (or tweel) was made when the warper tied on in such a way as to allow the shuttle, carrying the weft threads, to cross over two and under two warp threads. This produced the characteristic checked pattern. The opening created by the up and down movement of the warp was called the 'shed', and before mechanisation, the length of it was 27 inches. This corresponded to the average weaver's ability to pass the shuttle from one hand to another. Even after the invention of the flying shuttle and the advent of power looms, bolts of cloth still measured 21 yards by 27 inches, and anything broader was called 'broadcloth'.

Finishing. Weavers sent cloth back to the mill to be finished and the first part of this process often involved dyeing. Passed down through hundreds of generations, Border recipes for particular colours depended very much on the sort of native plants mentioned by James Locke in his letter to the owners of Buckholm Mill. For example, alder bark and docken roots produced black, dandelions gave magenta and bracken produced a pale yellow. Wholesalers from Holland specialised in more exotic colours such as Jamaican indigo, cochineal red and saffron from the stamens of crocuses.

Once cloth was dyed, it was carefully stretched on tenterhooks and when dry, 'lookers' examined it for flaws. As irregularities in the weave were spotted or knots found by feeling for them, the lookers circled the area with chalk so that it could be repaired. Next, the cloth was scarted with the heads of a plant called wild teazel to raise the nap and make it more full and warmer. Teazels were grown as a commercial crop in the countryside around Gala and Selkirk (and still grow there wild) and when cut, the heads were mounted on frames and drawn across the cloth in a brushing motion. The nap was then sheared to make it even. Only then was a piece of tweed cloth finished and suitable for sale.

CARLISLE CRACKERS

In 1831 Jonathan Carr walked from Kendal to Carlisle to make his fortune. He started a small bakery whose biscuits became so popular and distinctive that Queen Victoria granted him a royal warrant in 1841. Carr's Table Water Biscuits were originally a more refined version of hardtack ship's biscuit. In order to avoid spoiling in the variable temperatures of a long sea voyage, it was important that biscuits contain as little fat as possible. Carr's pioneered a technique of baking which used water as a binding agent and the result can still be enjoyed today.

In 1849 the world changed. The railway reached Galashiels, went on to Hawick and Carlisle, and in 1862 the Waverley Line, named after Sir Walter Scott's novels, was opened. The effect of this was radical, opening links between the Borders and the entire British rail network, allowing the rapid and widespread export of tweed to urban and, eventually, foreign markets, as well as the import of finer wools to make a variety of luxury fabrics. It is difficult to underestimate the impact of the railway. Transport by road with cart and packhorse was slow, seasonal and very expensive. By rail it was quick, regular and dependable. Even on the smallest country station platform dizzying new horizons opened; at Hassendean Station, near Hawick, it was possible to buy a ticket and board a train which would take passengers to London, Paris and the European capitals.

The railway even created communities. At Riccarton Junction a true railway village was built to house those who worked on the line. A branch of the Co-op was eventually built not on the street but on the station platform. However, despite the ease of rail transport the community felt enclosed. Riccarton became notorious for sporadic outbreaks of friction, and even violence which required the presence of the police to damp down. Workers at the village were kept busy for the Waverley Line had a number of difficult sections as it snaked through the hill country south of Hawick in awkward bends and steep gradients.

The squabbles at Riccarton were as nothing compared to what happened when the railway track itself was being built. Thousands of navvies (short for 'navigators', originally coined for the men who dug Britain's canals) were employed in throwing up embankments, making cuttings through hillsides and building impressive viaducts such as Leaderfoot Bridge and Shankend. There was little machinery and the vast bulk of this was achieved by sweated manual labour with pick, shovel and barrow. It was back-breaking work and by the time pay day arrived these men had developed a powerful thirst and a need to let off steam. Border newspapers carried advertisements warning local people that on the date the navvies were due to be paid "some disturbances were likely to take place". Much of this was predictable and avoidable, but a serious incident took place at St Boswell's on the Fair Day of 18th July 1849. A large crowd of navvies from the gangs laying the track between Kelso and St Boswell's had gathered around a fight outside Mr Brown's Inn. About 400 men watched an unequal contest as one man bludgeoned another into unconsciousness. The police waded through the crowd, stopped the fight and took the winner off to cool off in the cells. Immediately the navvies rioted (they were mostly Irish, but many Highlanders and Englishmen also joined the gangs) and for two drink-fuelled days they repeatedly attempted to rescue the prisoner, breaking the windows of the lockup and assaulting the policemen. This was too much for one young Borderer. William Lauder of Whitelee was employed as a shepherd at Old Melrose and he may have known some of the beleagured constables. Very unwisely he felt he could not longer stand by and watch them being attacked, and he rushed into one of the melees. The navvies set on the young man, throwing him to the ground where his head was, literally, kicked in. A few hours later he died of multiple fractures of the skull.

At this point the military were mobilised and with the villagers of Lessudden, armed and angry, they belatedly put an end to the rioting. Sixteen navvies were arrested and taken to Jedburgh Jail, but ultimately none of them were charged with Lauder's murder. On September 4th, probably acting on information received, constables arrested three navvies in Belford in North Northumberland and charged them with mobbing, rioting and murder. One man, Thomas Wilson, was convicted of murder and condemned to death. Outside Jedburgh Jail carpenters began to build a scaffold and a professional hangman was brought from Glasgow. On the dull and rainswept morning of October 25th Wilson was led out, his hands tied behind his back, onto the wooden platform to face the noose. Fearful of attacks and an attempt at rescue by bands of navvies, the town magistrates had sworn in 200 special constables and requested the armed attendance of detachments of the 21st Regiment of Foot. With bayonets fixed they surrounded the scaffold. Allowed a few final words, Wilson was said to have made a dignified speech, claiming his innocence and asserting that he would not go "before my God with a lie in my mouth". The crowd of 3,000 listened in hushed silence. Many were sympathetic and had raised a petition for a reprieve a few days before. There was more than a suspicion that the guilty men had escaped to North America in the interval between William Lauder's murder and Wilson's arrest. But it was all too late and as the black flags flapped in the rain and the provost and magistrates of Jedburgh looked on, Wilson was hooded, the noose tightened around his neck and the trapdoor dropped open.

This sad incident aside, the human cost of building the Border railways has gone largely unrecorded, but the engineering achievement can still be seen, and it was considerable. By the time the Lauder Light Railway opened in 1901 (it branched off the main Waverley Line at Fountainhall) a rail connection was made to every town and many villages. The only hindrance to the smooth running of the Border network turned out to be political, and a matter of old politics at that. The existence of the border itself discouraged the North Eastern Railway Company (English) from establishing a good working relationship with the North British Railway Company (Scottish). Taking its line as far as Kelso, where practicalities drew the railway border, the North Eastern built one station in Scotland at Sprouston. This was deeply resented by the North British management and they retaliated by refusing to publish details of connecting trains to England in their timetables. This petty animosity lasted right up to 1948 when British Rail amalgamated all of the different railway companies.

RAILWAY TIME

Britain is a long, thin country oriented on, broadly, a north/south axis. Distances from east to west are much shorter and this accident of geography made the imposition of standard time easier. In the early 19th century time was a local matter and it varied from town to town (understandably if they lay some distance to the east or west of each other) and also between Scotland and England. That meant that if it is was 3pm in Hawick, it might be 3.15pm in Berwick. For early train travel, these discrepancies became very important as timetables were compiled. People travelling from, say, Kelso to Berwick wanted to be sure to catch their onward connection south.

The Astronomer Royal, Sir George Airy, decided that Greenwich Mean Time, the time on the meridian at the Royal Observatory at Greenwich, should be adopted throughout Britain — even when, as in the case of Penzance and London, there really was a significant time difference. For a long time GMT was called 'Railway Time'

Such difficulties were incidental to the textile industry in the Borders. What mattered to manufacturers was the huge improvement in access to their markets, and the hosiery merchants of Hawick benefited particularly. While Galashiels had concentrated on the production of outerwear, Hawick had developed a successful trade in stockings and underwear.

In 1771 a local magistrate, Bailie John Hardie, took the sort of initiative characteristic of the Board of Trustees for Manufacture when he introduced stocking knitting frames into Hawick. Four were set up at 37 High Street and workers trained to operate them. In essence these were mechanical knitting frames able to make a 16 and a half inch piece of cloth out of linen, coarse worsted, and eventually lambswool. These pieces were seamed, footed and formed into the sort of stockings men wore below knee breeches. Hardie's frames knitted enough to satisfy local demand, but the innovation turned out to be invaluable in that Hawick workers were trained in a marketable skill which might be exploited and expanded. In 1780 John Nixon, a Nottingham stockinger, bought out Hardie's business and soon employed 65 people. 13 men worked the frames while 42 women spun the necessary yarn. By 1791 Hawick's annual output rose to 4,000 pairs of stockings, a substantial trade but still firmly local. What stimulated output massively was the outbreak of war in Europe. The urgent need to supply stockings for tens of thousands of British soldiers fighting in the Napoleonic Wars made Hawick's output rocket. In 1816, after the French defeat at Waterloo, 328,000 pairs were produced on 500 frames. But when hostilities ceased and soldiers were demobbed, demand naturally fell. Merchants and employers attempted to reduce the price paid to stockingers by 6d a dozen. A series of protracted strikes followed and one of the leaders, John Hogg, was imprisoned by the authorities.

At the beginning of the 19th century conditions for a rapid surge of growth in the hosiery industry in Hawick were very favourable. Cheviot sheep produced the right sort of hard wearing wool for warm stockings and labour was initially cheaper than in the older production centres of Glasgow and South Yorkshire. Advances in technology also ensured a plentiful supply of yarn at the right time, and the ambitions of the Emperor Napoleon created a ready market. By 1838 trade had recovered from a post-war slump and more than a million pairs of stockings were produced in Hawick that year. And in the 1840s the area saw an in-migration of English hosiery workers in search of jobs. These men, incidentally, brought the game of cricket to the Borders and Hawick and Wilton is one of the oldest clubs in Scotland.

By the middle of the 19th century Scottish hosiery production was centred in the Borders. And 60% of all of the 2,605 stocking frames in Scotland were working in Hawick. Serious competition, particularly on price, came from Nottingham and South Yorkshire but with the same alacrity as their Gala counterparts the Hawick merchants clambered aboard the bandwagon set rolling by Walter Scott and designed much of their output in tartan. High quality lambswool was used and this also helped to overcome the attractions of cheaper hose from the south.

The business was organised between merchants, factory owners and home workers. Sometimes two and even all three could be combined. Willie Laidlaw spun his own yarn on a hand jenny, knitted stockings on his frame and sold them himself, along with, it is alleged, illicit whisky. Because the carding and yarn spinning processes had in fact become largely concentrated in mills built by the Teviot and its fast-flowing tributary, the Slitrig, the industry was controlled by the mill owners. They bought domestic wool and imported finer stuff on the new railway, and when stockings were made, they sold them on to retail outlets. But the work of weaving was still overwhelmingly domestic, either done at home or in premises known as frame shops which were owned or rented by workers. Like the heckling sheds of the linen industry, these places operated as informal co-operatives. In 1857 80 existed in Hawick and more in Denholm, Langholm, Selkirk and Jedburgh — and even as far afield as Lochmaben, Dumfries and Lockerbie. Typically each shop took its output to the mill warehouses for 'the count', and after much agitated argument a price was agreed, cash handed over and the next week's supply of yarn taken away. On a Saturday night Hawick pubs were a favoured place for the shop to meet and divide up the cash. After all, landlords were never short of change. In prosperous years the weekend sometimes stretched as far as the following Tuesday or Wednesday. The Hawick stockingers were famously independent-minded, even thrawn, and like the linen hecklers before them, well informed about the world and how it worked.

TELFORD'S BRITAIN

Along with James Small, Thomas Telford could fairly claim to be a Borderer who had changed the face of the land. Born near Langholm, he served his time as a stone mason and through his own self-taught efforts rose to become an engineer and architect who worked all over Britain. Ferociously energetic he seemed able to juggle many projects at once. Not only was he responsible for 900 miles of roads and 120 bridges in the Highlands, in 1818 alone, he was involved in building the Menai Straits bridge, Holyhead Harbour, the London to Holyhead road, the Glasgow to Carlisle road, the Caledonian Canal, the Gloucester Canal, harbours at Dundee and surveys for a road from Glasgow to Portpatrick.

Buried in Westminster, Telford had made his own long road from the Border hillsides where his father was a hird.

In the middle of the 19th century fashions changed and Hawick was forced to change with them. Trousers were becoming increasingly popular, displacing breeches and dispensing with the need for stockings. Horse-riding needed breeches, train riding did not. To meet a new demand, the mills developed new lines, altering their methods and machinery to turn out men's (and ladies') woollen combinations, undershirts, and wide body belts known as 'cholera belts'. At 16 and a half inches across the old stocking frames were too small and new, wider machinery meant more concentration on factory production. Mill owners could more readily afford to replace obsolete frames than individuals, but even so, change happened only slowly. Indeed some mills opted to stay with domestic production since they believed it was a guarantee of higher quality. Lyle and Scott waited until 1893 to introduce power frames in their mill.

Hawick combinations and vests enjoyed two signal advantages over the competition. Lambswool garments were warm and in an era when central heating was unknown and trains particularly cold, this was a prime consideration. And since combinations were worn next to the skin, the weave needed to be smooth so as not to itch. Merino wool from Australia and New Zealand and fine German wools arrived in bulk by rail and were much prefered to the rougher Cheviot for underwear production. Comfort and a snug fit were also helped by the Hawick habit of making fully fashioned garments in different sizes, and since they were washed frequently, they also needed to be unshrinkable. Good photographs exist of workers pulling underwear onto flat body-shaped frames and steam pressing them.

Increasingly Hawick mills became aware of the importance of branding and marketing. Lyle and Scott promoted 'Ellan Ess' underwear, Innes, Henderson (later called Braemar) had 'Henderwick' and Peter Scott had the 'Pesco' brand. Between 1882 and 1888 eight new mills opened in Hawick, almost doubling the number of manufacturers and drawing more and more workers directly into the mills and away from domestic production. The population of Hawick quadrupled in the first half of the 19th century and in the boom years that followed 1860 people left the land and farming to come into the town and work in its mills. It must have been a bewildering transition, moving from the quiet farms of Teviotdale to the bustle of a growing town; the press of people after the windswept hills, the shattering racket of power looms after the wheeling cries of the whaups and the distant bleat of ewes. James Small's swing plough had brought the heavy horses with it and its efficiency ramified into every corner of farming, slowly reducing the need for large plough teams and their bairns to help with cultivation. Mechanisation in agriculture pushed rather than drove people off the land, and despite the starkness of the change, many were glad to take jobs in the clatter of the mills.

While Hawick can claim to have grown into the most industrialised of the Border towns, it has clung on to a poignant remnant of an agricultural past. The great scholar, J.A.H. Murray of Denholm, who edited the first Oxford English Dictionary was much interested in Border dialects. In 1873 he mourned the disappearance of the old dialect of the country districts, particularly in matters of pronunciation. Words like 'you' and 'me' had been spoken all over the Tweed Basin as 'yow' and 'mei', but in Galashiels, Melrose and Kelso, Murray noted that this version had vanished and expected it be generally extinct in one or two generations. But in Hawick, it has endured into the 21st century, perhaps because of the heavy concentration of in-migration from the countryside in the busy mid 19th century. Large groups of contemporaries transfered 'yow' and 'mei' from the hillside to the mill in a short period and it became the accepted pronunciation of the whole town.

JIMSIE

Homburg hatted, bearded, suited and knighted, Sir James Augustus Henry Murray returned to his native village of Denholm. The son of a weaver, largely self-taught, he had succeeded brilliantly at the centre of British intellectual life, having been appointed as the founding editor of the Oxford English Dictionary in 1879 and feted as a great and innovative scholar. As he walked across Denholm village green, he was stopped by an old lady who peered at his substantial figure for a moment before saying, "Mercy mei Jimsie, is that yow?"

Accommodation for Victorian mill workers resembled that of much of industrial Britain. It was crowded and often insanitary. For the fast-growing towns the old wells and streams would not longer suffice as a supply of usable water. New sources were urgently needed and at Selkirk the issue spiced local politics to the point of disrupting the 1866 Common Riding. 'The Pumpers' favoured the cheaper option of pumping water up from the Ettrick even though the river was polluted with effluent and an increasing amount of industrial waste from the mills on Dunsdale Road. 'The Gravitationists' prefered the more expensive but much healthier method of obtaining fresh water from an upland reservoir, and ultimately they triumphed. Because Galashiels was the last major Border town to invest in a clean water supply and drainage system, in 1915, the inhabitants acquired the indelible nickname of 'the pail-merks'. Before the First World War, on two days a week households left out a full pail of sewage for collection from their doorsteps. Even by the Second World War at least one of the mills still had to install inside toilets for their workers. Wakefield Mill provided only a set of squalid outside sheds with a pail in each cubicle, and because no chemicals were used the smell was apparently eye-watering. It took sustained pressure from the Transport and General Workers Union to force Wakefield Mill to pay for decent toilets.

Mill-work was hard. Every day except Sunday the lamp-lighters were first out of their beds. Generally 14 year-old girls, they arrived at the mill lodge at 5.45am sharp. There they were given lamps and their job was to have the production flats lit for the workers by 6am. Time-keeping was draconian. Each mill's hooter was differently tuned and they first blared out over the rooftops at 5.55am. If workers were not inside the mill gates by the time of the second hooter at 6am, they were locked out and their pay docked for the day. At 5.55pm the same sequence took place and the gates were opened at 6pm. In the winter-time without street lighting and in bad weather it was a remorseless grind for six days of every week. But holidays were not unknown and days off were granted for Common Ridings and other events. However, it was not until the 20th century that paid leave of any duration was conceded. As in the rest of Victorian Britain discipline in the mills was severe and summary. Since a man stood to lose not only his job if he was consistently late, inefficient or insubordinate, but usually also his tied home, few in Hawick or Gala dared to object to anything and simply got on with it.

Sanderson and Murray ran the largest skinworks in Europe and could process 20,000 sheepskins in a week. After the sorting and washing, the skins had their wool pulled off by hand. Sitting on a long row of benches with bins in front of them, men tore out the wool with their fingers. It was a difficult and unpleasant job. Although the wool had been washed, tics often remained embedded in the fleece and if someone got one under a fingernail, it quickly became infected. And there was also a remote danger of contracting anthrax. The chemicals used in the washing were powerful and the men wore 5 layers of aprons to protect their legs and laps but they found that the skin on their hands became paper-thin and easily perforated. In her excellent history 'Guid Auld Galashiels', Margaret Lawson remembers that when the pullers accepted a sweet, they took it on the backs of their hands to avoid putting their fingers near their mouths.

The gulf between the lives of mill workers and mill owners was immense. And in comparatively small towns such as Gala, Selkirk and Hawick these sharp contrasts were daily evident. There existed great rivalry between mill-owning families and they expressed it not so much in the running of their businesses but in the splendour of their houses. Perhaps the most impressive is Glenmayne, on the opposite bank of the Tweed from Abbotsford, but other magnificent houses went up at Kingsknowes, Netherby and Abbotshill. One family, the Cochranes, built no fewer than six grand villas. At Hawick the mill owners' houses were slightly more modest, and it appears that the town's wealthy families preferred to export their ostentation. One was so fond of holidaying in the south of France that they eventually made their stay permanent.

Owners were sometimes philanthropic and the Sanderson family gifted a fever hospital and the playing fields at Netherdale to Galashiels. A nephew, John Hayward, possessed real civic awareness and in 1930 he came up with the idea of a Gala Day to rival the ancient Common

Ridings of Selkirk and Hawick. However Hayward insisted that his workers do unpaid overtime to make up for the hours lost on the holiday of the Gala Day, and the philanthropy of the Sandersons seems to have stopped at the mill gates. Inside them wages remained low, sanitation poor and safety a low priority.

As they gazed up at these opulent houses on their daily trudge to and from the mills, Border textile workers did not believe themselves to be on the lowest rung of the social ladder. Even though many of them were only first or second generation townspeople, they looked down on those who had stayed on in the countryside. 'Fresh in frae fer oot' was a phrase that encapsulated their view, a mixture of mild derision and pity. In the agricultural Borders this was a radical shift in attitudes achieved over a very short period.

Part of the reason for this change was the sense that those who lived in the relative isolation of the countryside were missing something. In another phrase they were 'hicks off the heidrig'. They had limited access to the social life of the growing towns, and in particular to the busy pub culture which grew up in the middle of the 19th century. Stocking-makers used Hawick's pubs on a Saturday night to divide up the week's wages and also to spend a good deal of their cash. Whisky was cheap at 1/3 to 1/6 a quart and in Hawick landlords served a generous dram. Employers and the Kirk disapproved of strong drink and argued that it caused absenteeism from work and all manner of social laxity. The Temperance Movement began in Scotland in 1819, well before any similar initiative in England and by mid-century Temperance Societies (and even Temperance Hotels in most Border towns) and their junior branches, the Band of Hope, were established in several places.

A holy alliance between the Kirk and the Temperance Societies forced through a defining piece of social legislation. The Forbes-MacKenzie Act of 1853 imposed opening restrictions on pubs for the first time. Apart from a loophole allowing 'bona fide travellers' to drink in hotels, the new laws imposed total closure on the Sabbath, and laid down that pubs must stay open no later than 11pm on a weekday. This was later brought forward to 10pm. Before 1853 there were no limits on opening hours and a man could spend a great deal of time propping up a bar in a Border town.

The 1848 Temperance Review made interesting reading in Langholm. Its report on that year's common riding described the old ceremony of crying the fair as 'buffoonery'. The correspondent went even further when he defamed the Fair Crier who stood 'on the back of an old rugged steed which, like the Fair Crier himself, had seen better days'. The riders who inspected the boundaries of the Langholm Common were, allegedly, 'half seas-over' when they set out, and barely able to stay in the saddle by the time they returned. Surrounding all of this intemperate invective was, suprisingly, a good deal of information on the 19th century ceremonies and how they had evolved from much earlier beginnings.

The modern Langholm Common Riding appears to have largely been the initiative of one man. After accommodations had been made with the Maxwell family and the Dukes of Buccleuch, the geographical extent of the common was defined by 1759. Archibald Beattie was the town crier and drummer, and for 50 years after that date, he walked the bounds to see 'gif they were clear'. Better known as 'Bauldy', he took upon himself a simple mission. He and his cronies wanted to check that no encroachment of the common had taken place, the boundary markers had not been moved and that surrounding lairds and their flocks or herds remained outside those markers. This is the essence and genesis of all of the Border common ridings.

Because it was his job as town crier, Bauldy Beattie also 'cried the fair'. This insititution and its date in mid-July (the loss of 11 days in the adjustment from the Julian to the Gregorian calendar in 1752 made the traditional date 26th and not 15th July — now the date is the last Friday of July) is at least as old as the habit of inspecting the bounds of the common and probably much older. On common riding morning in the little market square, a man stands on the hind quarters of a strong horse which is steadied by its rider. When, with paper in hand, he cries the Langholm Fair, and describes its purpose and ceremony eloquently;

"Now, Gentlemen, we're gan frae the Toun,
And first of a' the Kil-Green we gan roun';
It is an ancient place where clay is got,
And it belongs tae us by Right and Lot;
And then frae there the Lang-Wood we gan through,
Where every ane may breckons cut and pu';
And last of a' we to the Moss do steer,
To see gif a' oor Marches they be clear;
And when unto the Castle Craigs we come,
I'll cry the Langholm Fair and then we'll beat the drum.

Now, Gentlemen, what you have heard this day concerning going round oor Marches, it is expected that every one who has occasion for Peats, Breckons, Flacks [turf], Stanes or Clay will go out in defence of their property, and they shall hear the Proclamation of the Langholm Fair upon the Castle Craigs."

And when the riders and foot procession return from the marches, there is a second fair crying;

"Now, Gentlemen, we have gane roun' oor hill,
So now I think it's right we had oor fill;
Of guid strong punch — 'twould mak us a' to sing,
Because this day we have done a guid thing;
For gangin' roun' oor hill we think nae shame,
Because frae it oor peats and flacks come hame;
So now I will conclude and say nae mair,
And gin ye're a' pleased I'll cry the Langholm Fair.
Hoys, Yes! That's yae time!
Hoys, Yes! That's twae times!!

Hoys, Yes! That's the third and last time!!!

This is to give notice;

That there is a muckle Fair to be hadden in the muckle Toun o' Langholm, on the 15th day of July, auld style, upon His Grace the Duke of Buccleuch's Merk Land, for the space of eight days and upwards; and a' land-loupers, and dub-scoupers, and gae-by-the-gate swingers, that come here to breed hurdrums or durdrums, huliments or buliments, hagglements or bragglements, or to molest this public Fair, they shall be ta'en by order of the Bailie and Toun Council, and their lugs be nailed to the Tron wi' a twalpenny nail; and they shall sit doun on their bare knees and pray seven times for the King and thrice for the Muckle Laird o' Railton, and pay a groat to me, Jamie Fergusson, Bailie o' the aforesaid Manor, and I'll away hame and hae a bannock and a saut herrin' to my denner by way o' auld style."

So far as anyone can remember no-one has been nailed by the ear to the door of the town hall. Perhaps that is because it is now difficult to distinguish a hurdrum from a durdrum.

Horses became a part of the Langholm Common Riding in 1816 when races were introduced on the Castleholm, an area of haughland inside the common where the River Esk meets the Ewes Water. Soon after this three local men decided to ride with the fair crier and his friends, and the year after that more riders appeared to form a mounted cavalcade. In 1817 it was decided to ask a young man to lead the procession and the ceremonies. At that time the commissioned officer in a British army cavalry troop who carried the colours was called a 'cornet' and Langholm, Hawick and Lauder adopted the title for their leading figure. Of the four ancient common ridings, only Selkirk retained the prosaic term 'Standard Bearer'. The flags carried by modern cornets generally feature the town coat of arms and other items of local iconography. But Langholm has many emblems, most carried by the foot procession and some the product of 19th century innovation. A barley bannock, or 'Banna', is nailed (by a twalpenny nail) with a salted herring to a wooden platter which is mounted on a long pole. They represent the basic elements of bread and salt, the products of the earth the townspeople sought to protect. And as at most common ridings a spade is carried aloft and used to cut and cast up turf so that the bounds can be clearly marked. When Musselburgh's Turf Cutter cuts a sod, he throws it up in the air and roars "It's a' oor ain!" A giant thistle is also carried in the procession at Langholm and it seems to be nothing more complicated than an emblem of Scottishness for a town lying only a few miles from the English border. And other 19th century introductions are the Floral Crown and the heather besoms (brushes) which are rhythmically hoisted up into the air in time with the band in front. While their historical significance might be slight, they add much to the exuberance and festivity of the day. The Cornet's colours for the year are, eccentrically, always taken from those of the winning jockey in the Derby.

THE COMMON RIDING CALENDAR

Because the order of each summer's common ridings is printed on the soul of native Borderers, it can be difficult to find the sequence written down anywhere. The dates are by no means fixed and since, for example, the Selkirk Common Riding day can have a variance as large as six, here is the sequence listed under the heading only of months;

June
  Hawick Common Riding
  Selkirk Common Riding
  Peebles Festival
  Melrose Festival
  Braw Lads Gathering at Galashiels

July
  Jethart Callants Festival
  Duns Reiver's Week
  Kelso Civic Week
  St Ronan's Festival Innerleithen
  Langholm Common Riding

August
  Lauder Common Riding
  Coldstream Civic Week

This calendar is designed so that none of the festivals clash significantly and the principals from each town can arrive with their horses to support their neighbours. It makes for a hard riding summer.

All of the Border common ridings have a decidedly Victorian look and feel and are punctuated by the likes of "Hip, hip, hurrah" and 19th century songs whose general popularity has long faded, but their traditional place in the celebrations frozen them in time. Hawick Cornets wear top hats and green tail coats, bowlers are popular and the Langholm Cornet sports Shepherd's check breeches and brown gaiters. Rosettes or favours are worn by almost everyone. What helped to fix the common ridings in Victorian aspic was the arrival of the railways. Cheap and dependable travel persuaded many exiles to return to their home town every summer to celebrate. "Souters aye come back tae Selkirk when the roses bloom in June" runs an emotional song. And such is the force of tradition that the Langholm Town Band still marches to the station to welcome the exiles home even though trains ceased to run more than 30 years ago. Nevertheless rail travel brought a dimension of sentimentality to the celebrations and strengthened an ingrained resistance to change and adaptation. The industrialising growth of Border towns in the second half of the 19th century also cemented the popularity of the common ridings by simply adding numbers and a powerful sense of shared experience to their support. It is no accident that the three oldest and most strongly rooted are in mill towns; Hawick, Selkirk and Langholm. And in an era before paid holidays, the mill owners helped to institutionalise these celebrations by setting aside a day or two's holiday in the summer. It allowed employees to let off steam and the townspeople to remember that through their ancient privileges, they had status and dignity of their own. For these ceremonies are not something sterile to be walked through or 'enacted'. They are genuinely of, by and for the people. The young man who is the focus each year is selected from those who support the common riding and the town. Money, status and education matter much less than an honest affection for the place and a loyalty to it. Partly for that reason the rituals remain rigid and anachronistic — they are designed to accommodate whoever occupies a leading role, no matter what skills at speechifying or leadership they may or may not have. Each year the same words and phrases are read out by Standard Bearers and Cornets (sometimes from typed cards stuck inside a bowler hat), the same routes taken by the rideouts, the same flags carried and the same tears wept for all that experience in one place. Aside from sitting well on a horse, no special skill is needed to be a principal at a common riding. In fact sheer ordinariness seems, hearteningly, to be most important. The ceremonies are about a whole community and while they carry those centrally involved, they also seem fresh and never lose the power to move. Acting like an annual check on change and a stimulus to memory, the Border common ridings mark the years, the steady heartbeat of life's passage, acting as a reference point for a community and offering a simple thing — the chance to rejoice in being a Borderer.

More sharply, the annual festivals define something of what it means to come from, say, Hawick, Coldstream, Duns or Langholm. Even though they share many characteristics and an outsider would detect little difference in the ceremonies of both ancient and modern common ridings, the natives of each town believe them to be utterly different, unique to that place, heart-piercingly moving, and almost inexplicable. When a Hawick man was recently asked to explain what the common riding meant to him personally, he shook his head and replied simply; 'It's better felt than telt'.

Border towns believe themselves to be passionately and sometimes irreconcilably different, and their separate identities depend not on geography, wealth or size, but on two polarising cultural magnets — one peaceful, one aggressive. In addition to the history and lyricism of the common ridings, there runs the powerful and sustained tradition of Border rugby. Unlike in England and the rest of Scotland, this is not a game played exclusively by the middle classes. As in South Wales all sorts of people play in the Borders, and the criteria for involvement continue to be based on ability and enthusiasm rather than income or education. And such is the strength of Border rugby and its identification with each town that when a young man says that he 'played for Kelso', no-one need ask which sport.

Statistics support the notion that rugby is truly populist and popular in the Borders. A survey made in 1993 showed that on each winter Saturday 167 teams turned out. That means more than 2500 participants, to say nothing of officials, committee members and helpers, and on the terracing stood an estimated 10,000 supporters. When all of that involvement was added together it produced a surprising quotient — something more than one in eight Borderers watches, plays or enables rugby. The recent professionalisation of the game and the removal of star players from club sides has resulted in a reduction in regular support and although some venerable clubs, like Walkerburn, are struggling to field teams, these trends have been counterbalanced by the surge in women's rugby, the extension of the fixture list and the use of substitutes. It will take more than economics to shift rugby far from the heart of civic identity in the Borders. Details often confirm cultural characteristics and recently the towns have begun to replace worn-out street signs in the colours of their rugby teams. Melrose's are now yellow and black, Gala maroon, Jedburgh royal blue and so on.

The historical beginning of these passions is usually located in the 1870s when most of the Border clubs were founded, but to accept that dating would be to ignore the real origins of rugby and its close ties with the people of particular places. And to ignore the determinant hand of a man who shaped so much of what defines the modern Border country, Walter Scott.

In late November 1815 an informal dinner was arranged by the Duke of Buccleuch at the newly rebuilt Bowhill House. Across a candlelit table, no doubt after a convivial glass or two of port, a ploy was hatched. Duke Charles' brother-in-law, the Earl of Home, would captain a team in a 'football' match to be played on a grand scale over the flat fields of Carterhaugh, immediately to the south of Bowhill. It was decided that Home would lead the men of Ettrick and Yarrow, almost all of whom were Buccleuch tenants and likely to heed the call, against a team of townsmen from Selkirk augmented by strong contingents from Hawick and Gala. The date of Monday 4th December was set, hands shaken and preparations put in train.

The day dawned sunny and very cold. About 100 callants had marched the 12 miles from Hawick to muster at Bailie Clarkson's house in Selkirk where each was issued with a strong dram and a twig of pine to pin to their bonnets or shirt fronts. Then they marched in 'braw order' down to the Ettrick to meet the Gala boys. At Carterhaugh bands were playing and a booth, generously supplied by the Duke, was dispensing refreshment. In what seems to have been an overwhelmingly military atmosphere the companies, detachments and platoons of shepherds and farmers from the valleys filed onto the field to be given sprigs of heather and to form up in a body opposite the townsmen. This solemn confrontation probably took place somewhere near the modern settlement of Gillkeekit.

At 11am Duke Charles and his aristocratic retinue appeared at Carterhaugh, having ridden down from nearby Bowhill House. And then an amazing passage of pomp and circumstance took place. The ancient war-banner of the Scotts of Buccleuch was produced. The last time anyone had seen it was at the funeral of Earl Walter in 1633. Evidently the family war-cry of 'Bellendaine!' had been embroidered under the old yellow and blue arms of the Scotts and was still legible. That this hallowed relic of serious business should be produced for a football match seems to have disconcerted no-one. The banner was handed to Sir Walter Scott's eldest son, also Walter, who then rode up and down the lines of Ettrick and Yarrow men to the stirring accompaniment of, of all things, bagpipes playing 'ceol mor' or war-music. Two thousand spectators are said to have cheered and Sir Walter's heart was, according to his biographer, Lockhart, bursting with pride at the spectacle. A song entered Scott's swelling heart, but sadly, its chorus shows him at less than his best;

> "Then up with the Banner, let forest winds fan her,
> She has blazed over Ettrick eight ages and more;
> In sport we'll attend her, in battle defend her,
> With heart and with hand, like our fathers before"

It is difficult to know what to make of all this. The relationship between war and sport seems completely formed by 1815, the invention of 'tradition' unblushingly accepted (highland bagpipes, instead of traditional cauld-wind pipes, and Border *clans*?) and the further connection between rival teams and rival places also appears to be secure, to say nothing of popularity. And the similarity between Duke Charles and a modern millionaire who buys a football team to act out his own sporting ambitions is more than incidental.

Although advertised and reported as 'football', the game itself was much more like the sort of handba played all over the Borders, and particularly in the towns. Jedburgh, Hawick, Selkirk, Ancrum, Lilliesleaf and Duns are only the recorded venues and the sport was likely much more prevalent. Walter Scott's fondness for unbroken historical continua may have tempted him to call it football since that was the game famously played by Wat Armstrong and his reiving family, as well as the Earl of Bothwell below Carlisle Castle. James Hogg was also at Carterhaugh on December 4th 1815 playing, of course, for the shepherds' team, and his energetic espousal of 'manly exertions' might also have persuaded contemporaries that they were watching and playing football. And given the very wide area over which it was envisaged that play would range, it may well be that some sort of kicking or hacking was involved. The goals were marked-off stretches of the rivers Ettrick and Yarrow and they stood almost a mile apart. Teams, however, numbered several hundred a side and no doubt there were opportunities for players to take a breather or two. They will have needed a rest since the match lasted from 11am until dusk at approximately 4pm.

Just as at the Jethart handba the game began when the ba was thrown up in the air. This was done at Carterhaugh by Duke Charles, who must have got smartly out of the way before the huge teams collided in an immense scrum. Probably spurred on by the aristocratic favour shown to the shepherds' team, the townsmen managed to move play towards the opposition goal at the Ettrick. Near the bank, a Selkirk mason, Rob Hall, broke free of the maul, sidestepped his way past several men and plunged into the freezing river to score a hail or a goal. As the Selkirk, Hawick and Gala men roared their approval, he is said to have stood in midstream holding the ba high over his head.

Half-time was called and it provided an opportunity for some chicanery. The morning had not gone according to the script. Duke Charles' team were losing and their prospects for the afternoon were not encouraging. The townsmen played ba often and clearly knew what they were doing. An embassy was despatched to the Gala contingent with Walter Scott as chief negotiator, and a deal of some sort was quickly done. Much to the outrage of Selkirk and Hawick, the Braw Lads of Gala exchanged their pine twigs for sprigs of heather and joined the Duke's team for the second half. It worked a treat and the shepherds quickly scored a hail in the Yarrow with George Brodie of Greatlaws on the Ale Water doing the heroic deed.

Conveniently dusk began to fall on Carterhaugh and there was said to be no time left to play a deciding half. The Selkirk men were furious, felt cheated and with their Hawick allies they pursued the Gala men after the match and those unwise enough to become detached from the main group were rewarded with bloody noses and cracked heads. And when Walter Scott's carriage rashly took a route through Selkirk's Market Place on the way to Abbotsford, enraged players stopped it to accuse the Sheriff of Selkirkshire of match-fixing. Quickly producing his purse, Scott defused the incident by dispensing two guineas so that the Selkirk team might enjoy a dram at his expense. But not before being denounced as 'jist an auld Tory ballad-monger' by one of the Scotts of Selkirk.

The Carterhaugh match was not rugby as we know it now, but it can unquestionably be seen as its close cousin. Many of the elements still present at Border grounds on a Saturday afternoon were there in 1815; passion, the close identity with place, skill, heroics and hard-fought competition. And perhaps at Carterhaugh the familiar cry of 'Dirty Gala!' was born.

Eight years later at Rugby School William Webb Ellis had a rush of blood to the head when he picked up a foot-ball and ran with it in his hands, thereby inventing the game of rugby in an instant. Although widely believed, this tale bears all the marks of apocrypha. What really happened at English public schools in the early 19th century was that the handba-style mauling games (the Eton wall-game still survives and closely resembles play at Jedburgh) were slowly becoming organised. Rules were agreed, time limits set, pitches defined and ball design evolved. An oval ball was generally thought to favour good handling and reasonably accurate kicking in what used to be called foot rushes. But in 1863 it was football, or more correctly Association Football, which prompted a tighter codification of the rules of rugby. At the Freemasons' Tavern in London, in 1863, the Football Association was formed and its first published code outlawed handling and hacking with the feet. Some clubs decided not to join and to continue to play to the old mixture of rules, and in 1871 Richmond, Blackheath and other London clubs joined together in the Rugby Football Union.

Late Victorian Britain became extremely keen on mass sport, both for spectators and participants. Before that period the idea of energetic recreation had simply not existed, for the good reason that it had not been thought desirable. Work itself was sufficiently tiring and the last thing most men and women wanted to do when they were not at work

was to tire themselves further. But the urbanisation of industrial revolution Britain changed these circumstances. Factory and mill workers
were enabled and encouraged to take exercise in the health-giving open
air. Employers made organised sport possible with the introduction of
a five and a half day week, and the games which ordinary people
played tended to be not the handba of Carterhaugh or Jedburgh but the
codified, time-limited games of the Engish public schools attended by
their employers. Football grounds were laid out and on Saturday
afternoons huge crowds regularly turned out to support their town or
city teams. The church smiled on all of this as an expression of muscular
Christianity, and before the concept existed, a cohesive community spirit
was partly created for the expanding towns by the focus of a football
team.

In 1871 three young Langholm men introduced the game which had
been codified by the Rugby Football Union only a few months before.
William Scott, Alfred Moses and William Lightbody had all been
educated at English public schools where they had learned to play
rugby. Their passion could just as easily have been football, but it may
be that the strong tradition of handba in the Borders persuaded the
new rugby to flourish instead.

A game was advertised in Langholm for 31st December 1871 by the
three men. So many came to play that William Scott simply divided the
crowd into two halves and after marking out a pitch, they kicked off.
Following their public school instincts and English example, the three
founded a club, the Langholm Rugby Football Club. English influence
helped the game to spread further and out of the Hawick and Wilton
Cricket Club, originally instigated by textile workers from Nottingham-
shire and Yorkshire, the Hawick Rugby Football Club emerged in 1873.
It can be no historical accident that organised rugby clubs first appeared
in Border mill towns where comparatively large numbers lived in a
concentrated area and predictable time off work could be forthcoming.

That same year the first fixture between Hawick and Langholm took
place — but not before both teams of 20 a side had agreed on the rules.
At issue was the definition of a goal. Should one be scored when the
ball was kicked over or under the crossbar? On a previous Saturday
Langholm had played Carlisle and they had settled on under rather
than over. Although the Hawick players ultimately agreed to follow
that example, Langholm were forced to accept an ironic draw in this
first match because their goalkicker sent his final conversion over the
bar.

The Scottish Rugby Union was formed in 1873 and immediately
dominated by teams created by the former pupils of Edinburgh and
Glasgow fee-paying schools. In late Victorian Scotland the middle classes
took less trouble to hide their disdain for the lower orders. And the
lower orders in the Borders were a constant irritant to the FPs of the
SRU. In his excellent 1994 article on Border rugby, Frank Coutts did a
simple calculation to demonstrate how that friction manifested itself.
Between 1871 and 1914, 118 international matches were played between
Scotland and the other countries and yet only 11 Borderers were selected
to represent their country in all that time — despite the fact that Border

teams regularly defeated city opposition. In the face of such blatant prejudice reportedly great players such as Speirs Black of Kelso had little chance of advancement, but fixtures between Border clubs and city teams retained an extra edge for most of the 20th century. Even as late as the 1960s Border players continued to have difficulty in forcing their way into Scotland teams at any level.

At a meeting of the Border clubs at St Boswells in 1891 a discussion was had on "the great dissatisfaction which exists in the South with the present state of matters, and the best way to secure redress of grievances and the furtherance of rugby would be easier promoted through the formation of a South of Scotland Rugby Union." Ten years later, in spite of stone-faced disapproval from the Scottish Rugby Union, the Border League came into being. Langholm, Hawick, Gala, Jedforest and Melrose combined to create the first competitive rugby union league anywhere in the world. They were briefly joined by Carlisle and then later by Kelso and Selkirk to make the number of clubs seven for most of the 20th century. Peebles was invited to join in 1996.

What fuelled the friction between the Border clubs and the Scottish Rugby Union was specifically the fear of professionalism. From an early date football had paid players and in 1895 St Helen's, Wigan and others formed a breakaway union in the north of England which eventually became known as rugby league. Because Border players were not drawn from the middle classes, it was thought in Edinburgh that the temptation of cash was therefore greater in the south and the danger of professionalisation ever present. A Border League might be a step on the road to rugby league. Perhaps rugby union's snobbery would have been slightly less reprehensible, if not acceptable, had it manifested itself only in the exclusion of Border players from the national team. But surely the greatest disfigurement was the disgraceful ban imposed on players who went south to turn professional after giving sterling service to their amateur clubs. Even though almost all of these were Borderers, the Border clubs meekly went along with this SRU ban, to their undying shame. One irony is that many successful middle class rugby internationalists made far more money out of their playing days and the kudos they gave them than any Border rugby league player ever did. A former Scotland centre-threequarter who made a small fortune in the Edinburgh money market once declared that business was just like rugby, "a contact sport".

THE CHAMPIONSHIP YEAR

At the time of writing the oldest Border rugby club languishes at the foot of Division Five of the Scottish league tables, played 7 won 1. But once they were kings. In the 1958/59 season Langholm was the champion club of Scotland and, uniquely in Britain and Ireland, they remained undefeated throughout the season. The wealthy and fashionable London Scottish travelled to Milntown to play a challenge match and were soundly beaten despite fielding six internationalists. It was an astonishing achievement for one of the smallest Border clubs with, probably, the smallest catchment area for players. And something, in the professional era, which will never happen again.

> *What carried Langholm through several close matches was a desire to win whatever the odds and a tremendous team spirit among the players, who cared passionately about their native town. Many were also common riding stalwarts and the Langholm stand-off, Jimmy Maxwell, was Cornet in 1955. Only three internationalists were selected from the championship team; Christie Elliot, E.J.S. Michie and Jimmy Maxwell. Despite being a gifted and charismatic player who orchestrated Langholm's success, Maxwell was capped only once for Scotland (torrential rain poured throughout the match day and the slippery ball and underfoot conditions made play a lottery and supplied the Scotland selectors with an excuse to drop the Langholm stand-off) and the resilience of SRU snobbery underlined once again.*

At Dovecote Park in Selkirk Robert Clapperton supervised the construction of a photographic studio. Few of the builders can have had much idea of what it was to be used for. The studio's doors opened for business in 1867, only 25 years after David Octavius Hill and Robert Adamson began their pioneering partnership in Edinburgh. Like them Clapperton was a superb photographer with a painterly eye for composition and the technique and determination to set up his cumbersome kit at any outdoor location which might offer a promising shot. His grainy black and white views of the Ettrick, Yarrow and Tweed valleys are suffused with a gentle lyricism, and when the light was good (as it almost always was — Clapperton must have been a patient man) the atmosphere can be intense. Early photographers used long exposures and landscape was attractive to them because it generally stayed still. People were more problematic, and inclined to blur out of focus, but that did not discourage Clapperton or his brother John, who opened a studio in Galashiels at the same time. Said to be 'an authority on Galashiels customs and mannerisms', he was clearly interested in the lives and work of ordinary people, few of whom would or could have paid him to take their picture. When they stood still for long enough, photographs of them were often pin-sharp and vivid. But much more than that, they represent something entirely new. A turning moment in history. These pictures show for the first time what ordinary Borderers actually looked like, and equally engaging, what their towns, villages and farms looked like as men and women went about their quotidien business.

Disappointingly there are few early close-ups of faces. Absolute stillness was required for that, and often in studio portraits neck-braces were used throughout the long exposures. In any case the Clappertons were often concerned to show architecture and landscape as well as people. What is striking in the many townscapes is the sense of street life. Except for horse and cart, no traffic existed to drive men, women, children or animals to one side or indoors and out of sight. There is a wide shot of thirty or forty adults and children strung out across the Edinburgh road at High Buckholmside in Gala. That seems to have been where John Clapperton came across the group, and asked them not to move for a minute or two. Another view of Gala, this time of the Volunteer Hall and taken some time after 1874, shows two bunneted and white-bearded old men standing in the roadway. One looks directly at the camera with open curiousity while the other, his head inclined forward and back turned, is blethering in his ear. Behind them two pony and trap rigs are clopping along the streets. Sometimes Robert Clapperton appears to have used people to give scale to his townscapes and a shot taken in 1880 in Kirk Wynd in Selkirk, shortly before the demolition of some adjacent houses, places four men part-way up the brae, and old lady keeking out at an entry.

Ordinary Borderers come suddenly into focus towards the end of the 19th century. A magnificent group portrait of about 150 workers was taken in 1890 when the Strang-Steel family bought Philiphaugh House and had it refurbished. Wearing homburgs foremen stand at the back, and in bunnets, waistcoats and aprons, the tradesmen stare rigidly at the camera. A slightly later picture shows a group of ten estate workers. Sitting on a trestle in the centre is a grim-faced factor or foreman (he wears the only tie) while on either side of him, perching on two wheelbarrows, are gardeners, joiners and foresters holding grapes, handsaws and an axe. Unusually at least two of the men are smiling.

NO SAFE HARBOUR

On October 14th 1881 the Berwickshire fishing port of Eyemouth suffered a disaster from which, arguably, it has yet to recover. In the teeth of hurricane-force winds and mountainous seas half of the fishing fleet was lost and 189 men drowned. Some of them died within a few yards of the harbour, pulled into the deeps by the tremendous undertow, their boats dashed to smithereens on the jagged rocks.

But this was a disaster which could have been much mitigated, even avoided. In 1881 Eyemouth lacked a deep water harbour accessible no matter what the tide, and it did not receive the investment to build one in time. The reason for this was rooted in ancient practices. For many centuries, long after the habit had withered elsewhere, Eyemouth Kirk had claimed a tithe, 10% of all the earnings of local fishermen. And because the stipend was so low, the ministers refused to abandon the anachronistic tax. Led by William Spears, called the 'Kingfisher', local families campaigned long and hard to have the tithe removed. Opposing them was an obdurate young minister, the Rev. Dr Stephen Bell.

Finally the matter was resolved in a compromise. Eyemouth bought out the tithe for a once-only payment of £2,000. But the cash had to be borrowed and over time interest doubled it. It was not paid off until 1878. During all that period the Eyemouth debt (and the resulting bankruptcy of the harbour trust) disabled investment in the harbour from government sources.

By August 1881 the Fishery Board was at last persuaded and plans were drawn up for a deep-water, asylum harbour, and the local economy looked set to leap forward. But it all came too late to save the 189 fishermen who drowned only two months after the announcement. And in fact so crippled was the Eyemouth fleet that a new harbour was not built until the 1960s.

On the day following the terrible storm of October 1881, an old man was seen sittiing on the beach, weeping and in great distress. It was the Kingfisher, William Spears, and he was being comforted by another old man, the Rev. Dr Stephen Bell.

The photographs of the Clappertons and others represent an immediate richness and offer a pungent and truthful sense of the Victorian past. But even though the images are eloquent, their people are mute and the words and thoughts of ordinary Borderers will wait until the early 20th century to find recorded expression. What the old men in Galashiels were saying might be irretrievable but how they said it is not. The great lexicographer, J.A.H. Murray of Denholm, published 'The Dialect of the Southern Counties of Scotland' in 1873. As a consequence of the advent of standardised education and the beginnings of mass communication through the telegraph, the railways and widely circulating newspapers, Murray believed that the local dialects in the Borders would quickly be lost. 1873 turned out to be too early a date to despair, and not only has Hawick's ordinary speech remained distinctive but also what Murray called the 'natural grammar' of the Borders dialect has remained audible. Certainly colourful local words, many of them describing a fading rural economy, have withered but basic forms such as 'oo' for both 'we' and 'us', or 'thir' for 'these' and 'thae' for 'those' are still is everyday use and show few signs of corruption.

And what appears to have grown in the latter years of the 20th century is confidence. No longer do dialect speakers compromise their speech when they talk to outsiders, on the telephone, or to Borderers who have been educated at private schools or in the cities. There appears to be an attractive assumption that everyone understands, or should. The likelihood is that modern natives of Galashiels would not only have understood the old men at the Volunteer Hall in the 1870s, but they would have sounded like them too.

Towards the end of the 19th century Border towns were beginning to acquire statutory powers to stiffen the heightened independent identities confered by the common ridings and the more recent surge in the popularity of rugby football. W.E. Gladstone's Liberal government introduced state-funded schooling and in 1872 the Education Act Scotland made provision "to amend and extend the law of Scotland on the subject of education in such a manner that the means of procuring efficient education for their children may be furnished and made available to the whole people of Scotland". The appointment of teachers had been removed from the presbyteries of the Church of Scotland and given to school boards, and a series of structures and examinations, like the Higher Leaving Certificate, were put in place. The new education legislation did much to accelerate the decline of the 'parish state' which had governed the lives of most Scots since the Reformation.

In 1843 the Church of Scotland had schismed over the central issue of patronage; whether or not local landowners or the kirk sessions should appoint ministers. The so-called Disruption impacted less in the Borders than the rest of Scotland, but it did open a wide fissure in the dour monolith of the parish state. Small groups had been seceding from the 1730s onwards, but the split of 1843 took place on an unprecedented scale, and it fatally weakened the power of the established kirk. If the population of a town could ultimately choose which church it wished to attend then the stranglehold of monopoly could no longer harness community pressure to enforce its judgements, and the courts of the kirk session could be safely ignored.

Reform acts in 1868 and 1884 extended the franchise to an electorate of 506,550 in Scotland, although the ability to vote was heavily hedged by property qualifications. And democracy at a local level also helped diminish somewhat the pervasive hegemony of the Kirk. The most comprehensive transfer of direct power, if not influence, took place in 1892 when the Burgh Police Act became law. It enabled towns to control broad swathes of popular cultural activity. This included the regulation and licensing of all sorts of premises, from public houses to billiard halls and gambling, and it allowed a wide variety of practice from town to town — from complete abstinence in Kirkintilloch to a movement to ban ice-cream shops in Lerwick. However, no-one who remembers the grey severity of the Scottish sabbath can argue that the Church of Scotland lost its influence in these matters, but the new legislation did erode its power to act directly.

While Border towns grew and became vigorous in the late 19th century, life on the land changed more slowly. The quiet revolution begun by James Small's plough led to the organisation of farm work around horse power. Ploughmen, or horsemen, became the focus of the rural labour force in the lower-lying arable areas of the Borders, and the hinding system was general. Farmers hired hinds for a term of one year, or sometimes six months. At the hiring fairs held in the towns, both workers and employers would negotiate pay and conditions and agree on a handshake and a drink in a nearby pub. An annual sum of cash was the basis of a contract but what were known as 'gains' or payments in kind were also important. These included the likes of several tons of potatoes, pasture for a cow, a pigsty, coal, corn or flour and sometimes other, more specific items. Hinds hung on to the convention of gains because they were inflation-proof and to a society often remote from towns and villages, convenient. Housing also figured large in the contract and the tenancy of an unfurnished cottage was almost always included. Farmers in Roxburghshire and Berwickshire used women to do all of the work not associated with horses, and hinds were bound to provide a female worker known as a bondager to single and shaw root crops, milk cows and make butter and cheese, do weeding and a variety of other back-breaking jobs. Bondagers were usually members of a ploughman's family, but a 'wumman worker' sometimes had to be contracted independently. The hinding system lasted a long time, well into the 20th century, and it has not quite outrun living memory.

In the hill farms of the Borders the pre-eminent figure was the shepherd. These men were all-rounders whose work extended well beyond tending sheep. Occasionally their cottages were remote and their gains mainly consisted of a 'pack' of sheep which belonged to them and not their employer. Packs could be large at 40 or more animals and it often used to be said that the hird's ewes always had twin lambs, while the farmer's had just the one.

While the grip of the Kirk slackened, towns grew and hinds and hirds bargained with farmers, the economic apex of Border society proved very resilient. The great landowners, their estates and their influence still bulk large in the landscape — even now at the outset of the 21st century. This stands in high contrast with the rest of Britain where anonymous trusts, companies and syndicates have taken over ownership of vast tracts of the Highlands, and the pressures on English dukes and earls (particularly those without lucrative urban properties) have forced many to sell land and open their houses to the public.

With 270,000 acres the Duke of Buccleuch is the second largest landowner in Scotland (behind the Forestry Commission) and the largest private landowner in Britain. The Duke of Roxburghe is also very wealthy, with much high-value arable land, and others such as the Marquis of Lothian have substantial holdings. A few dwindled. In 1874 Lord Lauderdale had 24,000 acres in fertile Berwickshire but only 8,100 by 1970.

This quiet omnipresence was backed by active participation in Border politics. For 43 years between 1900 and 1975 either the Duke of Buccleuch or the Duke of Roxburghe was convenor of Roxburgh County Council. Each also variously held the offices of Sheriff Depute, Commissioner of Supply and Lord Lieutenant. It was not until the reorganisation of local government in 1974/75 that the control of the aristocracy was finally ended. The participation of Border aristocrats in parliamentary politics has been notable in the second half of the 20th century. Sir Alec Douglas-Home of Coldstream was Prime Minister, the Earl of Ancrum Chairman of the Conservative Party and the Duke of Buccleuch MP for Edinburgh North in the 1970s. Visitors to the Borders sometimes remark on the persistence of a habit of deference, an unwillingness to be outspoken, a liking for paternalism and conservatism, the repetition of the mantra of 'it's aye been'. Given the immense power of the great landowners, such characteristics should not be wondered at.

As the 19th century drew to its close, the Scottish Border country would have seemed a recognisable, even familar place to modern eyes. Although peripheral housing has developed and spread, the centres of towns were then much as they appear now, the only general change being the removal of railway stations and the occasional construction of large supermarkets. A century ago there were even wild fluctuations in employment caused by decisions made in the U.S.A. In 1890 the federal government introduced protectionist tariffs against the import of woolen cloth from the Borders which threw thousands out of work in Galashiels.

In the world beyond the Tweed valley, 1900 represented only a new way of reckoning the date, and not a new dawn of any sort. Edwardian Britain and the enormous empire controlled from London carried on doing business, and when change came, it came slowly. Borderers fought in imperial wars and mass communication made those seem increasingly vivid. Photographers recorded a parade held in Kelso in 1900 to celebrate the fall of Pretoria in the Boer War. Buildings in the town square are hung with union jacks and a cart carries the effigy of the defeated Boer leader, General Cronje, who appears to be wearing an incongruous top hat. Behind the crowds a bonfire waits to be lit. This was a scene repeated in a thousand towns all over Britain and it describes an imperial world picture which took most of the 20th century to fade and disappear.

The Edwardian Borders is no longer remembered at first hand. The children of the crowds lining Kelso Square can recall, just, what their parents told them of their lives, but they were not there to experience it. The slaughter of the First World War marks a far more emphatic end to 19th century Britain than a simple change of date. And it also marks a significant shift in the tone of this story. Up until 1914 the lives of ordinary Borderers were played out in the shadowy background, a supporting cast for the powerful and the wealthy, people whose thoughts had to be guessed at or even imagined. After 1914 living memory begins and from then until the present day, the past will be recorded in the following pages by those who lived it. It is the best sort of history.

13

Oo

In recording the interviews which make up a substantial part of what follows, I was struck by how often older Borderers used the word 'oo' for both 'we' and 'us'. It seemed that for much of the 20th century ordinary people often did things in groups, or thought of themselves as part of a group rather than as an individual, and therefore tended to offer opinions and judgements in the plural first person pronoun. "Oo always went tae Melrose tae the fancy dress parade and fair enjoyed it". "The Edinburgh folk thought oo were a' stupid, slow like". "Oo never worried aboot the weather for common ridin' mornin'. Oo had to gaun, rain or no'."

It is difficult to say whether or not that signifies a strong sense of family and community, a lack of personal confidence, or merely a slowly dying habit from the past. Perhaps the long history of many of the common ridings, the shorter experience of town rugby teams, mill-working in large groups and farm-working in gangs at the harvest, the singling and the haymaking, as well as the shared tragedies of two world wars, have contributed to this. In any case the use of 'oo' rings a clear — and attractive — note across the sweep of the 20th century Border country.

Many of the interviewees who generously gave me and others their time and their memories are women, the daughters, wives and mothers of ordinary people. In the history of the Borders these are new voices, unheard until the 20th century. Often when they reflected on an eventful posterity, what stuck in the minds of all of the interviewees — of both genders — were pungent details, the sorts of things which bring history alive, cause tears or laughter, and weave remote and sometimes impersonal trends or statistics into the vivid fabric of real lives.

The 19th century concluded emphatically — in August 1914. The short Edwardian postscript to the Victorian age was brought to an end by gunfire. Another Balkan war had led to the assassination of the Austrian Archduke, Franz Ferdinand on 28th June when he and his wife were on a state visit to Sarajevo, the capital of Bosnia. The gunshots from Serbian nationalists ignited a fast-burning fuse of ultimata and military mobilisations which drew Britain quickly into war with Germany, and eventually with the Austro-Hungarian and Ottoman Empires.

The scale of what happened in the First World War, the Great War, was immense, immediate and unprecedented. Before war was declared on August 5th huge numbers of soldiers were set on standby for embarkation to France, amongst them the King's Own Scottish Borderers. Soon afterwards, territorials, or volunteers, were also mobilised.

Jenny Corbett of Selkirk can remember the shock of 5th August 1914;

"I would be 11 years old. I was in Leith, my mother belonged to Leith, and so I was at my grannie's for my holidays. My uncle Peter came flying in and said something to my grannie who said, "Haud yer tongue in front o' the bairn". But anyway he went on and all her four sons congregated at their mother's, and I was sitting in the corner.

She stayed not far from Leith Docks and there you could see some of the sailors being shanghaid down to the docks. They had their hands tied behind their backs. To say that I was terrified is putting it mildly.

My father came through on the Saturday and although I was supposed to be there for my school holidays, oh, I wanted nothing else but to be back in Selkirk. Of course there was a rumour that there was a Zeppelin coming and I've got a hazy recollection of something in the sky.

When I got home, I was greetin', and my mother says, "What's wrong?". And my father says, "she got an awfu' fright with a' the terrible carry-on in Leith". And my half-cousin, John Ford, put me on his knee and said, "Dinnae worry Jenny, the Germans'll never get to Selkirk".

I went to see the volunteers. They were older men. My uncle Rob was one and he had been in the Boer War. They were mustered at the Volunteer Hall. We stood on the pavement to watch them march away and my mother saw a wee laddie that used to come to us from the butcher's. My mother says, "Oh mercy Drew, you're surely no' gaun away to be a sodger." And he says, "Ee ken, Mrs Beattie, I was aye an unlucky wee devil. I just joined the volunteers so that I'd get a fortnight's holiday. And now I'm away to fight the Germans. But never you worry yourself, we'll be back by Christmas."

A lot of people congregated at the banking at the Toll to see the train coming from Selkirk Station, crossing the field to Bridgehaugh. And we were standing there with dishtowels, pillowslips and everything, waving to the volunteers. It was three days after war was declared."

Some young Borderers found themselves in action quickly. At the first battle of Ypres in October 1914 Andrew Wilson of Galashiels stood on one side with the 4th Battalion of the King's Own Scottish Borderers and, in an extraordinary historical twist, amongst the German forces ranged opposite was the 16th Bavarian Reserve Infantry (List) Regiment and its new recruit, Private Adolf Hitler.

Mae Wilson was 7 years old when her brother found himself in Flanders as hostilities began;

"When he went away to the war, Andrew was just newly 20. He got killed at the very beginning. It was the big battle at Ypres, and those sort of places. I don't know if I'm pronouncing it right or not. The Somme and all those.

They had nothing to fight with, you know, they hadn't enough [ammunition] to keep going and there were thousands killed in the first week. Thousands. Then, of course, Gala was just a little place and, oh, they were always there with the telegrams. It was just delivered with a telegram boy. It wasn't any different, nothing special.

Both my brothers won the Military Medal. After Andrew was killed, my other brother, Jim, was called up and he went through the war. Mind, he got shot in the leg. But they didn't have to take his leg off, he still had it.

When the men got sent home on leave, they weren't clean. Lice and things. Your folk had to clean you. It was an awfu' life.

Jim and Andrew were close, there was two years between them, but when Jim came home at the end of the war he couldna' bide and he left for New Zealand. Andrew said he joined the army for excitement, but he got too much."

JAMES DOUGLAS AND THE COSSACK

In 1916 James Douglas of Jedburgh enlisted in the Army Service Corps. Because he had ten years experience as a chauffeur, he was immediately posted out to Mesopotamia to act as a driver. Douglas' first mission was to take a party of Secret Service agents into Armenia to rescue stranded allied consuls. At that time much of the Middle East formed part of the hostile Ottoman Empire and when Douglas' party was captured by Turkish soldiers, they quickly realised that their fate would be grisly. Presumably in retaliation for a lack of co-operation and certainly as a form of dreadful cruelty, the Turks led out one of the party each morning to be shot. Finally, only Douglas was left. Finding an unlocked door, he escaped and soon became lost in the trackless wastes of the Caucasus plateau. Hungry and alone, Douglas wandered for some days before a figure on horseback appeared and began to gallop towards him brandishing a sword. But instead of cutting down the Border soldier, the Cossack stopped and, in English, asked him where he was going. It turned out that the rider had returned from emigration to Canada to join the Russian revolutionary forces. The Cossack told the astonished Douglas where he could jump a train heading westwards. Eventually captured and imprisoned for a year in Moscow, he was repatriated in a prisoner exchange for a Russian admiral. This was the first news his wife had had in two and a half years.

On his return to Jedburgh, Douglas was not allowed to sink back into the modest existence he craved. In 1921 on the KOSB barracks' parade ground in Berwick he was awarded the Distinguished Conduct Medal, the Military Medal, and, mysteriously, a medal for gallantry from the former Czar Nikolas of Russia. James Douglas and his family moved to Abbotford in 1928 to become chauffeur to the Maxwell-Scotts and eventually he did a tour of duty as a guide for visitors to Sir Walter Scott's house until retirement in 1958.

Jenny Corbett remembers the early phase of the war;

"It was a wee while before news of the first casualties came through. There was no wireless, no-one had the phone and you used to get it [news] by what we called Reuters. These messages were sent [to Selkirk] and we were sent at dinner-time to read the noticeboards and report to the school where the teachers used to shift these wee flags on a great big map.

There was a postman stayed next door to us, and I mind him saying to my mother one day, 'Ee ken, Mrs Beattie, I used to like my job, but no' now. As soon as I get one of those buff envelopes into my hand, I say to myself that's a sair heart for somebody.'

They got a little buff envelope to say that somebody was killed in action, missing or wounded. That was all. If they were missing, they might turn up, if they were wounded then somebody would surely write. They could go a long time without any [further] correspondence, no nothing, except the worry.

An awful lot of women were back in the mills at that time, doing mens' jobs. And when I was a pirn-winder I was sent up to Bridgehaugh Mill and it was all married women who were there. They were all soldiers' wives or mothers. And they used to send Belle Brown and me to their different houses in the morning, after the post had been. You were always feared that some woman's mother would give you a buff letter. Sometimes their mothers (who were looking after the house and the bairns) would look hard at you and say, "Tell her the post's not been yet". If anyone got bad news, it was bad news for everybody because in the first part of the war, it was the local battallions that were all together, just laddies.

And then there were casualties in the navy. On a ship sailing near Madagascar, there were two Selkirk men and one of them I had known since he was a laddie. The ship was torpedoed and the laddie couldn't swim. As he was drowning he roared to the other man, 'Jimmie, Jimmie, tell my mother'".

As the war ground on and casualties mounted, it crept nearer to the Borders. The Germans adopted a policy of blockade and they used their U-boats to attack merchant shipping in an attempt to starve Britain into surrender. Mary King was born in 1905 and lived near the Berwickshire coast between 1914–18;

"Every Monday mornin' there wis a big boat yaised tae come up. Frae where we were at Northfield ee could see it comin' frae the Newcastle wey up tae Leith and it wis called 'The Pathfinder'. Ah always remember its name. And it wis stovin' black reek oot and a submarine chasin' it and firin' at it. But it didnae get it. 'The Pathfinder' got away frae him. That wis a bit o' excitement.

And ah'll tell ee another thing. There wis a Saturday mornin' and there wis an awfy piece o' firin', gun firin', and ma mother and her neighbours went off up this path and ower the Bell Hill tae see what it was. And it wis a submarine bombin' a boat laden wi' monkey nuts. And it wouldnae sink. And they were shootin' the sailors as they were comin' doon the ropes, killin' some o' them."

Jenny Corbett recalls the state of morale amongst Borderers as it became clear that both sides had settled down to a murderous war of attrition;

"But no-one thought the war was wrong or should not be fought. They all knew that they were fighting for something. I never heard anybody really resent it. You see we had a lot of Belgian refugees, and we heard about the atrocities. But mind, it must have been hard sometimes to hold your tongue.

I remember we used to have a laddie from Ettrickbridgend to board at our house when he went to the High School. He was killed in the war, only 21, and for years afterwards I used to visit his mother. Tommy was an only child and she used to like me to talk about him and the times he boarded with us. He and I used to sit together on the fender with a plate of tatties and mince and two forks.

One of his pals in the artillery regiment said that he had simply been blown to bits with his gun. And years later his mother and I were speaking about him and she said, 'Ee ken, Jenny, if I only knew he had been buried.' It's stayed with me forever, that.

When the armistice was declared oo all stopped working and went to the kirk. The Lawson Memorial Kirk was full to the door, and it was the biggest, and that was where oo went. They just had prayers and that was it. Oo went back to our work in the afternoon.

But there was no celebration, the way they celebrated in some of the big towns, parties in London out in the streets. There was never anything like that here — because this was a much smaller community, and all the time you were thinking that it was finished, you could still see all the laddies that weren't coming home. There were no jollifications, no nothing."

THE STORE

The first Chartist co-operative store in Scotland was opened in Hawick in 1838. The Chartists got their name from a six point charter which listed a series of political demands — almost all of which are now accepted. Early glimmers of the co-operative movement began amongst the weavers in Ayrshire and Govan in Glasgow. Textile workers appear to have been more disposed to radical political thought and an early role for Hawick in the co-op movement is not surprising.

Many generations of Borderers knew the Co-op as simply 'the Store' and used all of its departments as regular shoppers. The annual dividend or 'divi' could be valuable, depending on how much a family had purchased at the Store. A divi book was marked up, using carbon paper between flimsy pages, and then its details copied into a series of central ledgers kept by each society. By 1867 Scotland had around 130 societies but during the 20th century the number slowly contracted as mergers took place. Close ties existed between the temperance movement and the Store and until 1958 no society which sold alcohol in its shops was admitted to the Scottish Co-operative and Wholesale Society.

Despite heavy competition from more glamorous private supermarket chains, the Store remains strong in the Borders and the Co-op Bank is flourishing.

Individual recollection is naturally partial but the tone of what Jenny Corbett, Mae Wilson and Mary King had to say is borne out by the crushing weight of statistics. The King's Own Scottish Borderers recruited mainly from the Scottish Border counties, including Dumfriesshire, Kirkcudbright and Wigtown. In the Great War they lost 6,859 men killed and 20,577 wounded. That adds up to more than 10% of the entire population of men, women and children in the 6 counties of the south of Scotland. While not all KOSBs were Borderers, these figures take no account of local men who enlisted in the navy or in other regiments. The likely total of killed and wounded is almost certainly higher. Each town and village has a First World War memorial carrying what seems to be an impossibly long list of names, of men who travelled the ghost road home. Small communities were shattered by the scale of the slaughter, and even at a distance of three generations, the sense of heavy loss is palpable.

The demands of the war economy meant full employment in the mills of Hawick, Gala and Selkirk. Soldiers were kitted out with the warm woollen underwear of the sort developed by the Hawick hosiery industry; long johns, combinations and cholera belts. For some men this sort of protection against the cold was new and its issue created a post war market amongst those lucky enough to survive the trenches. Stimulated by military contracts Hawick also began to diversify into outerwear. The cardigan got its name from the reckless 7th Earl of Cardigan who led the charge of the Light Brigade into the valley of death in 1854 in the Crimean War. At first it was made up as a knitted jacket with buttons up the front to give soldiers some comfort in the bitter winter winds that blew off the Russian steppes. Incidentally the charge of the Light Brigade was part of the battle of Balaclava, which bequeathed another garment much used by British soldiers — and children. In the First World War cardigans were produced in great numbers in Hawick, as were khaki pullovers or jerseys. These urgent needs accelerated gradual change into a decisive shift from the manufacture of underwear to outerwear.

In Selkirk Jenny Corbett remembers that the looms were very busy between 1914 and 1918;

"I was a weaver for 15 years. I was first on a four-box Hattersley [loom] with a maximum of three shuttles working. It was all plain work. This was the First World War years and we often made tartan stuff for soldiers' kilts. Sometimes it was plain tartan and sometimes it was finer for officers' wear. And other times it could be shirting or anything like that. You made fairly decent wages at that. It was piece-work and we were on from 7.30am to 12 o'clock. We got an hour off for dinner. We started back at 1pm and went on to 5.30pm...

I never liked it, standing there doing all this plain work, the shuttles going clickety-clack. It could have driven me crazy. But I always had a good memory and in my mind I would be reciting or singing, going places — all the time keeping my eyes on the weaving."

After the First World War ended in 1918 the school leaving age was raised to 14, but improvements in schooling itself did not automatically, or even speedily, follow. The collage of memories below tends to take little notice of the curriculum, which appears to have deviated only occasionally from the standard three Rs, and it is coloured much more by what happened around the classroom and the school day. And between 1910 and 1930, the power and summary sanctions exercised by teachers will surprise modern sensibilities.

Mary King has the earliest recollection;

"Ah went tae St Abbs School, ah think, in 1911... there wis two rooms but ah cannae mind o' the numbers o' pupils — the school aye seemed tae be full onywey. It was quite a big class ah wis in, there wis a lot o' children these days on the farm... the classes at St Abbs School were quite big.

Ah can remember the headmaster — McCulloch. Oh, what a monster of a man that was. Now ah wisnae in his room until ah wis twelve. He used tae dance wi' fury, ken, go roond screamin'. And he had two girls, his own girls, in the class, one called Anne and the other wis called Daisy. And Daisy had an awfy scarred face, she'd been burned at some time or other. And ah remember if he wis shoutin' at them he'd haul them oot the seat by the hair o' the head, his own girls. He wis a terrible man, terrible. Oh, the children were terrified of him. Oh, he yaised the belt a' right. Oh, ah got the belt. Ah cannae mind what for. There would be a raw o' us and oo'd be asked something, and if ah couldnae answer ah'd get the belt or the cane, whatever it wis. He used the cane an' a'. He struck ye on the hand. Oh, it wis sore. He yaised the belt or the cane quite a lot."

Margaret Paxton was born in 1905 at Gattonside, across the Tweed from Melrose. She went to school at Kirkton, near Hawick.

"[There were] two teachers, the gentleman teacher and the lady teacher. The gentleman was the head teacher. They called him Maister Turnbull. Oh, it was quite a good school Ah learned a lot at that school. Well ee ken, ah think it wis wi' me bein' older ah thought it wis a better school... At Kirkton the pupils stayed till they were fourteen. There used to be about three classes in the room. And the like o' the schoolmaster's class, there would be maybe four. And the schoolmaster sent out a minister out o' there, out o' his class — one o' his pupils became a minister later on. Oh. he was very bright, John Wilson they called him.

Ah like-ed arithmetic, ah did like arithmetic. It wis him Maister Turnbull that made iz... Ah didn't know anything about arithmetic when ah went tae Kirkton, so he says, 'I'll learn you'. So it wis subtraction. 'Well,' he says, 'come in and sit down.' And he said, 'D'ye see these four window panes?' Ah said, 'Yes'. 'Well, take two away. How many's left?' Ah said, 'Two'. And that's the way ah learned subtraction. Ah did enjoy it. Then he used tae read a story in the afternoon, the maister. Everyone o' us used tae go and listen tae him. So ah liked Kirkton School and got on well there".

ANNE REDPATH

A Border painter rather than a painter of the Borders, Anne Redpath's early career is marked by a streak of native determination to succeed in her chosen calling — and never to compromise. Probably taking a vibrant sense of colour from her father, Thomas, who was a designer with Robert Noble and Co in Hawick, she attended the Edinburgh College of Art at the beginning of the First World War. Her father wanted her to take a safer route and train as a teacher, but they struck a bargain that she would attend Moray House College at the same time. By feigning illness when classes clashed, and working very hard, Anne somehow managed to gain qualifications at both.

Her singular talent was recognised early and several bursaries came her way. Married in 1920 to James Michie, the couple moved to a much more exotic location, St Jean, Cap Ferrat on the French Riviera near Nice. Anne was profoundly influenced by the light and the vivid colours of the Mediterranean coast and they informed her style for many years.

But their time in France was cut suddenly short. They returned to Hawick and James Michie was forced to seek work in London. The marriage suffered, but Anne refused to sacrifice her independence as a painter, and to support her children she managed to survive on the income from sales of her pictures.

In 1949 Anne Redpath moved to Edinburgh, and after exhibiting in London in 1952, found herself established and recognised. Honours followed but they were not allowed to colour Redpath's Border origins and she remained a modest and unaffected person. At her funeral in 1964 the reporter from The Edinburgh Evening News noted that as well as the great and the good, cabbies, waiters, dustmen and students came to the graveside to pay their respects.

There is a power in Anne Redpath's paintings which seems to grow out of the experience of her life. And if there is no such thing as art, but only artists, then she deserves to be seen as one of Scotlnd's greatest.

In Selkirk Jenny Corbett first went to school in 1908 and did well enough to have ambitions of further education;

"I was quite a good scholar, though I say so myself, and when I was 13, getting on for 14, we got the school holidays on the Friday. Now at that time [1916], the Selkirk High School was fee-paying, and every year maybe 4 or 6 pupils from Knowepark School who had shown some ability, and if they passed what we called the qualifying exams and got good reports, they got to the High School free of charge. Along with another three I was to go to the High School. On the Saturday my father had been at the bowling green, and he came in as large as life and said, "I've got a job for ee". He says, "You're starting at Gairdner's Mill on Monday".

Now, you talk about the feet being taken from me. I had no idea what the mills were like. My mother had been in service and my father was a souter, a shoemaker. But it was 11 shillings a week. In 1916 11 shillings was a lot of money. And I suppose they had no thought of giving you a further education. That would just likely be a waste of money. And so. I nearly had a fit.

However, on the Monday I had to chum a lass [to the mill] who lived further up the Back Row. To this day I can feel this terrible feeling of being cut away from everything. It took me a long, long time to forgive my mother and father."

Annie Guthrie's father fought at the Dardanelles in the First World War with the King's Own Scottish Borderers and despite contracting asthma, he received no pension, suffering from bouts of ill health all his life. Annie was born in 1911 at Angelraw, near Greenlaw;

"There wis jist one teacher that ever bothered me. Now that was at Ashkirk School [between Selkirk and Hawick]. And they hadnae realised that ah wis short sighted. And it wis a map, and he took me out and ah wis tae point out this thing on the map. Well, tae be quite honest ah couldnae see it, ee see. But the teacher didn't know that. And of course he had got right cross and jist took ma head and knocked the blackboard clean over wi' ma head. He gripped me by the shoulders and jist gave me a shove and pushed the blackboard over. And of course ah said when ah went home. Ma father went tae the teacher and, 'Well,' he said, 'why couldn't she see? Why couldn't she point out the thing?' And it dawned on them, and then of course they got iz glasses. Ah didnae have glasses before then".

Dave Welsh was born in 1919 at Morebattle, and moved to Cessford soon afterwards. He first went to school at Caverton Mill;

"We walked a little over two miles to school, which of course we never thought anything about. There were kids used to come from Marchcleuch and much further up. It was two rooms, my auntie was the head teacher and as far as I can remember there was a Miss Elliot who used to teach what would be more or less the primary. They took kids up to the age of 14. And any of them that were any good had the opportunity to get on their bicycles and go to Kelso High School.

I took diphtheria and was off school a long time, and missed the qualifying exam to go to Kelso High School. Consequently in those days there was no going back. You couldn't sit it. That was it, you'd had it. So I left school at nearly 15 and went into the blacksmith's shop. The rest of the family were being educated at Kelso High School, which in those days was a bit expensive. It was hard in the blacksmith's shop — but you just had to get on with it. I would think fathers would be the worst possible to serve an apprenticeship with."

Annie Reid also went to Caverton Mill school, had the opportunity to sit the qualifying exam and cycled to Kelso on a Monday, boarded and came home on Fridays. Wintertime sometimes made for difficult travelling on the hilly seven-mile journey;

"It could be quite miserable drying wet clothes at the living room fire, even boots or clogs and gaiters — wellies came later. When the snow plough hadn't been along it was hard going, but I hated the frosty weather with cart tracks hard frozen. Many a spill we got when, having chosen a nice smooth cart track for the bike wheels, it was suddenly crossed by another track frozen solid. The sudden bump tended to catapult us over the handlebars. But worst of all cycling home wearily, carrier laden with bag of books etc, these ruts caused the gas lamps to go out. How often we had to get off to relight them with numb fingers. Then we would run out of carbide or flood it and the major operation of refilling would take place by the side of the road either in darkness or if lucky by the light of someone else's lamp. And oh that smell of wet carbide — I can smell it yet! Sometimes roads were 'blawn up' and we couldn't go to school, at least to Kelso High School. Often when younger the snow plough was sent with us to Caverton Mill School. I remember it must have been 1921 or 1922 my father took me by cart to Kirkbank station to get the train to Kelso so that I could sit an exam at KHS."

Jean Fleming began school at Morebattle in 1929;

"At dinner-times or play-times the big boys used to sit in the sun opposite the doctor's house and they would hold a scrap of paper under a piece of thick glass until the paper was scorched. The girls mainly played 'beds' [hopscotch] or skipped, although we had singing games as well, like 'the big ship sails through the alley-alley-o'. We played 'piney' or 'keppy, clappy, roly-pirn, backy' and this we would play against the wall, up in the air, or bouncing the ball on the ground.

Our gym teacher in those days was 'Wattie Clappie', arriving on a motorbike and wearing a soft leather helmet, and I can remember he had a bushy moustache. The teacher of the middle room was Beatrice Craig. She used to take us all into her room to learn 'Away in a Manger' and 'Good King Wenceslaus'. Donald Craig was our headmaster, who came to Morebattle in July 1906, I believe. He taught in the big room. I have school photos taken at the Old School, showing the thatched roof of the house round the corner from the shop, and the flag-pole in the corner of the play-ground. However I was soon to move to a new school being built down at the bottom of the village.

I can recall how we were all marched down to this lovely new building on 10th September 1931. My word, what a different world it was — there was so much space. Our new infant room seemed huge and the windows were so low we could see everything going past — the windows of the old school were high and we couldn't see out of them at all, but the new ones turned out to be partitions which would open on hot sunny days and that was an extra bonus if somewhat distracting. On the corridor side there were cupboards going all the way along. At the end of the corridor there was a fireplace with tiles showing farm animals. It is still there after all these years. The country children who could not go home for dinner used to give Miss Swanston their tin bottles of tea wrapped in a sock, and she would range them round the cosy fire to keep them warm to give out at dinner-time."

The new school at Morebattle was designed by the innovative Edinburgh architectural partnership of Reid and Forbes. In high contrast to Victorian habits of mind, their designs encouraged the outside world into the school and incorporated features such as large, accessible windows and airy classrooms. Part of the reason for the new openness was medical. In the 1920s tuberculosis still carried off significant numbers of young people and it was thought that the disease would shrivel in the 'sunshine and fresh air' features of schools such as Morebattle. Reid and Forbes also designed the new Kelso High School, Chirnside School and the new Leith Academy.

GOTTERDAMMERUNG

The two greatest racers ever prouced in the Borders both died when their vehicles left a German grand prix circuit and smashed into a stand of trees. At Hohenstein in 1937 Jimmie Guthrie of Hawick was riding in the German motorcycle grand prix when his Norton swerved into a clump of young trees and down into a ditch. He died from multiple injuries. At Hockenheim on April 7th 1968 Jim Clark of Chirnside was lying in seventh place in an unimportant Formula Two race when his Lotus flew off the track and hit a copse of trees. He died instantly.

At the time of their deaths both Borderers were at the summit of their sports. Jimmie Guthrie was reigning European Champion and Jim Clark had been World Champion twice and won the Indianapolis 500.

Guthrie developed a taste for motorbikes as a dispatch rider in the First World War, and on returning to Hawick he joined the local motorcycle club. Driving a vehicle belonging to Carr's, the makers of table water biscuits, Guthrie had an accident at Howdenburn. Admonished by the Sheriff, he was told that 15 mph was much too fast on that stretch of road.

The Hawick club sponsored Guthrie in his first TT race on the Isle of Man, and he began to win races regularly. Competitive motorcycle racing was heavily sponsored by a now defunct British industry, names such as AJS, Greaves, Ariel, Norton and Triumph, and cash prizes were substantial. Jimmie and his brother, Archie, built up a prosperous motor and general engineering business in Hawick, and racing success did much to enhance it.

Guthrie was 40 when he died and observers believe that his bike was forced off the track by a German rider who moved into his path to block him.

Jim Clark was born in Fife before his family moved to farm in Berwickshire. With his interest in motor racing kindled by the local Young Farmers Club, Clark was encouraged by Ian Scott Watson of Greenlaw, who lent him his Porsche. And at the disused Charterhall airfield, he drove it to victory in the Border Motor Racing Club trophy. A team was formed and they adopted the name 'The Border Reivers'. Hitting the headlines as the first driver to win a sports car race at an average speed of more than 100 mph, Clark began to dominate. When he moved up to Formula One in 1960, a glittering career quickly unfolded. Out of 72 grand prix races entered, Clark won 25 and was World Champion in 1963 and again in 1965. A punctured tyre is believed to have been the cause of his death at Hockenheim.

When Jean Fleming and her classmates marched down the hill to their new school in 1931, the economic slump known as the Great Depression was beginning to deepen. In the two years that followed more than a quarter of all working people in Scotland found themselves unemployed. The effects were felt most acutely in the industrial west of Scotland where the boom in wartime production quickly tailed off and, for example, shipbuilding did not experience a surge, despite the fact that much merchant tonnage had been sunk between 1914 and 1918. As total purchasing power declined, the demand for consumer goods slowed dramatically and the Border textile mills suffered. Jenny Corbett remembers;

"When oo struck the very bad time, the 1932 [Depression], and there was very, very little work, and we were signing on the buroo — oo ca'ed it the buroo then. We got half a crown a day. Now, they [the mill owners] worked it out so that we could get a wee bit in the mill. When we were on short time, they were very good.

Saturday at that time was considered a full day as far as the buroo went and so they worked it so that we did Monday, Tuesday and Wednesday in the mill and then we were off Thursday, Friday and Saturday. And we had to go and stand outside [the buroo], sometimes at 7pm on a Friday night, the rain coming down in buckets, and there would be a queue along to the bowling green. And we had to stand there and then go in and we got 7/6.

It was a rule that everybody paid their mother and father a pound a week board... whether you were working or not. And you didn't get into debt, or God help ee. So this night when oo came out, there were four o' oo — a' in signing. And when oo came oot, they said, 'Have ee made your board?', 'Oh well, jist'. And between the four of us we had fourpence halfpenny. So, there was a sweetie shop and oo went along and looked in the window. And there were big sweeties called Toffee Turtles and they were twopence ha'penny a quarter, and so we decided they would be the lastiest sweeties oo could get. Oo got 5 Toffee Turtles each. And that was the sweeties for the week. That was 1932 and there were about 4 years depression around that time. I would be about 29, near 30.

We would be an awful lot idle. And this aunt would say, 'Give me a hand with the washing and the ironing'. And you got sixpence a time and your tea. But ee see, though those times were so terribly hard, we learned an awful lot, learned to make do, to use what you had and be jolly thankful that you had it. Now that has stood me, and others that I know, in good stead all through life."

Walter Elliot was born in 1934, lived his early life in the Ettrick Valley but was too young to remember the Great Depression of the 1930s. However, his father, who was a self-employed fencer and woodcutter, passed on a vivid story;

"He could mind in the 1930s comin' doon tae Selkirk and there were 5 or 6 men askin' for a job. There was a wood bein'cut at Inner Huntly and there was this chap who came up, and tae get his money, he lived in a tent a' through the winter. And he came back doon tae Selkirk on the Saturday night tae spend time wi' his family, and then walked back up on the early Monday morning. And he jist lived in a tent that was packed with hay, and he jist more or less crawled in there at night. So these were bad times."

High unemployment in the Border towns went on into the 1930s and it was only the gathering threat of another European war which ultimately brought a modest revival.

Farming became very depressed by the late 1920s and early 30s. Britain had become dependent on cheap, imported food and produced only 25% of its needs at home. In addition farming and rural issues had slipped a long way down the political agenda in an urban-centred British economy which had grown accustomed to looking outwards to the Empire for raw materials. Land prices had bottomed out at a level where massive transfers of ownership began to take place. Between the two world wars 40% of all land in Scotland changed hands with the overwhelming proportion of new owners being the sitting tenants of large estates. The latter were severely eroded by the need to pay heavy death duties, partly because of war casualties, and many widely landed families were forced to give up much of what they had held for many generations. In the Borders national trends were muted, and by a mixture of good management and good fortune several very large estates survived. Some, like the Roxburghe Estates, even increased their holdings.

In 1932 a Border farmer, another Walter Elliot, was appointed Minister for Agriculture. Recognising that British stock farming was on the brink of collapse and the rest of the sector not far behind, he moved to restrict food imports and created the system of agricultural marketing boards which stabilised the situation by, essentially, fixing price-floors.

MANLY SUPPORT

Generations of men have reason to be grateful to the Hawick firm of Lyle & Scott. Y-fronts were a largely unspoken (at least in polite company) revolution in gentlemen's underwear, and a huge improvement on the unstructured and eventually baggy combinations turned out by the hosiery mills. But contrary to popular belief, Lyle & Scott did not invent the Y-front or jockey shorts, as they were sometimes known. In 1936 the company negotiated to buy the British licence to manufacture a design patented by Messrs Cooper and Co of the United States.

For ordinary workers life on Border farms ground on, almost unchanging. Mechanisation had yet to make its seismic impact after the Second World War, and people and horses still used their muscles to cultivate the land, putting in day after hard day in the fields. The old hinding system survived more or less intact and bondagers continued to be hired at the yearly fairs as an adjunct to a ploughman's fee. In 1921 there were 21,772 female farm workers in Scotland, and the principal attraction of these antique arrangements for employers was cost; a bondager generally earned half a ploughman's fee. This was particularly important in Berwickshire where arable farming could be so intense as to require a large labour force to work it and at the likes of the Duns or Earlston hiring fairs, it was difficult for a ploughman to get a single fee, that is, one without a 'wumman worker'. The principal attraction of the old bargains for the hinds and their dependents were the 'gains' or payments in kind. Housing, food allowances, pasture for a cow and a pack of sheep were all inflation-proof and immune from the vicissitudes of the stormy economic climate of the 1930s.

By the 1920s and 30s bondagers were almost exclusively members of a hind's family. Mary King remembered how work began for her in 1918;

"... ah wis bonded tae ma father at Temple Hall frae the age o' thirteen. Well, ye were bonded tae the ploughman. You were his worker, ah expect that's what bein' a bondager wid mean. Ah never thought much aboot it. But ye aye talked aboot the bondagers. It wis aye ma faither ah wis bonded tae. Ah worked beside him. Ah didnae sign any papers, nothing like that. Ma faither would arrange it. Ah would never be consulted. Ah wid jist be telt, 'Ye're gaun tae work oot'. And that wis that."

Housing conditions for farm workers improved only slowly, Because hinds moved from farm to farm very frequently at the end of a year's term — Mary King recalls her father moving every year for a little more cash — and farmers wanted to keep costs down, particularly if they themselves were tenants, there was rarely any pressure or incentive to upgrade farm workers' cottages. Mary King's family lived a term at Northfield farm, near St Abbs;

"At Northfield, oh, there were nae toilets. Ee jist had dry closets. There was a raw o' pig styes, oo ca'ed them pig craives. There wis a row o' them, one for each house. And the toilets were often at the back o' that. Ee had tae pass the pigs tae get tae the toilet. Oh, there wis one dry toilet for each house. Oh, oo never shared wi' onybody else, no' that ah mind aboot. No, ah never mind o' that, no. Oh, it would be ma mother likely that cleaned oot the toilet. Ma faither widnae dae it! Oh, ma mother wis the worker. Ah've nae idea if the toilet wis cleaned oot once a week, ah've nae mind o' that at all. It wis a terrible job that.

Oh, ma faither had a rare garden at Northfield. He wis a great gardener. He took a great pride in his garden. He grew tatties mainly, and cabbage and leeks — onything for the pot. Oh, ma mother saw tae the flowers. The garden wis in front o' the hoose. Oh, it wis a big garden, every house had its garden.

Well, the very first hoose, nearest the farm place, wis the shepherd's hoose. And the next yin wis the byreman: he wis important because he had the cows tae look after, and milk them tae, likely. Then the rest o' the hooses would be workers — ploughmen, very likely there'd be six ploughmen. And of course there wis a big hoose at the farm for the grieve. Well, we didnae ca' them grieves, we called them stewards. But they ca' them grieves in East Lothian, ah think. It wis the steward in Berwickshire. Well, the steward daist oversaw the workers and what wis tae be done and a'thing like that. He gave them their orders every mornin'. They a' assembled in the stable in the mornin'.

Now at this time o' the year, the end o' February, it's beginning tae get longer light now and it's light at six o'clock on the first o' March.

And that wis when ee went your hours — frae six in the mornin' tae six at night. And that wis frae the first o' March tae the autumn, after the harvest wis in. Ye see, the hours wis irregular in the harvest time, because they often went shifts. Ee see, they'd the old fashioned binders and there were often three horses in them. And they had tae have shifts for tae rest the horses, 'cause it wis a big strain on the horses. And then in the autumn and winter, oh, well, they would start when it wis daylight. They had tae wait on the light. If they were goin' tae be ploughin', well, ee didnae need an awfu' lot o' bright light for tae start tae plough. But if ye were daein' somethin' like shawin' or onythin' like that ee'd need mair light tae see what ee were daein'."

Mary King again;

"Oh, there wis a guid range o' work the bondagers did, right enough. Oh, oo did shawin' turnips and plantin' tatties and howkin' tatties, oh, oo did that. Hard work, ye ken. Shawin' wis a back-breakin' work. On the winter mornins, well, often at a tattie pit, where they had tatties stored in pits, ye'd have tae go oot and ye selected the tatties. Ye put the guid yins intae different bags, the other yins — for sale or for plantin' or for somethin' like that. And ah've seen it terrible cauld.

And, ee see, oo never wore trousers. Ah never saw a woman wi' trousers until the Land Army in the Second World War."

THE VOICE

Arguably the most famous Border voice in history belongs to the rugby commentator, Bill McLaren. A former Hawick player whose career was cruelly cut short by a life-threatening attack of tuberculosis, he was forced to take up commentating and rugby journalism at a comparatively early age. This has allowed him to hone his skills and knowledge to such a pitch that for at least two generations, McLaren has been the pre-eminent rugby commentator in the world. Although his preparation is meticulous and his memory encyclopaedic, it is his unashamed passion for the game which most animates his words and make him an authority. And also his voice. Difficult to describe, it is not a resonating bass whose principal attractions are depth and vibrato. Nor is it light and mellifluous, a version of the soft-spoken tongue of the Border. Perhaps the adjective — but certainly not the connotation — of 'tweedy' can be applied. Like a tough, rich and beautifully designed bolt of Border tweed, McLaren's voice adorns the national rugby stadia of the world.

It is surprising, with such a valuable asset at his disposal, that Bill McLaren has chosen not to become involved in the lucrative world of voice-overs for television advertising. Perhaps he feels unable to sum up much passion for soap powder or financial services.

The term 'bondager' fell out of use with the passage of the Agricultural Wages (Regulation) (Scotland) Act of 1937, and the arrival of the trouser-wearing girls of the Women's Land Army signalled a practical end to the life so eloquently recalled by Mary King. The Land Girls did whatever jobs needed doing and generally ignored time-honored conventions. There was, as everyone said, ' a war on'. Driving lorries and repairing them when they broke down, taking over men's work, and importing what was seen as urban sophistication, these women must have made the straw-bonnetted bondagers feel like relics from a bygone age.

The hinding system itself was swept away by another piece of clumsily titled legislation. The Essential Work (Agriculture) (Scotland) Act of 1941 was known more succinctly as 'the Stand Still Act' and it ended annual feeing for a fixed term by fobidding farm workers to move at the end of a year. Housing quickly improved because farmers found it difficult to attract and keep workers if their living conditions were poor. For the first time in many generations the rural population in the Borders began to take on a settled look.

In the towns workers faced different issues. The tweed mills of Galashiels and Selkirk found it difficult to recover their markets in the 1930s, and Jenny Corbett, like every other weaver interviewed, is clear about the reasons why. Like so many managers and proprietors in British manufacturing, the mill owners failed to modernise their businesses to cope with the demands of a changing market, failed to invest and reinvest, and ultimately, failed.

"The bosses were the gentry. They lived big. They had houses, and all those big houses at the other side of the water [the Ettrick] were all manufacturers' houses. And some of those houses down the Gala road.

But nobody really resented it in those days. They were looked up to. Folk touched their hats when they were passing them. But it wasn't servile. It was respect — which is different. Looking back now, I don't think it was strange at all. There aye has to be a heid yin, somebody with money, or you can't carry on a business.

The mills are a' away. Instead of giving themselves a grand time, and all their families, they should have put more into the mills to modernise the machinery. It was too old fashioned to weave the new style of cloth that was wanted. To us weavers it was sticking out a mile. The looms weren't adapted for some of the things and they made a trial out of what could have been a pleasure. At that time you never thought about it, but now I keep thinking back about what happened. I used to respect these folk [the mill owners] but now I've learned more, and I can see where the mistake was made. And you see, there are some of them are poorer craturs than what I am. And you just say to yourself, well, how the mighty have fallen... the money that they made — if it was ill gotten, it was ill spent."

Mae Wilson of Gala can recall a lack of investment in basic facilities. There were no flush toilets and the mill could be very cold in winter;

"I was a darner at Wakefield Mill, and there was an awful lot of unemployment at Wakefield... sometimes we only worked one day a fortnight. Wakefield was, I think, really the worst... Provost Heyward, he was one of our bosses, and his brother was older, Bert. And they were the two bosses. And then there were the older men, who had been bosses. That was what was wrong, there were too many bosses and not enough for anything else."

In Hawick the picture was different. In the 1920s and 30s the old hosiery mills were adapted to turning out an increasing volume of knitted goods, aimed particularly at the women's fashion market. Jumpers were made plain at first with round necks and a narrow choice of colours. But in 1934 Pringle's took a radical step in appointing Otto Weisz as chief designer. An Austrian, he brought innovative thinking to the knitwear business. Mills had relied on senior craftspeople to come up with design, colour and pattern, but Weisz was less interested in process than the product and he introduced new colours, and a variety of necklines and cuts. The other Hawick manufacturers were forced to respond by appointing their own designers. A virtuous circle of competition increased quality and classic outfits such as the ladies' twin-set emerged. Hawick diversified so successfully that by the end of the 1930s the production of outerwear far outstripped underwear.

Underlying economic trends are more easily discerned in retrospect. In the 1930s the life of the Border towns seemed attractive to outsiders. The Orcadian writer, Edwin Muir, was commissioned by the London publishers, Heinemann and Gollancz, to write a travel book about Scotland. H.V. Morton's 'In Search of Scotland' of 1929 had been a great success and J. B. Priestley had recently written 'English Journey'. In contrast to the patronising and probably apocryphal whimsy of Morton (at Melrose he claims to have talked to a 'bow-legged man' about the Duke of Buccleuch's hounds before meeting a leggy and flirtatious American girl who wore tartan garters (!) and spouted a stream of cliches), Muir takes a cold-eyed view of much of Scotland. But he liked the Borders and makes some worthwhile points;

"Galashiels is a typical border town, clean, bright, and with a stir of atmosphere which tells that it has a life of its own. The streets are low and broad; there is a satisfying amount of room in the centre of the place, where the Gala Water, artificially compressed within a stony gulley, foams over a miniature fall. Round green hills rise on every side, and in certain of the streets one can see them over the low roofs, when they look much nearer than they actually are. These hills, with the cattle grazing on them, give the town an appearance of having been dropped complete into a pastoral landscape, where it pursues a life at once cut off and autonomous. One gets a somewhat similar impression from the little towns which decorate medieval and early Renaissance Flemish landscapes.

These little border towns, such as Galashiels, Selkirk, Kelso and Hawick, have all this curiously wakeful and vivid air. I say 'curiously' for most of the other small towns I have seen in Scotland are contentedly or morosely lethargic, sunk in a fatalistic dullness broken only by scandal-mongering and such alarums as drinking produces; a dead silence punctuated by malicious whispers and hiccups. But the border towns have kept their old traditions more or less intact, and wherever that happens it is a sign that common life is still vigorous... .

They had not broken with their past like Montrose or Kirriemuir, leaving nothing but a vacuum; they have an industry, the weaving of tweeds and other woollen cloths, which, being essentially local and distinctive, has survived the intensifying onset of Industrialism that has eaten into the core of other communities. Perhaps too, their geographical position, the fact that for centuries they existed almost on the frontier of a hostile foreign nation, strengthened their individuality as units, and impressed upon them so strongly the need for united effort, yet it has not disappeared. The essential virtues of a nation generally gather at their greatest strength not at its centre but at the places where it is most powerfully and persistently threatened: its frontiers. The Border formed a rampart against English invasion for centuries, and it is still the part of Scotland which is least Anglicised. As soon as one is within sound of the Tweed one can feel the presence of history, in the landscape and in the faces and manners of the people. Over the rest of Scotland one has to dig for history beneath a layer of debris left by the Reformation and the Industrial Revolution.

The history of the Borders has accordingly a greater feeling of depth than that of the rest of the Lowlands."

Edwin Muir visited Abbotsford and hated it. But in the passage above he shows himself to be a true heir of Walter Scott. Both men saw the Borders overwhelmingly in terms of its history, rather than its potential, what it could produce or the enjoyment afforded by the landscape or the climate. Muir either did not know or chose to ignore what happened in the Borders before 1286 and his comments suggest that it was the medieval heritage which prompted his enthusiasm about pre-Reformation history. In any case the passage offers insights still pertinent today.

MATCHSTICK TOWN

In the early 1960s Marjorie Ellison worked as a receptionist in the Castle Hotel in Berwick Upon Tweed. As a pretty young teenager she was sometimes sketched by one of the guests, particularly if it was a rainy day and there was nothing else to do. The middle-aged man made several portraits of Marjorie but she remembered that " I didn't think anything of it… I tore the pictures up and put them in the bin."

The artist was L.S. Lowry and recently £1.9m was paid for one of his paintings. Northern industrial street scenes were a favourite subject and his 'matchstick' figures have become justly famous. First coming to Berwick on holiday in the 1930s, the painter fell in love with the town and at one point considered buying Lion House, which is situated on the ramparts. In all, Lowry painted at least 25 pictures in Berwick which have been clearly identified, but the likelihood is that many more exist. One of the most famous is of a shelter out at Berwick Pier. In 1998 Lowry enthusiasts were outraged when the council announced plans to demolish it and they successfully campaigned to have it restored. Now, a Lowry Trail is to be set up around the town, based on a similar arrangement at the French Mediterranean town of Collioure, where the painter, Henri Matisse, lived and worked.

If only Marjorie Ellison had known.

Meanwhile the storm clouds that drove the designer, Otto Weisz, to seek a new life and career in Hawick were beginning to darken over Europe. Dave Welsh remembers;

"What influenced me was the newsreels. They were American, and very good, especially about the rise of Hitler. And when you saw these buggers... well.

And we had a chappie who was sort of station master up at Sprouston and he was an ex-soldier — with the Northumberland Fusiliers. Of course we used to spend a lot of time meeting the 7 o'clock train from Kelso, especially on the dark nights, and he would regale us with tales of the First World War. And your hair would be standing on end. I mean it would be pretty bloody dreadful — because, that would be only 7 or 8 years after the First World War had finished. What a bloody awful business it had been. That impressed me more than anything. That, and these 'March of Time' newsreels.

In those days very, very few folk read a daily paper. There was a real lack of information. 'The Weekly Scotsman' was the thing for anybody who was inclined to read what was going on. It gave you some sort of indication of what was going on in the world. Local papers gave some information as well, if you go far enough back.

You saw these buggers goose-stepping over Europe and you thought, my God, it's coming, it's coming."

Dave Welsh again;

"I remember going to the Empire Exhibition at Bellahouston Park [Glasgow] and buying the paper as we came out late that evening. I thought how the hell is this happening? I'm getting the next day's paper and it's still the day before! I can still remember, it must have been round about September 1938. I got the Daily Express and the headline was, 'There Ain't Gonna Be No War'. And I never bought the bloody Daily Express after that in my life.

If anybody went to the pictures and read a newspaper then you realised that there was something going on in Europe that was decidedly unhealthy. And when Hitler marched into Czechoslovakia and Chamberlain said, 'Oh, it's a little country we don't know very much about.', you began to realise that there was some bloody treachery going on here".

The blitzkreig that overran Poland a year later persuaded many in Britain that a similar fate awaited. Hitler's bombers would mount devastating raids across the North Sea and when war was formally declared on 3rd September 1939, there was a sense of immediate threat, even in Border towns. Alison Brunton of Kelso;

"I remember very clearly when War was declared. I was six years old, my mother had recently died and I was in the care of an aunt and my grandparents. My father, Jock Gray (later to become Pipe Major) was already enlisted in the Territorials (4th Border Battalion KOSB) and when the call came he had to go.

On that particular night I was at home with my aunt, rather than at my grandparents' home. This would be nearer to my school in Kelso. As can be appreciated this was a very upsetting, tearful time for the womenfolk and my aunt was no different and as the evening wore on she had the support of another lady who was also to become an aunt to me. This aunt (to be) was the cook at the Kelso Cottage Hospital and looking back, seemed to take charge of the situation and thought the best thing to do under the circumstances was to take my aunt and myself to the nurses' home at the Cottage Hospital to spend the night there. We would all be together and of some comfort to one another and give each other support as and when it was needed. Not an easy night for the older folks, the mums, dads, brothers and sisters of the lads that had to go away to war so very quickly.

My memories of that night were of my aunt and myself squeezed into a single bed in the Nurses Home. I didn't sleep all that well and everything seemed to be in darkness and I can't remember where I got my breakfast."

As soon as war was declared women and children were speedily evacuated from Scotland's cities and industrial towns and many were put on trains bound for Border stations. The family of Brodie Robertson at Galalaw, near Kelso, were involved at the outset;

"At the beginning of September 1939, the new High School near Poynder Park [in Kelso] was due to be open for the first time, but was delayed for a couple of days as war with Germany was about to break out and the evacuated children from Edinburgh had to be sorted out as they arrived from Kelso Station. All the likely houses in the district that might have spare bedrooms had already been examined by officials to see how many children could be accommodated in each.

The farmhouse at Galalaw just outside the West Lodge at Floors [Castle] was no different from other big farmhouses in the Borders, and had two big bedrooms standing empty, so we were allocated three boys aged seven, ten and twelve along with their teacher Jean Yule along with her sister Mary, who was to prove a boon as a help in the house.

They all came from Leith Walk School. The children were taught in St John's Church Hall in Kelso. Any other spare halls in Kelso were needed for teaching. Providing food for them could not have come at a better time of year because it was harvest time and the number of rabbits that fell to the sticks of the Kelso people at the finishings (the small area that was left in the middle of the cornfield where the binder was cutting) was enormous. It was quite common at the end of the day to see dozens of boys going back into Kelso with eight or ten rabbits strung from their handlebars or frames. It must have been the best fed town in the UK at that time of year. My mother, of course, took advantage of the surplus food and, being a cookery teacher herself at one time, disguised the rabbits in all different ways such as stewed, roasted, casseroled and sometimes mixed with pigeon in a pie but in no way were we to mention the word 'rabbit' to the evacuees. This food went on for at least a month and who could blame my mother, for by now she had ten mouths to feed, but the oldest boy was not to be fooled and complained of a sore stomach. My mother took him to the medicine chest and told him he needed a good clean out. "In that case", said the boy, "what you'll need is a blinkin' ferret".

The Christmas holidays came along and as no German bombs had fallen in the middle of Edinburgh, the children went home to their parents."

The organisation of the war economy was seen as a key advantage and food production in blockaded Britain quickly made a priority. The 'Restrictions on Engagements Order of 1940 prevented farm workers from leaving the land, and a range of incentives was offered to farmers to enhance cropping and output. For staple foodstuffs, prices were fixed and for ploughing up grassland, a subsidy of £2 per acre was offered, and eagerly taken up. Wheat and barley acreage doubled during the war and the extra labour needed for cultivation was supplied by the Women's Land Army. By 1945 nearly 80,000 had enlisted, and for many it was a life-changing experience. German and Italian prisoners of war were also used and some lived in the steadings of Border farms.

Highly visible economies and sacrifices were made during the early part of the war, and the lack of iron railings caused Brodie Robertson difficulties when the Galalaw cattle were being driven to Kelso's fat stock mart;

"Fat cattle and sheep were mostly walked there and during the war the iron garden railings along the streets were removed and melted down to help the war effort. My job was to go in front of the cattle and close all the garden gates. On one occasion going down Roxburgh Street, a bullock went up a narrow back stairs and got stuck in the communal lavatory headfirst. In the excitement he did his business in all the wrong bit. On another occasion we were taking cattle to the mart and when driving them through the Square and up Bridge Street, one decided to go into the British Linen Bank, now the Bank of Scotland. It went behind the counter and when it saw its mates disappear up Bridge Street it was one mighty job with a stick in my hand to prevent it from jumping through a plate glass window. The Manager of course hit the roof, and it didn't help matters when I told him the cattle belonged to the bank.

Taking sheep to the mart and crossing Kelso Bridge, the one man in front was going to have difficulty in guiding them up the Station Brae, so the shepherd at the back, just beyond the Tollhouse, sent his collie dog to 'get away bye'. And the collie, quite naturally thought the parapet of the bridge was just an ordinary dyke, and over he went. And as there was just the right amount of water in the river, swam to the far side and carried out his orders as if there was nothing wrong."

Borderers volunteered to join up in large numbers, but many initially feared that the appalling experience of 1914–1918 would be repeated, with trench warfare on a near-static western front. But the defeat at

Dunkirk and the fall of France changed all prospects. And in fact the casualties of the KOSBs turned out, over the whole course of the war, to be less than a fifth of the total for the Great War. When Hitler gained control of the Western European seaboard in 1941, the threat of invasion appeared to be very real and the Local Defence Volunteers or Home Guard were formed. Men too old, young or unfit for conscription, or in reserved occupations, were called to arms and while no-one doubted their seriousness of purpose, their attempts at training for battle have stuck with a smile in the memories of Borderers such as John Ogilvie of Kelso;

"… we watched the Home Guard drilling outside the Drill Hall which was their Headquarters, and laughing at 'Tacks' Anderson doing his sentry duty stint in his slippers as he didn't like boots! The Home Guard were holding manoeuvres with the Army and a gang of us were watching them at Orchard Park. One patrol was looking for the 'Enemy' who were hiding in Tucky Lynch's tattie shaws, which were very high. The patrol could not find them but Tucky was leaning out of her window enjoying the fun and she shouted, 'You're all ******* blind, they hiding in the ****** tatties.'

After Charterhall aerodrome opened, four of us youngsters decided to walk there to see the aircraft situation. There was George Pringle, wee 'Chicken' Tait, Jim 'Schnozzle' Fairbairn and myself. Every hill would surely be the last and eventually we arrived at Charterhall. Talk about security!! We were at the south end of the 'drome and there was a long line of drainage pipes waiting to be dug under the ground and they were of such a diameter we could walk through them onto the airfield without being seen! There was a solitary aircraft standing there and we clambered all over it, had a look at the cockpit where 'Schnozzle' was pulling levers and switches. The undercarriage locks must have been secure or he might have dropped the whole lot on top of us! I found out later that this aircraft was the new Beaufighter and then was still on the secret list. Security, what a laugh! We headed home to find the Police were looking for us, as not realising the time, we had been away nearly all day."

Charterhall was one of two airfields in Berwickshire used by the RAF. The other was at Whinfield, north of the Tweed, near Norham, and both formed the headquarters for 54 OTU (Operational Training Unit). Because of the number of fatal crashes invoving trainee pilots, the RAF knew Charterhall as 'Slaughterhall'.

Army camps dotted the Border landscape but the largest was at Stobs, in the hill country south of Hawick. Built to hold 100,000 men at any given time, it was huge, and after being used to induct National Servicemen after the war, it was finally closed in 1959. But perhaps the most important strategic wartime installation in the Borders was mostly manned by women. In 1943 ICI opened a massive munitions factory at Charlesfield, near St Boswells. One of only two designed to produce large volumes of incendiary bombs, it had made almost 24,000,000 by the end of the war. Mae Wilson worked there;

"But oh, ah'll never forget at Boswells, ee ken, where the munitions was. There were too many darners in the mill, and ah had tae go away. I was sent to this place to be assessed. And I had this sort of dullness on my lung, but I said nothing and I went to Boswells to work. But I didn't tell my own doctor ah was away tae Boswells. So he comes into the house and sees me and says, 'Are you not working?' 'Aye' ah says, 'at Boswells'. Oh, he nearly exploded. He says, 'And what in all the earth are you doing there?' 'Look', he said, 'if you get some of that powder in your lungs, you'll not get any money for it.' He was right enough for I never told them about it. However, it didn't do me any harm.

It was making bombs, incendiary bombs, but we had a few accidents. One was a pretty big one. Something had fallen and struck a machine and we had a big fire. But then, ee see, we knew it was coming to the end of the war.

I did like Boswells, the factory, but it was a long day. Ee was away frae the hoose at 4.15am [Mae was still living in Gala with her parents]. Oo got a' kinds o' women in the munitions. Oo got some country folk in to work with us, but oo got on fine wi' them. But there was this one specially. She was ca'ed Rose and she was a right tough guy. She was drunk every Friday night.

The factory was really a bit of a farm, but there was aye a policeman and a policewoman at the gate. You had to pass them and, of course, a lot of them [the workers] were pinching that good nylon. I was terrified. I wouldn't touch it. I wasnae wantin' lifted. They made it into pyjamas and all that sort o' thing."

As the course of the war began to turn and the allies became more organised, the Borders was used by free Polish, Czechoslovakian and other Eastern European troops as a location for their camps and for training exercises. Shedden Park in Kelso was used as a tank depot by the Poles and the danger involved even in training is remembered in a memorial on the flanks of nearby Roxburgh Castle where a fatal accident took place. When the Yalta Conference of 1945 placed Poland in the Russian sphere of influence, some Polish servicemen elected to stay where they were stationed in the Borders. Their influence has been significant, both on the rugby field and in the community in general. Working backwards from the letter 'Z', Polish and other Eastern European names are flecked through the pages of the Borders telephone directory; Ziolkowski, Zawadski, Zawadecky, Wykowska, Wichary, Poloczek, Poklekowska, Mazur, Goldsztajn (pron. Goldstein) and many others.

PREFABS AND CRUDENS

Homes for heroes in 1945 may have been modest affairs but their inhabitants found them well designed. In most Border towns groups of prefabricated houses were quickly assembled, services and roads supplied and garden plots laid out, complete with garden sheds closely resembling Anderson shelters. Made out of smooth asbestos sheeting (long before anyone had anxieties about it) for high insulation, prefabs were only one storey but they contained a magical innovation

> *for ordinary families. Gas-powered refrigerators were installed complete with ice cube trays and a set of cylindrical plastic pods for making ice lollies.*
>
> *Like most temporary structures the prefabs lasted well beyond their planned lives and many in the Borders were still inhabited in the 1960s. By that time more traditional bricks and mortar council housing had been built and in at least three Border towns the name of the builder was attached to the dwellings. 'The Crudens' became an address as well as a construction company.*
>
> *Ordinary people welcomed these well-designed houses, but many were found to be too small. From the 1930s to the 1960s Border families tended to remain extended rather than nuclear, and often three generations squashed into two or three bedrooms. If genders were mixed that could lead to a living room being turned into a bedroom. Nevertheless the houses were warm, weathertight and did not involve an outside journey to the toilet.*

Only twenty years separated the end of the First World War and the outbreak of the Second, and in 1944 and 1945 when people began to think of the aftermath, memories were fresh. Millions of soldiers and civilians were determined that not only would there never be another world war, but that there would never be another post-war world like the depressed and impoverished 1920s and 1930s. Dave Welsh served in the RAF and recalls the mood of servicemen;

"The soldiers had been around, and they thought they wanted something a bit better than before. There was a general feeling that we can't have these fellas who ran the country before the war — who got us into the whole thing.

In the Borders, to be brutally frank, [people thought] the fellas in the Big Hoose knew how to run things. But [it turned out that] they didn't know how to run things. How could you sort it out? Only one way and that was politically. And eventually this is how it did change.

What raised a lot of interest was the Beveridge Report during the war. That got everybody thinking — that this is what we need to get back to, a health service, free at the point of entry, and the education system. These were the two main things, and they brought a radical change in the Borders. You got onto a doctor's panel and that was it. I believe that there were quite a few doctors didn't fancy it. But it was all a tremendous change from before the war."

For the general election of 1945 the wartime coalition dissolved into the Conservative, Labour and Liberal parties. Partly because the Conservatives appeared to be lukewarm about the prospects for the implementation of the Beveridge Report (and partly because many returning soldiers believed that Churchill had prolonged the war unnecessarily), the Labour Party won a landslide victory. In Scotland they took 37 seats and 48% of the vote, and it seemed that the New Jerusalem was at hand.

However, Labour candidates have never fared well in the conservative Border country. Since the beginnings of the Labour movement and the final extensions of the franchise, only Conservatives and Liberals have represented the area, and the differences between them seemed a matter of inherited memory rather than a function of any current policy. Dave Welsh recalls;

"It [conservatism] was a natural thing. Nobody thought of anything different to it. I've heard the Auld Man [his father] in days gone by on about the Liberals — they were a terrible thing! He used to tell me the story of a gentleman farmer near Morebattle who farmed a tiny place, tiny for a man of his connections to the Earls of Lauderdale. The Auld Man remembered when there was this election and the polling place was in Morebattle. And of course all the transport was pony and cart and it was decked out to take the conservative voters. But ah! There was one Liberal! A ploughman who let it be known that he was a Liberal. Aye. He had to walk, and pass them by. An indication of what went on.

The local toffs were very Conservative. They more or less told you; 'Awfully nice chap, this Conservative man'. And when the Labour candidates came, they were even worse than the Liberals. There was always this Liberal tendency in the Borders — and they were the danger. They could have been elected. The mill towns were Liberal, but the mill owners would have a big lot of influence on how people voted. It was just this lack of education and information. People just didn't have it".

Walter Elliot became interested in politics at an early age, devoting his considerable energies to the cause of the Scottish National Party;

"When oo were canvassing I met a Tory in the street, just an ordinary working man, worked in the mills. And oo got on aboot politics, and I said to him, 'Would you rather have ten shillings on your wages or get the Duke to say good morning to you?' He thought about it for a while, and then said , ' I think I'd rather get the Duke to say good morning tae iz.'… Well, I just can't understand that mentality.

In the past the folk that worked with their hands tended to be the radicals; the weavers, the men and women in the mills, where there was an associated bunch o' them — rather than on the estates where there were ones or twos or threes. People didn't congregate and possibly speak aboot things. The mill workers tended to discuss things."

WALLACE, WINNIE, WENDY AND WALTER

The chairman of the Selkirk branch of the Scottish National Party, Walter Elliot, raised money in 1967 to pay for the erection of a plaque outside the Auld Kirk. The legend would state that William Wallace had been proclaimed Guardian of the Realm of Scotland in 1298 in the old kirkyard.

Following Winnie Ewing's stunning victory at the Hamilton by-election, Elliot determined to invite her to unveil the plaque at the common riding of 1968. However the non-party political town council insisted that the occasion was not to be used as a platform for a political speech, and the suggestion of Mrs Ewing was politely declined. Instead, it was thought, surprisingly, that the noted nationalist firebrand, Miss Wendy Wood of the Scottish Patriots, would be a more suitable choice.

> *And so, after the casting of the colours on common riding morning, the official party made their way up the Kirk Brae for the ceremony and the speeches. Wendy Wood began with what she must have thought were some innocent, and appropriate, remarks praising the souters o' Selkirk and attacking the Earl o' Home in the manner of the common riding song. Provost Len Thomson bristled. A well known Conservative, he took Miss Wood's remarks as an attack on the former Tory Prime Minister, and he objected to her effrontery in making a political speech. Bristling herself, Miss Wood then launched into what she considered to be a political speech, and the Provost gathered all his civic dignity about him and marched out of the kirkyard. Much encouraged by this the speaker found it difficult not to connect the career of William Wallace with the cause of Scottish Nationalism. Such was the cut and thrust of Border politics.*

At the 1950 general election when Clement Attlee's Labour government hung on by a whisker in the teeth of a surge in the Conservative vote, the Borders, against national trends, ejected a Tory and elected a Liberal M.P. Because Attlee's majority was fragile, the government was forced to call another election within a year. Winston Churchill's Conservatives triumphed and Archie MacDonald lost Roxburgh, Selkirk and Peebles to Commander C.E.M. Donaldson. Described as 'a mild, unimpressive man', he continued to live in London and made little effort to find a home in the constituency. Always known formally as 'Commander' Donaldson, he held the seat in 1955 and despite the energetic efforts of a young Tam Dalyell for the Labour Party, he increased his majority over the Liberals to more than 10,000 in 1959. After the end of food and clothes rationing in 1954, and the obvious growth of the British economy, the Prime Minister, Harold MacMillan, was able to coin a resonant phrase during the election campaign whe he announced to voters, 'You've never had it so good'. Rising standards of living confirmed the basic truth of the claim and the Conservatives swept back to power with an increased majority, which included Commander Donaldson.

The fact that a Border laird succeeded Harold MacMillan in 10 Downing Street appears to have done little to bolster Donaldson's standing. Alec Douglas Home's government looked vulnerable in the changing atmosphere of the early 1960s, and there were ominous rumblings about the competence of the sitting M.P. in the Borders. Hector Monro had failed to get the Conservative nomination for the Dumfries by-election, and as a former rugby player (for Langholm) he was thought to be highly electable. And Donaldson had appeared to premiate the interests of his party above those of his constituency when the Beeching Report was published. In the Borders the M.P. spoke against axing rail services, including the Waverley Line, but when he came to vote at Westminster, he supported the cuts and walked into the government lobby.

In spite of these difficulties the dour and durable Donaldson retained sufficient support in the Roxburgh, Selkirk and Peebles Conservative Association to hang onto his party's endorsement for the 1964 election. But it was to prove a hard fight. The dynamic young Liberal candidate slashed his majority to a narrow 1,739. David Steel had switched from building up the Edinburgh Pentlands seat to take on the Borders because he was reluctantly convinced that it was more winnable. And then fate took a hand to prove his judgement ultimately correct. At the comparatively early age of 63, Commander Donaldson was admitted to St Thomas Hospital in London for a minor operation, and while under anaesthetic, he died of a heart attack.

The by-election was set for March 1965 and Steel began to plan his campaign. A local grandee, Robin McEwen of Marchmont House in Berwickshire, was selected for the Conservatives. Good-looking, relatively young and qualified as a barrister, he seemed a formidable opponent. But Steel fought a well-organised and thoroughly modern campaign which pushed the Conservatives into pulling in big guns to support their man. One of them, Sir Gerald Nabarro, shot himself and his party in the foot when he pronounced himself unsurprised by depopulation from the Borders. Why, Lord Napier and Ettrick used to employ 14 domestic servants, and now, only had 1, poor fellow. Perhaps equally unsurprisingly, McEwen's health appeared to fail him during the campaign and his wife, Brigid, was forced to turn up alone at meetings to read out his speeches.

At the declaration of the result at Jedburgh Town Hall, the figures showed a huge turnout of 84% and Steel storming to victory by 4,607 votes to become, at 25, the youngest M.P. in the House of Commons. Since that famous night the Borders has remained stubbornly Liberal, refusing, just as it had with Commander Donaldson, to change its allegiance easily. Much later, Berwick Upon Tweed elected a Liberal M.P. to complete the party's hold on the Tweed Basin. And despite the fact that since 1945, however talented and dedicated, their M.P.s have never formed, and rarely aspired to form part of a Westminster government, the outsider nature of the Liberal Party seems to fit well into a wide streak of independence which has characterised the Borders and Borderers for many generations. The dogged, and sometimes cussed differentness of the Liberals, until more recent times, seemed to appeal to ancient instincts. Borderers wanted to be unlike those to both the north and the south and found a way of expressing that politically.

NEW ABBEY

The most spectacular example of religious architecture to rise in the Borders since the golden age of the medieval abbeys stands in Eskdale, near Langholm. The Samye Ling Tibetan monastery is a gorgeous structure with a golden pagoda-style roof complete with dragons and much brightly painted wood. Golden buddhas seem to be everywhere. Founded in 1967, it is home to 100 monks and lay people, as well as many thousands of annual visitors. Akong Tulku Rinpoche and another Tibetan abbot fled the Chinese invasion and somehow fetched up in the Borders.

Engagingly, the centre runs a cafe called the Tibetan Tea Rooms and efforts are being made to raise funds to build a stupa, a monument at the entrance whose energy will transform "the causes of pollution, war, famine, poverty and disease and create conditions of balance and peace for the planet and all beings."

Policies of an apolitical sort were formulated in the immediate post-war
era which could, by their singular nature, only impact decades after
they were initiated. And they have had a radical effect on the Border
countryside. In 1920 the Forestry Commission was formed to oversee
the re-afforestation of Britain after the depredations of the First World
War. New planting went in at Glentress, near Peebles, Kershope, near
Newcastleton and at Kielder in Northumberland. Because they were
well adapted to open sites with poor, acidic and peaty soil, Sitka spruce
was used. However, many of the early plantings failed until the device
of ribbon ploughing was developed. This created deep furrows for better
drainage and banked up the soil into thick and warm dreels which
protected the saplings' roots and allowed them to take a firm hold.
Unfortunately ribbon ploughing has been a partial cause of unexpected
difficulties in the Border river-system. More efficient rainwater run-off
from the high ground swells the burns and rivers so quickly after a wet
spell that a powerful force of water is produced which, in turn, erodes
the river banks in an unprecedented way. The lower Teviot has been
particularly badly affected.

By the end of World War II 5% of the land area of the Borders had
been afforested, but in the late 1940s the pace of planting accelerated
dramatically. At the beginning of the 21st century a huge area, 14.5%,
has been ploughed and planted with trees, the overwhelming mass of
them evergreen softwoods. And most of those a single species, Sitka
spruce.

In the period immediately following the Second World War, little
thought was given to any sort of amenity. Trees were seen simply as
another crop, only with a long timescale for ripening. Particularly in
the area south of Hawick, in Wauchope Forest and in the large forests
in the Tweed Valley between Peebles and Hawick, evergreens were
planted in regular rectilinear blocks of 1200 acres. And because of their
hardiness, Sitka spruce was often prefered, with some admixture of
larch, Norway spruce and Douglas fir. Fifty years on the effects of this
enormous change have been mixed. At first forestry provided much
needed jobs and special housing was built to accommodate workers,
but as mechanisation increased, the jobs melted away. But the new
planting did make productive use of large areas of windswept and
barren land in the upland areas.

However, the massive increase in planting has changed the face of
the Borders substantially. Densely packed in geometric blocks on
hillsides, the black-green woods are forbidding and sterile, giving an
unnatural shape to the landscape while making quite different places
seem oddly similar. And when a plantation is clear-felled, the effect
can be brutal. In more recent times these harshnesses have been
softened by fringing the new woods with hardwoods and planting in
sympathy with the grain of the land. Future generations will be grateful
for that.

HOMING

Since the 1960s the salmon population has been declining rapidly. Comparisons of relative catch sizes show a disastrous fall in numbers, perhaps as much as 90%. As with much in the life of the Atlantic salmon, the reasons for this remain mysterious.

It appears that fairly high numbers of young salmon leave the east coast rivers of Scotland, but only a small percentage of them return. "Something is happening to them out at sea", said Dr John Baxter of Scottish National Heritage, in September 2001," but we are not certain what it is."

A range of causes for the decline have been advanced; climate change making the ocean warmer, netting off the east coast by English fishermen, and large-scale infestation by sea lice from escaped farm salmon.

The situation became so acute that on the Tweed fishermen agreed to a voluntary catch and release policy to increase the population of young fish. As a direct consequence, the 2000 mile Tweed river system saw an extra 4,000,000 eggs spawned in 2001. Scientists will have to wait three or four years while the salmon swim in the North Atlantic to see if more will find their way home.

Posterity was also much in the mind of the men from the Ministry of Agriculture in the immediate post-war years. Determined to avoid a slump similar to that experienced after the Great War, and also to make an austere Britain less reliant on food imports, they decided that farming ought to be subsidised and, in essence, removed from the market. In 1947 the annual price review system began and it set price-floors in such a way as to allow farmers some predictability in planning their businesses. Mechanisation had been encouraged in the war economy and it now gathered pace as farmers realised that they had cash to invest in plant.

Harry Ferguson was an Ulster Scot who had developed a tractor with a three point linkage at the back end. This device allowed the power of the tractor's engine to be transfered to whatever implement was attached behind. In the past, early tractors had merely pulled implements with more power but less precision than the big horses. Ferguson's tractor became affordable and widely available after the Second World War, and well over 500,000 'wee grey Fergies' were made by the Standard Motor Company of Coventry. And some still chug happily around Border farms today.

The effect of the Fergie was to bring horseworking to an end, and by the late 1950s it was unusual to see Clydesdales in the fields of Border farms. And when horseworking ended all of the associated skills and crafts began to wither. Dave Welsh saw the changes happen;

"The smiddy [at Sprouston] was hard work, and pretty constant. Maybe 120 to 150 horses from the farm places around would be shod and when they were being worked, that would be every six weeks or so. Some of them were not very co-operative, leaned on you. At times when there wasn't so much on the go, we'd make shoes and hang them on hooks around the wall. I mind the smiddy elders, the old men who came in to blether and sit smoking their pipes. Likely the daughter-in-law or the wife wanted rid of them from in front of their fire. They argued all the time, 'Aye that would be when oo was at Kersknowe, no, Kersquarter, or no, maybe Redden.' Argued about bloody anything.

The smiddy began to tail off. And it was a question of did we want to adapt to machinery, maintenance, that sort of thing. Eventually we stopped altogether in the 1960s."

Post-war austerity was sharpened by the long and bitter winter of 1947 and the uncomfortable fact that the economy looked as though it was sliding towards a slump similar to that which followed the Great War. Blocked roads exacerbated food shortages, the freezing conditions cut electricity supplies (many of the more remote Border valleys had to wait until the 1950s and 60s before an electricity supply was made available), and while the temperature dropped the unemployment total in Britain climbed to 2 million. But the American Marshall Plan injected massive amounts of aid into the ruined European infrastructure, and regeneration gathered pace very quickly. By the late 1940s consumer demand had revived and British companies were looking to foreign markets and what became known as a series of 'export drives'.

In Hawick the knitwear manufacturers showed real marketing acumen by courting early forms of celebrity endorsement. In 1949 the actress, Deborah Kerr, was persuaded to remember the Border origins of her surname and she wrote, slightly awkwardly, something which must have delighted the Pringle's management;

"It gives me great pleasure to tell everyone how tremendously admired my twin sets have been here in Hollywood, not to mention how useful they have been to me personally... thank you for some lovely cosy days."

Otto Weisz had become managing director at Pringle and the company used this sort of glamour-associating publicity very adroitly. The menswear market was no doubt impressed by the fact that Edmund Hillary was wearing a Hawick jumper when he led the conquest of Mount Everest in 1953. Two years later Lyle & Scott employed Christian Dior to design a range of knitwear, and several brandnames began to enjoy recognition and success in both domestic and overseas markets. After the Second World War Hawick was reckoned to be the highest dollar earner per head of population in Britain, and in 1953 80 to 90% of her high quality woolen output went to North America. By the early 1960s the textile industry experienced acute labour shortages and branch factories opened in Border towns with no history of manufacturing; Kelso, Earlston, Duns and Eyemouth. Companies were also expanding overseas and Turnbull's of Hawick opened a shop in the fashionable Via Tornabuoni in Florence which was still trading in the early 1980s.

However, far sighted Border politicians were concerned that textiles, even when successful, and a contracting agriculture provided too narrow an economic base for the area, and the experience of James Stewart, a local businessman who became Provost of Kelso, offers a concise paradigm of how one community approached these issues;

"The population [of Kelso] has been fairly stable. In 1921 it was down to 3,500 and then it gradually went up to almost 4,000 in 1950. People were dependent almost entirely on agriculture and the various services that were needed for agriculture. In the past we had very few industries, only John Hogarth Ltd at Kelso Mill, Andrew Dun & Sons' bone mill at Maxwellheugh, George Henderson with the foundry and nail factory and Middlemas & Son making aereated waters. That was about all the manufacturing industry we had.

I joined the town council in 1955 because... actually because I always rather admired the people who did these jobs. I remember the Provosts, Arthur Middlemas and John Hill, and John Tully. I thought that it was only right that we should try to put something back into the town. Of course at first I just took a back seat. Then, after two or three years I was appointed Hon Treasurer of the burgh. I found that tremendously interesting. We levied the rates at that time. We did our best with housing and kept the rates at a reasonable level. The officials of the town council were part time in those days, both the Burgh Chamberlain and the Town Clerk. We operated from a requisition from the county council who looked after the major services like education and roads and so on.

Council housing was the main task of the council from about 1925 onwards. The first schemes were at the Tofts, a scheme at the top of Roxburgh Street, one at Hillbank Terrace and at Inch Road. In Maxwellheugh there was Springwood Terrace and then in my time on the council we had the prefabs which were built at the end of the war. We then built quite a number of houses, at Inchmyre and elsewhere. We invoked the help of the Scottish Special Housing Association and really got on with a large programme. I remember opening the 2000th house owned and built by the town council. I was very proud of the revenue account because we were one of the few authorities to balance that account. It meant slightly higher rents but we took no more from the general ratepayer than the statutory amount.

When I joined the town council our great problem was to alter the economic base, to make Kelso more industrial. We didn't make much progress until the act of 1965; the [result of the] government white paper on the Scottish economy, 'A Plan for Expansion 1965 to 1970'. That was followed by the Percy Johnstone Marshall report on the Borders. The whole thing co-ordinated with the appointment of a full-time Town Clerk in 1965. This was Mat Carlaw and he did a tremendous job for Kelso.

As I said, we wanted to broaden the economic base. The population was only expanding through people coming in from the country, and we needed to create industry. We also took up a Glasgow overspill arrangement but never really made progress with that.

Following the government white paper where the Borders were made a development area, the town council purchased the Pinnacle Hill estate. We were very successful in attracting industry there, so much so that the population increased by 25% between 1965 and 1975. This was really quite phenomenal. I feel that we led the Borders in this.

At Abbotseat the council housing was of such a high standard that many people thought it was private housing. And at Barony Park the town council bought the old auction mart, laid in the services and sold off plots to a private developer. This was a very successful operation indeed.

Our next move was to try to modernise our housing and also other property in the middle of the town. We tried to re-develop the housing lying between Woodmarket and Horsemarket. We couldn't quite manage that but there is a good new development at Rutherford Square with its sheltered housing and a day centre.

One building in the town I've always liked is the Town Hall. It's really a splendid piece of architecure with its clock tower. I can recall the curfew bell being rung each night at 8pm. And on the first Monday of every month when the Town Council met, it was rung at 6pm. When the last meeting of the town council took place in 1975 I arranged for it to be rung for the last time.

I think Kelso lost out on the reorganisation of local government which happened as a result of the Wheatley Commission in the 1970s. The town lost its individuality. That was unavoidable… Before that we were running the town with local people and local officials and I think the record of Kelso Town Council from 1892 to 1975 was very good. I would deprecate this [change] very much and I said at the time that we would lose quite a lot. But there you are, that's progress."

OFF THE RAILS

On a bitter night in January 1969 the last passenger train ever to travel the Waverley Line from Edinburgh to Carlisle and beyond was approaching Newcastleton. The engine driver braked. Up ahead he could see that a large crowd had shut the level crossing gates across the tracks, blocking the route south. Two or three hundred from the old railway village had been led by their minister, the Rev. Bryden Maben, to make a last, grim protest at the closure of the line.

The crowd refused to disperse and when the police, who had driven down from Hawick, attempted to push back the level crossing gates, scuffles broke out and the minister was arrested. The young David Steel was aboard the train, and he persuaded the crowd to move off the track if the police would agree to release the Rev. Bryden Maben without charge. They did, and they did, and the last train rumbled on into history.

The designation of the Borders as a development area was certainly helpful, but it was not the singular achievement it has sometimes been made to appear in retrospect. After 1965 the whole of Scotland, with the sole exception of well-set Edinburgh, was made a development area. The gruff but powerful Labour Secretary of State for Scotland, Willie Ross, used the new government's reliance on Scottish votes to extract the funds for spectacular growth in identifiable public expenditure north of the border — and, it turned out, north of the Borders. Between 1964 and 1973 it rose by 900%. And every part of Scotland appeared to benefit substantially from this bonanza, except the Borders. In order to tackle its particular problems, the Highlands and Islands got a Development Board and a large budget. New towns were established in central Scotland at Livingston and Irvine, new universities at Strathclyde, Heriot Watt, Stirling and Dundee, and three more further education colleges at Hamilton, Ayr and Falkirk. By 1973 10,000 civil servants were working at St Andrew's House in Edinburgh and injecting significant cash into the local economy, and the Forth and Tay road bridges were completed to supply a cohesive infrastructure for the central belt. At Longannet at massive pit was opened up with the potential to employ 10,000 workers, a nuclear reactor was built at Dounreay and an aluminium smelter at Invergordon.

By contrast no initiatives of comparable scale took place in the Borders. In fact the transport infrastructure was seriously weakened by the closure (and immediate slighting) of the Waverley Line in January 1969, and the continuing inadequacy of the A7 trunk road as it wound its picturesque way around the heather-covered hillsides. The central hospital for the Borders at Peel near Galashiels remained a scatter of wartime wooden huts linked by covered, outdoor walkways. Sometimes patients were wheeled to surgery through heavy rain blown horizontal by the wind. Peel had no gynaecological or maternity departments, and despite a determined, dedicated and dogged staff, its survival stood as an unhappy monument to how badly the Borders missed out in the public spending boom of the late 1960s. In point of fact the new Borders General Hospital was not opened until 1988.

Old-fashioned politics no doubt played a part in the relegation of the Borders to the back of the queue in the 60s. Anxious to protect the Labour heartlands of the Central Belt, Willie Ross concentrated his spending in and around constituencies which might return Labour MPs at general elections. With its new devotion to the Liberals, and the Tories running a close second (at the 1966 election David Steel's majority was reduced to 2,211), the Borders offered little prospect of political return on government investment. And since the sitting MP was unlikely to become the member of a party in government, it was difficult for him to exert much pressure for big projects to be sited south of Edinburgh. Nevertheless, the fact that the Highlands and Islands succeeded (and continues to succeed) so well despite only a very small Labour representation shows that party politics was not entirely determinant. And the Borders also suffered from statistics. Unemployment figures were generally significantly lower than the Scottish national average because of a substantial retired population and the sad habit of young people being forced to seek qualifications and find work outside the Tweed Basin.

The Official Guide to the County of Roxburgh of 1972 is a fascinating document. And it helps to explain something of why the Borders seems to have been dismissed in the Sixties as a never-never land. Or perhaps an aye-been land. Determinedly old-fashioned, it describes a moment, frozen in time. But not in 1972. The dated and downbeat presentation suggest 1952 — at the latest. On the cover, congealed in picturesque aspic, is Queen Mary's House in Jedburgh and on the first page of copy is a tired black and white still of Scott's View. As Lord Lieutenant of Roxburghshire, His Grace the Duke of Buccleuch K.T., P.C., G.C.V.O., LL.D. writes a bland introduction, while on page 43, he heads the list of council officials. Immediately below him is the name of the Convenor of the County Council, His Grace the Duke of Roxburghe D.L., J.P. Such text as there is begins with an extended historical essay followed by what might be described now as a guide to Borders heritage — common ridings, traditions and so on. Astonishingly the section on sport begins with foxhunting and shows a picture of a pack of hounds 'patiently waiting to move off from the meet'. The heading 'Football' actually means rugby, 'the most popular game in Roxburgh', and it merits less than half the space given to hunting and fishing. The sole scintilla of modernity is to be found on page 38 in the shape of an advertisement for the Jedburgh precision toolmaker, L.S. Starret, the only organisation that appears to be looking to the future rather than the past. Incidentally it is also the only company to advertise that it can be contacted by telex.

At the back of the county guide lists of statistics offer an occasional insight. In 1972 the council was responsible for the registration and licensing of motor vehicles, and during the year to 31st August 1970, 18,681 vehicles were licensed in Roxburghshire, all bearing the KS index mark. Allowing for a substantial proportion of commercial vehicles in that total, and also the fact that some Borderers bought their cars outwith the county, it looks as though mass car ownership had arrived by 1970. In the same section the number of electors was reckoned at 31,877, and therefore a high ratio of ownership seems likely.

STATELY RATES

Many of Britain's stately homes opened their doors to the public in the 1960s and 70s. In 1992 the Duke of Roxburghe took access a stage further and offered Floors Castle for hire and on 9th April 1992, the going rates were published in The Scotsman. Here they are;

Location fees
  Dining-room from £500
  All state rooms from £750

Daytime rate
  Morning coffee, buffet lunch, afternoon tea, castle guide-book and service charge… £44 (per person)

Evening rate
  Four-course gala dinner, castle guide-book and service charge… £44 (per person)

Fireworks
  Dependent on requirements: e.g. five minute finale with special effects and musical soundtrack… from £1850

Musical entertainment
  Pipers… from £50
  Highland dancers (minimum of 3)… from £75 (each)
  Toastmasters… from £75
  Pianists and Clarsach players… from £120

> *Classical trio/quartet... from £300*
> *Regimental pipe band... from £600*
>
> *Clay pigeon shooting*
> *(minimum of 15 participants)*
> *Full day per head... £100*
>
> *Private barbecue and picnics*
> *Barbecues (minimum of eight people)... £22 (per person)*
> *Picnics (minimum of eight people)... £15 (per person)*
> *Off-road vehicles, fly-fishing, archery, hovercraft driving, croquet etc also available.*

Cars changed lives in the Borders by, literally, expanding the horizons of ordinary people. But another innovation tended to drive them indoors. By 1970 television ownership was near-universal, and while it supplied both information and entertainment, it did inhibit and diminish communal social life. The expansion of the imaginary community of television did produce one attractive historical quirk. When Border Television replaced Tyne-Tees and Scottish Television as the regional ITV channel in the Tweed Basin in 1961, the orientation of its masts recreated the shadow of an ancient polity. Carlisle and Cumbria rejoined Galloway and the Scottish Borders in the nightly news programme, Border News and Lookaround. Alick Cleaver, Derek Batey and Mary Marquis read news items which drew together communities divided centuries before by the frontier, and they did their best to recreate a sense of mutual interest which had been forgotten since the days of the Reivers and the macMalcolm kings.

In the 1960s Border TV's programme-makers attempted to run with the grain of Border society and a series based on the well known inter-town rivalries was broadcast. Taking the form of a quiz and also a competition between musicians and performers, it was entitled, without a trace of innuendo, 'Cock o' the Border'. However, it proved impossible to avoid solecism. When a Scottish town was pitched against an English town, the northerners were stumped when asked to name the dates of the English bank holidays such as Whitsun or the football grounds of English soccer teams.

Despite such lapses, Border Television serves its difficult area with much tact, and its regional programmes remain popular, outperforming the BBC both south and north of the line.

In the early 1970s Border News and Lookaround began to report on fundamental changes taking place in the textile industry. Consolidation of ownership was led by Joseph Dawson Ltd of Bradford, later Dawson International. They bought out Pringle's and Braemar of Hawick, while Courtaulds took over Lyle & Scott. In 1972 Hawick textile workers came out on strike to protest at the changes which, they correctly predicted, would prejudice their jobs. In a fluctuating market most of the independent Border manufacturers became subsidiaries of larger companies whose headquarters and whose focus lay beyond the Tweed and Teviot valleys. In what now seems a spiral of decline, mills were closed, production 'rationalised', and perhaps the lowest point came in

February 2000. For a figure coyly placed 'between five and ten million', Dawson International sold the Pringle brand to the Fang Brothers of Hong Kong. 140 people lost their jobs and another 60 were transfered to a different Dawson company.

In the 1960s Hawick was voted the best dressed town in Britain, its citizens regularly wore the best of woolens and tweeds (usually purchased in the annual mill sales) and the shops in the High Street bustled. Now, property in Hawick can be bought within the limit of a normal credit card and the old air of confidence and vivacity has gone. A comparison with Melrose is both poignant and pointed. In the comfortable lee of the Eildon Hills, a prosperity has settled on the place which expresses itself in speciality cookshops, galleries, a small theatre and a busy restaurant. No new industry has come to bring high incomes to Melrose, the well-planned pensions of the retired middle classes have created this enclave, pushed property values to Edinburgh levels and made it seem a world away from its near-neighbour down the A7.

Electronic industries have partly filled the gap in the Borders economy left by the shrinkage of textiles and the mechanisation of agriculture. But the central difficulty continues to revolve around control. Most electronics manufacturers of any scale turn out to be parts of large companies, often based in other countries. That can make for baffling, devastating decisions of a summary nature. The fragility of this sort of 'inward investment' was pointed up in 1999 when Viasystems, a U.S. based electronics company, abruptly decided to close its factory in Selkirk with the loss of 1,000 jobs. Based thousands of miles away, it was much easier for the Viasystems management to take a harsh business decision than if they had been headquartered in Selkirk or a nearby town.

PRINTED CIRCUITS

Not all of the electronics businesses in the Borders arrived through 'inward investment'. Some were originated in the area. Two Gala men, Robert Currie and Ken Mill, had the idea of developing a workable industrial process for making printed circuits. The theory of printing a circuit rather than creating it with wires and valves had been around for 20 years or so, but in a room above the British Linen Bank in Galashiels High Street, Currie and Mill turned it into a reality.

After a rapid phase of development, the two men disagreed over the direction the business should take and they dissolved their partnership. Robert Currie founded Exacta Circuits in 1962 before emigrating to the USA in 1965 to work in electronics and with the NASA space programme. By 1971 Exacta had expanded out of Galashiels into a purpose-built factory on the edge of Selkirk. This eventually became the ill-fated Viasystems, was then taken over by Signum, which has now gone into receivership.

Meanwhile Ken Mill set up BEPI Electronics. After a period of expansion he sold the company to the Pye Group which then became part of the multinational Philips International Group.

Although Exacta and BEPI no longer exist as independent companies, their founders did much to establish a skill-base in the Borders which encouraged other electronics businesses to come to the area.

Two years after the publication of the guide to Roxburgh, the county was abolished. The Wheatley Commission reported on the reorganisation of local government and recommended that the Borders be joined to Edinburgh and the Lothians in a new southeastern region. After a hard fight, that proposal was overturned and a two-tier system of districts (based on the old counties of Roxburgh, Selkirk, Peebles and Berwickshire) and a region with offices at the old county headquarters at Newtown St Boswells. With these changes the Dukes departed. 1975 saw the end of threequarters of a century of aristocratic hegemony in local government in the Borders and the beginning of a slow march towards party politics. Independent councillors are still elected, but now more and more Liberals, Labour, Conservative and SNP candidates are standing and being elected. In 1986 another reorganisation swept away the districts and focused the voters' attention solely on the regional structure.

Too much and too little took place in the Borders at the end of the 20th century. Too little investment was made and too many textile mills closed, and too little was done to diversify into other industrial sectors. Too many young people are still forced to leave and seek further education outwith the area, where no independent university has yet been established. And too little has been done to attract that talent back. Too many business decisions affecting the Borders have been taken elsewhere and too little done to grow and encourage enterprise native to this place, and committed to it in every meaningful sense.

In the latter decades of the 20th century the story of the Borders has been one of slow decline, and now the best hope of rapid regeneration rests with the current attempts to connect with the booming economy of Edinburgh. Invigorated by the opening of the Scottish Parliament in 1999, the city is expanding and its well-heeled middle classes are seeking the sort of property available in the Borders. The in-migration of people with resources and connections hardly amounts to a policy for industrial renewal but their presence would inject cash and demand services. But there is a difficulty with transport infrastructure. The A7 remains sub-standard and there is no rail link, except to Berwick Upon Tweed. While strenuous efforts are being made to re-establish the mode of transport most favoured by commuters, it will take a long time for the trains to come back down the Gala Water valley, if they come at all. And it cannot have escaped the notice of some that there is a nugget of the purest historical irony rattling around inside all of this. In the referendum of 1979, which failed to produce a Scottish Parliament, the Borders voted no. Fearful of domination by the politics of the Central Belt a generation ago, Borderers are now forced into the position of needing urgently to connect with them and their fruits.

14

Postscript

Within a generation 'history' has been replaced in common usage by 'heritage'. The phrases 'Our National Heritage' or even 'Border Heritage' wrap up easier, slacker and less demanding packages of ideas than the spikier, more combustible 'National History' or 'Border History'. Prominent in the heritage package are the looming shapes of the big houses, palaces, castles and the parks around them. Bowhill, Floors, Mellerstain and the rest supply the cornerstones of what many people think of as our heritage, and those curious about Border history are almost always given a list of these places and their opening times. For inside their walls sit the comforting, paternalistic stories of the wealthy people whose names and exploits decorate that heritage. Since the grand houses of the titled opened to the public in the 1960s and 70s, thousands have trooped around them, shepherded by ropes and plastic carpet protectors, looking up at the iconic, anonymous portraits of forgotten marquises gorgeously robed, often staring into the middle distance with a confident air. As well they might. For who they were is much less important than what they represent. Amongst the glass cases of bric-a-brac and the brocaded furniture, visitors search not so much for coherence or information but more for reassurance and out of curiousity.

But such visits are emphatically not a study of our history or even a good place to start. They are merely tourism. The big houses and the estates of the Borders were and are important, but they are not representative of our heritage, our history or indeed *our* anything. They belong to those landowners and their families and, quite legitimately, they tell their stories, but they are in no meaningful sense ours. After all, the literal meaning of 'heritage' is 'something which can or may be inherited'.

Sweeping aside the distracting debris of aristocratic collections of locks of hair, trinkets and knick-knacks, there is an immense story to be comprehended in the Borders. This book is a first draft of that story, an attempt to set out markers in the landscape, to bring important but ignored figures out of the shadows and to reconstruct or record a memoir of what the day-in, day-out business of life was like for Borderers since the Old Peoples first ventured north after the retreat of the last Ice Age. Inevitably this huge canvas remains patchy, with areas of brilliant colour bordering opacity or even darkness.

Even so, what this first draft has shown can be surprising, and often counter-intuitive.

We were not always Borderers. After the Roman Empire fell in the west and Britannia was abandoned in 410AD, native British Celtic society reasserted itself rapidly and powerfully in the lands between the Antonine and Hadrian's Walls. And when the warbands of the Northumbrian kings overran the Tweed basin, our ancestors found themselves at the centre of power in Britain, and in no sense a frontier people. Mid-Britons rather than Borderers.

The birth of the idea of Scotland in the ambitions of Gaelic kings, and the contemporary rise of a successful English dynasty from Wessex promised trouble somewhere. But in general these rivals clashed further south and the macMalcolm kings — primarily the brilliant David I — planted the seeds of a golden age in the Borders. Guided by monkish enterprise, the early medieval economy surged and left the unsurpassed marks of ruined greatness at Kelso, Jedburgh, Melrose and Dryburgh. When its outlook was international, when trade and ideas flowed through Berwick, the Borders found itself in touch with the heartbeat of European intellectual and mercantile life. John Duns Scotus, Michael Scot and others did not dream on the borders of anything. Far from accepting marginal roles, they travelled easily to the centre of European culture and took the names of their native places with them. And when Italians and Flemings came here to buy wool, they left their names and observations.

Only when the border became a frontier of material difference did our history begin to turn sour. After the death of Alexander III in 1286, centuries of warfare and waste followed. Much of what was built was thrown down, and the conditions for the rise of the Border reivers were created. Peace offers little drama and warfare confers glory of a sort. The early bards converted the militarisation of the frontier into poetry and the ballad tradition grew stronger as life became more desperate. Historically the border was bad for the Borders, but great poetry compounded our difficulties by premiating the martial over the creative, the dramatic over the everyday and, in many important ways, the past over the future.

The ballads sparked the creative imagination of the young Walter Scott and his overpowering talent set a cultural tone which still endures and finds doleful expression in the phrase 'it's aye been'. Of all the difficulties facing the Borders in the 21st century, aye-beenery may be the most intractable.

Scott's wizardry and his obsession with matters martial drew down a mist which has shrouded much of our real — rather than imagined — history until the 20th century. The undoubted greatness of James Small was just the sort of muddy, practical tale to be drowned out by what Sir Walter himself called 'the big, bow-wow stuff'.

But in his encouragement and promotion of the infant tweed industry, Scott showed how the power of poetry, and the romance of historical fiction, could be forward-looking and lay down a fertile ground for the creation of wealth and jobs. Since his death in 1832 what the Borders has needed is not less of Scott but more of his showmanship, assurance and flair. For a flickering moment his writing put the Borders back in the centre of creative life. And if this can happen once, it can happen again. More than fragile inward investment, the Borders needs ideas — ideas which have their beginnings and endings in these hills and river valleys, and which can reach out and touch the lives of anyone. For with the creation of the Scottish Parliament, the border is hardening again and if this book shows anything, it shows how dangerous that can be. And also it shows how our posterity was far from marginal. But if we are not circumspect, our future might be.

The sole legacy worth having from the appalling Border reivers is a thrawn sense of independence. Let us use that to ignore the imaginary line which has divided Borderer from Borderer for centuries, let us incorporate Berwick, Carlisle and north Northumberland into our way of thinking if not our new polity. Let us understand who we were so that we may recognise who we really are.

Bibliography

This is a select bibliography. It is arranged in sections which correspond approximately with the chapter headings, but many books did not fit into my own particular compartments and also covered lengthy periods. These are generally to be found under 'General'. In compiling this bibliography I looked through all my notes in search of what was useful and might intrigue or stimulate a reader anxious to delve deeper into the history of the Borders. Sadly, I wasted a great deal of time on material that was useless, incomprehensible, frivolous, or daft and naturally that has been excluded. Also absent are references to periodicals or works which are extremely difficult to find. Just as the foregoing was intended for the general reader, so this reading list is aimed at those who have access to a local library, and not a university. In each section there are several books listed which are in print, often the latest in their particular field, and available to buy in bookshops or through the addictive internet retailers and bookfinders. I recommend them all. Finally I want to repeat my thanks to those who allowed me to quote from their work.

1. General.

The Borders Book, ed. Donald Omand, 1995.
The Royal Commission for Ancient and Historical Monuments, the volumes for the Borders are Berwickshire, 1909 and 1915, Roxburghshire, 1956, Selkirkshire, 1957 and Peeblesshire, 1967.
The Scottish Borderland — The Place and the People, ed. Richard Allan and Isobel Candlish, 1988.
The Border, ed. J. Ivy and P. Clack, 1983.
A History of the Border Counties, Sir George Douglas Bart. 1899.
The Border History of England and Scotland, G. Ridpath, 1776.
The History and Antiquities of Roxburghshire, Alexander Jeffrey, 1838.
History of Selkirkshire, T. Craig-Brown, 1885.
The Border Country, A Walker's Guide, Alan Hall, 1993.
Discovering the Borders, Alan Spence, 1992.
Calendar of Border Papers, ed. J. Bain, 1894.
Highways and Byways in the Borders, Andrew and John Lang, 1913.

Edinburgh, Lothians and the Borders, John Baldwin, 1985.

The Nature of the Borders, Scottish Natural Heritage Pamphlet, no date.

Warfare and Fortifications in the Borders, John Dent and Rory McDonald, 2000

Christian Heritage in the Borders, John Dent and Rory McDonald, 1998.

Galloway, Andrew McCullough, 2000.

Carlisle, Sydney Towill, 1991.

Carlisle, An Illustrated History, D.R. Perriam, 1992.

Carlisle, The Border City, Pitkin Guide, no date.

Berwick Upon Tweed, F.M. Cowe, 1998.

Berwick, Frank Graham, 1987.

Historical Sites of Northumberland and Newcastle Upon Tyne, G.L. Dodds, 2000.

A Historical Guide to Jedburgh, ed. Tom B. Dobson, 2000.

Guid Auld Galashiels, Margaret Lawson, 1997.

Kelsae, A History of Kelso from Earliest Times, Alistair Moffat, 1985.

Companion to Hawick, R.E. Scott, 1970.

The Place-Names of Roxburghshire, J.S.M. MacDonald, 1991.

The Churches and Graveyards of Roxburghshire, G.A.C. Binnie, 2001.

Scottish Place-Names, W.F. H. Nicolaisen, 1976.

The Celtic Place-Names of Scotland, W.J. Watson, 1926.

The Dictionary of Place-Names in Scotland, Mike Darton, 1992.

Dictionary of British Place-Names, Andrew M. Currie, 1994.

Scottish Festivals, Sheila Livingstone, 1997.

Scottish Folklore, Raymond Lamont-Brown, 1996.

Scottish Customs, Sheila Livingstone, 1996.

Scotland — A New History, Michael Lynch, 1991.

A History of the Scottish People, T.C. Smout, 1969.

An Historical Atlas to Scotland, 400 to 1600, ed. Peter McNeill and Ranald Nicolson, 1975.

A History Book for Scots, Walter Bower's Scotichronicon, ed. D.E.R. Watt, 1998.

The Scottish Nation, Tom Devine, 1999.

Scotland Before the Industrial Revolution, Ian D. Whyte, 1995.

Scottish Country Life, Alexander Fenton, 1976.

The Drove Roads of Scotland, A.R.B. Haldane, 1997.

Scottish Historical Documents, ed. Gordon Donaldson, 1970.

Scottish Elites, ed. Tom Devine, 1994.

The Nature of Scotland, ed. Magnus Magnusson, 1991.

Scottish Animal and Bird Folklore, Malcolm Archibald, 1996.

The Scots Herbal, Tess Darwin, 1996.

The Scots Kitchen, F. Marian McNeill, 1929.

In Search of Scotland, H.V. Morton, 1929.

Scottish Journey, Edwin Muir, 1935.

Scotland the Brand, David McCrone, 1998.

The National Museum of Scotland has published an excellent series of booklets on aspects of Scottish history. All of them are highly informative;

Going to School, Donald J. Witherington, 1997.

Farming, Gavin Sprott, 1995.
Sporting Scotland, John Burnett, 1995.
The Scots in Sickness and in Health, John Burnett, 1993.
Spinning and Weaving, Enid Gauldie, 1995.
Feeding Scotland, Catherine Brown, 1996.
Going to Bed, Naomi Tarrant, 1998.
Going to Church, Colin McLean, 1997.
Leaving Scotland, Mona McLeod, 1996.

Chambers Scots Dictionary, ed. William Grant, 1929.
Scots Dialect Dictionary, Chambers, 1911.
Collins Encyclopaedia of Scotland, ed. John Keay and Julia Keay, 1994.
The Oxford Companion to Scottish History, ed. Michael Lynch, 2001.
The Oxford Companion to British History, ed. John Cannon, 1997.
The Isles, Norman Davies, 1999.
Europe, A History, Norman Davies, 1996.
Mysterious Britain, Janet and Colin Bond, 1971.
Last of the Free, James Hunter, 1999.
Time in History, G. F. Whitrow, 1989.
Money — A History, ed. Jonathan Williams, 1997.
A Taste of History, ed. Maggie Black, 1993.
The Weather, ed. Richard Whitaker, 1996.
The Story of Philosophy, Bryan Magee, 1998.
Britain's Wildlife, Plants and Flowers, Readers' Digest, 1987.
The Oxford Companion to English Literature, ed. Margaret Drabble, 1999.

2. The Wildwood.

Early Settlers in the Borders, John Dent and Rory McDonald, 1997.
The Manor Valley, ed. Trevor Cowie, 2000.
The Whitlaw Mosses, Michael Robson, unpublished thesis, 1984.
Ancient Scotland, Stewart Ross, 1991.
Wild Harvesters, Bill Finlayson, 1998.
Scottish Woodland History, ed. T.C. Smout, 1997.
Farmers, Temples and Tombs, Gordon Barclay, 1998.
Life and Death in the Prehistoric North, Stan Beckensall, 1994.
Settlement and Sacrifice, Richard Hingley, 1998.
Art, Ritual and Death in Prehistory, ed. Stephen Aldhouse-Green, 1996.
Facing the Ocean, Barry Cunliffe, 2001.
The Enchanted Forest, Yvonne Aburron, 1993.
The Pagan Religions of the British Isles, Ronald Hutton, 1991.
Healing Threads, Mary Beith, 1995.

3. Language and Silence.

Britannia, Shepherd S. Frere, 1967.
Roman Cavalry, Karen Dixon, 1994.
The Illustrated Gaelic-English Dictionary, Edward Dwelly, reprinted 1994.
Vegetius, Epitoma Rei Militaris, ed. A.L. Jenkins, 1892.
The Outpost Forts of Hadrian's Wall, R. Ambleton, 1983.

The Trimontium Story, Walter Elliot, 1995.
A Dictionary of Roman Military Terms, Frank Graham, 1989.
Warlords and Holy Men, A.P. Smyth, 1984.
Agricola, Tacitus, ed. J.G.C. Anderson, 1922.
Roman Britain, John Wacher, 1980.
Christianity in Roman Britain to AD500, Charles Thomas, 1981.
The Carvetii, N. Higham, B. Jones, 1985.
Late Celtic Britain and Ireland, Lloyd Laing, 1977.
The Hillforts of Southern Scotland, J.S. Rideout, O.A. Owen, E. Halpin, 1992.
Between and Beyond the Walls, ed. R. Miket, C. Burgess, 1984.
Hadrian's Wall, D.J. Breeze and B. Dobson, 1976.
Wild Men and Holy Places, Daphne Brook, 1994.
The North Britons, a Pre-history of a Border People, Richard Feacham, 1965.
Place-Names of Roman Britain, A.L.F. Rivet and C Smith, 1979.
Life and Letters on the Roman Frontier, Alan K. Bowman, 1994.
Arthur and the Lost Kingdoms, Alistair Moffat, 1999.
Scotland: The Making of the Kingdom, A.A.M. Duncan, 1975.
A Gathering of Eagles, Gordon Maxwell, 1998.
Corruption and the Decline of Rome, Ramsay MacMullen, 1988.

3. Romanitas.

The Age of Arthur, John Morris, 1973.
Invaders of Scotland, Anna Ritchie and David J. Breeze, 1991.
Angels, Fools and Tyrants, Chris Lowe, 1999.
The Gododdin of Aneirin, John T. Koch, 1997.
Arthur's Britain, Leslie Alcock, 1971.
Bede's Ecclesiastical History of the English People, ed. B. Colgrave and R.A.B. Mynors, 1969.
Bede: History of the English Church and People, ed. Leo Shirley-Price, 1978.
The Earliest English Kings, D.P. Kirby, 1991.
The Kingdom of Northumbria, N.J. Higham, 1993.
Holy Island, Frank Graham, 1987.
The Age of Bede, ed. Betty Radice, 1965.
Celt and Saxon, ed. K. Jackson, N. Chadwick, 1963.
The Celts, N. Chadwick, 1970.
Anglo-Saxon England, Sir Frank Stenton, 1971.
Brito-Roman and Anglo-Saxon, Ian M. Smith, 1984.
Yeavering: An Anglo-British Centre of Early Northumbria, Brian Hope Taylor, 1977.
Anglo-Saxon Art, David M. Wilson, 1984.
Language and History in Early Britain, Kenneth Jackson, 1953.
The Kingdom of the Scots, G.W.S. Barrow, 1973.
A History of Wales, John Davies, 1990.
The Son of Prophecy, David Rees, 1997.
The English Settlements, J.N.L. Myres, 1986.
The Anglo-Saxons, ed. James Campbell, 1982.

The Encyclopaedia of Anglo-Saxon England, ed. Michael Lapidge, 1999.
The Anglo-Saxon Chronicle, ed. Michael Swanton, 1996.
Northumbria in the Days of Bede, Peter Hunter Blair, 1976.

5. Both Sides the Tweed.

St Cuthbert, Dominic Marner, 2000.
Walter Elliot, unpublished papers on Old Melrose.
Pilgrimage in Medieval Scotland, Peter Yeoman, 1999.
The Churches and Graveyards of Berwickshire, G.A.C. Binnie, 1995.
Kingship and Unity, G.W.S. Barrow, 1981.
The Age of Conquest, R.R. Davies, 1987.
The Making of Wales, John Davies, 1996.
The Lindisfarne Gospels, Janet Backhouse, 1981.
The Book of Kells, Ian Zaczek, 1997.
Scandinavian Scotland, Barbara Crawford, 1987.
Viking Scotland, Anna Ritchie, 1993.

6. All the Faithful Sons of Holy Mother Church.

Liber de S. Marie de Calchou, The Bannatyne Club, 1846.
Liber de S. Marie de Dryburgh, The Bannatyne Club, 1847.
Liber de S. Marie de Melros, The Bannatyne Club, 1837.
The Flower of the Forest, ed. J.M. Gilbert, 1985.
Historic Melrose, Patricia Dennison, Russel Coleman, 1998.
Melrose Abbey, Marguerite Wood, J.S. Richardson, 1932.
Dryburgh Abbey Guidebook, Marguerite Wood, J.S. Richardson, 1948.
Scottish Abbeys, S. Cruden, 1960.
Scottish Medieval Churches, Richard Fawcett, 1985.
Hunting and Hunting Reserves in Medieval Scotland, J.M. Gilbert, 1979.
The Normans in Scotland, R.L.G. Ritchie, 1954.
Medieval Scotland, Peter Yeoman, 1995.
Scottish Abbeys and Priories, Richard Fawcett, 1994.
Scottish Castles, Christopher Tabraham, 1986.
Scottish Medieval Churches, Richard Fawcett, 1985.
A Medieval Chronicle of Scotland, trans. Joseph Stevenson, reprinted 1991.

7. The Battlelands.

Robert the Bruce and the Community of the Realm, G.W.S. Barrow, 1988.
Scotland — The Late Middle Ages, Ranald Nicolson, 1974.
Border Bloodshed, Alastair MacDonald, 2000.
Flodden, Niall Barr, 2001.
Seige of Carlisle, Isaac Tullie, 1840.
The Illustrated Border Ballads, John Marsden, 1990.
Smailholm Tower, Christopher Tabraham, 1993.

8. Riding Times.

The Steel Bonnets, George MacDonald Fraser, 1971.
The Last Years of a Frontier, D.L.W. Tough, 1928.
The Border Reivers, Godfrey Watson, 1974.
The Border Reivers, Keith Durham, Angus McBride, 1991.
The Native Horses of Scotland, Andrew F. Fraser, 1987.
The Harvest of the Hills, Angus J.L. Winchester, 2000.
The Selkirk Protocol Books, ed. Walter Elliot and Tessa Maley, 1993.
The Protocol Book of Sir Ninian Brydin, ed. Walter Elliot and Tessa
    Maley, 1995.
History of Northumberland, Cadwallader J. Bates, 1895.
Bloodfeud in Scotland, K. Brown, 1986.
The Protocol Book of Robert Wedderop, ed. Walter Elliot and Tessa
    Maley, 1993.
Ride with the Moonlight, Michael Robson, 1987.

9. Dangerous Rapture.

The Scottish Covenanters, I.B. Cowan, 1976.
Scottish Covenanter Stories, Dave Love, 2000.
Scotland and the Union, David Daiches, 1977.
The Deil's Ain, Roy J.M. Pugh, 2001.
The Coldstream Guards, Charles Grant, 1971.
Scotland's Chronicles of Blood, Norman Adams, 1996.

10. Day In, Day Out.

Scots Cooking, Sue Lawrence, 2000.
A Tour in Scotland, Thomas Pennant, 1772.
Farm Servants and Labour in Scotland, ed. Tom Devine, 1984.
Riot, Revelry and Rout, John Burnet, 2000.
An Ingenious Mechanic, Michael Robson, 1989.
The Statistical Account of Scotland, 1791–99, vol III, The Eastern Borders,
    reprinted 1979.
A Break with the Past, Michael Robson, 1990.

11. Walter Scott and the Kindred Ground.

Walter Scott, David Daiches, 1971.
Sir Walter Scott, Rev. J.A. Carruth, no date.
The Journal of Sir Walter Scott, ed. W.E.K. Anderson, 1972.
The Ragged Lion, Allan Massie, 1994.
Mungo Park, Mark Duffil, 1999.
Water Music, T. Coraghessan Boyle, 1983.

12. The Singing Country.

Grace Darling, W.A. Montgomery, 1974.
Carlisle Citadel Station, Dennis Perriam, David Ramshaw, 1998.

The Lost Railways of the Scottish Borders, Gordon Stansfield, 1999.
Waverley, Roger Siviter, 1996.
A Century of the Scottish People, T.C. Smout, 1986.
The Border Hosiery and Knitwear Industry, Clifford Gulvin, 1979.
A Border Woolen Town in the Industrial Revolution, Karen McKechnie, 1968.
The Scottish Hosiery and Knitwear Industry, Clifford Gulvin, 1984.
The Tweedmakers, Clifford Gulvin, 1973.
A History and Industrial Archaeology of the Galashiels Woolen Mills, Agnew Prize Essay, Alison A. Nawrocha, 1969–70.
From Dawn to Dusk, Betty Little, 1997.
Bowhill Guidebook, 1999.
Selkirkshire in Old Photographs, Ian W. Mitchell, 1989.
Victorian and Edwardian Borderland, Peter Adamson and R. Lamont Brown, 1981.
The Border League Story, Laing Speirs, 2000.
The Championship Year, John G. Smith, 1999.

13. Oo.

Maxton 2000, Charles Denoon, 2000.
Scotland in the 20th Century, ed. Tom Devine, 1996.
Kelso, History in Focus, ed Robin Robeson and Alastair Campbell, 2001.
Langholm with the Lid Off, Wattie Bell, 1996.
A Souter's Bairn, Jenny Corbett and Avril Jack, 1993.
The Story of a Community, Dingleton Hospital, 2000.
Who Owns Scotland Now? Auslan Cramb, 1996.
The Arts in Berwick, C.G.W. Green, 2001.
Against Goliath, David Steel, 1989.

I am very grateful to the editors of the following books for allowing me to quote from them;

The Bondagers, ed. Ian McDougall, 2000 (extracts have been taken from pp 7–8, 16–17, 18–19, 25, 42–43 and 66).
A Kalewater Miscellany, ed Douglas Hall, 1999.
Wartime Memories of Kelso, ed. Willie Turnbull and Bill Pattison, 2001.

Index to Notes

Index of Names and Places

Rule Brittania 294
Rule of St Benedict 158
Rulehaugh 228
Runes 126
Rupert, Prince 276
Russia 332
Rutherford 287
Rutherford, John 287
Rutherford, Samuel 275
Rutherford, Will (Wull the Hird)
  6, 14
Rutherglen Fair 320

Safeways 29
Sais, The 50, 105
Salamis, Battle of 50
Salmon People, The 39
Salmon Queen, The 31
Salutation Inn 9
Samhain 58
San Gimignano 258
Sanderson and Murray 359, 360
Sandstell 31
St Abbs 390
St Abbs School 383
St Aidan 109, 110, 118, 121, 148,
  156, 337
St Albans 86
St Andrew 189, 226, 251
St Andrews 173, 271
St Andrews, Bishop of 155, 239
St Anthony 129
St Audrey 226
St Augustine of Canterbury 108,
  113, 212
St Augustine of Hippo 124, 125
St Bartholomew 154, 226
St Bernard of Ponthieu 145, 148
St Bernadine of Siena 227
St Boisil 119–121, 130, 148, 156,
  159
St Boswells 34, 130, 159, 258, 353,
  398, 399
St Boswells Fair 59, 192
St Bothan 159
St Christopher 226
St Columba 33, 89, 109, 148
St Columbanus 112, 113
St Cuthbert 7, 31, 85, 86, 94, 111,
  117–127, 130, 133, 138, 148,
  155–157, 159, 161, 165, 167, 172,
  181, 187, 222, 226, 233

St Cuthbert's Isle 122
St David 105, 226
St Etheldreda 226
St Gabriel 227
St George's Cross 9, 11, 226, 251
St Gorgian 90
St Helen's 369
St James the Great 226
St James the Less 226
St James' Church 167, 173, 294
St James Hotel 342
St Jean, Cap Ferrat 384
St Jerome 124, 125
St John of Beverly 183
St John the Evangelist 120, 127,
  146, 148
St John's Church Hall 396
St Joseph Cupertino 227
St Kentigern 89, 113, 125, 129, 156
St Lo 151
St Mark 126
St Martin of Tours 87, 111
St Matthias 226
St Mary 110, 146, 148, 155–157,
  225
St Mary's Loch 336
St Modan 110
St Nicholas 167
St Ninian 109, 111
St Patrick 86–89, 96, 97, 109, 226
St Paul 129, 226
St Paulinus 108
St Peter 226
St Ronan's Games 333
St Ronan's Well 333, 334
St Thomas Aquinas 166
St Thomas a Becket 161, 212
St Thomas' Hospital 403
St Tobias 118
St Waltheof 164–166, 180, 226
St Wilfrid 121–123, 127, 183
Sampson, Agnes 281
Samye Ling 403
Sandyknowe Farm 324
Santiago de Compostela 226
Sarajevo 377
Saxons 76, 78, 94, 95, 104
Scandinavia 23, 79, 332
Scenes of Infancy 330
Schiehallion 53
Scone 153
de Scope, Sir Gafrid 217